INTRODUCTION TO ASTEROIDS
The Next Frontier

Clifford J. Cunningham

Published by:

Willmann–Bell,Inc.
P.O. Box 35025
Richmond, Virginia 23235 ☎ (804)
United States of America 320-7016

Publishers and Booksellers

Serving Astronomers Worldwide
Since 1973

Library of Congress Catalogin-in-Publication Data

Cunningham, Clifford, 1955–
    Introduction to asteroids.

    Bibliography: p.
    1. Planets, Minor   I. Title.
QB377.C86 1987   523.4'4   87–12047
ISBN 0-943396-16-6

Printed in the United States of America
87 88 89 90 91 92 10 9 8 7 6 5 4 3 2 1

FOREWORD

During the past two decades, new and varied methods of studying asteroids, both observationally and theoretically, have greatly increased our knowledge of these small bodies. A spectacular development is the work of Alvarez *et al* that an asteroid impact caused the extinction of the dinosaurs and other life 65 million years ago. It has served to bring asteroid research into contact with several other scientific disciplines and it has generated great public interest in the subject of asteroids.

The Infrared Astronomy Satellite, with its discovery of solar system dust bands likely of asteroidal origin, and its detection of thousands of asteroids, has proved the value of Earth-orbiting telescopes for asteroid research Its success is all the more remarkable since asteroid observations were not even considered until after IRAS had been launched.

This book covers these and other developments, reviewing our over-all knowledge of asteroids as of early 1987, while providing a historical perspective to put it into context. Its synoptic view shows us how diverse and fascinating the study of asteroids has become.

Tom Gehrels

DELLA SCOPERTA

DEL NUOVO PIANETA

CERERE FERDINANDEA

OTTAVO TRA I PRIMARJ DEL NOSTRO SISTEMA

SOLARE.

PALERMO
1802

NELLA STAMPERIA REALE.

ACKNOWLEDGEMENTS

Grateful thanks go to all those people in the Profiles chapter, many of whom furnished me with papers in advance of publication; and particularly to the scientists at the Lunar & Planetary Laboratory and the Planetary Science Institute who provided much invaluable information during a series of personal interviews in Tucson.

I am indebted to the following libraries for providing me with research material: The Canada Institute for Scientific and Technical Information, Library of Congress, Metropolitan Library of Toronto, McDonald Observatory, University of Waterloo, Princeton University and the University of NewBrunswick.

A special thanks to those who helped ensure the accurate interpretation of the data presented in this book by reviewing chapters prior to publication: Luis Alvarez, Richard Binzel, William Clemens, Dale Cruikshank, Jack Drummond, Richard Greenberg, Eleanor Helin, Lucy McFadden, Steve Ostro, Ettore Perozzi, Frederick Pilcher, Eugene Shoemaker, Charles Sonett, Gordon Taylor, Ronald Taylor, Edward Tedesco, David Tholen and Vincent Zappala. Any remaining errors in the text are solely my responsibility.

Thanks also to those who provided valuable source material: Arthur C. Clarke, Patrick Moore, David Levy, David Allen, Tapio Korhonen of Turku Observatory, Jost Jahn, Alan Hildebrand, Richard G. Marsden of ESA, Arthur Sweet of the Geological Survey of Canada, Bill Frickey, and Murray Kaitting for his two photos of the author. Several original papers in foreign languages appear for the first time in English in this book. Translations were generously provided by Peter and Ilsidore Kautsky and Sonja Kroisenbrunner (German text), Gabrielle Niccolli (Italian text), and Mike Bolan (French text).

My special gratitude to Dave Tholen for a wealth of data from his PhD thesis, and many hours of friendly conversation. And a unique thanks to Rick Binzel, who gave me my first taste of big-telescope time on asteroids at McDonald Observatory.

Most importantly, thanks go to three men without whose support this book would have not been possible. Peter Kautsky, who tirelessly typed the manuscript of this book into a word processor; Tom Gehrels, who kindly wrote the Foreword; and Perry Remaklus, president of Willmann-Bell, who gave me the opportunity to write this book on asteroids.

TABLE OF CONTENTS

INTRODUCTION

> The judgment of contemporaries is always subject to severe limitations. The long-range judgment of posterity is unknown.
>
> S. Chandrasekhar, 1984

Most amateur astronomers have never seen one; most professional astronomers hope they never have to see one. But these small objects, variously known as planetoids, minor planets or asteroids, are increasingly being viewed as key to our understanding of the origin of the solar system.

Even more surprising, they have had an impact (quite literally) on the study of evolution, paleontology, geology, the future planning of space colonies and space manufacturing, the length of the astronomical unit, the mass of the planets and questions in general relativity—even the nature of time itself.

This book was written to present the latest scientific findings on these varied topics, and at the same time fill a void in the literature. The landmark opus *Asteroids,* edited by Gehrels, was published in 1979. While it will remain a useful volume for many years, its technical nature puts it beyond the level of all but graduate students and professional asteroid researchers. It is clearly impossible for any one person to improve upon what nearly 70 scientists collaborated on to produce in *Asteroids*. In writing this book, it was my intention to update our fast-moving understanding of the asteroids, especially covering topics that were not considered in *Asteroids*. And at the same time present this wealth of technical data at a level accessible to the advanced amateur and undergraduate, although I trust that this synthesis will also be useful to those who study asteroids at the professional level. In short, I have striven to follow the precepts of Robert Blake (1984):

> The author must be widely read, he must be able to convert the discoveries of others into lucid prose and he must have some sort of "vision" which he wishes to put across. But he cannot expect to make an 'original contribution' in the doctoral thesis sense of the words.

In a book such as this, I believe it is most important to enable the reader to trace the sources of ideas back to the original papers. As a result, I have referenced (and read) every one of the hundreds of sources required. An important byproduct of this research has been the discovery that several widely-held beliefs about asteroid work are erroneous. For example, asteroid families were first identified in 1888 (not 1918), the first asteroid lightcurve was measured around 1810 (not 1901), and the binary nature of asteroids was first investigated in 1802 (not 1901).

The majority of professional astronomers have long regarded planetary science in general, and the study of asteroids in particular, as much less glamorous pursuits than stellar structure or galactic evolution. In response to a question about this attitude, Professor John Lewis of the University of Arizona had this to say:

> Who needs astronomers! The overwhelming majority of all astronomers, for obvious historical reasons, were trained to do stellar or deep space astronomy. They regarded a full moon as the bane of their existence; the planets were things that fogged their plates. They had no training in anything with a temperature below $2,500°\,K$, so what is a planet to them? Noise. Of course one man's noise is another man's data.
>
> The planetary sciences got its impetus not from astronomy, curiously enough, but from celestial mechanicians, people like Kant and Laplace; and from the realm of chemistry, the work of Harold Urey and Gerard Kuiper. It wasn't until 1960, when it became possible to launch spacecraft to escape velocity, that those people became organized into a community and started cloning themselves in large numbers. Planetary science is still in the exponential growth phase, which will continue past the turn of the century.

A glance at the accompanying histogram clearly shows this growth. It plots the number of citations of asteroid papers that have appeared in the annual *Astronomy and Astrophysics Abstracts* for each year since 1969. Three plateaus are evident—close to 80 papers per year for the first three years; then, largely as a result of the first international asteroid conference, the number doubles to 160; the second international conference again spurred the volume of papers in to the 200–240 range; and the Asteroids Comets Meteors conference in 1983 marked a peak of 274 papers.

Citations are sure to increase now that asteroid conferences are being scheduled every few years—Uppsala in 1985 and Tucson in 1988. These conferences are always quite serious scientific gatherings, of course, but they are also a fertile ground for amusing anecdotes. At a Division of Planetary Science meeting in Pittsburgh in 1981, the possibility of asteroidal satellites was being discussed. David W. Dunham reportedly said that "if Hebe turns out to be a binary then we already know its name—Jebe!" (The heebie-jeebies, for those not familiar with American slang, is a term descriptive of intense nervousness or the jitters). A true classic occurred at the Symposium on the Origin of the Solar System held in Nice in 1972. Among others, two prominent astronomers—Fred Whipple and Paul Pellas—were present. Whipple's paper was entitled "The Strange Case of Pallas," but a hastily prepared updated version of the program changed the title into "Whipple: The Strange Case of Pellas." The next day, a joking participant added a new line to the posted program: "Pellas: The Strange Case of Whipple." The biggest laugh at the Asteroids Comets Meteors II conference in Uppsala, Sweden (June, 1985), came when Tom Gehrels explained the procedures used in the Spacewatch project to find asteroids. To find a moving object (asteroid) in a CCD scan, "we get rid of all the junk—stars and galaxies." Vermin of the skies in reverse!

Before any of the 677 scientific papers referenced in this book could be written, it was necessary to collect data at the telescope. Like others, I have spent many hours using, and occasionally pampering, sometimes balky photometers on long, cold winter nights to gather the precious photons reflected by fragments of rock millions of kilometers away. But I'll let David Levy (1983) describe the feelings shared by dedicated asteroid observers toward the end of a marathon session on Kitt Peak in Arizona:

> Only two hours are now left until dawn, and with the pace of our work, I wonder how we shall ever make it. Sitting next to me is a tiny refractor I carry, and with it I take occasional glances at the mountaintop sky. But even with this diversion I am beginning to tire. After all, we have been working for five straight nights. Tomorrow will be the last of this run. I think of the long nights that observers earlier this century have spent in their domes. I think of Milton Humason at the focus of the 100-inch Hooker reflector on Mt. Wilson. I recall Clyde Tombaugh telling me of the nights at Lowell, patiently preparing his plates for the long dark spell of each lunation as he searched for the elusive 'Planet X.' And I look at the observer beside me as he checks the position of our next asteroid with care. I am awake now. In company such as this, second wind comes easily.

> Toward dawn we have to be especially careful, because that is when the sky condition may change. On cue, the wind picks up. Our dome slides toward the south so that we can watch

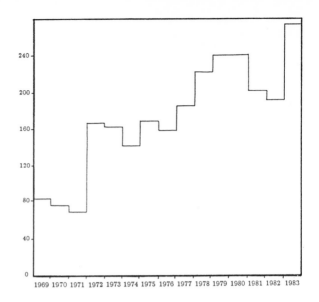

Fig. I–1. *Number of citations of asteroid papers in* Astronomy and Astrophysics Abstracts *1969–1983.*

asteroid 201 Penelope as she whirls rapidly on her axis. And finally, another check on 1620 Geographos, an Icarus-type asteroid that is not too far from Earth. Earlier we saw it moving through the aperture of the photometer as it dashed across the sky.

> Thanks to a special reduction program, our observing continues well into the brightening sky. But soon, even the asteroids become too faint to see. We take the last of our readings and close down. In opposite order from the set-up procedure that seemed to have taken place so long ago, the equipment is brought to a state of rest. The shutter closes—it seems so long since it opened half a day ago.

> Over the Rincon Mountains far to the east, the sky is now brightening rapidly, but because of the altitude, it is not very red. The brightening localizes, and then suddenly, a green spark marks the end of the Sun's eclipse by the bulk of the Earth. And as the green quickly turns to yellowish red, we know that the long night's journey into day is finally over.

After three years of researching this book at conferences, libraries, observatories and universities in Europe and North America, I will leave the last (hopeful) word to the ancient Roman architect-engineer Vitruvius.

> I have tried as best I can to explain this difficult material clearly in writing, but this is not an easy explanation, nor is it comprehensible to everybody unless they have had some experience in this kind of thing. But if anyone has not understood well enough from what I've written, when he looks at the real thing he will realize at once how it has all been designed with ingenuity and precision.

HISTORY 1

As to the satellites of Mars, and the swarm of asteroids, they seem to be too small to retain an atmosphere sufficient for the support of beings like ourselves. If they had a course to run, it has probably been concluded long ago.

George Searle, 1890 discoverer of 55 Pandora

PHASE 1: The Visual Search

The existence of a planet in what we now call the asteroid belt was first suggested by Johannes Kepler when he wrote "Inter Jovem et Martem interposui planetam" (Between Jupiter and Mars I placed a planet) (Kepler, 1596).

According to Heward (1912), Kepler postulated the existence of an unseen world while assisting Tycho Brahe in preparing the Rudolphine astronomical tables. "Tycho's very exact observations of the places of the planets suggested to Kepler that Jupiter was very much farther away from Mars than accorded with his sense of just proportion of distances. All through his life Kepler had been dominated by a sense of analogy; he believed with unwavering faith that unity of design was an ordinance of the Creator's plan. Hence he concluded that, though invisible to the eyes now, a large planet existed in this region."

In 1766, Titius von Wittenburg developed an empirical formula for planetary distances. The rule takes the form $Y = .4 + .3(2^{n-1})$, where $n = 0, 1, 2 \ldots$ for $n = 0, Y = 0.4$, which corresponds to the orbit of Mercury in astronomical units.

Take heed of the distances of the planets from each other, wrote Titius in 1772, and note that in almost every case they are separated from each other in proportion to their increase in size. If the distance from the Sun to Saturn is reckoned as 100 parts, then Mercury is 4 such parts away from the Sun; Venus is $4 + 3 = 7$ thereof; Earth $4 + 6 = 10$; Mars $4 + 12 = 16$. But now notice that from Mars to Jupiter there is a deviation of this exact proportion. From Mars there follows a space of $4 + 24 = 28$ such parts which to date no main planet or satellite has been observed. Are we to assume that the Divine Creator has left this space empty? Of course not! We may be confident that this space is occupied by hitherto undiscovered moons of Mars.

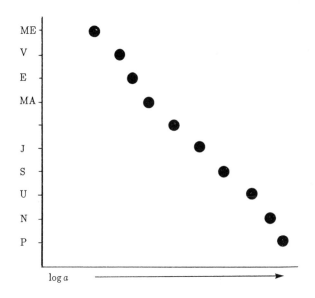

Fig. 1–1. *A diagrammatic version of Bode's Law, with the planets from Mercury (top) to Pluto plotted versus the logarithm of their semi-major axes. The fifth place is occupied by the minor planets.*

Johann Bode, director of the Berlin Observatory at the time, used Titius' relationship to promote the case for an unknown planet. So much so, in fact, that the formula has become known as Bode's Law (Fig. 1–1). When the planet Uranus was discovered by William Herschel, it was noticed that its distance from the Sun conformed to the formula, a fact which led Baron Franz von Zach to believe Bode's Law was correct.

The 29-year-old Hungarian met Herschel in London in 1783, just two years after the discovery of Uranus. While no specific documents exist to prove it, the two men must have discussed the vindication of Bode's Law, and the curious gap between Mars and Jupiter. Herschel invited von Zach to observe with him at Datchet, and the young astronomer was accompanied by his friend Count Moritz von Bruhl, an amateur astronomer and ambassador to Great Britain of the Elector of Saxony. As we shall soon see, this connection launched von Zach's career. Just two years after meeting Herschel, von Zach went so far as to predict the position of the missing planet: distance from the Sun 2.82 AU; eccentricity 0.14; orbital period 4.74 years; inclination 1°36'; heliocentric longitude of perihelion 192°6'.

"Of the supposed planet between Mars and Jupiter I'll talk to you in person and show you what kind of calculations I have been occupying myself with. I seem to have all the elements of this yet unknown planet except one, that is the epoch longitudinis." (von Zach, 1789).

After several years of fruitless searching, the baron organized a meeting, at which six astronomers gathered on 11 September 1800. Among those present at the observatory of Johann Schroeter in Lilienthal near Bremen were Wilhelm Olbers and Karl Harding, both destined to find an asteroid within four years. At this historic meeting, the baron proposed the formation of a society of astronomers, 24 in all, each of whom would look at a specific section of the zodiac to search for the missing planet, while producing a new star chart of his sector.

> They voted Schroeter for their president and me (von Zach) they honored as secretary of the astronomical society. Everybody was assigned a zone 15 degrees in length and 7 to 8 degrees from north to south in width for inspection. Almost everybody took it with delight except Sniadecki in Krakau and Wurm in Blaubeuren (Von Zach, 1801).

The proposal was accepted, and letters outlining it were sent to astronomers in other countries, including Father Guiseppe Piazzi in Palermo, Italy, where he was the director of the Palermo Observatory established by the King of Naples in 1790. At the time the 54-year-old Piazzi was already updating an existing star catalogue by Wollaston. Replete with inaccuracies, the catalogue had to be checked star by star, a task Piazzi was performing with a 1.5 meter vertical circle to determine star positions on the night of 31 December 1800.

He saw in the constellation Taurus a light which was not in the catalogue. The next night, he found it had shifted position, and the next night it had moved again. On 24 January 1801, with the Napoleonic invasion of Italy very much on his mind, Piazzi wrote this historic letter in his Sicilian dialect to Barnaba Oriani in Milan:

> Although the current political circumstances have interrupted all our correspondence, I hazard nevertheless to write to you, impatient as I am to give you news which you will not find unpleasant. On the first day of January, I observed in Taurus an 8th magnitude star which, the following night advanced approximately 3'30" towards North and about 4' towards Aries. By verifying my observations on the 3rd and 4th of January, I found more or less the same movement. On the 5th, 6th, 7th, 8th and 9th of January the sky was overcast. I again saw the star on Jan. 10th and 11th

Photo. 1–1. *Johannes Kepler (1571–1630), German astronomer and assistant to Tycho Brahe. In 1596, he published Mysterium Cosmographicum, in which he adopted Plato's theory of five nesting regular solids. Each could be fitted alternately inside a series of spheres to create a 'nest' which described the distances of the planets from the Sun. In the space between Mars and Jupiter, Kepler postulated the existence of an unseen planet. (Mary Lea Shane Archives of the Lick Observatory).*

and, subsequently, on the 13th, 14th, 17th, 18th, 19th, 21st, 22nd and 23rd of January. Its RA in my first observation was 51°47', with a declination of 16°8'19" from the 10th to the 11th, from a position of retrograde motion it became direct. And on the 23rd of January I observed RA 51°46' with a declination of 17°8'. I have announced this star as a comet. But the fact that the star is not accompanied by any nebulosity and that its movement is very slow and rather uniform, has caused me many times to seriously consider that perhaps it might be something better than a comet. I would be very careful, however, about making this conjecture public. When I have gathered a greater number of observations I will then attempt a calculation of the elements. In the meantime it would please me very much if you took it upon yourself to observe it, informing me of your thoughts on it and of any one else who may have seen it.

The following day he wrote a similar letter to Bode in Berlin. Piazzi continued to observe the moving light until February 11, when poor weather and illness forced him to discontinue observations.

Photo. 1–2. *Giuseppe Piazzi (1746–1826), Italian monk and astronomer, director of Palermo Observatory from 1790–1826. In the 1790s Piazzi used the favorable climate at Europe's southernmost observatory to plot the positions of all the fixed stars. For this purpose he had commissioned a 1.5 meter vertical circle from Ramsden, and with it discovered the first asteroid, Ceres, on 1 January 1801. In 1803 he published his first star catalogue containing 6,748 stars, and followed this in 1813 with another 7,646 stars. (Mary Lea Shane Archives of the Lick Observatory).*

Photo. 1–3. *Karl Gauss (1777–1855), German mathematician who devoted much of his time between 1800 and 1810 to astronomical problems. In 1801 he solved the orbit of Ceres, permitting it to be found again. He also worked on the theory of perturbations, which was used by Le Verrier and Adams in their calculations toward the discovery of Neptune. (Mary Lea Shane Archives of the Lick Observatory).*

Bode received Piazzi's letter on 20 March and soon concluded that the search for the missing planet was over. "Unabashed by speculative scorn, he had scarcely read Piazzi's letter, when he concluded that it referred to the precise body in question." (Clerke, 1887). The discovery announcement was made in the *Monthly Correspondence*, which was edited by Baron von Zach, in the summer of 1801.

But the astronomers of the day were presented with a conundrum—the newly discovered planet was lost. Piazzi, anxious to publish the first orbit himself, was reluctant to send positional data to anyone. On 30 May Bode received a second letter from Piazzi simply telling him that the 'comet' had been followed until 11 February. Piazzi did send his data to Joseph-Jerome Lalande in Paris, however. After receiving it, on 31 May Lalande's colleague Johann Burckhardt calculated both circular and parabolic orbits for the object. In mid-June Burckhardt first determined an elliptical orbit.

Bode did not receive Piazzi's observations until 11 June, and Piazzi's own analysis was published shortly thereafter, concluding it had a circular orbit with a mean distance of 2.69 AU. Ephemerides for the latter part of 1801 were published by Burckhardt, Olbers and Piazzi,

but they ranged over 5° in the sky. The mathematical problem posed by the object Piazzi had named Ceres was of the sort which Newton had said belonged to the most difficult in astronomy.

Among the subscribers to von Zach's journal was a young man in Brunswick, Karl Friedrich Gauss. Perhaps the greatest mathematical genius in history, Gauss easily developed the techniques necessary to compute the orbit of Ceres. In November, he published the orbital elements: semi-major axis 2.77 AU; eccentricity 0.08; inclination 11°. How did he do it? Remarkably enough, we don't know! According to Taff (1985), Gauss did not use the method he later published. This is how Gauss himself expressed his solution to the problem in 1809.

Some ideas occurred to me in the month of September in the year 1801 which seemed to point to the solution of the great problem. Just about this time the report of the new planet, discovered on the first day of January of that year with the telescope at Palermo, was the subject of universal conversation; and soon afterwards the observations made by that distinguished astronomer Piazzi from the above

Photo. 1–4. *William Herschel (1738–1822), a German-born English astronomer who discovered Uranus in 1781 from his backyard in the city of Bath. Herschel's solar system research included the discovery of two satellites of Uranus and two of Saturn. In 1801 he conducted the first scientific investigation of Ceres and Pallas-objects that he coined the term 'asteroids' to describe. (Mary Lea Shane Archives of the Lick Observatory).*

Photo. 1–5. *Franz von Zach (1754–1832), Hungarian baron and director of Seeberg Observatory. Prompted by his belief in Bode's Law, which predicted a planet between Mars and Jupiter, von Zach had already computed most of the orbital elements of the missing planet by 1791. Unsuccessful in his search for it, he organized a group popularly known as the Celestial Police. In 1805 they published their only report, bearing the seal of the society (seen below), on the first three asteroids. (Mary Lea Shane Archives of the Lick Observatory).*

date to the eleventh of February were published. Nowhere in the annals of astronomy do we meet with so great an opportunity, and a greater one could hardly be imagined, for showing most strikingly, the value of this problem, than in this crisis and urgent necessity, when all hopes of discovering in the heavens this planetary atom, among innumerable small stars after the lapse of nearly a year, rested solely upon a sufficiently approximate knowledge of its orbit to be based upon these very few observations. Could I ever have found a more seasonable opportunity to test the practical value of my conceptions, that now in employing them for the determination of the orbit of the planet Ceres, which during these forty-one days had described a geocentric arc of only three degrees, and after the lapse of a year must be looked for in a region of the heavens very remote from that in which it was last seen? This first application of the method was made in the month of October, 1801, and the first clear night, when the planet was sought for as directed by the numbers deduced from it, restored the fugitive to observation. Three other new planets,

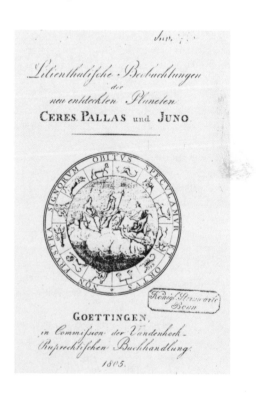

subsequently discovered, furnished new opportunities for examining and verifying the efficiency and generality of the method. Several astronomers wished me to publish the methods employed in these calculations immediately after the second discovery of Ceres; but many things prevented my complying at the time with these friendly solicitations. The methods first employed have undergone so many and such great changes, that scarcely any trace of resemblance remains between the method in which the orbit of Ceres was computed, and the form given in this work.

Armed with the search ephemeris, several astronomers began to search for Ceres. Baron von Zach had at his disposal the finest observatory in Germany, financed by his patron, Duke Ernst II of Saxe-Gotha who had hired von Zach on the recommendation of von Bruhl. Seeberg Observatory was a massive construction of native stone divided into five compartments ranged side by side, the central one being surmounted by a tower with a revolving dome. The instruments included a transitcircle, a Dollond achromatic 4-inch refractor, a zenith-sector and a pendulum clock. The main instruments were mounted upon piers of porphyry which were based upon the bedrock of the mountain. (Armitage, 1949). It was here that von Zach made the first recovery of Ceres on 7 December 1801. As there were four small stars near the predicted position, he was not able to confirm the rediscovery. A break in the clouds on 18 December allowed another look. One of the stars was missing, but it was not until the early morning hours of 1 January 1802 that von Zach was able to conclusively identify the elusive Ceres (Von Zach, 1802). Independently, Ceres was found again by Olbers on 1 January 1802. Thus it is this third date most often quoted as the rediscovery date of Ceres (Combes, 1975).

The story of the missing planet might have ended here. Gauss had his pension increased by the Duke of Brunswick, enabling him to marry in 1805 at age 28. He was already established as the greatest mathematician in the world, and went on to even greater triumphs when he laid the foundations of the theory of electro-magnetism and invented the electric telegraph. "If the minor planets have nothing else to their credit, let it always be remembered that they converted Gauss from a mathematician to an astronomer, to the lasting benefit of our science," declared J. G. Porter (1950), president of the British Astronomical Association.

Bode was vindicated in his belief of the existence of another planet, and lived another quarter century. Baron von Zach had no need to organize his planet search committee, as the lone object of his search had already been found by accident. On behalf of the King of Sicily, the Secretary of State wrote Piazzi commending him on his discovery. Instead of striking a commemorative medal, as the King had originally proposed, the letter agrees to buy another instrument for the Palermo observatory.

Photo. 1–6. *Heinrich Wilhelm Olbers (1758– 1840), German doctor and astronomer. He is best known for his formulation of Olber's Paradox: if we accept an infinite, uniform Universe, why is the whole sky not covered by stars shining as brightly as our Sun? Olbers discovered the second asteroid, Pallas, and the fourth, Vesta within seven years of attending von Zach's first meeting of the Celestial Police. He also developed the first theory of the origin of the asteroids. (Mary Lea Shane Archives of the Lick Observatory).*

Olbers continued to observe Ceres in order to provide Gauss with enough positional data for a more precise orbital calculation. On 28 March 1802, he discovered another moving object near to Ceres in the sky. A second planet, named Pallas, had been found. Gauss, rather disparagingly, referred to Ceres & Pallas as "a couple of clods of dirt which we call planets" (Bell, 1937).

Nonetheless, he spent a great deal of time on Pallas. In 1804 the Paris Academy offered a prize of a gold medal weighing one kilogram for a theory of the perturbations on Pallas by the planets. The closing date was set for 1806, but as no one solved the problem it was extended to 1 October 1816 for double the prize. In the event, the prize was never awarded, although Gauss did solve the problem after the deadline. Marsden (1977) details how he did it.

During the last quarter of 1810 Gauss made a numerical integration of the orbit of Pallas as perturbed by Jupiter over the interval 1803 to 1811. The integrations were performed in the orbital elements themselves, the equations for the variations of the elements being written in the so-called Gauss form, i.e., in terms of components of the forces rather than partial derivatives of the single disturbing function, for the force component equations are easier to evaluate numerically.

Gauss realized that by studying the motion of Pallas over only eight years he had not really solved the problem, and in August 1811 he began his most extensive work of producing a theory of 'general perturbations' on Pallas, valid for all time. This basically involved a double harmonic analysis of the force components in the variation-of-elements equations, the components being evaluated at 12 points for the position of Pallas in its mean orbit and at 48 points for the relative positions of Pallas and Jupiter. The first iteration for the solution occupied him some two months, and as in the case of Ceres, an approximate 2:5 resonance with Jupiter yielded some of the largest terms (although the 1:2 terms were of the same order). In the second iteration, begun in April 1812 but not completed until July 1813, he also considered the effect of the extremely close 7:18 resonance with Jupiter, and his final expressions for the elements contained a total of more than 800 terms (Brendel 1906). Gauss then had to calculate the perturbations by Mars, but he had his student Friedrich Bernhard Nicolai calculate those by Saturn; and with the help of Johann Franz Encke general tables for the motion of Pallas were completed at the end of 1817.

The most careful observer of these first two asteroids was William Herschel. Piazzi became one of Herschel's most enthusiastic correspondents, and once visited his observatory at Slough, near Eton in England, where "he had the doubtful privilege of falling off the ladder at the side of Herschel's great reflector and breaking his arm." (Asimov, 1972). It is interesting to note that the first discoverer of a planet since prehistoric times met the first discoverer of an asteroid (Cunningham, 1984a).

Herschel was the first to write a scientific paper on these newly discovered objects, which he proceeded to name. Both Ceres and Pallas, he wrote, "resemble small stars so much as hardly to be distinguished from them. From this, their asteroidal appearance, if I may use that expression, therefore, I shall take my name, and call them Asteroids; reserving for myself, however, the liberty of changing that name, if another, more expressive of their nature, should occur." (Herschel, 1802). But while Herschel was actively observing the new planets from England, Von Zach was fuming, as expressed in a letter he wrote 9 April 1802 from Seeberg (near Berlin in Prussia, now East Germany).

Oh, if no one in our fatherland discovers and observes Ceres and Pallas, I will feel ashamed to be a Hungarian baron, because they're being observed in Poland! From Sniadecki I received the observation of Ceres from Cracau and now I hope to receive some on Pallas from there. But won't any arrive from Ofen, Tirnau, Erlau or Carlsstadt? Will Ceres and Pallas remain invisible for my fellow wise and worthy countrymen? Oh! If I could only get to Ofen on a magic wish, just for one minute, so that I could set up and focus the telescope on these two curious visitors of heavens (Balazs & Szecsenyi-Nagy, 1984).

But Poland was not the only 'foreign' country where the asteroids excited professional interest. In 1802, the Russian celestial mechanician V.I. Shugert published a work on the perturbations on the orbit of Ceres caused by Jupiter. It was the first of many investigations into the perturbed movement of asteroids.

Within five years two more asteroids were found— Harding, observing at Schroeter's observatory, found Juno in Pisces on 1 September 1804; and Olbers found his second asteroid on 29 March 1807. Named Vesta, it proved to be even brighter than the three which preceded it. So bright, in fact, that Schroeter made the first observation of an asteroid without a telescope. "We both afterwards saw this planet several times, with our naked eyes, when the sky was clear, and when it was surrounded by smaller invisible stars, which precluded all possibility of mistaking it for another. This proves how very like the intense light of this planet is to that of a fixed star." (Schroeter, 1807).

In a letter to Bode, dated 3 April 1807, Olbers tells of his discovery and describes his search technique.

With great delight, dearest friend, I hasten to tell you that I was lucky enough to find yet another planet belonging to the family of asteroids, on 29th March. This time, however, the discovery was no mere chance. According to my hypothesis concerning asteroids, I have, as you know, concluded that all asteroids, of which there are probably a large number, must pass through the northwestern portion of the constellation Virgo and the western portion of the Whale. Regularly each month, therefore, I checked a particular section of these two constellations, having first thoroughly acquainted myself with the star content and choosing whichever happened to be suitably placed.

Olbers' selection of these two regions of the sky was based on his theory that the asteroids were fragments of a planet which had been burst asunder (Olbers, 1803). Even though the fragments were at various inclinations, they all diverged from the same point. Thus, according to his theory, they ought to have two common points of reunion, nodes, through which all the fragments must pass. Even though he continued his search until 1816, no more fragments were found.

Olbers' theory was at odds with one propounded by Huth (1807). He believed that "these tiny planets were as old as all the others, and it seemed more probable to him that the matter which formed the planets had coagulated into many small spheres in the space between Mars and Jupiter. In fact he would not be surprised if Ceres and Pallas had at least ten co-planets."

Meanwhile, very little was known about the asteroids aside from their orbits. The Scottish physicist Sir David Brewster, writing in 1811, proposed a particularly imaginative theory to account for the supposed atmospheres around Ceres and Pallas.

> It is a very singular circumstance, that while two of the fragments, Juno and Vesta, are entirely free from any nebulous appearance, the other two fragments, Ceres and Pallas, are surrounded with a nebulosity of a most remarkable size. Now, the Comet of 1770, if it is lost, must have been attracted by one of the planets whose orbit is crossed, and must have imparted to its nebulous mass; but none of the old planets have received any addition to their atmospheres; consequently, it is highly probable that the Comet has passed near Ceres and Pallas, and imparted to them those immense atmospheres which distinguish them from all the other planets. (Moore, 1976).

This 'nebulosity' was originally reported by Schroeter, and it is interesting to note that it was still accepted as fact as late as the mid-nineteenth century (Alexander, 1851).

The next few decades was a very sad period in the history of asteroid astronomy. Schroeter's observatory, where the so-called 'celestial police' had first met in 1800, was destroyed along with all his unpublished observations in 1813. It fell victim to an invading French army, whose soldiers plundered the brass telescopes, believing them to be made of gold (Moore, 1983). Before the next asteroid was discovered, all the main characters in the discovery of the first asteroids had died: Schroeter (1816), Herschel (1822), Bode and Piazzi (1826), Von Zach (1832), Harding (1834), and Olbers (1840).

The fifth asteroid was not discovered until 1845, when Karl Hencke, a postmaster in Driesen, Germany, found Astraea. By 1850 ten were known, and many astronomers thought the list was nearly complete. After recording the discovery of three more asteroids in 1851, the Council of the Royal Astronomical Society stated that such a rate of increase among the known members of the solar system "can hardly be expected to continue very long.

The continuing search for asteroids in the 19th century was largely left to amateur astronomers. A case in point is Hermann Goldschmidt. He was an artist living in Paris, and, at the age of 45, attended a lecture on astronomy by the great Le Verrier. His enthusiasm aroused, Goldschmidt purchased a two-inch telescope with the proceeds of the sale of his portrait of Galileo. Using the Berlin star charts, he discovered the 21st asteroid, Lutetia, in 1852. He went on to find a dozen more.

Scientists in Russia concentrated on devising theories of motion of the minor planets. Noted among them are D.N. Perevoschikov in Moscow, M.F. Khandrikov and R.F. Fogel in Kiev, D.I. Dubyago in Kazan, O.A. Baklund, G. Tsepel, and P.F. Barkevich in Odessa who in 1868 published his theory of the motion of Juno. (Putilin 1953)

Meanwhile, the foundations were being laid for the physical investigation of asteroids. In 1868, Daniel Kirkwood noted several gaps in the asteroid belt. Even now, the origin and dynamics of the Kirkwood gaps is an important and active area of asteroid study (see Chapter 5).

In Germany, the first spectroscopic studies of asteroids were being conducted by Hermann Vogel (1874), not to be confused with his brother Eduard, who was an enthusiastic computer of comet and asteroid orbits (Ashbrook, 1970b). Vogel's visual observations led him to infer that Vesta had an atmosphere.

> Of the planetoids, I have, until now, observed spectroscopically only Vesta and Flora. Vesta was observed on February 3, 1872. The spectrum was altogether very weak. With relatively large accuracy, only one line could be recorded, which after repeated measurements was identified as F. In addition and as confirmation of the observation, the mark in the telescope was focused on the dark line in the spectrum of Vesta and then was adjusted to Alpha Leonis, where the mark showed exactly the wide line of hydrogen in the spectrum of this star. In addition, two lines in the spectrum of Vesta were perceived, one of which was quite dark and wide, the other being weaker and less wide. The wavelength of the first line is 577 microns, and the second 518 microns. It may be that the occurrence of these lines may be a result of the planet's surrounding atmosphere. Flora was observed spectroscopically at the time of opposition on a few evenings in October, 1873. Nothing besides a weak continuum spectrum, in which the colors could hardly be made out, could be recognized.

The first extensive photometric observations of asteroids were made by Henry Parkhurst at Harvard Observatory in the 1870's, 80's and 90's. Despite his careful observations, Parkhurst, who was employed as a stenographer for the Superior Court of New York City, found no light variability in any asteroid. A variation he suspected in the light of 40 Harmonia he attributed to the asteroid "passing over a chimney on the three evenings in question." (Parkhurst, 1890).

And E. E. Barnard (1895) published the results of his micrometer observations of the first four asteroids. While the diameters he derived are known to be too small, they were the best available until the 1970's.

The rapid growth in the numbers of asteroids, and the ensuing work involved in computing their orbits before the days of computers, led to the first specific plan of cooperation among professional astronomers. In 1863, it was agreed that the Observatory of Paris should observe the asteroids from full moon to new moon, while the Observatory of Greenwich was assigned those from new moon to full moon. In the following year, the National Observatory in Washington joined in the effort (Dreyer and Turner, 1923; Gould, 1856).

9

Photo. 1–7. *Maximilian Wolf (1863–1932), German astronomer, director of Konigstuhl Observatory from 1896–1932. By applying his photographic expertise to astronomy, Wolf discovered more than 200 asteroids. His most important discovery was made in September, 1903, when he found 588 Achilles, the first Trojan asteroid. (Mary Lea Shane Archives of the Lick Observatory).*

Even so, many astronomers felt the asteroids were more of a nuisance than they were worth. "Their supervision," wrote Rudolph Wolf, "requires an unduly prodigious amount of time. In fact even now the value of a new discovery is hardly in proper proportion to the additional work it causes." (Ley, 1963). They came to be called vermin of the skies, probably from a German astronomer who called it a "plague of minor planets." By 1890, 300 were known—literally a "celestial cluster within our own solar system" (Kirkwood, 1892)—but the second phase in asteroid research was just about to begin.

PHASE 2: The Photographic Search

The second phase was begun by Max Wolf of Heidelberg in 1891. Using an astronomical camera, he made a total of 231 discoveries, eclipsing the pre-photographic record of 53 asteroids set by Johann Palisa in Vienna (Pilcher and Meeus, 1973).

Wolf's method was described in some detail by Holden (1896). Using portrait lenses of five and six inch aperture, with foci of 25 and 30 inches, respectively, Wolf exposed plates in duplicate. Plate A was exposed for one hour, then Plate B was exposed for another hour, and finally Plate A was exposed for an hour. In this way, part of the space

occupied by the trail of the asteroid on A was vacant on B, and vice versa.

To compare the plates, both were laid on a retouching frame, on top of one another, and examined with a magnifying glass. For asteroids brighter than magnitude 12.6, Wolf found that a field of 70 square degrees was available under good conditions.

While Wolf proceeded apace to reap a rich harvest of celestial rocks, others began using the new photographic process. In 1898 a landmark discovery was made by G.Witt, director of the Urania Observatory in Berlin, and Felix Linke, who was in charge of checking the position of the guide star. The story was related by Linke 50 years later (Linke, 1948):

> In 1896 Witt began to photograph the minor planets. He did not intend to discover additional bodies—his scientific goal was to find known planetoids which had not been observed for some time, so that he could provide material for a better determination of their orbits, a job which was handled with great zeal and diligence by the Berliner Astronomisches Recheninstitut (now the Kopernikus-Institut). Witt had only a rather primitive instrument for this purpose. The clockwork drive worked middling well only for certain areas in the sky, the areas we used to photograph, but even there it was hardly possible to neglect checking on the guide star for more than a few seconds. Its position had to be constantly corrected. I had volunteered for this job in 1897 and did many of the exposures myself. We exposed our plates for two hours and always developed them at once so that they could be checked the following morning ...'
>
> For the purpose of finding Planetoid Eunike (No. 185) which had not been seen for years, we centered the plate on the star β Aquarius during the night from August 13 to August 14, 1898, and I exposed the plate for two hours. Eunike had to be in that area. The temperature was tropical even during the night, the only refreshingly cool place was the dark room. Next morning, after the plates had dried, the plate was checked and it was found that both Eunike and another known planetoid had been registered, so that the goal of this particular observation had been reached. But a third and longer line drew our attention. It was so long (0.4 millimeters) that we first thought it to be a flaw in the emulsion, but it was too clean to be that, hence we suspected an actual object with a high rate of apparent motion, a comet. Since the evening of August 14 was again clear, we could look for the suspicious object with the 12–inch refractor of the Urania Observatory, at that time the largest telescope anywhere in Prussia. A few quick mea-

surements proved that it had such an unusually fast movement as had never been observed for a Minor Planet. Its appearance spoke against the thought that it might be a comet; it was a tiny dot of light without any appendages ...

The Observatory at Kiel, at that time the central clearing house for new astronomical discoveries, attached the temporary designation 1898DQ on the new asteroid. When its orbit was announced a mere 13 days after discovery, it surprised everyone—its perihelion was far inside the orbit of Mars. The first Mars-crossing asteroid had been discovered. To emphasize its unique nature, the new object was given a male name—Eros.

Eros was also the object of the next major advance in our knowledge of asteroids. Early in 1901, Oppolzer discovered that its brightness varied, although its period of rotation was not accurately known for some time. It was announced as a few hours by Oppolzer, as about five hours by Cerulli, and as two and half hours by Deichmuller. The double period, corresponding to about five hours, was confirmed by Bailey (1913), who also found five other asteroids to be variable.

Yet a third line of research is associated with this remarkable asteroid, which has been called the Halley of minor planets by Brian Marsden. In 1912, A. R. Hinks was awarded the Gold Medal of the Royal Astronomical Society for his determination of the solar parallax from observations of Eros. The parallax was described as the most important constant in astronomy "as giving the scale of the solar system and the base line from which the stellar universe is surveyed." (Dyson, 1912).

Meanwhile, advances were being made in the photographic and theoretical branches of asteroid work. Joel Metcalf (1906, 1907) developed a photographic technique "just the opposite of Wolf's method, for he follows the stars so that they are points on the photographic plate and the asteroids are trails, while I have followed the asteroids and the stars are trails."

Metcalf found that the method produced sharp images, and provided a gain over the old method of two magnitudes. It also permitted more accurate measurement of the object's position with reference to comparison stars.

On the theoretical side, Henry Russell (1906) published a classic paper on the light variations of asteroids. The mathematical foundation for all future asteroid research on light curves, it showed that it is always possible (theoretically) to determine the position of an asteroid's equator, but it is not possible to determine its shape. "We can determine by inspection of its light curves whether or not they can be accounted for by its rotation alone," wrote Russell, and "the light curve of a planet at phases remote from opposition may aid in determining the markings on its surface." These very topics still account for a great deal of modern asteroid work (see Chapter 8).

The year 1906 was particularly memorable for celestial rock hounds for another reason. On February 22, Wolf discovered an asteroid which moved in the same orbit as Jupiter, 55.5° preceding the giant planet. It was recog-

nized by C. V. Charlier (1906) of Lund Observatory that this object, named Achilles, was in a stable orbit first postulated by Lagrange in 1772. Before the year was out, another such asteroid was found, this one leading Jupiter by 55.5°. It was named Patroclus, thus beginning the family of Trojan asteroids (see Chapter 15).

The following decade saw a flowering of statistical analysis which the large number of photographic discoveries had made possible. Samuel Barton (1916) published a statistical survey of the elements of 806 asteroids. Kester and Alter (1919) suggested an analogy between the solar system and the atom, "the grouping of orbits of electrons, as assumed by Bohr, may be due to perturbations in some manner similar to those that Jupiter produces on the asteroids."

But the most important analysis was done by Kiyotsugu Hirayama (1918), who discovered that asteroids are really rather sociable animals after all, not the vermin that most astronomers regarded them as. Hirayama's families, groups of asteroids probably of common origin, have been key to our understanding of the evolutionary history of asteroids and the solar system (see Chapter 11).

Photo. 1-8. *Yrjo Vaisala (1891–1971), Finnish astronomer who began a survey of asteroids at Turku Observatory in 1935, of which about 100 have received permanent designations. Vaisala was a skilled optician: he improved methods for testing large objectives, and did some early work on multiple-mirror telescope design. By 1957, he had discovered 808 minor planets.*

Working at Simeis Observatory in the Soviet Union, P.F. Shajn became the first woman to discover a minor planet. The 1928 find received the designation 1112 Polonia.

The most important development in the 1920's was N. T. Bobrovnikoff's study of asteroid spectra in 1929. In the photographic region the spectra of 12 asteroids were shown to be deficient compared to GO stars. He found Ceres to be bluer than Vesta, in agreement with modern results.

1932 was another landmark year for asteroid discoveries. Amor was found in March, and Apollo was discovered in April. Prototypes of the Apollo-Amor class, these were the first asteroids found whose orbits crossed that of Earth. In a prescient statement, M. Davidson (1932) wrote that the "discovery of planet 1932 HA (Apollo) will assist in throwing some additional light on the past history of our solar system."

In 1935, Yrjo Vaisala began an asteroid survey at Turku University in Finland that was to last until 1957. Vaisala, who died in 1971, discovered 808 asteroids, only some of which have since received permanent designations. All such discoveries are distinguished by the letter T. Recently, some 50 asteroids were given Finnish names, honoring the work of Vaisala and Liisi Oterma.

The technique that would begin to unlock the solar system's history ushered in the third phase of asteroid research before the decade was out.

PHASE 3: Photoelectric Photometry

Aside from inconclusive measurements made on the first four asteroids by Calder (1936), the first photoelectric light curve of an asteroid was published by F. E. Roach and Laurence Stoddard of the Steward Observatory, University of Arizona in 1938. Appropriately enough, the object of their work was the most studied of all asteroids, Eros. Using a photoelectric quartz cell, galvanometer and amplifier, they found the predicted amplitude of 1.5 mag.

But it was not until 1949 that a systematic photometric study of asteroids was organized by Gerard Kuiper. Begun at McDonald Observatory in Texas, it consisted of two parts:

1. A systematic survey with a 10-inch $f/7$ telescope, to obtain approximate magnitudes of all asteroids down to magnitude 16.5;

2. Detailed photometry of all asteroids brighter than about 10. (Groeneveld & Kuiper, 1954, Kuiper et al, 1958).

The Indiana Asteroid Program, which for more than a decade provided photographic magnitudes of asteroids, was also initiated by F.K. Edmondson in 1949.

The late 1940's also saw a rebirth of the very practical problems of keeping track of the 1600-odd asteroids. "The minor planet programme was very badly disorganized" at

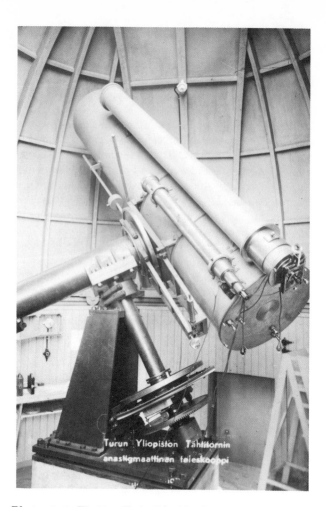

Photo. 1–9. *The 50cm Turku Schmidt telescope used in Vaisala's asteroid survey. Discoveries were made using the "double point method." A photograph of a star field was taken through the Schmidt; a short while later, the telescope was shifted slightly and a second exposure was taken on the same plate. Each object was then represented by a double point: stars appeared as vertical pairs and asteroids as pairs at some angle due to their movement.*

the end of World War II (Herget, 1950). "The Rechen Institute had moved from Berlin to Heidelberg, but about half of its staff and material remained in the Russian zone. The observatories formerly engaged in this work were not at all able to return to it; and at first the quality of photographic plates was poor or a supply unobtainable." The International Astronomical Union established a minor planet center at Cincinnati Observatory, which began publication of the *Minor Planet Circulars* in 1947. The Institute at Leningrad also began publishing the *Ephemerides of Minor Planets* in 1947, and both these publications continue to be of great value in the 1980's.

The relationship of asteroids to other smaller solar system objects also began to be addressed at this time. "The existence of the huge cloud of comets finds a natural explanation if comets (and meteorites) are considered as minor planets escaped, at an early stage of the planetary system, from the ring of asteroids." (Oort, 1950).

The first occultation of a star by an asteroid (Vesta) was made by Gordon Taylor in 1958, and an attempt to develop a classification system for asteroids was proposed by Miller (1956).

The 1960's saw a continuation of the photoelectric and theoretical investigations begun in the previous decade. The state of our knowledge about asteroids was well reviewed by Newburn (1961), just at the time when space missions to asteroids were first being seriously considered. But the most significant developments were in technology—computers and more sophisticated instruments set the stage for the next phase of asteroid research.

PHASE 4: The Educated Asteroid

So much is known about asteroids that many of them have taken on individual identities. They have been scrutinized by the most sophisticated astronomical instruments, analyzed by the most powerful computers, and categorized by the most diligent clerks of science. Even Scrooge would be pleased at the thoroughness of it all.

The fourth phase of asteroid research began in 1968, when Icarus was used in a game of celestial boomerang—radar signals were sent out, bounced off Icarus, and returned to Earth. This represented our first contact, albeit indirect, with an asteroid.

Important new advances were made yearly. Spectrophotometry of asteroids was begun in 1969 with Vesta, and the reflectivity of an asteroid, Icarus, was first determined with the polarimetric method in 1970. The first infrared diameter of an asteroid was also made in that year.

The first international conference on asteroids was held in Tucson in 1971. The study of asteroids had come of age. There were about 140 participants at the five-day meeting, which became the 12th Colloquium of the International Astronomical Union. An important outgrowth of the conference was a book, *Physical Studies of Minor Planets* (ed. Gehrels), the first scientific book on asteroids.

Classification of the asteroids into the two broad classes C and S was developed in the early 1970's by Bowell and Chapman. By the end of the decade six types had been recognized.

Ceres had the distinction of being the first asteroid from which radio emissions were detected, in the year 1973. The 1970's also saw an explosive growth in UBV data on asteroids—from only 50 objects in 1971 to 735 by 1979. And in 1976 the first speckle interferometry of an asteroid (Vesta) was conducted.

The first Aten asteroid was found in 1976, the distant asteroid-like object Chiron was discovered in 1977, and a spate of observations in the late 1970's led to renewed speculation on the existence of satellites of asteroids.

This renaissance in the scientific investigation of asteroids culminated at the end of the decade in the second asteroid conference, also held in Tucson. The result was a 1,181 page opus, *Asteroids* (ed. Gehrels), by far the most important and comprehensive book ever published in this

Photo. 1–10. *Gordon Taylor, British astronomer at the Royal Greenwich Observatory, former president of the British Astronomical Association. In 1958 he made the first observation of the occultation of a star by an asteroid, Vesta. Taylor's predictions of asteroid occultations are now used to plan major observing expeditions.*

field of study. The prime reference source on asteroids, the Tucson Revised Index of Asteroid Data (TRIAD), was included in the book. Maintained at the University of Arizona, TRIAD contained all known physical parameters for the 2,118 asteroids known at the time.

By the end of the 1970's technical advances made photoelectric photometers available to astronomers outside the professional community, thus aiding the growth of light curve and rotational data on the asteroids (Hall & Genet, 1984).

This contribution is recognized in a cogent summary of the latest asteroid research presented at the Indian meeting of the IAU by Chapman (1985). But technical advances were not limited to earthbased observatories, setting the stage for the fifth phase of asteroid research.

PHASE 5: Telescopes and Spacecraft

The current phase of asteroid studies was launched on 26 January 1983, when the Infrared Astronomy Satellite (IRAS) was placed into orbit around the Earth. Detailed data from IRAS was released in 1986, and will help us to better understand the asteroid belt, now numbering more than 3,700 bodies (Fig. 1-2).

13

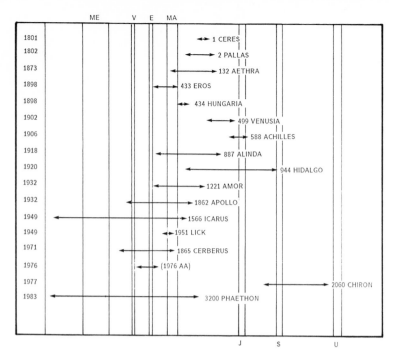

Fig. 1–2. *The expansion of the range of orbits covered by the asteroids since they were discovered in 1801. The range of orbits covered by planets from Mercury to Uranus are indicated along the bottom. Adapted from Combes & Meeus (1976).*

Preliminary discoveries include 3200 Phaethon, the parent of the Geminid meteor shower, and three dust rings in the asteroid belt that may be created by asteroidal collisions (Robinson, 1984). Beyond IRAS, which ceased operations in late 1983, is the much-heralded Space Telescope. Although little time will likely be available for asteroid work with it, the Space Telescope could confirm or deny the existence of asteroidal satellites.

Like the Space Telescope, Hipparcos is scheduled for launch in the late 1980's. An astrometric satellite, Hipparcos will also be able to search for binary asteroids. In situ measurements, in the form of a fly-by, orbiter, lander or even sample-return mission will increase our understanding by orders of magnitude.

Mining the asteroids, and eventually a manned mission to one of these "clods of dirt", will open the sixth phase early in the 21st century. Perhaps some 19th century astronomers would be pleased to know that the heavens may yet be less cluttered with vermin.

ORIGINS 2

They are small planets; whether the fragments of a stupendous world shattered by internal convulsions or external violence, or formed as other planets were, no one can tell.

John Davis, 1868

I view the asteroid belt as a kind of zoo, where planetesimals from all parts of the solar system have been preserved (in a unique dynamically safe refuge). Understanding how these 'rare beasts' arrived in this refuge will provide insight into the dynamics of accretion.

Eugene Shoemaker, 1984

Measured against the 15 billion year history of the Universe, the Sun and its attendant planets, comets and asteroids are still youngsters—grandchildren, if you will, of the massive stars that died more than 5 billion years ago. But it is the product of those ancient nuclear fires— metals and radioactive elements—that became the material from which were created the asteroids.

The following scenario of the formation of the asteroids and meteorites is based on interviews with Drs. Stuart Weidenschilling, Donald Davis and Charles Sonett, and papers by Davis *et al* (1985), Greenberg & Chapman (1984), Chapman & Davis (1975), Weidenschilling (1977), Shoemaker (1977), Herbert & Sonett (1979), Heppenheimer (1978), Napier & Dodd (1974), Opik (1976), Narayan & Goldstein (1985), and Cameron (1979). While many of the details are speculative, and a fully quantitative understanding is not yet available, the concepts involved are fairly well established.

An interstellar cloud, possibly several light years across, began collapsing after being shocked by the explosion of a nearby supernova. Matter would form a thin disk in the mid-plane of this primitive solar nebula for about 10 million years, after which the inflow of material would end. When the density of this material reached a critical value, it became gravitationally unstable, allowing small bits of matter to contract to form larger bodies a few kilometers across.

By the time these proto-asteroids, known as planetesimals, formed, the Sun had already grown to its full mass, perhaps 30% more massive than it is now. Meanwhile, the planetesimals were growing by accretion. Originally, there was up to 2 Earth masses of material in the asteroid belt. The total mass is now 1,000 times smaller, only 5% of a lunar mass. Accretion time of how long it takes to grow a

body the size of Ceres depends on how much mass there is in the region for Ceres and other bodies to accrete.

If you take the asteroids as they exist today and smear those out to 1 km size bodies which then accreted to form the present belt, it would take a time in excess of the age of the solar system to grow a body as large as Ceres. So it seems clear there was on the order of one Earth mass originally, but what happened to the missing mass? Mass removal would have to be completed by the time Vesta's crust formed, which has been estimated at several tens of millions of years after solar system formation. One possible mechanism is to have the asteroidal orbits 'stirred up' and allow them to collisionally erode down to dust size particles where radiation forces, the Poynting-Robertson effect, (which causes small particles to spiral inward from the belt) or other effects could remove the mass. The most recent models, however, indicate only a modest amount of collisional evolution since velocities were pumped up, which suggests it is likely that whatever mechanism stirred up the velocities also depleted the mass in the asteroid belt. What that mechanism was we still don't know.

In the meantime Jupiter was forming by accreting 10 to 20 Earth masses, which resulted in a sudden increase in the perturbations of bodies orbiting in that part of the solar nebula. These planetesimals were thus scattered through the solar system, primarily in the area between Earth and Jupiter.

Collisional studies suggest you could not pump up the velocities of the asteroids to what they are today simply by physical collisions. The way to do it without destroying the asteroids is to have more massive objects pass through the belt and use gravitational perturbations through close encounters to stir up the encounter velocities to their current value of 5 km/sec., from about 1 or 2 km/sec. But

Photo. 2–1. *Charles Sonett of the University of Arizona has been studying possible heating mechanisms in the early stages of asteroidal formation. Passing through a stage similar to T–Tauri stars, the Sun apparently caused two modes of heating in the proto-asteroids, but why some melted and others did not is still unknown.*

timing is crucial. Too early Jupiter formation would have led to premature orbital stirring, preventing asteroid accretion; too late formation would have allowed the planet building process in the belt to proceed much further than it did.

It has been proposed that an Earth-sized planetesimal was flung into the asteroid belt by Jupiter. Its ultimate fate would be to collide with Jupiter or be ejected from the solar system, but it could have made several thousand orbits through the belt before this happened. Pallas likely attained its high (34°) inclination by a close encounter with one of these Jupiter scattered planetesimals (JSPs). Alternatively it may have passed through a secular resonance with Jupiter. Resonances played an important role in the formation of the solar system, being instrumental in the creation of the Kirkwood gaps. Indeed, the presence of Jupiters' mass so near the asteroid region may have prevented the asteroids from accreting to form a fifth planet.

In this early era of solar system formation, the Sun was spinning up to 50 times faster than it is now, with a consequent increase in mass loss via the solar wind. This rapidly rotating Sun also "wound up" the interplanetary magnetic field spiral and induced electromagnetic heating in the proto-asteroids. Recent data indicates that kerogens, tar-like substances common in early carbonaceous material, tend to break down, increasing the temperature

to produce elemental carbon. It forms very thin layers over individual grains. Enough of it will create a conducting path, which can cause heating or turn it off if the conductivity is too high. If something is too conductive it can not be heated— in a toaster it is not the cord that gets hot, but rather the toaster wires. They have more resistance than the cord, so that is where the heat gets dumped.

It is known from the Apollo program that the solar wind can cause very large electrical induction on the Moon. In the proto-asteroids, the rapidly-spinning Sun caused two modes of heating. In eddy current heating, currents were induced in the planetesimals due to being exposed to the fluctuating solar magnetic field. The inside got very hot and essentially formed a short circuit, with the heat moving towards the outer parts of the object with time. As the induced fields grew very large, they exerted a pressure (the magnetic field has a pressure similar to a gas pressure that goes as the square of the field strength) that pushed back on the solar wind, thus limiting the process.

The other mode of heating is a version of unipolar induction. Consider the Faraday disk as an analogy. A copper disk with an axle that is spun with a magnetic field across it will get so hot that it will become luminescent. Put a brush (a current take-off) on the axle and another one on the edge of the disk, so that current flows from the axle through the disk. An asteroid is like the disk, except that it is three-dimensional, and the solar wind provides the two brushes. The field lines will cut through the planet, and closes in the solar wind which is in relative motion and provides the basis for unipolar induction. It will heat the asteroid and create a bow wave in front of it. Depending on the Suns' evolution, this heating mechanism may have been periodic.

The problem changes dramatically if the radioactive nuclide aluminum 26 (half-life 720,000 years) was present. The radioactive heating would add to the electrical heating. As time goes on the electrical heating, looked at by itself in the presence of aluminum, is less than it would be without the aluminum. This is due to the short-circuit effect caused by rising temperature and conductivity. In the interior is a highly conducting material, and outside that is a crust which is not as conducting. So all the heat gets dumped into the crust, therefore tending to quench the temperature.

It has been recognized for many years that the properties of meteorites required a heating episode in ages past. Tschermak (1875) was the first to suggest cosmic volcanism as the heating source; it was not until Fish *et al* (1960) showed radioactivity was the likely heating agent that meteorites were widely believed to have originated in planetesimals of asteroidal dimensions. The effects of this heating are bound up with theories on the formation of the meteorites. Their original locations are called parent bodies, and estimates of the cooling rates of various meteorites permits an estimate of the sizes of their parent bodies. The parent bodies of mesosiderites (a type of stony-iron meteorite) were about 150 km diameter, the pallasite parents 50 km, and the iron parents less than 30 km., perhaps less than 10 km. Consider the formation of an object 100–200 km in diameter, which long ago was destroyed in a collision

Photo. 2-2. *A rendition of two asteroids colliding, by artist and astronomer William Hartmann of the Planetary Science Institute in Tucson. Asteroid collisions over the eons have been of fundamental importance in creating the asteroid belt as we see it today.*

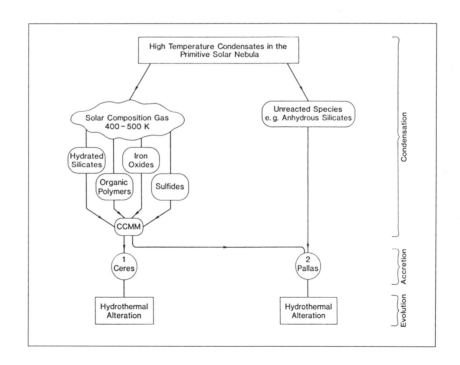

Fig. 2-1. *One likely model of the evolution of Ceres and Pallas. Both formed with a major component of carbonaceous chondrite matrix material (CCMM), but either because of their heliocentric distances or heterogeneities in the solar nebula, Pallas acquired a higher abundance of magnesium-rich silicates than Ceres. Larson et al, 1983.*

that showered the Earth, Moon and Mars with meteorites.

Heating of the chondritic planetesimal causes the metal component to sink, forming a molten core overlaid by a partial melt zone. Liquid basalt rises up through this zone to the surface crust, eventually replacing the original crust by a layer several kilometers thick. After solidifying, this basalt crust becomes denser than the mantle it covers. A large impact will puncture the crust, fracturing it so severely that it will sink to the core in about 12 hours.

These blocks of basalt will float at the core/mantle interface like icebergs at the air/ocean interface, occupying a layer 25 km thick. Liquid iron, at about 1150°C, will then penetrate into the cracks, forming the metallic network seen today in mesosiderite meteorites. On a time scale on the order of 100–1000 years, the mesosiderites cooled to about 750°C, with much slower cooling thereafter. Millions or billions of years later, the mesosiderites were freed from their imprisonment by a collision that totally disrupted their parent body, perhaps leaving only the core to survive as a metallic asteroid.

Modeling of the conditions in the early solar system that permitted formation of the asteroids has come a long way since Olbers, early in the 19th century, proposed the explosion of a fifth planet to explain their presence. One of the major outstanding problems is to explain why some asteroids melted and others did not. Why is it that some asteroids melted and others located in basically the same region did not melt and differentiate? Research is underway to model the conditions that caused different size and different composition asteroids to melt, and that terminated the planet-forming process which was underway in the belt.

METHODS OF INVESTIGATIONS 3

I think that scientists are capable of stating answers to any question that is asked. The problem is whether those answers are believable. I think we basically couldn't believe any answer concerning the physical nature of the asteroids a few years ago.

Clark Chapman, 1978

At the disposal of the modern asteroid researcher are seven techniques that enable almost every aspect of an asteroids physical characteristics to be determined. Two of these, photometry and occultations, are accessible to the amateur astronomer, some of whom have made valuable contributions to our knowledge of the asteroids.

RADIOMETRY

An asteroid of a particular visual magnitude may be either small but highly reflective or large but very dark. However, the infrared brightness is higher in the latter case, both due to the larger size and higher temperature a dark body attains by absorbing more of the incident sunlight.

If the total sunlight striking an asteroid is denoted A, called the Bond albedo, the absorbed insolation is defined as $1 - A$. The standard radiometric model assumes a slowly rotating, spherical, airless body whose surface is in thermal equilibrium with the absorbed insolation. The surface material is assumed to have low thermal conductivity, so that none of the absorbed insolation is re-radiated by the dark hemisphere. And the photometric properties are assumed to match those of the dark, dusty surface (Brown et al, 1982, 1973, 1977).

Making all these assumptions permits a quantitative application of the radiometric method, resulting in diameters and albedos of the asteroids being found. In practice, observations are made at 10 and 20 microns, windows into the infrared that our atmosphere is transparent to at high altitudes like Mauna Kea in Hawaii or Mt. Hopkins near Tucson, sites of major infrared telescopes.

Departures from the standard model have been found (see the Physical Characteristics section of Chapter 13). Eros likely has a rocky surface, which contradicts the low-conductivity assumption, and it is also elongated, in contradiction of the sphericity assumption. Another kind of asteroid that causes problems is the metallic variety, which has high conductivity.

The radiometric method was developed in 1970 by David Allen specifically for Vesta, which thus became the first asteroid with an infrared diameter (Allen, 1970). "A couple of years earlier," wrote Allen (1984), "I happened to look at Vesta through the 12–inch Northumberland refractor at Cambridge University. On that night the asteroid was near opposition, and I could elongate binaries of expected separation 0.3–0.4 arc second. It was, in fact, one of those nights on which dreams are built.

"When Vesta swung into view and settled, I was struck by the fact that it appeared resolved—not quite a disk, but certainly less sharp than the nearby stars. Using Barnard's diameter, I derived 0.3 arc second for its angular diameter—too small to appear resolved in a 12-inch. This experience set me wondering whether a better diameter-measuring technique could be found.

"The fact that the better technique showed Vesta to be larger than Barnard's value actually worried me for a while. Could the preconceptions have colored my analysis? It was with relief that I read Joe Veverka's paper in Icarus, Vol. 15, 1971, page 11, confirming the larger diameter by his polarimetric method." According to Allen, the radiometric method had a rocky beginning. "At first the method wasn't believed. Later it was adopted, in my opinion, rather over-enthusiastically. I was always conscious of the uncertainties, but these were somewhat glossed over in more recent work. The fact that occultation diameters disagree with radiometric values by more than the quoted uncertainties seems to confirm my opinion."

POLARIMETRY

Like the radiometric method, polarimetry can be used to define an asteroid's surface structure, albedo, diameter and compositional class. The method is based on the variation with phase angle of linear polarization of sunlight reflected from the asteroid. The polarization of light was first noted by Thomas Young in 1817, although bees have used the polarization of skylight to help them navigate for eons.

Thinking of light as an electromagnetic wave, it consists of electric and magnetic fields that are perpendicular to each other and the direction of motion. The direction of the electric field is called the polarization direction. Linearly polarized light has a constant polarization direction.

A polarization-phase curve is negative at small angles, but rises linearly at angles greater than 15°. Fig. 3–1 compares the curves of four asteroids with the Moon. The important parameters in such a plot are P_{min}, the depth of the negative branch; α, the inversion angle where the polarization changes sign; and h, the slope of the ascending branch measured in percent per degree. There is a linear relationship between an asteroid's geometric albedo and the slope, h. This slope-albedo law, first discovered in 1967, is the basis of the polarimetric method. It is an empirical, not a physical, law.

The first polarization measurements of asteroids were made photographically by Lyot in 1934, but it was not until 1955 that reliable photoelectric measurements were made by Provin. The modern era of polarimetry was begun by Tom Gehrels and Joseph Veverka in 1968, who observed, respectively, Icarus and Flora.

According to Dollfus and Zellner (1979), P_{min}, α, and h, together with the albedo, are related to surface structure texture. For main belt asteroids, P_{min} is a good indicator of taxonomic type, and can, with some caution, be used as an indicator of albedo. It ranges from 0.3% for high-albedo E–type asteroids to about 2% for dark C–type asteroids. Laboratory work has simulated observed polarization-phase curves with samples of powder grains about 100 microns in diameter, less than 10% being in the form of 10 micron or finer dust particles.

PHOTOMETRY

By far the most widely used technique in asteroid research, photometry is the measurement of light intensities in three broad spectral bands—ultraviolet, blue and visual. The impetus for modern photometric work was begun under the direction of Gerard Kuiper in the 1950's. UBV photometry is now available for about 2,000 asteroids.

The infrared is also covered by photometry, in the so-called J, H and K bands (1.25, 1.65 and 2.2 microns). The first JHK photometry of asteroids was performed by Johnson *et al* (1975) on Ceres, Pallas and Vesta. These IR colors complement UBV photometry (0.3 to 1.1 microns), and are used in conjunction with laboratory data on meteorites. It is particularly useful in the classification of asteroids into their various spectral types.

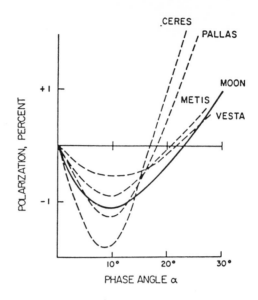

Fig. 3–1. *A comparison of the polarization curves of the Moon and four asteroids. Note that from Earth few asteroids can be observed at phase angles larger than 30 degrees. Veverka, 1971.*

Beginning in the 1970's, it became possible to measure the spectral reflectivity of asteroids from 0.3 to 1.1 microns with higher resolution than in the UBV system. This technique is termed spectrophotometry. No data are yet available on asteroids from .115 to .195 microns (Butterworth & Meadows, 1985), but ultraviolet spectra of 28 asteroids in the range .21 to .32 microns were obtained by the International Ultraviolet Explorer satellite. Data derived from narrow-band photometry are usually expressed in a relative reflectance vs wavelength curve normalized to unit reflectance at 0.56 microns, close to the V bandpass. Smith (1985) gives a list of IR reflectances of 41 asteroids. The technique is based on the principle that the visible colors of minerals are due to the broad absorption bands caused by charge transfers and electronic transition within crystals. The wavelengths of these bands are determined by the structure of the crystal lattice, as well as the identity of the elements in the crystal. The detection and analysis of these bands, often called colorimetry, began in 1929, although the first measurement of the color index (difference between photographic and visual magnitude) of an asteroid was made by Hertsprung (1911).

But the breakthrough came in 1970, when a spectral reflectivity curve of Vesta was obtained by Thomas McCord (Fig. 3–2). The first narrowband spectrophotometry of a non-main-belt asteroid was done in 1973, on the asteroid 1685 Toro, an Apollo. An eight-color survey of 405 asteroids, one of the most important data sets now available to asteroid scientists, was completed by David Tholen in 1984.

Photometry and spectrophotometry provide a wealth of data: magnitude, phase coefficient, albedo, diameter, surface composition, rotation period, shape, pole position. Due to the power of the technique, and the availability of photometers, amateur astronomers have been able to do

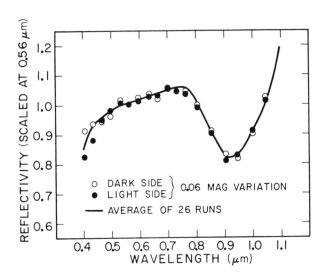

Fig. 3–2. *Spectral reflectivity of 4 Vesta. Individual runs on approximately opposite sides of the asteroid are plotted on the mean curve of 26 runs. Mt. Wilson 152 cm reflector, February 16, 1970. Chapman et al, 1971.*

In the figure: REFLECTIVITY (SCALED AT 0.56 µm) on vertical axis, WAVELENGTH (µm) on horizontal axis.

○ DARK SIDE ⎫ 0.06 MAG VARIATION
● LIGHT SIDE ⎭
— AVERAGE OF 26 RUNS

Year of First Detection	Asteroids	
	Mainbelt	Near-Earth
1968-79	1 Ceres	1566 Icarus
	4 Vesta	1685 Toro
	433 Eros	
		1580 Betulia
1980	7 Iris	1862 Apollo
	16 Psyche	
1981	97 Klotho	1915 Quetzalcoatl
	8 Flora	2100 Ra-Shalom
1982	2 Pallas	
		12 Victoria
		19 Fortuna
		46 Hestia
1983	5 Astraea	1620 Geographos
	139 Juewa	
	356 Liguria	
	80 Sappho	
	694 Ekard	
1984	9 Metis	2101 Adonis
	554 Peraga	
	144 Vibilia	
1985	6 Hebe	1627 Ivar
	41 Daphne	1036 Ganymed
	21 Lutetia	1866 Sisyphus
	33 Polyhymnia	
	84 Klio	
	192 Nausikaa	
	230 Athamantis	
	216 Kleopatra	
	18 Melpomene	

TABLE 3–1
RADAR-DETECTED ASTEROIDS

important work in this field. Telescopes as small as 8–inches can be used on the brightest asteroids, while instruments in the 12– to 16–inch range can rather easily do photometry on asteroids that have scarcely been touched by professional researchers.

RADAR AND RADIO

Radar is an acronym for "radio detecting and ranging", and was first applied to asteroids in 1968, when Icarus made a close approach to the earth. Radar can yield information on the physical and chemical properties of asteroid surfaces, its size, albedo, shape and spin. More than 40 asteroids have been detected by radar, (Table 3–1) and it is expected that 60 will have been observed by the late 1980's (Jurgens and Bender, 1977).

In practice, two giant radio telescopes are used to study asteroids. The Goldstone 210–foot telescope, which made the pioneering detection of Icarus, operates at 3.54 cm. The world's largest radio telescope, the Arecibo 1000–foot dish, uses the 12.6 cm wavelength band. Such large collecting areas are necessary to receive the incredibly weak signal reflected from the asteroid. Typically, the transmitted beam power is 400–450 kw, while the received signal is on the order of 10^{-23} watt. Analysis of this echo power reveals a wealth of information about the asteroid.

Since asteroids rotate, signals reflected from them will exhibit the well-known Doppler shift: the frequency of the signal will be shifted in one direction by the approaching limb, and the opposite direction by the receding limb. Thus, the width of the echo will be broader than the original signal. Measurement of this bandwidth, B, permits an estimate of the asteroids' diameter, D:

$$B = \frac{4\pi D \cos \delta}{\lambda P},$$

where P is the synodic rotation period, δ is the radar's declination, and λ is the operating wavelength (Ostro, 1983; 1985; Fig. 3–3).

The actual signal transmitted by the radio telescopes is in the form of circularly polarized waves. This form of wave is chosen because it permits a determination of the asteroid's geometric albedo. Two parallel receivers measure the echo power in the same rotational sense of circular polarization as transmitted (*sc* sense), as well as echoes in the opposite (*oc*) sense. The geometric albedo, p, is simply:

$$p = \frac{\sigma_{oc} + \sigma_{sc}}{4},$$

where σ is the radar cross section (usually about one-tenth the physical cross section). The ratio of *sc* and *oc* radar cross sections yields the important circular polarization ratio. This ratio is related to the overall degree of centimeter-to-meter scale roughness of the asteroid's surface. Further analysis permits an estimate of the asteroid's bulk density and the metal-to-silicate weight ratio, thus shedding some light on its chemical properties. A related form of inves-

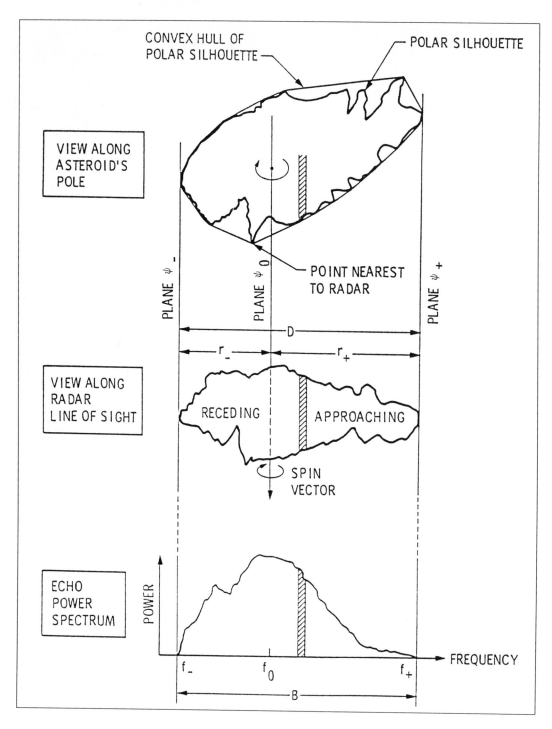

Fig. 3-3. *Geometric relationship between a rotating asteroid and its radar echo power spectrum. The asteroid's diameter is indicated by D, and the full width of the echo received from the asteroid is the bandwidth, B. Ostro, 1985a.*

tigation is radio astronomy. Instead of beaming a signal to the asteroid, large radio telescopes listen to the natural emission coming from it. Only about 10 asteroids have been detected in this way, the first one being Ceres (Briggs, 1973). The wavelengths used in radio asteroid work are somewhat smaller than in radar: between 3 mm and 3.7 cm.

According to Dickel (1979), asteroid radio emission is of thermal origin and arises a few centimeters below the surface. Its intensity depends on the inward conduction of heat from the Sun and the outward transfer of this radiation. Most of this is, as you might expect, in the infrared, but a small fraction is in the form of radio waves.

Radio data provide information on the thermal properties of the surface materials, and some indication of layering. Models designed to fit the observed data are dependent on such things as the thickness of dust overlying a rocky surface. The microwave emission of large main-belt

Photo. 3–1. *The Zeiss 40cm double astrograph at the Crimean Observatory in the Soviet Union. Astrographs are multiple-lens refracting telescopes designed to photograph large areas of the sky in a single exposure. The double astrograph shown here is used by Dr. Chernykh to photograph asteroids.*

asteroids is currently being studied by the Very Large Array radio telescope in New Mexico. The continuum spectra of an asteroid can yield estimates of radius, regolith depth, density and bulk composition (Lowman & Webster, 1984).

SPECKLE INTERFEROMETRY

An interferometer is a device for measuring small angles by using the principle of interference. Since the light from an asteroid can be considered as a wave, alternate reinforcement or cancellation of these waves cause interference, which can be measured to yield an estimate of the size of the object.

First proposed by Labeyrie in 1970, speckle interferometry permits a telescope to deliver optimum performance. Speckle data consist of a series of short exposure photographs at large image scales. On time scales short enough to freeze turbulent motions in the atmosphere, a telescope behaves like a multiple-aperture interferometer. Normally, resolution is limited to one arc second, but this method achieves diffraction-limited resolution. For a 1.5 meter telescope, this is 0.09 arc second, while a 5 meter can see detail as fine as 0.02 arc second, corresponding to about 30 km on most asteroids.

Because speckle interferometry is able to resolve the asteroid, by following the changing size, shape, and orientation of the projected body as it rotates it is possible, with a few simple and reasonable assumptions, to derive the asteroid's size, shape, and direction of its spin axis in one or two nights. If the asteroid is a triaxial ellipsoid that is smooth and featureless on a large scale, then the ellipsoid always projects as an ellipse, and the transformation between projected ellipses and ellipsoid yields simultaneous solutions for the three axes dimensions and the angles which lead to the direction of its rotational pole. Thus, one of the greatest attractions about speckle interferometry is that, independent of other techniques, it is capable of directly determining the dimensions and pole of an asteroid from just a few hours of observation. Such observations are currently being undertaken by Steward Observatory at the University of Arizona.

A sophisticated speckle camera, used on the 1.5 meter Danish telescope at the European Southern Observatory, was described by Bauer and Weigelt (1983). Their image processing system is sketched in Fig. 3–4. The camera contains a magnetically focused image intensifier, with a gain of 3×10^6. Magnified speckle images are focused on the cathode of the image intensifier with the aid of microscope objectives. The images, after passing through a selected interference filter, are recorded with a 16–mm motion picture camera or a 35–mm camera. Both can be used to record individual photon events. The interferograms are recorded at a rate of 10 or 30 frames per second (1/20 or 1/60th of a second). The films are usually reduced digitally using a 512×512 pixel video memory and PDP 11–34 computer.

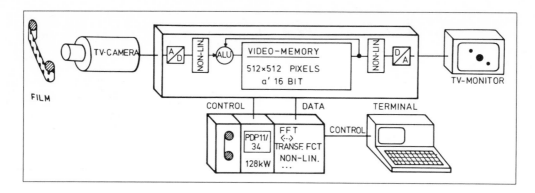

Fig. 3–4. *Structure of the image processing system of the digital speckle interferometry experiments. A/D: analog to digital converter, NON–LIN: nonlinearities by a look-up-table, ALU: arithmetic logical unit, D/A: digital-to-analog converter. Bauer & Weigelt, 1983.*

OCCULTATION

When an asteroid passes in front of a star as seen from earth, it casts a narrow shadow on our planet (Fig. 3–5; Millis *et al*, 1983). But unlike total solar eclipses, the occultation track can not be precisely predicted very far in advance. Occultations are the only reliable, direct method of determining an asteroid's size and shape.

Even though several occultations of stars by asteroids brighter than magnitude 12.5 occur each night, predictable events occur much more rarely, perhaps less than 10 a year.

To predict an event, the path of an asteroid is compared with the known positions of stars from a variety of catalogs. But an uncertainty of only 0.2 arcsec in the predicted position results in an occultation track on the earth uncertain to at least 300 km. (Millis and Elliot, 1979). Photographic astrometry can determine a much more precise track, but in practice this must be done near the time of occultation, providing only a few hours notice for observers who must travel accordingly. The fascinating story of how an 18-inch astrograph was established at Lowell Observatory in 1984 is told in Hoag (1985). The 30-year-old lens is now being used to predict asteroid occultation tracks accurate to 0.01 arc second, and was instrumental in permitting observations that showed Ceres was smaller than previously believed.

The first visual observation of an asteroid occultation was made from Sweden in 1958, involving Vesta. The first photoelectric observation of an occultation was made of Pallas in 1961, from India. The first photograph of an asteroid occultation was made of Metis from South America in 1979. Maley (1982) lists the circumstances of all 29 occultations seen up to that time.

Even now, most occultation observations are visually made by amateur astronomers, who are conveniently much more widely distributed than professional astronomers and their observatories. Prior to 1978, only two occultations had been observed at more than one site, a necessary condition for a diameter determination.

In addition to the visual estimates, an increasing number of photoelectric observations are being made. Since the tracks of occultations almost invariably miss major

observatories, it has been necessary to create a portable photoelectric observatory. This usually takes the form of a 14-inch Schmidt-Cassegrain telescope and a photometer, with a suitable recording device such as the M.I.T. portable digital data system. Developed by Baron and Dunham (1983), it has high time resolution and accurate absolute timing, and is equipped with two strip chart recorders.

It has also been suggested that a charge-coupled device (CCD) is capable of taking a series of short exposure images that can be viewed as a movie—a potentially useful technique for occultation observations.

Once an occultation diameter has been determined, the following equation permits the visual geometric albedo (p) to be derived:

$$2\log D = 6.244 - \log p - 0.4V(1,0)$$

where $V(1,0)$ is the absolute magnitude. Occultations can even provide some constraints on the asteroids' pole of rotation (Kristensen, 1984).

GRAVITY

Occasionally, two asteroids pass close to one another. Their gravitational interactions permit their masses to be measured, and combined with diameter estimates, densities can then be inferred.

This method was first recognized by Gauss as early as 1802, when he obtained the first reliable orbital elements of Ceres and Pallas (Schubart, 1971). Which are in a 1:1 resonance eventhough they do not approach one another. The gravitational effects caused by the total mass of the asteroid belt were sought without success in the early 20th century.

The perturbations caused by a close approach of two asteroids was studied mathematically by Crum (1918), but the first search for close encounters between asteroids was done by Fayet in 1949, who noted 13 pairs of close approaches near common opposition. One of these involved 4 Vesta and 197 Arete, which Hertz (1968) discovered approach each other within 0.04 AU every 18 years. This allowed him to make the first mass determination of an asteroid (Vesta) due to its effects on Arete's orbit. More recently, Lazovic and Kuzmanoski (1979) measured the perturbing effects of asteroid 215 upon 1851 during a particularly close encounter. They also studied the durations over which such effects are noticeable for approaches within 60,000 km.

According to Schubart & Matson (1979), there is a similar interaction between Ceres and Pallas, and Ceres and Vesta. The masses of all three have been determined by the gravitational method, which depends on very precise positional measurements by a branch of astronomy known as astrometry. Astrographs with multicomponent lenses or catadioptric systems of the Schmidt or Maksutov type have fields of several degrees and reach a limiting magnitude of 17 on plates of scale 1 to 3 arcmin/mm. (Photo 3–1). These short-focus instruments are occasionally complemented by use of large long-focus telescopes, which can reach magnitude 21. Computerized reduction of the plates, which usually contain stars whose positions are well-known, yield the asteroid's position.

The gravitational method will not attain wider applicability until asteroid-dedicated spacecraft are launched. The passage of such a craft, or a probe released by it, near an asteroid would produce a measurable deflection of its trajectory. An extensive application of the gravitational method will have to await the 21st century.

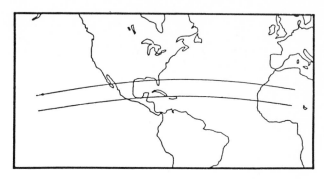

Fig. 3–5. *The occultation track of BD +8° 471 by Ceres on Nov. 13, 1984, discovered by Millis et al, 1983.*

NAMES AND NUMBERS 4

Perhaps the most frequently asked question about asteroids is, "How many are there?" The first attempt to
answer this question estimated the number brighter than
photographic magnitude 20.0 to be 57,200 (Stroobant,
1920). Walter Baade attempted to answer this question in
1934. Based on photographic plates taken with the 2.5 meter Mt. Wilson telescope, he estimated that some 44,000
asteroids brighter than photographic magnitude 19.5 exist.

This is more than 10 times the number of asteroids that
have received permanent designations (Fig. 4–1). In 1939
an even greater number was calculated by Putilin (1952).
Down to a magnitude limit of 21.5, he arrived at a total of 139,000 asteroids! While other astronomers claimed
that only a small increase in the numbers of asteroids with
decreasing magnitude should be expected, Kuiper *et al*
(1958) gave strong support to Baade's conclusions. They
based their statistical count of the total number on absolute magnitudes. In this method an 80 km asteroid is
assumed to be magnitude 9.0; an 8 km asteroid, magnitude 14.0; an 0.8 km asteroid, magnitude 19.0 (Fig. 4–2).
Kiang (1962) synthesized the disparate number estimates
of Stroobant, Baade and Johnson (who in 1951 estimated
4,000 asteroids brighter than 17.0), correcting their errors
and reducing the data by a uniform procedure. He developed a logarithmic expression that gives the number of
asteroids brighter than magnitude p, down to magnitude
20:

$$\log N(p) = 1.12 + 0.375(p - 10)$$

The observed and projected numbers of asteroids versus
B(1,0) for three different ranges of distance from the Sun
are shown in Figs. 4–3, 4, & 5 (Zhou & Wu, 1983).

According to Ishida *et al* (1984), there are 10 billion
asteroids larger than 0.1 km diameter, and a total mass of

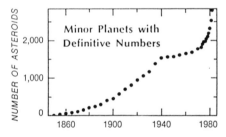

Fig. 4–1. *Minor planets with definitive numbers, between 1850
and 1982. Meeus, 1983.*

2.2×10^{21} kg, assuming an average density of 3 g/cc. The
asteroids smaller than 25 km contain only 5 percent of the
total mass, but in number account for all but one in 10^7
asteroids. Spacecraft observations could refine or modify
these figures (see American plans section of Chapter 16).

Since 1970 the number of provisional designations of
minor planets has averaged more than 700 per year. From
1972 to 1980 only 300 asteroids received permanent numbering. During 1982 a record 293 made the permanent list
(see Tables 4-1, 2 & 3). The Infrared Astronomy Satellite
made 11,449 asteroid sightings, but it is unlikely that many
of these will receive permanent numbers, as orbit determinations cannot be made for them. Davies *et al* (1984),
working with IRAS data, found no evidence for a significant population of undiscovered asteroids at high ecliptic
latitudes brighter than magnitude 16.

Keeping track of all this flying debris is a major task.
Astronomers were lamenting the situation many years
ago. "The rapid and continuous multiplication of discoveries, since the invention of the photographic method for
their detection, has introduced an embarrassment of riches

27

TABLE 4–1 FREQUENCY OF ASTEROID DISCOVERIES			
Years	Total Numbered Planets	5 Year Periods Numbered Planets	Annual Mean
1801–1850	13	13	0.26
1851–1855	37	24	4.8
1856–1860	62	25	5.0
1861–1865	85	23	4.6
1866–1870	112	27	5.4
1871–1875	157	45	9.0
1876–1880	219	62	12.4
1881–1885	253	34	6.8
1886–1890	302	49	9.8
1891–1895	409	107	21.4
1896–1900	463	54	10.8
1901–1905	582	119	23.8
1906–1910	707	125	25.0
1911–1915	813	106	21.2
1916–1920	939	126	25.2
1921–1925	1052	113	22.6
1926–1930	1158	106	21.2
1931–1935	1376	218	43.6
1936–1940	1539	163	32.6
1941–1945	1563	24	4.8
1946–1950	1568	5	1.0
1951–1955	1616	48	9.6
1956–1960	1649	33	6.6
1961–1965	1684	35	7.0
1966–1970	1779	95	19.0
1971–1975	1966	187	37.4
1976–1980	2321	355	71.0
1981–1985	3357	1036	207.2

Table 4–1. *Frequency of Asteroid Discoveries. Data from Combes (1976), supplemented by data from Frederick Pilcher.*

TABLE 4–2 FIRST MINOR PLANET DISCOVERIES				
Location	Year	Planet	Discoverer	City
Europe	1801	1 Ceres	Piazzi	Palermo
America	1854	31 Euphrosyne	Ferguson	Washington
Asia	1861	67 Asia	Pogson	Madras
S. Hemisphere	1901	475 Occlo	Stewart	Arequipa
Africa	1911	715 Transvaalia	Wood	Johannesburg
Oceania	1971	1806 Derice	—	Perth
Photographically	1891	323 Brucia	Wolf	Heidelberg
By artifical satellite	1983	3200 Phaethon	IRAS	

Table 4–2. *First Minor Planet Discoveries. Data based on a table by Combes (1976).*

TABLE 4–3 DISCOVERY PLACES OF 1940 NUMBERED MINOR PLANETS			
	Quantity	Percent	Discovery Period
Per Hemispheres			
Northern Hemisphere	1793	92.42	
Southern Hemisphere	147	7.58	
Per Continents			
Europe	1507	77.68	
America	236	12.16	
Asia	17	0.88	
Africa	179	9.23	
Oceania	1	0.05	
Per Observatories			
Heidelberg	654	33.71	1891–1956
Simeis, Ukrainian S.S.R.	132	6.80	1913–1948
Nice, France	118	6.08	1885–1948
Uccle, Belgium	98	5.05	1925–1954
Vienna	97	5.00	1875–1923
Turku, Finland	95	4.90	1936–1948
Johannesburg (RO)	87	4.48	1911–1953
Alger	61	3.14	1916–1952
Clinton, NY, USA	48	2.47	1861–1889
Bergedorf	42	2.16	1914–1972
CRAO (Partizanskoye)	34	1.75	1966–1972
Marseille	32	1.65	1853–1899
Taunton, MA, USA	31	1.60	1905–1910
Palomar (PLS inclusive)	30	1.55	1949–1974
Johannesburg (LS)	29	1.49	1924–1935
Pula[1]	28	1.44	1874–1880
Indiana	26	1.34	1949–1964
Dusseldorf	24	1.24	1852–1890
Berne	24	1.24	1961–1974
Ann Arbor, MI, USA	21	1.08	1863–1877
Paris[2]	21	1.08	1854–1913
La Plata	17	0.88	1921–1952

[1] Presently in Yugoslavia, formerly Pola in Austria-Hungary.
[2] Not included are the 14 discoveries by Goldschmidt, who observed at his residence, and not at the Paris Observartory.

Table 4–3. *Discovery Places of 1940 Numbered Minor Planets. Data from Combes (1976).*

Photo. 4–1. *Paul Herget, American celestial mechanician and director of the Minor Planet Center from 1947–1978. As custodian of the asteroids, Dr. Herget collected more than 170,000 precise positions of asteroids and published them in 4,390 Minor Planet Circulars. He personally computed new and improved orbital elements of 800 asteroids; and he compiled the Names of Minor Planets with their name sources, discoverers and dates. (Mary Lea Shane Archives of the Lick Observatory).*

which makes it difficult to decide what to do with them. Formerly the discovery of a new member of the solar system was applauded as a contribution to knowledge. Lately it has been considered almost a crime." (Metcalf, 1912). The first organization to keep track of the asteroids was the Rechen-Institut in Berlin-Dahlem, under the direction of Bauschinger, which undertook the job in the 1890's. By 1911 the Rechen-Institut began to provide ephemerides accurate between 30' to 60' (this contrasts to an accuracy of about 5' today). In 1917 it began publishing the minor planet ephemerides in a separate publication, *Kleine Planeten*. And in 1926 a series of *RI Circulars*, containing urgent and current data, was instituted.

At the end of World War II, both publications ceased, and the IAU established the Minor Planet Center in 1947. Under the leadership of Paul Herget of Cincinnati Observatory, the Center began the critical work of putting minor planet astronomy back into shape. In addition to working on some 200 poorly determined orbits, Herget began using the new technology of computers, although at first he had to scrounge time on IBM computers owned by businesses (Marsden, 1980).

Three kinds of activities pursued by the Center were outlined by Herget in 1971, but apply equally well today: the publication and distribution of the *Minor Planet Circulars* (successor to the *RI Circulars*); the collection and maintenance of a complete file of minor planet observations; and the computation of orbital elements and ephemerides. Herget slowed the pace of asteroid numbering considerably. He "was very careful in assigning numbers," wrote Brian Marsden in 1984. "He was concerned with finding previously numbered asteroids that had become lost, and only gave out 100 new numbers during the first 18 years he ran the center."

Meanwhile, the Institute for Theoretical Astronomy in Leningrad began issuing the *Ephemerides of Minor Planets* in 1946. A successor to *Kleine Planeten*, it originally contained ephemerides for all asteroids for a 50-day interval centered on the opposition date, but this was expanded to 70 days in 1971. Ephemerides under the direction of Victor Shor of bright asteroids have also been given for a six-month period in each year except 1971.

A more important change relates to the elements of the asteroids. As the result of a recommendation by IAU Commission 20 in 1976, high-precision osculating elements for a current standard epoch were made available with the 1980 *Ephemerides*. Prior to 1980, the published elements were not 'standardized' to a particular epoch, thus making it difficult for most astronomers to utilize them fully in making orbital predictions. The *Ephemerides* has grown with the number of asteroids—from 163 pages in 1971 to 300 pages in 1984.

When Herget retired in 1978, the directorship of the Minor Planet Center was assumed by Brian Marsden, who transferred the Center to the Harvard-Smithsonian Center for Astrophysics in Cambridge, Massachusetts. "The principal task of the Minor Planet Center," wrote Marsden in 1979, "is to increase the number of objects for which reliable orbital data can be provided." According to Marsden

Photo. 4–2. *Victor Shor, deputy chairman of the editorial staff of* the Ephemerides of Minor Planets *in Leningrad. The* Ephemerides *are published by the Institute for Theoretical Astronomy, whose minor planet section is headed by Yu. V. Batrakov, vice-president of the asteroid Commission 20 of the IAU.*

in 1984, most asteroids brighter than magnitude 16 have already been discovered. "Unless new, sustained observing programs are begun that can discover and adequately follow up fainter objects, the rate (of new discoveries) is not likely to exceed that of recent years." The *Minor Planet Circulars* are now issued on a more frequent (monthly) basis, and much reference material has been made available through the use of modern computers. Details are given in Appendix I.

NOMENCLATURE

Astronomers have had great fun over the years attaching monikers to their favorite chunks of space rock. Dignified names of the early 19th century gave way to whimsy in the 20th century, and only recently have some stricter controls been placed on a once-popular sport.

Politics has dogged the naming of asteroids from the very beginning. Before Ceres was generally adopted as the name of the first asteroid (it was known as Hera in Germany), Pierre Laplace expressed a preference for the name Juno, but Piazzi rejected this (Kirkwood, 1888). Instead he named it Ceres Ferdinandia in honor of King Ferdinand IV of Naples and Sicily. This followed from a precedent begun by William Herschel, who named the planet he discovered Georgium Sidus, in honor of his patron, King George III of Great Britain. While the British continued to refer to the Georgian planet until 1850, everyone else adopted Johann Bode's suggestion of the name Uranus.

While one controversy ended in 1850, another began the same year. The players were B. A. Gould, editor of the *Astronomical Journal*, W. C. Bond, director of Har-

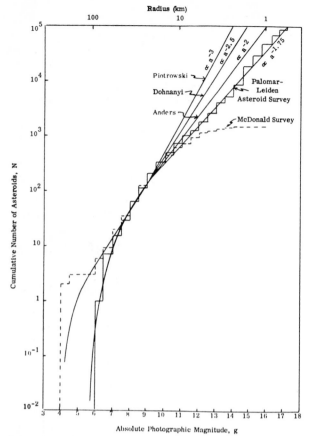

Fig. 4-2. *Cumulative asteroid distribution, according to various authors and surveys. Figures on the curves are power-law exponents. Implicit in accepting any of the three steeper curves is the assumption of a systematic selection process in the surveys. Soberman et al, 1971.*

Photo 4-3. *Brian Marsden, director of the Minor Planet Center at the Smithsonian Astrophysical Observatory in Cambridge, Massachusetts. His interest in orbital work goes back 40 years. "The vagaries of the English climate had impressed upon me the value of trying my hand at calculating the motions of the planets rather than actually trying to look at them." His office is now the worldwide clearing house for asteroid and comet discoveries, and he is the one responsible for computing their orbits.*

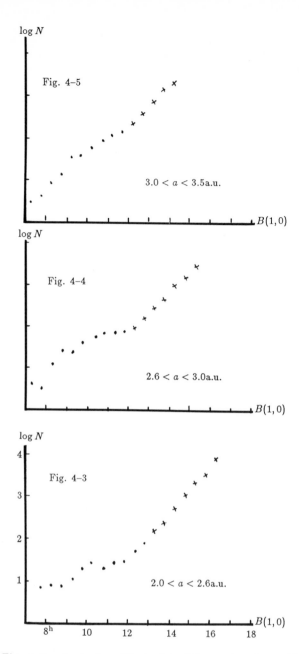

Fig. 4-3, -4, -5. *Logarithmic plots of the number of asteroids in three different zones versus B(1,0). Zhou & Wu, 1983.*

vard College Observatory, and J. R. Hind, discoverer of the 12th asteroid. "Mr. Hind," wrote Gould, "has selected the name Victoria, with a star surrounded by a laurel wreath for a symbol. Such nomenclature is at variance with established usage, and is liable to the objections which very properly led astronomers to reject the name Ceres Ferdinandea."

Bond countered, stating that "Victoria was the daughter of Pallas, and one of the attendants of Jupiter, and, therefore, the name appears to fulfill the required conditions of a mythological nomenclature." To this Gould adds a note to the effect that Pallas was "a giant—not the goddess, who is believed to have left no children." Nonetheless, Bond, recognized as the highest authority on astronomy in America, prevailed.

In his defense, Hind printed a letter in the *Astronomical Journal* saying that "the name Victoria was submitted to the approbation of astronomers on mythological grounds, and not exclusively as marking the country where the discovery was made. I foresaw the objections which you have advanced, and, therefore, devised a symbol which would apply equally well to Victoria or to another name—Cleo—which I had in view in case the general feeling of astronomers was against the latter. I would at once reject any name that is not founded in mythology. It seems to have been forgotten that Her Majesty's name is derived from the goddess, who cannot thereby lose her celestial rights." Partly as a result of this controversy, European astronomers conferred in person and by mail in order to lay down some principles. Piazzi, Olbers, Harding and Hencke had started the custom of using female names from mythology, so it was decided to continue this practice.

But controversy continued to dog the naming of asteroids, as evidenced by this pungent comment from the pen of Sir John Herschel (1866). "Many of the names of the asteroids appear to us very unhappily chosen. Thus, confusion is very likely to arise in printing or speaking, between Iris and Isis, Lutetia and Laetitia, Thetis and Metis, Pallas and Pales. Is it too much to hope that the discoverers of the interfering members of these pairs will reconsider their names?" As a glance at Tables 4–4 and 5 readily show, Herschel's plea was ignored.

According to Edward Holden (1896), no one was more happy in choosing names for asteroids than C. F. H. Peters. "Immediately after returning from the transit of Venus expedition, he discovered two planets—Adeona and Vibilia—in one night. Adeona is the patroness of homecoming, and Vibilia the patroness of ways—of journeying. The name of his asteroid Miriam (who was the sister of Moses) was chosen in defiance of rule, and of malice aforethought; so that he could tell a theological professor, whom he thought to be too pious, that Miriam, also, was a 'mythological personage'."

Holden goes on to decry the departures from mythology that became more frequent after 1875. "Some of them have a right on a list of heavenly bodies, but many of them, at least, read like the Christian names in a girl's school. Although the matter of nomenclature is a minor one, it is worth while to keep it as impersonal as possible in the

TABLE 4–4 NOMENCLATURE SIMILARITIES			
1221 Amor	337 Devosa	794 Irenaea	189 Phthia
774 Armor	1328 Devota	14 Irene	432 Pythia
—	—	—	—
965 Angelica	673 Edda	7 Iris	997 Priska
64 Angelina	207 Hedda	42 Isis	1359 Prieska
—	—	—	—
265 Anna	221 Eos	497 Iva	1792 Reni
1668 Hanna	433 Eros	1627 Ivar	1371 Resi
—	—	—	—
1157 Arabia	718 Erida	89 Julia	907 Rhoda
1087 Arabis	636 Erika	816 Juliana	437 Rhodia
—	—	—	—
43 Ariadne	1346 Gotha	1387 Kama	1796 Riga
1225 Ariane	1049 Gotho	1357 Khama	1180 Rita
—	—	—	—
1474 Beira	424 Gratia	1175 Margo	244 Sita
1249 Deira	984 Gretia	1434 Margot	689 Zita
—	—	—	—
1487 Boda	723 Hammonia	1348 Michel	1170 Siva
998 Bodea	40 Harmonia	1376 Michelle	140 Siwa
—	—	—	—
1071 Brita	699 Hela	1549 Mikko	299 Thora
1219 Britta	1370 Hella	1185 Nikko	1685 Toro
—	—	—	—
1246 Chaka	101 Helena	638 Moira	1266 Tone
1671 Chaika	1075 Helina	1257 Mora	924 Toni
—	—	—	—
1106 Cydonia	173 Ino	1347 Patria	131 Vala
579 Sidonia	85 Io	1601 Patry	262 Valda
—	—	—	—
395 Delia	1838 Ursa	894 Erda	908 Buda
560 Delila	351 Yrsa	167 Urda	1158 Luda
—	—	—	—
526 Jena	1209 Pumma	1107 Lictoria	1120 Cannonia
789 Lena	1928 Summa	12 Victoria	1444 Pannonia
—	—	—	—
1132 Hollandia	381 Myrrha	99 Dike	1314 Paula
1269 Rollandia	632 Pyrrha	307 Nike	537 Pauly

Table 4–4. *Nomenclature Similarities. Based on a table by Pilcher & Meeus (1973). In 1985, Commission 20 of the IAU recognized this situation as serious. "Names proposed for minor planets will not be accepted if they are too nearly similar to those of other minor or major planets or natural satellites."*

TABLE 4–5 IDENTICALLY NAMED OBJECTS	
Minor Planet	Satellite
85 Io	Jupiter I
52 Europa	Jupiter II
1036 Ganymed	Jupiter III
203 Kallisto	Jupiter IV
38 Leda	Jupiter XIII
113 Almathea	Jupiter V
106 Dione	Saturn IV
577 Rhea	Saturn V
593 Titania	Uranus III
1810 Epimetheus	Saturn XI

Table 4–5. *Identically Named Objects. Table from Pilcher & Meeus (1973).*

future. The abuses to which a contrary course might lead are only too evident."

But the lowest point was reached in 1885, when an asteroid was actually put up for auction! The notice appeared in the astronomical journal *Observatory*: "Herr Palisa, being desirous to raise funds for his intended expedition to observe the total solar eclipse of Aug. 29, 1886 will sell the right of naming the minor planet No. 244 for 50 pounds." According to Herget (1971), the offer was not accepted until Palisa had discovered two more asteroids, 248 and 250. It has since borne the name Bettina, wife of Baron Albert von Rothschild. The lucky Baroness also proposed the name Valda, the 262nd asteroid, also discovered by Palisa. The faintest pretense of restraint was thrown to the wind in the years following Holden's plea. 1033 Simona is named after the daughter of the discoverer, G. Van Biesbroeck; his son Edwin got asteroid 1046; and another of his children received 1045 Michela. Monarchs became acceptable, with 1128 Astrid named in honor of the Queen of the Belgians and 1246 Chaka, former King of the Zulus! Names have been given to asteroids in honor of mountains (1317 Silvretta), cities (2104 Toronto); animals (1320 Impala); rivers (1323 Tugela); islands (1399 Teneriffa); bays (1394 Algoa); presidents (1550 Tito); countries (1554 Yugoslavia); flowers (1095 Tulipa); trees (1060 Magnolia); operas (1047 Geisha); ballets (815 Coppelia); composers (2266 Tchaikovsky); observatories (2830 Greenwich); and all the Atens are named after Egyptian gods.

More appropriately, scientists have been commemorated: 1000 Piazzia (Guiseppe Piazzi, discoverer of the first asteroid); 1001 Gaussia (Karl Gauss, whose computations led to the rediscovery of 1 Ceres); 1002 Olbersia (Heinrich Olbers, discoverer of Pallas); 2000 Herschel (William Herschel, who made the first scientific study of Ceres and Pallas); 1999 Hirayama (K. Hirayama, who first studied families of asteroids); 1123 Shapleya (Harlow Shapley, director of Harvard Observatory); 1134 Kepler (Johannes Kepler, who first postulated the existence of a planet between Mars and Jupiter); 1217 Maximiliana (Max Wolf, who began the photographic discovery of asteroids); 2732 Witt (Gustav Witt, discoverer of Eros); 2905 Plaskett (John S. Plaskett, founder of the Dominion Astrophysical Observatory in Victoria, B.C., Canada); 2001 Einstein (Albert Einstein); and 1983 Bok (Bart Bok). An alphabetical list of 2,785 asteroid names was presented by Kelly (1986).

Until 1898, most asteroids had female names. But with the discovery of 433 Eros, masculine names have been given to asteroids which cross the orbit of Mars. According to A. C. D. Crommelin, writing at the time of Pluto's discovery in 1930, Eros was not the first name suggested for the 433rd asteroid. "The name Pluto is excellent; it has not been used for an asteroid; it was suggested for Eros before the latter name was suggested (see Observatory for the end of 1898 and beginning of 1899) but it was rejected as being too gloomy a name for a planet so full of hope; but it is quite suitable for a planet lost in darkness." (Moore, 1984).

The first asteroid given a masculine name was 59 Elpis, but not without a fight. Leverrier, director of the Paris Observatory, did not want this asteroid named at all. He proposed a new nomenclature in 1860 whereby the name of the discoverer would be attached to the number of the asteroid. Many prominent astronomers, including Herschel, Airy and Hind, protested. In the ensuing confusion, the asteroid, not content with being a generic no-name variety, was given two names! Von Littrow, director of the Vienna Observatory, named it Elpis after a Samian who had erected a temple to Bacchus. But in 1862 Leverrier allowed the asteroid's discoverer, J. Chacornac, to name his find. Chacornac permitted Hind to select the name Olympia, which was used for a short time (Herget, 1968).

The naming of asteroids has been put on a firmer footing in recent years. To quote *Minor Planet Circular 4845*, "...if the discoverer is deceased, or if a minor planet remains unnamed ten years after it has been numbered, a name could appropriately be suggested by identifiers of the various apparitions of the object, by discoverers at apparitions other than the official one, by those whose observations contributed extensively to the orbit determination, or by representatives of the observatory at which the official discovery was made. In such a case, the selection of a name shall be judged by a committee of three, consisting normally of the President and the Vice President of Commission 20 and the Director of the Minor Planet Center, and a final decision shall be made not less than six months following the announcement of the numbering of the minor planet." The nature of the proposed name is also subject to approval. "All names proposed for minor planets will be reviewed for suitability, even when names are proposed by discoverers. The review will be done as indicated in the 1979 Commission 20 resolution, except that in the case of a name proposed by the discoverer the six-month waiting period for a newly numbered object can be reduced to two months. Names shall be limited to a maximum length of sixteen characters, including spaces and hyphens." (IAU Trans, 1982).

The first asteroid to be discovered in the same orbit as Jupiter was 588 Achilles in 1906. Max Wolf gave it a male name, at the suggestion of J. Palisa. Later the same year, another such asteroid was discovered, and was named 617 Patroclus. Both Achilles and Patroclus were heroes of the Trojan War c 1400 BC, and thus it became natural to refer to asteroids in Jupiter's orbit as Trojans.

But things got confused from the beginning—Achilles was discovered at the L4 point, which precedes Jupiter by some 55.5°, while Patroclus occupies the L5 point, trailing Jupiter. As more Trojans were discovered all the objects at L5 should have been Trojan heroes, and all the ones at L4 Greek heroes. But the naming of Patroclus ruined the logic of the situation; he is among the Trojans, while 624 Hektor lurks among the Greeks (Ley, 1963). Other heroes of Troy include 884 Priamus, 1172 Aeneas, 1173 Anchises and 1208 Troilus. Greek heroes (who were the victors) include 659 Nestor, 911 Agamemnon, 1143 Odysseus, 1404 Ajax, 1437 Diomedes and 2146 Stentor.

Photo. 4–4. *Frederick Pilcher, chairman of the physics department at Illinois College and eminent amateur astronomer. Professor Pilcher has observed more than 1,300 asteroids; many have received names he proposed, including 1801 Titicaca, 1426 Riviera, 2542 Calpurnia and 2137 Priscilla, named in honor of Bart Bok's wife.*

Despite all the rules and regulations, politics is still very much a part of the naming of asteroids. In late 1983, Frederick Pilcher suggested that the name 2807 Karl Marx be rescinded. "This extension of the cold war into the sky is intolerable," he wrote. This prompted a reply by Brian Marsden, director of the Minor Planet Center. As an exposition on the current policy of the naming of minor planets, it is worth quoting at length.

> Let me comment on Prof. Pilcher's remarks concerning the name 2807 KARLMARX and the supposed denial of the rights of discoverers to name their discoveries. I deplore as much as he does the use of the minor-planet names for purposes of propaganda, but occasional appearances of political or ultra-nationalistic names are far from new, and many such names have most decidedly been proposed by the discoverers of the planets concerned. After all, 12 VICTORIA was christened by its English discoverer as long ago as 1850, and all the indications are that 852 WLADILENA was named by its discoverer a few months after Vladimir Lenin's death in 1924. There are also instances where discoverers have named minor planets to honor political figures or ideals, only to want to change the names when the figures or ideals became out of favor! Such changes have not been permitted, and I think that most astronomers would not wish the names of minor planets to be as impermanent as those of airports, streets and other manmade constructions. A name proposed by a discoverer has traditionally been rejected only if it was felt to be too nearly similar to that of another minor planet, in bad taste or deliberately obscene.

However, the unprecedented rate at which new minor planets are becoming eligible for naming has clearly made it desirable to try to eliminate the more offensive proposals. The IAU Working Group on Planetary System Nomenclature, which was set up a decade ago principally to name features on solar-system bodies, explicitly prohibits the use of names of political or religious figures. IAU Commission 20, which oversees the Minor Planet Center, feels that it would be inappropriate to adopt the WGPSN rules outright—this would preclude the possibility of naming a minor planet for a living person, for example—but it did in 1982 form a committee to examine the suitability of each name that is proposed. The committee, which consists of the President and Vice President of the Commission and the Director of the Minor Planet Center, would be very happy not to receive blatantly political proposals and those that glorify military adventures. We are currently deliberating on several such proposals, not all of which have been submitted by the Russians. There is of course a long-established tradition to confer on a particular class of minor planet the names of participants on both sides of the Trojan War, and what makes 1489 ATTILA acceptable is that the passage of 15 centuries has reduced that once absolutely despicable character to a joke. Certainly, none of the present members of the committee would ever wish to see minor planets immortalizing the 1939 leaders of Germany and the U.S.S.R., but in the centuries to come even the most heinous exploits of those murderers will be considered laughable.

The committee, which currently does not have a representative in a communist country, tried to be objective with regard to the proposal for 2807, and several months elapsed before all three members were convinced that, just one century after the individual concerned had died, he had in fact made an appropriate and valid contribution to human thought that could reasonably be acknowledged. The citation that accompanied the naming of 2807 on MPC 8065 mentioned his work in what we thought was a satisfactorily informative and factual manner, and in this respect it was obviously preferable to the Soviet citation that had accompanied the original proposal. It should be remembered that one of the purposes of the IAU is to encourage cooperation and to foster friendships among astronomers all over the world. One could probably find someone somewhere and at some time in history who would object to the name of any minor planet, from 1 CERES on. Just consider that for every ten (say) people who may dislike a particular political or military name there will be one who disapproves when a discoverer names a minor planet for his mistress! The IAU itself takes a dim view of those who sell names for profit, whether they be entrepreneurs who think they have the right to name stars or legitimate discoverers of minor planets who are well aware of the right traditionally accorded to them. But what can one really do, other than perhaps try not to immortalize those who have, in recent memory, been directly responsible for causing death, injury and destruction or for promoting hatred among either individuals or nations.

"Less hurried contemplation," wrote Pilcher shortly afterward, "show that this (rescinding of political names) is a bad precedent, and will lead to chaos if carried on extensively. In a future and saner age the historical records would have to be searched and the original names reassigned."

NUMBERING SYSTEM

The system of numbering asteroids in order of their discovery was made by Rudolf Wolf in 1851. By that time 15 were known, and a curious system of symbolic notation had arisen (Table 4–6). An important discourse on this matter by Gould (1854) is worth quoting.

> As the number of the known asteroids increases, the disadvantages of a symbolic notation analagous to that hitherto in use increase much more rapidly even than the difficulty of selecting appropriate names from the classic mythology. Not only are many of the symbols proposed inefficient in suggesting the name of which they are intended to be an abbreviation; but some of them require for their delineation more artistic accomplishment than an astronomer is necessarily or generally endowed with." In modern parlance, which tends to be more concise if less polite, the system was useless because most astronomers can't draw!

Gould's paper marked the introduction of a new notation: a circle containing the number of the asteroid in the chronological order of its discovery. Since 1931, the official method of designating a minor planet has been to use its number, followed by the name, without comma between and with no parentheses or other marks surrounding the number. Parentheses are still used in text references, but omitted from tabulations.

Planet.	New Symbol.	Date of Discovery.	Old Symbol.
Ceres,	①	1801, January 1,	⚳
Pallas,	②	1802, March 28,	⚴
Juno,	③	1804, September 1,	⚵
Vesta,	④	1807, March 29,	⚶
Astræa,	⑤	1845, December 8,	
Hebe,	⑥	1847, July 1,	
Iris,	⑦	" August 13,	
Flora,	⑧	" October 18,	
Metis,	⑨	1848, April 25,	
Hygea,	⑩	1849, April 12,	
Parthenope,	⑪	1850, May 13,	
Clio,	⑫	" September 13,	
Egeria,	⑬	" November 2,	
Irene,	⑭	1851, May 20,	
Eunomia,	⑮	" July 29,	

Table 4–6. *Asteroid Symbols. There have been three name changes since this table was published by Gould (1854). The new versions are 5 Astraea, 10 Hygiea and 12 Victoria.*

In the pre-photographic days, a newly discovered asteroid was immediately given a name and number. But this often led to a new object being identified with one already numbered. Therefore, it was decided on 15 July 1892 to institute a system of provisional designations. Each asteroid was identified by its year of discovery followed by a capital letter, beginning with A. In the following year, the rule was changed. Double letters were used consecutively, regardless of when the year changed, so that 1893 AP was followed by 1894 AQ. As chronology was not preserved in this system, another numbering system was introduced in 1914, whereby the year of discovery was followed by a small letter. A third system was invented by the Russian astronomers at Simeis when they were unable to communicate with the outside world during World War I. It used a Greek symbol *sigma* followed by a number.

All three systems were abolished at the suggestion of E. C. Bower of the U.S. Naval Observatory in 1925. The designation adopted then remains in use today. It consists of dividing the year into 24 half-month intervals, designated alphabetically. Thus the first asteroid discovered in 1990 will be known as 1990 AA, provided the discovery takes place between Jan. 1 and Jan. 15. The next one will be called 1990 AB, if found in the same interval. From Jan. 16–31, the first discovery will be called 1990 BA (Table 4–7). If more than 25 discoveries are made in the same half-month interval, the alphabet at the latter place is repeated with the index 1, and with more than 50 discoveries with index 2. Thus, the 57th asteroid found between October 1 and 15 in 1931 is 1931 TG2. (Pilcher & Meeus, 1971).

Nomenclature for asteroids that were discovered prior to 1925 thus presents a problem, especially if the original designation was erroneous. A system was devised by W. Strobel to handle this situation: provisional designations begin with the letter A, followed by the final three digits of the year of observation, and lastly two letters indicating the half month and order within that half month (for example A920 BA for the first asteroid found between January 16 and 31, 1920).

TABLE 4–7				
CONVENTION FOR NUMBERING ASTEROIDS				
A	Jan. 1-15	1	O	July 16-31	14
B	Jan. 16-31	2	P	Aug. 1-15	15
C	Feb. 1-15	3	Q	Aug. 16-31	16
D	Feb. 16-29	4	R	Sep. 1-15	17
E	Mar. 1-15	5	S	Sep. 16-30	18
F	Mar. 16-31	6	T	Oct. 1-15	19
G	Apr. 1-15	7	U	Oct. 16-31	20
H	Apr. 16-30	8	V	Nov. 1-15	21
I=J	May. 1-15	9	W	Nov. 16-30	22
K	May. 16-31	10	X	Dec. 1-15	23
L	June 1-15	11	Y	Dec. 16-31	24
M	June 16-30	12	Z	not used	25
N	July 1-15	13			

Table 4–7. *Convention for Numbering Asteroids. Table from Pilcher & Meeus (1973).*

A separate system of provisional designations was used for asteroids discovered in the Palomar-Leiden survey. Some 2,403 objects found in the PL survey had orbits computed, but not in most cases accurate enough to permit recovery (Van Houten *et al*, 1984). All asteroids located in this survey are assigned a number followed by the letters PL. Some have been identified with objects given provisional designations on the Bower system, and have subsequently been given permanent numbers. For example 1931 BD = 4645 PL = 1812 Gilgamesh.

The number of independent discoveries which received provisional designations was 5,000 in 1934; 10,000 in 1952; 20,000 in 1975 and 30,000 by 1981. The percentage of asteroids for which orbits are known is correlated with their discovery date. For objects found on plates exposed around 1910, the figure is 75%; around 1940 it drops to 50%; in 1971, 25%; and less than 10% after 1978. There are an average of 4 independent discoveries (i.e., provisional designations) for each numbered asteroid (Kresak, 1984).

In order to avoid the admission to the list of permanently numbered asteroids too many faint members that might not be recoverable in the future, Stracke (1941) proposed a new rule-number new asteroids fainter than magnitude 16 in aphelion only if they have been observed in two oppositions. The IAU adopted a formal resolution on the matter of permanent designations in 1948: "Permanent numbers shall, as a rule, be assigned to a new minor planet after it has been observed in two oppositions and a satisfactory orbit has been obtained. In the case of a planet that approaches the Earth within the orbit of Mars, a permanent number may be assigned after a single opposition, provided that the planet was well observed and that a satisfactory orbit was obtained." The rules were later strengthened to three oppositions.

A discrepancy regarding discovery dates persisted until rather recently. As an example, the asteroid 1137 (provisional designation 1929 WB) was first noted in the second half of November. But after it received this designation, it was also found on a plate taken 27 October. This latter date is listed as the official discovery date. The reverse situation applies to minor planet 1634. It was first photographed on 14 May 1928 at Simeis, then by Reinmuth

seven days later (1928 KB). It was observed again by C. Jackson on 25 July, 2 August and 19 August 1935. The latter date (1935 QP) is the official discovery date, and the official discoverer is Jackson.

On 20 August 1979, I attended a meeting of IAU Commission 20 in Montreal which defined the discovery as the earliest apparition at which an orbit useful in the establishment of identifications was calculated. In the case of a double designation during the same apparition priority is given in order of announcement of discovery, unless the double designation follows from an orbit computation using the observations made according to the second announcement (Gilmore & Kilmartin, 1984).

Another quirk that can lead to endless confusion is the practice of asteroid renumbering. A selection of such cases is given in Table 4–8. One of the worst cases occurred in 1877. On 1 October of that year, James Watson discovered his 21st asteroid, to which he assigned the number 175. A telegram announcing the discovery was sent out by the Smithsonian Institution, but was somehow lost. His own confirmation of the discovery by letter did not reach Europe until several weeks later, too late for follow-up observations. The Austrian astronomer Palisa, not aware of Watson's discovery, found an asteroid on 2 October, which he also labelled 175.

It was soon noticed that Palisa's object was the same as asteroid 161 Athor, so the number was still available. But then Peters at Clinton, New York recorded an asteroid on 14 October which also was labelled 175 and given the name Iduna. When the mess was finally untangled, Iduna was given the number 176, and Watson's 175 was confirmed and named Andromache (Leuschner, 1936).

THE CASE OF THE MISSING ASTEROID

As early as 1903, Edward Pickering was concerned about missing asteroids. "Of the five hundred asteroids so far discovered, sixty-eight have not been seen during the last five years, while the last observation of twenty-five of them was from ten to thirty-five years ago. Evidently there is a great danger that many of them will be lost, and then it will be impossible to decide when one is observed whether it is new or not. Finding missing asteroids is evidently much more important than discovering new ones." The asteroid sleuths have been very busy in the last few years—their diligence, in fact, may soon put them out of business. In 1979, 20 asteroids were listed as lost, with orbits so poorly determined they could not be found (Zhuravlev and Kiryushenkov, 1982). Now, only three remain on the list: 719 Albert, 724 Hapag, and 878 Mildred, (Table 4–9). It was even discovered by West *et al* (1982) that 330 Adalberta never existed. Noted photographically by Max Wolf in 1892, it was found that both his measured positions refer to galactic stars. Differences in limiting magnitudes of his plates simulated a moving object.

TABLE 4–8
CHANGES IN THE ASTEROID NUMBERING

Asteroid(s)	Explanation
525–1171	In 1958 they were found to be the same object. Number 525 was then assigned to another asteroid.
715–933	They were found to be the same in 1928. The number 933 was assigned to another asteroid. It is not clear if Hirayama in 1933 repeated the whole classification or simply added to the previously identified families the asteroids with numbers between 951 and 1223; in this last case the 933 of Hirayama is different from that of other authors.
864–1078	This case is the same as for 525 and 1171.
1095–1449	From 1966 on the number 1095 was assigned to another asteroid, because of the identity of the old 1095 and 1449.
1125	From 1957 on this number was given to a new object. The old one was recovered in 1987.

Table 4–8. *Changes in the Asteroid Numbering. Table from Carusi & Valsecchi (1982).*

The search for these shy asteroids was aided greatly by the publication of a computer-readable catalogue with 43,500 positions of lost and unnumbered asteroids (Minor Planet Center, 1981). Some 2,000 of these unnumbered objects were identified with numbered ones; 120 asteroids are now on the 'critical list' (Table 4–10).

A recent meeting of IAU Commission 20 addressed itself to the missing asteroids. "Commission 20 encourages the accurate measurement of positions of minor planets from the extensive plate collections such as those at the Budapest, Goethe Link, Johannesburg, Lowell, Simeis and Turku observatories. Specifically, there is a need for measurement of plates of unnumbered minor planets for which only approximate positions were previously available. Further, in order to support the current efforts to recover the few remaining lost minor planets or to make a linkage with a possible accidental rediscovery, Commission 20 encourages the early reexamination and remeasurement of all existing plates that contain or may contain images of those lost planets and the prompt publication of the results in the *Minor Planet Circulars*." The value of searching old plates was clearly shown by Borngen & Kirsch (1983), who found 600 asteroid images on Schmidt plates taken at the Schwarzschild Observatory. Of these, less than 10% were already-known objects. After extensive analysis, 1973 UT5, one of the asteroids recorded several times, was given the permanent number 2424 Tautenberg.

The methods used to find lost asteroids are detailed in Ashbrook (1970a), Kristensen (1981), Schmadel & Kohoutek (1982) and Schmadel (1980). As an example, consider the asteroid 1370 Hella. It was discovered by Reinmuth in Heidelberg on 31 August 1935, and received the preliminary designation 1935 QG. Up to November 1 of that year, it was observed six nights. Nonetheless, it could not be located at subsequent oppositions for two reasons.

TABLE 4–9				
Asteroid Number	Year Last Observed	Mag.	Inclination	Eccentricity
473	1901	11.2	27.78	0.256
719	1911	16.9	10.82	0.540
724	1911	14.8	11.77	0.254
878	1938	16.6	2.02	0.231
1026	1923	14.6	5.39	0.180
1179	1936	15.1	8.74	0.175

Table 4–9. *Lost Asteroids. Data from Zhuravlev & Kiryushenkov (1982). Since this table was prepared, three of the asteroids have been recovered: 1179 Mally and 1026 Ingrid in December, 1986, and in January 1987 the recovery of 473 Nolli was announced (its semimajor axis is 0.3 AU smaller than previously computed).*

Firstly, the last observations used in the orbit computation yielded a rather large deviation in declination so that the ephemeris corrections in 1938 and 1945 were far too large. Secondly, Hella has an orbital period which causes perihelion passages to occur under rather poor observing conditions in northern latitude summers. In the 50 years after it was first seen, Hella made 13 revolutions around the Sun, corresponding to 31 oppositions. In all this time, it was not even seen accidentally, as no unnumbered object has been matched with it. Ephemerides for Hella were discontinued in 1969, and it was supposed to be hopelessly lost. All the old plates were remeasured on the basis of more accurate positions and proper motions of stars, and an additional observation from 1935 was discovered. On the very first attempt to "reseize" Hella, it was found with the 1 meter Schmidt telescope of the European Southern Observatory by H.-E. Schuster in 1979. It was only 10.7 minutes of right ascension and 1° 15' of declination from the computed position.

Table 4–10. *Critical List of Asteroids. Table from the 1987 edition of the Russian* Ephemerides of Minor Planets, *lists asteroids observed at fewer than five oppositions, or not at all in the last decade.*

№	Число наблюденных оппозиций	Год последних наблюдений	№	Number of observed oppositions	Year of last observations	№	Число наблюденных оппозиций	Год последних наблюдений	№	Number of observed oppositions	Year of last observations
353	>5	1975	2101	3	1984	2800	3	1982	3101	3	1984
473	1	1901	2135	3	1984	2868	3	1983	3102	2	1984
719	1	1911	2148	3	1979	2876	3	1983	3103	2	1984
724	1	1911	2198	3	1979	2895	3	1983	3119	3	1984
878	2?	1938?	2202	2	1980	2899	3	1983	3122	3	1984
879	>5	1976	2210	3	1980	2904	3	1983	3144	3	1984
880	>5	1976	2212	3	1980	2914	3	1982	3148	3	1984
881	>5	1976	2218	3	1980	2915	3	1983	3160	3	1984
998	>5	1975	2229	3	1980	2926	3	1983	3161	3	1984
1009	3	1982	2257	3	1980	2935	3	1983	3162	3	1984
1025	>5	1976	2260	3	1980	2937	3	1983	3169	3	1984
1026	1	1923	2272	3	1980	2940	3	1983	3178	3	1985
1134	>5	1973	2285	3	1979	2948	3	1983	3192	3	1984
1138	>5	1975	2327	3	1980	2964	3	1983	3198	3	1985
1179	2?	1936?	2335	3	1980	2966	3	1982	3199	2	1984
1205	4	1976	2340	3	1983	2968	3	1982	3200	2	1984
1226	>5	1973	2368	3	1983	2974	3	1983	3204	3	1984
1230	>5	1975	2373	3	1980	2977	3	1983	3206	3	1985
1316	3	1983	2420	3	1981	2986	3	1983	3211	3	1985
1372	>5	1976	2444	3	1981	2994	3	1983	3212	3	1984
1373	>5	1974	2449	3	1981	2999	3	1984	3217	3	1984
1538	3	1984	2462	3	1981	3004	3	1984	3218	3	1984
1580	>5	1976	2503	3	1981	3013	3	1984	3225	3	1984
1647	>5	1973	2539	3	1981	3014	3	1984	3245	3	1984
1657	>5	1974	2551	3	1981	3017	3	1983	3252	3	1985
1709	5	1976	2552	3	1981	3018	3	1984	3254	3	1985
1710	5	1975	2596	3	1982	3022	3	1984	3255	3	1985
1750	4	1974	2608	2	1982	3025	3	1984	3270	2	1985
1818	5	1974	2619	3	1982	3037	3	1984	3271	2	1985
1871	4	1974	2629	3	1982	3040	3	1984	3273	3	1985
1876	4	1974	2645	3	1982	3041	3	1984	3274	3	1985
1883	4	1974	2663	3	1982	3043	3	1984	3284	3	1985
1917	4	1976	2669	3	1982	3044	3	1983	3287	3	1985
1919	5	1976	2671	3	1981	3046	3	1984	3288	2	1985
1921	3	1980	2695	3	1982	3057	3	1984	3289	3	1985
1981	2	1976	2703	3	1982	3073	3	1984	3302	3	1981
2059	2	1977	2706	3	1982	3075	3	1984	3304	3	1984
2061	3	1985	2758	3	1982	3079	3	1984	3307	3	1984
2062	3	1978	2765	3	1982	3080	3	1984	3309	3	1985
2063	3	1984	2791	3	1982	3086	3	1984			
2076	3	1977	2799	3	1982	3087	3	1984			

		TABLE 5–1				
		LARGE-SCALE STRUCTURE OF THE ASTEROID BELT				
		Source: Zellner *et al*, Reproduced by permission from Icarus				
Zone	Description	Number in TRIAD	Mean a	Limits for a	Limits for e	Limits for i
AAA	Apollo-Amor-Aten	36	1.831	—	$q = a(1 - e) \leq 1.30$	—
HU	Hungarias	30	1.900	$1.78 \leq a \leq 2.00$	$e \leq 0.18$	$16° \leq i \leq 34$
MC	Mars crossers	29	2.285	—	$q \leq 1.666$	—
FL	Floras	421	2.230	$2.10 \leq a \leq 2.30$	(Limited by MC)	$i \leq 11°$
PH	Phocaeas	62	2.368	$2.25 \leq a \leq 2.50$	$e \geq 0.10$	$18° \leq i \leq 32°$
NY	Nysas	44	2.448	$2.41 \leq a \leq 2.50$	$0.12 \leq e \leq 0.21$	$1.5° \leq i \leq 4.3°$
I	Main belt	316	2.391	$2.30 < a \leq 2.50$	(Limited by MC)	$i \leq 18°$
PAL	Pallas zone	4	2.755	$2.500 \leq a \leq 2.82$	(Limited by MC)	$33° \leq i \leq 38°$
IIa	Main belt	455	2.614	$2.500 \leq a \leq 2.706$	(Limited by MC)	$i \leq 33°$
IIb	Main belt	298	2.761	$2.706 < a \leq 2.82$	(Limited by MC)	$i \leq 33°$
KOR	Koronis zone	86	2.873	$2.83 \leq a \leq 2.91$	$e \leq 0.11$	$i \leq 3.5°$
EOS	Eos zone	144	3.014	$2.99 \leq a \leq 3.03$	$0.01 \leq e \leq 0.13$	$8° \leq i \leq 12°$
IIIa	Main belt	189	2.933	$2.82 < a \leq 3.03$	$e \leq 0.35$	$i \leq 30°$
THE	Themis zone	165	3.145	$3.08 \leq a \leq 3.24$	$0.09 \leq e \leq 0.22$	$i \leq 3°$
GR	Griquas	3	3.243	$3.10 \leq a \leq 3.27$	$e \geq 0.35$	(No test)
IIIb	Main belt	480	3.140	$3.03 < a \leq 3.27$	$e < 0.35$	$i \leq 30°$
CYB	Cybeles	51	3.431	$3.27 < a \leq 3.70$	$e \leq 0.30$	$i \leq 25°$
HIL	Hildas	34	3.952	$3.70 < a \leq 4.20$	$e \leq 0.03$	$i \leq 20°$
T	Trojans	35	5.203	$5.05 \leq a \leq 5.40$	(No test)	(No test)
Z	No zone	6	—	—	None of the above	—

		TABLE 5-2			
		AVERAGE ORBITAL ELEMENTS			
Minor planets	a	e	i	q	Q
1–100	2.701	0.164	7.97	2.258	3.144
101–200	2.788	0.144	8.85	2.386	3.182
201–300	2.781	0.134	8.05	2.408	3.154
301–400	2.779	0.141	9.25	2.387	3.171
401–500	2.785	0.147	10.05	2.376	3.194
501–600	2.863	0.149	10.29	2.436	3.290
601–700	2.899	0.151	10.99	2.461	3.337
701–800	2.823	0.149	10.97	2.402	3.244
801–900	2.760	0.144	9.49	2.363	3.157
901–1000	2.859	0.171	10.61	2.370	3.348
1001–1100	2.788	0.158	9.03	2.347	3.228
1101–1200	2.802	0.152	9.44	2.376	3.228
1201–1300	2.842	0.137	9.31	2.453	3.231
1301–1400	2.772	0.149	10.83	2.359	3.185
1401–1500	2.770	0.149	8.54	2.357	3.183
1501–1600	2.724	0.155	10.66	2.302	3.146
1601–1700	2.657	0.171	7.74	2.203	3.111
1701–1800	2.704	0.136	7.32	2.336	3.072
1801–1900	2.819	0.141	9.13	2.421	3.216
1901–2000	2.643	0.164	9.87	2.218	3.068
2001–2100	2.612	0.164	9.13	2.166	3.058
2101–2200	2.732	0.140	8.83	2.367	3.098
2201–2300	2.824	0.164	7.35	2.385	3.263
2301–2400	2.776	0.148	7.83	2.381	3.170
2401–2500	2.689	0.140	6.99	2.315	3.062
2501–2600	2.685	0.136	6.07	2.324	3.047
2601–2700	2.714	0.136	7.71	2.352	3.077
2701–2800	2.706	0.133	6.79	2.349	3.063
2801–2900	2.644	0.131	6.97	2.302	2.986
2901–3000	2.694	0.134	7.76	2.338	3.051
Mean					
1–1000	2.804	0.149	9.65	2.385	3.222
General Mean					
	2.785	0.150	9.40	2.368	3.201

Table 5–2. *Average Orbital Elements. Data from Coombes (1976), supplemented by data from Frederick Pilcher. In intervals of 100 asteroids, average values of the orbital elements are given: a (semi-major axis), e (eccentricity), i (inclination), q (perihelion), Q (aphelion). Units of astronomical units are used for a, q, and Q; i is in degrees.*

ORBITAL CHARACTERISTICS 5

The Greek gods had won out in their contest
with the astronomers—Andromache had escaped!
But her freedom did not last for many years.

A. O. Leuschner, 1936

The best known characteristic of asteroids is that they orbit the sun between the planets Mars and Jupiter. The first indication this is not entirely true came on 14 June 1873, when James Watson discovered 132 Aethra. Although it was followed for only three weeks and then lost for 49.5 years, the orbit calculated by Watson showed its perihelion was inside the aphelion of Mars. Since then many different asteroids have been discovered that do not lie in the main asteroid belt. Various categories, each named after an archetype of its class, are shown in Table 5–1 (Zellner *et al*, 1985).

Apollos, Amors and Atens, collectively called Earth-crossers, will be covered in Chapter 13. The distant Trojan and Hilda asteroids will be the subject of Chapter 15. The mean orbital elements of the first 3,000 asteroids are given in Table 5–2 compiled by Frederick Pilcher.

The apparent motion of asteroids in the sky is usually direct, that is, from west to east. But when an asteroid near opposition is overtaken by the Earth, moving with higher relative velocity, its normal direct motion can become temporarily retrograde (east to west). Such motion is also exhibited by Mars, Jupiter and all other planets beyond Earth. But the Amor asteroids present a unique case. They may have an angular velocity at perihelion opposition greater than that of Earth, in which case they appear to move from west to east (direct opposition motion) rather than the familiar retrograde loops. This has the curious consequence that an Amor asteroid can come to opposition not only one, but three times during a close approach (Pilcher, 1984).

The close proximity of Earth-crossing asteroids to us does not mean they are more easily observed than the distant Trojans. The Aten asteroid 1984 QA, for example, will not be observable again until the year 2040. It came within 4 million kilometers of Earth in August, 1983, but was not discovered until August, 1984. It also has an unstable orbit, so that it will either impact on one of the planets or be ejected from the solar system within 10,000 years.

ORBITAL ELEMENTS

Computation of an asteroid orbit requires the determination of six elements. Five elements are needed to describe the size, shape and orientation of the ellipse itself. The sixth gives the asteroid's position at a particular time, usually when it passes perihelion.

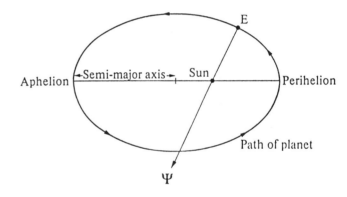

Fig. 5–1. *Plan of an elliptical orbit. If the eccentricity of an orbit is denoted e, and the semi-major axis is denoted a, then the distance between the sun and the perihelion point is a(1 − e). From N. T. Roseveare, Le Verrier To Einstein, 1982. Reprinted by permission of Oxford University Press.*

The size and shape of the ellipse (Fig. 5–1) are given by the length of the semi-major axis, a, and the eccentricity, e, which is defined as c/a, where c is the distance from the sun to the center of the ellipse. If e is less 1, the orbit is an ellipse. If it is equal to 1, the orbit is parabolic, while values higher than 1 signify a hyperbolic orbit. All asteroid orbits are elliptical. Robert Richardson (1967), who computed the orbit of Icarus along with Seth Nicholson, tells an amusing story about Walter Baade, discoverer of Icarus. "He said the only time he had tackled the orbit of an asteroid he got an eccentricity greater than 1. This is ridiculous, since asteroids don't move in hyperbolic orbits. Baade said it made him so mad he never tackled an orbit again. Three years later at the meeting of the IAU in Rome, Baade read a paper that led astronomers to double the size of the universe. But he was baffled by asteroids!" The remaining three orbital elements are shown in Fig. 5–2. The inclination, i, gives the angle between the plane of the asteroid's orbit and that of the earth, the ecliptic. When this angle is greater than 90°, the motion becomes opposite to that of the planets and is said to be retrograde. No asteroid exhibits this motion.

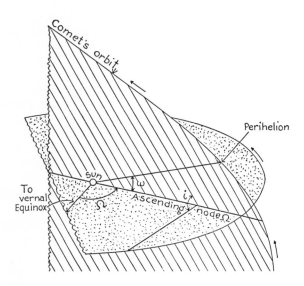

Fig. 5–2. *The geometrical relationships of the orbital elements. Watson, 1956.*

The fourth element, Ω, is the longitude of the ascending node. It is the angular distance measured eastward in the plane of the earth's orbit, from the vernal equinox to the point where the asteroid crosses the ecliptic from south to north.

The fifth element, ω, is called the argument of perihelion. It defines how the major axis of the ellipse is oriented in its orbital plane by giving the angle between the ascending node and the perihelion point, measured in the direction of motion. Another term that may be encountered is the longitude of perihelion, π. It is equal to $\omega + \Omega$, the sum of the two angles not in the same plane.

Some exceptional asteroids include:

1985 PA the highest inclination at 74°.

1383 Limburgia the lowest inclination at 0.014°.

311 Claudia the lowest eccentricity at 0.0031.

3200 Phaethon the highest eccentricity at 0.8979; the smallest perihelion distance at 0.13504.

2060 Chiron the largest perihelion distance at 8.5 AU.

279 Thule the only asteroid at the 4/3 resonance.

944 Hidalgo the first asteroid found in a typical cometary orbit (Fig.5–3).

1373 Cincinnati the only nonresonant stable asteroid the orbit of which passes close enough to Jupiter to suffer strong perturbations.

1685 Toro the only Apollo object involved in a double resonance with two terrestrial planets, Venus and Earth.

1951 Lick the only Amor object not crossing the orbit of any planet, being situated between Earth and Mars.

Hermes made the closest known approach to Earth; 800,000 km or 0.006 AU on 30 October, 1937.

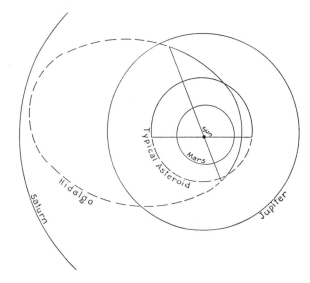

Fig. 5–3. *The orbit of 944 Hidalgo compared to that of a typical asteroid. Hidalgo is the only asteroid in a typical cometary orbit— its aphelion reaches almost to the orbit of Saturn, and it has a high inclination of 42.5 degrees. Watson, 1956.*

The histograms in Figures 5–4 and 5–5 show the distribution of eccentricities and inclinations of the asteroids. For e less than 0.10 there is an increasing number of orbits as e increases; from 0.10 to 0.20 there is a plateau with two maxima; and for e greater than 0.20 the number falls off. The double maxima seems to violate an empirical rule formulated by Plummer (1916) that predicted a single maxima in the eccentricity distribution. Among the numbered asteroids, the primary maxima lies between 0.10 and 0.12, with a secondary between 0.16 and 0.18. But Palomar–Leiden Survey (PLS) asteroids, which generally includes smaller asteroids than those in the numbered list, have a primary maxima between 0.16 and 0.18, with a secondary between 0.12 and 0.14. (Beck, 1981). With the exception of Hidalgo, the eccentricities of long-period asteroids are consistently small.

In 1862 Simon Newcomb noted that the perihelia of asteroid orbits were concentrated on one side of the sun.

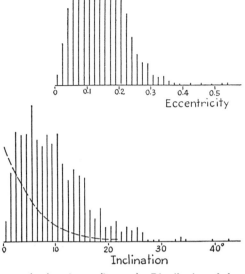

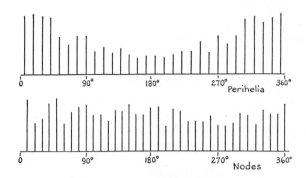

Fig. 5–6. *Distribution of the nodal points of the asteroids. The upper plot shows how the perihelion positions of asteroid orbits are turned with respect to the long axis of Jupiter's orbit. The lower one shows the directions in which asteroid orbits cross the Earth's orbital plane. Watson, 1956.*

Fig. 5–4. *(top) and* 5–5 *(bottom). Distribution of the eccentricties and inclinations of the asteroids. The dashed line shows the distribution of inclinations after correction for the possibility that an orbit will have a low inclination; small tilts are relatively frequent. Watson, 1956.*

While partly a selection effect due to seasonal influences affecting the likelihood of discovery, much of it is due to a tendency for the asteroid orbits to parallel Jupiter's orbit. The directions of the nodal points, where the asteroid orbits cross the ecliptic, show no such clustering (Fig. 5–6; Watson, 1956).

With the exception of Hildalgo, the eccentricities of long-period asteroids are consistently small. Inclinations are also related to orbital period: for periods less than 3.6 years, there are few high inclinations; between 7 and 10 years, the inclinations are all low, while for periods near 12 years there is a large scatter of orbital tilts.

Thus the shapes and orientations of asteroidal orbits depend upon their periods, which in turn indicate the closeness with which they approach the orbit of the giant planet Jupiter. The effects created by the gravitational influence of the solar system's largest planet in the asteroid belt form the topic of the next section.

RESONANCES

The term resonance originated in acoustics, where the audible resonances of musical instruments have been known since antiquity. A note struck on a piano can set a violin string vibrating, for example.

The music of the spheres is analogous to this. With Jupiter as the celestial piano, and the asteroids as violin strings, a complex series of resonances have been established. These relationships were first noted by Daniel Kirkwood. "The first statement Kirkwood made of the asteroid gaps, apparently, and also of the gaps in the rings

of Saturn, was before the Buffalo meeting of the American Association for the Advancement of Science, in August 1866." (Hogg, 1950). Based on 87 asteroid orbits, his results were published briefly in 1867 and more fully in 1868, when he listed 97 asteroids ranging from Flora at 2.20 AU to Sylvia at 3.49 AU.

A histogram of the asteroids (Fig. 5–7) clearly shows several gaps. Kirkwood calculated the orbital periods of these gaps and designated them t. In accordance with Kepler's Third Law, he found they were related to the orbital period of Jupiter, T, by the relationship

$$\frac{t}{T} = \frac{a}{Ae^{3/2}}$$

where a is the gap and A the distance of Jupiter in A. U.

Kirkwood found for t/T the following data: A period equal to 1/2 that of Jupiter is 3.2776 AU and that 4/9 = 3.0299 AU; 3/7 = 2.9574 AU; 2/5 = 2.8245 AU; 1/3 = 2.5012 AU; and 2/7 = 2.2569 AU.

To account for these intervals, Kirkwood formulated a gravitational hypothesis. "A planetary particle at the distance 2.5—in the interval between Thetis and Hestia—would make precisely three revolutions while Jupiter completes one (the 1/3 resonance); coming always into conjunction with that planet in the same parts of its path. Consequently its orbit would become more and more eccentric until the particle would unite with others, either interior or exterior, thus forming the nucleus of an asteroid. Even should the disturbed body not come in contact with other matter, the action of Jupiter would ultimately change its mean distance, and thus destroy the commensurability of the periodic times. In either case, the primitive orbit of the particle would be left destitute of matter."

This means that in the first gap the asteroids have a period one-half that of Jupiter, in the second gap four-ninths, and so on. As shown in Fig. 5–7, eight major resonances are now recognized. Asteroids were first found at resonant positions in the following years: 1875: Hilda at 3/2 1888: Thule at 4/3 1908: Achilles at 1/1 1918: Alinda at 3/1 1918: Griqua at 2/1. Three of these resonances are not gaps at all, but concentrations of asteroids: the Hilda

Photo. 5–1. *Daniel Kirkwood (1814–1895), American astronomer and professor of mathematics at the University of Indiana. As early as 1857, Kirkwood noticed that three regions of the minor planet belt were devoid of asteroids. In 1866, he announced the discovery of what became known as the Kirkwood gaps, and he went on to do preliminary work on asteroid families.*

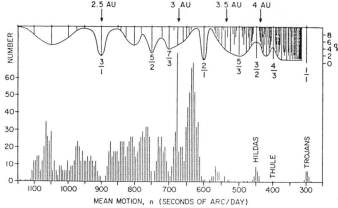

Fig. 5–7. *Frequency distribution of the asteroids between the Sun and 1/1 resonance with Jupiter. Resonances are indicated on top of the diagram as vertical solid lines of length inversely proportional to their order. The location of the Hildas, Thule and the Trojans are indicated. Greenberg & Scholl, 1979.*

$$\sigma = Q\lambda - P\lambda - J + (P - Q)\overline{\omega},$$

where Q and P are integers, λ and λ_J are the mean longitudes of the asteroid and Jupiter, and $\overline{\omega}$ is the longitude of perihelion of the asteroid (Chapman *et al*, 1978).

While most common commensurabilities depend on the asteroid's orbital eccentricity, inclination-type resonances are also possible, although they tend to be much weaker. Mathematically, this is due to the fact that terms occur at one lower power of the eccentricity than of the inclination. This power is the difference $P - Q$, and is called the degree (denoted by q). Its relative strength at different resonances is shown along the top of Fig. 5–7.

Asteroids can even be in resonance with one another. Opik (1970) examined the effect of Ceres on Pallas, which have nearly identical mean distances from the Sun, mean angular motions and periods of revolution. This 1/1 commensurability results in conjunctions approximately every 2,640 years (the last one being about 313 years ago). Opik concludes that the two asteroids are little affected by resonance, having retained their orbital characteristics since their formation in the same "ring of diffuse matter." The stability of a resonance is determined by the phase angle, σ. If it librates about some angle, usually 0 or 180°, the resulting resonances will be very stable. Such is the case for 4/3, 3/2, and 2/1. At 1/1, the phase angle librates about 60°, a case that will be considered in Chapter 15.

As an example, consider the asteroid 1362 Griqua at the 2/1 resonance. In 1970, Brian Marsden did a study of Griqua's orbit. Fig. 5–8 shows the oscillations of the phase angle for a period of 3,000 years. Griqua librates about 0° with an amplitude of 100° to 120° in a period of close to 400 years. The numbers at the maxima and minima of the curve show the least distances from Jupiter in AU. These take place when the libration is near its extremes. Marsden concluded that Griqua's nodal period is 34,000 years. Liu and Innanen (1985) have found that the resonant phenomenon becomes more pronounced as the orbital eccentricity of the asteroid increases. In addition,

group at 3/2, Thule at 4/3 and the Trojans at 1/1. Percival Lowell caught the essence of it best when he stated "If the asteroids were numerous enough we should actually behold in the sky a replica of Saturn's rings, altered only by the perspective of our different point of view." (Lowell, 1917).

The early interest in resonances stemmed from the ability to deduce fairly accurate masses of the objects involved. In the late 19th century, for example, Simon Newcomb used perturbations in the orbit of the asteroid Polyhymnia to find the mass of Jupiter to be 1/1047.35 that of the sun. This is nearly identical to the modern value of 1/1047.355.

One modern goal of theorists is to formulate a theory of the origin of the resonances, and why some generate gaps and others concentrations of asteroids. Milani *et al* (1985) have found "a difference in the local topology between the 2/1 Hecuba gap and the 3/2 Hilda group based purely on gravity." While much research remains to be done, it appears there is a "protection mechanism in the asteroid motion" that permits clustering at some resonances and gaps at others.

Resonances such as 2/1 are called commensurabilities, wherein Jupiter's and the asteroids' orbital periods have a ratio of small whole numbers. In such a case, the asteroid and Jupiter repeat their relative positions (eg conjunctions) at certain longitudes. For such a resonance, a phase angle is defined to be

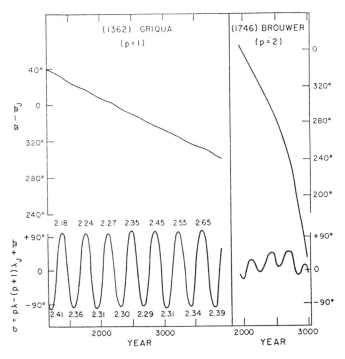

Fig. 5–8. *Oscillations of the phase angle in the orbit of 1362 GRIQUA, librating about the 2/1 resonance and 1746 BROUWER (right). The figures at the maxima and minima of the curve indicate the least distances from Jupiter. Marsden, 1970. Reprinted by permission of the* Astronomical Journal.

the variations of the elements a, e and i are larger in the regions of the resonant zone which lie just inside or outside the boundary of the libration region.

While the mathematical theory of resonances is beyond the scope of this book, it is important to understand the basic principles and their shortcomings. Most models have been based on the three-body problem (Sun-Jupiter-asteroid), which is a reasonable approximation since the disturbing influence of Jupiter far exceeds that of the other planets (Giffen, 1973).

In the study of planetary motions, the theory of secular perturbations can be used over intervals of 10^5 years. This theory fails in the case of commensurable motion, however, due to the presence of the infamous small divisors in the series expansions of the perturbations. The alternative of numerically integrating the equations of motion directly also fails for long time intervals due to cumulative round-off errors.

Thus, almost every theoretical and numerical study of the asteroid resonances rely on the so-called averaging principle. It was first introduced by Lagrange and Laplace, and was explicitly stated by Gauss, who replaced each planet by a ring of mass whose density at each longitude was inversely proportional to the planet's velocity at that longitude.

Following an extension of this idea by Poincare in 1902, J. Schubart developed a model in the 1960's for the investigation of commensurable motion at a resonance. This averaging principle remains an intuitive assertion which is, strictly speaking, untrue. According to V. I. Arnol'd, "This principle is neither a theorem, an axiom, nor a def-

inition, but a physical proposition. Such assertions are often fruitful sources of mathematical theorems."

The averaging principle is used simply because it is too expensive to study unaveraged equations of motion. The averaging process eliminates short-period variations, making the equations tractable. With this caveat in mind, we can now look at the four theories put forward to explain the Kirkwood gaps.

Collisional Hypothesis

The Kirkwood gaps are created by collisions between asteroids according to this hypothesis. These collisions result either in destruction of the asteroid in the gaps, or an orbital change that sends them out of the gaps.

In 1975, T. A. Heppenheimer investigated this problem by a Monte Carlo simulation of collisions at the 2/1 commensurability. The evolution of 50 fictitious asteroids was followed, and all remained in the gap even after numerous collisions. He also concluded that the fragmentation of gap asteroids by collision is only slightly faster than for nonresonant asteroids outside of the gaps, again militating against the collisional hypothesis.

Stanley Dermott and Carl Murray provided further evidence militating against this hypothesis in 1981. They found there is no significant tendency for low-magnitude objects to be further away from the resonances than high-magnitude objects. Such a tendency was predicted by the collisional hypothesis. Binzel (1986) has also concluded that inter-asteroid collisions are not an important process in clearing the Kirkwood gaps.

Cosmogonic Hypothesis

This hypothesis suggests the gaps represent regions where asteroids failed to form during the early history of the solar system. This highly speculative hypothesis was examined by Heppenheimer in 1978. On the assumption that planetesimals break up at velocities exceeding 100 m/sec, his model predicted that Jupiter would increase the eccentricities, and therefore velocities, of the planetesimals at the resonant positions. The surrounding nebula would decrease the eccentricities outside these areas, thus allowing the planetesimals to remain in stable orbits without breaking up.

This model suffers from severe initial constraints, however. It requires an appropriate density, mass and temperature for the nebula, and implies that all asteroids are formed in almost circular orbits in a thin disk. It also requires the Hilda asteroids, which are in resonant motion, to be formed at a different place. And since low eccentric orbits behave like nonresonant orbits, asteroids with small eccentricities should be visible in the Kirkwood gaps, a prediction not supported by observation.

Dermott & Murray (1983) conclusively eliminated the cosmogonic hypothesis. They showed that the resonant locations in the asteroid belt must have formed after the asteroids dispersed from the disk in which they accreted.

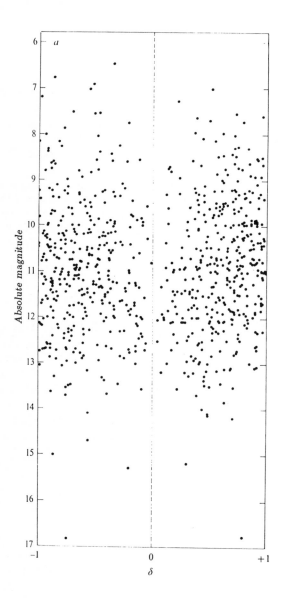

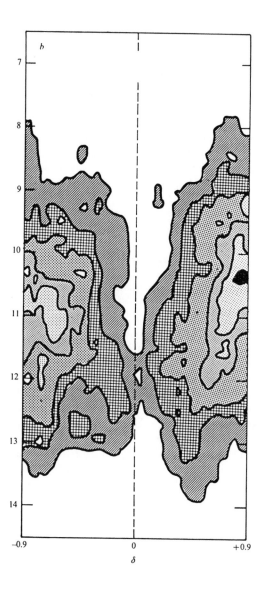

Fig. 5–9. *(left) and* **–10** *(right). A plot of absolute magnitude versus delta (a measure of the displacement from the nearest strong resonance) for 757 asteroids between 2.5 and 3.28 AU from the Sun which are not members of families. The apparent lack of asteroids with large absolute magnitudes is a selection effect. Dermott & Murray, 1981. Fig 5–10: A smoothed number density contour plot of the data points in Fig 5–9. The continuously increasing number density as delta increases implies that the effects of resonance pervade the entire asteroid belt. Dermott & Murray, 1981. Reprinted by permission from Nature, Vol. 290, pp 664.*

Statistical Hypothesis

Just as a pendulum spends the majority of its time away from the bottom of its swing, or equilibrium point, so asteroids near commensurabilities undergo large variations in their semi-major axes, spending most of their time outside the gaps.

While this hypothesis was considered by Brendel in 1924 and Brown in 1928, it was not put to a numerical test until 1969, when Francois Schweizer used a modern computer. He calculated the orbits of 185 asteroids around the Hecuba gap at 2/1, 20 orbits at 5/2, and 13 orbits around the Hestia gap at 3/1, as well as four orbits inside of gaps.

In each case, he took the osculating mean motion n_0, which performs nearly sinusoidal oscillations around a mean value x with a period on the order of several hundred years. While quite a short time scale, it is thought his results are valid up to at least 10^5 years. When Schweizer plotted the distribution function for n, the result still showed Kirkwood gaps. If asteroids really crossed the gaps, this time averaged plot would have filled them in.

Dermott & Murray (1983) showed that the Kirkwood gaps "cannot possibly be a statistical phenomenon." For it to be tenable, most asteroids near a gap must be librators, but observations show the regions where they should exist are almost devoid of asteroids.

Gravitational Hypothesis

The gravitational hypothesis, the most widely accepted explanation for the origin of the Kirkwood gaps, says the gaps are formed by purely gravitational interactions with Jupiter.

Both Stanley Dermott and Carl Murray in 1981 and 1983, and Jack Wisdom in 1982 and 1983 have provided strong evidence to support the gravitational hypothesis. In the first study, 757 main-belt, non-family asteroids were used. To analyze the properties of asteroids and their orbits, Dermott and Murray defined a parameter δ as the measure of the displacement of an asteroid from the nearest strong resonance. An exact resonance corresponds to $\delta = 0$, while $|\delta| = 1$ is the greatest displacement from resonance that an asteroid can have.

A direct plot of absolute magnitude, B(1,0) versus δ is shown in Fig. 5–9. Figure 5–10 shows a smoothed number density contour plot based on the same data. Since the number density increases continuously as d increases, this implies the effects of resonance pervade the whole distribution of main-belt asteroids.

Dermott and Murray showed that observational selection produces an excess of high magnitude, low inclination asteroids. Thus, they reduced their data set to 144 asteroids, constituting a bias-free set, from which they concluded there is no magnitude-frequency distribution change near the Kirkwood gaps. This result was mentioned as tending to disprove the collisional hypothesis.

More importantly, they found the tendency for both eccentricity and inclination to increase with increasing $|\delta|$ is a fundamental property of the Kirkwood gaps (Fig. 5–

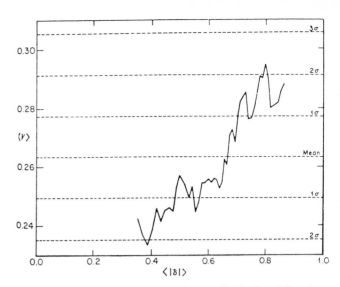

Fig. 5–11. *A plot showing the tendency of both E' and I' to increase with increasing $|\delta|$ indicates the effects of gravitational forces acting on individual asteroids, as a possible mechanism for the origin of the Kirkwood gaps. Dermott & Murray, 1981. Reprinted by permission from Nature, Vol. 290, pp 664.*

11). Since the magnitude of the gravitational disturbing function acting on an asteroid increases with e and i, this result strongly suggests that Jupiter's gravitational effect creates the Kirkwood gaps.

They conclude that at least some of the Kirkwood gaps have been formed since the time of formation of the solar system, and that they are not simply regions of small asteroid number density since the effects of resonance pervade the entire asteroid belt. They confirmed and extended these conclusions in 1983. Fig. 5–12 shows quite dramatically the lack of asteroids at resonant positions in the belt, particularly at 3.3 AU and 4.0 AU where resonances overlap. The few asteroids that remain in a libration region tend to have eccentricities much higher than the average of their neighbors.

Near the 3/1 commensurability, for example, only two asteroids are known with librating orbits: Alinda ($e = 0.55$) and Quetzalcoatl ($e = 0.58$). According to the gravitational mechanism, large eccentricities can be expected for librating orbits whose rate of change of perihelion longitude is near zero. As shown by Scherbaum & Kazantsev (1985), this is precisely what is found. Wisdom (1982) used a set of 300 'test asteroids' in the neighborhood of the 3/1 commensurability to determine if gravitational influences over a period of 2 million years could produce a gap. Such a gap formed, but was narrower than the actual one. Using improved computational techniques, he repeated the test.

"Of the 300 test asteroids in the random distribution, 89 were found to have chaotic trajectories and only 11 were quasiperiodic librators. All but five of the chaotic trajectories became Mars crossing within 300,000 years and only one had not reached an eccentricity of 0.3 within 1 million years. The predicted gap is now in satisfactory agreement with the full distribution of real asteroids." (Wisdom, 1983). As Fig. 5–13 clearly shows, the boundaries of the chaotic zone discovered by Wisdom match the boundaries of the real 3/1 Kirkwood gap quite well.

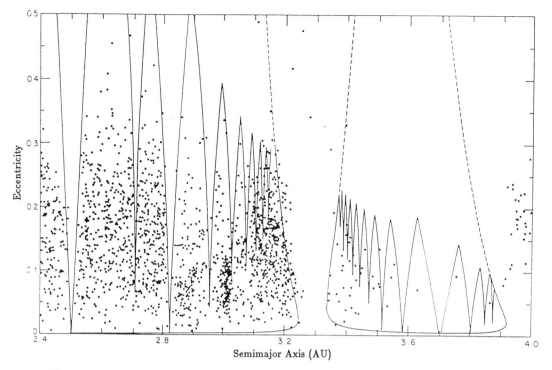

Fig. 5-12. *Distribution of the osculating eccentricities of all asteroids with 2.4 < a < 4.0 AU listed in the TRIAD file. The solid lines represent the libration width associated with the leading eccentricity term in the expansion of the disturbing function. All resonances in the $p/(2p+1)$, $p/(p-1)$ and $3p(3p+1)$ series, and the 8:3 resonance at 2.70 AU, are shown. Resonance overlap occurs where the solid lines meet. In the region of resonance overlap the libration widths of the 2 : 1 resonance of 3.3 AU and the 3 : 2 resonance at 4.0 AU are represented by dashed lines. Dermott & Murray, 1981. Reprinted by permission from Nature, Vol. 301, pp 204.*

Several important conclusions result from this work.

1. Chaotic orbits are common, contrary to the results of previous work: collision probabilities with the Earth and Mars appear adequate to remove the asteroids with chaotic orbits within the age of the solar system.

2. Sudden large increases in the eccentricity of asteroids occur near the 3/1 commensurability, and likely others as well.

3. The outer boundary of the chaotic region corresponds precisely to the boundary of the 3/1 Kirkwood gap, thus showing that the gravitational hypothesis can adequately explain the gap.

This line of research has been explored further by Murray (1986), who found extensive chaotic regions in the vicinity of both the 2/1 and 3/2 resonances. In the central region of the 2/1 resonance is an area where asteroids will become Jupiter crossing, whereas no such central area exists at 3/2. He suggests that this difference in the high-eccentricity regions may explain why asteroids are found at the 3/2 resonance but absent at 2/1.

Before leaving the subject, mention must be made of secular resonances and libration of the argument of perihelion, ω. Secular resonances arise if the rate of the node or perihelion of an asteroid matches a frequency of one of the fundamental, long-period oscillations of the planetary system. Several such resonances are known, and all

are greatly depleted in asteroids. Secular resonances may have caused the present distribution of eccentricity and inclinations of the asteroids (Scholl and Froeschle, 1985). They will be considered further in Chapter 13.

While not usually classed as a resonance, the argument of perihelion, ω, of an asteroid can librate about 90° or 270° when a combination of e and i exceeds a critical value. Only 1373 Cincinnati and the Mars crosser 1974 UB exhibit such behavior, both librating about 90°. In the case of Cincinnati, the period of libration is 11,000 years.

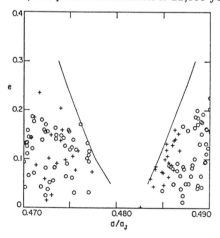

Fig. 5-13. *Boundaries of the chaotic zone that define the 3/1 Kirkwood Gap. Numbered asteroids are denoted by circles; PLS asteroids by plus signs. Wisdom, 1983. Reproduced by permission from Icarus.*

COMPOSITION
AND TAXONOMY   6

There was a time—and very recently—when the idea of learning the composition of the celestial bodies was considered senseless even by prominent scientists and thinkers. That time has now passed. To step out onto the soil of asteroids, to lift with your hand a stone on the moon, to set up moving stations in ethereal space—what could be more extravagant!

Konstantin Tsiolkovsky, 1911.

CLASSIFICATION

There are several different classification schemes for asteroids, some based on observational parameters like albedo, others based on shared spectral characteristics. Unlike the old days, when all asteroids looked the same, they now come in all shapes, sizes and colors to suit every taste.

Classification schemes, however, are useful only as long as they help bring order and understanding to a chaotic situation. On some level each asteroid is unique. As data become more complete, scientists are faced with potentially arbitrary decisions as to how much variety can be permitted in a given type, and how different an asteroid can be before it defines a new type.

The most widely used classification system employs single-letter designations, and was developed in the early 1970's. Beginning with just the C and S types, it has now grown to 14 classes (Table 6-1). Each letter relates to the inferred composition of an asteroid, or a feature of its spectral reflectivity: C (carbonaceous), S (stony), M (metallic), F (flat), R (red) and so on. The D, P, F, and A classes were only recognized between 1979 and 1983. Figs. 6-1 to 6-5 indicate the IR domain of each class.

The vast majority of asteroids are types C and S. The paper by Bowell *et al* (1978), which set up the five basic classes, recognized 190 C-types, 141 S-types, 13 M-types, and only 3 each of the E and R class, with 55 considered unclassifiable. More than 650 asteroids now have types assigned to them, including 15 D-class (Tedesco *et al*, 1983a), and only 1 R-class. This single asteroid, Dembowska, is now believed to be unique, and the asteroids originally assigned to the R-class were re-classified as type A.

The A-class was first recognized by Veeder *et al* (1983),

TABLE 6-1		
Type	Visual Geometric Albedo	Spectral Reflectivity
T	Very low (0.042)	Similar to D-class
P	Low (0.05)	Similar to M hence pseudo-M or P
D	Low (0.05)	Very red longward of 0.7μm
F	Low (0.065)	Flat
B	Low (0.065)	Similar to C-class
G	Low (0.065)	Similar to C-class
C	Low (0.065)	Neutral, slight absorption blueward of 0.4μm
S	Moderate (0.09-0.24)	Reddened, typically an absorption band at 0.9 to 1.0μm
M	Moderate (0.07-0.21)	Featureless, sloping up into red
A	Moderate (0.12)	Rises steeply to 0.7μm then slopes downward
Q	High (0.21)	Identical to ordinary chondrites
V	High (0.25)	Vesta; strong absorption band at 0.95μm
R	High (0.25)	Very red; bands deeper than S
E	Very high (0.33)	Featureless; flat or sloping into red

Table 6-1. *The Tholen Taxonomic Classification.*

who presented JHK data and some UVB observations by David Tholen and Ed Tedesco to distinguish them from the S-types.

Some asteroids in the original classification system have multiple-letter designations. Type CMEU, for example, means the asteroid could be any one of these classes. Since C asteroids are the most numerous, it is listed first as being the most likely possibility by default.

David Tholen (1983) has more recently produced a far more comprehensive and logical asteroid taxonomy based

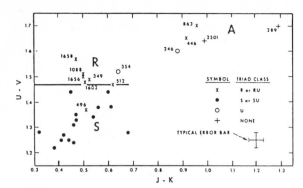

Fig. 6–1

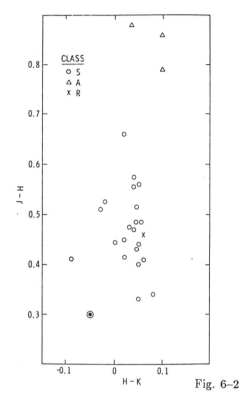

Fig. 6–2

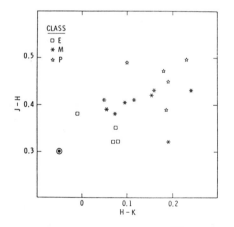

Fig. 6–3

Photo. 6–1. *David Tholen, assistant astronomer at the University of Hawaii. While at the University of Arizona, he observed hundreds of minor planets for the eight-color survey, and subsequently developed a new classification system for the asteroids.*

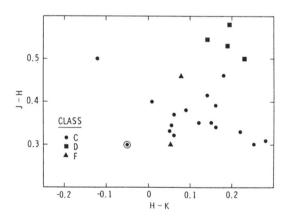

Fig. 6–1 *through* **–4.** *The color domains of various types of asteroids. A closed dot surrounded by a circle indicates the color of the Sun. Fig. 6–1 is from Tedesco et al, 1983a. Figs. 6–2 –3 & –4 are from Veeder et al, 1983.*

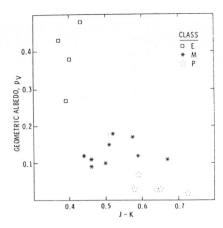

Fig. 6–5. *A plot of asteroid colors in magnitudes versus geometric albedo, for the same asteroids in the color-color plot of Fig. 6–3. Veeder et al, 1983. Reprinted by permission of the* Astronomical Journal.

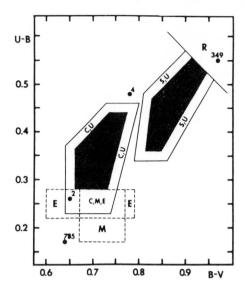

Fig. 6–6a. *Domains of asteroid types distinguished by UBV colors, with four representative asteroids. This was the system used in the TRIAD file in 1979. Zellner, 1979. Reprinted from* Asteroids *by Tom Gehrels by permission of the University of Arizona Press.*

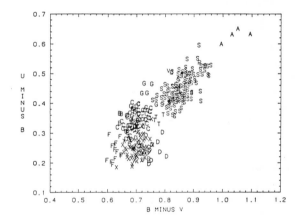

Fig. 6–6b. *A similar plot in the new classification system developed by David Tholen is devoid of rigid boundaries. Each letter represents an individual asteroid. Tholen, 1984b.*

on the eight-color survey. Using 405 objects with high-quality data, he found that seven major classes and seven minor classes account for all the sample asteroids. Multiple designations, such as EMPC, also occur in this system. The first letter here represents the most likely taxonomic class. The old system of rigid boundaries (Fig. 6–6a) hase also been eliminated in the new system (Fig. 6–6b). Something that fell just outside of a boundary used to be given a U (unidentifiable) designation, ignoring the possibility of measurement error.

His system is based on the concept of numerical taxonomy or cluster analysis, which evaluates the affinity between taxonomic units and orders these into taxa accordingly. This method was first employed by Pike (1978) using 22 asteroids and Davies *et al* (1982), using a data set of only 82 asteroids. The resulting taxonomy recognizes gross spectral differences; classes are "suggested by gaps or abrupt density changes in the distribution of objects in the seven-dimensional color space and one-dimensional albedo space." (Tholen 1984b) Of necessity, several papers published prior to the Tholen system have been used in this book, a point to keep in mind to avoid confusion.

Much confusion has arisen over the use of C as an asteroid class. The term C was derived from their spectral similarity to some carbonaceous chondritic meteorites and the fact that both the asteroids and meteorites have low albedos. But meteorites are classed according to their chemical composition, while asteroids are classed spectrally. C–type asteroids do not necessarily have carbonaceous surfaces or compositions (Lebofsky, 1980). According to Wasson (1985) there are several reasons why the spectra of asteroids are not readily matched by the laboratory spectra measured on meteorite powders or mixtures of minerals:

1. At each wavelength, the spectrum tends to be dominated by the most strongly absorbing component.

2. The degree of absorption varies with grain size.

3. Common meteoritic materials are opaque having no absorption features.

4. Space-weathering tends to produce darker materials with less-pronounced absorption features than meteorite powders.

5. Regoliths consist of mixtures more heterogeneous than most meteorites.

In Tholen's system, types E, M and P are spectrally degenerate; that is, their spectra cannot be distinguished from one another. Differences do show up in thermal radiometry, but aside from this case all asteroid types are recognized by visual photometry. No new asteroid type has been recognized by JHK photometry alone that visual photometry doesn't also recognize. While it is still some-

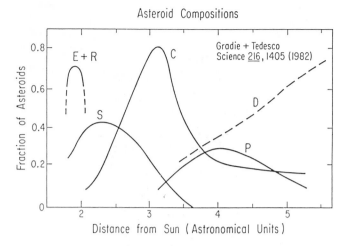

Asteroid Compositions

Fig. 6–7. *The distribution of compositional types as a function of distance from the Sun, based on a sample of 1,373 asteroids. Gradie & Tedesco, 1982. Copyright 1982 by the AAAS.*

what contentious, it appears that the best way to classify an asteroid is to have high-quality data spanning 0.3 microns (atmospheric cutoff) to 3.0 microns (onset of thermal radiation), along with a geometric albedo at some wavelength in that range.

Aside from all the technical squabbles over spectra, composition, albedos and colors, there is a very dramatic way in which the asteroids can be distinguished. Gradie and Tedesco (1982) showed that each type dominates a different region of the asteroid belt, with at least six major compositionally distinct regions (Fig. 6–7). They infer from this that the asteroids formed at or near their present locations, and this should provide insights into the conditions present in the solar nebula at the time the solar system formed.

The other major way to classify asteroids involves the identification and interpretation of specific spectral features that are characteristic of specific minerals or mineral types. As explained by McFadden *et al* (1985), mineralogy is controlled by initial chemistry, temperature and pressure, so the presence of the same absorption bands on different asteroids implies they underwent a similar evolution. The strength of an absorption band is a function of particle size, which may be controlled by primary processes such as cooling rate or secondary regolith-forming processes (i.e., collisions). In addition to knowing what physical processes may produce the observed features, this method also requires sufficient spectral resolution and wavelength coverage to distinguish different types of asteroids (Gaffey & McCord, 1979). Being more subjective than the single-letter system, this system has resulted in an avalanche of categories.

Chapman *et al* (1978) took 35 different visible and near-IR spectral types and grouped them into 16 categories with significantly different mineralogical compositions. Using the Gaffey & McCord list, King *et al* (1983) have classified 113 spectra into 14 groups. Within each group, a wide range of albedos exist, in contrast to the method described earlier. Feierberg *et al* (1982) have examined the spectra of S–type asteroids, dividing them into nine groups, desig-

nated Sa to Si. These correspond to different proportions of olivine and pyroxene, and the fraction of silicates like iron, magnesium and calcium.

SURFACES OF ASTEROIDS

The successful acquisition of observational data for asteroid surfaces does not by itself always lead to immediate scientific results.

H. P. Larson, 1977.

While a geologist-astronaut standing on the surface of an asteroid would be greeted by a treasure trove of minerals to study, most people would find the prospect bleak indeed. The horizon would appear much closer than it does on the earth or the Moon, even on the largest asteroids. Aside from this, it would probably appear similar to the Apollo 11 landing site—numerous craters of varying sizes, with flat to rolling terrain, possibly with a light coating of dust, and generally gray in color. Temperature, about 150 Kelvin, atmosphere, none.

Impacts of smaller objects which have continued at certain levels of activity since the formation of the asteroids create a layer of fragmental rocky debris known as regolith over the entire surface of the asteroid. Models to elucidate the nature of the regolith have characterized studies of asteroidal surfaces since the early 1970's (Table 6–2).

According to Housen (1981), the amount of regolith determines whether or not an asteroid can yield a significant amount of so-called brecciated meteorites that are found on the Earth. A breccia is simply a rock composed of broken rock fragments (the regolith) cemented together by finer-grained material. An estimate of regolith depths on an asteroid can be used to help model the size of parent bodies for meteorites.

While every study prior to 1981 considered regolith development to be due solely to crater ejecta, Horz and Schaal (1981) claim that asteroidal regolith may be completely dominated by spallation processes. Before considering this important aspect, a brief review of the ejecta process is in order.

Models of asteroidal regoliths must specify the mass distribution of the impacting bodies, their impact velocity, size of crater produced, the amount of regolith lost into space due to an impact, and the degree to which the regolith is churned or "gardened". Various studies have shown that regoliths are quite variable in depth, whether or not the effects of large craters are included.

Regolith depth increases with the asteroid's size because larger bodies have a greater gravitational pull, thus limiting the amount lost in space. But for sufficiently large asteroids (about 300 km), the amount of regolith will tend to decrease. In this large domain, crater diameters decrease with increasing gravity. As ejecta blanketing decreases, gardening increases. To give some numerical estimates, small objects are thought to have regoliths ranging from dust coatings to layers a few meters thick, depending on the asteroid's strength. An asteroid 300 km in diameter

TABLE 6–2		
Surface Processes on Asteroids		
Type	Process	Effect
External	Cratering and Spallation	Produces regolith blocks craters spallation scars, facets, edges etc., grooves (?) May compact regolith.
Surface	Gravity	Produces downslope movement of loose material.
Internal	"Volcanism"	On some C objects, may produce release of volatiles (e.g. H_2O vapor). On larger objects may produce lava flows.

Table 6–2. *Surface Processes On Asteroids. Table from Veverka & Thomas (1979). Reprinted from Asteroids by Tom Gehrels by permission of the University of Arizona Press.*

will have 3.5 km of regolith, but asteroids 500 km or larger have only 1.2 km. (Housen *et al*, 1979). These are only averages though, and it is expected that major variations occur among otherwise similar asteroids. Webster & Lowman (1984) have inferred a regolith-like surface layer on 15 Eunomia, based on microwave continuum spectra, only 1 cm deep. The theory of Horz and Schaal says there is an effect which is an order of magnitude more important than any considered by these ejecta theories. An object hitting an asteroid will send shock waves through it. These may reach the other side of the asteroid with sufficient magnitude to cause spallation—that is, whole chunks or plates of the surface may be fractured, increasing regolith. The mass contained in these "spall products" exceeds that created by the actual crater volume.

Further, the seismic energy released by such an impact will shake the asteroid, possibly leading to an interesting twist in the gardening mechanism—coarse grains may form a matrix through which fine grains percolate to the bottom. This theory accounts quite neatly for the coarse-grained nature of asteroidal surfaces inferred from the meteorite evidence, as well as the time meteorites are thought to sit on the surface. This can be estimated by measuring the amount of solar wind gases that have been implanted in the meteorite. The ejecta theories postulated crater production rates 2 to 3 orders of magnitude larger than the lunar ones, while the Horz and Schaal theory predicts roughly equivalent rates. The spall deposits essentially take the place of rapid ejecta creation, both of which tend to bury already existing regolith, and thus shield it from the solar wind.

Another surface feature that may be present on many small asteroids are grooves. It is thought that a nearly catastrophic impact will create fractures, from which regolith will be ejected by steam derived from dehydration of carbonaceous material. Such an ejecta mechanism will create grooves that have been seen on the Martian satellite Phobos (Thomas & Veverka, 1979; Fig. 6–8).

Even though the surfaces of asteroids are not directly visible from the Earth, a combination of laboratory and

Photo. 6–2. *Dmitrij Lupishko, deputy- director of the Astronomical Observatory at Kharkov University in the Soviet Union. Dr. Lupishko uses the 70 cm reflector of the Institute of Astrophysics in Tadzhik to conduct photometric studies of asteroids.*

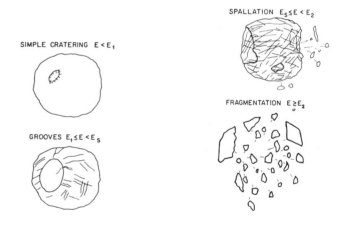

Fig. 6–8. *Schematic diagram showing the results of different types of impact involving progressively higher energies. Beginning with an isolated crater, the next step is a crater plus associated fracturing, followed by spallation. The final case is complete fragmentation. Thomas & Veverka, 1979. Reproduced by permission from Icarus.*

observational methods can draw some educated inferences concerning the nature of an asteroid's surface properties.

Employing polarimetry, Dollfus *et al* (1979) concluded that M–type asteroids have a surface texture that is a powder of small metallic fragments with grain sizes between 20 and 50 microns. It was later shown by Feierberg *et al* (1983) that this powder is mixed with a significant amount of fine silicate dust, thus ruling out a pure metallic surface.

Turning from the microscopic to the macroscopic, Schober *et al* (1980) show that small-scale features in lightcurves are indicative of surface features. They employ a simple equation to transform differences of magnitudes and times to the actual geometric extent of surface features:

$$\Delta m = -2.5 \log \left(A + \frac{\Delta A}{A} \right),$$

where $A = \pi D^2 / 4$ is the area of the asteroid, ΔA is the increase of the projected area, D is the diameter and Δm is the magnitude difference of the observed lightcurve feature. Using the relation $L = \Delta A^{1/2}$, we get the linear extension L of a surface element that causes the bump or dip in the lightcurve. Using the asteroid 337 Devosa as an example, they note that a 0.02 magnitude bump in the lightcurve corresponds to a surface feature some 6 or 7 km in extent, perhaps craters or mountains (Fig. 6–9).

Lupishko *et al* (1983) have taken exception to the widely-held assumption that asteroid surfaces are homogeneous. They show that average reflectivity variations can reach 0.15 mag, in contrast to the conclusion of Degewij *et al* (1979), who state that albedo variations are negligible. According to Lupishko, we can distinguish 10 gradations in polarization, 50 in color and 500 in albedo, if the size and shape of the asteroid is known.

Using albedo as the most sensitive parameter we have for detecting heterogeneity on surfaces of asteroids, they present a mathematical treatment that allows the contribution of albedo spots to be removed from a lightcurve (Fig. 6–10). The resulting lightcurve is due to non-spherical shape alone. Thus, many asteroids may not be single geologic units, a basic assumption of the crater ejecta regolith theories. Employing speckle interferometry, Drummond *et al* (1984b) discovered a bright spot on 532 Herculina. Some 75% brighter than the rest of the asteroid, it extends over a diameter of 55° of the asteroid's surface. Asteroids with the greatest differences between opposite sides are given in Table 6–3.

Unlike these other methods, radar provides a direct means of measuring the surface topography and roughness of asteroid surfaces. For all the asteroids measured so far, most of the echo power is in the OC polarization (see Methods of Investigation chapter). Estimates of the circular polarization ratio range from 0.00 to 0.40. This is similar to the lunar value, implying similar decimetre-scale morphologies for both. S–types tend to be slightly rougher (0.14) than C–types (0.08) at centimeter to meter scales. It has also been found that the ratio for S–types decreases slightly with asteroid size, which is consistent with the theory that predicts thinner, rockier regoliths on

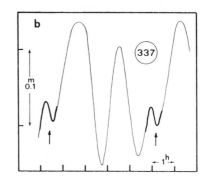

Fig. 6–9. *A smoothed lightcurve of 337 Devosa, showing features that can be associated with small- scale characteristics on its surface. Schober et al, 1980.*

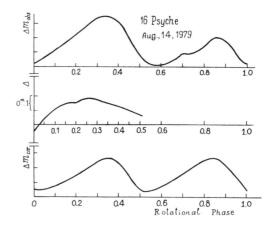

Fig. 6–10. *Separation of the contribution of albedo spots and shape to the light curve of 16 Psyche. The lower curve corresponds to a photometrically-homogeneous surface. It is due to non-spherical shape and was obtained by correcting the magnitudes of opposite sides of the asteroid by $\Delta/2$, with the appropriate sign. Lupishko et al, 1983.*

smaller asteroids (Ostro *et al*, 1985).

To look at a few examples, the circular polarization ratio of Pallas (0.05 ± 0.02) indicates nearly all the echo must be due to single-reflection backscattering from surface elements which are very smooth from centimeter to meter-scale within the top few meters of the regolith. At the other extreme is Vesta (0.40 ± 0.11), which has substantial decimetre-scale structure near the surface. For near-Earth asteroids, the distribution of ratios overlaps the high end of the distribution for main-belt objects, implying they are much rougher than large asteroids at centimeter to meter scales. (Ostro, 1985a).

MINERALOGY

Our knowledge of the composition of asteroids is due largely to recent spectroscopic observations, and similarities between them and laboratory spectra of meteorites. Olbers, in 1805, was the first to suggest that meteorites are asteroidal fragments, but this was apparently a revision of his earlier views.

Table 6-3. *Asteroids with the greatest differences in brightness between opposite sides. Columns give asteroid number, name, compositional type, phase angle in degrees, dm (amplitude), dmax (maximum observed difference in magnitudes), P(h) the rotational period in hours, pv (geometric albedo), and D(km) the diameter. Table from Lupishko et al (1983).*

TABLE 6–3 ASTEROIDS WITH THE GREATEST DIFFERENCES IN BRIGHTNESS BETWEEN OPPOSITE SIDES							
Asteroid	Type	α	dm	dmax	P(h)	pv	D(km)
4 Vesta	V	2.0	0.10	0.10	5.342	0.255	555
9 Metis	S	2.7	0.11	0.09	5.064	0.118	168
16 Psyche	M	4.6	0.32	0.17	4.196	0.094	249
23 Thalia	S	1.6	0.18	0.15	6.15	0.200	118
29 Amphitrite	S	3.3	0.13	0.10	5.39	0.147	200
32 Pomona	S	1.7	0.20	0.10	9.443	—	269
43 Ariadne	S	2.8	0.13	0.09	5.751	0.130	85
49 Pales	CG	3.1	0.18	0.12	10.42	—	175
304 Olga	CMEU	3.0	0.20	0.16	18.36	—	68
337 Devosa	EMP	7.8	0.19	0.15	4.610	—	107
471 Papagena	S	3.8	0.11	0.10	7.113	0.163	145

Already in 1795 Dr. Olbers held a talk in the museum of Bremen about the so-called rain of rocks and had mentioned the following idea. It is not impossible that heavy parts of other planets, particularly the Moon, could be thrown down to our Earth. These "sinister stones" were at that time explained as coming from volcanoes.

Since then it has been established through Howard's research that these rocks are not of volcanic origin; a thunderous explosion accompanies these meteors. There have been at least 14–15 examples in the last decade. It takes great forces to propel these heavy bodies, which is why only a few of these masses which are thrown off the Moon fall on the Earth. Accordingly the Moon would have to lose part of its own mass, because it would have to lose many stones in order for a few to hit the Earth. And would there not have to be a lot of such heavy parts of satellites circling the Earth? Why would those objects not be visible in our powerful telescopes, since fireballs are large objects and the observations of Ceres and Pallas show us that these bodies, which are lighted by the Sun, can be quite small in diameter? These falling stars are obviously of cosmic origin, so might they not be small Earth satellites? (Olbers, 1803).

In the 1960's, an authority as eminent as Opik argued that the idea of an asteroidal origin for meteorites must be completely renounced. But virtually all experts now agree with Olbers, and specific asteroids can now be tentatively identified with certain types of meteorites found on Earth. Before looking at the evidence, some familiarity with the different types of meteorites is needed, but Bell *et al* (1984c) caution that the statistical distribution of meteorite types reaching Earth has no relation to the abundances of mineralogically similar main-belt asteroids.

STONY METEORITES: These are composed mostly of silicates, and are the most common type observed to fall. They are of two types.

CHONDRITES: These are the most common type, and are similar in composition to the early solar system. They contain chondrules, millimeter-sized spherical objects that likely were created in the solar nebula as molten drops. Chondrites are further divided into three groups. Carbonaceous chondrites are the most primitive and are composed mostly of olivine. (C–type asteroids got their name from this group). Enstatite chondrites contain large amounts of metallic iron along with their chondrules. Ordinary chondrites, the third group, consist primarily of the minerals olivine and pyroxene, and have large chondrules. These are related to the S–types.

ACHONDRITES: The second type of stony meteorites, the achondrites lack chondrules, and are generally much younger than other meteorites. They are divided into nine groups. Vesta's reflectance at visible and IR wavelengths is a near- perfect match to that of basaltic achondrites.

IRON METEORITES: Primarily composed of the nickel-iron minerals kamacite and taenite. Irons are divided into 12 groups based on abundance of trace elements such as germanium and gallium. About 600 such meteorites are known and are the M–asteroid prototypes.

STONY-IRON METEORITES: These transition meteorites are composed of both silicate minerals and metal, and may be related to A–type asteroids. These are the rarest variety, and are divided into four groups. Pallasites contain metal with grains of olivine. Mesosiderites contain metal and the silicate minerals pyroxene and plagioclase. Siderophyres contain networks of metal enclosing granular aggregates of pyroxene. Lodranites are composed of aggregates of metal, olivine and pyroxene.

The spectral trend from Vesta (type V) to type S to R to A corresponds to a compositional trend from pyroxene to olivine. (Veeder *et al*, 1983). Here is a synthesis of the compositions of the major types (Fig. 6–11):

C–TYPES: Asteroids with low visual albedos (0.04), having flat, featureless spectra have been classified as C–

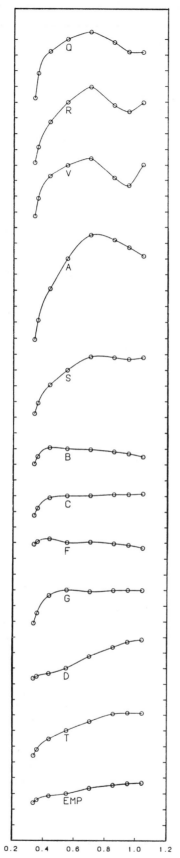

Fig. 6–11. *Spectral characteristics of seven types of asteroids, from 0.3 to 1.1 microns. Tholen, 1984b.*

types; 75 percent of the objects in the main belt are members of this type. While the C stands for carbonaceous–type, no C–type asteroid spectrum has been matched in all details with any meteorite spectrum. This difference is likely due to what is termed aqueous alteration—water has altered the surface material. Tholen (1985) has divided the C class into four sub-classes. F asteroids show no UV absorption; G asteroids have a very strong UV feature; B asteroids are spectrally similar to classical C–types, but have albedos twice as high.

The dark materials covering these asteroids consist of silicate clay minerals (montmorillonite, chlorite and serpentine) intermixed with opaque materials including magnetite and finely-divided carbon-rich compounds. Aqueous alteration has been observed to remove iron from clay materials in carbonaceous chondrite matrix material (CCMM), yielding magnetite. The most important spectral feature associated with this matrix material is a strong absorption band at 3 microns, which has been detected on several C–type asteroids. The spectral characteristics of magnetite have also been detected on 324 Bamberga. This important result not only explains the difference between carbonaceous chondrite meteorites and this C–type asteroid, but also accounts for its low albedo (Feierberg *et al*, 1981; Gradie and Veverka, 1980). Based on 3 micron spectrophotometry of 14 large C–type asteroids, Feierberg *et al* (1985) conclude that their compositions reflect a range of temperatures, either in the solar nebula during accretion or in their interiors after formation. They detected the presence of water (in hydrated phyllosilicates) on nine asteroids, but the other five were found to be anhydrous (i.e., lacking water). They suggest that such anhydrous C–types have olivine as a silicate component, and further propose a mechanism to account for this marked difference among C–types.

Heating by radioactive decay in the interiors of the original population of C asteroids would have driven off the water from the hydrated minerals, leaving the carbonaceous matter behind. The minerals in the outer layers were thus subjected to aqueous alteration, resulting in objects with a differentiated structure. The current population of C–types are fragments of these parent bodies, although the largest asteroids (Ceres, Pallas and Hygiea) may have preserved their original mantles.

S–TYPES: There is currently great debate among various researchers as to the true nature of the S types. While they were long associated with stony-iron meteorites, some now believe they resemble ordinary chondrites, the most common type of meteorites. According to Feierberg *et al* (1982), they have olivine/pyroxene ratios between 1 and 10. Finely divided metallic iron, probably less than 20% by weight, is also indicated.

But Gaffey (1984) presented a persuasive corpus of data that shows the S types cannot, in general, be the ordinary chondrite parent bodies. Feierberg *et al* suggested that the metal abundance was enhanced by some regolith process, but Gaffey showed that only the most metal-rich members of the chondritic group can undergo such a process to yield an S-type spectrum. The relative abundance of mafic silicates in S–types is not consistent with such metal-rich material. In a detailed study of 8 Flora, Gaffey concluded "that the presence of a steeply reddened, elemental NiFe signature in the spectral reflectance curve of Flora (and the other S asteroids) indicates the presence of an abundant coarse-grained metal phase in the parent material. Such a petrology is characteristic of the differentiated metal-rich meteorites but is unknown—and by definition, essentially impossible—in the chondrites. Flora is thus the exposed residual core of a magmatically differentiated and collisionally disrupted body." He also showed (Gaffey, 1986) that metal grains found in chondritic bodies are coated with an optically thick surface layer that suppresses the NiFe spectral contribution. "Known regolith processes cannot reasonably produce an S–type spectrum" from these assemblages, again leading to the conclusion that S–type represents metal-rich, differentiated bodies. Wetherill (1985), commenting on this debate, wrote that it "is the author's guess that in some way the surficial spectrophotometric data are providing the correct mineralogy (olivine, pyroxene, metal) of ordinary chondrites, but not the correct proportions of these minerals." In his view, ordinary chondrites are derived from S–type asteroids near the 3:1 Kirkwood gap, the largest of which are 11 Parthenope, 17 Thetis and 29 Amphitrite. He found that the predicted meteorite orbits closely match those found for observed ordinary chondrites, and the total flux is in approximate agreement with the observed rate of fall. But as Gaffey (1985) aptly puts it, "past experience in exploring new regimes (Hell hath no fury like an unjustified assumption) suggests that the issue cannot be considered completely closed until actual samples of a number of S–type objects have been studied in detail." While on the subject of Amphitrite, Bell *et al* (1985) report that its mineralogy may correspond to lodranites. Its major spectral features indicate nickel-iron metal, a band near 0.95 microns due to pyroxene and olivine absorptions, and a band at 1.95 microns due to pyroxene alone.

Dermott *et al* (1985), in a plot of U-V color versus semimajor axis for 191 S–types (Fig. 6–12) conclude that asteroids closer to the Sun than 2.4 AU are much redder than more distant ones. They interpret this as indicative of two distinct sub-classes of S–type asteroids, although some question has been raised that it may merely be a geometric effect since objects at smaller heliocentric distances are usually observed at higher phase angles as well. Fig. 6–13 further indicates that the surface properties of S–types are size dependent. The division between those asteroids with and those without substantial regoliths occurs at about 20 km. diameter.

E–TYPES: A very high albedo class (> 0.23), the surfaces of E–type asteroids consist of colorless translucent, iron-free silicates such as plagioclase, forsterite or enstatite. Their composition is similar to that of the enstatite achondrites (Zellner *et al*, 1977). 44 Nysa is the best known E–type asteroid.

D–TYPES: This type (formerly called RD), exhibits low albedos and very red spectral curves. They consist of clays (90%), magnetite, carbon black and an opaque

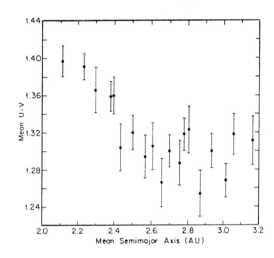

Fig. 6–12. *Variation of the mean U–V color of 191 S–type asteroids with mean semi-major axis. (10 asteroids in each sample). The one sigma error bars were estimated from the variance of each sample. Dermott et al, 1985. Reproduced by permission from Icarus.*

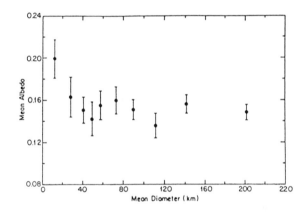

Fig. 6–13. *Variation of the mean albedo of 100 S–type asteroids with mean diameter (10 asteroids in each sample), which suggests that the surface properties of these asteroids are size dependent— the division between those with and without substantial regoliths occurs at about 20 km. Dermott et al, 1985. Reproduced by permission from Icarus.*

carbon-rich substance similar to kerogen. Kerogen-like substances compose the bulk of the organic material in some carbonaceous chondrites (Gradie & Veverka, 1980).

No meteorites with D–type spectral characteristics are known, but it is thought that the minerals producing this spectral curve are widespread in the solar system, extending from the main belt to at least Saturn. The dark hemisphere of Saturn's satellite Iapetus provides an excellent spectral match to the average D–type infrared colors (Bell *et al*, 1984a).

Most D–types are Trojans, but 336 Lacadiera in the inner belt was identified in 1984 (it had formerly been classed as a C).

M–TYPES: These moderate-albedo (0.07-0.23) asteroids have been associated with enstatite chondrites or stony-irons. A pure metallic surface, indicative of iron meteorites, has now been ruled out. They are composed of a metal-silicate mixture (Feierberg *et al*, 1983). Lupishko & Belskaya (1985) postulated that the microstructure of a metallic asteroid surface might be due to the presence of a magnetic field capable of orienting ferromagnetic particles on the surface. In a detailed photometric study of the M asteroid 16 Psyche, they found no such preferred direction, thus reinforcing the Feierberg *et al* results.

A–TYPES: Only three of these rare, high albedo (> 0.16) asteroids have been studied in detail. 246 Asporina, 289 Nenetta and 446 Aeternitas appear to be nearly pure olivine, with less than 10% pyroxene and a possible large fraction of metal. They are likely mantles of differentiated parent bodies that have been exposed by fragmentation and are related to pallasite meteorites (Cruikshank & Hartmann, 1984). A–types are probably remnants of larger differentiated objects which have been eroded down to the core/mantle interface zone where olivine crystals and nickel-iron metal coexist (Bell *et al*, 1984b). It has also been discovered by Cruikshank *et al* (1985) that S–types with colors near the A–type region are compositionally related to the A's. These include Amalthea and Eleonora.

P–TYPES: Little is known about this low-albedo (0.065) class; P asteroids are spectrally indistinguishable from M and E asteroids (Tholen, 1985). Its largest member is 87 Sylvia (diameter 282 km).

Q–TYPES: This type was identified by Tholen (1984b) based on 8-color and albedo criteria. The three known examples are all Earth-approachers. Their visible and near-IR spectral albedo properties are identical with laboratory measurements of ordinary chondrites.

V–TYPES: Only two asteroids are currently known in this class. Vesta was long thought to be unique, but the identification of an Amor asteroid with an identical spectrum led Tholen (1985) to create this new class.

The mineralogy of asteroids is intimately connected with the place of origin of the meteorites, which objects scientists are able to examine in great detail in the lab. As mentioned earlier, meteorites are believed to be fragments of asteroids. This parent-body scenario requires that the orbit of a fragment be gravitationally altered, so it can intersect the earth's orbit. The length of time allowed for this transition is set by the so-called cosmic ray exposure ages of stony meteorites—the longer a fragment travels from the asteroid belt to the vicinity of Earth, the more cosmic rays will hit it. Assuming a constant flux of cosmic rays from the universe, the time it has spent in space can be computed.

For eucrites, this cosmic-ray exposure age is 10^6 to 10^7 years. While Vesta is the only large, intact asteroid whose properties are compatible with the eucrites, no dynamical mechanism has been discovered to deliver eucrites on such a short time scale (Feierberg *et al*, 1980). Assuming a 10.68 hour period, the surface of Vesta consists of two nearly equatorial spots of diogenite (pyroxene and a lower relative abundance of feldspar); while the rest of the surface consists of relatively dark eucrite (pyroxene and plagioclase). The smaller of the two equatorial spots appears

to have an olivine-rich center. On a hemispheric scale, the pyroxene/feldspar abundance ratio varies from 0.2 to 0.8 (Fig. 6–14; Gaffey, 1985).

Even more puzzling are the most common meteorites of all, the ordinary chondrites. No asteroid has been identified as a source body of these objects. Olivine-rich achondrites, on the other hand, are expected to be much more prominent in our meteorite collections than they are.

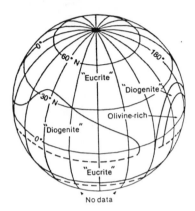

Fig. 6–14. *A map of the surface composition of Vesta, showing areas rich in calcium-aluminum silicates (eucrites) and magnesium-iron silicates (diogenites). Adapted from a diagram by Michael Gaffey; Sky & Telescope Dec. 1983.*

The case of the enstatite achondrites is much more promising though. Nysa's shape, its association with smaller fragments of similar composition, and the proximity of the metal-rich asteroid Hertha suggest they all came from a single differentiated parent body. Differentiated asteroids are formed when a body of initially chondritic composition is melted, with a resulting gravitational separation of minerals, the denser ones forming a central core. Nysa may be the largest surviving fragment of a silicate crust, broken away from the iron-core body Hertha in a cataclysmic event. An ejecta speed of only 100 m/sec is required for the fragments in the Nysa 'family' to be thrown into a Kirkwood gap, from where objects are believed to be perturbed into Earth-crossing orbits.

This is only one example of how scientists are trying to construct models based on the compositions of asteroids in families and gravitational perturbations caused by Jupiter and Mars to produce the observed flux of various types of meteorites on Earth (Zellner *et al*, 1977). It should be noted that not all meteorites come from asteroids—some may come from Mars (Wood & Ashwal, 1981). These are the so-called SNC meteorites, represented by shergottite, nakhlite and chassignite achondrites; all exhibit relatively young isotopic ages ranging from 0.6 to 1.3 billion years. It has been postulated that fragments on the order of 15 meters in diameter were ejected from Mars, and that the SNC meteorites are the result of a collision between these bodies and small asteroidal debris. But Wetherill (1984) concludes it much more likely that only small fragments are ejected from Mars, which are themselves the SNC meteorites that fall to Earth. Feierberg & Drake (1980) examined five different origins for the shergottites, concluding that Vesta is the most likely source.

INTERIORS

Our knowledge of the interiors of asteroids is very sketchy. An early attempt to model the interior of Ceres was presented by Hodgson (1977), who considered both a differentiated and undifferentiated case. In the latter, a frozen interior containing a mixture of carbonaceous and/or basaltic materials is covered with a regolith of denser material, from which ice has evaporated. In the differentiated model, two further zones are predicted towards the center—a shell of refrozen water ice that migrated from the core, encasing a core of concentrated materials.

However, Watson (1977) states that if water ice exists in asteroids, it would only be found in the spaces between rock fragments rather than in a homogeneous layer. The degree to which this empty space, or porosity, is present in an asteroid is governed by three factors: uniformity of rock sizes, shape of the rocks and the packing of the rocks. Asteroids composed of rounded rocks of similar shape will have higher porosity than one with irregular rocks of varying sizes. Generally high porosity can be expected due to the low gravity of asteroids, and the lack of mineral solutions that fill in the pore spaces of terrestrial rocks.

King and King (1979) proposed that most asteroids (i.e., C–types), have a core of chondrule-free volatile-rich CCMM. This is overlaid by a mantle of chondrule-rich carbonaceous materials, which is covered by the thin layer of regolith whose properties are observable from Earth. They do not believe that radioactive heating was very important in the interior development of such asteroids (Fig. 6–15).

The various types of differentiated meteorites have been related to their depth of formation in parent bodies, whose fragments are the asteroids we see today. Basaltic achondrites erupted from magma-chambers in the mantle into the surface, while pallasites are derived from the core-mantle boundary. Irons came from the cores, which became exposed to impact when the parent body was catastrophically fragmented. Mesosiderites also formed in differentiated parent bodies, but their depth is not known.

The identification of asteroids with differentiated or undifferentiated parent bodies is made on the basis of their observed compositions. Those asteroids derived from differentiated parents should be either olivine-free or pyroxene-free and feldspar-free, and may be either metal-rich or metal-free. If derived from undifferentiated parents, an asteroid is expected to contain all four of these minerals. The origin of these parent bodies and the sources of heat needed to cause differentiation was considered in chapter 2 (Feierberg *et al*, 1982).

COSMIC DUST

The close association of asteroids and cosmic dust was suspected by Fesenkov (1942), but was only clearly revealed by IRAS in 1983 when it discovered dust rings in the asteroid belt. But the investigation of this 'cosmic dust' began more than a century ago, when the British exploration ship

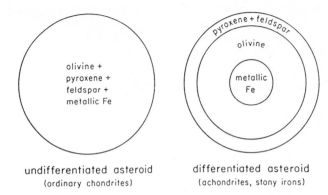

Fig. 6–15. *Cross sections of idealized meteorite parent bodies. Ordinary chondrites are derived from undifferentiated asteroids and contain finely intermixed grains of olivine, pyroxene, feldspar, and metallic Fe. Differentiated asteroids are formed when a body of initially chondritic composition is melted and there is gravitational separation of minerals according to density. The different types of differentiated meteorites can be understood in terms of depth of formation in their parent bodies. Feierberg et al, 1982.*

Challenger recovered mud samples from the sea floor in the 1870's. After running a hand magnet through the mud, the researchers found minute spheres, which they identified as having come from outer space.

According to Brownlee (1981), these cosmic deep-sea spheres (Photo 6–1) are highly degraded samples of interplanetary dust that were melted in the atmosphere and later modified chemically in the ocean. Tens of thousands, up to 3mm in diameter, have been collected. While comets may be the primary source of cosmic dust, asteroids are believed to contribute a significant portion of the 10,000 tons of material smaller than 1 mm diameter that falls to the Earth's surface each year.

The sea-floor is a good place to collect samples of these larger examples of cosmic dust—a cubic meter of sea-floor mud contains all the particles that fall onto a square meter of surface area in 500,000 years. But scientists are also very interested in dust smaller than 100 microns, which can be collected by high-flying aircraft. These minute particles do not burn up or even melt in the atmosphere. They decelerate from their cosmic velocity of 15 km/sec to only 1 cm/sec at an altitude of 100 km.

The first micrometeorites were collected from the atmosphere in 1970 during a balloon flight, but since 1974 a U–2 aircraft has collected more than 500 particles under direction of the NASA Ames Research Center. Most of these particles are black aggregates of sub-micron size grains. The individual grains, ranging in size from 10 microns to 100 angstroms or less, are usually iron-magnesium silicates or iron sulfides.

At an even smaller level, the grains are, in turn, aggregates of carbonaceous materials and crystalline silicates, similar in elemental composition to carbon-rich meteorites. The material that comprises the most common type of cosmic dust has not been found in meteorites, thus bridging an important gap in our knowledge of the true constitution of the asteroids.

Electron microscopes have revealed tiny crystals of silicate and carbide minerals in forms never seen in mete-

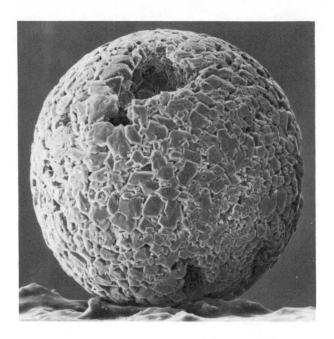

Photo. 6–3. *A melted spherule of extraterrestrial matter, collected from the deep ocean floor. Most of the crystals seen here are the minerals olivine and magnetite, both likely prominent constituents of asteroids. Photo courtesy of Donald Brownlee.*

orites. They resemble material formed directly by solidifaction from vapor, a process which may indicate formation during the origin of the solar system or earlier (Brownlee, 1984).

The deep-sea spheres, on the other hand, occur in three types: (Brownlee *et al*, 1983) Stony (S)—composed of olivine and glass and have chondrule-like textures. Iron-Nickel sulfide (FSN)—composed of magnetite and pyrrhotite: have not been found larger than 25 microns. Iron (I)—composed of iron-nickel metal, magnetite and wustite; are not analogs to anything in meteorites. According to Clayton *et al* (1986), the I–type contain oxygen richer in heavy isotopes than any natural sample ever analyzed. They interpret this as indicating the spheres are not spherical droplets produced in space by the collision of asteroids.

The chemical composition of the spheres indicates that 80 per cent of them came from material similar to primitive carbonaceous chondrite meteorites (Photo 6–3). A link has been noted between climatic changes and elevated concentrations of cosmic dust about 15,000 years ago. Both iridium and nickel in the ice were found to be one to two orders of magnitude higher as compared with present levels. These concentrations are thought to reflect higher concentrations of cosmic dust in the interplanetary environment, rather than evidence of impact events (La Violette, 1983).

The study of cosmic dust entered a new phase with the launch from the space shuttle in April, 1984 of the Long Duration Exposure Facility (LDEF). In addition to many other experiments, LDEF exposed various targets to impact by cosmic dust. It has not yet been returned to Earth for study.

Here is a brief outline of the cosmic dust experiments:

1. Chemistry of micrometeoroids—designed to collect micro-meteoroid residue in and around impact craters formed in sheets of pure gold and pure aluminum. The gold collector is expected to record 165 craters larger than 5 microns, 52 larger than 10 microns, and 9 larger than 50 microns (Horz *et al*, 1981).

2. Interplanetary dust—four impact sensors, spaced at 90° intervals around LDEF, will obtain data on particle mass and velocity (Singer *et al*, 1981). Study of impact craters—craters resulting from impact on various metallic and glass samples will be used to determine the mass, density, velocity and direction of cosmic dust (Mandeville, 1981).

3. Dust debris collection—will use thin metal foils to collect cosmic dust, at least as fragments suitable for chemical analysis (Mandeville, 1981).

MAGNITUDES   7

The inhabitants of Glauke became tired of Nature's uniform gray and chose to repaint their planet, first with a dark primer during April, and then with a new bright color, which they completed around mid-May. Later that month, the planet began peeling off to reveal the old gray again.

Alan Harris, 1983

In the 19th century, magnitudes of asteroids were determined by comparison with the Bonner Durchmusterung (BD) star atlas. Most of this early work was done by Friedrich Argelander and Muller. The practice of tying in with the BD, the Cordoba Durchmusterung (CoD) and the Cape Photographic Durchmusterung (CPD) was continued even after the advent of photography.

The photographically discovered asteroids were fainter than the chart limit of magnitude 9.5, so the scale had to be extended. For this purpose a scale was usually made of images of a single star with different exposure times. An alternate procedure was to compare a new asteroid with known ones on the same plate. Most asteroid magnitudes down to 16 were determined by these methods until photoelectric magnitudes became available in the 1950's.

On the basis of the McDonald photographic survey, Gehrels redetermined the magnitude system, which "was direly needed because some of the values were off about three magnitudes. That system was adopted by the IAU in 1958 and used until 1985." Even by the early 1970's, UBV color data were available for only 50 asteroids. By the end of that decade, the number had risen to 735, and the data base continues to increase rapidly.

Three different magnitudes are now used in asteroid research:

Opposition magnitude: This is the actual brightness of an asteroid that you can see through a telescope. At opposition, the asteroid is at its brightest. There are two kinds of opposition—perihelic and aphelic, the former being the closer and brighter. Asteroids with a high inclination, however, reach their greatest brightness at the oppositions occurring close to the nodes of their orbits. These special cases are called nodal oppositions. The mean opposition magnitude is defined to be

$$B(a,0) = B(1,0) + 5 \log a(a-1)$$

where B(1,0) is the absolute magnitude (see below) and a is the semi-major axis of the asteroid's orbit. This approximation, however, holds only for nearly-circular, zero-inclination orbits. The true average opposition magnitude

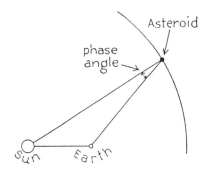

Fig. **7–1.** *The phase angle at which we see an asteroid. Most asteroids cannot be observed from Earth at phase angles greater than 30°. Watson, 1956.*

typically differs from this by several tenths of a magnitude, but in the case of Earth-crossers can reach a full magnitude.

To calculate a more nearly correct value, Knezevic & Zappala (1982) proposed a revised formula which incorporates the median distance of the asteroid from the Sun instead of the geometrical mean distance a. While the revised formula can still be in error by up to 0.4 magnitude, it is notably more accurate than the canonical formula, although it has yet to come into wide use.

Reduced magnitude: The brightness of an asteroid if it were placed 1 AU from both Sun and Earth. This is analogous to the absolute magnitude of a star, which is its brightness at a distance of 1 parsec. The reduced magnitude can be calculated by subtracting the correction factor $5 \log r\Delta$ (where r is the heliocentric distance and Δ is the geocentric distance), from the observed magnitude. The reduced magnitude is also referred to as the corrected magnitude.

Absolute magnitude: This is determined by plotting the reduced magnitude versus the phase angle (the solar elongation of the Earth seen from the asteroid.) This geometrical relationship is shown in Fig. 7–1. The absolute magnitude is the intercept of the extrapolated linear phase relation at 0°. A plot of the phase function of Mas-

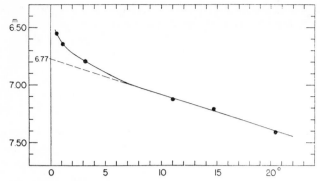

Fig. 7–2. *The phase function of 20 Massalia (spring, 1955). Abscissae, the phase angle in degrees. Ordinates, the observed magnitudes, V on the (U, B, V) system, reduced to unit distances from the sun and earth. This plot shows the first discovery of the opposition effect, where an asteroid at small phase angle gets markedly brighter. Gehrels, 1956.*

salia from Gehrels' 1955 paper is shown in Fig. 7–2, with the absolute magnitude of 6.77 indicated.

It is interesting to note that at very small phase angles, the Earth will transit the Sun as seen from the asteroid; as seen from the Earth, the asteroid will pass through the Earth's penumbra. As shown by Tholen (1984a), such an aspect will typically dim the asteroid by an incredibly small 0.0004 magnitude! The plot of Massalia shows the important opposition effect. This particular plot, in fact, was the first proof of such an effect for an asteroid. This surge in brightness at phase angles less than 7 or 8° is very similar for all asteroids, and is close to 0.3 magnitude.

The first quantitative explanation of the opposition effect was given by H. Seeliger in 1887. In a study of Saturn's rings, he assumed the particles in the rings are large enough to cast shadows. At opposition, each particle hides its own shadow, thus producing a marked increase in brightness.

However, the opposition effect does not disappear if the particles involved are transparent, so a more complex mechanism appears to be at work. Shkuratov (1983) has shown that certain irregularities at the microscopic level on the surface of an asteroid can act as concentrating lenses. The amplitude and width of the opposition effect "characterize the ability of particles and details of the microrelief to focus light onto the underlying scattering layers of particles." He suggests that the opposition effect should be highly sensitive to the fusing of soil particles (agglutination).

The absolute magnitude defined above is designated V(1,0), and is the one used in the literature most frequently. In 1979 Bowell and Lumme defined a new kind of absolute magnitude designated V(0°). In effect, it takes the opposition effect into account, and the relationship is simply expressed

$$V(0°) = V(1,0) - 0.32 mag.$$

This new form of the absolute magnitude (designated H) was adopted by the IAU in 1985. Combined with a switch from using B magnitudes to V magnitudes, new

absolute magnitudes will be one magnitude brighter than old ones.

The distribution of opposition and absolute V(1,0) magnitudes for the first 1900 numbered asteroids is shown in Table 7–1. In this table, compiled by Combes (1977), the opposition magnitudes are photographically determined. Most asteroids are 0.8 mag. brighter when observed visually than photographically.

Minor Planets	Mean Values			V(1,0)
	m_{min}	mo	m_{max}	
1–100	10.9	11.9	12.8	8.6
101–200	12.3	13.2	14.0	9.7
201–300	13.4	14.2	14.9	10.7
301–400	13.1	13.9	14.7	10.5
401–500	13.3	14.1	14.9	10.7
501–600	13.6	14.4	15.3	10.8
601–700	14.0	14.9	15.7	11.2
701–800	13.9	14.7	15.5	11.2
801–900	14.5	15.4	16.2	12.0
901–1000	14.4	15.4	16.3	11.9
1001–1100	14.7	15.7	16.5	12.2
1101–1200	14.9	15.8	16.6	12.4
1201–1300	15.1	15.9	16.7	12.4
1301–1400	15.1	15.9	16.8	12.5
1401–1500	15.3	16.2	17.0	12.8
1501–1600	15.2	16.2	17.2	13.0
1601–1700	14.9	16.0	16.9	12.9
1701–1800	15.4	16.3	17.0	13.0
1801–1900	15.7	16.4	17.3	13.2

TABLE 7–1
AVERAGE MAGNITUDES

Table 7–1. *Average Magnitudes. In intervals of 100 asteroids, the brightest, faintest and mean photographic magnitudes of the first 1,900 asteroids are given. The average absolute magnitudes in the V band are listed in the final column. Data from Combes (1977).*

The slope of the linear portion of the phase curve in Fig. 7–2 is called the phase coefficient, and in the case of Massalia is 0.031 mag/degree. This important parameter, designated β, is defined as the slope of the phase curve between 10 and 20° of phase angle.

The formula defining absolute magnitude has changed through the years, a fact which must be kept in mind when comparing published values. Until 1979, the absolute magnitude in the blue band, designated B(1,0) was defined by Gehrels to be

$$B(1,0) = B(1,\alpha) + 0.584 - 0.188|\alpha|0.545 - 8\beta.$$

for $\alpha < 8°$ where $\beta = 0.023$ mag/deg was the phase coefficient used for all asteroids. Absolute magnitudes obtained by this method have been referred to as 4° absolute magnitudes, because the correction at 4° is 0.

This method was superseded in 1979, as detailed by Gehrels and Tedesco. For $\alpha < 7°$ the revised formula is:

$$B(1,0) = B(1,\alpha) + 0.538 - 0.134|\alpha|0.714 - 7\beta.$$

In this new format, a value of $\beta = 0.039$ is assigned to asteroids with an undetermined value of β. This value represents a weighted mean: C–asteroids have a mean value of 0.041, while others have a value of 0.032, with C–asteroids in the majority at 76%. To convert from the old to the new system, a correction of -0.10 magnitude was applied by Gehrels and Tedesco.

PHASE COEFFICIENT

The physical meaning of phase coefficients is somewhat obscure, despite its wide use in the literature. In a 1971 study of this matter, Joseph Veverka stressed that typical values of β (0.025 to 0.035 mag/°) cannot be interpreted unambiguously. This is because the coefficient may depend as much on the photometric properties of a particular area on the asteroid's surface as on the degree of large-scale surface roughness, which is what β ostensibly relates to.

It has been shown that β cannot provide any information on the mineralogical composition of an asteroid, nor does it contain any data about whether a surface is particulate. Veverka further showed that albedos cannot be derived from phase coefficients, and that irregularly shaped asteroids with rough surfaces do not have a unique value of β.

Ten years later, however, Lumme and Bowell (1981) came to a conclusion they characterized as somewhat contrary to Veverka. For low albedo objects, such as most asteroids, the opposition effect and the so-called linear part of the phase curve are caused by different phenomena. While the opposition effect is caused by porosity, the linear part is mainly due to roughness.

A few definitions are in order here. Lumme and Bowell considered in their theory the surface of an asteroid to be composed of particles themselves defined as the scattering elements. The porosity was defined as $1 - D$, where D is the volume density (the fraction of the volume occupied by particles).

Roughness is a term that includes both large-scale and small-scale roughness. On the large scale are features such as hills and canyons, caused by fragmentation or collision with meteorites. Small-scale roughness is due to the distribution of small numbers of particles, with abrupt changes in surface slope between each clump. Essentially, a porous surface produces a much steeper opposition effect than a rough surface.

While the part of the phase curve at angles greater than 7° has been considered by most researchers to be linear, Bowell and Lumme have shown that between 10° and 20°, the phase curve is non-linear by about 0.01 mag. Thus, the use of the term "so-called linear part of the phase curve."

Taking the asteroid 69 Hesperia as an example, they showed that depending on the interval over which the phase coefficient was calculated, the resulting value could be in error by 20%.

This is one of the reasons they developed the multiple-scattering theory. Phase curves can be completely described by Q and $V(0°)$ rather than β and $V(1,0)$. The multiple scattering factor, Q, is the ratio of multiple scattered light to total scattered light at 0° phase angle.

For values of Q between 0.05 and 0.35, approximate photometric albedos and diameters can also be computed:

$$p(0°) = 1.252Q + 0.039$$

$$\log d = k - 0.5 \log p(0°) - 0.2V(0°)$$

where k is a wavelength-dependent constant. For d in km, $k = 3.122$ for the V band and 3.248 for the B band. Due to the low albedo of C-type asteroids, this method does not apply for them.

The albedo referred to here is the geometric albedo, defined as the ratio of the flux received from an asteroid to that expected from a perfectly reflecting disk of the same size at zero phase angle. An albedo of 0.1 indicates 10% of the incident light is reflected. 44 Nysa has the highest albedo of any asteroid: 0.49.

The Bond albedo is defined as the total incident light reflected by a spherical body. It is equal to the phase integral multiplied by the ratio of its brightness at zero phase angle to the brightness it would have if it were a perfectly diffusing disk. Table 7–2 gives values for the phase integral, q, and the Bond albedo, A for the three main classes of asteroids, along with V-band values of Q and the geometric albedo, p.

TABLE 7–2 MAGNITUDE PARAMETERS			
Object	Q	p	q	A
C	0.04	0.052	0.33	0.017
S	0.15	0.196	0.47	0.092
M	0.15	0.179	0.47	0.084

Table 7–2. *Magnitude Parameters. For the three main types of asteroids are listed Q (multiple scattering factor), p (geometric albedo), q (phase integral) and A (Bond albedo). Data from Lumme & Bowell (1981). Reprinted by permission of the Astronomical Journal.*

There is a close numerical relationship between Q and β where $Q = 0.821 - 30.76\beta + 267.6\beta^2$ for $\beta > 0.015$ mag/deg.

With reference to Fig. 7–4, it is possible to derive the value of Q for a particular asteroid graphically.

Phase coefficients are also color dependent, but only slightly. As shown in Fig. 7–3, taken from a 1967 paper by Gehrels, the values for Vesta differ in U, B and V. The slight decrease in β with increasing wavelength may be due to an increase in the amount of multiple scattering at long wavelengths. In a study of the wavelength dependence of the phase coefficients of various powdered samples of meteorites, Gradie & Veverka (1986) found them to be qualitatively similar to that of the Moon and S– and C–class asteroids. They attribute the difference in phase coefficients of C-type (0.0359 in the V band) and S-type (0.0293) asteroids as due to compositional differences, not necessarily differences in surface roughness.

One other effect to mention is phase reddening. H. L. Giclas in 1951 was the first to note that asteroids be-

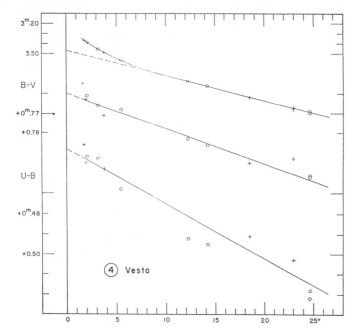

Fig. 7–3. *Phase functions of Vesta. Abscissas, the orbital phase angle in degrees. Ordinates, top curve, the observed magnitudes (V on the UBV system) reduced to unit distances from the sun and earth; middle curve, the B–V colors. Crosses are for observations made before and circles for after opposition. Gehrels, 1967. Reprinted by permission of the Astronomical Journal.*

come slightly redder as phase angle increases. It is believed due to differential albedo effect: at longer wavelengths, the albedo increases and there is an accompanying increase in Q. There are wide variations of phase reddening among the asteroids.

THE NEW MAGNITUDE SYSTEM

There has been considerable debate in the last few years over the appropriate formula to use for computing the absolute magnitude of an asteroid. According to Brian Marsden, writing early in 1985, "The magnitude-formula debate seems to have concluded with the idea that we have a 'two-tier' system: one in which a fairly sophisticated formula (with 14 constants!) is used to derive the absolute magnitudes and phase coefficients, while a simplified formula (with no more than 4 constants) is used in the computation of ephemerides. This way future improvements can easily be introduced in the determination of the values for an individual object, but we won't always be up in the air as regards getting the "latest" formula whenever we want to calculate an ephemeris." This new magnitude system was formally adopted at the IAU Commission 20 meeting at the November 1985 General Assembly. It is this magnitude system that was used in the IRAS asteroid data reductions. IRAS observed asteroids at much higher phase angles than is possible from Earth; with the new formula, magnitudes can be predicted at large phase angles using data from small phase angles, and vice versa.

The new formula for the prediction of the apparent magnitude of a minor planet is

Photo. 7–1. *Edward Bowell, an astronomer at the Lowell Observatory in Arizona, whose astrometric work nets about 4,000 asteroid positions a year. With Kari Lumme of the University of Helsinki he laid the theoretical groundwork for the new magnitude system of asteroids, which was adopted by the IAU in 1985.*

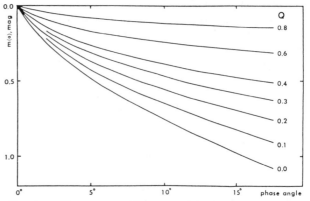

Fig. 7–4. *Phase curves with a range of Q values. As the multiple scattering factor increases, the slope of the phase curve decreases. The maximum slope occurs as Q tends to 0. Bowell & Lumme, 1979. Reprinted from Asteroids by Tom Gehrels by permission of the University of Arizona Press.*

$$5 \log r\Delta + H - 2.5 \log[(1 - G)\overline{\phi}_1 + G\overline{\phi}_2],$$

where r and Δ are, respectively, the heliocentric and geocentric distances (in AU), H is the absolute magnitude (in the V band unless otherwise specified) at solar phase angle $\alpha = 0°$, G is termed the slope parameter, and $\overline{\phi}_1$, $\overline{\phi}_2$ are two phase functions approximated by

$$\overline{\phi}_i = \exp\{-A_1[\tan(\alpha/2)]^{**}B_i\}$$

where $i = 1, 2$, $A_1 = 3.33$, $A_2 + 1.87$, $B_1 = 0.63$, and $B_2 = 1.22$.

The IAU also formally adopted a slope parameter (G) to replace the phase coefficient. The resulting phase function and its first derivative are both continuous, neatly eliminating the discontinuity inherent in the old system at $7°$. (Tholen, 1986).

LIGHTCURVES AND ROTATION RATES   8

The discovery by Dr. von Oppolzer that the light of Eros is variable suggests some photometric problems of great interest. If, as seems probable, we assume that the variation is due to the rotation of the planet, we can, from measures of its light determine the time of rotation, and the direction in space of the axis of rotation.

Edward Pickering, 1901

One common property of all asteroids is that they rotate, and as they do so their apparent brightness varies. Photometry can reveal the asteroids' rotational period since the lightcurve repeats every revolution. Throughout a single opposition, the observed amplitude of the lightcurve can vary as the viewing geometry changes (Fig. 8–1), and the shape of the lightcurve itself can vary enormously from one opposition to another (Fig. 8–2).

While different studies of the same data have come to conflicting conclusions, the latest evidence points to five trends:

1. M asteroids rotate faster than S asteroids, which rotate faster than C asteroids.

2. There is an excess of slowly rotating asteroids of small and intermediate size.

3. Large asteroids rotate faster than small asteroids, the trend being linear.

4. Smaller asteroids have a greater range of rotational amplitudes.

5. There is a pronounced change in rotational properties between 120 and 250 km.

The fact that asteroids exhibit lightcurves was not definitely established until 1901, when E. von Oppolzer noted brightness variations in Eros. There were, however, previous reports of rotational variation, the earliest being a 27 hour period ascribed to Juno by Schroeter about 1810 (this period is approximately a multiple of four of the true period). (Kirkwood, 1888). The problems associated with modeling this remarkable light variation of asteroids led to an equally remarkable suggestion. A group of astronomers

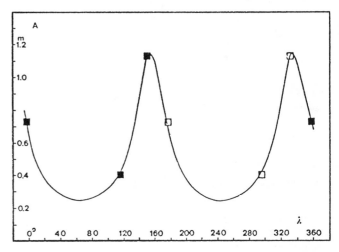

Fig. 8–1. *Plot of the light curve amplitude of 216 Kleopatra versus ecliptic longitude. Open symbols represent values obtained by adding or subtracting 180° Zappala et al, 1983a. Reproduced by permission from Icarus.*

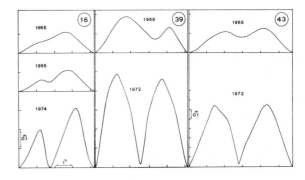

Fig. 8–2. *Free-hand light curves of the asteroids 16 Psyche, 39 Laetitia, and 43 Ariadne at different oppositions, showing the change in amplitude and, sometimes, poorly defined secondary extrema. (Zappala et al, 1983b).*

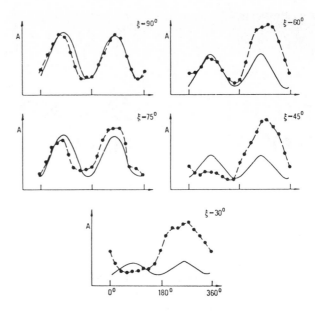

Fig. 8–3. *Laboratory lightcurves obtained for the largest fragment at different aspect angles (dotted line). The reference curve (solid line) is that computed theoretically for a triaxial ellipsoid. Barucci et al, 1983.*

considered "the advisability of suggesting experimental studies of the reflection and diffusion of light by rocky surfaces, possibly by means of aeroplane" (Leuschner, 1916). Periods or amplitudes have now been determined for more than 500 asteroids. Lightcurve data used to be maintained in the TRIAD file at the University of Arizona, but more recently Alan Harris at JPL has been correlating the latest results. The particular form of an asteroids' lightcurve can be due to its irregular shape, eclipses or occultations of a binary system, or albedo differences on the surface. A study of lightcurves from several oppositions can yield the orientation of the axis of rotation (pole position), and the interrelationships between lightcurves type, diameter and shape can provide important insights about asteroidal origins.

Most lightcurves have two pair of extrema (that is, double maxima, double minima), but a few have three. It is difficult to determine unambiguously whether an asteroid is singly or doubly periodic, the most famous case being Vesta, the brightest asteroid. Its period is either 5.3 hours, or double that, 10.6 hours. The supposedly well-known periods of several large asteroids (Europa, Berbericia, Aspasia and Diotima) have recently been halved by recent observations (Zappala *et al*, 1985). It is also possible for an asteroid to change the number of extrema from one opposition to the next.

In recent laboratory studies, Fulchignoni and Barucci (1984) showed that the presence of a large crater on the surface of model asteroids does not affect the shape of the lightcurve as long as its albedo is the same as the surrounding area. Other laboratory work on lightcurves has revealed some interesting trends. The largest fragment derived from the Barucci *et al* (1983) impact experiment described in chapter 10 had its lightcurve measured by SAM—the System for Asteroid Models. This system allows the variation of the aspect, obliquity and phase angle by mechanical movements, the reflected light being recorded by a photometer. Fig. 8–3 shows that at an aspect angle of 90°, the lightcurve is characterized by one maxima and one minima, clearly showing that the same object can change the number of its lightcurve extrema. Dr. Barucci relates an amusing anecdote about SAM.

> During my work on laboratory simulations, after thousands and thousands of lightcurves taken with different models, I took my colleague and friend Marcello Fulchignoni and put him near the support for the model. Then I asked him to turn around constantly. So ... I took the first 'human head lightcurve." The unusual asteroid (half very dark and the other half with mountains and craters) showed the nicest lightcurve that we know from the literature!

AMPLITUDES

The lightcurve amplitudes of asteroids range from a few hundredths of a magnitude to the enormous variation of 2.03 magnitude noted for the Earth-approaching asteroid Geographos. Most asteroids have an amplitude of 0.2 magnitude, with few exceeding 0.4 magnitude. Small ampli-

Photo. 8–2. *M. Antoinetta Barucci, an Italian astronomer at the Istituto di Astrofisica Spaziale in Rome. Her laboratory work on the shapes of asteroids and their corresponding lightcurves follows the pioneering work on J. L. Dunlap.*

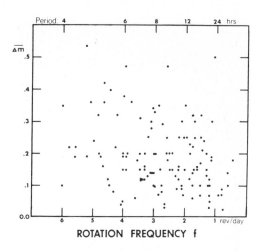

Fig. 8–4. *A plot of mean amplitude versus rotation frequency for 134 asteroids, which is interpreted as indicating there is no correlation between shape and spin rate. Tedesco & Zappala, 1980. Reproduced by permission from Icarus.*

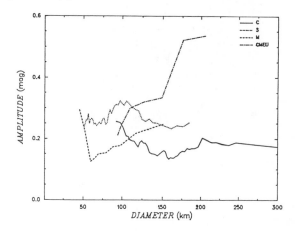

Fig. 8–5. *Running mean of amplitudes plotted versus mean diameter for taxonomic types C, S, M and CMEU, based on a data set of 218 asteroids. Both C and S types exhibit peak amplitudes at about 100 km. Lagerkvist, 1983.*

tudes result from polar aspects, while large amplitudes correspond to more equatorial aspects.

Tedesco & Zappala (1980) examined the relationship between rotation, amplitude, diameter and type (Fig. 8–4). For a sample of 30 S–type asteroids, an amplitude of 0.193 ± 0.017 was found; for 26 C–types, the average amplitude was 0.181 ± 0.024 magnitude. They conclude there is no significant difference in amplitudes for C and S asteroids, and that the mean amplitude in the size range 20 to 50 km is greater than that for larger asteroids. With the exception of objects between 150 and 250 km, there is no correlation between spin rate and amplitude. Within that range, however, spin rate increases with increasing amplitude.

Lagerkvist (1983), however, finds there is a correlation between type and amplitude (Fig. 8–5). For all diameters, the amplitudes of S asteroids are larger than those of C–types, and both show a maximum amplitude at about 100 km. Type CMEU asteroids have much larger amplitudes than the others plotted, a trend that increases with diameter. Correlations have also been noted between amplitudes and orbital elements of asteroids (Cunningham, 1985d).

In Fig. 8–6 is plotted mean amplitudes versus B(1,0) for $\Delta m < 0.70$ magnitude, and $B(1,0) < 14.0$ magnitude (Cunningham, 1984b). Only three asteroids fainter than magnitude 10.5 have amplitudes less than 0.15 magnitude, but the trend for fainter asteroids to have higher amplitudes is due to a photographically-induced selection effect. There is an observational bias to detect short period, large amplitude asteroids, and this bias increases for fainter objects, because of the reliance on photographic photometry (denoted by x's) for asteroids fainter than 11. While the photoelectric method can distinguish amplitudes smaller than 0.01 magnitude, the photographic method is limited to variations larger than 0.17. As a result, low-amplitude

Photo. 8–3. *Marcello Fulchignoni, director of the Institute of Space Astrophysics in Rome. With Dr. Barucci, he developed SAM, the System for Asteroid Models, to study the lightcurves of asteroids.*

Fig. 8–6. *A plot of mean amplitudes versus B(1,0) for 350 asteroids. Cunningham, 1984b.*

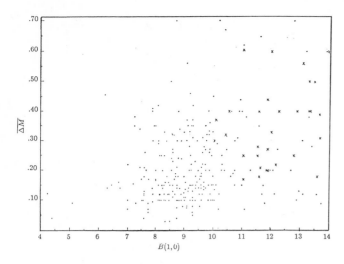

Photo. 8–4. *Edward Tedesco of the Jet Propulsion Laboratory has been a major participant in two landmark asteroid surveys: the eight-color survey at the University of Arizona, and the Infrared Astronomy Satellite survey of asteroids.*

Photo. 8–5. *C.-I. Lagerkvist, a Swedish astronomer at Uppsala University, has done an extensive survey of asteroids by means of photographic photometry. Sweden has become a European center of minor planet studies due to his efforts in organizing asteroid conferences in Uppsala.*

objects are under-represented (Binzel, 1984b).

Since amplitude is somewhat diagnostic of shape (Burns & Tedesco, 1979), as an asteroid becomes fainter and smaller (left to right in Fig. 8–6), it is more likely to be less spherical. Note also in Fig. 8–6 a void bounded by $0.48 < \Delta m < 0.59$ and $9.5 < B(1,0) < 13.0$. While it may be due to a selection effect since most amplitudes are only determined from one apparition, it may be statistically significant and related to the evolutionary history of the asteroid belt.

The Apollo asteroids with known amplitudes, all of which are too faint to appear in Fig. 8–6, have a mean amplitude of 0.630 magnitude. Binzel found that the mean amplitudes of Earth and Mars crossers is significantly larger than main-belt asteroids of comparable sizes, indicating that the main-belt objects are less elongated. In his study of small asteroids, Binzel found that the mean amplitude of asteroids from the smallest up to 90 km. is nearly equal, but there is a significantly smaller amplitude for those asteroids between 91 and 120 km (Table 8–1). This may indicate a discontinuity that represents a separation between primordial asteroids and those produced by catastrophic collisions. There is also a trend toward larger sample variance with decreasing diameter, indicating that smaller asteroids may have a greater range of amplitudes.

PERIODS

It was noted by Alfven (1964) that the spin periods of most of the planets and asteroids are very approximately equal—around 8.5 hours. As recently confirmed by Komensaroff (1984), the spin angular momentum of asteroids, planets and stars all closely follow a power law relationship to their mass.

Most asteroids have a rotational period between 6 and 13 hours, with extreme values of $2^h 27^m$ for Icarus and 80^h for 182 Elsa. The observed lightcurve period of 288 Glauke is 2 months, but this object may in fact be a binary system, the two month period being the precession of the spin axis (Harris, 1983a). Precession has not been observed in the lightcurve of any single asteroid. The approximate axial alignment time for asteroids is $6 \times 10^{-9} R^{-2}$ year, where R is the diameter in km (McAdoo and Burns, 1974). Including Glauke, 15 asteroids with periods greater than 40 hours are now known. A plot of rotational frequency versus diameter for 217 asteroids is given in Fig. 8–7.

Many statistical studies have been made in an attempt to correlate rotation rates with compositional type, and diameter. Each effort has reached conclusions that differ with the others. The data presented here is based on the three most recent investigations which attempted to disentangle and reinterpret the confusing situation which developed in the literature.

The distribution of spin rates in five different diameter ranges is shown in Fig. 8–8. In order to eliminate observational bias, objects observed by photographic photometry, and those asteroids in families, are distinguished by the shaded area labelled NF–NP. The best-fit Maxwellian

TABLE 8-1
MEAN LIGHTCURVE AMPLITUDE FROM PHOTOELECTRIC OBSERVATIONS

Diameter Range (km)	N	Mean Amplitude	Sample Variance
0–30	17	0.246	0.041
31–60	35	0.249	0.021
61–90	44	0.249	0.017
91–120	49	0.175	0.011

Table 8–1. *Mean Lightcurve Amplitude from Photoelectric Observations. Data from Binzel (1984b). For four ranges of size, the number (N) of measured asteroids is listed, along with their mean lightcurve amplitude and sample variance. Reproduced by permission from Icarus.*

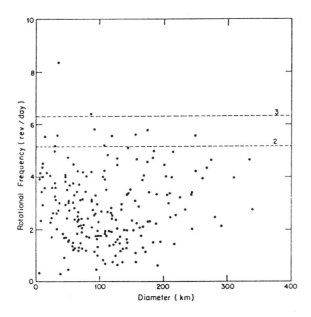

Fig. 8–7. *Rotational frequencies and diameters of 217 main-belt asteroids with reliable rotational periods. All data are from the file maintained by Harris. Ceres, Pallas, Vesta, and Hygeia are included in the data set, but since their diameters are >400km they are not shown here. The dashed lines are the rotational limits of the gravitationally bound "rubble piles" described by Weidenschilling (1981). The numbers 2 and 3 refer to their densities in grams per cubic centimeter. Dermott et al, 1984. Reproduced by permission from Icarus.*

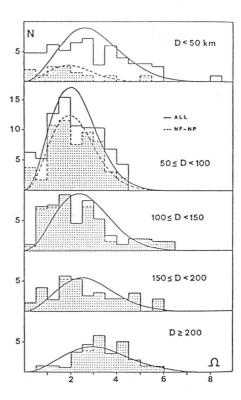

Fig. 8–8. *Maxwellian distributions for all asteroids are based on a sample of 253. Of these, 180 are non-family, non-photographically observed asteroids. Farinella et al, 1981b.*

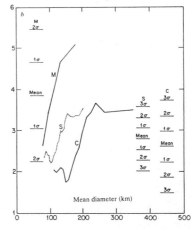

Fig. 8–9. *Mean rotational frequency versus diameter for 117 asteroids with measured albedos. Sigma values for each type are shown on the right. The larger the sigma value, the more significant is the data, so small bumps in the curves have little relevance. Dermott et al, 1984. Reproduced by permission from Icarus.*

curves are also plotted in Fig. 8–8. If the spin rates of the asteroids were not dependent on any orbital or physical parameters, they would form an equilibrium population based on random processes. This is what the Maxwellian curve represents, and any significant departures from it indicate possible interrelations with other factors, such as type or diameter.

Two basic conclusions were drawn from these plots by Farinella *et al* (1981b). Firstly, the excess of slow rotators is limited to intermediate and, in particular, to small asteroids. Secondly, at least from 50 km up, the average spin rate increases for larger objects. Dermott *et al* (1984b) question the validity of this analysis, while still agreeing with their conclusions. They claim that when uncertain data are removed, there is a broadening of the distribution

from a Maxwellian. That is, the 'excess' of slow rotators is about the same as the 'excess' of fast ones. "What appears to be indicated is a superposition of two or more populations, each of which may obey Maxwellian statistics, but with different means."

Fig. 8–9 plots the mean rotational frequency against mean diameter for different types. This clearly shows that M objects rotate faster than S–types, which rotate faster than C–types. At any one mean diameter, S–types rotate faster than C–types by a factor of 1.48 rev/day. By considering a set of 134 main-belt asteroids of all types, it was found that the mean rotational frequency increases lin-

TABLE 8–2		
ASTEROIDS WITH DETERMINED		
ROTATION PERIODS		
B(1,0)	Total	Photo	Lower Limit
4–5	2	–	–
5–6	1	–	–
6–7	6	–	–
7–8	32	–	–
8–9	82	–	5
9–10	117	1	1
10–11	63	9	7
11–12	90	16	6
12–13	46	6	1
13–14	39	10	2
14–15	14	3	1
15–	23	1	–
Total	515	46	23

Table 8–2. *Asteroids with Determined Rotation Periods. Asteroids in a range of absolute blue magnitudes (B(1,0)) are tabulated in the total column. Some of these were determined by photographic photometry, and others only have a lower limit of rotation period known.*

TABLE 8–3		
ASTEROIDS WITH KNOWN		
PERIODS OR AMPLITIUDES		
Type	Number	Earth Crossers	Mars Crossers
C	172	2	–
S	225	12	3
M	23	–	–
E	5	–	–
U	44	9	–
Other	84	1	1
Total	553	24	4

Table 8–3. *Asteroids with Known Periods or Amplitudes. The total number of asteroids with known periods or amplitudes are divided according to taxonomic class. The number that are Earth-crossing or Mars-crossing are also listed.*

early from 2.1 rev/day (11.1 hrs) for 60 km objects, to 3.7 rev/day (6.5 hrs.) for 230 km objects (Dermott & Murray, 1982).

The tendency for slow spin rates between 50 and 150 km was first noted by Tedesco & Zappala (1980), who suggested that 150 km diameter may mark the transition between "primordial" and collisionally evolved (fragmented) asteroids. But Dobrovolskis & Burns (1984) have offered a much different explanation—cratering impacts. They note that the ejecta from an impact thrown out in the direction of rotation escapes more easily than that expelled in the opposite direction. This 'momentum leakage' operates only in the intermediate size range, and may tend to slow down the rotation of such asteroids.

Asteroids with known periods or amplitudes as a function of absolute magnitude and compositional type are shown in Table 8–2 and 8–3. Out of 515 asteroids with known periods in 1986, 46 have been determined only by photographic photometry, and 23 have only a lower limit

TABLE 8–4	
APOLLO/AMOR	
ROTATIONAL PERIODS	
Asteroid	Period (hrs)
1566 Icarus	2.27
1984 KD	2.4
1980 AA	2.7
3199 Nefertiti	3.01
1862 Apollo	3.06
1979 VA	3.55
1978 CA	3.75
3200 Phaethon	4
1915 Quetzalcoatl	4.9
1983 RD	4.93
1620 Geographos	5.22
1580 Betulia	6.13
1865 Cerberus	6.80
2608 Seneca	8.0
1864 Daedalus	8.57
1982 XB	9.01
1685 Toro	10.19
2100 Ra-Shalom	19.79
2201 Oljato	24
887 Alinda	73.97
1982 DV	75
3102 1981 QA	148

Table 8–4. *Apollo-Amor Rotational Periods. Apollo-Amor asteroids seem to be divided into two types according to their rotational periods. Most have periods less than 12 hours, but a few have very long periods.*

to their periods listed. Approximately equal numbers of C– and S–types have been measured, with only 24 Earth-crossers and 4 Mars-crossers included in the total data base of 550 objects in 1986. The number of asteroids with known periods as a function of diameter are shown in Fig. 8–10. Most objects less than 10 km in the histogram are Apollo-Amors. (Cunningham, 1984b).

While on the subject of Apollo-Amors, consider the rotational periods in Table 8–4. The bimodal distribution is quite striking—a few with long periods of 1 to 6 days, and several with periods shorter than half a day. A much larger sample will be needed to strengthen the statistical significance of this distribution, but the evidence seems to distinguish two distinctly different types of Earth-crossers. This bimodal distribution is similar to comet spin statistics, and suggests that at least some of them may be extinct comets (Harris, 1985).

POLE POSITIONS

While several methods have been used to determine the pole orientations of asteroids, only two techniques have gained wide acceptance in the 1980's: photometric astrometry and the analytic method. The mathematical details of these methods can be found in Taylor (1979) for the former, and Zappala (1984) and Pospieszalska-Surdej & Surdej (1985) for the latter. Photometric astrometry converts observed synodic periods into consistent values for a sidereal period, pole orientation and sense of rotation. The mean synodic period is the average of the synodic periods of an asteroid over its entire orbit, and the uniquely determined value of this mean leads to a sidereal period

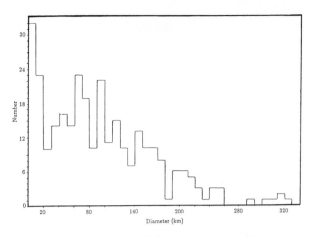

Fig. 8–10. *A histogram of the number of asteroids in ten-km bins, for a sample of 328 objects with known periods. Cunningham, 1984b.*

Photo. 8–6. *Paolo Farinella, an Italian astronomer at the University of Pisa, who conducts theoretical and laboratory work on orbital problems in asteroid research.*

Photo. 8–7. *Ronald Taylor, a high school teacher in Tucson, Arizona. At the University of Arizona, Professor Taylor pursues his reseach into pole determinations of asteroids.*

and pole position. In order to apply this method, it is necessary to have 6 to 10 high-quality lightcurves from one opposition that span a wide range of phase angles; and at least one high-quality lightcurve, over a full period, from 4 more oppositions. Practical examples can be found in Taylor & Tedesco (1983) and Tedesco & Taylor (1985).

It has its limitations, however. Photometric astrometry leads to spurious results if the asteroids' terminator is not considered, because the epoch and maximum and minimum light shift with respect to the maximum and minimum projected area. Both photometric astrometry and radiometry require several months of data to determine an asteroids' sense of rotation (prograde or retrograde). Speckle interferometry, on the other hand, allows this to be measured with only a few hours of data. Assuming the asteroid is a smooth triaxial ellipsoid, it presents a series of ellipses that change in size, shape and orientation as it rotates. The asteroids' axial dimensions and direction of its spin axis, including the sense of rotation, can be found from a least squares analysis of this ellipse series (Drummond *et al*, 1985a; 1985b).

The analytic method is based on the assumption of a triaxial shape, and on the relationships among aspect angle, lightcurve amplitude and magnitude at maximum brightness. A unique value of the pole coordinates can only be found for asteroids with high orbital eccentricities and/or inclinations. Several pairs of observations, obtained in different oppositions, produce a set of pole coordinates, whose weighted mean is adopted as the value defining the direction of the rotational axis. Magnusson (1986) has successfully combined the two methods to determine pole positions and the sense of rotation of 20 main belt asteroids.

Neglecting scattering effects leads to an overestimate of the geometrical ratios (a/b and b/c), thus leading to an error in the pole determination. Zappala *et al* (1984b) have developed a method to correct the input data of amplitudes and magnitudes at maximum brightness. Preliminary results led to differences of 2 to 4° for small values of b/c in the asteroids 16 Psyche and 63 Ausonia, and 8 to 9° for 39 Laetitia whose b/c is about 2.

The coordinates of the poles of 37 asteroids are given in Table 8–5 (Cunningham, 1985a). Based on a small data set of 17 pole positions, Burns and Tedesco (1979) concluded that the pole directions are randomly oriented in space, suggesting the system of asteroids have evolved collisionally. Using a set of just 22 asteroids with pole positions, Barucci *et al* (1986) concluded the opposite. "Most asteroids appear to have poles in the intermediate latitudes with respect to the ecliptic plane. For most of them the angle between the pole and the normal to the orbital plane lies between 70° and 35°." Any significant deviation from this observed Maxwellian distribution will have major implications for the evolutionary history of the asteroids. It is expected that about 75 asteroids will have pole coordinates known by the late 1980's permitting a more extensive statistical analysis.

TABLE 8–5 Part 1	Pole Coord. λ	β	Ref.
2 Pallas	49	6	7
2 Pallas	200	37	5
2 Pallas	44	4	58
2 Pallas	228	43	41
2 Pallas	211	38	6
2 Pallas	54	-6	29
3 Juno	71	49	10
3 Juno	101	29	58
3 Juno	110	40	29
4 Vesta	139	47	20
4 Vesta	126	65	20
4 Vesta	333	39	43
4 Vesta	151	49	47
4 Vesta	350	40	47
4 Vesta	57	74	10
4 Vesta	14	80	8
4 Vesta	103	43	50
4 Vesta	120	65	29
4 Vesta	325	55	29
5 Astraea	332	-9	46
5 Astraea	148	9	46
6 Hebe	5	50	22
6 Hebe	344	30	58
6 Hebe	145	15	19
6 Hebe	355	50	29
7 Iris	11	41	45
7 Iris	193	15	19
7 Iris	184	55	8
7 Iris	15	25	29
7 Iris	195	15	29
8 Flora	157	10	19
9 Metis	191	56	57
9 Metis	2	26	58
9 Metis	186	43	58
9 Metis	156	15	19
9 Metis	348	76	10
12 Victoria	242	17	27
15 Eunomia		-90	54
15 Eunomia	250	74	9
15 Eunomia	106	-73	29
15 Eunomia	351	-61	29
15 Eunomia	164	52	33
16 Psyche	225	5	62
16 Psyche	40	23	58
16 Psyche	217	31	53
16 Psyche	222	4	25
16 Psyche	223	37	57
16 Psyche	36	-21	29
16 Psyche	217	-14	29
20 Massalia	30	54	31
20 Massalia	20	80	29
20 Massalia	200	80	29
20 Massalia	10	78	27
20 Massalia	207	51	2

TABLE 8–5 Part 2	Pole Coord. λ	β	Ref.
22 Kalliope	19	-11	29
22 Kalliope	199	14	29
22 Kalliope	215	45	40
22 Kalliope	214	42	58
22 Kalliope	13	17	58
28 Bellona	93	18	58
28 Bellona	285	37	58
29 Amphitrite	142	50	58
29 Amphitrite	165	45	53
29 Amphitrite	308	40	58
29 Amphitrite	320	45	53
29 Amphitrite	160	53	30
29 Amphitrite	135	-15	29
29 Amphitrite	320	-25	-29
31 Euphrosyne	317	4	2
31 Euphrosyne	178	72	31
31 Euphrosyne	315	5	31
37 Fides	100	5	29
37 Fides	280	-5	29
39 Laetitia	114	28	54
39 Laetitia	111	56	31
39 Laetitia	128	38	30
39 Laetitia	116	49	58
39 Laetitia	121	37	37
39 Laetitia	130	10	19
39 Laetitia	103	61	9
39 Laetitia	129	30	29
39 Laetitia	324	35	29
41 Daphne	186	-40	29
41 Daphne	335	-33	29
41 Daphne	19	35	2
41 Daphne	159	32	2
41 Daphne	157	28	1
41 Daphne	15	36	1
43 Ariadne	248	20	3
43 Ariadne	73	25	3
43 Ariadne	75	35	30
44 Nysa	100	60	49
44 Nysa	99	49	58
44 Nysa	295	54	58
44 Nysa	265	55	49
44 Nysa	94	59	28
44 Nysa	288	63	28
44 Nysa	100	50	57
44 Nysa	105	30	19
44 Nysa	358	84	8
44 Nysa	105	57	29
44 Nysa	300	61	29
52 Europa	0	37	3
63 Ausonia	120	-30	29
63 Ausonia	305	-30	29
63 Ausonia	127	38	58
63 Ausonia	298	28	58

TABLE 8–5 Part 3	Pole Coord. λ	β	Ref.
129 Antigone	331	30	2
129 Antigone	20	50	29
129 Antigone	180	72	29
192 Nausikaa	130	40	38
216 Kleopatra	71	21	28
216 Kleopatra	72	20	29
216 Kleopatra	235	34	29
216 Kleopatra	67	15	58
216 Kleopatra	231	31	58
281 Lucretia	90	33	18
354 Eleonora	355	36	33
354 Eleonora	3	28	7
354 Eleonora	159	22	29
354 Eleonora	339	2	29
354 Eleonora	0	35	26
354 Eleonora	357	38	58
433 Eros	23	37	12
433 Eros	16	12	18
433 Eros	17	10	39
433 Eros	15	9	32
433 Eros	29	22	61
433 Eros	4	45	36
433 Eros	349	62	56
433 Eros	2	53	24
433 Eros	9	38	42
433 Eros	353	13	4
433 Eros	10	46	8
433 Eros	13	28	55
433 Eros	22	9	48
433 Eros	304	48	60
511 Davida	302	29	59
511 Davida	291	37	14
511 Davida	122	10	19
511 Davida	306	34	11
532 Herculina	132	-59	13
624 Hektor	324	10	15
624 Hektor	152	29	58
624 Hektor	314	15	58
624 Hektor	144	10	28
624 Hektor	322	-4	28
624 Hektor	315	10	35
624 Hektor	315	16	34
624 Hektor	151	27	34
624 Hektor	134	-15	29
624 Hektor	330	-30	29
704 Interamnia	70	10	23
1566 Icarus	49	0	21
1580 Betulia	140	20	52
1620 Geographos	200	60	17
1620 Geographos	60	-60	17
1685 Toro	200	55	16

Table 8–5. *Pole Positions. The pole positions of asteoids measured from 1931–1986 are given, followed by references to the 62 papers in which the data appeared. Often there are two solutions which are equally likely, which explains the dual pole positions quoted for some asteroids from the same reference. In general, only recently-determined positions are reliable.*

Sources: 1. Barucci, 1983; 2. Barucci et al, 1985; 3. Barucci et al, 1986; 4. Beyer, 1953; 5. Binzel, 1984; 6. Burchi & Milano, 1983; 7. Burchi et al, 1985; 8. Cailliatte, 1956; 9. Cailliatte, 1960; 10. Chang & Chang, 1962; 11. Chang & Chang, 1963; 12. Drummond et al, 1984a; 13. Drummond et al, 1984b; 14. Drummond & Hege, 1985; 15. Dunlap & Gehrels, 1969; 16. Dunlap et al, 1973; 17. Dunlap, 1974; 18. Dunlap, 1976; 19. Gehrels & Owings, 1962; 20. Gehrels, 1967; 21. Gehrels et al, 1970; 22. Gehrels & Taylor, 1977; 23. Harris & Burns, 1979; 24. Krug & Schrutka-Rechtenstamm, 1936; 25. Lupishko et al, 1980; 26. Lupishko et al, 1981; 27. Lupishko & Bel'skaya, 1983; 28. Magnusson, 1983; 29. Magnusson, 1986; 30. McCheyne et al, 1985; 31. McCheyne et al, 1985; 32. Millis et al, 1976; 33. Piironen et al, 1985; 34. Pospieszalska-Surdej & Surdej, 1985 35. Poutanen et al, 1981; 36. Rosenhangen, 1932; 37. Sather, 1976; 38. Scaltriti & Zappala, 1976a; 39. Scaltriti and Zappala, 1976b; 40. Scaltriti et al, 1978; 41. Schroll et al, 1976; 42. Stobbe, 1940; 43. Taylor, 1973; 44. Taylor et al, 1976; 45. Taylor, 1977; 46. Taylor, 1978; 47. Taylor, 1979; 48. Taylor, 1985; 49. Taylor & Tedesco, 1982; 50. Taylor et al, 1985; 51. Tedesco & Taylor, 1985; 52. Tedesco et al, 1978; 53. Tedesco & Sather, 1981; 54. Van Houten-Groeneveld & Van Houten, 1958; 55. Vesely, 1971; 56. Watson, 1937; 57. Zappala & Van Houten-Groeneveld, 1979; 58. Zappala & Knezevic, 1984; 59. Zappala & Knezevic, 1985; 60. Zessewitsch, 1931; 61. Zessewitsch, 1937; 62. Zhou & Yang, 1981.

SIZES 9

If you call La Gallienne a minor poet you might
just as well call a street lamp a minor planet.

Edward Marsh

At least six distinct techniques have been used to estimate asteroidal diameters, some now only of historical
interest. Nineteenth-century measurements converted into
km are listed in Table 9–1.

DISKMETER

The first attempt to measure the size of asteroids was made
on April 1, 1802, by none other than Sir William Herschel,
discoverer of the planet Uranus. He described his method
before a meeting of the Royal Society in May of that year.

> Having placed a lucid disk at a considerable
> distance from the eye, but so that I might view
> it with perfect distinctness, I threw the image
> of Mr. Piazzi's star (Ceres), seen in a 7-feet
> reflector, very near it, in order to have the pro-
> jected picture of the star and the lucid disk side
> by side, that I might ascertain their compara-
> tive magnitudes (sizes).
>
> I soon perceived that the length of my gar-
> den would not allow me to remove the disk-
> micrometer, which must be placed at right an-
> gles to the telescope, far enough to make it
> appear no larger than a star; and, not having
> disks of a less diameter prepared, I placed the
> smallest I had, as far from me as the situation
> of the star would allow.
>
> Then, bringing its image again by the side of
> the disk, and viewing, at the same time, with
> one eye the magnified star, while the other eye
> saw the lucid disk, I perceived that Ceres, was
> hardly more than one third of the diameter of
> the disk.' (Herschel, 1802).

It is interesting to note that the angular diameter of
Ceres varies from 0.27 to 0.69 seconds of arc—extremely
small values. This extraordinary observation required Herschel to place the lucid disk 54 meters from his eye! He
repeated the experiment with Pallas, the only other asteroid known at the time. His diameter estimates, 161 miles
(259 km) for Ceres and 147 miles (236 km) for Pallas, were
unfortunately very much smaller than the true values.

A modern version of Herschel's lucid disk was developed by Camichel in 1953. His diskmeter produced a small

TABLE 9–1			
HISTORICAL DIAMETER MEASUREMENTS (KM)			
Author	Ceres	Pallas	Juno	Vesta
Schroeter	2,526	3,258	2,222	536
Herschel	259	236		
Argelander	362	254	169	435
Bruno	365	275	185	370
Galle	637			
Knott	1,014			
Muller	950	708		946
Lamont		1,074		
Pickering		269	151	513
Stone			200	344
Madler				467
Secchi				724
Tacchini				1,417
Millosevich				1,014
Harrington				837
Barnard	767	489	193	385
Bauschinger	772	584	292	834

Table 9–1. *Historical Diameter Measurements (km). A variety of diameters were quoted by scientists in the 19th century for the first four
asteroids.*

artificial bright disk in the telescope's eyepiece. By viewing a nearby star, an observer could adjust the brightness,
color and blurring to match its image. Switching to the
asteroid, the brightness and color was then set to match
its observed characteristics, thus leading to an estimate
of its apparent size. According to Dollfus (1971), this instrument was used by Camichel on the Pic-du-Midi 60 cm
refractor and by Gerard Kuiper on the 5–meter Palomar
reflector to measure some asteroids.

MICROMETER

After Herschel's pioneering work, the next major advance
in diameter work was done in 1894, when E. E. Barnard
used a filar micrometer on the 90 cm refractor at Lick and
the 100 cm refractor at Yerkes. His estimates for the first
four asteroids were much better than Herschel's, but still

too small: Ceres (770 km), Pallas (490 km), Juno (195 km), Vesta (390 km).

Like the lucid disk method, Barnard's micrometer method had a modern counterpart. The double-image micrometer was used on Vesta and Pallas by several French astronomers in 1967 and 1969. Their Vesta measurements agreed with Barnard, but the diameter of Pallas was twice as large.

INTERFEROMETER

An interferometer with a double slit was used on Vesta by M. Hamy with the 60 cm coude refractor in Paris in 1899. Based on eight nights of observation, he estimated Vesta's size to be 400 km, similar to Barnard's measurement.

The interferometric principle too has experienced a modern revival. First proposed by Labeyrie in 1970, the technique of speckle interferometry has revolutionized the way astronomers measure the sizes of both stars and asteroids. Speckle data consist of a series of short exposure photographs at large image scales. On time scales short enough to freeze turbulent motions in the atmosphere, less than 0.05 seconds, a large telescope behaves like a multiple-aperture interferometer. Normally, resolution is limited to one arc second, but this method allows angular details to be observed at the smallest scale permitted by theory. Typical errors quoted in speckle work are 0.01 arc second or even less.

POLARIMETRY

By observing the polarization of an asteroid's light at different phase angles, a so-called polarization-phase curve can be plotted. Fig. 9–1 illustrates the main aspects of such a plot: the depth P_{min} of the negative branch, and the slope h, usually measured in percent per degree of the ascending branch.

This slope is related to the asteroid's geometric albedo, although it is insensitive for albedos less than 0.05. This slope-albedo law, first noted in 1967, is the basis of the widely-used polarimetric method. Zellner *et al* (1974) gave the equations needed to compute asteroid radii:

$$\log a = -\log h - 1.78.$$

$$2 \log r = 5.642 - 0.4 V(1,0) - \log a.$$

As an example, if the geometric albedo in the V band for Ceres is $a = 0.068$, and $\log a = 1.17$, the diameter for Ceres is 1,050 km.

While the polarimetric method does not depend on a physical model of the asteroid, as the radiometric method does, it is based on a laboratory-derived empirical relation, the cause of which is not fully understood. Also, it is only applicable to asteroids which can be observed at large

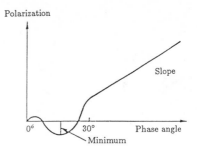

Fig. 9–1. *A polarization phase curve. The polarimetric method is based on Fresnel's law which states that unpolarized light becomes polarized after reflection. The amount of polarization depends on the phase angle which is the angle Sun-asteroid-Earth. Scholl, 1982*

phase angles, beyond the inversion (typically 18° to 24°). Only about 100 asteroids have had their polarization-phase curves plotted.

RADIOMETRY

This technique, which has provided us with most asteroidal diameter estimates, is based on sound physical principles but is subject to uncertainties in our knowledge of the asteroids' physical characteristics. The visible brightness of an asteroid is proportional to the product of the geometric albedo and the square of the diameter. For asteroids of the same size at the same distance, one of lower albedo will naturally be fainter in the visible. But in the infrared, the lower albedo object will be hotter. This thermal emission is proportional to the product of one minus the Bond albedo and the square of the diameter.

This complementarity of the dependence of brightness on albedo in the two spectral regions is the basis for the radiometric method. The exact relationship between the geometric and Bond albedos, however, is an unknown which must be modeled. As explained by Morrison and Lebofsky (1979), for a typical dark asteroid, the diameters and geometric albedos are quite insensitive to this relationship. The main factor that determines infrared brightness is the diameter itself, so an IR magnitude is quite good by itself in getting at the diameter.

Unlike the polarimetric method, which consumes a great deal of observing time, the radiometric method is quite efficient. Even an instantaneous difference in visible and IR magnitudes is adequate to determine the asteroid diameter to within 10%.

Using occultation measurements of the diameters of Pallas and Juno, Voyager spacecraft diameter of Jupiter's satellite Callisto, and IR photometry of these objects with the 3 meter IR telescope in Hawaii, Brown *et al* (1982) have revised the radiometric asteroid scale. As a result, the diameters given in the TRIAD file must be reduced by 5% to bring them into agreement with the new calibration. Albedos similarly have to be increased slightly, by 10%. A new theory by Lebofsky (1985) similarly calls for a size reduction, although for substantially different reasons.

Photo. 9–1. *Benjamin Zellner of the Space Telescope Science Institute in Baltimore, Maryland. With David Tholen and Edward Tedesco, he developed the eight-color asteroid survey.*

Photo. 9–2. *Larry Lebofsky of the University of Arizona was instrumental in developing the asteroid thermal model used to analyze data collected by IRAS. From ground-based observations he detected evidence for water of hydration on several asteroids.*

OCCULTATION

The only reliable, direct method of determining an asteroid's size is by observing an occultation. Even though several occultations of stars by asteroids brighter than magnitude 12.5 occur each night, observable events occur much more rarely, perhaps less than 10 a year.

The list of asteroids with occultation diameters is rapidly growing: Ceres, Pallas, Nemausa, Cybele, Thisbe, Ursula, Patientia, Davida, Aglaja, Athamantis and others. Two Pallas events have been recorded from more than one site: seven sites noted an occultation on 1978 May 29; and the 1983 May 29 occultation resulted in more than 120 timings, the best observed to date. The two occultations gave similar results: 538 ± 12 km in 1978, 523 ± 5 km in 1983. The observed occultation chords from the 1983 event, shown in Fig. 9–2, show how the diameter and shape of an asteroid can be defined by this method.

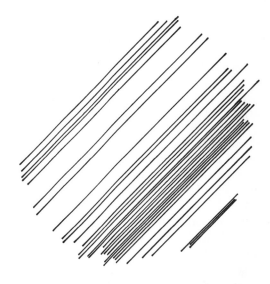

Fig. 9–2. *The occultation chords of the 1983 Pallas occultation, adapted from a plot of 54 chords by Marie Marr and David Dunham. The occultation of 1 Vulpeculae by Pallas was seen by more than 100 persons from the southern United States.* Sky & Telescope, *Sept. 1983.*

SIZE DISTRIBUTION

A perusal of the literature on asteroid diameters in the last 15 years might give you the impression that the asteroids are rapidly changing objects, expanding and contracting every year or two. In general, as our understanding has grown, the asteroids have shrunk.

As an example, consider Pallas, one of the best observed asteroids. In 1971, its diameter was believed to be 920 km. As the result of the 1979 occultation of a star by Pallas, this was revised downward to 538 km, and the 1983 occultation further shrunk its size to 523 km. Perversely, the latest value is closer Barnard's 1894 estimate (490 km) than the 1977 value was (Taylor, 1983).

The largest asteroid, Ceres, has had similarly disparate diameter estimates. In 1977 it was 1,003 km. By 1979 it

TABLE 9–2			
ASTEROID DIAMETERS IN KM			
1 Ceres	932	24 Themis	236
4 Vesta	528	16 Psyche	236
2 Pallas	523	13 Egeria	233
10 Hygiea	414	88 Thisbe	232
704 Interamnia	321	65 Cybele	230
511 Davida	318	216 Kleopatra	224
52 Europa	277	624 Hektor	223
3 Juno	271	165 Loreley	217
451 Patientia	267	19 Fortuna	215
31 Euphrosyne	257	7 Iris	211
15 Eunomia	248	532 Herculina	208
324 Bamberga	243	702 Alauda	206
107 Camilla	239	2060 Chiron	200
87 Sylvia	238	250 Bettina	200
45 Eugenia	237		

Table 9–2. *Asteroid Diameters in km. Modern measurements indicate 29 asteroids have diameters larger than 200 km. These figures are generally accurate to about 5% in most cases, although the distant Chiron may be larger.*

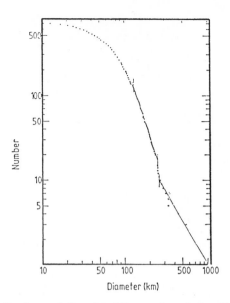

Fig. 9–3. *A cumulative plot of the number of asteroids having diameters greater than 125 km listed in TRIAD. The two lines represent linear regression fits to the area over the size range larger than 260 km, and between 248 and 130 km. Hughes, 1982.*

had grown to 1,025, but by 1982 it had shrunk to 953 km. due to a recalibration of the radiometric technique. This diameter was shrunk even further by an occultation on 13 November 1984. The diameter of Ceres is now believed to be 932 km.

One of the worst cases is 65 Cybele. In the 1979 TRIAD file it is listed at 311 km., but an occultation by Cybele in that year gave a value of 230 km. (Taylor, 1981). But what exactly is meant by a diameter, since most asteroids are not spherical?

Herculina is thought to be a prolate spheroid, with dimensions of 278 by 181 km, as deduced by speckle interferometry (Drummond and Hege, 1983). An irregularly shaped object will appear to have a different size, depending on its orientation to the observer. Unless otherwise stated, the diameters quoted in various books and papers assume sphericity. On this basis, Herculina in TRIAD has a diameter of 219 km. The best estimates for all asteroids larger than 200 km. are given in Table 9–1.

Two important studies of asteroidal diameters were published in 1982. Stanley Dermott & Carl Murray showed that the rotational frequency of main-belt asteroids depends on both type and diameter. And a study by David Hughes related the size of asteroids with their collisional history, in conflict with the Demott-Murray paper. In general, rotational frequency increases with diameter, from a minimum of 11.1 hr at 60 km. diameter to 6.5 hr. at 230 km. In other words, the rotational period decreases with increasing diameter. Fig. 9–9 in Chapter 8 shows that there are discontinuities at diameters 125 km (for C asteroids) and 105 km (for S asteroids). This was interpreted as distinguishing between primordial asteroids and their collisional products. Hughes, however, puts this transition zone at about 250 km.

By plotting the number of asteroids versus diameter, he noted four distinct regions obeying slightly different power

laws. Donnison & Sugden (1984), however, showed that this mathematical treatment suffered from "a number of important defects." By using a technique known as maximum likelihood estimation, they found the size distribution of asteroids can be successfully modeled by a single straight line. A rigorous examination showed the apparent lack of fit in the range $240 < D < 248$ is statistically insignificant (Fig. 9–3). Ishida *et al* (1984) also examined the size distribution of asteroids based on a survey of 2,700 Schmidt telescope images taken from Japan. Like Hughes, they required different indices to model the distribution by an inverse power relation. As in other aspects of asteroidal statistics, this highlights the fact that different mathematical treatments on similar data yield different results.

Paolicchi *et al* (1981) also suggested a transition region between 200 and 250 km. based on the effects of major collisions between asteroids. Above 250 km., the mass of the larger asteroid is sufficiently high to prevent fragments from achieving escape velocity, while below 200 km. fragments can become asteroids in their own right.

Ceres may be the largest asteroid, but identifying the smallest is like measuring the smile on a Cheshire cat. The smallest ones we can see are the Earth approaching asteroids due to the very fact they get close enough to see. The largest Apollo is 1978 SB at 8 km, while the smallest ones seen so far are only 0.1 to 0.2 km. across. The Spacewatch telescope is able to detect asteroids only 30 meters across. Objects smaller than this can be considered meteors. There is some evidence to suggest that smaller asteroids may be concentrated towards the ecliptic plane (Mikami & Ishida, 1986).

The first four asteroids are occasionally referred to as the Big Four. As can be seen from Table 9–2, this is a

misnomer. Juno, the third asteroid discovered, is probably only the 8th largest. The term Big Four was first suggested by Morgan Sanders, an active asteroid observer in Baltimore in the 1930s (Rice, 1937).

MASS AND DENSITY

The first estimate of the total mass of the asteroid belt was made in 1901 by J. Bauschinger and P. V. Neugebauer. Based on Barnard's diameter measurements of the largest asteroids, estimated mean densities, and derived diameters of smaller asteroids, their mass estimate was 3×10^{-9} solar mass. At the time, only the first 458 asteroids had been found, but their figure was nonetheless a gross underestimate.

This was largely due to Barnard's diameters, which were too small. A 10% increase in diameter results in a 33% increase in mass; a 5% diameter error translates into a 0.4 g/cc uncertainty in density. Significant progress in this study was not made until 1977, when L. Kresak estimated the total mass of all asteroids to be 3×10^{24} g.

Fig. 9–4. *The distribution of planets, satellites, asteroids, comets, and meteorites in the solar system as a function of their relative masses (expressed as log M). (From NASA Publication TM X–64677.)*

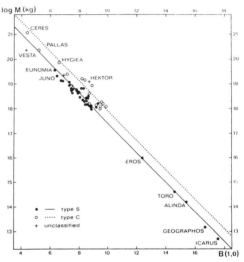

Fig. 9–5. *Masses of asteroids from the list of Chapman et al (1975), log M, plotted against their absolute magnitude B(1,0). Kresak, 1977.*

He found that the three largest asteroids contain 55% of the total mass, the Trojans, Hildas and Thule 3 to 4%, the major Hirayama families 1.5% and the Earth-crossers only 0.0001%. A comparison of asteroidal masses with other objects in the solar system is shown in Fig. 9–4.

Table 9–3 gives the masses and densities of the asteroids. The combined mass of all asteroids smaller than Ceres is equal to approximately 1.5 Ceres' mass, while the total asteroid belt represents only 3% of the Moon's mass, or a mere 0.04% of Earth's mass (Glass, 1982; Schubart & Matson, 1979).

To determine the mass of an asteroid whose diameter is known, Kresak used the formula $M = 1/6\pi dD^3$, where d is

	TABLE 9–3		
	MASSES AND DENSITIES		
Asteroid	Mass (grams)	Mass (10^{-10} solar units)	Density (g/cc)
Ceres	1.18×10^{24}	5.9 ± 0.3	2.7 ± 0.14
Pallas	2.16×10^{23}	1.08 ± 0.22	2.6 ± 0.9
Vesta	2.76×10^{23}	1.38 ± 0.12	3.3 ± 1.5
all others	1.30×10^{23}	0.65	

the density. For S–type asteroids, a density of 3.5 g/cc was adopted, while C–type asteroids have an assumed density of 2.6 g/cc (Fig. 9–5). The Earth, by comparison, has a density of 5.5 g/cc. A more recent estimate of the mass of the asteroids, by D. W. Hughes in 1982, is based on the assumption that all 740 asteroids he considered have a density of 3.5 g/cc. As a result, his figure of 4.76×10^{24} g is higher than the currently accepted figure of 3.0×10^{24} g.

It has been recognized since the 19th century that the gravitational action of the minor planets on the motion of Mars is appreciable (Bryant, 1889). Data from the Viking landers on Mars will permit a more direct and accurate determination of asteroidal mass. In particular, the masses of Ceres and Pallas can probably be improved by a factor of two, and a Vesta mass from a future lander mission will likely be accurate to within a few percent. A spacecraft on any main-belt or planet-crossing asteroid would also be capable of providing excellent mass determinations of other asteroids (Williams, 1984). (See also the Determination of Astronomical Constants section of Chapter 13).

SHAPES   10

The surest scientific payoff of observations of an occultation is a very direct and unambiguous measurement of the asteroid's size and shape.

Alan Harris, 1983

Of all the known physical characteristics of asteroids, their shapes are the most poorly defined. It appears that only a few are spherical, the remainder being ellipsoidal or irregular. Four methods have been used to establish asteroidal shapes.

RADAR

Ideally, this method can determine an asteroid's shape, but both its rotational period and pole must be known for the data to be interpreted unambiguously. In the absence of extensive data derived from other methods, radar can still provide constraints on an asteroid's shape.

SPECKLE INTERFEROMETRY

Astronomers at Steward Observatory in Tucson began a speckle program in 1981 to observe asteroids of various types to check the assumptions and results obtained by other methods. The results have been spectacular.

Photo 10–1 shows intensity contours superimposed on the seeing-corrected power spectra of 433 Eros. The first frame shows a star for comparison. The next seven frames show Eros at different light-curve phases. These differ from the star in two ways: the energy falls off more rapidly (i.e., the object is resolved) and it does not fall off uniformly (which indicates the object is more highly resolved—longer—in a particular direction).

To process the data, elliptical contours are fit to each of these energy distributions to extract the semi-major and -minor axes, and the position angle for each observation. This set of values is used to determine the actual dimensions and pole of the asteroid.

Photo 10–2 clearly shows the oblong-shaped Eros rotating in space. The bottom half of each frame is the actual data, while the top half is the triaxial ellipsoid solution for that data. The first frame shows three circles, the inner one corresponding to $0''.3$, the middle to $0''.1$ and the outer one to the diffraction limit of $0''.05$. Because the power spectrum is a reciprocal space (frequency), large dimensions are close in while smaller dimensions are further out (Drummond *et al*, 1985a).

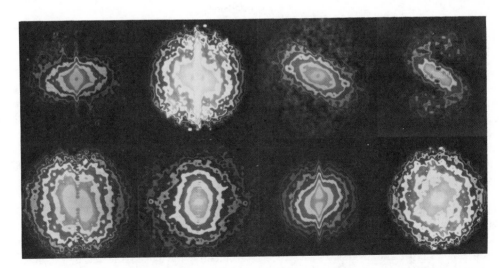

Photo 10–1. *Intensity contours of the asteroid Eros, resulting from speckle interferometry observations. The first frame shows a star for comparison; the others show Eros at various phases in its lightcurve. Photo courtesy of Dr. Jack Drummond and Icarus.*

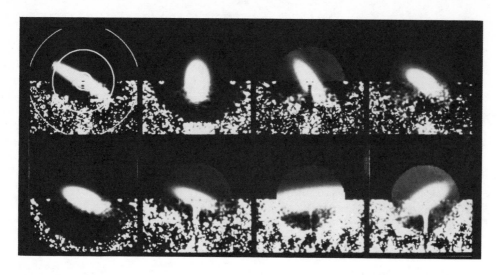

Photo. 10–2. *Speckle images of Eros, showing the oblong-shaped asteroid rotating in space. Photo courtesy of Dr. Jack Drummond and Icarus.*

OCCULTATION

The profile of an asteroid can be defined by a large number of chords, but this requires an equally large number of observing sites. Since there are few portable photoelectric telescopes, only an occultation by a bright asteroid is likely to produce enough chords for a reliable shape determination.

Even a large number of observations at a single occultation event provides no information about the asteroids' three-dimensional shape. This requires prior knowledge of the asteroids' pole position and a second occultation at a different aspect angle. Four parameters must be known to actually determine the lengths of the three axes of a triaxial ellipsoid: the projected outline of the asteroid from a position not along the rotational axis; the rotational phase; the angle between the rotational axis and the line of sight; and the lightcurve amplitude for that particular pole orientation (Dunham *et al*, 1984).

LIGHTCURVES

According to Heward (1912), the light variations of Vesta led Olbers, in the early 19th century, to speculate on the shape of that asteroid. "These variations led Olbers to infer that Vesta could not be globular, that it must surely be an angular mass of rock, whose larger flattened sides when turned towards the Sun give back more light than the smaller angle could reflect when thus placed." A modern investigation relies not on the light variations caused by the orbit of the asteroid around the Sun or its varying distance from the Earth, but on the lightcurve resulting from the asteroids' rotation.

By far the most widely used technique, it is a synthesis of laboratory work on model shapes and inversion of actual lightcurves. The simplest model used is a triaxial ellipsoid, with the axes $a > b \geq c$, where a is the semi-major axis of the long side, b that of the intermediate and c the short

length, or axis of rotation. As the asteroid rotates, its projected area will vary from πac to πbc, and its magnitude will vary according to the relation $\Delta m = 2.5 \log(a/b)$. (Gehrels, 1970). Since the rotation axis will usually be tilted to the line of sight, the actual Δm will be smaller than this, and it will change as the aspect changes from one night to the next. Thus, c can be estimated, along with a/b and b/c ratios (Burns & Tedesco, 1979).

Astronomers at the Planetary Science Institute began a four-year program in 1981 to study the shapes of large, rapidly rotating asteroids. The basic data set consists of more than 200 lightcurves. They have selected 16 large asteroids with periods less than 6 hours as the best candidates for testing the hypothesis that rubble-pile asteroids assume quasi-equilibrium shapes expected according to the laws of fluid mechanics. Their goal is to obtain lightcurves at 10° intervals of ecliptic longitude, thus spanning 60–100% of the range of each asteroid's pole position (Levy *et al*, 1984).

An important development in our understanding of how to interpret the shape of an asteroid from its lightcurve was made in 1984 by Steve Ostro & Robert Connelly. Their lightcurve inversion method yields a 2-dimensional convex profile which, under certain conditions, has a precise mathematical relationship to the real 3-dimensional shape. Assuming the asteroid to be convex means that any line segment connecting two points on its surface will be inside the asteroid. Convex profiles for two asteroids, and the parent light curves, are shown in Fig. 10–1.

CAUSES OF SHAPES

Johnson & McGetchin (1973), suggest that the largest asteroids may have been affected by radiogenic heating early in their history, as well as impact erosion, thus explaining their sphericity. Rotational distortions on the order of 10% have also been invoked by Stanley Dermott (1979), who

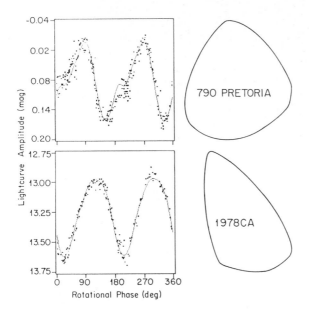

Fig. 10–1. *Convex profiles of two asteroids and their parent lightcurve. In each plot, the symbols are the lightcurve data and the curve is a model lightcurve derived from the convex-profile inversion. The profiles are shown at rotational phase 0°. Ostro & Connelly, 1984. Reprinted by permission from Icarus.*

calculates that C–type asteroids such as Ceres, which are probably composed of weak materials, cannot have surface features higher than 1km. The resulting brightness variation (Burns and Tedesco, 1979) can be as high as 0.04 mag., which, fortunately for the theory, is the actual observed amplitude.

According to Lambert (1983), the figures of highly fractured asteroids with deep regoliths should approximate equilibrium ellipsoids. Solutions for the relationships between rotational rate, angular momentum, and figure for such bodies were given by Chandrasekhar (1969). As an asteroid increases its spin rate, its shape will become more oblate. For a density of 2.5 gm/cc, the minimum rotational period is 3.94 hours.

While heating, impact erosion and rotational distortions have affected the shapes of large asteroids, objects whose size is less than 100 km are believed to be the product of collisions. Farinella *et al* (1982) state that shapes are significantly modified through collisions because the probability of colliding with a massive, high-velocity object is large, and there is little chance for the resulting fragments to coalesce after impact.

For asteroids of intermediate size (100-300 km), self-gravitation is likely the prime shape-determining agent. This is not a new idea. "It is therefore probable to admit that the asteroids are bodies of irregular form, possibly representing accumulations of independent block heaps." (Vsessviatsky & Filippov, 1935) According to Farinella, these "rubble pile" asteroids are probably quite common since the majority of asteroids have never been molten.

LABORATORY EXPERIMENTS

Until recently, little laboratory work has been done to model the shapes of asteroids, the pioneering study having been done by J. L. Dunlap in 1971. Twelve models were made with a Styrofoam center covered with a thin layer of Plasticene and finally dusted with powdered rock. The model was rotated by a stepper motor, and the reflected light measured by the same sort of photometer actually employed at the telescope. Variations of a cylinder with hemispherical ends were used in the experiments.

Fig. 10–2 shows the close match between the observed light curve of Geographos, and the laboratory curve produced with the model, of which one end and part of one side were darkened with graphite powder to better match the asteroids' reflectivity. He noted the laboratory lightcurves were much smoother than actual lightcurves, with variations of less than 0.004 mag., indicating that surface texture is the major source of small amplitude features.

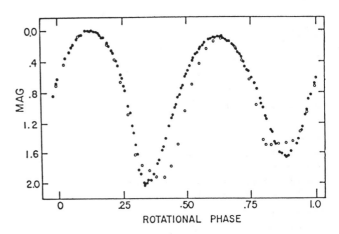

Fig. 10–2. *Comparison of model to telescopic observations: Geographos, August 31, 1969; open circles: model. This pioneering work by Dunlap (1971) showed that at least some asteroid lightcurves could be reproduced in the laboratory using simple models.*

Fujiwara *et al* (1978) was concerned with the shape of fragments produced in high-velocity impact experiments. While the mean relative velocity of asteroid impacts is 5 km/sec, the tests were made at slightly slower velocities: 2.6 and 3.7 km/sec. A similar study by Barucci (1983) was made at 10 km/sec; and Bianchi *et al* (1984), using completely different collisional parameters of mass, composition and shape of both projectile and target, obtained results comparable to Fujiwara's study.

Based on a study of fragments produced by the impacts, both studies found the average ratio of $a : b : c$ is given by the simple relation $2 : \sqrt{2} : 1$ (Fig.10–3). Very few elongated or spherical fragments were created, and all had a c/a ratio greater than 0.2. In comparing the shapes of Laetetia, Eros, Hektor and Geographos, it was found that their c/a values were near the limiting one, but fell within the distribution of c/a and b/a produced by the laboratory fragments. Since these asteroids have a large

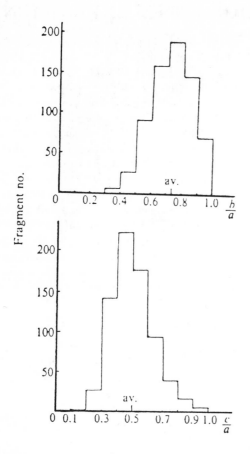

Fig. 10-3. *Histogram for b/a and c/a. Av. is the average value. The average ratio of a: b: c is approximately given by 2: square root 2:1. The distribution of shapes of asteroidal-like fragments in the laboratory is shown in this histogram for b/a and c/a. Fujiwara et al, 1978. Reprinted by permission from Nature, Vol. 272, pp 602.*

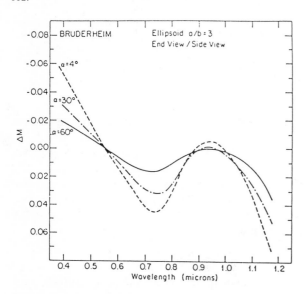

Fig. 10-4. *The phase dependence of color effects for a Bruderheim meteorite ellipsoid. As the phase angle increases, the difference in spectral contrast between the end and side views of the ellipsoid changes considerably. Few asteroids are as elongated as this example. Gradie & Veverka, 1981.*

magnitude variation, their small c/a ratios were expected as indicative of their highly irregular shapes.

While this agreement between observation and theory was most important, it is thought to be applicable only to small asteroids. According to Fujiwara, highly irregular rocky objects larger than 300–500 km radius will gradually change their shapes into spheres. As an example, they site Vesta, with b/a and c/a ratios near 0.9, with unity indicating sphericity. Paolicchi *et al* (1983) have proposed doing experiments with targets composed of rock agglomerate to better understand "rubble pile" asteroids—those of intermediate size not studied previously.

Gradie & Veverka (1981) considered an ellipsoidal object with axes $b = c$, $a/b = 3$, which corresponds to a light curve amplitude of 1.2 mag. The Earth-approaching asteroid Eros is thought to have such an elongated shape. Samples of the ordinary chondrite meteorite known as Bruderheim were used to simulate the spectral reflectance properties of Eros.

As shown in Fig. 10-4, the difference in spectral contrast between the end and side views of the ellipsoid changes considerably as the phase angle increases from 4 to 60°. Their study also showed that the side view of an ellipsoid is slightly redder than a smooth sphere would appear. They predict that most asteroids should appear redder at maximum than at minimum light, and caution observers to be wary of color variations with amplitude less than 0.03 mag. Such variations are likely caused by the non-spherical geometry of the object, rather than com-

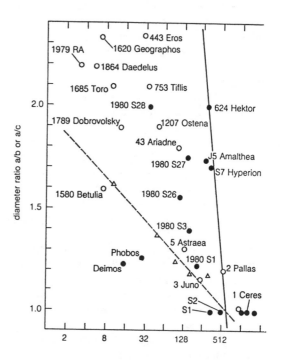

Fig. 10-5. *The shape irregularity of asteroids as a function of size (km). Closed circles denote direct shape measurement of a/c; Open circles are based on light curves which reveal a/b. Triangles are averages from asteroid lightcurves a/b. Several satellites of Mars, Jupiter and Saturn are shown for comparison. From William K. Hartmann, Moons and Planets, second edition. Copyright by Wadsworth, Inc., reprinted with permission.*

Photo. 10–3. *Stuart Weidenschilling (left) and Don Davis, with a model of the Martian satellite Phobos at the offices of the Planetary Science Institute in Tucson. The results of their lightcurve survey of large, rapidly rotating asteroids was published in 1987.*

positional variations that have come to be rather quaintly termed "spots". You're more likely to find an asteroid of unusual shape than one covered in polka dots.

Zappala (1980), using simple models like a triangular prism, was able to create light curves in the laboratory similar to those actually observed. He cautions that rotation periods derived from the two maxima and two minima assumption may be incorrect. For example, a pyramid-shaped model gave two maxima and two minima in only 180° of rotational phase. Several asteroids, such as 44 Nysa, exhibit such a light curve, "and therefore their published rotation periods should be treated with care. Several peculiarities of the light curves, such as humps, inflections or flat parts, are generally considered as evidence of macroscopic features on the asteroid surface. This interpretation may be true for the majority of asteroids, but in some cases these peculiarities may represent an alarm signal for the correct detection of the rotation period."

More recently, Catullo *et al* (1984) examined the size dependence of the axial ratios of fragments in laboratory impact experiments as a function of lightcurve amplitude. They concluded that small asteroids (less than 100 km) have very similar amplitude distributions to fragments larger than 1 gram. The distribution for large asteroids (greater than 200 km) was completely different, supporting the view that they are roughly spheroidal. The most interesting results relate to the third class of asteroids studied, the Apollo-Amors. The experiments showed that 25% of the Apollo-Amors are much more elongated than every fragment larger than 1 gram generated by impact. To see

if these asteroids correspond to a 'low mass tail' of the fragment distribution, they selected 600 fragments smaller than 1 gram, and showed that they do indeed represent a class of more elongated objects. Even so, the Apollo-Amors are still over-abundant in highly elongated objects, a phenomenon that may be due to an unknown physical effect. Recent results by Capaccioni *et al* (1986) have ruled out the possibility that the odd shapes of the Apollo-Amors are simply a consequence of their being small-sized fragments of large parent bodies.

SHAPES OF SOME ASTEROIDS

A combination of theoretical and laboratory work has come up with shapes and associated dimensions of a few asteroids (Fig. 10–5). Here is a brief survey:

1 CERES: Spheroidal to within a few percent, with topography as high as 10 km, but probably no higher than 1 km. Can be fit by an ellipse 907 × 959 km.

2 PALLAS: Nearly spheroidal.

4 VESTA: Ellipsoid (580 × 530 × 470km). Speckle data by Jack Drummond (*Sky & Telescope*, June, 1987) indicates that dark areas predominate on one side of the asteroid to such an extent that a minimum in its light curve occurs when its maximum cross-section faces Earth. Brightness variations in its 5h 20.5m period thus appear to be controlled by its albedo survace features, not its shape.

81

Photo. 10–4. *Vincent Zappala, an Italian astronomer at Torino Observatory who developed the analytic method of determining an asteroid's pole. His lightcurve work has revealed several ambiguous rotational periods.*

3 JUNO: Elliptical (288 × 230 km).

51 NEMAUSA: Triaxial ellipsoid (85 × 70 × 67 km).

1620 GEOGRAPHOS: Successfully modeled as a cylinder with hemispherical ends (1.5 km wide, 4.0 km long).

9 METIS: Triaxial ellipsoid (245 × 190 × 110 km).

22 KALLIOPE: Triaxial ellipsoid (215 × 160 × 130 km).

39 LAETITIA: Triaxial ellipsoid (255 × 150 × 85 km), with major topographic structures revealed by repetitive small-scale features in the lightcurve.

93 MINERVA: $a/b = 1.1$; $a/c = 1.7$; pancaked shaped.

216 KLEOPATRA: Triaxial ellipsoid, but possibly a binary system with nearly contact components.

433 EROS: Prolate or cylindrical (14.1 × 14.5 × 40.5 km).

8 FLORA: Spheroidal, within 10%.

624 HEKTOR: Four models have been proposed-biaxial ellipsoid, with axial ratos $a/b = a/c = 2.02$; an ellipsoid with ratios $a/b = 2$, $a/c = 2.63$; a dumbbell, due to partial coalescence of two nearly spherical objects of comparable size; a binary model consisting of two tidally elongated, nearly contact ellipsoids. Its dimensions are roughly 150 × 300 km.

1685 TORO: Elongated and irregular ($a = 2.6$, $b = 1.68$ km).

1580 BETULIA: Prolate spheroid with a topographic feature of size comparable to the radius (3 km). See Fig. 10–5.

6 HEBE: Nearly spherical.

532 HERCULINA: Ellipsoid (263 × 218 × 215 km).

To avoid complications, the various forms of ellipsoids have not been distinguished here. Since the reader may encounter these in some technical papers, definitions are given in the Glossary for the following terms: Darwin ellipsoids, Maclaurin spheroids and Jacobi ellipsoids.

FAMILIES   11

On examining the distributions of the asteroids with respect to their orbital elements, we notice condensations here and there. In general, they seem to be due to chance. But there are some which are too conspicuous to be accounted for by the laws of probability alone.

Kiyotsugu Hirayama, 1918

Daniel Kirkwood, of Kirkwood gap fame, was the first to call attention to the similarity in the orbital elements of certain asteroids. He listed four pairs of asteroids which had nearly identical values of inclination, eccentricity, longitude of perihelion and longitude of ascending node. (Kirkwood, 1888).

He speculated that these similarities were not coincidences, but resulted from the break-up of primordial bodies. While he stopped short of formulating a framework of 'families', it is interesting to note that each of his four pairs are now considered to be members of four different families (Kirkwood, 1890).

Contrary to popular belief, the first person to recognize the existence of families was W. H. S. Monck of Dublin. Referring to Kirkwood's asteroid pairs, Monck extended the search to discover that "many pairs not strictly adjacent in this respect (mean distance) exhibit similar traces of a common origin." He noted over a dozen pairs, and then took the final step in the synthesis. "A glance at the list will show that the resemblance frequently extends beyond a single pair and embraces what may be called a family—a circumstance which is known to occur in the case of comets also." (Monck, 1888).

Just as the gaps in the asteroid belt are linked to the name Kirkwood, so are the families of asteroids associated with the name Kiyotsugu Hirayama. Beginning with his first paper in 1918, Hirayama used the term family to express his belief that "an asteroid was broken into a number of fragments at a certain epoch." Initially he found only three families—Themis (22 members), Eos (21 members) and Koronis (13 members).

The 'classical' Hirayama families number only five. He added Maria and Flora in 1923, although several others of a somewhat doubtful nature were also listed. "We can enumerate five or more families, although with some degree of uncertainty owing

1. to the smallness of the numbers

2. to the indefiniteness of the boundary

3. to the poor density."

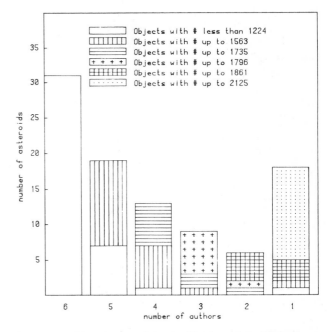

Fig. 11–1. *Synoptic view of the classifications of the family Eos. The ordinate represents the number of asteroids assigned to the family by the number of authors at the bottom of each column. The symbols refer to the limits of the data samples: 1,224 objects for Hirayama, 1,563 for Brouwer, 1,735 for Arnold, 1,796 for Williams, 1,861 for Carusi & Massaro, and 2,125 for Kozai. From Carusi & Valsecchi, 1982.*

These very problems still plague the study of families.

In an excellent review, Carusi and Valsecchi (1982) examined the seven different classification schemes that have developed over the years. The Eos family (to be considered in more detail presently) illustrates the problem (Fig. 11–1). While 31 members have been recognized by six authors, only 19 have been confirmed by five authors. Altogether, some 95 asteroids have been assigned to the Eos family. While 31 seem definite, the membership of the others depends on whose computational methods you accept.

To understand why such discrepancies exist will require a short digression into celestial mechanics. In Hirayama's 1918 study, he looked for clusterings in semimajor axis a, eccentricity e and inclination i. These are the so-called osculating elements. In an osculating (i.e., ideal) orbit,

TABLE 11-1					
HIRAYAMA ASTEROID FAMILIES					
	N	a'	e'	I'	Albedo
Koronis	42	2.875 ± 0.018	0.049 ± 0.006	2.12 ± 0.08	0.17 ± 0.05
Eos	74	3.015 ± 0.006	0.071 ± 0.008	10.20 ± 0.28	0.09 ± 0.04
Themis	62	3.136 ± 0.025	0.152 ± 0.009	1.42 ± 0.22	0.07 ± 0.03

Table 11–1. *Hirayama Asteroid Families. The number of asteroids in three families are given, along with their proper orbital elements and average albedo. Table from Dermott et al (1984). Reprinted by permission from Nature, Vol. 312, pp 505.*

the perturbing forces of the other planets are suppressed. The asteroid is assumed to move in an ellipse subject only to the gravitational attraction of the Sun.

In reality, of course, the asteroids are perturbed in their orbits by the other planets (Fig.11–2). To accurately define a family, these effects must be taken into account, by the appropriately named proper elements. These are distinguished from osculating elements by the prime symbol (e.g., e'). (Table 11–1; Dermott *et al*, 1984). Hirayama later used these proper elements in his studies of the families, giving a detailed treatment of the subject in Hirayama (1923). In his brief review of earlier attempts to detect asteroid groups, it is apparent that he was unaware of Monck's paper based on the osculating elements.

To complicate matters further, four different methods for calculating proper elements have been devised and used by those searching for asteroid families. This has contributed somewhat to the different family memberships in the literature. But the problem of computing proper elements is so complex that a new calculation of the elements seems necessary (Zappala, *et al* 1984A). The widely differing criteria used for including or rejecting an asteroid from family membership are the other major source of confusion.

With the above caveats in mind, the reader is referred to Kozai (1979), who lists each numbered asteroid assigned to 72 different families. In addition, the Palomar-Leiden Survey (PLS) has nearly doubled the number of asteroids with known proper elements, and these have been used in family studies (van Houten, *et al* 1970). Among both the numbered and unnumbered asteroids, nearly half are believed to be members of families. Thus, an understanding of the dynamics and physical properties of families is crucial to forming a clear picture of the asteroid belt as a whole.

PHYSICAL CHARACTERISTICS

The term 'family' of asteroids means different things to different people. It can either be a genetically related group, as proposed by Hirayama, or merely a statistical association. It was recognized by Williams (1971) that the Hungaria and Phocaea regions are not large families but segments of the asteroid belt isolated by resonances. The most widely used technique for distinguishing the various possible origins of families has been UBV photometry, although the eight-color survey of nearly 600 asteroids has

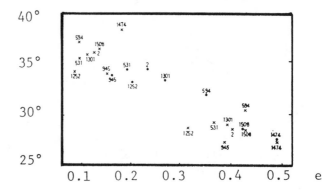

Fig. 11–2. *Variations of the eccentricities and the inclinations for asteroids belonging to Pallas family. Kozai, 1978.*

also proven useful in this regard. The albedos of nearly 40% of the asteroids in the prominent Hirayama families are now known (Tedesco *et al*, 1985). This technique compares the UBV colors of family asteroids with so-called 'field asteroids'—those objects of the surrounding population not believed to be family members.

If the two sets of asteroids are noticeably different, it is thought to be indicative of an origin by the breakup of a primordial body. Similar UBV colors suggest either that the family formed from a heterogeneous (i.e. undifferentiated) parent body whose composition is the same as the field asteroids, or the family was formed by other processes (possibly multiple parent bodies) (Gradie *et al*, 1979).

The first attempt to correlate asteroid families and classes gave rather inconclusive results. Based on a study of 10 families each with five or more classified members, Hansen (1977) found a correlation for only four families. Gradie *et al* (1979) found that most of the homogeneous families in the inner belt are composed of S–types, while in the outer belt C–types predominate. In between, they are equally common. Of 48 families used in their analysis, 26 have members of similar spectral type, while 9 are dominantly composed of one type but have one member of different type. The remaining 13 are dissimilar, having two or more types present. It is also known that most large S–type asteroids are not members of families. Those that are members have lightcurves with larger amplitudes than non-family S–types (Gaffey, 1985b).

Despite its importance, little has been done to follow up these initial studies. The collisional evolution of fami-

	TABLE 11–2 HIRAYAMA FAMILIES PRODUCED BY DISRUPTION OF PARENT BODIES GREATER THAN 200 KM DIAMETER		
Family	Minimum Parent Size in km*	Largest Remnant Diameter in km	Second Largest Remnant Diameter in km
1 Themis	300 (G) 294 (Z)	24 Themis – 249	90 Antiope – 138
24 Nysa/Hertha	200 (G)	135 Hertha – 70	44 Nysa – 66
106 Undina	272 (Z)	94 Aurora – 190 92 Undina – 184	490 Veritas – 127
113 Meliboea	209 (Z)	137 Meliboea – 153	788 Hohensteina – ~123
124 Budrosa	380 (G) 134 (Z)	349 Dembowska – 145	558 Carmen – 64
124 Leto	200 (G) 134 (Z)	68 Leto – 128	236 Honoria –67
132 Concordia	250 (G) 224 (Z)	128 Nemesis – 190	58 Concordia – 103
138 Alexandra	270 (G) 232 (Z)	54 Alexandra – 177	70 Panopaea – 153

Table 11–2. Hirayama Families Produced by disruption of Parent Bodies Greater than 200km Diameter. Table courtesy of Donald Davis of the Planetary Science Institute. Note (*): (G) indicates size estimate from Gradie et al (1979) and (Z) indicates size estimate from Zappala et al (1984a).

lies, however, has finally been addressed in some detail by Zappala *et al* (1984a).

Using a set of 73 families, they first examined the mass distribution of the members of each family. The ratio of the largest family member to the total observed mass of a family is plotted against the diameter of the largest member in Fig. 11–3. The plot is divided into three broad groups according to the diameter of the largest asteroid— 25 families with D greater than 100 km, 26 families in the range 50–100 km, and 22 with D less than 50 km. At the small end of the scale, almost all have a mass ratio less than 0.5, while the larger range exhibits a larger ratio. Intermediate families show a bimodal distribution.

They interpret this plot in terms of gravitational reaccumulation. If a family was formed by the collisional mechanism, it would be natural to expect the parent body to be broken up into fragments. But if the ejection velocity of the fragments was low enough, some of them may have come back together (i.e. reaccumulated) to form the largest member and possibly other smaller ones (Table 11–2). The gravitational effect is most pronounced in the large range—the percentage of bodies retaining more than 80% of the original mass is 40% versus 27% for the intermediate range. Over long periods of time, it is also expected that an excess of large-size members will develop as the small asteroids shatter one another. This process is thought to be responsible for the three dust bands discovered in the asteroid belt by IRAS. See Chapter 16.

In their study, Zappala *et al* also looked at the velocity distribution. Fig. 11–4 shows a plot of mean ejection velocity versus diameter of the largest fragment, showing no strong correlation. They interpret this as consistent with laboratory impact experiments which show that ejection

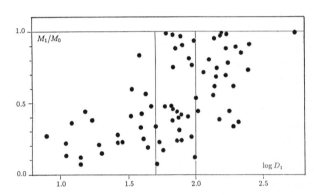

Fig. 11–3. *Mass distribution of the members of asteroid families: a plot of largest remnant mass (M1) to total mass (M0) ratio versus largest remnant diameter (d1) for all 73 families listed by Williams. Vertical lines divide the plot into three subsamples. For the large size region, the majority of families have a mass ratio larger than 0.5, while the opposite is true for small ones. Zappala et al, 1984a. Reproduced by permission from Icarus.*

velocity depends on the energy delivered to the target by the collision, not on the target's size. The strip between the two lines defines those families for which gravitational re-accumulation effects were most important. The largest 'large family members' close to this strip are 70 km in diameter, implying that this mechanism was unimportant for smaller sizes. It is unknown why families do not occur in the lower left corner of the plot, i.e. those with small main members and ejection velocities less than 60 meters per sec. But it is important to note that ejection velocities much larger than 100 meters per sec are not found. This supports the collisional mechanism as the origin for the families—higher velocities would have dispersed the

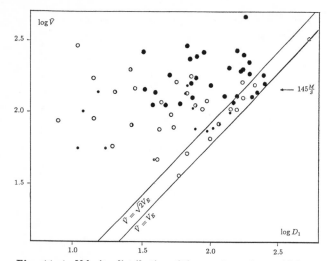

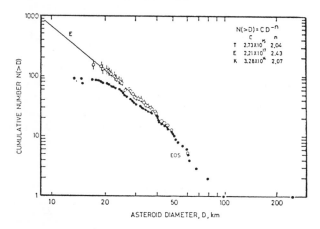

Fig. 11-4. *Velocity distribution of the members of asteroid families is shown in this log-log plot of mean ejection velocity versus diameter of the largest remnant. Full dots: assymetric families; open dots: dispersed families; half-full dots: intermediate cases; smaller dots: families with only three members. Diagonal lines bound the region diagnostic of self-gravitational reaccumulation. Zappala et al, 1984a. Reproduced by permission from Icarus.*

Fig. 11-5. *Cumulative size spectra of the Eos family. Solid circles, observed objects; open circles, data corrected for the detection bias. The straight line E is fitted by a power function. Fujiwara, 1982. Reproduced by permission from Icarus.*

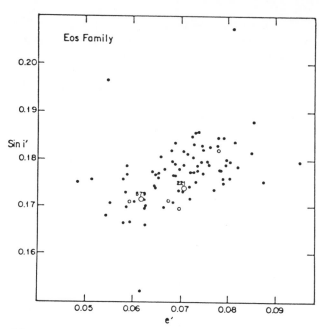

Fig. 11-6. *The distribution of Eos family members in proper element space. Open circles represent the largest members (Gradie 1978).*

2. Spallation with fragments ejected from the impact site and the opposite point of the target. The Thetis and Anahita families are typical.

3. Complete breakup with the target crushed into small fragments, leaving only a small core. The Eos and Themis families represent this type.

Fujiwara (1982) confirmed the complete fragmentation of the Eos and Themis parent bodies, as well as the Koronis parent. He computed the impact energy/parent mass to be about 10^8 ergs/g in each case. It is thought that 221 Eos, largest member of its family, is a spheroid, consistent with the view that gravitational reaccumulation formed the larger family members as rubble pile structures with equilibrium figures (see also the section on causes of shapes in Chapter 10).

Binzel (1986) has noted that asteroid families do not appear to be located near resonances, so there is no evidence that they induce increased catastrophic collision probabilities.

PARTICULAR FAMILIES

The number of families is too large to consider in detail, but a brief survey is in order, with particular attention on the well-studied Eos family. These profiles have been prepared from papers by Gradie *et al* (1979), Tedesco (1979), Gradie and Zellner (1977) and Carusi and Massaro (1978).

EOS: The most compact family, it is one of the three original families identified by Hirayama. Eos is the only high inclination group among the rich families and contains only two PLS asteroids. The three largest members are

fragments instead of allowing them to continue their association in space.

Kresak (1977), who looked at the mass distribution of families, concluded that families composed of a large body and numerous smaller collisional fragments do not exist, or are very rare. He further stated that no evidence in favor of the collisional hypothesis can be drawn from the magnitude distribution of families.

Evidence of three types of fragmentation processes in the asteroid belt, resulting in families, were found by Ip (1979), who calculated the random velocity of each member relative to the largest body in six selected families.

1. Surface cratering with fragments ejected from the impact site and the target remaining almost intact. This type is represented by the Flora and Psyche families.

221 Eos (98 km), 579 Sidonia (80 km), and 639 Latona (68 km). See Figures 11–5 and 11–6. There are approximately 60 asteroids in the family, whose parent body was at least 180 km in diameter.

The UBV colors of the Eos family are shown in Fig. 11–7. In the outer belt, where Eos is located ($a = 3.01$ AU), nearly all the large field asteroids are C–type. Clearly, the Eos members do not include any classical C objects. Of the 20 Eos family asteroids classified by Tholen (1986b) nearly all are S–type, with one possible M type (798 Ruth). Table 11-3.

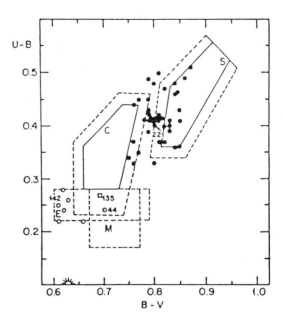

Fig. 11–7. *The UBV colors of the Eos family (filled circles) and the Nysa family (open circles). The object 135 Hertha is indicated by the square. Data are from Gradie (1978), Zellner et al (1977), and Zellner et al (1985).*

TABLE 11-3	
CLASSIFICATION	
OF	
EOS FAMILY MEMBERS	
Minor Planet	Class
221 Eos	S
339 Dorothea	S
529 Preziosa	S
562 Salome	S
579 Sidonia	S
639 Latona	S
651 Antikleia	S
653 Berenike	S
661 Cloelia	S
775 Lumiere	S
798 Ruth	M
1087 Arabis	S
1105 Fragaria	ST
1148 Rarahu	S
1434 Margot	S
1604 Tombaugh	EMPSCU
1711 Sandrine	S
2052 Tamriko	S
2111 Tselina	S
2345 Fucik	S

Table 11–3. *Eos Family asteroids observed in the eight color survey. Data courtesy of Tholen (1984b).*

While the two largest members are nearly identical, the smaller members display a small but continuous range in albedo and color. The geochemical makeup of the parent body has thus not been reconstructed, but it was at least 180 km in diameter.

According to an analysis of the rotational frequency distribution of the Eos family, Binzel (1986) found that it is consistent with a Maxwellian distribution. This implies that it is collisionally evolved and therefore near the age of the solar system. The Koronis family (see below) does not fit such a distribution.

THEMIS: The major family in the outer ring, containing more than 100 asteroids. Among the distant, rich families, Themis has the smallest proper inclination and largest proper eccentricity. Most of its members are B–types (essentially C asteroids with slightly higher than normal albedos; Tholen, 1984b), and are believed to have originated in a parent body at least 300 km in diameter. Among its members are 24 Themis (type C; 220 km), 90 Antiope (type C; 130 km), 222 Lucia (type BU, 55 km), 268 Adorea (type FC, 123 km), and 171 Ophelia (type C; 113 km).

The Themis family contains two asteroids which may be interlopers: 223 Rosa (type EMP), and 515 Athalia, whose S–type eight-color spectrum is inconsistent with its low albedo. Of the hundreds of objects studied by Tholen in the eight-color survey, this is a unique case, and has been assigned the classification I for inconsistent.

KORONIS: The only rich family with low eccentricity and low inclination, it consists of about 60 asteroids in the outer belt, between 2.8 and 2.9 AU. This family represents the fragments of a highly homogeneous S–type parent body some 90 km in diameter. It may play an important role in the evolution of fragments into Earth-crossing orbits due to its location adjacent to the 2:5 Kirkwood gap.

Binzel (1986) found that Koronis asteroids have a significantly higher mean lightcurve amplitude than nearby non-family asteroids. Since observations were obtained at random ecliptic longitudes, this implies that the spin vectors of these family members have similar low obliquities. Since the observed asteroidal fragments do not appear to have had their rotation rates (and therefore angular momenta) significantly affected by the event that created the family, such a preferential alignment of their rotation axes is not unlikely. The small dispersion of rotational frequencies in the Koronis family further support the idea that it is less collisionally evolved, and therefore younger, than the Eos family.

MARIA: Located at $a = 2.25$ AU, it is separated from the main belt by its 15° inclination. Most of its members are S–types.

HYGIEA: Contains at least 56 numbered asteroids, but PLS asteroids comprise 67% of the total membership.

NYSA and HERTHA: Close neighbors separated by a narrow gap in inclination. Both are composed of single large asteroids 70 km in diameter and many objects smaller than 20 km in diameter. All members fall in or close to the E and M–type domains. The juxtaposition of high-albedo E and A types here with many dark F asteroids "presents a major puzzle" according to Zellner *et al* (1985a). The families are adjacent to the 1:3 resonance at 2.50 AU, and thus may be an important source of Earth-crossers (Fig. 11–5).

FLORA: The richest family, containing more than double the average number of asteroids in the other Hirayama groups. At least 162 numbered asteroids have been assigned to this complex family. Nearly all the members have reddish UBV colors compared to only half for the field asteroids. The nearly spherical shape of Flora (160 km diameter) suggests that it is not a collisional fragment. It has been theorized that the family was created by the fragmentation of a binary or multiple object, of which Flora was the largest.

HUNGARIAS: Actually a region just inside the main belt (1.8 to 2.0 AU) consisting of Williams' families 190 to 191, and other objects. They all have inclinations greater than 16°. Of the Hungarias studied by Tholen (1984b), most if not all the family's 190 members turned out to be E types (Table 11–4).

TABLE 11-4 HUNGARIA REGION ASTEROID CLASSIFICATION	
Minor Planet	Class
434 Hungaria	E
1103 Sequoia	E
1919 Clemence	EMP
1920 Sarmiento	EMP
2048 Dwornik	E
1019 Strackea	S
1355 Magoeba	EMP
1453 Fennia	S
1509 Esclangona	S
1025 Riema	E
2001 Einstein	EMP
2083 Smither	EMP
2131 Mayall	S
2272 1972 FA	S
2449 1978 GC	E
2491 1977 CB	EMP
2577 Litva	EU
2735 Ellen	SDU
1981 LA	TS
2035 Stearns	E

Table 11–4. *Hungaria region asteroids observed in the eight color survey. Data courtesy of Tolen (1984b).*

SATELLITES   12

> After what has just now been shown, with regard to the size of these new stars, there can be no great reason to expect that they should have any satellites. The little quantity of matter they contain would hardly be adequate to the retention of a secondary body.
>
>   William Herschel, 1802

The possibility of asteroids having satellites was first mentioned by Sir William Herschel, who made the first search for them in 1802. Neither Ceres nor Pallas, the only two asteroids known to him, showed any evidence of a binary nature. Nearly a century passed before Charles Andre (1901) suggested that the lightcurve of Eros may be caused by the mutual eclipses of a binary object because it so closely resembled the lightcurve of the eclipsing binary star β-Lyrae.

The preliminary observations we were able to make of the luminous variability of Eros led me to believe that, contrary to what is generally accepted, this variation was double. The curve of light from Eros is similar to that of Beta Lyrae and U Pegasi; like them, it shows that the variable light from this planet, like that of these two stars, is due in part to a pronounced elliptical form, and in large part to successive and reciprocal occultations of two objects which move around their common center of gravity in an orbit which is probably elliptical. Because of the relative displacement of the Earth and Eros, the system of the orbital plane changes progressively in relation to us; soon the plane would no longer meet Earth, and all the periodic variations in light would disappear and in this way, eros would return to being like the other small planets. With respect to its value, I would say that the period of rotation of the satellite of Eros is close to that of Phobos (7 hours 39 minutes); the eccentricity is nearly the same as the lunar orbit (0.0549); the average density of the system differs slightly from that of Mars (2.28); and the semi-major axis, expressed in the radius of the planet, resembles very closely that of Phobos, when measured with the radius of Mars.

The lightcurve of Nysa has been compared to the contact binary W Ursa Majoris, while Ophelia, Pales and Hestia resemble Algol-like lightcurves. But Cellino et al (1985)

have concluded that asteroids considered binary candidates on the basis of lightcurve similarities to eclipsing binaries can no longer be considered as such. "The reason is that equilibrium shapes, at least for the secondary components, always present a significant elongation, and this would rule out the flat shape of the light curve maxima which on the other hand were the determining factor for choosing these objects." Their examination of the lightcurves of 10 asteroids is based on a theory developed by Leone et al (1984), which provides constraints on admissible values of the mass ratio and density, and a qualitative description of the light curve morphology in specific cases.

H. J. Schober (1982) lists nine lightcurve effects which may indicate a possible binary nature:

1. Lightcurve maxima sharper than minima (e.g. 129 Antigone).

2. Complex lightcurves (e.g. 24 Themis, 29 Amphitrite, 51 Nemausa).

3. Increase in amplitude with increasing solar phase angle (e.g. 349 Dembowska, 944 Hidalgo).

4. Lightcurve with two maxima and minima per rotation cycle at one opposition, but only one of each at another (e.g. 532 Herculina).

5. Triple maxima and minima per rotation cycle (e.g. 1580 Betulia, 337 Devosa).

6. Contact binary lightcurves (e.g. 44 Nysa).

7. Nonperiodic irregular features in the lightcurves, or showing up with periods different from the rotation rate (e.g. 37 Fides).

8. Color variation during rotation, if not interpreted as a spotty surface (e.g. 48 Doris).

9. Slowly spinning asteroids (e.g. 1689 Floris-Jan, 288 Glauke).

One early study of lightcurve evidence for binary asteroids was made for Ophelia. Wijesinghe & Tedesco (1979) showed mathematically that Ophelia's lightcurve can be modeled on the basis of a binary system with a separation of 100 km, diameter ratios of 1:2.96 and an orbital period of 13.146 hours.

Tedesco (1979) suggests that binary asteroids are not uncommon, and that the difficulty in distinguishing photometrically between an elongated object and a close binary is the reason more evidence for them is not apparent.

Fig. 12–1 shows the four binary phenomena that can be superimposed on an asteroid's rotational lightcurve. Support for the idea that slowly spinning asteroids are actually tidally evolved binaries was provided by Alan Harris (1983). The dynamical argument is that a massive satellite of a rocky asteroid (10–100 km diameter) will evolve outward to 10–15 radii in 4.5×10^9 years, at which time the orbital period is several days. If the satellite mass is greater than 0.1 of the primary, the spin period and rotational period will become synchronized.

Such a state may not have been reached for a more extreme mass ratio, however. In this case, the satellites' orbit may be quite eccentric, causing the primary's spin axis to precess. Harris suggests that the 2–month period found for Glauke may in fact be such a precession, while the lightcurve that is normally seen as caused by rotation is being masked.

While lightcurves can give some hint as to an asteroid's binary nature, the prime evidence for satellites rests on occultations of stars. The primary occultation caused by the asteroid passing in front of a star is sometimes accompanied by one or more "secondary" events, which may be caused by one or more satellites. At some observing sites, only secondary events are seen. Attention has focused on seven candidates:

HEBE: P. D. Maley observed an occultation of a 3.6 magnitude star by Hebe on 5 March 1977. The shadow path was 900 km south of his Texas site, but he noted a 0.5 sec. secondary event, which was interpreted as a 20 km diameter satellite (Dunham & Maley, 1977).

PALLAS: While double star observers as early as 1926 (Binzel, 1978) reported Pallas as a double object, it was not until 1980 that evidence for a large satellite was published. Speckle interferometry (Hege *et al*, 1980) indicated a satellite between one-third and one-sixth the size of Pallas may be in orbit around it. A recent radar search, however, has not detected any such satellite (Showalter, 1982). Occultation evidence for a Pallas satellite was collected by Richard Radick on 29 May 1978 (Kerr, 1980). A 28.16 second primary occultation was followed 3 seconds later by a secondary event that lasted about 50 milli-seconds, indicating the presence of a body about 1 km wide. The well-observed Pallas occultation of 29 May 1983 did not indicate any secondary component (Dunham *et al*, 1983).

HERCULINA: The best and most widely-touted evidence for binary asteroids was collected 7 June 1978, when 532 Herculina occulted a star (Fig. 12–2). According to James McMahon (1978), who observed the occultation visually, seven distinct events occurred, ranging from 0.5 sec-

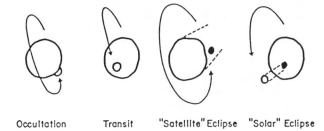

Occultation   Transit   "Satellite" Eclipse   "Solar" Eclipse

Fig. 12–1. *The four types of occultation, transit, and eclipse phenomena that could complicate asteroid lightcurves. Eight sets of events per synodic period occur, since two nodal passages occur. These could be rare and discrete for widely separated pairs with high orbital i; they could be discrete, but occur every revolution period for pairs with widely separated pairs with heliocentric and satellite orbits lying in the ecliptic plane; and they could be non-discrete and continual for closely spaced pairs. In the extreme case of contact binaries, they become identical with topographic effects. Hartmann, 1979. Reprinted from Asteroids by Tom Gehrels by permission of the University of Arizona Press.*

onds to 20.6 seconds in the case of the primary event. The longest secondary event, 97 seconds before the primary, lasted 4 seconds, indicating a 45 km. diameter satellite 977 km. from Herculina. Such a visual detection by itself is not sufficient evidence, but a simultaneous photoelectric observation was made by Edward Bowell and Michael A'Hearn at Lowell Observatory. They recorded a 5.3 sec. occultation, although the asteroid was a mere 2.5° above the horizon. A third observer, Keith Horne, did not see any secondary events.

Even though some scientists have written papers showing that Herculina's satellite was probably formed by collision and ejected into orbit about the asteroid (Donnison, 1979), others are skeptical that such a satellite even exists (Reitsema, 1979). Drummond *et al* (1984b) found no evidence for a satellite of Herculina from speckle interferometry data.

What is needed is a photoelectric record of a "well-behaved" secondary event (Kerr, 1980). Well-behaved means that the combined brightness of the asteroid plus star must drop sharply at the start and rise sharply at the end of an occultation. Also, the brightness must drop to that of the asteroid alone, thus ruling out any spurious instrumental effects, atmospheric phenomena, or passing object like a plane. The Herculina observation of the secondary does not meet this criterion: the brightness fell and rose more slowly than the primary event, and dawn twilight prevented Herculina's light being distinguished from the sky background.

MELPOMENE: The Herculina results prompted the first organized search for a minor planet satellite on 11 Dec. 1978. As reported by David Dunham (1979), three photoelectric and one visual record of secondary events may have been caused by several satellites.

KLEOPATRA: Two amateur astronomers, Gerry Ratley and William Cooke, set up two visual observing sites 0.6 km. apart on the night of 10 October 1980. While both were in the wrong location to see the primary oc-

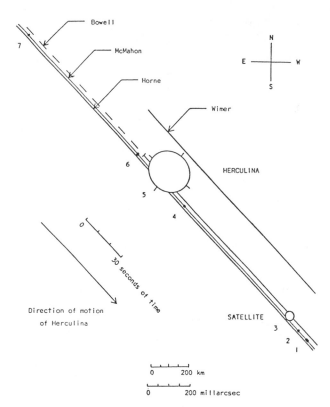

Fig. 12–2. *Spatial relationships for observations of the occultation by Herculina on June 7, 1978. The solution for Herculina corresponds to an ellipse having an axial ratio of 0.87. Black rectangles represent unexplained secondary extinctions observed by Bowell. Wimer observed at Fresno. McMahon, 1978.*

Photo. 12–1. *Hans Schober, director of the Institute for Astronomy at the University of Graz in Austria, has determined the rotational properties of numerous asteroids.*

Photo. 12–2. *Richard Binzel of the Planetary Science Institute in Tucson, a major proponent of asteroidal satellites, and an expert on small asteroids in the main belt. His discovery that Crocus is likely a precessing asteroid lends support to the binary asteroid concept.*

cultation by Kleopatra, they each saw a secondary event lasting 0.9 seconds and coinciding within 0.7 sec. (Kerr, 1980). They also reported a change from the bluish color of the asteroid to the reddish appearance of the star during the event.

METIS: Chinese astronomers have reported a satellite orbiting Metis based on photographic evidence. A slight bulge in Metis' image, noted seven times over a period of several months, seems to indicate the presence of a 60–km. satellite orbiting 1,110 km from Metis. Visual secondary events noted in a Metis occultation in Venezuela in 1979 tend to corroborate these findings (Kerr, 1980). A visual search for a satellite of Metis was conducted by David Kring of the University of Indiana in 1983, but no conclusive evidence was found.

LUCINA: On 18 April 1982, French astronomers observed an appulse by 146 Lucina at the Meudon Observatory with a long-focus video camera attached to a 102 cm telescope. Their equipment permitted not only photometry of short events but astrometry from the same recording. They observed a short extinction (0.6 sec.) which could be interpreted as due to a satellite of Lucina, at least 5.7 km in diameter at a distance of 1,600 km from Lucina (Arlot *et al*, 1985).

According to Van Flandern *et al* (1979) and Wallentinsen (1979), satellites of asteroids can be dynamically stable, although for many years astronomers did not believe this to be true. While the gravitational sphere of influence of an asteroid extends to some 100 times its own diameter, it is expected that most satellites of asteroids will be near the so-called "tug-of-war" distance from the primary. This distance is given by $S = a\sqrt{M}$, where a is the asteroid's orbital semi-major axis and M is the mass ratio, in the sense asteroid/Sun. All known natural satellites are well within S or within a factor of 2 of near-unity tug-of-war ratios. For Herculina, $S = 1,181$ km. and its sphere of influence extends more than 30,000 km. Its suspected satellite, at a distance of 977 km., is within both these limits.

TABLE 12–1							
DISTANCE OR DIAMETER IN KM							
$(a-1)$AU	1	10	50	100	250	1000	10000
1.1	0.014	0.138	0.689	1.379	3.447	13.788	137.88
2.0	0.001	0.017	0.069	0.138	0.345	1.379	13.79
3.0	0.001	0.007	0.034	0.069	0.172	0.689	6.89
4.0	–	0.005	0.023	0.046	0.115	0.460	4.60
5.0	–	–	0.017	0.035	0.068	0.345	3.45

Table 12–1. *Distance or Diameter in km. This indicates, for example, that a 1,000-km diameter asteroid at a distance of 5 AU subtends an angle of 0.345 arcseconds. Table from Schober (1982).*

All satellites larger than 100 m in diameter are thought to be safe from collisions with other objects that might knock them out of orbit. Such a collision would not be expected on time scales shorter than the age of the solar system. Tidal forces, however, should have a noticeable effect in the case of Herculina. The ratio of Herculina's volume to its satellite is about 107 to 1, making the satellite very large relative to its primary compared with other solar system examples. Additionally, tidal forces must be very strong in the Herculina system. These facts led Hodgson (1978) to question why such forces had not synchronized the asteroid's rotation period and the satellite's orbital period. Both the Earth-Moon system and the Pluto-Charon system exhibit such tidal locking, and are the only two cases with comparable volume ratios. Two improbable solutions were proposed to account for this situation: either the satellite was captured by Herculina, or a collision with another object enlarged the satellite's orbit. One possible end result of tidal forces is that the satellite of an asteroid will fall onto the primary—the complex lightcurve of Themis has been interpreted as indicative of major topographic features, possibly tidally-decayed satellites.

An extreme case would be a binary system with nearly equal masses. This could form a contact-binary, which would appear dumbbell-shaped. Geographos has been proposed as a possible example (Van Flandern et al, 1979), and crater evidence from both the Earth and Moon has been used to support this scenario. In the Clearwater Lakes craters in Canada, a pair of craters 32 and 24 km in diameter were formed simultaneously 31 km apart. A single asteroid would not likely have split in two to form the craters, but a binary asteroid could have done it (Weissman, 1985). Multiple crater chains on the moon may have been caused by asteroids with several satellites (Kerr, 1980).

It is thought that a binary system could form as the result of a collision of one asteroid with another. Such a scenario is unlikely to result in binary systems for either large or small asteroids, however. (Only fragments smaller than 25 metres, flung out by the creation of a 10 km crater on Ceres, would exceed its escape velocity of 460 m/sec. (O'Keefe & Ahrens, 1985)). Sufficiently massive projectiles to create a binary from a single large asteroid are rare, while the allowed range of impact energy causing fragmentation without escape becomes narrower for small bodies. For asteroids of intermediate size (50–150 km), however, fairly frequent collisions could create gravi-

tationally bound fragments. Zappala et al (1980) note that the short periods and large amplitudes exhibited by intermediate size asteroids may signal the presence of binary objects, as tidal synchronization would slow the rotation period of the primary.

Strong support for the existence of binary asteroids was recently presented by Binzel (1985), who showed that 1220 Crocus is likely in a state of forced precession. The Earth is an example of a body in such a state, where the torque exerted by the Sun and the Moon induces a precession with a period of 25,800 years. In the case of Crocus, data reveal two different amplitudes (0.87 and 0.15 magnitude), the larger of which is associated with precession, the smaller with rotation. The precession period of 30.7 days is best accounted for by a satellite orbiting Crocus with a period of 22–31 hours, and a diameter of 6–9 km.

While the crater and lightcurve evidence is suggestive, and the occultation data tempting, only direct evidence in the form of a photograph will be truly convincing of the existence of minor planet satellites. In a Spacewatch telescope survey of nine asteroids, published in Icarus in 1987, Gehrels found no evidence for binary asteroids. Both the U. S. Space Telescope and the Hipparcos astrometry satellite of the European Space Agency will be able to provide such evidence in the late 1980's or early 1990's. Table 12–1 shows the arc-second separation for a range of distances or diameters in the asteroid belt. The separation of Herculina from its suspected satellite is 0.87 arc seconds, well within the ±0.002 (±.005) resolution of Hipparcos. For comparison, the Pluto-Charon separation is 0.9 arc seconds, a resolution that Earth-based telescopes rarely exceed (Schober, 1982).

APOLLOS,
AMORS AND
ATENS   13

The conjecture that the evolution of comets
is linked with that of asteroids, because the
Apollo or Amor asteroids could be dead cometary
nuclei, has not received a final answer.

A. H. Delsemme, 1977

DISCOVERIES AND ORBITAL CHARACTERISTICS

To those who travel beyond the Earth, space holds many
dangers and unknowns; those of us on the planet's surface rarely suffer more than a sunburn from events beyond
Earth. There is, however, a lurking (albeit remote) danger
of an asteroid striking our planet.

While the majority of asteroids exhibit stable orbits
between Mars and Jupiter, hundreds, or even thousands,
have orbits that bring them much closer. These near-Earth
asteroids fall into three classes: Apollos, Amors and Atens.
They can be distinguished on the basis of a (semi-major
axis), Q (aphelion distance), and q (perihelion distance).

> **ATENS:** An asteroid with semi-major axis
> smaller than Earth's which overlap the orbit
> of Earth near their aphelia. Atens includes all
> asteroids with semi-major axis < 1.0 AU and
> the aphelion distance ≥ 0.983 AU, where 0.983
> AU is the perihelion distance of the Earth.

> **APOLLOS:** An asteroid that travels inside
> the orbit of the Earth. They are defined by
> semi-major axes ≥ 1.0 AU and perihelion dis-
> tance q ≥ 1.017 AU, where 1.017 AU is the
> aphelion distance of the Earth.

> **AMORS:** An asteroid with perihelion a little
> outside the Earth's orbit. They are defined on
> the basis of perihelion distance, 1.017 AU <
> q ≥ 1.3 AU. These objects make relatively close
> approaches to the Earth, but do not overlap
> the Earth's orbit. Some, however, are known
> to cross the orbit of Jupiter.

The significance of the Apollo/Amor boundary is really
just a matter of convention, as some Amors have perihelia that oscillate back and forth across 1.0 AU. Fig. 13–1

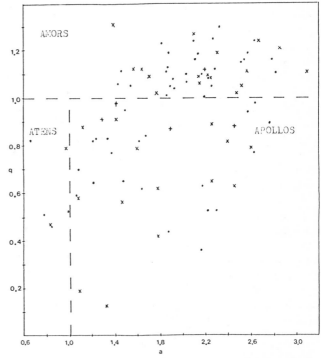

Fig. 13–1. *A plot of perihelion distance versus semi-major axis of
the Earth-approaching asteroids. Ranges of inclination are denoted
as follows: less than 15° (·); between 15° and 40° (x); greater than
40° (+).*

shows the distribution of Apollos, Amors and Atens. As
of mid–1987, 46 Apollos (7 lost), 47 Amors (3 lost) and
7 Atens are known. Of the Apollo-Amors, 56 are earth-
crossers. Seventy-three main-belt asteroids (excluding the
Amors) are now known to cross the orbit of Mars. A study
of 14 of these Mars-crossers by Hahn and Rickman (1985)
revealed a wide variety of orbital characteristics. Some,
such as 1983 SA, 1983 XF and 1984 BC are in cometary,
chaotic orbits. Others, like 1981 FD, are in a stable libra-

	DISC	A	E	I	PERI	APH	H
TABLE 13–1 PART 1 **APOLLOS AND AMORS** **SORTED BY PERIHELION DISTANCE**							
3200 Phaethon	1983	1.27	.890	22.0	0.140	1.100	16.0
1566 Icarus	1949	1.08	.827	22.9	0.187	1.97	16.5
2212 Hephaistos	1978	2.16	.835	11.9	0.357	3.97	14.0
1974 MA	1974	1.78	.762	37.8	0.423	3.13	14.0
2101 Adonis	1936	1.87	.764	1.4	0.443	3.30	18.5
2340 Hathor	1976	0.84	.449	5.9	0.464	1.22	20.2
2100 Ra-Shalom	1978	0.83	.436	15.8	0.469	1.20	16.2
1986 WA	1986	1.50	.701	29.3	0.449	2.56	16.0
1954 XA	1954	0.78	.345	3.9	0.509	1.05	19.0
3362 Khufu	1984	0.99	.468	9.9	0.526	1.417	18.0
1982 TA	1982	2.30	.771	12.1	0.527	4.07	15.0
1984 KB	1984	2.22	.762	4.6	0.528	3.914	15.5
1864 Daedalus	1971	1.46	.615	22.1	0.563	2.36	14.9
1865 Cerberus	1971	1.08	.467	16.1	0.576	1.58	16.9
1986 PA	1986	1.06	.442	11.1	0.591	1.529	18.0
Hermes	1937	1.64	.624	6.2	0.617	2.66	18.0
1981 Midas	1973	1.78	.650	39.8	0.622	2.93	17.0
2201 Oljato	1947	2.17	.712	2.5	0.626	3.72	15.7
3360	1981	2.46	.744	22.0	0.628	4.22	17.0
1862 Apollo	1932	1.47	.560	6.4	0.647	2.29	16.2
1979 XB	1979	2.26	.713	24.9	0.649	3.88	19.0
2063 Bacchus	1977	1.08	.349	9.4	0.701	1.45	17.7
1959 LM	1959	2.15	.674	7.6	0.702	1.85	15.0
1983 LC	1983	2.63	.709	1.5	0.765	4.50	19.0
1685 Toro	1948	1.37	.436	9.4	0.771	1.96	14.1
2062 Aten	1976	0.97	.182	18.9	0.790	1.14	17.4
2135 Aristaeus	1977	1.60	.503	23.0	0.794	2.40	18.2
1983 VA	1983	2.61	.692	16.2	0.805	4.416	16.5
1982 HR	1982	1.21	.322	2.7	0.820	1.60	19.0
2329 Orthos	1976	2.40	.658	24.4	0.821	3.99	15.1
6743 P-L	1960	1.62	.493	7.3	0.821	2.42	(Lost)
1983 TF2	1983	1.34	.387	7.8	0.823	1.862	17.5
1620 Geographos	1951	1.24	.335	13.3	0.827	1.66	15.8
1950 DA	1950	1.68	.502	12.1	0.838	2.53	15.9
1866 Sisyphus	1972	1.89	.540	41.1	0.872	2.92	13.2
1973 NA	1973	2.43	.638	67.9	0.878	4.04	14.4
1978 CA	1978	1.12	.215	26.1	0.883	1.37	18.0
1863 Antinous	1948	2.26	.606	18.4	0.889	3.63	15.8
1986 JK	1986	2.76	.678	2.13	0.898	4.621	19.0
2102 Tantalus	1975	1.29	.298	64.0	0.905	1.67	16.3
1982 BB	1982	1.41	.355	20.9	0.908	1.91	15.0
6344 P-L	1960	2.58	.635	4.6	0.940	4.21	(Lost)
1982 DB	1982	1.49	.360	1.4	0.953	2.02	18.5
1979 VA	1979	2.64	.627	2.8	0.982	4.29	16.3
1985 PA	1985	1.41	.303	55.55	0.986	1.841	15.5
1984 KD	1984	2.19	.540	13.6	1.009	3.386	17.0
1982 XB	1982	1.84	.446	3.9	1.017	2.70	19.5
3122 1981 ET3	1981	1.77	.422	22.2	1.022	2.52	14.5

Table 13–1. *Apollos and Amors Sorted by Perihelion Distance. All the Apollo-Amor asteroids discovered by late 1986. Their discovery dates are followed by semi-major axis (A), eccentricity (E), inclination (I), perihelion (PERI), aphelion (APH), and absolute blue magnitude (H). Four asteroids have been lost. Data provided by Eleanor Helin and Brian Marsden.*

	DISC	A	E	I	PERI	APH	H
2608 Seneca	1978	2.48	.586	15.6	1.025	3.93	17.6
1980 PA	1980	1.93	.459	2.2	1.043	2.82	18.5
2061 Anza	1960	2.26	.537	3.7	1.048	3.48	16.7
1980 AA	1980	1.89	.444	4.2	1.053	2.73	19.5
1986 LA	1986	1.54	.317	10.8	1.056	2.033	18.5
1917 Cuyo	1968	2.15	.505	24.0	1.063	3.23	15.2
1943 Anteros	1973	1.43	.256	8.7	1.064	1.80	15.8
1915 Quetzalcoatl	1953	2.52	.577	20.5	1.069	3.99	19.0
1983 RD	1983	2.09	.486	9.5	1.073	3.00	17.0
1981 QB	1981	2.24	.518	37.1	1.079	3.39	16.0
1980 WF	1980	2.23	.514	6.4	1.084	3.38	18.5
1980 Tezcatlipoca	1950	1.71	.365	26.8	1.085	2.33	14.1
1221 Amor	1932	1.92	.434	11.9	1.087	2.76	18.1
1983 RB	1983	2.22	.507	19.4	1.096	3.18	16.0
1972 RB	1972	2.15	.487	5.2	1.101	3.23	19.0
887 Alinda	1918	2.49	.558	9.2	1.102	3.88	14.2
3288 Seleucus	1982	2.03	.457	5.9	1.104	2.96	15.5
1985 TB	1985	2.57	.567	26.8	1.114	4.036	15.5
2202 Pele	1972	2.29	.512	8.8	1.116	3.46	16.3
1985 JA	1985	1.64	.321	36.8	1.117	2.172	16.5
1580 Betulia	1950	2.19	.489	52.0	1.122	3.27	14.5
1982 YA	1982	3.70	.697	34.5	1.122	5.08	16.5
1627 Ivar	1929	1.86	.397	8.4	1.124	2.60	12.9
3199 Nefertiti	1982	1.57	.284	32.9	1.128	2.01	15.0
1977 VA	1977	1.86	.394	3.0	1.130	2.60	17.5
433 Eros	1898	1.46	.223	10.8	1.133	1.78	10.7
1985 WA	1985	2.84	.602	9.7	1.133	4.558	19.0
4788 P-L	1960	2.55	.545	10.8	1.16	3.93	(Lost)
1986 DA	1986	2.81	.585	4.3	1.166	4.457	16.0
1986 NA	1986	2.12	.450	10.3	1.168	3.083	20.0
3352 McAuliffe	1981	1.88	.368	4.8	1.186	2.57	15.9
3102	1981	2.15	.448	8.4	1.186	3.118	16.0
719 Albert	1911	2.58	.540	10.8	1.188	3.98	(Lost)
1983 LB	1983	2.29	.478	25.4	1.194	3.43	17.5
1983 SA	1983	4.23	.714	30.7	1.208	7.19	13.5
1986 RA	1986	2.88	.577	18.0	1.219	4.551	15.5
1036 Ganymed	1924	2.66	.537	26.4	1.232	4.09	9.4
1980 YS	1980	1.82	.321	2.3	1.232	2.40	16.5
2368 Beltrovata	1977	2.10	.413	5.3	1.235	2.97	15.6
1916 Boreas	1953	2.27	.450	12.8	1.251	3.30	15.1
2059 Baboquivari	1963	2.65	.525	11.0	1.257	4.05	14.7
1982 FT	1982	1.77	.283	20.4	1.271	2.277	15.0
3271	1982	2.10	.395	25.0	1.272	2.932	17.0
1979 QB	1979	2.33	.442	3.4	1.299	3.36	17.8
1951 Lick	1949	1.39	.062	39.1	1.305	1.48	14.5

TABLE 13–1 PART 2
APOLLOS AND AMORS
SORTED BY PERIHELION DISTANCE

tion around the 2/1 resonance. The story of Apollo-Amor asteroids goes back to 14 June 1873, when James Watson discovered asteroid 132 Aethra. Even though it was lost after only three weeks observation, Watson's orbital calculations showed that its perihelion was inside the aphelion of Mars, the first time an asteroid was found to deviate from the main belt.

Twenty-five years later, Gustav Witt discovered the earth-approacher 433 Eros, which has since become one of the best observed asteroids. Eros has a mean distance from the Sun less than the mean distance of Mars, and can pass as close as 22.5 million km from Earth (Fig. 13–2).

Further discoveries came slowly: 719 Albert in 1911, 887 Alinda in 1918 and 1036 Ganymed in 1924. Then in 1932, two startling discoveries were made. Eugene Delporte found an object that passed only 16.1 million km from Earth. Later called 1221 Amor, it is one of the intrinsically faintest asteroids.

Less than six weeks later, 1862 Apollo itself was discovered. Karl Reinmuth found it during a photographic search for main-belt asteroids. It was only observed from April 24 to May 15, when it passed a mere 11.3 million km from Earth. The orbit of the fast moving object was found to cross the orbits of both the Earth and Venus, and it thus became the prototype for all other such asteroids.

Just four years later, in 1936, an even closer approach was made by 2101 Adonis. A few days before it was found, Adonis came within 2.4 million km of our planet. But the record for closest approach is held by Hermes, which literally skimmed by at 800,000 km, only twice the Earth-Moon distance.

The discoveries of Apollo asteroids are strangely bunched in time. After an initial flurry in 1932–37, there was a gap until 1948–51, and another interval until 1959. No more were found until 1971. During the 1948–51 period, five Apollos were found. 1566 Icarus and 1620 Geographos were both discovered with the Palomar National Geographic Sky Survey 48–inch Schmidt, while the other three were found in the course of a proper motion program with the 20–inch astrograph at Lick. One of the Lick discoveries was 1685 Toro, whose resonant motion will be considered shortly. The 1959 discovery, simply known as 1959 LM, was discovered on plates taken at the Boyden Observatory in South Africa, but the images were not even noticed until 1960.

The drought was ended by Tom Gehrels in 1971, during a survey for Trojan asteroids, ironically the most distant class. Only an object of 16th magnitude on photographs taken with the 122 cm Schmidt, 1971 FA was the first in a surge of Apollo asteroid discoveries. In 1982 alone, four Apollos and five Amors were located. This rapid discovery rate has been due almost entirely to the Palomar Planet-Crossing Asteroid Survey, begun in 1973 by Eleanor Helin and Eugene Shoemaker. The survey is primarily conducted with the 46 cm Schmidt camera, with a four-to-five night observing run scheduled each month when the brightness of our Moon does not interfere.

As many as 70 'survey fields', out of a total of 250, are photographed each night, taken in 20–minute and 10–

Photo. 13–1. *Eleanor Helin of the California Institute of Technology, who initiated the near-Earth asteroid survey in 1973. Using the Schmidt telescope at Palomar in California, she has added greatly to the number of known Apollos and Amors. In 1976, she discovered the first Aten asteroid.*

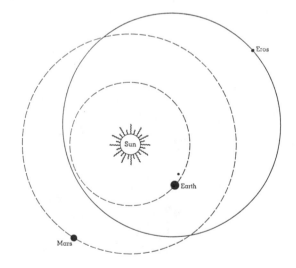

Fig. 13–2. *The asteroid Eros in its eccentric (off-center) orbit crosses the orbit of Mars and approaches close to the earth. Nourse, 1975.*

minute exposure pairs. The short-exposure plates are examined stereoscopically the same night, in case a newly discovered asteroid is recorded on the film. The longer exposure is scanned with a binocular microscope for trailed

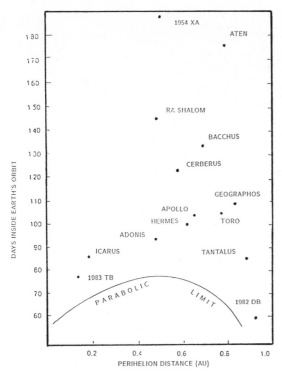

Fig. 13-3. *The time spent inside earth's orbit versus perihelion distance for a selection of Earth-crossers.*

images, with the shorter exposure serving as a comparison. Threshold detection is visual magnitude 15.5. If an object is found, positional data is relayed by telephone to Brian Marsden and J. G. Williams, who compute the orbit and provide ephemerides for further observations.

All astronomical discoveries provide some excitement, a case in point occurring on 15 Nov. 1979, when Helin and her colleague Schelte (Bobby) Bus found an unusual Apollo asteroid, 1979 VA. Its discovery circumstances were related in a letter written by Helin to George Wetherill, who had visited the observatory on the night before discovery.

You may be aware by now that on the night of November 14/15th a new Apollo (1979 VA) was found. Drat! So wish you could have been present to see how it happens. After Bobby and I took 2 pairs of films, I developed them, feeling the sooner developed, the sooner I could scan them. Well, still in the dark room, with film just out of the wash, I took a quick look (the films in their holders on the light box). My eyes ran over the negatives quickly, but stopped short on one 20 min. exposure, for there, with the hand lens, my eyes focused in on a dark short trail. My heart started pounding as I looked closer, thinking it was just too sharp and bright. Was it a piece of emulsion which had floated onto the film, or—was it real? I tried moving the tiny image—it didn't move! I looked still more carefully and satisfied myself that it was indeed a real, trailed image. I rushed for the companion film, and after fum-

bling to get wet films oriented properly, I located the corresponding trail (half as long as the 10 minute exposure), and to my amazement, found the object to be moving prograde (direct). Hurried measurement of the two images told me it was moving somewhere in excess of a degree a day and was startlingly bright. I rushed up to inform Bobby and have him come take a look. He was excited as I was, for this was really the first time an object has truly been found in the darkroom. In less than 2 hours from when the first set of films were photographed, we were back on the position and photographing a third position—quickly developed, and reconfirmed! I phoned Marsden and Williams before 11:00 p.m., as well as placing calls to others who had asked to be informed as soon as possible after a discovery, so preparations could be made to get on other telescopes to acquire a variety of physical observations during discovery apparition. Well, the rest is documented in the IAU Circulars. Many more observations and results will be appearing soon. As you can see, the orbit is very cometary like, and has perhaps the largest *a* and *Q* of any other known Apollo. Preliminary orbital computations indicate it has a record high aphelion. So much for the saga of our latest discovery—the only regret is that you missed being present, and really only by one night. In any case, I'm sure your visit brought us the luck we needed!

The most exclusive class of Earth-crossers are the Aten asteroids. The prototype of this class was found by Helin on 7 January 1976. Its 0.5 mm trail on a 20-minute exposure indicated a motion of some 2° per day. One week later, at its closest approach, Aten passed 18.3 million km from Earth. Aten was tracked for five months, until it had faded to magnitude 19, thus allowing the orbit to be well determined. Surprisingly, it had an orbital period of less than one year and hence a semi-major axis of less than 1.0 AU. Only seven Atens are known, and their estimated population of 100 is less than the Amors or Apollos.

Like the main-belt asteroids, Earth-crossers also experience resonant motion, a concept explained in Chapter 5. More than half of these asteroids overlap the Earth's orbit only part of the time, as is shown for the case of 1915 Quetzalcoatl in Fig. 13-4. During 1,400 years, this Apollo asteroid crosses the orbit of the Earth nine times. The four cycles of libration shown in the diagram are due to the asteroid's 3/1 commensurability with Jupiter.

In addition to the resonances listed in Chapter 5, Apollo asteroids have their own set of resonances with the inner planets. These are listed in Table 13-2, after a paper by Janiczek *et al* (1972). The last asteroid on the list, Toro, has been extensively investigated by Janiczek *et al* (1972), Ip & Mehra (1973), and Williams & Wetherill (1973).

Toro is a most interesting case, as its orbital period

TABLE 13–2
POSSIBLE RESONANCES AND ENCOUNTERS IN THE INNER SOLAR SYSTEM

Minor planet	Period Yr	Semi-major axis A.U.	Eccentricity	Major planet	Multiple major planet mean motion i	Multiple minor planet mean motion j	Possible encounters
Eros (433)	1.76	1.4581	0.2229	Venus	1	3	
				Earth	4	7	Yes
Alinda (887)	3.99	2.5158	0.5436	Venus	2	13	
				Earth	1	4	Yes
				Mars	8	17	Yes
				Jupiter	3	1	
Ganymed (1036)	4.33	2.6584	0.5424	Venus	1	7	
				Earth	3	13	Yes
				Mars	10	23	Yes
Amor (1221)	2.67	1.9223	0.4358	Venus	3	13	
				Earth	3	8	Yes
				Mars	12	17	Yes
				Jupiter	9	2	
Icarus (1566)	1.12	1.0777	0.8267	Venus	5	9	Yes
				Venus	6	11	Yes
				Venus	11	20	Yes
				Earth	8	9	Yes
				Earth	17	19	Yes
				Mars			Yes
Betulia (1580)	3.25	2.1949	0.4928	Venus	3	16	
				Earth	4	13	Yes
				Mars	11	19	Yes
Geographos (1620)	1.39	1.2440	0.3353	Venus	4	9	Yes
				Earth	5	7	Yes
				Earth	13	18	Yes
				Mars			Yes
Ivar (1627)	2.55	1.8642	0.3967	Venus	1	4	
				Earth	2	5	Yes
				Mars	17	23	Yes
Toro (1685)	1.60	1.3679	0.4360	Venus	5	13	Yes
				Earth	5	8	Yes
				Mars	20	17	Yes

is exactly 8/5 that of the Earth, and nearly 13/5 that of Venus, since Venus and the Earth have a near commensurability of 8/13 in their periods. As the argument of perihelion of Toro precesses, its orbit can intersect the orbits of the Earth and Mars, and it can pass closer to Venus than is currently possible. Table 13–3 lists Toro's close approaches to the three planets from 1970 to 2025.

Fig. 13–5 illustrates the push-pull mechanism at work between Toro, Venus and Earth. The upper plot shows Toro's variable orbital period. Between 1600 and 1850 AD, its average value is 1.5994 years, which is the 13/5 commensurability with Venus. This libration has a period of 180 years. A transition occurred between 1850 and 1900, during which time it came under the influence of Earth's 8/5 commensurability. With an average orbital period of 1.6000 years, Toro is now experiencing a libration period of 150 years. This will last until 2200 AD.

The lower plot in Fig. 13–5 is the difference in longitude (critical argument) between Toro, Venus (broken line) and Earth (solid line) at Toro's perihelion approaches. This so-called libration function indicates the variation in the mean motion of Toro.

Toro's dance with Venus and Earth (shown in Figs. 13–6 and –7) will eventually end. If it does not impact on either planet, a single close encounter with Mars will knock it out of commensurability on a time scale of about three million years.

The Spacewatch Telescope

The first idea of having a dedicated asteroid telescope dates from the early 1970's. The concept of a survey telescope, which was originally going to be a big Schmidt, dates from 1977–78, but the current concept of using a CCD scanning camera on a specially designed telescope was proposed in 1979. According to Tom Gehrels, who has led the effort to build the telescope, the principal reason for abandoning the big Schmidt concept pertained to the limiting magnitude for fast-moving objects (i.e. Earth-crossers). A 70–minute exposure on an object that does not move has a limiting magnitude of 21, but for fast-moving objects you begin to notice movement at 7/10 of a minute. After that there is no further integration, just a trail, which reduces the limiting magnitude to only 16. The main advantage of the Schmidt, being able to cover a wide area of the sky at one time, will also diminish as arrays of CCD's are developed to cover more sky.

"I myself was an old-fashioned devotee of the big Schmidt," explained Gehrels. "I was very nicely along

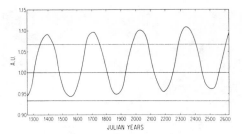

Fig. **13–4.** *Secular variation of radius to the ascending node of the orbit of 1915 Quetzalcoatl, based on forward and backward integrations of the motion of the asteroid by Marsden. About four cycles of libration of the mean motion of the asteroid about the 3:1 commensurability are represented. Extreme values of aphelion and perihelion distances of the earth are shown by horizontal lines lying equal distances above and below 1 AU. Shoemaker et al, 1979. Reprinted from Asteroids by Tom Gehrels by permission of the University of Arizona Press.*

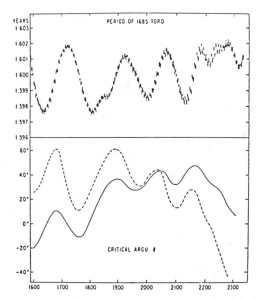

Fig. **13–5.** *(a) Variation of the orbital period of 1685 Toro. The irregular variation between 2200 AD and 2350 AD is due to the breakdown of the libration patterns. (b) The difference in longitude (critical argument) between Toro, Venus, (broken line) and the Earth (solid line) at Toro's perihelia of retarding close approaches every eight years. Ip & Mehra, 1973. Reprinted by permission of the Astronomical Journal.*

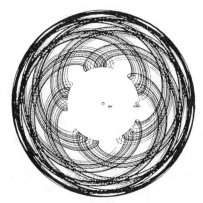

Fig. **13–6.** *The orbit of Toro from 2000 to 2200 plotted in a coordinate system rotating with Venus and scaled at each time to the heliocentric distance to Venus. Janiczek et al, 1972. Reprinted by permission of the Astronomical Journal.*

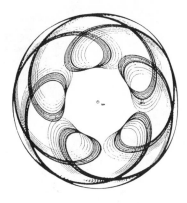

Fig. **13–7.** *The orbit of Toro from 1800 to 2000 plotted in a coordinate system rotating the Earth and scaled at each time to the heliocentric distance to Earth. Janiczek et al, 1972. Reprinted by permission of the Astronomical Journal.*

with that—I even had the corrector plate. I could have very quickly had a big Schmidt and I would have loved it. So I came around the hard way." Observations began with the Spacewatch telescope in May, 1983, with regular asteroid observations commencing on 22 April 1984. Unique to such a large project in asttronomy is the fact that part of the cost of Spacewatch, with its 0.9 meter telescope on Kitt Peak, is being raised from the public sector. The telescope itself is a real veteran: originally set up on the University of Arizona campus in 1919, it was moved to Kitt Peak in 1963. It is still the only Newtonian and the only telescope with a glass mirror on Kitt Peak, although the instrument has been completely refurbished with an electronic drive.

The CCD used is an RCA 53612, which consists of a 320 by 512 array of pixels. The pixel, which covers 1.3 arcseconds with the telescope optics of Spacewatch, is a silicon light-sensitive metal-oxide-semiconductor 29.5 micrometers square. The integration time can be as short as 3.3 seconds, in which time 163,840 diodes have to be read out into a computer, each with a brightness number of 10 bits for gradations in the light intensity (Gehrels and Binzel, 1984). Unlike the usual stare mode used in CCD work (Fig. 13–8), Spacewatch uses the scan mode. The telescope is set at a fixed hour angle and as the sky drifts by the charge will be shifted out at the same rate (Fig. 13–9). When each object is on the 512 array during a 3.3 sercond integratinon time, the image stays just 6.5 milliseconds on each 30 micrometer pixel. This rate is held for five minutes after which the scan is repeated. Such a dual scan results in 298 million bits which have to be intercompared by by the computer to detect a moving object. As the CCD array is aligned with right ascension and declination in the sky, the result is a long strip, 7 arc minutes wide and typically 5° long. On a given night, the scope scans three regions three times. A computer will then compare the scans, eliminate all the fixed stars, and pick out the moving objects. Real-time data acquisition will produce a list of moving objects, and determine if any of them are known asteroids.

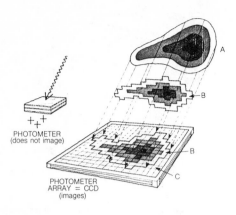

Photo. 13–2. *Eugene Shoemaker of the U.S. Geological Survey and the California Institute of Technology, is shown with the blink comparator used in the near-Earth asteroid survey which he began with Eleanor Helin in 1973.*

Fig. 13–8. *CCD explained: Thin-film semiconducters can be made to accumulate charge when struck by photons (left)—the 'photometer principle.' An array of such photometers, right, is called a charge-coupled device or CCD. In this simplified example, a celestial object (A) creates an image of itself (B) on the CCD surface (C). Photometers within CCD are called 'pixels,' for 'picture elements.' Diagram courtesy of Carisse Graphic Design Ltd.*

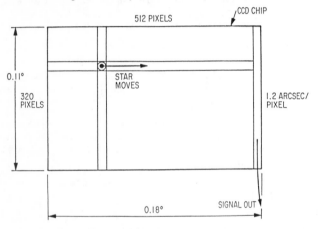

Fig. 13–9. *Schematic illustration of a Spacewatch CCD scan, using a chip 512 × 320 pixels. Diagram courtesy of Tom Gehrels.*

The magnitude limit with the 0.9 meter is 19.6. Astronomers can either scan to a fainter magnitude or increase sky coverage by a factor of four by driving it backwards, instead of keeping it still.

Data from a night are transmitted via microwave from Kitt Peak to the University of Arizona in Tucson. On the mountain, a computer compresses the data by a factor of four by discarding the background. Each raw image consumes one-third of a megabyte of computer storage; with compression, one scan will fit into about 2.5 megabytes. On campus is a 300 megabyte disk drive to handle the data. Once an asteroid is located, all that is known is a position in terms of how many pixels from the starting position it is. To determine its actual coordinates, astrometry must be done based on the positions of known 9th magnitude stars in each strip. For this purpose, the disk drive also handles Sky Map, a compilation of many star catalogues including SAO and AGK3.

Each month, Spacewatch scans nine regions in the two-week period between last quarter and first quarter moon,

Photo. 13–3. *Tom Gehrels, a Dutch-born American astronomer at the University of Arizona, where he heads the Spacewatch project for new, small asteroids. Dr. Gehrels is well known for organizing two asteroid conferences in Tucson in the 1970's, which provided much of the impetus for the modern investigation of asteroids. In 1955, he discovered the opposition effect.*

the so-called "dark time." Each region is repeated four times per month. With a 3 or 4-day arc, an approximate ephemeris can be prepared so the new asteroids can be observed again a week to a month later. In the case of the fast-moving Earth-crossers, astronomers at other observatories may even be notified the same night for follow-up observations. It is predicted that in a single scan six objects will be seen, only one or two of which are known. In its first two years of asteroid observatrions, 69 new asteroids were discovered by Spacewatch, although none were Earth-crossers. Of these, good orbits were derived for 16, including one Trojan, one Hilda, and one asteroid at the 2/3 resonance. Astrometry is done for about 10 asteroids per month, from a list submitted by Brian Marsden.

During the period each month when the moon is too bright for asteroid work, Spacewatch is used by R.S. McMillan *et al* to search for large planets orbiting other stars. The instruments on the telescope do not have to be changed, the siwtch from the CCD camera to the doppler accelerometer being accomplished by having two separate Netonian "ports." By making accurate observations of the change in the doppler shift of stellar absorption lines, scientists can detect differences in the speed of the stars as precise as 3m/sec., which might indicate the gravitational presence of planets.

Spacewatch will provide better statistics on the population of Earth-crossing asteroids and faint comets; locate asteroids that are easy to get to with spacecraft for surveys or mining; and act as an early-warning system for asteroids on a collision-course with Earth. Chunks of rock as small as 30 meters, which can be detected by Spacewatch, could cause a major catastrophe if they hit a populated area. Even a 100 meter object would have an impact energy of 1,000 Hiroshima-class bombs (Gehrels & McMillan, 1982). "You can never be certain," explained Gehrels in a National Geographic interview. "There might be an asteroid out there that could impact Earth just 30 years from now. It would be criminal if we didn't attempt to find it, so we could at least try to avoid the collision." (Frederick, 1984).

PHYSICAL CHARACTERISTICS

The composition of the Earth-crossing asteroids has been the subject of a great deal of study since the mid 1960's. A knowledge of their physical characteristics is essential to an understanding of their origins, and the interrelation between comets, asteroids and meteorites.

As shown in Fig. 13–11, most Earth-crossers fall into the well-known C and S compositional types. In the more recent eight-color survey, Tholen (1984b) examined 17 earth-approaching asteroids. All but two of them (2100 Ra-Shalom and 1979 VA) are reddish, the remainder being S or Q types. Lucy McFadden (1983), on the basis of 24-color spectrophotometry of 17 Earth-crossers, concluded they are composed of basically the same kinds of materials found in the surface material of main belt asteroids, but the distribution of these materials is different in near-Earth asteroids. No near-Earth asteroid exhibits the spectral characteristics of known geological units on the Moon, Mercury, Mars or the satellites of the outer solar system. Strong UV and near-infrared absorption bands are present on 75% of the near-Earth asteroids, but only 40% of the main-belt asteroids have these features (Mc-

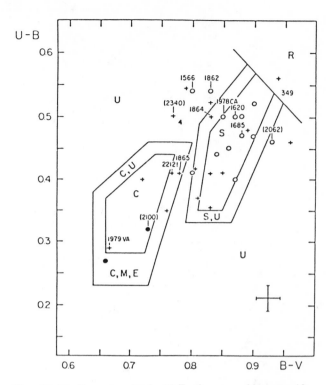

Fig. 13–10. *Two-color plot for 32 Earth- approaching asteroids from Tedesco et al. (1981c): Atens (numbers within parenthesis), Apollos (numbered) and deep Mars-crossers. Open circles are used for objects with albedos > 0.065, and (+) symbols where the albedo is unknown. A (!) following a number indicates an association with a radar meteor stream as reported by Drummond (1982). The boxes define the locations of various taxonomic types. Degewij & Tedesco, 1982.*

Fadden *et al*, 1985).

McFadden claims that on the basis of visible and infrared spectral reflectance there may be more silicate minerals with strong absorption bands in these regions and fewer minerals that absorb light at all wavelengths compared to the majority of main-belt asteroids. Differences in surface texture might also enhance such strong absorption bands, but if this is the case, we presently can't conceptualize these textures to simulate them in the laboratory. Near-Earth asteroids may exhibit higher spectral contrast and albedo by virtue of their being fresh, relatively unweathered material, consistent with the view that they are younger fragments of parent bodies that had weathered surfaces.

McFadden *et al* (1984) were able to distinguish four groups of near-Earth asteroids on the basis of their spectral data (Fig. 13–12).

Group A: Olivine and pyroxene assemblages dominated by olivine, except for 1915 Quetzalcoatl which is predominantly pyroxene.

Group B: Dominantly olivine, with an additional unspecified 'reddening agent.' This agent may be finely dispersed, fine-grained carbon or metallic particles, but fine-grained olivine cannot be ruled out.

101

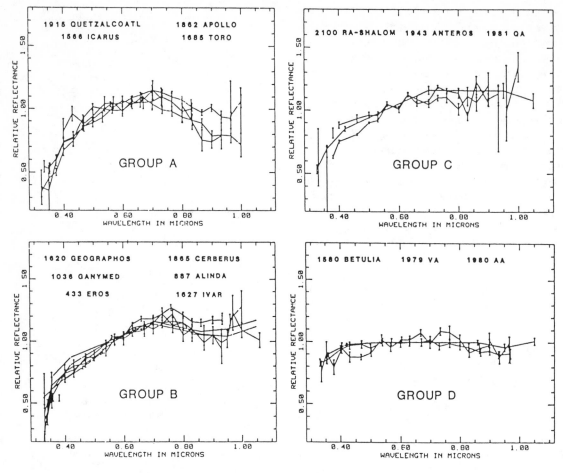

Fig. 13–11. *Spectra of the four groups of near-Earth asteroids identified by McFadden et al, 1984. Reproduced by permission from Icarus.*

Group C: Likely composed of silicates, opaque minerals, and either low iron abundance or small particle size.

Group D: High-iron olivine, small grains of magnetite or carbon that are transparent in the IR, silicates and large particle-size opaques are indicated.

Surface characteristics have revealed discrepancies in the classification of some Apollo, Amor and Aten asteroids. In a 1979 paper, Lebofsky *et al* reported on radiometric observations of three Earth-crossers, and compared them to data on other such asteroids.

For both 1580 Betulia and 2100 Ra-Shalom, the radiometric albedo is much higher than the polarimetric one, and is also inconsistent with the classification from UBV colors. They proposed rocky surfaces for these asteroids, so that a significant thermal flux is radiated by the nightside of the asteroid. In the case of 1978 CA, radiometry and polarimetry indicate it is C–type, while UBV colors suggest it is S–type. Similar overestimates of albedo indicate Eros has a rocky surface.

It appears that small, Apollo-type asteroids lack a layer of surface dust, or regolith, that main-belt asteroids apparently have. This is attributed to their lower gravitational pull, so that when another object hits them, residue escapes. Lack of this low-thermal inertia material accounts for the unusual thermal fluxes.

It is interesting to note that Betulia and Pallas both travel in highly inclined orbits, and both have similar compositions. Two other similarities with main-belt asteroids have been noted. Quetzalcoatl and portions of Vesta have the same spectral features. Vesta is believed to be basaltic, having lava on its surface. And Dembowska, which may also be basaltic, has been compared to the Apollo asteroid Toro. This well-observed asteroid has already been mentioned earlier in this chapter with regard to its orbital motion.

Ostro *et al* (1983), found from radar observations made with the giant Arecibo telescope that Toro's regolith has a porosity comparable to that of lunar soil. The surface is much rougher than the Moon at 10 to 100 meter scales, and is marked by variations in optical albedo. A rocky surface is indicated, in agreement with data on other Apollos.

In addition to comparing them with main-belt objects, scientists have looked carefully at laboratory spectra of meteorites, finding some analogs. Quetzalcoatl compares with a certain basaltic meteorite; some spectra of Toro match the reflectivity of a typical chondrite, as does 1862 Apollo and 1980 AA. Two carbonaceous chondrites compare well

102

with 2100 Ra-Shalom.

    This does not prove, but suggests that these asteroids may be the parent bodies of the meteorites (Simonenko & Levin, 1983). The absence of many meteorite analogs among the asteroids suggests that parent bodies have been fragmented into objects smaller than those now detectable, or that their sources are few in number and located in regions where asteroids have not been detected. Greenberg & Chapman (1983), however, take the opposite view. They argue that the observed distribution of meteorite classes can be derived from cratering processes on main-belt asteroids, relegating the Earth-approachers to a minor role.

DETERMINATION OF ASTRONOMICAL CONSTANTS

The gravitational influence of the Sun and planets on the asteroids can be used to determine the values of many important solar system constants:

1. Planetary mass

2. Moon/Earth mass ratio

3. Solar parallax

4. Astronomical unit

5. Dynamical oblateness of the Sun

    In addition to this, the determination of the equator and equinox of the celestial coordinate system can be established with the aid of asteroids. While spacecraft are becoming increasingly important in solar system work, asteroids will remain an important source for the values of fundamental constants. The Earth-crossing asteroids have been the prime tools in this connection. Shortly after the discovery of Eros, Chandler (1898) wrote that "It is manifest that this little object is destined to play a role in our astronomy of very great importance. It opens up, at a stroke, an unexpected and royal road to the problem of the solar parallax, as well as those of nutation, the Moon's mass, and aberration."

Planetary Mass

In 1873, G. W. Hill published a list of 12 asteroids which exhibit large perturbations in longitude due to the gravitational influence of Jupiter. He suggested these objects as being particularly suitable for the determination of the mass of Jupiter (Table 13–4).

    Several studies were conducted in the 1960's using the first seven asteroids in Table 13–4, culminating in a paper by Klepczynski in 1969. He gathered 3,250 observations of Hygiea, Themis, Euphrosyne and Europa, deriving the reciprocal mass of Jupiter from each. His data, together with that developed previously, are given in Table 13–5 (Klepczynski, 1974). Combining all seven results gave a value of 1047.364 ± 0.005, in close agreement with an asteroid-derived value of 1047.35 determined by Simon Newcomb in the 19th century.

TABLE 13-3 CLOSE APPROACHES 1970-2025 TORO				
J.D.	Year	Venus A.U.	Earth A.U.	Mars A.U.
2441535.5	1972		0.14	
2442810.5	1976		0.37	
2444460.5	1980		0.16	
2445730.5	1984		0.34	
2446410.5	1985			0.34
2447380.5	1988		0.18	
2448650.5	1992		0.29	
2450295.5	1996		0.22	
2450365.5	1996	0.42		
2450560.5	1997			0.40
2451410.5	1999			0.17
2451570.5	2000		0.24	
2453215.5	2004		0.26	
2453285.5	2004	0.38		
2454490.5	2008		0.20	
2456135.5	2012		0.30	
2456205.5	2012	0.34		
2457410.5	2016		0.16	
2458090.5	2017			0.34
2458945.5	2020			0.28
2459060.5	2020		0.33	
2459125.5	2020	0.33		
2460330.5	2024		0.13	

Table 13–3. *Close approaches 1970–2025. Close approaches of the asteroid Toro to the planets Venus, Earth and Mars from 1970 to 2025. Table from Janiczek et al (1972). Reprinted by permission of the Astronomical Journal.*

TABLE 13-4 HILL'S LIST OF MINOR PLANETS		
Minor planet	Coefficient	Period
10 Hygiea	14676	98
24 Themis	14606	92
31 Euphrosyne	28997	99
52 Europa	6584	68
48 Doris	5087	72
57 Mnemosyne	12956	103
65 Cybele	13145	94
49 Pales	11639	62
62 Erato	13655	83
76 Freia	32244	121
86 Semele	10861	65
90 Antiope	28568	104

Table 13–4. *Hill's List of Minor Planets. A list of 12 asteroids proposed by G. W. Hill in 1873 which, because of the commensurability of their mean motion with that of Jupiter, suffer large perturbations in longitude. The amount of this orbital inequality is known as the coefficient, and is expressed in arcseconds (one arcsec is 1/3600 of a degree). The period of the inequality is given in years. Table from Klepczynski (1969). Reprinted by permission of the Astronomical Journal.*

| TABLE 13-5 |
| DETERMINATIONS OF MASS OF JUPITER |
| USING THE HECUBA GROUP OF MINOR PLANETS |

Minor Planet	Observations Mass	Reciprocal Error	Mean	Year	Investigator
10 Hygiea	1849–1966	1047.351	0.006	1969	Klepczynski
10 Hygiea	1932–1967	1047.314	0.031	1970	Chernykh
24 Themis	1853–1964	1047.359	0.010	1969	Klepczynski
31 Euphrosyne	1854–1964	1047.372	0.006	1969	Klepczynski
48 Doris	1857–1967	1047.340	0.024	1969	Zielenbach
49 Pales	1857–1968	1047.340	0.013	1971	Dogett
52 Europa	1858–1964	1047.337	0.027	1969	Klepczynski
57 Mnemosyne	1859–1965	1047.356	0.004	1968	Fiala
65 Cybele	1861–1966	1047.387	0.004	1967	O'Handley
76 Freia	1864–1971	1047.366	0.007	1971	Klepczynski, Janiczek and Fiala

Table 13-5. *Determinations of Mass of Jupiter Using the Hecuba Group of Minor Planets. The minor planets proposed by Hill are members of the Hecuba group, whose mean motions are commensurable to Jupiter's in the ratio 2:1. Table from Klepczynski (1974).*

It was recognized as early as 1900 that Eros could be used to determine the mass of Mars, and its motion was eventually employed to find the mass of Venus and Mercury as well. Contrary to expectations, however, these planetary values were very poorly determined from Eros data.

Icarus has also been used for Mercury, due to its close approach to that planet just prior to the well-observed 1968 opposition. Jay Lieske and George Null quote a value for the inverse mass of Mercury from Icarus data as 5,934,000 ± 65,000, in close agreement with a radar-derived value of 5,935,000 ± 45,000. In an investigation of the asteroid 944 Hidalgo, Brian Marsden (1979) found that a reciprocal mass value for Saturn of 3498.5 reduced the relatively large orbital residuals in Hidalgo's orbit substantially. The adopted value at that time was 3501.6 for the ringed planet. The smaller residuals obviated the need to introduce nongravitational forces to explain Hidalgo's motion.

Photo. 13-4. *Kitt Peak, Arizona, the mountain-top site of the national observatory of the United States. The largest telescope on Kitt Peak, a 4-meter, is housed in the tallest dome at right. The Spacewatch telescope is in the dome at left. Photo by the author.*

Moon-Earth Mass Ratio

The close approaches of Apollo asteroids to the Earth-Moon system are especially important for the determination of the mass of that system due to the enhancement of their effects on the computed positions. The first calculation of this kind was performed by G. Witt in 1905, using the asteroid 433 Eros.

But it was not until the late 1960's that the true value of u, the Earth-Moon mass was found. Based on Eros data, the following values were calculated in the first half of the century: $1/m = 328370 \pm 68$ Noteboom (1921); 328390 ± 69 Witt (1933); 328452 ± 43 Rabe (1950) where m is the combined mass of the Earth and Moon.

To obtain more accurate values, it was suggested that Icarus (Herrick, 1953) or Triberga (Brouwer & Ashbrook, 1951) be used instead. Icarus passes closer to the Earth than Eros, thus magnifying the gravitational effects to be measured, and Triberga has an orbital period that would avoid any dependence on the fundamental system of star positions, a dependence suffered by Eros.

By the 1960's, however, it was known from radar work that the value should be close to 328900. In 1966, Schubart found from observations of 1221 Amor that the Earth + Moon mass was fairly consistent with the radar results. He used 227 observations obtained from 1932 to 1964, to get $1/m = 328895$.

Schubart's method was applied by Zech to the Eros data used by Rabe in 1950. For this purpose he made use of 37 positions from 1926 to 1945 given by Rabe, and got the result $1/m = 328894 \pm 30$, in excellent agreement with Schubart's value. Rabe himself independently discovered the conceptual error he made in 1950, and gave a revised value of 328890 ± 16 in a 1967 paper.

The value of the Earth/Moon mass is an important quantity when computing the orbit of an Apollo asteroid. Brian Marsden (1970) at first thought that 887 Alinda was subject to non-gravitational forces due to strongly systematic residuals in his orbit determination. But it quickly became evident that the trouble was due to an error in the adopted value of the Earth-Moon system. The cumulative effect at the approaches of Alinda to Earth every four years was very noticeable, but when a mass consistent with the radar data was used, the residuals vanished.

Solar Parallax And The Astronomical Unit

Because asteroids are observed from different locations on the Earth's surface, rather than its center, the resulting parallactic displacements on the sky are inversely proportional to the geocentric distance. Objects such as Apollo-Amors that closely approach Earth are thus ideal tools for determining the solar parallax and the astronomical unit, which are related through the definition of the solar parallax as the angle subtended by the Earth's equatorial radius at a distance of 1 AU. As the asteroid gets closer, the parallax gets larger and easier to measure. Using the trigonometric method, familiar through its use by land surveyors, the AU can be calculated from the measured values of the solar parallax and the Earth's radius (Rabe, 1971).

Another method of determining the astronomical unit is based on a relation between the AU, denoted by A, expressed in kilometers, and the ratio m of the mass of the Earth-Moon system to the solar mass. According to this so-called dynamical method, mA^3 equals a constant. As detailed in the last section, close approaches of asteroids to the Earth permit a calculation of the Earth-Moon mass, and thus of the astronomical unit and solar parallax.

Before Eros was discovered, Newcomb had calculated the solar parallax to be 8.790, but at a meeting in 1896 of the directors of the principal national ephemerides, he accepted a value of 8.80 to be used by everyone. Witt (1908), the first to use Eros to measure the parallax, found a larger value: "According to this there is no doubt the presently accepted value of the mass of the Earth-Moon system needs a quite sizable correction." Noteboom tried twice to better those numbers, but his results only showed that the perturbations of Eros' orbit by Mercury can be neglected (Schmadel, 1981).

Discordant values of the solar parallax were quoted over the years and are shown in Table 13–7. Both Hinks and Spencer-Jones employed the trigonometric method, while Witt and Rabe used the dynamical method. While the Witt and Rabe values agreed closely, the Spencer-Jones result caused great consternation. It was based on an ambitious Eros parallax programme of 1930–31, which employed several telescopes, including two in South Africa and a 26–inch refractor and 13–inch astrographic telescope at Greenwich.

The difference became even more troublesome when radar data in the 1960's indicated a value between the two, 8.7940. This led to new investigations, which resulted in

| | \multicolumn{4}{c}{TABLE 13–6} |
| \multicolumn{5}{c}{GRAVITATIONAL EFFECTS BY ASTEROIDS ON MARS} |
Number	Short Period Amp (m)	P (year)	Long Period Amp (m)	P (year)	Accel (m/year²)
1	160	1.6	850	10	315
	165	2.4	90	8.3	
2	29	1.6	210	10	80
	60	2.4	50	8.4	
3	3	1.6	28	14	6
	7	2.7			
4	95	2.0	5,200	52	76
			135	4.2	

Table 13–6. *Gravitational effects by Asteroids on Mars. The first four asteroids have both short and long period effects on the orbital motion of Mars. The acceleration due to their gravitational effects is given in the last column; Ceres has by far the largest effect. These motions have been detected by the Viking space craft. Table from Williams (1984). Reproduced by permission from Icarus.*

| \multicolumn{3}{c}{TABLE 13–7} |
| \multicolumn{3}{c}{MEASUREMENT OF SOLAR PARALLAX} |
| \multicolumn{3}{c}{1875–1950} |
Asteroid Used	Parallax	Author
Flora	8.889	Galle (1875)
Juno	8.765	Lindsay & Gill (1877)
Victoria	8.8017	Gill (1894)
Victoria	8.8010	Gill (1897)
Sappho	8.7960	Gill (1984)
Victoria	8.8249	Auwers (1897)
Sappho	8.7965	Gill (1897)
Iris	8.8114	Elkin (1897)
Iris	8.779	Auwers (1897)
Eros	8.803	Witt (1908)
Eros	8.807 ± 0.003	Hinks (1909)
Eros	8.806 ± 0.004	Hinks (1910)
Eros	8.7988 ± 0.0006	Witt (1933)
Eros	8.790 ± 0.0013	Spencer-Jones (1941)
Eros	8.7984 ± 0.0004	Rabe (1950)

revised values of the Earth-Moon mass and corresponding changes in the solar parallax. The dynamical and radar results were finally reconciled, with the accepted modern value of $\pi = 8.794148 \pm 0.000007$.

The reasons for the discordant trigonometric result of Spencer-Jones, however, were not finally revealed until 1982, when R. d'E. Atkinson published the results of an investigation he made in 1953.

Why was the value 8.790 ± 0.0013 too small by four times its claimed probable error? According to Atkinson, the error analysis used was faulty, and should have resulted in an error of 0.0059, not 0.0013. He also suggested that if all the telescopes used in the Eros programme had been properly calibrated, the solar parallax would have been nearly correct, but with a probable error substantially larger than the published one.

The currently accepted value of the astronomical unit is 149,598,640±250 km., which represents the mean distance of the Earth from the Sun.

Photo. 13-5. *Lucy McFadden of the Goddard Spaceflight Center in Maryland is an expert on the mineralogy of near-Earth asteroids and meteorites.*

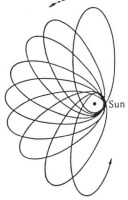

Fig. 13-12. *A precessing elliptical orbit. It takes the planet Mercury 260,000 years to precess one full revolution; eccentric Earth-crossers such as Icarus and Phaethon also exhibit such orbital precession. From N. T. Roseveare, Le Verrier To Einstein, 1982. Reprinted by permission of Oxford University Press.*

The Sun And Relativity

Even the esoteric subject of relativity theory has seen some input from observations of Apollo asteroids. It concerns both the possible variability of the Newtonian gravitational constant G, and a determination of $J2$, the quadrupole moment of the Sun, which is a measure of the oblateness of the Sun. A spherical Sun would have $J2 = 0$.

The possibility of solar oblateness has become important due to its relativistic implications. In 1859 Le Verrier announced an anomalous advance in the perihelion of Mercury's orbit. Fig. 13-13 shows the type of orbit resulting from such a precession. In the case of Mercury, the ellipse takes 260,000 years to precess through one full revolution. If the Sun were oblate, 4" of the 42.98" per century ad-

vance in perihelion would be explained. Thus, the 43" per century prediction of Einstein's theory of relativity would introduce a small discrepancy in Mercury's orbit (Dicke, 1965).

Using radar and optical observations of the position of the Apollo asteroid 1566 Icarus, Jay Lieske and George Null (1969) attempted to determine the value of J2. Like Mercury, Icarus exhibits a relativistic advance of perihelion of some 10" per century due to its high eccentricity (Gilvarry, 1953), given by the equation

$$\Delta w'' = \frac{3\overset{''}{.}838}{a^2\sqrt{a}(1-e^2)}.$$

where a is the astronomical unit and e is the eccentricity (Sitarski, 1983).

Unfortunately, almost all the 154 photographic positions of Icarus were made during the months June and July. Such a concentration seriously limited the relativistic data Lieske and Null were able to obtain. Nonetheless, they quoted a value of $J2 = (1.8 \pm 2.0) \times 10^{-5}$.

While such an uncertain value could not be used as a discriminant between competing relativistic theories, it is interesting to note that an asteroid was used to determine $J2$, and to briefly consider subsequent developments.

In 1982, physicists Henry Hill, Philip Goode and Randall Bos challenged Einstein's theory of relativity based on data of the Sun's core. Their observations indicate the Sun's core bulges at the equator and is flattened at the poles. The irregular gravitational pull of the Sun's oblate core would account for some of Mercury's precession, and that of Icarus as well.

Two spacecraft missions have been proposed to determine $J2$ accurately, thereby providing a test between Einstein's theory and its sole remaining rival, the generalized theory of John Moffat (Mease *et al*, 1982; Moffat, 1981). Plans for Starprobe to make a hairpin turn around the Sun in 1994 have been shelved for the present, but Khatib *et al* (1985) have since proposed an Asteroid Lander Mission to either Icarus or Phaethon. The idea is to land a transponder on one of these asteroids. Ranging positions are currently accurate to 50 km, but with a transponder this could be reduced to 3 meters. Making an accurate measurement of the precession of an asteroid has acquired increased urgency due to two recent revelations that appear to support Moffat's theory. The precession in the double star system DI Herculis is 0.65° per century, compared with the 4.27 predicted by Einstein's theory (Guinan & Maloney, 1985; Moffat, 1984). And Fischbach *et al* (1986) report the discovery of anti-gravity (the fifth fundamental force of nature), also a consequence of Moffat's theory.

Remarkable as it may seem, an improved knowledge of the mass of the asteroids is essential for a better understanding of both gravity and time itself. At the heart of the matter is the question, are the fundamental constants of physics really constant?

It has been the goal of some physicists in the last few decades to link the values of "local" physical constants to the evolutionary expansion of the universe. These cosmic effects may affect either gravitational or atomic physics. The consequences are startling—there may be two different

Photo. 13–6. *George Wetherill, director of the department of Terrestrial Magnetism at the Carnegie Institution in Washington D.C., pioneered the dynamical study of near-Earth asteroids and their origins.*

types of time. An atomic clock may not measure the same time as a pendulum clock.

If there is a link between the evolution of the universe and physical constants, there should be a measurable change in the gravitational constant G (its rate of change is called G dot, and written $\dot{G}$). In an attempt to detect such variability, Hellings *et al* (1983) used data from the Viking spacecraft that landed on Mars in 1976. They found that the characteristic time for variations in the ratio $\dot{G}/G$ is $0.2 + 0.4 \times 10^{-11}$ per year, or about 500 billion years. The true value may in fact be zero, in which case only one type of time exists and the constants really are constant.

The uncertainty is where the asteroids come into the picture. Despite their small mass, Ceres, Pallas and Vesta have a significant effect on the orbit of Mars. Reasenberg (1983), who gives an excellent account of solar system tests on the constancy of G, calls this uncertainty "gravitational noise." Table 13–6 lists the perturbations in Mars' longitude caused by the first four asteroids. Ceres, Pallas and Vesta dominate with amplitudes of 0.8 km (10–yr. period), 0.2 km (10 yrs.) and 5 km (52 yrs.), respectively. The large Vesta term results from a near commensurability (2/1) with Mars (Williams, 1984).

Hellings *et al* also had to take into account the other 200 large asteroids, dividing them into two groups. Both the inner (S) and outer (C) belt asteroids were treated as point masses, with the three large asteroids considered as individuals. The effect of the other 2,000 or more asteroids was found to be negligible, but the density of the C group is uncertain by 30%. Depending on the assumed density of the two groups, the $\dot{G}/G$ ratio ranged from -0.18×10^{-11} to $+0.55 \times 10^{-11}$. Clearly, the density, and thus the mass, of the 200 largest asteroids has a major impact in this important relativistic experiment. Twentieth century physicists can certainly sympathize with the 19th century astronomers who decried the "vermin of the skies." While on the subject of gravity, it may come as a surprise that even pure mathematics has seen some use for asteroids. Gerver (1984) has developed a heuristic solution of

the five-body problem (see Chapter 15 for an explanation of the three-body problem), such that the five bodies move faster and farther apart without colliding. It consists of a triangle of three stars and an asteroid that passes near each one, transferring some of its momentum on each pass. To maintain the asteroids' momentum, a fifth object (planet) orbits one of the stars in a direction opposite that of the asteroid, giving it a gravitational boost at just the right time. The net result is that the asteroid moves ever faster around the stars, which move further and further apart. Within a finite time, the stars are an infinite distance apart.

Celestial Coordinate System

Due to the star-like images of minor planets, it was recognized early in this century that they were particularly well suited for the determination of the equator and equinox of the celestial coordinate system.

The basic idea is to obtain a vast quantity of precise positional measurements of asteroids relative to the stars. The difference between the observed and calculated positions of an asteroid will be related to changes in the positions of the celestial equator and equinox. In particular, local errors are known to occur in the fundamental system of reference, known as FK4 (Fourth Fundamental Catalogue). If the computed asteroid positions are based on definitive orbits, their deviation from a large number of accurately observed positions will reveal these local distortions.

The most severe limitation to using just the four terrestrial planets for this purpose is their small range of inclinations. As explained by Brouwer (1935), "the seriousness of this limitation is that it is impossible to determine from the observations the two corrections" delta RA and delta DEC. To end the guess work, Brouwer proposed a programme of systematic observations of 14 selected minor planets distributed nearly uniformly between declinations +30° and −30°.

Between 1935 and 1948, some 7,000 observations of these minor planets were obtained at Allegheny, Yale New Haven, Yale South Station and Leiden. It was not until the 1970's that Pierce (1971) analyzed this body of data. He determined local corrections for 54 small areas of the Yale Zone Catalogues and 60 areas in the General Catalogue by Boss. While Pierce described his results as rough estimates, it has since been learned that his results were quite accurate. During working on the new FK5 catalogue, Walter Fricke (1982) found that Pierce's systematic corrections were in complete agreement with the transformations needed to go from FK4 to FK5. An observing program involving 34 minor planets, designed to improve the fundamental coordinate system, is currently underway at the University of Texas.

An even larger such effort is underway in the Soviet Union, where 30,000 observations have been collected at 32 observatories since 1949. Both this, and 2,200 observations of the asteroid Nemausa from 1943–1977 at Copenhagen, Leiden and Santiago, are in agreement with Pierce's results. Based on this important study of asteroids, the right ascensions of the new FK5 define the zero point as closely as possible to the true intersection of the ecliptic and equator (Koroleva & Orelskaya, 1982).

As pointed out by Fricke, there is a growing demand for an accurate dynamical reference frame in the fields of planetary dynamics, space navigation, geodesy, geophysics, and a link between FK5 and the radio astrometric extragalactic reference frame. The value of asteroid observations can truly be said to extend beyond the confines of the solar system to the realm of the galaxies.

SOURCES

> We have the basis to expect that when the comets are located in remote areas for a significant period of time, their comas can condense, if not completely then at least significantly making similar to stars. Then they become asteroids.
>
> William Herschel—from his collected Scientific papers

The birth and death of Apollo asteroids can tell us much about the history of the solar system, the evolution of comets, and the development of life on Earth (a matter considered in the next chapter).

The first question that arises is "where do they come from?" Serious study on this began in the early 1950's, when Ernst Öpik calculated the population of Apollo asteroids at the origin of the solar system.

In 1951 and 1963 studies, he concluded the Apollos have not been in their present near-Earth orbits since they formed. Starting with the seven Apollos known in 1963, and a collision rate with Earth of one per 100 million years, the extrapolated population at the beginning of the solar system was in the trillions. The total mass of these hypothetical Apollos was 1,000 times the mass of the Sun! Thus, the vast majority of Earth-crossers must have been injected from other parts of the solar system. Since the number of craters produced on the Earth and Moon have been fairly constant over the last 3×10^9 years, this injection must have been acting to maintain the steady-state population we see today from the earliest times.

The obvious place to look for asteroids injected into these orbits is the main asteroid belt between Mars and Jupiter. A qualitative understanding of the processes involved can be gained from the block diagram in Fig. 13–14. This study, by Wetherill & Williams (1968), offers Mars-crossing asteroids as a possible source of Apollos and the meteorites that impact Earth.

To maintain the observed Apollo population would require hundreds of times more Mars-crossers. The actual ratio, however, is in the range of 10 to 60, so only a few percent of the Earth-crossers can have originated from this source.

Since the late 1960's, attention has focused on two sources of Apollos: resonances in the asteroid belt, and comets. In the former case, two kinds of resonances are

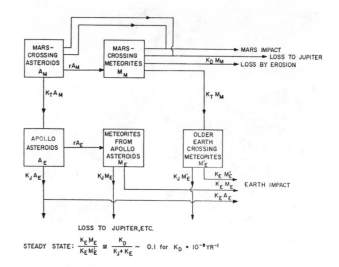

Fig. **13–13.** *Block diagram indicating the processes involved in the production of meteorites from Mars-crossing and from Earth-crossing (Apollo) asteroids. A steady state of 0.1, for the assumed mean lifetime of collisional destruction (Kd), means that ten times as many meteorites formed in Mars-crossing orbits compared to Earth- crossing orbits. Wetherill & Williams, 1968. Copyright by the American Geophysical Union, reprinted with permission.*

involved. The Kirkwood gaps are, as the name implies, depleted in asteroids. The gaps considered as sources of Apollos are at 2/1, 5/2 and 3/1 commensurabilities with Jupiter. In addition, secular resonances known as $\nu5$, $\nu6$ and $\nu16$ are areas of space similarly devoid of asteroids (Fig. 13–15).

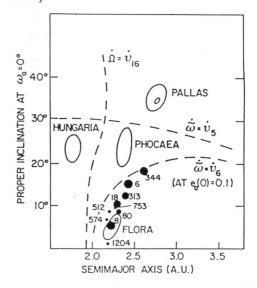

Fig. **13–14.** *Observed distribution of large asteroids in the inner portion of the asteroid belt and in the vicinity of the $\nu6$ resonance. The large open "ovals" approximately define the limits of the Hungaria, Flora, Phocaea, and Pallas regions of the asteroid belt. Wasson & Wetherill, 1979. Reprinted from Asteroids by Tom Gehrels by permission of the University of Arizona Press.*

This naturally leads to the suggestion that whatever asteroids occupied these areas, or whatever collisional fragments got thrown into these areas, were ejected, possibly into Earth-crossing orbits.

TABLE 13–8			
INITIAL ORBITS			
Objects	a	e	i
1204 Renzia	2.26	0.29	2°
313 Chaldaea fragment	2.32	0.30	12°
Phocaea region fragment	2.20	0.25	23°
Comet Encke	2.21	0.85	12°
Hypothetical extinct comet $q = 0.92$AU	2.56	0.64	5°
Hypothetical extinct comet $q = 1.50$AU	2.80	0.46	6°

Table 13–8. *Initial Orbits. Real and hypothetical orbital elements used to derive the number of Earth-crossers in Table 13–9. Table from Wetherill (1979). Reproduced by permission from Icarus.*

TABLE 13–9		
STEADY-STATE DISTRIBUTIONS		
INJECTION RATE = 15 OBJECTS, MILLION YEARS		
Initial Orbit	Amors	Apollos
	$1.0 < q < 1.3$	$q < 1.0$
1. 1204 Renzia	840	331
2. 313 Chaldaea fragment	1611	661
3. Phocaea region fragment	2181	274
4. Comet Encke	1195	769
5. Extinct comet, $q = 0.92$	685	233
6. Extinct comet, $q = 1.50$	495	222
7. Same as 1, no Jupiter encounters	1152	515
8. Same as 1, $1/2\nu6$ amplitudes and no Jupiter encounters	1457	359
9. Same as 4, no Jupiter encounters. Estimated number brighter than $V(1,0) = 18$	1200	926
(Shoemaker, 1977)	600 ± 400	750 ± 300

Table 13–9. *Steady-State Distributions. If 15 objects per million years are injected into the initial orbits indicated at left, a certain number of Apollo and Amor asteroids will be produced in a steady-state distribution. Table from Wetherill (1979). Reproduced by permission from Icarus.*

In 1973, Zimmerman and Wetherill published a study on the 2/1 resonance. They postulated that collisions between asteroids in the vicinity would inject fragments up to 500 meters in diameter into the gap with velocities between 50 and 200 m/sec. Resonant perturbations with Jupiter will cause such an object to build up its eccentricity to 0.3 or 0.4.

A second collision will then become likely, either with another fragment or an asteroid. Close approaches to Jupiter's orbit will slowly decrease the semi-major axis of the orbit and cause the perihelion to descend. Eventually, the fragment will cross the Earth's orbit, becoming an Apollo, Aten or Amor. Wetherill has followed the subsequent evolution of such orbits, and found them to be consistent with orbits calculated for meteorites that were observed falling to Earth.

Typical fragments in this study became Earth-crossing in less than 10^4 years, and their calculated flux rate at the Earth of 8×10^8 grams/year was also in agreement with observational data on meteorites.

A similar collision mechanism, this time with the $\nu6$ secular resonance, was used in Wetherill's landmark 1979 analysis on steady-state populations of Apollo-Amor objects. In this case, close encounters with Mars produced a set of Mars-crossing orbits whose evolution was calculated. These, together with the orbit of comet Encke (the only active comet in an Apollo-like orbit) and the orbits of two hypothetical comets, are listed in Table 13–8.

The population of Apollo-Amor asteroids produced by these orbits is given in Table 13–9, for the arbitrary injection rate of 15 per 10^6 years. This rate was chosen to match the estimated populations of Apollos and Amors, namely 750 and 600 respectively. Wetherill estimated the number of asteroids greater than 1 km in diameter in adequate proximity to both the $\nu6$ resonance and Mars aphelion at 5,000, with an approximate collision lifetime of 10^9 years. Using these data, a steady-state production of 5 per 10^6 years results; about 30% of these will evolve into Apollo-Amor orbits, a factor of 10 too low to account for the observed population. Thus, he concludes that the majority of Apollo objects do not originate in this way at all, but are former comets.

The $\nu16$ resonance might cause large amplitude oscillations in inclinations, analogous to those in eccentricity produced by $\nu6$. The $\nu5$ resonance may also be important, although it only occurs at high inclinations. The $\nu6$ resonance is probably an effective producer of Earth-crossers due to its proximity to the densely populated Flora family. However, it seems likely that the 3/1 resonance is the most significant asteroidal source of Apollo-Amors, supplying 10 to 20% of the observed objects (Wetherill, 1985). This important conclusion is based on the fact that predicted meteorite orbits from 3/1 closely match those actually found; about 10% of the ordinary chondrites may come directly from the asteroid belt, the remainder by subsequent fragmentation of Earth-crossers. Wisdom (1985) has confirmed that at least some asteroidal debris injected into the dynamically chaotic zone near the 3/1 resonance can be transported to Earth.

Perhaps we must look beyond the asteroid belt to the realm of the comets for the prime source of Apollo asteroids. The close relationship of comets and asteroids has been recognized for many years. "It is becoming increasingly clear that there is no essential difference between comets and asteroids. It seems now that asteroids may be comets which have lost their gaseous envelopes ("dead comets"), or fragments of a single giant comet." (Bobrovnikoff, 1929). Indeed, it was postulated by Alexander (1851), in his study of the similarity of asteroid and comet orbital elements, that the data indicated "a common origin of all the bodies concerned."

Recent theories allow for two-way traffic on the road between comets and asteroids: comets may originate as asteroids, and Earth-crossers may be former comets. The former case, as developed by O'Dell (1986) is based on the controversial postulate that comets are a "renewable resource". Among the startling conclusions that O'Dell reaches is that the Oort cloud exists only in the minds of astronomers. In his view, the one-kilometer asteroids (which number 10^6) can be perturbed into Jupiter-crossing orbits. Many of these will be flung into the outer solar system, where they will acquire a mantle of interstellar frost. Such an object, returning to the inner solar system, would exhibit the characteristics of a comet.

Most comets just make one pass near the Sun and escape from the solar system, but a few are deflected into elliptical orbits with periods of less than seven years. To convert such a comet into an Apollo object, two changes must take place. First, its orbit must alter further, and second, it must become asteroidal in appearance. Almost all short-period comets have aphelions beyond the orbit of Jupiter, but all known Apollos have aphelions within that orbit. Only comet Encke has an aphelion that overlaps the Apollo range at 4.1 AU.

As long ago as 1963, Opik put forward the hypothesis that the terrestrial planets can perturb the comets in close encounters, either ejecting them from the solar system or pulling them further inside Jupiter's orbit. The Earth and Venus would be the main agents of this action.

Yamada (1982) examined the orbital evolution of comets into Apollo-like orbits. His analysis is based on the restricted three-body problem, here involving Venus, Earth and comet. A well-known mathematical property of this problem is the Jacobi constant, or Tisserand invariant. As the name implies, it is a quantity that remains unchanged, and was first considered in minor planet work by Klose (1928).

In this case, it is defined as $C = 1/a + 2\sqrt{a(1-e^2)}\cos i$ where C is the Jacobi constant; a, e and i are respectively the comet's semi-major axis, eccentricity and inclinations. No matter how drastically the comet's orbit is changed by Venus or Earth, the value of C will remain the same.

As shown in Fig. 13–16, most Apollo-Amor objects have C values in the range 2.7 to 3.0. Among a variety of hypothetical short-period comets Yamada examined, every one in about the same range has an orbit that enters or grazes the orbit of Earth or Venus, irrespective of aphelion distance. This remarkable agreement leads him to conclude that a cometary encounter with Earth or Venus can perturb an Encke-like object into an Apollo-Amor orbit. The Apollo asteroid 2212 Hephaistos (1978 SB) may be such an object, as suggested by its similarity to Encke's orbit (Fig. 13–17).

The fact that we only observe one comet in an Apollo-like orbit is not a cause for concern. According to a review article by Wetherill (1979b), a single Encke-like comet every 65,000 years would supply Apollos at a rate of 15 per million years, the rate needed to maintain the steady-state population. The size of cometary cores and Apollos is also comparable.

While much has been written on the relationship between comets and asteroids, the most recent conclusion is that no extinct cometary nucleus has been recognized as such (Degewij & Tedesco, 1982). Three possibilities exist. Extinct cometary cores are either:

1. Indistinguishable from asteroids;

2. Mostly small, dark objects that remain undiscovered;

3. The fraction of near-Earth objects which are extinct cometary cores is much smaller than believed.

At least five good candidates for an extinct comet are

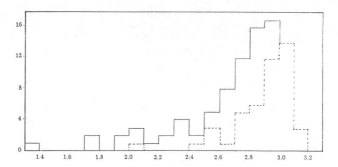

Fig. 13–15. *Distribution of Jacobi constants of the Apollo-Amor asteroids. Amor asteroids are contained below the dashed line.*

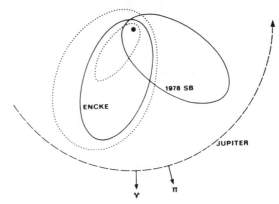

Fig. 13–16. *A comparison of the orbits of the Apollo asteroid 1978 SB and Comet Encke. Dashed line—the orbit of Jupiter, with the directions of vernal equinox and perihelion indicated by arrows; dotted lines—the approximate boundaries of the Taurid meteor stream associated with P/Encke. Kresak, 1979. Reprinted from Asteroids by Tom Gehrels by permission of the University of Arizona.*

known. The Mars-crossing asteroid 1984 BC travels in an orbit typical of short period comets, crossing the orbits of both Mars and Jupiter. Immediately after its discovery by Helin and Dunbar at the Palomar Schmidt, it was observed by Lebofsky with the Infrared Telescope Facility on Mauna Kea, Hawaii. It appears to be very dark, as would be expected of a comet nucleus that has lost its gas and dust. And its diameter of about four km is also well within the range exhibited by comet nuclei (Anderson, 1984).

A second possibility is 3200 Phaethon (diameter 4.7 km), whose orbital elements are virtually coincident with the mean orbital elements of the Geminid meteor stream. It has been variously classified as type S (Cochran & Barker, 1984), type F (Tholen, 1985), and type B (Green et al, 1985). Cochran & Barker found no cometary-type emissions, but they note that if such emissions had been found, it would not have showed that a comet had evolved into an asteroid, but rather that a comet had been misclassified as an asteroid.

To date, the evidence seems to indicate Phaethon is not an extinct comet. Its rapid rotation of 4 hours suggests it is a rocky body, since an icy comet nucleus would probably fragment if spun this rapidly. Infrared data taken between 1 and 20 microns supports this idea—Phaethon appears to have a surface that conducts heat like bare rock. Davies (1985) hypothesizes that the Geminids may be a relic of an ancient collision that knocked Phaethon out of a stable orbit in the main belt and forced it sunward through subsequent gravitational perturbations. Alternatively, it may have arisen from a smaller collision that occurred after Phaethon was already in an Earth-crossing orbit.

Drummond (1982) proposed a tentative link between 2201 Oljato and several meteor streams. According to Davies (1984), the Pioneer Venus spacecraft, currently orbiting that planet, has provided further support for this suggestion. During its first five years of operation, the spacecraft detected 31 variations in the interplanetary magnetic field, in which it rises to a peak and falls off over a period of a few hours. Close to 25% of these events correlate with material coming from Oljato, which may have a tail of material millions of kilometers long. The rate at which material must be leaving Oljato to sustain this tail is 5 kg of gas per second, only about 10% of the rate expected for an active comet. Russell *et al* (1984) suggest that this solid debris, too faint to be observed from Earth, outgasses at this rate for roughly 20 days after perihelion. Another asteroid Drummond associated with meteor streams is 2101 Adonis. Radar results indicate Adonis is very different from other asteroids and active comets. Ostro (1985b) suggests it may be an extinct cometary nucleus.

Hidalgo, the most widely accepted candidate for being an extinct comet, is 60 km in diameter. While rather large for a cometary nucleus, at least one comet is thought to be 75 km in diameter. Hidalgo's short-period orbit is the prime reason for identifying it with a cometary origin, but it also has UBV variations over its surface six times larger than that found for most asteroids. Degewij and Tedesco, in their 1982 review, suggest this color spot may be related to an early phase of strong outgassing activity.

Hidalgo is a type D asteroid, the predominant type among the Trojans. While it may be an extinct comet covered with this type of material, Hidalgo may simply be an escaped Trojan. Hidalgo has a dynamical lifetime of 100,000 years after which it will become an Amor. Shoemaker (1985) also lists four other Jupiter-crossers as likely former comets: 1983 VA, 1982 YA, 1983 SA and 1983 XF. Thus, with the proviso that there is as yet no experimental proof, the birth of asteroids in Apollo-like orbits is now fairly well understood on the basis of dynamical and collisional mechanisms. Their demise, however, is much more exciting, and is the subject of the next chapter.

THE GREAT EXTINCTION DEBATE 14

I really cannot conceal my amazement that some paleontologists prefer to think that the dinosaurs, which flourished for 140 million years, would suddenly, and for no specified reason, disappear from the face of the earth in a period measured in tens of thousands of years. I think that if I had spent most of my life studying these admirable and hardy creatures, I would have more respect for their tenacity and would argue that they could survive almost any trauma except the worst one that has ever been recorded on earth—the impact of the C–T asteroid.

Luis Alvarez, 1982

It seems that the 26 million year periodicity of extinction events is largely fortuitous. The evidence for impacts of meteorites or asteroids with the Earth is largely equivocal at the moment, and the role of such events in causing major mass extinctions is far from universal.

A.A. Bray, 1985

Modern science has seen a cross-fertilization of ideas between many disciplines, but few as disparate or unusual as that now underway between physics, paleontology, geology and astronomy. But far from coinciding, these ideas have created a great debate where fellow scientists publicly rebuke one another at conferences or in popular science magazines (eg Jastrow, 1983). It all centers on a cause for the extinction of the dinosaurs and other life forms 65 million years ago.

On a human time scale, the threat of an asteroid hitting the Earth seems unthinkably remote. But it was recognized as early as 1958 that the effects of such a collision would be catastrophic to life on our planet. The area of lethal action, wrote Opik nearly 30 years ago, "would correspond to the complete annihilation of land life, including the soil which will be covered with a layer of hot ashes. Marine life may survive." In commentary for this book, William Clemens, a paleontologist and noted opponent of the asteroid extinction theory, remarked that "Opik's description of the effects of an impact is interesting. He makes a point that appears to have escaped a

number of our colleagues in the physical sciences. If an impact-generated catastrophe was that severe, how could any plants or animals survive? Many species of both marine and terrestrial organisms survived the end of the Cretaceous. Thus, one is directed to the conclusion that either Opik was in error in his model or such an event did not occur at that time."

MASS EXTINCTIONS

In 1980, Luis Alvarez *et al* published a paper entitled "Extraterrestrial Cause for the Cretaceous–Tertiary Extinction," in which they proposed an asteroid as the agent of destruction. The evidence came from a thin layer of clay near Gubbio, Italy, which was deposited when the extinction occurred 65 million years ago. Neutron activation analysis (NAA) of 28 elements in the sample showed very similar patterns of abundance variation, except for iridium, which was 1,000 times higher than the background level (Fig. 14–1).

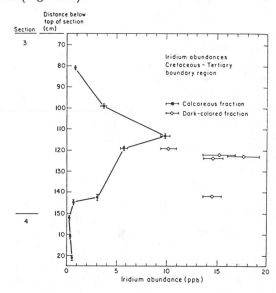

Fig. 14–1. *Typical iridium profiles across the Cretaceous/Tertiary boundary. The marked enhancement is approximately 110 cm below the top section of this sample from the North Pacific. Alvarez et al, 1982.*

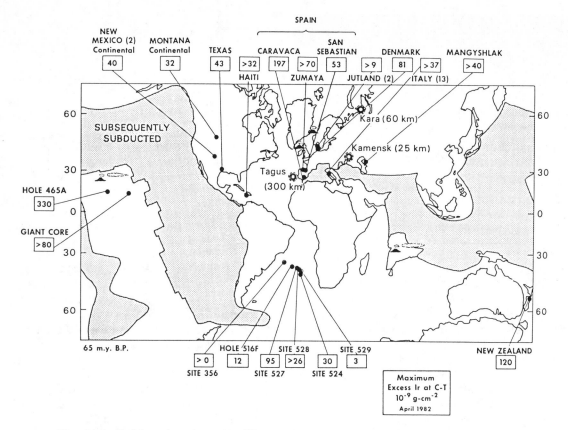

Fig. 14–2. *Positions of continents 65 million years ago and integrated iridium values (small filled circles). Shaded area is oceanic crust subsequently subducted. Craters (large circles, with diameters in parentheses) and volcanic areas (smoking triangles) are candidates for the impact site. Alvarez et al, 1982.*

In NAA, a sample of material from the clay layer was bombarded by neutrons inside a 1,000 kilowatt reactor to make it radioactive. The spectrum of energies of the gamma rays emitted from the sample, sensed by a germanium detector, provided a unique signature for each isotope created. From this data, Alvarez was able to deduce which elements were originally present and in what quantity (Fisher, 1983).

To test whether this was merely a local anomaly, similar sediments were examined in Denmark. The results were even more striking-iridium concentrations almost 10,000 times above normal. Even in distant New Zealand, iridium was found to be more prevalent in the transition zone (Fig. 14–2). In the same New Zealand deposits, Brooks *et al* (1984) found enrichments of copper, iron and nickel, as well as iridium.

Alvarez *et al* rejected the hypotheses that the iridium arrived on Earth from a supernova, or passage of the Earth through the arms of the Milky Way. Since the platinum metals, including iridium, are some 1,000 times more abundant in meteorites than on Earth, they concluded that an asteroid impact was the best explanation (Fig. 14–3).

Even more striking, this so-called Cretaceous Tertiary (C/T) boundary layer is correlated with the mass extinction of the dinosaurs and other life forms. The top of the Cretaceous is a limestone containing a rich abundance of flora and fauna. The contact is a very thin clay layer,

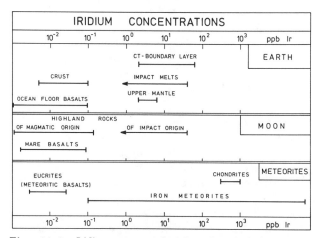

Fig. 14–3. *Iridium concentrations in endogenic igneous rocks from Earth, Moon, and eucrite parent body, C/T boundary, and impact-generated rock from Moon and Earth, in units of parts per billion. The meteorites have the highest abundances. Palme, 1982.*

the boundary, containing few specimens. This clay layer is overlain by more layers of limestone, reflecting the increasing prevalence of life in the Tertiary. (Photo 14–1; Sweet & Jerzykiewicz, 1985). The ecological niches emptied by the extinctions were reoccupied in the matter of a fraction of a million years (Hsu *et al*, 1982). At least 10^{17} grams of material was distributed world-wide, now represented by this thin layer of clay (Kyte and Wasson, 1982). The

Photo. 14–1. *Luis Alvarez, Nobel laureate and physicist at the Berkeley Radiation Laboratory. Dr. Alvarez originated the theory that an asteroid impact on the Earth 65 million years ago led to the extinction of the dinosaurs and other life forms.*

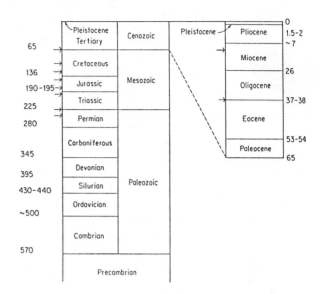

Fig. 14–4. *Geologic time scale, with dates shown in millions of years before the present. The ten extinction events noted by Raup & Sepkoski are indicated by arrows.*

iridium layer represents a brief interval, perhaps as little as one year, essentially instantaneous on a geologic time scale. It has been found not only in marine sediments, like Gubbio, but in deposits in New Mexico (Orth *et al*, 1982). The broad alluvial plains that existed in New Mexico 65 million years ago provided a suitable environment to receive and preserve the ash or dust fallout from the impact. The material accumulated in ponds and swamps, where the acidic reducing environment transformed the fallout into the kaolinite clay seen today (Pillmore *et al*, 1984).

A contrary view is presented by Officer and Drake (1985), who conclude the iridium deposit was formed over a period of 10,000 to 100,000 years. They suggest that the deposit was the result of a long period of volcanic activity, rather than a single impact, citing observations that airborne particles from an eruption of Kilauea were enriched in iridium by up to 20,000 times the concentrations found in normal Hawaii basalt. "The effect of this intense volcanism would be global cooling, intense acid rain and increased ultraviolet radiation. These effects would produce the selective extinctions," both by directly killing exposed animals and by destroying many of the plants they ate (Officer, 1986).

Searches for the impact site have turned up several possibilities (including the Tagus Plain off Portugal), but so far nothing definite has been found. Fig. 14–2 shows the positions of the continents as they were 65 million years ago. About 20% of what was then the surface of the Earth has been destroyed by subduction, so an impact on this

area will never be found. The seas of the late Cretaceous were somewhat similar to modern tropical waters. Warm seas were far more extensive and there were no polar ice caps. (Milne & McKay, 1982). An impact crater may not even exist. While unlikely, the asteroid may have broken up before it reached the surface, a scenario that would explain the very high content (20%) of extraterrestrial matter in the boundary. If the asteroid had survived all the way to the ground, the impact materials would have been diluted to a much greater extent (Kyte & Wasson, 1983).

Additional support for the asteroid theory came in 1983, when Kastner *et al* (1984) announced the detection of the clay mineral smectite in samples taken at Stevns Klint, Denmark and from a core in the Pacific Ocean. Smectite is a common decay product of glass such as might have been produced by a large asteroid impact. Asaro and Michel analyzed the samples and found high concentrations of iridium. The samples also had unusual amounts of platinum, gold, nickel and cobalt, all common elements in meteorites. Layers of smectite have already been found in 36 places around the world, indicating the debris was evenly spread around the Earth. Kastner's two smectite samples were also extremely pure, suggesting it was deposited by a single catastrophic event. However, in a French study noted by Officer & Drake (1985), it was found that iridium-enriched material at Stevns Klint started 40 cm below the CT boundary, yielding an estimated time interval for deposition of 7,000 to 150,000 years. Rampino & Reynolds (1983), examining the clay mineralogy and smectite at Stevns Klint, conclude they were formed not by impacts but by glassy volcanic ash. A similar controversy

115

envelopes the study of potassium-rich feldspar spherules at various CT sites. Some researchers believe they were produced by the impact of a large asteroid, whereas others conclude they are of volcanic origin.

Two separate studies published in early 1984 used the sudden disappearance of shellfish fossils to bolster the asteroid theory. A team headed by Richard Benson analyzed 32,000 samples from drill holes made by the deep-sea ship Glomar Challenger. Each sample contained hundreds of crustaceans, called ostrapodes, each about one mm long. In the 30 samples covering the CT boundary period, some 30% of the ostrapode population became extinct. In the well-protected deep sea environment, this represents a major event, especially considering the suddenness of the change. The other study, by Alvarez et al, showed that a similar extinction of four different shellfish groups occurred at the same time in Denmark.

This event, whatever its origin, caused the extinction not only of the dinosaurs but many of the animal and plant species on Earth. It also appears to have been sudden. In one limestone formation in Spain, 90% of the species of tiny protozoans vanished in an extremely brief time (Smit and Hertogen, 1980).

It is just this issue, gradualism versus catastrophism, that has sparked a great debate among scientists. W. Alvarez et al (1984) point out, however, that both gradual and sudden turnovers of species are possible. But the supporting evidence for the impact is now seen by some as so strong that some recent papers critical of the idea have been dismissed as "pleasantly nostalgic."

Raup and Sepkoski (1984) suggested that the evolutionary clock may be periodically reset by extraterrestrial forces. If confirmed, such cyclical events would have a greater impact on the development of life than the slow forces of evolution.

As can readily be imagined, the controversy unleashed by the discovery of the iridium anomaly and the subsequent claim of Raup and Sepkoski has been little short of overwhelming, perhaps on a par with the debate that raged over continental drift for many years. As Maddox (1984) observed, "The models now proposed for periodic extinctions are lent credibility only because Raup and Sepkoski have put forward a conclusion that cries out for an explanation. Reflection will show that astrophysicists often have no other way in which to make progress." Hallam (1984), in criticizing the Raup and Sepkoski conclusion, is even more direct. "Before astronomers indulge in further speculations about the cause of mass extinctions they would do well to learn something about the rich stratigraphic record of their own planet."

What the two paleontologists did was determine the extent of 10 extinctions, and pin down their times of occurrence with greater accuracy than had been done before. These 10 events comprised three already well-known major extinctions, and seven other minor or previously unrecognized episodes (Fig. 14–4). Unfortunately, current methods of age determination and correlation do not have the level of refinement needed to test the asteroid impact hypothesis.

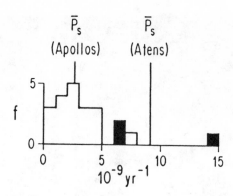

Fig. 14–5. *Frequency distributions of collision probability with Earth, Ps, for Apollo (open bars) and Aten (solid bars) asteroids. Mean impact probabilities for Apollos and Atens are shown with vertical lines. Shoemaker et al, 1979. Reprinted from Asteroids by Tom Gehrels by permission of the University of Arizona Press.*

The intervals between these events range from 19 to 31 million years, but average 26 million. These events represent periods when the background extinction rate of 200–300 species per million years increases by a factor of two to ten, leaving the planet depopulated of its life forms by as much as 96%.

Such repetitive events imply a similar cause. Massive radiation doses from solar flares, or passage of the Earth through dangerous sections of the Milky Way have been proposed. But again, Apollo asteroids are a distinct possibility, although the rate of one impact per 26 million years is four times higher than is believed to be the case. Collisions in this 10 km size range could be twice as frequent as asteroid collisions.

Further support for this periodicity was found by W. Alvarez and Muller (1984), who looked for evidence that craters on Earth also formed cyclically. Using a set of 16 craters with diameters larger than 5 km and ages whose probable error is less than 20 million years, they noted a period of 28.4 million years. This is not only very similar to the Raup & Sepkoski value, but is in phase with it.

Data on the impactor compositions at six of the seven periodic craters in the sample are more consistent with an asteroidal source than a cometary one, a fact which led Weissman (1985) to suggest the periodicity in the cratering and extinction records is a statistical fluke. "It is difficult to imagine a dynamic mechanism that would supply asteroidal impactors to the Earth with a 26–28 million year period. Although impacts may be occasionally, or even often, the major triggering event, it is still possible that there are other types of events that may also trigger extinctions." This has sparked a whole new controversy over the possible cause of such periodic events, and whether such a period actually exists. The Alvarez & Muller results were based on a list of 88 craters compiled by Richard Grieve (see also the next section on collisions), who questions the validity of using Fourier transform analysis in identifying patterns in such a small data set (Simon, 1984). Responding to this controversy, Raup and Sepkoski (1986) have recently done a further statistical analysis involving 11,800 genera, of which 9,250 are extinct. Their firm conclusion is that the "claim for a stationary periodicity with a spacing of

Photo. 14–2. *The Cretaceous-Tertiary boundary at the base of a coal seam in Alberta's Red Deer River valley is indicated with a pick. Photo courtesy of Dr. A. R. Sweet.*

approximately 26 million years is strong enough to merit further search for confirming evidence."

Broadening the controversy even further, Rampino and Stothers (1985) listed not only mass extinctions and impacts, but other geologic phenomena with periodicities near 33 million years. These include low sea levels, seafloor spreading and geomagnetic reversal. The suggestion that all these processes may be punctuated or at least modulated by episodes of cometary or asteroidal impact was the subject of lively disagreement at a Galaxy-Solar System Interaction conference in Tucson early in 1985.

To explain the periodicity, the truly far-out possibility has been raised that it is due to a dwarf star orbiting our Sun. Nicknamed Nemesis, it has been theorized that when the dwarf is at its perihelion (perhaps 3000 AU), its gravitational influence will disturb the Oort cloud of comets. The resulting million-year long shower of a billion comets through the solar system would greatly increase the chances of a major impact on the Earth (Overbye, 1984). A telescopic search is now underway to locate Nemesis, the prime candidates being 3,000 known red dwarfs stars.

Early in 1984, an informal workshop was held at the Lawrence Berkeley Laboratory in California to discuss these concepts. To quote Shoemaker and Wolfe (1984), "From 2,000 Monte Carlo simulations of the dynamical history of relatively distant hypothetical solar companions, we find that there is, at most, one chance in 1,000 that the sun had a companion star at the distance required for the apparent period of recurrence of mass extinctions and whose orbit was also sufficiently stable to cause a periodic sequence of extinctions over the last 245 million years. If the apparent strong periodicity of mass extinctions and correlated crater ages is not a statistical fluke, we are unaware of a satisfactory explanation for it." Kyte (1984) has also thrown cold water on the "Death Star" scenario. From a core sample taken in the North Pacific, he has derived a continuous record of iridium sedimentation from 32 to 66 million years. Kyte finds that the iridium excesses found are up to 100 times less than would be expected from a massive cometary incursion into the inner solar system that Nemesis would trigger. Hut (1984) has studied the

orbital stability of such a star. He believes its original orbital period was in the range of 1 to 5 million years, much shorter than the recent value of 26 to 28 million years; and the final escape of the star "might take place on a time scale of the order of a billion years" from now. The question of periodicity and the cause of them—by asteroids, comets, or passage through the galactic plane—is sure to continue for many years.

Iridium anomalies have been searched for at the Cambrian/Precambrian boundary 500 million years ago, Permian/Triassic boundary region, some 230 million years ago, and the Eocene/Oligocene boundary 34 million years ago. The PT boundary witnessed the most massive extinctions ever experienced, with at least half of all animal families killed off.

Asaro did not detect any anomaly at the Permian-Triassic boundary, but Xu *et al* (1985) did. As well as high levels of iridium, the boundary clay also had high concentrations of platinum group metals. The reason for one team finding iridium and another missing it is itself the subject of some debate, which has undermined the confidence of the procedures used (Bray, 1985). The clay layer between the ancient Precambrian and Cambrian boundary has also yielded an iridium anomaly, along with high concentrations of thorium, molybdenum, rubidium, osmium and gold. But its interpretation is also controversial as the two samples separated by 1,000 km in China, show differing anomalies. (Bray, 1985).

The E/O boundary does have an iridium anomaly. The additional presence of microtektites, thought to be produced when an asteroidal-sized body hits the earth, is strong evidence for a second impact event (Asaro *et al*, 1982).

McLaren (1983) has examined the evidence for indications of asteroidal impacts associated with mass extinctions. In addition to the Cretaceous event, he lists an extinction in the Devonian period 350 million years ago as the most likely such occurrence; an iridium anomaly at this boundary was identified by Playford *et al* in 1984. An even more ancient extinction, 446 million years ago in the late Ordovician period, may also be associated with an impact, although Wilde *et al* (1986) conclude that high iridium concentrations at the Ordovician-Silurian boundary were caused by terrestrial erosion of upper mantle rocks at their site in southern Scotland. Another OS boundary, on Anticosti Island in Canada yielded no iridium anomaly or microtektites.

While the impact of an Apollo-type asteroid with the Earth 65 million years ago is now generally accepted, its cause of the extinction is at the center of the debate. Clemens (1982) sees no clear evidence of a single-event cause of the mass extinctions. His evidence shows that, in the fossil-rich Badlands of Montana, dinosaurs died out before the impact. Recent explorations have shown that many small mammals associated with the post-impact period were actually alive in the earlier, Cretaceous period. There is even some evidence that dinosaurs in New Mexico lived on after the C/T boundary. Sloan *et al* (1986) unearthed dinosaur fossils from six locations in Montana within a geological strata that had been deposited after the CT event. He believes 70% of the kinds of dinosaurs living at the time survived the asteroid impact.

The implication is that something was happening, gradually, to change animal life on Earth well before the Cretaceous-Tertiary boundary. While a mass extinction undoubtedly occurred at the boundary, it seems that dinosaurs in Montana either left the scene 80,000 years before the CT boundary event, or survived after it. But Jablonski (1986) has assembled a persuasive body of evidence that arrives at a different conclusion. "Rather than simply accelerating or emphasizing trends already manifest during background times, the end-Cretaceous mass extinction was characterized by qualitative as well as quantitative changes in patterns of extinction and survival." As Raup (1986) states, "extinction episodes are biologically selective, and further analysis of the victims and survivors offers the greatest chance of deducing the proximal causes of extinction." Fassett (1982) goes as far as to state that the event that created the C/T boundary did not cause catastrophic, worldwide, mass extinctions. In contradiction of these results, Smit & Van der Kaars (1984) state that the Montana deposits have been misinterpreted. The postulated time span during which the diversity of dinosaurs decreased while the diversity of mammals increased simultaneously simply did not exist. They conclude that the iridium enriched layer and mass extinction were caused by a large impact. Bohor *et al* (1984) have examined a clay layer (it is 90% quartz; 25% of the quartz grains show lamellar, or scaly, features) from Montana with concentrations of iridium 200 times the local background level. The mineralogical features of the clay are characteristic of shock metamorphism and is "compelling evidence that the shocked grains are the product of a high velocity impact."

The Montana debate has been joined by Officer & Drake (1985), who question the interpretation of Bohor *et al*. Why, they ask, were the lamellar features not destroyed by annealing during reentry? They also note that several buried impact craters of Mesozoic age were found in the vicinity some years ago. The shock metamorphic features reported by Bohor *et al* are, according to Officer & Drake, characteristic of materials associated with meteor craters. Specifically, the lamellar features in quartz are seen in both normal tectonic metamorphism and shock metamorphism. But this is not the case, as is apparent in photomicrographs of quartz grains published in *Science* (8 May 1987). The appearance of lamellae in a grain from the Lake Mistastin, Labrador impact crater is similar to a grain for the C/T boundary in Colorado. But two other grains subject to tectonic deformation only have one set of lamellae, not two or more intersecting sets exhibited in the shocked quartz.

Clemens has recently shifted the controversy to Alaska with his study of 180 dinosaur bones hundreds of kilometers further north than the creatures had previously been found. There is considerable evidence that the Cretaceous environment of the North Slope of Alaska was much warmer than it is now; indeed, the Arctic Ocean was ice free and forests grew along its margins. Some have suggested the presence of dinosaurs so far north may have given them the adaptability to survive a long winter caused by an asteroid impact. But Clemens (1985) discounts the suggestion, although it indicates dinosaurs were adapted to deal with a high latitude light cycle.

It has also been claimed that less than a score of dinosaur species in 10 families existed in the late Cretaceous time. These roamed in only one geographic region of North America, a restriction that enhanced the possibility of extinction. Thus, a very small number of species extinctions could account for an immense number of familial extinctions, making it appear that the extinction was much greater than it really was (Schopf, 1982).

This scenario, however, is contradicted by other scientists, notably Russell (1982). In this view, the total diversity of life in existence 65 million years ago has been very poorly sampled. Places as widely separated as China and South America may contain large numbers of Cretaceous dinosaurs that have not yet been located. To summarize, Alvarez (1985) lists four questions where controversy continues:

1. Did the terminal-Cretaceous extinction precisely coincide with the impact event?

2. By what intermediate mechanisms could a massive bolide impact produce worldwide extinctions?

3. Which, if any, of the other known mass extinctions are marked by evidence for impact?

4. Are impacts and mass extinctions periodic, and if so, why?

On the last question, Benton (1985) lists four interpretations of the data:

1. Each extinction event was triggered by the same external impulse, acting directly (Raup & Sepkoski, 1984).

2. The cyclical pattern of extinction events correlates with some physical phenomenon that follows the same cycles (for example, fluctuations in sea level), and these are controlled by a third external variable (Fischer, 1984).

3. The events are caused by a variety of factors that relate to the internal dynamics of the biological system; each extinction event should be considered as an isolated event (Kitchell & Pena, 1984).

4. The apparent cyclicity is an artifact of the patchiness of the fossil record (Hoffman & Ghiold, 1985).

Whatever the consensus eventually turns out to be, it is interesting to muse that an asteroid may have aided the evolutionary steps leading to man by allowing mammals to develop free from the threat of dinosaurs.

PROJECT ICARUS

In 1967, a team of students from the Massachusetts Institute of Technology (MIT) were given the task of stopping Icarus from colliding with Earth.

An asteroid about one kilometer in size, Icarus was found to be on a collision course with the earth. In 70 weeks, it would likely plunge into the Atlantic Ocean, 1600 km east of Bermuda. The resulting tidal wave would wash

Initial orbit	Velocities (km/sec)			Number of Apollos		
	V	V_M	V_E	$\epsilon_{\text{Earth}}(\%)$	A_{MOON}	A_{EARTH}
1. 1204 Renzia	15.9	16.1	19.4	7.0	441	1482
2. 313 Chaldaea fragment	18.0	18.2	21.2	5.4	1008	3773
3. Phocaea region fragment	15.7	15.9	19.3	2.5	1119	3673
4. Comet Encke	19.2	19.3	22.2	7.2	804	3163
5. Extinct comet, $q = 0.92$	15.3	15.5	19.0	3.6	689	2198
6. Extinct comet, $q = 1.50$	19.8	19.9	22.7	2.4	665	2680

TABLE 14–1
STEADY-STATE NUMBER OF APOLLOS REQUIRED
REQUIRED TO MATCH OBSERVED CRATERING RATES

Table 14–1. *Steady-State Number of Apollos Required To Match Observed Cratering Rates. For objects considered in Tables 13–8 and 13–9, the geocentric velocity (V), lunar impact velocity (Vm) and earth impact velocity (Ve) are listed. Epsilon is the calculated fraction of the injected bodies which impact Earth. Lunar cratering rates imply an Apollo population only one-third that implied by cratering rates derived from the Quebec-Labrador area on Earth. Table from Wehterill (1979). Reproduced by permission from Icarus.*

away the resort islands, swamp Florida and inundate cities 2,400 km away with a 61 m wall of water.

If it missed the ocean and hit land instead, Icarus would create a crater 24 km in diameter and 8 km deep. The shock waves and pressure changes would cause earthquakes, hurricanes and heat waves of great magnitude.

The team considered four possible methods of preventing a collision with the earth.

1. A soft landing of rockets on the surface which would be ignited to perturb its orbit.

2. A nuclear charge implanted beneath the surface after a low-speed landing.

3. Disintegration with a hydrogen bomb delivered at high speed.

4. Perturbation of the orbit by detonation of a bomb near the surface delivered at a high closing speed.

The first two possibilities were ruled out because of lack of time and insufficiently powerful rockets. The third option was also dropped, as it was found that complete disruption of the asteroid would require a 1,000–megaton bomb, far larger than any in existence.

Thus, the scientists planned to intercept the asteroid and deflect it into a new orbit. For this purpose, they decided to launch six Saturn V–rockets, which were just then being built for the Apollo moon missions.

Each interceptor would carry a 100–megaton bomb and be launched from D–72 days to D–5 days. The rockets would first be sent into earth orbit. After one orbit or less, the S–IV B stage would be restarted and, together with the Apollo module carrying the bomb, would coast to the asteroid.

The terminal phase of the mission begins when the optical sensor on the craft detects the asteroid three hours before rendezvous. The radar system begins to supply distance information four minutes from intercept and at the five- second stage, the bomb is armed. Detonation was planned to occur within 30 m of the surface.

It was determined that this method of attack would result in an 86% reduction in damage on the earth and a 71% chance of no damage at all. Fortunately for humanity,

the Icarus mission was purely theoretical. As expected, it missed earth by 6 million kilometers in 1968. But in the scale of the solar system, six million kilometers is uncomfortably close. Icarus is due back in 1987.

COLLISIONS

Ast'roids—solar planetary debris. They orbit agelong, but are never free. In frigid void of silent starlit space, Lone meteoroid and blue-swirled orb did race. Overcome when greeting gravity hand, Downward meteor plunged o'er sea, o'er land. Streaking helplessly, traversing night sky, Dismayed bolide pleaded with sonic cry: "Please release me from gravity accursed." But to no avail, was shortly dispersed! His time had come, his destiny fulfilled. North yonder he lies, shattered and stilled. Till remains are found, enigma'll persist, And someday haunt future geologist.

For asteroids brighter than magnitude 18, it is expected that 3.2 Earth crossing objects per million years will hit the earth, at an average impact speed of 20 km/sec. (Fig. 14–5). Assuming equal numbers of C and S types, 8.7 C types and 3.3 S types capable of producing craters greater than 10 km diameter strike the earth every million years. But only one third of this total of 12 asteroids actually hit the continents (Shoemaker, 1983).

As we have seen from Wetherill's analysis in the previous chapter, an injection rate of about 1 body per 10 million years is likely. For each of his six orbits, the steady state number of Apollos required to match the observed cratering rates on the Earth and Moon was computed.

These results are tabulated in Table 14–1. The geocentric velocity is V, while Vm and Ve refer to lunar and terrestrial impact velocities, respectively. The Earth percentage is the calculated fraction of the injected bodies which impact Earth. The number of Apollos associated with the observed cratering rates is A. These quantities are related by the formula $A = kI(d)/E$ where k is the number of Apollos for an injection rate of 1 per million years, and $I(d)$ is the observed production rate per million

Fig. 14–6. *Distribution of known impact structures. Open symbols—craters with associated meteorite fragments; closed symbols—structures with shock metamorphic effects and in some cases iron-like anomalies. Grieve, 1982.*

years of craters with diameter larger than *d*.

The calculated lunar rates are in good agreement with the observed number of Apollos, but the terrestrial values are a factor of three higher. By using a more precise value of the terrestrial cratering rate, however, this discrepancy is reduced to a factor of two. Shoemaker *et al* (1979) have also postulated that, based on the difference between the terrestrial cratering rate in the last half billion years and the 3.3 billion year record on the Moon, there has been an increase in the population of Earth crossing asteroids. This enhancement in the last few 100 million years is attributed to the number or mass of stars passing near the Sun that perturb the Oort cometary cloud, an area far beyond the planets where comets exist. In any case, the calculated number of Apollos required by the observed cratering rate is in the range of the number observed.

Turning from the general to the specific, the map in Fig. 14–6 (Grieve, 1982) shows the locations of known and suspected asteroid impacts on the Earth. Because extensive ancient bedrock is exposed in Canada, more than 25 probable impacts have been documented there, including the enormous Manicouagan crater (Photo 14–3), 10 km deep & 100 km in diameter, which was formed 200 million years ago. This enormous impact melted 1000 cubic km of rock, and the effects of the event are still visible in rocks over an area of 20,000 square km (Grieve, 1982). The most recent very large impact formed the crater now filled by Lake Bosumtwi in Ghana some 1.3 million years ago.

The famous Meteor crater near Barringer, Arizona, was formed a mere 50,000 years ago (Photo 14–4). Such a fall, producing a crater 1.2 km wide, occurs once in tens of thousands of years. Most such relatively small craters have long ago been obliterated by erosion. This is apparent from

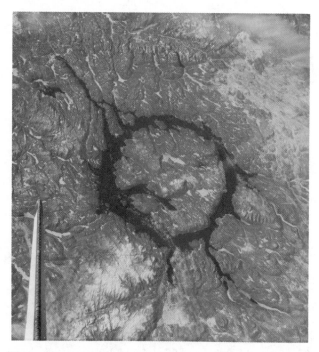

Photo. 14–3. *The Manicouagan crater in Quebec as seen from the space shuttle. Formed by an asteroid impact 200 million years ago, the crater is 100 km in diameter. The crater has been tentatively linked by Digby McLaren of the Geological Survey of Canada with an extinction of reptiles and amphibians in Nova Scotia at that time. Photo courtesy of NASA.*

Fig. 14–7—most small craters on Earth are also young, the large craters being much older.

The site of Sudbury, Ontario has twice been carved out by huge asteroids. The first impact, 1.8 billion years ago, is

120

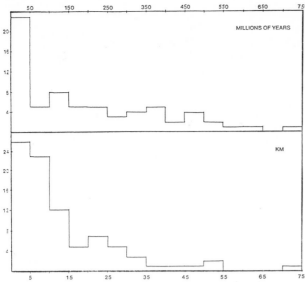

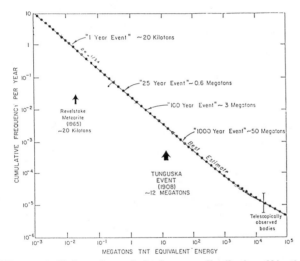

Fig. **14-7.** *Histogram of terrestrial crater ages (top) and crater sizes (bottom). In addition to the craters plotted here, 13 others associated with meteorites exist. All these are of recent origin, the largest being 1200 meters in diameter. Prepared from data in Grieve, 1982.*

Fig. **14-8.** *Estimated cumulative frequency distribution of kinetic energy of bodies colliding with the Earth. Year events indicate how often an object of that energy impacts the Earth. Shoemaker, 1983. Reproduced with permission, from the Annual Review of Earth and Planetary Sciences, Vol. 11, copyright 1983 by Annual Reviews Inc.*

also the largest (140 km) and oldest in North America (Dietz, 1964). The second impact occurred 35 million years ago, creating a 9km wide crater. The Sudbury Igneous Complex, as it is known to geologists, is a rich source of nickel, copper and platinum group metals. It is thought the impact caused a fracturing of the crust, generating magma in the deep crust which then filled the crater producing rocks of the igneous complex. The Complex itself is overlain by 1,800 meters of breccias, and the whole complex is underlain by rocks dated to 2.56 billion years. Faggart *et al* (1985), presenting new isotopic evidence, conclude this ancient rock was melted by an impact event 1.84 billion years ago.

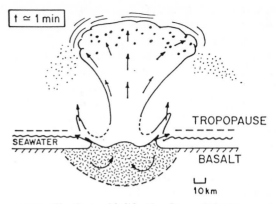

Fig. **14-9.** *The Crater Modification Stage of the impact of an asteroid on the Earth: A steam 'fireball' ejects condensed meteorite vapor to high altitude. The crater on the sea floor begins to collapse and large waves are generated near the edge of the final crater. Melosh, 1982.*

These prehistoric events far exceed any impacts recorded in recent times (Fig. 14-8). Even the relatively small Meteor Crater had an estimated energy equivalent to 15 megatons, about the same as the much publicized Tunguska bolide of 1908. That object was observed 1,000 km from its endpoint; trees were knocked down in a 40 km radius, with a fireball igniting dry timber up to 15 km from the endpoint. By comparison, the Revelstoke meteorite that appeared over British Columbia in 1965 was puny—only 20 kilotons. The nature of the Tunguska bolide is still a matter of debate. Sekanina (1983) concluded it was a rocky asteroid, probably a small Apollo some 100 meters across. But Levin & Bronshten (1986), by comparing how the breakup altitudes of fireballs and the Tunguska object were affected by approach angle, mass and terminal velocity, have reaffirmed the long-held belief it was a comet. A colorful rendition of the explosion, by Don Davis, can be found in Chaikin (1984). Some volcanic eruptions have far exceeded the Tunguska event. Mt. St. Helens (1980) in the United States blew its top with a total energy of 24 megatons. But the alltime record goes to Krakatoa (1883), with a blast of 33 megatons. The largest manmade nuclear explosion was a Soviet test of a 60 megaton bomb in 1961 (Jones & Kodis, 1982).

While the largest known Apollo asteroid is only 8 km in diameter, even such a relatively small object could cause great havoc if it impacted the Earth. The U.S. National Aeronautics and Space Administration's Scientific Advisory Council has warned that the collision of an asteroid as small as a house would produce as much energy on impact as several Hiroshima-class atomic bombs. Such an object, "coming in undetected, its impact and ensuing shock wave being mistaken for a nuclear explosion, could trigger a nuclear war," the council warned.

"If an asteroid collision were imminent, the orbital modification required could be calculated and a mission deployed to give the object the proper nudge. Once perturbed, the troublemaker would again recede into the background for many thousands of years," stated the report. Such a scenario has been a favorite subject in science fiction, notably in Arthur C. Clarke's book Rendezvous With Rama, and the movie Meteor.

To divert an asteroid 1 km in diameter would require the explosion of a nuclear warhead with a yield of 10 kilotons, only half that of the Hiroshima weapon. The asteroid could most effectively be diverted when at perihelion, but that may not be possible as such an object could escape detection until just a week before impact. One of the purposes of the Spacewatch project, described in the previous chapter, is to provide a more reliable early-warning system, thus averting a situation in which human civilization is added to the list of extinctions, of which the dinosaurs are the most notable example.

THE IMPACT SCENARIO

What would happen if the earth met a 10 km diameter asteroid? By almost any measure it would be a catastrophe. Since about three-quarters of the earth is covered by water, an impact into the ocean is most likely. The dynamics of large body impacts was a major topic at a conference at Snowbird, Utah in 1981 that resulted in a 528 page book. Papers by the following authors from that meeting were used in developing this scenario (Gault & Sonett, O'Keefe & Ahrens, McKinnon, Melosh, Croft, Toon *et al*, Lewis *et al*, Jones & Kodis, 1982), and Wolbach *et al* (1985).

Unlike pebble-sized objects that burn up in the atmosphere, swarms of which provide us with annual displays of meteor showers, a 10 km diameter asteroid would scarcely be slowed down by the atmosphere. At 25 km/sec, an oceanic impact would require 15 bolide diameters to stop the asteroid. However, it would likely be fractured by aerodynamic stresses, but there is only enough time between breakup and impact for the fragments to expand a kilometer or two.

Entering the atmosphere at 72 times the speed of sound, an intense shock wave preceded by a halo of ultraviolet radiation would be generated. Only a small fraction of the energy is transferred to the atmosphere by this primary shock wave. A quarter second before impact, the asteroid has an altitude of 5 km and a kinetic energy of 2.4×10^{30} ergs.

At 0.3 seconds after hitting the surface of the ocean (which at 5 km deep, is only half the diameter of the asteroid), the seawater has been raised to $100,000°$ K. The shock wave has already passed through the ocean to the seabed, while another shock wave is passing upward through the asteroid.

By 0.45 seconds, the asteroid has been slowed to 6 km/sec. Expansion of the vaporized material begins, an amount of water equal to the entire vapor content in the Earth's atmosphere, and three to four orders of magnitude larger than the water vapor in the stratosphere. Material on the order of 1,000 cubic kilometers expands into the upper atmosphere, reaching several hundred kilometers.

Between 1 and 4 seconds after impact, the shock wave creates a crater on the sea floor up to 70 km in diameter, with an energy equivalent to a magnitude 10.1 earthquake.

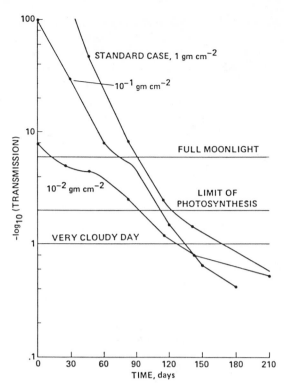

Fig. 14-10. *The logarithm of the transmission of visible light is illustrated as a function of time for various mass loadings. The transmission levels equivalent to three natural phenomena are indicated. For the larger two mass loadings, not enough light reaches the surface to allow vision for several months. Photosynthesis could not occur for any of these cases for about 3 months. Toon et al, 1982.*

Photo. 14-4. *Meteor crater, near Barringer, Arizona is much younger and smaller than Manicouagan— 50,000 years old and just 1.2 km in diameter.*

Within a minute, the crater has collapsed to a depth of 500 meters. But most of the action is at the surface, where ocean waves as high as the Rocky Mountains are moving outwards to devastate the coastal areas of the planet (Fig. 14-9). (It should be noted that there is no geological evidence for such a massive perturbation of the oceans).

Within a few hours, atmospheric flows generated by the impact are expected to distribute small particles worldwide, blocking out sunlight. The degree to which it would darken can be seen in Fig. 14-10. A very cloudy day corresponds to 1, full moonlight 8. The darkest night is about equal to 9. The absolute threshold for human vision is 10, while for cats it is 11. As is apparent from the diagram, for the most likely standard model, virtually no sunlight would reach the earth's surface for 3 months-no creature could see, no photosynthesis in plants could take place.

Meanwhile, a giant mushroom cloud, superheated to 2,200° C, rushes out to 1,900 km from the impact site. It knocks down all the trees and vegetation, which, after a few months of drying out gets ignited by lightning. Thousands of square kilometers of downed timber produce giant clouds of smoke and soot that plunge the Earth into darkness.

Sub-freezing temperatures over the entire planet, lasting perhaps 6 months, could result in 6 meters of snow covering the continents. Large quantities of nitric oxide would also be produced by the energy of the impacting asteroid, leading to a collapse of the ozone layer for several years. Subsequent rainout of the resulting strong acids would affect not only plants but calcium-shelled animals.

After the cooling period, a long period of heating would take place. In the case of an oceanic impact, this would be caused by the familiar greenhouse effect. For a land impact, ultraviolet radiation would pass unhindered by the now-depleted ozone layer, causing severe damage to a wide range of life forms (Fig. 14–11).

These extreme temperature changes—first a heating of the atmosphere by 15° C, then a cooling to sub-freezing temperatures, and finally another heating episode—combined with utter darkness for several months, is the essence of the mass extinction theory. Direct evidence that an asteroid packing an energy equivalent to 250,000 Mt. St. Helens eruptions hit the earth is the iridium found at the C–T boundary.

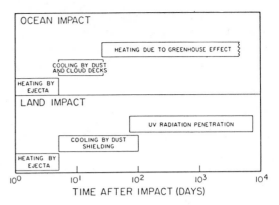

Fig. 14–11. *Relevant time scales for effects on the Earth's biota resulting from the impact of Cretaceous/Tertiary bolide in the ocean or on land. O'Keefe & Ahrens, 1982.*

"Still, the Jurassic period was all right while it lasted"

Fig. 14–12. *Dinosaurs flourished in the Jurassic period and seemed to become extinct about 60 million years ago at about the time-border between the Cretaceous and Tertiary geological ages. Palaeontologically there is still considerable debate as to whether the extinction was instantaneous. This Hector Breeze cartoon apeared in Private Eye and is reproduced by permission of the editors of that magazine.*

TROJANS, HILDAS AND CHIRON 15

The story of the Trojan asteroids is a fascinating one and there seems to be little doubt that there is a close relationship between them and the outer satellites of Jupiter.

Seth Nicholson, 1961

While most attention is focused on the near-Earth asteroids, the distant ones have been relatively neglected. Even the brightest of them, 624 Hektor, is only visual magnitude 14.7; and as time on large telescopes is scarce, so are data on the Trojans, Hildas and Chiron.

The Hilda asteroids are the most distant asteroids in the main belt, bounding it at 3.9 AU, location of the 3/2 resonance. Chiron is the most distant object yet designated as an asteroid, although its true nature is still somewhat uncertain. The location of the Trojans at the 1/1 resonance is not only unique, but an interesting problem in gravitational balancing.

Sir Isaac Newton, who formulated the law of gravitation in the 17th century, provided a solution to the "two-body problem." On the basis of this inverse-square law, Newton found that two bodies would revolve about each other in elliptic orbits, with the center of gravity at one of the foci of each ellipse. The "three-body problem", while seemingly a simple extension of this, has eluded a general solution (Hildebrand, 1984).

Consider a special case where two of the bodies have finite mass, and the third an infinitesimal mass. While it does not disturb the motion of the two massive bodies, it is controlled by their attractive forces. This special case also constrains the third body to be in the plane of the orbit of the first two, and they in turn are revolving about their center of gravity in circular orbits. The equilateral triangle solution of this three-body problem was formulated by Lagrange in 1772. He found that this configuration is gravitationally stable—if a perturbing force moves the third body away from the critical point at the vertex of the triangle, it will oscillate about that point, but will not move into a different orbit. These points, termed Lagrange points, exist in the orbits of all the major planets orbiting the Sun. But only in the orbit of Jupiter have asteroids been discovered at these points (Fig. 15–1); although in 1980 the Voyager spacecraft discovered three small satellites at the Lagrangian points of the Tethys-Saturn and Dione-Saturn

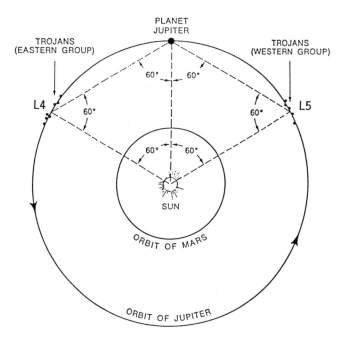

Fig. 15–1. *The location of the Lagrangian points in the orbit of Jupiter. It has been estimated there are 700 asteroids at the L4 location, but only 200 at L5. Knight, 1973.*

system. (The discovery of Trojans as a distinct class of asteroids was treated in Chapter 1).

Unfortunately this simple scenario is subject to several complex modifications. Lagrange's theory applies strictly to circular orbits, but Jupiter is in an elliptical orbit. Worse yet, the perturbing force I alluded to is not merely a theoretical problem—it is the planet Saturn. In addition to varying Jupiter's eccentricity from 0.03 to 0.06, it ensures that the Trojan asteroids rarely inhabit the Lagrange points. The difficult three-body problem has become a four-body problem! (Schubart, 1982; Wyse, 1938).

TROJANS

As an example, consider the motion of the most highly inclined Trojan, 1976 UQ. With an inclination of 39°, this Trojan varies its angular separation from Jupiter between

TABLE 15–1
TROJAN ASTEROIDS
AND THEIR
ABSOLUTE MAGNITUDES (H)

Trojans East of Jupiter			Trojans West of Jupiter		
Asteroid	H	Type	Asteroid	H	Type
588 Achilles	8.58	DU	617 Patroclus	8.17	P
624 Hektor	7.47	P	884 Priamus	8.89	D
659 Nestor	8.80	EMPC	1172 Aeneas	8.26	D
911 Agamemnon	7.88		1173 Anchises	8.91	P
1143 Odysseus	8.43	D	1208 Troilus	9.00	FCU
1404 Ajax	9.1		1867 Deiphobus	8.60	D
1437 Diomedes	8.30		1870 Glaukos	10.8	
1583 Antilochus	8.66	D	1871 Astyanax	11.2	
1647 Menelaus	10.2		1872 Helenos	10.2	
1749 Telamon	10.1		1873 Agenor	10.6	
1868 Thersites	9.6		2207 Antenor	8.87	D
1869 Philoctetes	11.2		2223 Sarpedon	9.41	DU
2146 Stentor	10.4		2241 1979 WM	8.66	D
2148 Epeios	11.1		2357 Phereclos	8.99	D
2260 Neoptolemus	8.95	DTU	2363 Cebriones	8.8	D
2456 Palamedes	9.6		2594 1978 TB	11.7	
2759 Idomeneus	9.77		2674 Pandarus	9.05	D
2797 Teucer	8.51		2893 1975 QD	8.99	D
2920 Automedon	8.83		2895 Memnon	9.9	
3391 1977 DD3	10.3		3240 1978 VG6	9.9	
3451 1984 HA1	8.1		3063 1983 PV	8.6	

Table 15–1. *The Trojan Asteroids. The Trojan asteroids are listed with their absolute blue magnitudes (H), and taxonomic type as given by David Tholen in his PhD thesis. There were 46 numbered Trojans by mid-1987.*

54 and 61° in a period of 167 years. Its perihelion also exhibits a period (5,800 years), with its longitude of ascending node moving counterclockwise (direct motion).

Another interesting case is 1749 Telamon. With an inclination of only 6°, it oscillates between 49 and 76° from Jupiter. Its period of perihelion is smaller, 3,600 years, but its longitude of ascending node moves clockwise (Bien, 1980).

The oscillating nature of the Trojan orbits can be seen in Fig. 15–2. Their perihelion distance from the Sun is equal to that of Jupiter at both ends of the path. A Trojan ahead of Jupiter will increase its lead, if its mean motion is faster than Jupiter's. As it moves further from the giant planet, the force of Jupiter's attraction and its direction relative to the asteroid's velocity change so that the mean motion of the asteroid decreases until it matches that of Jupiter. The asteroid's mean motion becomes less than Jupiter's, and the planet gains on it, until the difference in their speed reaches a maximum at 60°. Therefore the Trojan is rarely found at the Lagrange point itself (Nicholson, 1961). The first high-precision results designed to prove the existence of periodic orbits of large amplitudes about the Lagrangian points was given by Rabe (1961).

The distribution of orbital inclinations of 72 Trojans is shown in Fig. 15–3. About half these are on the permanently numbered list (Table 15–1). Fifteen Trojans with reliable orbital elements were found in the Palomar-Leiden Survey (two of which have permanent numbers),

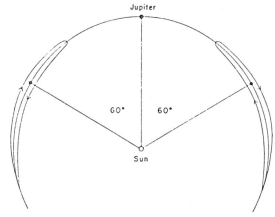

Fig. 15–2. *Paths of the Trojan asteroids librate with large amplitudes about the Lagrangian points 60 degrees from Jupiter. Nicholson, 1961.*

and 34 Trojans were found in a special survey made in 1973 (Degewij & Van Houten, 1979).

The total number of Trojans at the preceding point (known as L4) larger than 15 km diameter is estimated to be 700, while the following point (L5) contains only 200. The different number of Trojans in the two clouds may be a fossil remnant recording orbital conditions in the early solar system. According to Barber (1985), the effect was caused by the long-term gravitational perturbations of the system by Saturn. The magnitude-frequency distribution

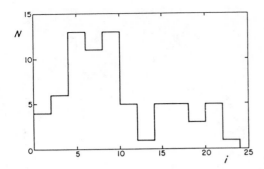

Fig. 15–3. *Distribution of the orbital inclinations of 72 Trojans. About half these are on the permanently numbered list. Degewij & Van Houten, 1979. Reprinted from Asteroids by Tom Gehrels by permission of the University of Arizona Press.*

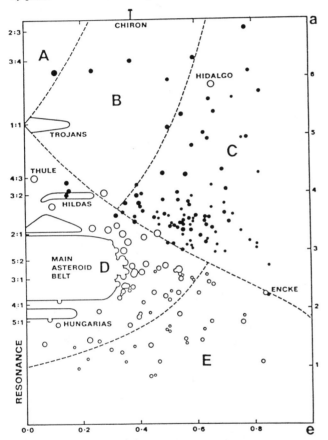

Fig. 15–4. *Short-period comets (solid circles) and asteroids (open circles) plotted in a diagram of semimajor axis versus eccentricity. Increasing circle size distinguish the objects as follows: diameter less than 1 km or a lost object; diameter 1 to 3 km; diameter 3 to 10 km; diameter 10 to 30 km; diameter > 30 km. A indicates the transjovian Region, B Jupiter's domain of weak cometary activity, C Jupiter's domain of strong cometary activity, D the minor planet region, and E the Apollo region. Kresak, 1979. Reprinted from Asteroids by Tom Gehrels by permission of the University of Arizona Press.*

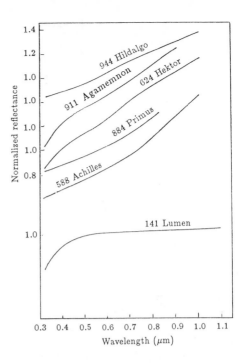

Fig. 15–5. *Reflectance spectra of four D– type Trojan asteroids and the unique asteroid Hidalgo, whose orbit carries it even beyond the Trojans. C–type asteroid, Lumen, is shown for comparison. Gradie & Veverka, 1980. Reprinted by permission from Nature, Vol. 283, pp 840.*

of the Trojans is similar to that of main-belt asteroids, but the distribution of inclinations may be bi-modal. Such a distribution is also exhibited by the faint PL asteroids, and may indicate the presence of two different populations—asteroidal and cometary, the latter causing the higher inclinations (Gehrels, 1977).

It was also argued by Rabe (1971) that some comets of the Jupiter group may have originated from the Trojan 'clouds'. The domain of the Trojans, indicated in Fig. 15–4, clearly falls within Jupiter's domain of weak cometary activity. According to Rabe, the Jacobi constant (explained in Chapter 13) of almost all asteroids is greater than 3, with the notable exception of the Trojans and some Hildas. Like these asteroids, the Jacobi constant of nearly all Jupiter group comets is less than 3. The extensive overlap of the two Jacobi distributions suggests a close dynamical affinity between the Trojans and comets. At least one comet, Slaughter-Burnham, has been captured into an orbit with temporary Trojan-like librations, but does the reverse process occur as proposed by Rabe?

Based on radiometric data, Cruikshank (1977) found that four Trojans, as well as two outer satellites of Jupiter, have very low albedos (0.02 to 0.03). Icy bodies have much higher albedos (0.4 to 0.7), and comets are widely believed to be quite distinct from the bright, icy comets.

The relationship between the Trojans and Jupiter's outer satellites has also been a subject of some debate. The Trojans may be escaped satellites of Jupiter, or they may have had their origin in the primeval Jupiter system. The satellites themselves may have been captured from the Trojan cloud (Kuiper, 1956). Like the Trojans, data on the small satellites of Jupiter are scarce due to their faintness. Only the sixth satellite (J6) is brighter than any Trojan.

With the exception of 1173 Anchises, both clouds of Trojans appear to share a similar taxonomy. The reflectance of most increases steadily with wavelength—the infrared reflectance of Trojans is exceptionally high, characteristic of D and P type asteroids. (Fig. 15–5; Gradie

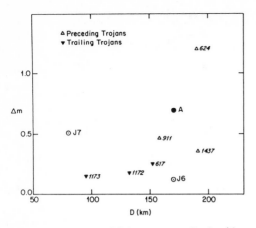

Fig. 15–6. *Comparison of light curve amplitudes (shapes) of several Trojan asteroids, and the Jupiter satellites Amalthea, J6 Himalia, and J7, Elara. The Amalthea point is calculated; others are from data in Degewij & van Houten (1979). D is the diameter of the object, Δ m is the amplitude of the lightcurve in magnitudes. Thomas & Veverka, 1980.*

Photo. 15–1. *Dale Cruikshank, an astronomer at the University of Hawaii, has researched the relationship between comets and distant asteroids. Comets at large distances from the sun apparently have crusts of low albedo, thus resembling asteroids.*

and Veverka, 1981). Among these outer objects, Smith *et al* conclude they are quite different from mainbelt objects. Hartmann *et al* (1982), using infrared data, (useful for distinguishing objects with rocky or dusty surfaces from those covered with frozen water or methane), also suggest that outer solar system objects "may constitute a generically related swarm of small bodies. Our measurements to date suggest close relationships among all of them."

The similarity of lightcurve amplitudes of three Jovian satellites with the Trojans (Fig. 15–6) may be further evidence of their close relationship (Thomas & Veverka, 1982). The most recent study (Tholen & Zellner, 1984), concludes that the colors of the outer Jovian satellites are C–type, while "The absence of D–class spectra among the outer Jovian satellites suggests that they were not derived from the same population as the outer-belt and Trojan asteroid populations."

A search has been underway since 1978 for Earth Trojans, asteroids which may be trapped in the Lagrangian points of our planet's orbit. On the basis of 18 plates taken between 1978 and 1982, Dunbar & Helin (1983) estimated the population of Earth Trojans to be 14 + 50% to a limiting magnitude of V(1,0) = 20. So far, none have been found, and they may in fact be nonexistent. To properly inventory any Sun-Earth population that may exist, Hildebrand (1984) proposed placing a telescope near the Trojan points, but sunward of them to take advantage of favorable illumination geometry and the opposition effect. This Optimized Reflection Search Asteroid Mission (OR-SAM) could travel in an elliptical orbit with aphelion of 1 AU, enabling it to survey all of the Earth's orbit.

HEKTOR: The best studied Trojan asteroid is 624 Hektor, which is also the largest highly elongated asteroid known. As a result of this shape, Hektor has one of the largest lightcurve amplitudes of any asteroid—its brightness can change by a factor of 3.1 during its 6.9 hour rotation.

Hartmann & Cruikshank (1978) proposed that Hek-

tor is a dumbbell-shaped asteroid 150 by 300 km in size, resulting from the partial coalescence of two spheroidal planetesimals. They suggested that the energy losses in a low-speed collision, which is possible in the Lagrangian cloud, may be sufficient to crush rock locally and at the same time prevent either rebound or complete fragmentation. Definite evidence that Hektor's amplitude is due to an elongated shape rather than albedo variations was presented by Hartmann & Cruikshank (1980).

Weidenschilling's (1980) calculations, however, show that the two components that comprise Hektor are not in contact. He showed that each component (98 by 65 by 60 km) has been gravitationally distorted into ellipsoids. Recent theoretical work on thermal lightcurves from irregular objects may better define the unusual character of this asteroid. (A list of the proposed models for Hektor are given in the Chapter on Shapes).

HILDAS

As mentioned in the previous section, some comets of the Jupiter group occupy the same types of orbits as the Hildas. According to Kresak (1979), a comet can be captured from a low eccentricity orbit between Jupiter and

Saturn (Region A of Fig. 15–4) and assume an orbit with aphelion well inside the orbit of Jupiter (Region D). Comet Oterma, for example, occupied this unstable 3/2 resonance from 1937 to 1963 until it was accelerated by Jupiter into another orbit. Some Hilda asteroids may be such captured comets.

Like the Trojans, the 31 numbered Hilda asteroids experience libration cycles (typically 250 to 300 years). Most members of the group avoid close approaches to Jupiter by a mechanism that is based on the near resonance of the mean motions of the asteroid and Jupiter. Most of the Hildas exhibit small or moderate values of proper inclination (Schubart, 1982).

Very few Hildas have been studied in detail. Degewij & Van Houten (1979) presented data to show that both 958 Asplinda and 1162 Larissa have high albedos (0.30 and 0.18 respectively), while 1512 Oulu has a low albedo (0.03). Only P, C, and D types are represented among the Hildas. Earlier published data indicating M and S types among the Hildas were erroneous. (Table 15-2).

Let S, J, T be three bodies whose masses are s, j, t, situated so as to form an equilateral triangle of side a; then the accelerations produced on T by S and J are

$$\frac{ks}{a^2} \text{ along TS}, \qquad \frac{kj}{a^2} \text{ along TJ},$$

or

$$s \cdot TS \cdot \frac{k}{a^3} \text{ along TS}, \qquad j \cdot TJ \frac{k}{a^3} \text{ along TJ}.$$

Let M be the centre of gravity of S, J, and G the centre of gravity of S, J, T; then by a well-known proposition the above accelerations compound into

$$(s+j) \cdot TM \cdot \frac{k}{a^3} \text{ along TM}.$$

Which is equivalent to

$$(s+j+t) \, TG \cdot \frac{k}{a^3} \text{ along TG}.$$

By symmetry the accelerations of S, J are

$$(s+j+t) \, SG \cdot \frac{k}{a^3}, \qquad (s+j+t) \, JG \cdot \frac{k}{a^3}$$

along SG, JG respectively.

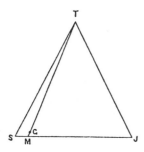

Now if the three bodies were rotating about G with uniform angular velocity ω, their velocities would be ωGT, ωGS, ωGJ, and their accelerations $\omega^2 GT$, $\omega^2 GS$, $\omega^2 GJ$, along TG, SG, JG.

Hence if ω^2 be equal to $(s+j+t) \cdot \frac{k}{a^3}$, the three bodies will continue to rotate uniformly about G under their mutual attractions.

It will be seen that the result holds whatever be the law of Force, provided it is merely a function of the distance, not of the direction.

Fig. 15–8. *This form of Lagrange's proposition was given by Crommelin (1906), shortly after the discovery of the first Trojan asteroid.*

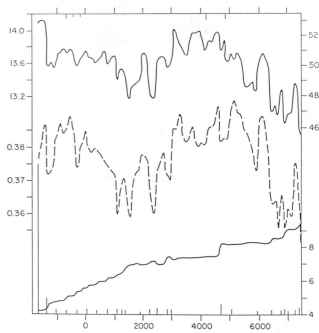

Fig. 15–7. *Orbital elements of the asteroid-like object Chiron. The variations in the orbital elements a (and P), e and i between the encounter with Saturn in −1664 and about the year 7400. The vertical lines inside the frame of the figure represent close approaches to Saturn (bottom) and Uranus (top). Only approaches D within 2 AU are marked, the lengths of the lines being proportional to $D^{-1} - 0.5$.*

CHIRON

During a systematic search for distant solar system objects with the Schmidt telescope at Palomar, Charles Kowal found the 'Mother Lode'. On November 1, 1977, he recognized a slow-moving object on three plates taken two weeks earlier. At photographic magnitude 18, it had moved just 3′ per day, much slower than the usual 8′ to 15′ daily motion of main-belt asteroids.

The discovery of 'Object Kowal', later given the permanent designation 2060 Chiron, created a sensation. While too small to be a planet, no other object had been found orbiting between Saturn and Uranus. Similarly, it was too big to be called a comet, so it was added to the list of asteroids for want of another name. Chiron is the first member of a new class of asteroids termed Centaurs, which name has been reserved for asteroids outside the Jovian system.

The orbit of Chiron is strange in an even more interesting way—it is chaotic, that is, unstable. Fig. 15–7 (Kowal *et al*, 1979) shows the variation in the period, eccentricity and inclination of Chiron's orbit between 1664 BC and 7400 AD. Currently, $P = 50.6832$ years, $a = 13.6954$ AU, $e = 0.3786$ and $i = 6.9229°$. In 7400 AD, the inclination will have increased to more than 9°, and the period will have decreased to less than 46 years. There is a good chance that Chiron will some day be in an orbit similar to that of a short-period comet, but before that occurs, it may instead be ejected from the solar system on a hyperbolic trajectory (Everhart, 1979; Kowal, 1979).

Chiron's origin is equally uncertain. In 1664 BC, Chiron passed within 0.1 AU of Saturn (about the distance of Saturn's moon Phoebe). Its orbital motion prior to that date is impossible to determine, but Hartmann *et al* (1981) speculate that "many such planetesimals may have formed from mixtures of ice and carbonaceous-like stony material near Jupiter or Saturn's orbit, and may have spent varying time in situations such as the Oort cloud, captured outer satellite orbits, and/or chaotic orbits like Chiron's." The similarity in infrared color index between Chiron and Phoebe tends to support this view.

Physically, Chiron is approximately 180–250 km in diameter. It has been classed as a C–type object (sub-class B), with a range of low-albedo mixtures of carbonaceous-rich, black silicate soil and icy grains thought to be present on the surface. Typical of other dark, stony objects it is believed to have an albedo in the range of 0.05 to 0.10, with $V(1,0) = 6.9$. Visually, it can reach magnitude 15 at perihelion, but there is some evidence it changed brightness abruptly a few years ago, possibly indicative of comet-like activity (Lebofsky *et al*, 1984).

TABLE 15–2 CLASSIFICATIONS OF HILDA ASTEROIDS	
Minor Planet	Class
153 Hilda	P
190 Ismene	P
334 Chicago	C
361 Bononia	DP
499 Venusia	P
748 Simeisa	P
958 Asplinda	—
1038 Tuckia	DTU
1144 Oda	D
1162 Larissa	P
1180 Rita	P
1212 Francette	P
1256 Normannia	D
1268 Libya	P
1269 Rollandia	D
1345 Potomac	EMP
1439 Vogtia	EMPFU
1512 Oulu	P
1529 Oterma	P
1578 Kirkwood	D
1746 Brouwer	D
1748 Mauderli	D
1754 Cunningham	P
1902 Shaposhnikov	EMP
1911 Schubart	P
2067 Aksnes	P
2246 Bowell	D
2312 Duboshin	D
2760 1980 TU6	EMP

Table 15–2. The Hilda asteroids observed in the eight-color survey. Data courtesy of David Tholen (1984b).

SPACE
MISSIONS   16

The proper way to exploit space was not to mine the planets, where you must grub deep into the crust to find a few stingy ore pockets. No, the asteroids had all the minerals man would ever need, in developing his extraterrestrial colonies and on Earth herself. Freely available minerals, especially on the metallic asteroids from the core of the ancient planet. Just land and help yourself.

Poul Anderson, 1960

Asteroids have figured in the visions of science fiction writers; the long-range plans of military analysts; the nightmares of 'space lawyers'; and the earth-orbiting telescopes of astronomers. They have been suggested as sites of 21st century farms, mining operations and battle stations, and even 'generation spaceships'. Taken together, these concepts have established the asteroids as the next frontier of human development.

TELESCOPES AND SPACECRAFT

In 1961, the American Rocket Society conducted a conference in New York City called Space Flight Report To The Nation (Grey & Grey, 1962). Twenty-four leaders of the U.S. space program attended, including Arthur Kantrowitz, director of the Avco-Everett Research Laboratories and William Pickering, director of the Jet Propulsion Laboratory.

In a panel discussion, Pickering stated that he did "not know whether any serious thought has been given to actual landings on the asteroids. I suppose if one could land on the Moon or on one of the planets, landing on one of the asteroids should not be much different. However, I believe by far the most interesting thing to do is to land on either Mars or Venus." Kantrowitz, apparently more intrigued with asteroids, queried Pickering. "I wonder why you consider that definitely more interesting? It might even be easier to land on one of these asteroids, because they do not have much gravity. Further, they do have a history similar to that of the planets, so that many of the same sort of scientific questions might be answered by landing on one of the asteroids." Pickering replied that "It is true that landing on one of the asteroids is simply a rendezvous

problem, and one could presumably accomplish it. I think the question really is whether or not an asteroid is a piece of meteoric material. I grant you that it would be an interesting thing to do, but I'd rather go to Mars or Venus first. I believe we have a lot more to learn there." The direction set by Pickering guided solar system exploration for the next 25 years. The United States has sent two landers to Mars and probed the atmosphere of Venus, but has not yet sent a spacecraft anywhere near an asteroid.

Some spacecraft have already gone to the asteroid belt, but they were just passing through. Pioneer 10 was first, in 1972, followed by Pioneer 11 in 1973, Voyager 1 and Voyager 2 in 1980. None of them passed near a known asteroid, and all survived the passage to the outer planets intact.

The year after the New York conference, Harold Goodwin (1962), director of NASA's Office of Program Development, wrote of a flight to the earth-crosser Hermes. "A fascinating possibility, but one that poses many problems, is an investigation of Hermes, preferably by a manned flight. In some ways, this would be an even greater feat than the first manned expedition to Mars." NASA even published a massive *Planetary Flight Handbook* which contained a series of charts and tables of trajectory data associated with one-way trips from Earth to Jupiter, Ceres and Vesta between 1960 and 1970 (Ross, 1966). While funds for such ambitious space missions seemed nearly unlimited in the 1960's, a much bleaker scene has faced the planetary exploration community in recent years. A NASA scientific advisory board, the Committee on Planetary and Lunar Exploration (COMPLEX, 1980) has recommended "that spacecraft exploration of asteroids should be undertaken and considers that it will produce a qualitative increase in our understanding of these bodies." COMPLEX established three scientific objectives for missions to the asteroids:

1. To determine their composition and bulk density.

2. To investigate the surface morphology including evidence for endogenic and exogenic processes and evidence concerning interiors of precursor bodies.

3. To determine the internal properties, including states of magnetization of several carefully selected on the basis of their diversity.

According to Helin & Hulkower (1981), a multiple asteroid rendezvous mission cannot be accomplished ballistically by a single spacecraft equipped with a payload capable of fulfilling the COMPLEX objectives. Either an ion drive (also known as a solar electric propulsion system) or a craft equipped with solar sails is needed. Development of a solar sail is being pursued by the World Space Foundation. Solar sails have an unlimited $\Delta - V$ capability, allowing asteroid survey missions of indefinite length (Henson, 1979). But more recently, it was discovered by Chen-wan Yen at JPL that a ballistic spacecraft can rendezvous with one or more main-belt asteroids. Employing ion propulsion as well, he has identified several multiple fly-by and rendezvous missions one of which could visit seven asteroids in 14 years (Friedman & Sagan, 1984).

An actual landing-sample return mission to an asteroid was studied as early as 1964. The target was a favorite one, Eros. The details of such a mission, designed to return about 100 kg of Eros surface material to Earth, were given by Meissinger & Greenstadt (1971). Since then, experience has been gained with the Viking robot landers on Mars, which will serve as a prototype for the first asteroid lander. A typical example of a shuttle-launched sample return mission is shown in Fig. 16–1 (Niehoff, 1978).

One peculiarity of 'touching down' on an asteroid deserves mention. Site selection will likely be done on the basis of where the pole is located—since surface gravity on Eros is only one-thousandth that on Earth, the spacecraft may bounce off after landing! This rather embarrassing incident can be avoided by landing at one of the poles (Fig. 16–2), where centrifugal effects are minimized.

To further minimize the bounce effect, it has been suggested that the craft anchor itself to the ground by using a winch or explosive pitons fired out on cables, but this method will not work on a regolith-covered object. If the lander is also a roving vehicle, the problems are increased. A configuration in the form of a mesh ball or series of loops like the Lunar rover wheel used by the Apollo astronauts might work; it could flatten itself against the surface, and use adhesives to 'glue' itself to the rocks (Lunan, 1979).

A manned mission to an asteroid was studied by Alfven & Arrhenius (1970) and Staley (1970). While the former study concluded that a person could not be 'lost in space' by jumping off an asteroid, Staley showed that such a danger does exist. In any case, a manned mission will require a major national commitment, as more than 20 space shuttle launches would be required to deliver enough propellant and materials into orbit for the spacecraft (Niehoff, 1977).

Here is a brief survey of fly-by probes and earth-orbiting telescopes that have either been completed or are being planned.

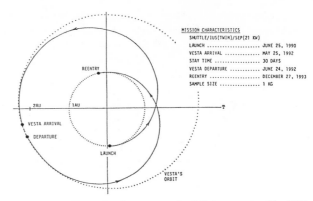

Fig. 16–1. *Example of a spacecraft visit to an asteroid: 1990 Vesta sample return mission to be launched by the Space Shuttle on June 25, 1990, arrive at Vesta May 25, 1992 and stay for 30 days, depart Vesta on June 24, 1992 and return to Earth with a 1 kg sample on December 27, 1993. Niehoff, 1978.*

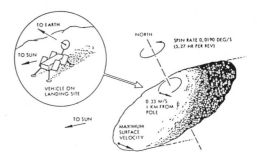

Fig. 16–2. *Landing site selection on rotating small asteroid; assumed diameter: 35 by 16 by 7 km. To avoid being flung off the asteroid, a position near the pole is indicated. Meissinger & Greenstadt, 1971.*

ASTEREX: A project of the European Space Agency, this mission was rejected by ESA's Science Program Committee in 1981. The proposed craft had a weight of 750 kg. Designed to carry an imaging camera, infrared spectrometer, and radar altimeter, Asterex would have had a three year lifetime.

AGORA: A revised version of Asterex, known as Agora (Asteroidal Gravity, Optical and Radar Analysis) was considered by ESA in 1983. It was recommended that a technological study should be carried out regarding the development of solar electric propulsion within Europe, and that a joint ESA-NASA study examine a possible collaborative asteroid mission. An Agora-like craft will likely be sent to the asteroids in the 1990's.

The AGORA spacecraft, while not approved by the ESA, serves as a prototype of what the first dedicated asteroid probe will be. Before considering the overall aspects of such a fly-by mission, here is an outline of the scientific payload, from the AGORA Assessment Study (ESA, SCI(83)5, Sept. 1983).

1. Imaging system. The objectives of the imaging system, which consists of a wide angle camera and a high resolution camera are (1) the size, shape and

volume of the asteroid; (2) mass; (3) surface properties including morphology (4) rotation period and pole orientation. At 500 km, the high resolution camera will have a resolution of 5 meters per pixel. Both cameras will employ several filters and polarizers.

2. Infrared spectrometer. This will provide information on lateral transport processes on regolith-covered asteroids; allow definition of mineralogical boundaries; characterize the chemical nature of the substrate; and allow identification of different classes of silicates and minerals.

3. Radar altimeter/Microwave radiometer. This device will measure the height of the spacecraft above the asteroid within a distance of 5,000 km to an accuracy of 100 m; the surface slope between 1 and 10 degrees to an accuracy of 0.5 degree; the brightness temperature with an accuracy of 0.5 degree Kelvin; and infer the temperature gradient for the upper 10 meters of the surface.

4. Gamma Ray spectrometer. This experiment measures elemental abundances for certain elements in the upper half-meter of the surface. The gamma rays, which originate from the decay of primordial radioactive nuclei and the interaction of cosmic rays, have energies which are characteristic of specific nuclei.

5. Test mass device. To determine an asteroid's mass, a reflector 20 cm in size will be released two days before the encounter. As it travels between the asteroid and the spacecraft, the perturbations can be measured to yield the asteroidal mass to an accuracy of 5%.

6. Magnetometer. It is not known if asteroids possess a magnetic field. This device will measure the ambient magnetic field during the rendezvous phase or put upper limits on its magnetic properties.

7. Dust Detector. Due to collision and fragmentation, asteroids are believed to be a major source of interplanetary dust. This detector will measure the mass and velocity of impacting particles with masses on the order of 10^{-12} grams or less.

Three types of asteroid-spacecraft missions are possible-fly-by, rendezvous or landing (with the possibility of sample return). The baseline AGORA mission called for rendezvous with at least three asteroids. In the case of a Vesta rendezvous, the craft was scheduled to go into orbit at an altitude of 100 km for at least 20 days. During this period, the asteroid would be completely mapped with a resolution of 3 km, with selected areas mapped at 1 km resolution (Fig. 16-3).

The mission planners concluded that the combination of an Ariane launch, a Mars gravity assist and chemical propulsion did not yield any possibilities for an asteroid mission. Only ion propulsion, which has an exhaust velocity 10 times higher than a chemical motor (30 km/s versus 3 km/s) will suffice. The lack of such a rocket motor is

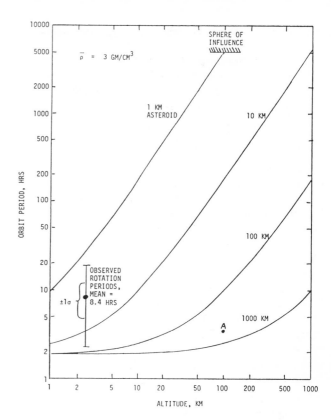

Fig. 16-3. *Orbital characteristics around asteroids. the point labelled A indicates the proposed orbital period of the AGORA spacecraft around Vesta. Niehoff, 1978.*

Photo. 16-1. *Laurel Wilkening of the University of Arizona has been a prime exponent of space missions to asteroids and comets.*

a major obstacle to sending a probe to the asteroid belt. The ion drive on Agora would be the prime consumer of power, needing about 4000 W at full thrust; the payload and other systems need only 300 W. Two solar arrays, 30 m by 3.3 m, were designed to generate nearly 25 kW of power (Balogh, 1984).

GALILEO: Our first close-up look at an asteroid was to have taken place on 6 December 1986, when the Galileo spacecraft, enroute to Jupiter, made a flyby of 29 Amphitrite. Originally, Galileo was to be launched by inertial upper stage booster from the space shuttle, which would have sent it through the asteroid belt more than once.

As a result, several potential asteroid targets were identified. But plans were then changed to use a Centaur rocket: the two-year shorter trip to Jupiter appeared to eliminate any chance of an asteroid flyby. It was only early in 1984 that mission planners realized Galileo could flyby Amphitrite, at a point 224 million km from Earth.

On 18 July 1984, 22 scientists met in Washington to assess the merits of an Amphitrite flyby. Changes in the basic mission were judged to be minimal—a delay in arrival time at Jupiter of three months and a 3% loss of scientific data. Additional mission costs of $15 million would not have to be expended until 1990–91. The potential benefits, on the other hand, were judged to be extremely significant. According to the working group report, "it should be possible to resolve the crucial debate as to whether S–asteroids are the collisionally-stripped cores of differentiated bodies, or less geologically evolved objects. The radiometric observations should provide a significant test and calibration of thermal models used to interpret disk-integrated measurements of asteroids made from Earth or from near-Earth spacecraft such as IRAS." Data bearing on the S–type debate was to have been provided by the Near Infrared Mapping Spectrometer (NIMS). "During the flyby NIMS will obtain a global map of Amphitrite in each of 204 spectral bands between 0.7 and 5.0 microns; there will be about 1000 resolution elements over the asteroid's disk. This approach can be expected to provide a very powerful tool for deciphering the petrologic history of the minerals on the surface of Amphitrite." Perhaps most exciting were the pictures Galileo's CCD camera could have taken. Up to 20% of the surface was to have been photographed at a resolution of 200 meters, with global coverage at a few kilometers resolution. Phase angles up to 120 degrees would have been available during the flyby. Assuming a flyby speed of 15 km/sec and a "miss distance" of 10,000 km, Galileo was scheduled to spend two hours within 100,000 km of Amphitrite (200 km diameter).

David Morrison, chairman of the Solar System Exploration Committee and member of the working group, wrote NASA administrator James Beggs in August 1984 to recommend approval of the flyby. "It will permit the U.S. to take the lead in asteroid studies, rather than forcing us to come in second or third to the Russians or Europeans. The alternative—to fly past this exciting object without even turning on the spacecraft instruments, thereby deferring our first exploration of the asteroids by nearly a decade seems indefensible." On 24 December 1984, Beggs formally approved the flyby. (Beatty, 1985; AW & ST 24 September 1984). On 28 January 1986, all these plans proved useless as the space shuttle that was to have carried Galileo exploded shortly after liftoff. It is unknown when Galileo will now be launched or whether a different asteroid flyby will become possible.

HIPPARCOS: An astrometric satellite scheduled for launch in 1988, this ESA earth-orbiting telescope will have as its primary task the accurate plotting of the positions of 100,000 stars. It will also be able to search for binary asteroids by direct imaging, with some 350 asteroids brighter than $B = 13.0$ being accessible (Schober, 1982). Hipparcos will be able to observe asteroids 100 km in diameter at a distance of 2 to 3 AU, corresponding to an apparent diame-

Photo. 16–2. *Artists' conception of a Mariner Mark II spacecraft, which is scheduled to study asteroids at close range in the 1990's.*

ter of 0.05 arc second. A secondary component is expected to be more than 0.1 arc second from the primary. Periodic variations from a smooth orbit, or even direct observations of a faint secondary, are possible if the same asteroid is scanned several times. From the observed orbital rates and absolute distances within the binary system, masses and densities could be determined (Cunningham, 1983a).

In 1984, some 8,000 stars between −30° and +30° ecliptic latitude were submitted by astronomers at the University of Texas to the Hipparcos project. Observations of selected minor planets with respect to Hipparcos stars with ground-based telescopes and the Space Telescope will allow the Hipparcos system to be referred to a dynamical system defined by the motion of the minor planets. Even a small number of such observations could make a significant contribution to the Hipparcos reference frame.

AMSAT: The West German branch of the Radio Amateur Satellite Corporation is planning to send a 300 kg probe to the asteroid belt, with a launch on the Ariane–4 rocket. DFVRL, the West German space agency, has completed a mission feasibility study; the Max-Planck Institute in Lindau is involved in developing the scientific payload; and AMSAT itself is working on the basic spacecraft design. Plans call for a 16 cm Ritchey-Chretien telescope to do infrared spectroscopy between 1 and 5 microns. It will employ a cryogenic refrigerator to provide 2,500 hours of operation at 80° Kelvin (Cosmovici *et al*, 1983; Ganoe, 1984).

EUROPEAN PLANS: When Agora was canceled, it was recommended that a technological study be carried out regarding the development of solar electric propulsion within Europe. An ESA-NASA study, called the Joint Working Group on Cooperation in the Exploration of the

Planetary System, began an assessment in 1984 of the Multiple Asteroid Orbiter with Solar Electric Propulsion. MAOSEP is in competition with two other candidates—a Titan Probe and Saturn Orbiter, and a Mars Surface Rover. The study on all three was completed by the end of 1985. A joint ESA/NASA primitive bodies science study group, co-chaired by Laurel Wilkening and Dieter Stoffler, held its first meeting in London in December, 1984.

Its consensus is that a comet nucleus sample return should have the highest priority, followed by mainbelt asteroid multiple rendezvous and flyby and comet coma sample return missions. Early in 1985, NASA stated that a mission of the Agora type will not be considered for inclusion in its planetary program, even in collaboration with ESA. As it is too expensive for ESA to develop alone, the Europeans began an assessment of a simplified asteroid rendezvous mission in the framework of a test flight for the electric propulsion module (EPM). One of the test flights of the upgraded Ariane rocket (Ariane 5) will be earmarked for the mission, thus reducing costs substantially. Both Ariane 5 and the EPM are scheduled for testing in 1995. Development of a simplified AGORA is likely, as it will be necessary to test the EPM and gain experience in low-thrust navigation and rendezvous techniques before a comet sample return mission can be performed (Cunningham, 1985b).

Meanwhile, ESA has approved construction of an Infrared Space Observatory. ISO consists of a cooled 0.6 m diameter telescope in a 3-axis stabilized spacecraft, and has a planned lifetime of 1.5 years. To quote from the phase A study (SCI (82)6), "For asteroids, very little is known about their spectrum above 5 microns. Clearly these studies would benefit enormously from both the high spectral resolution and very high sensitivity of an infrared instrument operating outside the Earth's atmosphere. The 1–5 micron spectrum of asteroids is specially interesting for a determination of their surface composition. Some ground-based data exists for the largest asteroids and a 1–5 micron camera array aboard ISO could substantially improve this data by extending the spectral range into regions of earth-atmospheric opacity and by increasing the number of samples. Broad-band photometry longward of 10 microns permits a determination of diameters and albedos. ISO could make such measurements for a large number of asteroids."

AMERICAN PLANS: The first of the Mariner Mark II outer planet/primitive body missions was scheduled to be launched in July 1990 (Photo 16–2). Known as the Comet Rendezvous Asteroid Flyby (CRAF) mission, it would have flown past 772 Tanete and the comet Kopff (Fig. 16–4), but a start on this project scheduled for October 1986 has been delayed at least one year for budgetary reasons. A July, 1991 launch would see a flyby of comet Kopff and 86 Semele (type C, 112 km). The CRAF spacecraft may be equipped with an 18.7 cm aperture Imaging Science Subsystem. If it were left on for weeks as CRAF passed through the asteroid belt, Gehrels (1986) has calculated that magnitude-density relations can be obtained for objects as small as a few meters. Studies

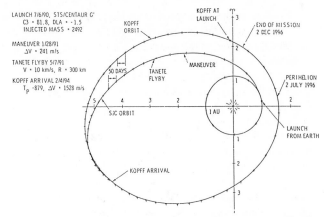

Fig. 16–4. *A proposed American space mission to comet Kopff, with a flyby of asteroid Tanete in 1991. Although this particular mission will not be performed, it is typical of the mission scenarios being envisaged for the Mariner Mark II spacecraft. Stetson et al, 1984.*

of such small asteroids are of primary importance, because "the magnitude-frequency law is basic for the understanding of origins, collisional fragmentation, tensile strength of the bodies, and interrelations of asteroids, comets and meteorites." The Mariner Mark II program will consist of 6 spacecraft, each weighing 1024.5 kg. As currently envisioned, the third in the series will be a Main Belt Asteroid Rendezvous mission (Stetson *et al*, 1984).

Still in the early stages of design is a Large Deployable Reflector. This 10-meter-class instrument will operate in the infrared and submillimeter domains (0.03 to 1 mm). Its resolution in the IR will be a ten-fold improvement over current equipment, and should thus greatly improve IR spectral studies of comets and asteroids (Field and Chaisson, 1985)

SOVIET PLANS: The latest Soviet strategy was stated in August, 1986 by Vyacheslav Dalebanov, assistant director of the Institute of Space Research of the USSR Academy of Sciences.

> In 1990 the USA plans to send a space probe towards Mars to study the planet from orbit. In the opinion of many Western scientists, co-ordinating the programme of this flight with the Phobos project, which will be realized two years earlier, would permit obtaining maximum scientific results.

> Sending a space probe into the asteroid belt appears to be no less interesting. A flight trajectory can be selected so that in a few loops around the Sun it will meet 10 to 20 minor planets. The most effective flight variant on which Soviet scientists are currently working, is to use, as in the Vera case, one space probe for several parallel missions. For example, the probe first flies to Venus or Mars, explores them and then turns back to the Earth. Within the Earth's pull, it makes a gravitational maneuver and sets out for the asteroid.

> The study of asteroids will apparently have to

be done from a fly-past trajectory. However, landing sounders on one or two of them could be attempted. Only yesterday such a project would have been thought fantasy. Today it is in the immediate plans of Soviet cosmonautics. Just as the Vera and Phobos projects, it will be international.

The Soviet Union is planning to launch a mission to the Martian moon Phobos in 1988. Viewed by some U.S. planetary scientists as a "poor man's asteroid mission", it could return data related to understanding small objects in the solar system. One craft will hover within 100 meters of Phobos and fire both laser and ion beams to vaporize surface material for analysis. It will also drop a lander that will have the ability to hop across Phobos' surface. A second craft will perform the same experiments at Deimos.

In 1991, the Soviets are planning to launch a twin spacecraft mission to Venus and Vesta. Once in space, the craft will separate; the dedicated asteroid vehicle will flyby Vesta and drop a lander onto its surface, which will carry a camera, gamma ray spectrometer and X-ray spectrometer (Couvalt, 1985).

SPACE TELESCOPE: While little time will be available for asteroid work on the space telescope (due for launch from the space shuttle in the late 1980's), observations will likely be made of a few specific targets. "The Planetary Camera will have a resolution for a typical main-belt asteroid of about 100 km, not high enough to yield geological structure. This resolution is clearly great enough, however, to search for albedo or color variations on the largest asteroids. For 1 Ceres, an image would include about a hundred pixels, for 4 Vesta and 2 Pallas, about 30. Based on some recent occultation photometry, it has been suggested that several asteroids may be double or multiple. The Planetary Camera can easily resolve this question; the suggested companion of 432 Herculina would be separated from it by more than 10 pixels." (Morrison, 1979).

MINING

> The economic development of the moon and the asteroids and Mars is very much going to be a main investment opportunity of the next century.
>
> Thomas Paine, former NASA administrator, 1986

Quite literally, the cutting edge of the next frontier will be the mining of asteroids. It has been estimated that a 200-meter asteroid contains more than $1 billion worth of platinum, and enough mass to build 50 ten-gigawatt solar power satellites (Williams, 1982).

The concept of mining asteroids is not new. In 1957, rocket pioneer Hermann Oberth wrote that "It is easier and cheaper, from the power-requirement viewpoint, to go and get such a planet (asteroid) as a raw-material source for further work than to bring everything up from Earth and build it there. The asteroids would be wonderful

Photo. 16–3. *John Lewis of the University of Arizona is director of the Arizona Center for Space Resources, which will coordinate efforts to exploit the asteroids as a natural resource in space.*

Photo. 16–4. *The discovery photograph of the earth-crosser 1982 DB. Comet du Toit-Hartley is also visible in the lower left. So far, 1982 DB is the only asteroid known which has any possibility of being economical compared to retrieving materials from the lunar surface. Even here there is only one mission opportunity in the next quarter century with a ΔV of less than 100 m/sec: a launch in 1998, returning in 2002. Cutler & Hughes (1985). Photo courtesy of Eleanor Helin.*

sources of raw materials and would play a large part in future space travel since they are easily accessible because of their weak gravitational force and their small size. The asteroids are obviously natural space stations." In an interview for this book, Dr. John Lewis of the University of Arizona explored the rationale for and practical problems of mining the asteroids.

> The whole business of the economic exploitation of asteroids is predicated upon there being asteroids that are energetically close to Earth. All of the factors that lead us to assess the exploitation of these asteroids as being economically feasible could not have been said before 1973, because there weren't any asteroids of that type known. The first logical necessity is that you discover asteroids that are nearby. Historically, this has been very difficult to do. Most of the Earth-approaching asteroids are very small—they need to get within a few million kilometers of Earth to be detected. They

TABLE 16–1
Allowable Return Mass of Processed Metals as a
Function of Ballistic Return Velocity Increment (Δv)

Return Δv (km/sec.)	Tons of Returned Mass per Ton of Invested Mass	Examples	Launch Date (or Frequency)	Round-Trip Travel Time
0.1	100	1982 DB at Special Times	2000–01	2 Years
0.2	49			
0.5	19.2	1982 DB, 1943 Anteros, 433 Eros, and 1982 XB	Occasionally	2–3 Years
1.0	8.9			
1.9	4.0	Phobos	Every 2 Years	2 Years
2.4	3.0	Lunar Surface	Frequent	7 Days
5	1.0	Martian Surface	Every 2 Years	2 Years
		1982 DB	September 2001	4 Months
		Several Near-Earth Asteroids	Frequent	1–5 Years

Table 16–1. *Allowable Return Mass of Processed Metals as a Function of Ballistic Return Velocity Increment (Δv). Table from O'Leary, 1983. Assume $\Delta v = 5$ km/sec. for the trip out from low Earth orbit, the same cryogenic rocket with exaust velocity 4kn/sec. is used for the return trip as for the trip out, the rocket is refuled with liquid oxygen (and possibly liquid hydrogen) obtained at the astroid, and the materials are aerobraked at the Earth prior to landing or orbit insertion.*

move at very high angular rates across the sky (up to 90° per day), so classical methods of search, such as time exposure, may not show them at all.

The second thing you need, which is absolutely crucial, is an approximate compositional characterization for each new asteroid. This means an infrared and visible reflectance spectrum. Since some of these asteroids are only visible for a couple of days, the spectroscopic effort has to be closely coordinated with the discovery effort. This could swallow up $1 million a year. The Space Science and Applications Office of NASA spends $1 billion each year, so that's only 0.1% of their budget and its an investment in their future.

But the way NASA is structured, there isn't any part of NASA that's responsible for space industrialization. What you have to do is build a constituency—find all the people who are interested in advanced propulsion techniques, aerocapture techniques, geochemical mapper missions, resources and strategic materials, solar power satellites and the use of large masses of material in low Earth orbit for structures. (To this end, the Arizona Center for Space Resources was established in 1985).

The metals that are clearly profitable to bring back from space are the ones that have the highest unit cost—$10,000 to $20,000 a pound—and that is the platinum group metals. These four metals (rhodium, ruthenium, palladium and platinum) are four of the five most hard-to-get materials on earth because their production is almost 100% derived from South Africa and the Soviet Union. The world's needs are concentrated in the West, because the uses of these metals are closely correlated with high technology. They are used as catalysts, corrosion-resistant coatings, and switches in microelectronics.

We are very dependant on Canada for many strategic metals. But the top two things on the list are also the two that Canada can't provide, and that is chromium and the platinum metals. There is a class of meteorites, whose parent body we have not yet identified, that contains chromium nitride. Every meteorite that falls on the Earth contains a higher concentration of platinum-group metals than the richest ore body on Earth. Not only that, in meteorites these metals reside in the iron-nickel-cobalt alloy phase, and this means in any process which simply crushes these meteorites and magnetically extracts the metal, it takes all the platinum-group metals as well. The carbonyl process can then give an ultra-pure dust of platinum-group metals. These metals are produced in exactly this way as a byproduct at the Sudbury refinery of International Nickel Company in Sudbury, Ontario.

In essence, the carbonyl process involves passing carbon monoxide over the asteroidal material. By adjusting the pressure and temperature, some metals will form gaseous carbonyls while other metals remain behind. By directing the carbonyls to an empty chamber with the proper pressure and temperature, solid metal will be deposited. Different metals are deposited at different temperatures and pressures, alloying very pure metal deposits to be obtained easily.'

137

The development of solar sails, which require no fuel and could be used for transportation between high Earth orbit and the asteroids, will make mining of the asteroids even more attractive. Lewis has found a variation of the carbonyl process in which solar sails can be made economically—a laser is used to decompose a metal carbonyl and deposit a very thin, reflective metal film on a thin support framework (Ganoe, 1984b).

If you are standing on the surface of an Earth-approaching asteroid, the amount of energy you need to return to Earth is so small you can almost forget about it. Take 1982 DB as an example—the speed you need to leave that asteroid is 0.06 km/sec. This means the amount of fuel you need is less than 1% of the mass of the payload you are returning. To get from the asteroid belt back to Earth, typical $\Delta - V$'s would be 4 km/sec. The energy that is required goes up as the square of the speed, so a departure speed nearly 100 times greater requires 10,000 times as much energy per pound of returned material (Fig. 16–5).

Just put this in economic terms. We know it costs $1,000 a pound to put a payload in orbit around the Earth from the ground. It is cheaper to bring it down from the Moon—a couple of hundred dollars a pound. If you bring it back from the asteroid belt it also costs several hundred dollars a pound. Mercury, Venus and Mars are hideously expensive. From 1982 DB, to bring a pound of payload back to low Earth orbit or the ground costs about 10 cents! (Table 16–1; O'Leary, 1983).

A mining spacecraft has to be capable of rendezvous and docking with the asteroid (the word landing is inappropriate-they are too small), lifting dirt off the surface, seiving it so it won't take anything bigger than your fist, crushing it all down into a fine powder, magnetically extracting the metal component and then loading this dust (less than 1 mm diameter) into a payload bay. It does this for a couple of years until the asteroid gets back to an energetically favorable position for a launch back to Earth, and launches the payload. Each miner could produce 100 tons per year for a lifetime of 10 years—that is only 5 ounces per minute, which means the crusher can be the size of a telephone.

The vehicle which returns to Earth would have a small solid-propellant rocket engine, and a cold-gas jet for attitude stabilization and midcourse correction. It will line up precisely to graze the Earth's atmosphere, and will have a large aerocapture heat shield, comparable in size to the space shuttle. The ram pressure passing through the atmosphere will be about 1 bar for 10 minutes. On the first grazing pas-

	TABLE 16–2 Approximate Chemical Composition (%) of Meteorites and Lunar Soil Samples		
Component	Ordinary Chondrites	Carbonaceous Chondrites	Lunar Samples
Silicates	75–86	76–90	98–100
Water	.2–.3	1–21	0
Free Metals	8.3–19	.1–3.5	0–1
Carbon	0	.1–3.8	0
Nitrogen	0	.01–.3	0

Table 16–2. *Approximate Chemical Composition(%) of Meteorites and Lunar Soil Samples. Table from O'Leary, 1977. Copyright 1977 by the AAAS.*

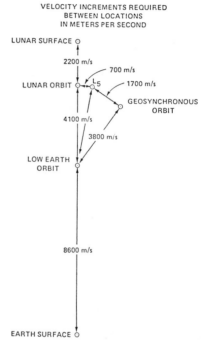

Fig. 16–5. *Velocity increments to transfer between points in space. At this scale, the DV needed to move from 1982 DB to Earth, 60m/sec, is too small to show. From Space Settlements, NASA SP–413 (ed. Johnson), 1977.*

sage, enough heat will be dissipated to slow down the payload so it is gravitationally captured by Earth. After a few passes the payload ends up in a circular orbit, and then there will be a small rocket burn to lift periapsis out of the atmosphere. The payload will then rendezvous with a space station, with the processing done alongside in a little factory. It will be possible to return materials reasonable economically by the mid 1990's.

The atmospheric breaking concept for cargo ships was first considered by Preston-Thomas (1952), who envisaged "a system in which fuel and cargoes are derived from satellites and asteroids. The crew of the original ship will build the necessary heavy equipment, stations and ships, originally at Deimos and later from material from any of the low-gravity bodies of the inner solar system.

Once we have a permanent manned presence in space," continued Lewis, "you want to supply the needs of those people from space. It costs $1,000 to lift a pound of water into orbit! It's crazy. But perhaps one-third of the Earth-approaching asteroids are carbonaceous. They have reflectance spectra that look just like C2 or C3 carbonaceous chondrites, which have up to 5% by weight of water (Table 16–2). You can get it out with a simple solar cooker. Those same asteroids are rich in carbon and nitrogen, extractable sulfur compounds, soluble sulfates and phosphates- all the things you need for life. There would be nothing in a carbonaceous asteroid that you would want to return to Earth, but there would be a lot that you would use in space.

After you extract the metals, there is quite a pile of non-metallic impurities in the iron— gallium, germanium, arsenic and antimony. The next generation of solid-state devices are going to be gallium-arsenide. The gallium-arsenide fabrication into large crystals appears to be something that would be a lot easier to do in zero G. So if you had your source of gallium and arsenic up there, and the zero G conditions, that is another area where industrialization will be important.

(The space-based gallium-arsenide market is expected to exceed $100 billion annually within 20 years; Kolcum, 1984).

If you have large amounts of iron and nickel in low Earth orbit with a device to make I-beams, all of a sudden you are in business to make solar power satellites cheaply. When SPS were being planned, nothing was known about near-Earth asteroids as sources of mass. Now the economics of SPS has to be reassessed.

The ability to deliver large amounts of material into Earth orbit is also of great interest to the military. Satellites or battle stations in orbit, as envisioned in the Strategic Defense Initiative (better known as Star Wars), will have to be protected, or "hardened", against attack. In the long run, this will require extraterrestrial materials. To this end, the Civilian Advisory Council on National Space Policy has called for an immediate program of asteroidal exploration "to gain new knowledge about these critical bodies." (Pournelle, 1983).

The popular "mass driver" concept, first proposed by Arthur C. Clarke (1950), is not necessary in this scenario. Essentially an electromagnetic catapult, a mass driver could either propel material from an asteroid to some location in space where it could be processed, or it could serve as a rocket engine by altering the orbit of an asteroid to a convenient one for mining (O'Leary et al, 1979). Wright (1982) has suggested a compact electromagnetic rotary mass launcher on 1982 DB that could send a mass stream of asteroidal material to the Earth approximately 2% of the time. Even though the technology is being developed, many scientists believe that the chunks of flying rock expelled by mass drivers will pose a hazard to other spacecraft, exceeding the 'natural population' of meteoroids. Unless the exhaust of rocks is vaporized, mass drivers in space may remain in the realm of science fiction.

The value of asteroids has not been lost on military planners. Fortunately, not all such plans have bordered on the lunacy of asteroid arsenals considered by Dandridge Cole, a planner for the Missile and Space Vehicle Department of General Electric. In the early 1960's, Cole identified asteroids as "an unusual weapon system," sharing with biological weapons the ability to pose as a natural catastrophe (David, 1980).

Lewis & Meinel (1983) advocate a vigorous program leading to asteroid mining. This will (1) reduce the vulnerability of the United States and NATO to disruption of its supply of strategic metals, (2) revive the space sciences community by creating a national goal of the sort that drove the Apollo program and (3) provide the large masses needed for shielding permanently inhabited space stations from cosmic rays. They further anticipate that shielding of military satellites, which cost $100,000 per kg, will stabilize that situation without introducing any new weapons into space.

SPACE LAW

Even though space law is still in its infancy, the exploitation of resources in space has been a matter of international concern for many years. The United Nations Outer Space Treaty (1967), since ratified by more than 100 countries, addresses itself to the matter:

> The exploration and use of outer space, including the moon and other celestial bodies, shall be carried out for the benefit and in the interests of all countries. Outer space, including the moon and other celestial bodies, is not subject to national approbation by claim of sovereignty, by means of use or occupation, or by any other means.

This has been interpreted by some legal experts as prohibiting the mining of asteroids. According to Walz (1981), the term 'celestial body' was left undefined in the UN Treaty. She suggests that conservationists could interpret any alteration of celestial bodies, such as mining, to be prohibited. Alternatively, White (1984) concludes that the treaty prohibits only national, not private, appropriation of space resources. Reijnen (1981) goes even further, stating that under "the present rules of space law, exploitation is only possible by multinational private enterprises which may set up standards for division of the benefits derived from their activities."

Even if private enterprise establishes a mining operation on an asteroid, its nation of origin may still be responsible for any mishaps, as stated in Article IV "States party to the Treaty shall bear international responsibility for national activities in outer space, including the moon and other celestial bodies, whether such activities are carried out by governmental agencies or by non-governmental entities."

The conservation idea was addressed, albeit in jest, by Wetherill (1979). "It is likely that the Apollos, together with a few comets, represents the only accessible source of nonterrestrial carbon compounds and water in nearby space, a source that requires about 25 million years to be replenished. Perhaps it would be better if the region of space occupied by the Apollo objects and their close relatives the Amor objects were declared an inviolable 'wilderness area'." More seriously, Drexler (1978) pointed out that the resources of space are effectively limitless. "A single asteroid, Ceres, contains resources enough to build a land area over 600 times that of Earth." In the same vein, O'Leary (1977) maintains that the "exploitation of one or more of the Apollo or Amor asteroids should cause no great concern for the long-term ecological integrity of the solar system because most of them are doomed to collide with Venus, Earth or the moon within a relatively short time frame."

In 1971 the Soviet Union introduced a Moon Treaty to the United Nations. Eight years later it was sent to the General Assembly for adoption, but the refusal by the United States to sign the Moon Treaty has rendered it useless. It would have limited the use, and forbid the exploitation, of natural resources from space, and denied any legal entity the capacity of owning any part of these resources:

> States party to this agreement hereby undertake to establish an international regime, including appropriate procedures, to govern the exploitation of the natural resources of the Moon as such exploitation is about to become feasible. Neither the surface nor the subsurface of the Moon nor any part thereof or natural resources in place shall become the property of any state, international, intergovernmental or nongovernmental organization, national organization or nongovernmental entity or of any natural person.

Even though only the Moon is mentioned in this extract, the treaty applies to all celestial bodies in the solar system excluding Earth.

Rothblatt (1981) has proposed the creation of a Universal Asteroid Development Organization, modeled along the lines of INTELSAT, an international satellite communications service whose benefits are shared by 140 countries. He shows that development of asteroidal resources will be hampered by either an international monopoly or a tax on such exploitation.

While the prospect of a grizzly old space miner setting up a private little operation on a small asteroid in 2050 has a certain appeal, such activities will likely be considered illegal and monitored closely. On the other hand, there are so many asteroids over such a vast volume of the solar system it may prove to be a difficult job. Let me tell you the story of the space cadet who was given an electronic hound dog to sniff out a platinum bootlegging operation on 1773 Rumpelstilz ...

SCIENCE FICTION

Asteroids have appeared in science fiction stories, television shows, and movies for 50 years, although rarely in starring roles. The prospect of mining asteroids was first considered in the 1930's and 40's by Clifford D. Simak (*The Asteroid Of Gold*, 1932), Stanton Coblentz (*The Golden Planetoid*, 1935), and Malcolm Jameson (*Prospectors of Space*, 1940), among others.

In 1939, Robert Heinlein wrote *Misfit*, a story about capturing an asteroid "to be used as a space station—a refuge for ships in distress, a haven for life boats, a fueling stop, a naval outpost." Heinlein even envisioned growing plants in the asteroidal soil, after it had been fertilized and treated with cultures of anaerobic bacteria. The concept of "asteroid farming" was taken up again 41 years later by O'Leary (1980), who states that food can be grown more cheaply and reliably in space than on Earth. "A three-kilometer carbonaceous asteroid could provide enough growing area to support 6 billion people."

An asteroid was the subject of Isaac Asimov's first published story, *Marooned off Vesta* (1939). *Lucky Starr And The Pirates Of The Asteroids* (Asimov, 1953) featured the heroic space ranger in a fast-paced adventure tale set on Ceres, which is attacked by pirates who control most of the asteroid belt. Earlier stories of interplanetary skulduggery set in the asteroid belt include *Asteroid Pirates* (1938) by Royal W. Heckman and *Asteroid Justice* (1947) by V. E. Thiessen. E. C. Tubb's *Asteroids* (1956) is a humorous short story about an interplanetary confidence trickster.

More recent stories dealing with asteroids include Poul Anderson's episodic novel *Tales of the Flying Mountains* (1970) and *Barnacle Bull* (quoted at the beginning of this chapter), and several short stories by Larry Niven (*At The Bottom of a Hole*, 1966; *The Adults*, 1967) about the "belters", as inhabitants of the asteroid belt are known. The concept of asteroids being occupied by pioneer prospectors is common in the genre, as in Robert Sheckley's *Beside Still Waters* (1953) and Poul Anderson's *Garden in the Void* (1952). The mining of asteroids was developed further in *The Third Millenium* (Stableford & Langford, 1985), a highly speculative look at the future of humanity during the next thousand years. They envision Von Neumann machines (self-reproducing devices) being sent out into the asteroid belt in the 2270's. Their job was to refine useful elements by using demolition bacteria, plasma torches and solar mirrors. These valuable ingots were later used by "microworld colonists" when the asteroids became inhabited. But the ultimate mining operation occurred in 2433, when Ceres was blown apart by fusion bombs!

Olber's idea of a fifth planet that exploded millons of years ago was well used in Raymond Z. Gallun's *A Step Further Out* (1950). He envisioned that the planet was home to an advanced civilization, whose artifacts could still be found by prospectors. Such fanciful speculations even found their way into what were ostensibly books of science. Witness this passage from the pen of rocket pioneer Hermann Oberth (1957). "No atmosphere has been found on any of them. It is possible, however, that remains of air, water, and gas have been retained in hollows because if an asteroid is actually a large planet which was never completed, the biggest of them would consist of blocks falling on top of each other with hollows and cracks between them. These would light the space traveler artificially and would perhaps make life possible so that Jules Verne's *Voyage to the Center of the Earth* might become a reality, though not on the Earth but on Ceres, Pallas, or Vesta."

One of the most imaginative explanations for the origin of the asteroids can be found in Jack Williamson's *Seetee Ship* (1951). In the story, a form of matter known as contra-terrene particles cause a violent explosion when brought in contact with ordinary matter. An explosion involving this altered matter and a planet beyond Mars created the asteroids, but the asteroid belt now contains both kinds of matter. Asteroids made of c-t matter pose a great danger to colonists and miners, but hold out the prospect of being a valuable power source. Conveniently, the technology needed to harness that power is found on a deserted alien spaceship.

The most famous use of an asteroid in science fiction literature was in Arthur C. Clarke's book *Rendezvous with Rama* (1973). Clarke envisions a thousand-tons of rock and metal destroying the Italian cities of Padua, Verona and Venice in the year 2077. Casualties and damage totaled 600,000 people and $1 trillion. In the story, this devastation prompted the formation of Project Spaceguard, which by 2130 kept track of 500,000 asteroids—none would ever be allowed to breach the defenses of Earth.

Icarus has been a popular subject. In *Icarus Descending* (1973), Greg Benford tells of a NASA mission sent to Icarus. *Summertime On Icarus*, a short story by Clarke (1960), tells about a crash and rescue on the asteroid as it nears perihelion. Slusser (1978), in an analysis of this story, opines that Clarke gives us the vision of a man suspended at the crossroads of life. "Perceptions of the inhuman machinery of the cosmos are linked in the hero's mind with analogies to familiar human things." The "blasted cinder" of Icarus was certainly an inspired setting for such cosmic considerations. The strange fates of humans marooned on asteroids were also the subject of *The Master of the Asteroid* (1932) by Clark Ashton Smith and *The Horror on the Asteroid* (1933) by Edmond Hamilton.

In his book 1984: *Spring*, Clarke calls attention to a fallacy common in science fiction.*

A number of writers have fallen into another gravitational trap by proposing that space travelers should use asteroids or comets to give them free rides. Some asteroids, they point out, have passed within a few thousand miles of the Earth and then gone on to cut across the orbits of the other planets. Why not hop aboard such a body as it makes its closest ap-

proach to Earth and then jump off at a convenient moment when passing Mars? In this way your spaceship would only have to cover a fraction of the total distance: the asteroid would do the real work ...

The fallacy arises, of course, from thinking of an asteroid as a kind of a bus or escalator. Any asteroid whose path took it close to Earth would be moving at a very high speed relative to us, so that a spaceship which tried to reach and actually land on it would need to use a great deal of fuel. And once it had matched speed with the asteroid it would follow the asteroid's orbit whether the asteroid was there or not. There are no circumstances, in fact, where making such a rendezvous would have any effect except that of increasing fuel consumption and adding to the hazards of the voyage. Even if there was any advantage in such a scheme, one might have to wait several hundred years before there was a chance for a return trip. No, interplanetary hitchhiking will not work ...

Nichols (1993) suggests that hollow asteroids may be the most popular spaceships of the future. "Communities living in asteroids could slowly and peacefully make their way to the stars"—a true generation starship. In literature, an asteroid that was revealed to be a spaceship was the subject of *The Wailing Asteroid* (1961) by Murray Leinster.

Asteroids have proved to be somewhat less peaceful to starships in television and movies, however. In *Star Wars—The Empire Strikes Back*, dodging an asteroid belt was a very dangerous exercise, and landing on one even more so. Our rocky friends lent their name to a popular 23rd century expression in the *Star Trek* television show (Go chase an asteroid!); and in *Star Trek: The Motion Picture* the starship Enterprise nearly collided with an asteroid. But the ultimate menace came in the movie *Meteor*, where an asteroid-like object was diverted from hitting the Earth by nuclear explosion.

The concept of an asteroid hitting Earth has reached such popularity that a game entitled *Asteroid* was developed in 1980 by Marc Miller and Frank Chadwick. But it is based on an interesting twist—the asteroids have been deliberately sent on a collision course by a mad scientist using thermonuclear mining charges!

*Reprinted by the permission of the author.

IRAS   17

The world is divided, as far as astronomy is concerned, into the lords of creation who gaze at the universe, and the grubbers after facts who look at the solar system. Most satellites are designed by the lords of creation. The original intention of IRAS was to reject anything that moved; in other words if it moved don't shoot it. This seemed to me a pity.

Jack Meadows, 1986 British IRAS scientist

Different products of the IRAS asteroid database will serve users having radically different needs. Essentially they will span the range from naive users, who are not familiar with asteroids but wish to learn some simple facts about them, to asteroid researchers wishing to conduct highly specialized investigations.

IRAS Workshop 2, 1983.

The Infra-Red Astronomy Satellite opened a new era in the study of asteroids. Launched on 26 January 1983 near Lompoc, California, it carried a liquid-helium cooled, 60 cm reflecting telescope. Designed to survey the entire sky between 10 and 100 microns, it exceeded expectations, enabling 96.4% of the sky to be observed four times and 70.0% of it six times (Steward *et al*, 1984). Detailed results from the IRAS mission were released in 1986.

During its 300–day lifetime, IRAS carried out a complete survey of the sky at infrared wavelengths, and also made some 14,000 additional observations of select sources. In all, it mapped more than 200,000 IR objects (Macdougall *et al*, 1984). But asteroids were considered only as a second thought. The first asteroid workshop was held at JPL in June, 1983, five months after IRAS was launched. Only 2–3 weeks notice was given to 150 scientists, about 40 of whom were able to attend.

Since then, several more workshops have been held at JPL. At these crucial meetings, chaired by Thomas McCord, ways to salvage asteroid data from the IRAS scans were developed, and plans were made to create an IRAS Database.

To identify an asteroid, IRAS compared what it observed with a "Known Objects" catalog. If the observed and predicted detections matched, the source was said to be "seconds confirming." The next stage involved the "New Source Database." A source found to have the same position as a source observed on a previous scan was termed "hours confirming." This two-stage process was designed to enhance the reliability of detecting genuine sources, and to reject fast-moving objects (such as Earth- and Mars-crossers).

The first criteria used to search among these "rejects" was the IR flux—sources too hot or too cold were eliminated. Next, only sources above a certain galactic latitude were accepted. The next step was to select pairs of sources if they were observed on different orbits of IRAS, and if their fluxes in each band agreed within certain tolerances. A listing of these pairs was produced for study by project scientists (Thomas, 1983).

Not everything went as smoothly as this, of course. To measure the flux of an object in the infrared, for use in attempting to identify it as an asteroid, you first need a "thermal model" to predict what its IR flux should be. To quote from the second IRAS workshop (1983), "We were surprised and disturbed to learn that no member of the asteroid community has been involved in the selection or computation of these thermal models." Participants at the early workshops were also frustrated by the lack of any real data on which to base their analysis. Nonetheless, a wealth of new and exciting data on thousands of asteroids is now available in the IRAS Asteroid Database.

According to the *Asteroid and Comet Survey* (ed. Matson, 1986), a total of 11,449 asteroid sightings were made by IRAS. Of these 7,015 were accepted, and they yielded data for 1,811 asteroids. At the seconds-confirming step, IRAS observed 3,993 accepted and 3,285 rejected sightings; at the hours-confirming step, there were 3,022 accepted

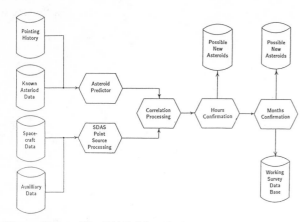

Fig. 17-1. *The IRAS Scientific Data Analysis System: a schematic of how asteroids were identified. From the IRAS Asteroid Workshop Number 1 (1983). JPL D–803.*

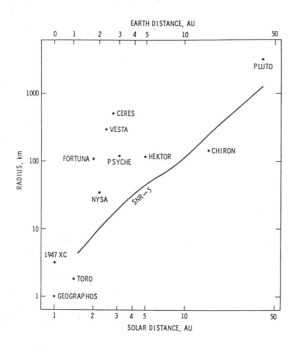

Fig. 17-2. *A selection of asteroids plotted according to their radius and distance from the Sun. A signal-to-noise ratio of 5 for IRAS is indicated; the survey cutoff was at SNR 3. From the IRAS Workshop Number 1 (1983). JPL D–803.*

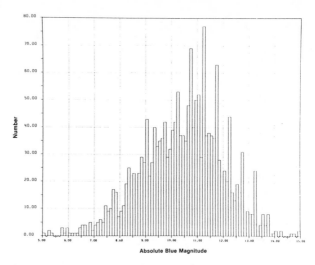

Fig. 17-3. *A histogram of IRAS sightings of asteroids according to their absolute blue magnitude. Few asteroids fainter than 13.5 were observed. From The IRAS Asteroid and Comet Survey (ed. Matson, 1986).*

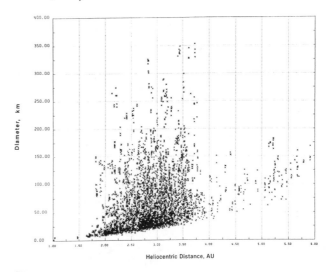

Fig. 17-4. *Asteroids surveyed by IRAS, plotted by diameter versus heliocentric distance. From The IRAS Asteroid and Comet Survey (ed. Matson, 1986).*

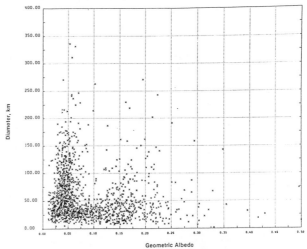

Fig. 17-5. *Asteroids surveyed by IRAS, plotted by diameter versus geometric albedo. From The IRAS Asteroid and Comet Survey (ed. Matson, 1986).*

and 780 rejected.

Asteroids were observed in four bands: 12, 25, 60 and 100 microns, although only the brightest ones were seen at 100. For the 4,380 asteroids observed only at 25 microns, just 1,324 were accepted. This is because useful color information is not available for discriminating against non-asteroids, and they usually have a low signal to noise ratio (the cutoff of the survey was at a SNR of 3; Fig. 17-2). Main belt asteroids have an infrared spectra peak at 25 microns, so those with high SNR are usually detected at either 12 or 60 microns or both. Of the 5,080 asteroids observed at all three wavelengths, fully 4,403 were accepted. A histogram of IRAS sightings of asteroids is shown in Fig. 17-3. The decreases in the number of faint asteroids is due to the SNR limit, and the incompleteness of orbital elements for small objects (Fig. 17-4).

The IRAS survey was biased against small very high albedo asteroids. Of the high albedo types, only 44 Nysa was detected several times at multiple wavelengths with a good SNR. The distribution of diameters versus albedos for the IRAS asteroids is shown in Fig. 17-5, and albedos versus heliocentric distance is shown in Fig. 17-6. In the IRAS data reduction, a guess of the diameter and albedo of an asteroid was made and used as input in the standard thermal model. These values were then iterated until both the visual magnitude and observed IR flux were matched by the model. The model is based on two large C-class asteroids (Ceres and Pallas). Thus, the resulting data may have to be revised in the future as more occultations and other ground-based observations are made of different types of asteroids (Lebofsky et al, 1986).

DISCOVERIES

One early result from IRAS that has potentially far-reaching implications is the discovery of a shell of particulate matter around the star Vega. The shell has an apparent diameter of 20″, corresponding to a distance from Vega of 85 AU and an orbital period of 554 years. It has been hypothesized that this shell is a ring of cometary bodies with a minimum mass of 15 earth masses, analogous to the Oort cloud around our Sun.

But there also appears to be an inner shell, only 2.4 AU from Vega, possibly as warm as 500° K. If the Vega system resembles the solar system at an earlier stage of its evolution, it may have developed an asteroid belt as well (Weissman, 1984). From an analysis of IRAS observations of 500 nearby stars (closer than 75 light years), Aumann (1985) concluded that 12 are orbited by solid material : ι–Eridani, γ–Dorado, β–Ursa Major, β–Leonis, α–Corona Borealis, γ–Serpentis, Vega, β–Pictoris, η–Eridani, Fomalhaut, G–196 and G–838. Non-IRAS studies have indicated three other stars—HL Tauri, R Monocerotis and Van Biesbroeck 8—may be surrounded by dust or larger bodies. According to Aumann, there is a good chance that half of the 2,000 nearby stars have material around them in significant quantities.

In our own solar system, IRAS discovered two pairs of zodiacal dust bands 10° above and below the ecliptic, parallel to the ecliptic equator (Fig. 17-7). This interplanetary dust was likely created by collisions in the asteroid belt (Neugebauer et al, 1984). Solar distances for the outer band pair are 3.2 AU for the northern band and 2.2 AU for the southern, while the inner band is at 2.3 AU (Low et al, 1984). The 1 AU difference between the outer bands may be due to a near 2/1 commensurability between the precession of the argument of perihelion and the nodal regression of particles in the bands. According to Sykes & Greenberg (1986), at a given ecliptic longitude, if the particles in the northern band are at aphelion, then the particles in the southern band appear as two lines varying sinusoidally in ecliptic latitude. If this is the case, the material orbits have a semimajor axis of 2.7 AU and an eccentricity of 0.19.

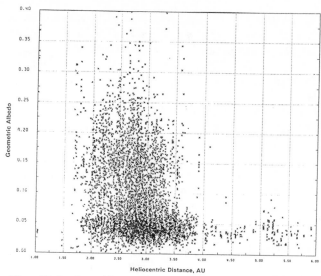

Fig. 17-6. *Asteroids surveyed by IRAS, plotted by geometric albedo versus heliocentric distance. From The IRAS Asteroid and Comet Survey (ed. Matson, 1986).*

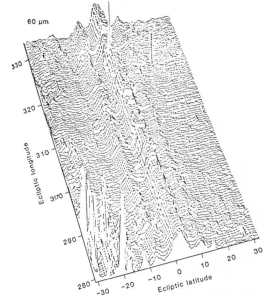

Fig. 17-7. *Zodiacal dust bands. IRAS data at a wavelength of 60µm taken from scans across the ecliptic plane near 300° ecliptic longitude were spatially averaged to 1° resolution and high-pass filtered in the direction perpendicular to the ecliptic plane to show the zodiacal dust bands. Intensity is proportional to the height of the projected three-dimensional surface. The three dust bands are found in the ecliptic and 10° above and 10° below the ecliptic, and run parallel to the ecliptic equator. The large peaks in the lower left of the map are due to the strong emission from the plane of the Milky Way. Neugebauer et al, 1984.*

Dermott et al (1984) have identified the asteroid families Eos, Themis and Koronis as the most likely source of this dust. "Although the total volume of the prominent Hirayama families is only a few percent of the total volume of the asteroid belt, the debris derived from the original catastrophic break-up of the present asteroids, or from the gradual comminution of the resultant family members, may be very much more prominent in the smaller size ranges." A contrary view is held by Gustafson (1985), who states that bands as bright as those observed could not emerge from the small end of the size distribution of the Hirayama families. He suggests that disruption of a 20 km diameter asteroid can lead to bands of the observed brightness 10,000 years later. Such bands are expected to last for a few tens of thousands of years, which is also the expected frequency of band formation. The major zodiacal bands so far discovered have surface areas of approximately $10^{19}\,cm^2$, but Skyes & Greenberg (1986) predict than another 30 band pairs whose surface areas exceed $10^{18}\,cm^2$ also exist. Almost a third of these are likely due to collisions between asteroids every 10,000 years less than 10 km in diameter. The remainder may result from more massive collisions; a more thorough analysis of IRAS data may reveal some of these bands.

A color-coded view of the dust bands can be found in *Sky & Telescope* magazine for March, 1986.

It has been discovered that cosmic dust particles (discussed in Chapter 6) accumulate solar flare tracks in their minerals. According to Sandford (1986), a study of these tracks can help discriminate between dust of cometary or asteroidal origin.

The zodiacal light is a permanent phenomenon that can be seen as a faint glow on a clear moonless night in the west after sunset and in the east before sunrise. It is shaped like a slanting cone and extends up to 20 degrees. The light is actually sunlight scattered by dust particles which were long thought to be of cometary origin. But the discovery of the IRAS dust bands associated with asteroids is evidence that at least some of the zodiacal light particles come from asteroids.

Dust injected into the interplanetary medium from asteroids arrives in the Earth's vicinity in nearly circular orbits. Particles emitted by the Eos-Koronis-Themis families completely cross the Earth's orbit in only 1.3% of the total infall time to 1 AU. Thus, the track densities found in such particles should exhibit a narrow range (spiked). A second possibility is that larger groups of asteroids produce the dust, in which case the density distribution should mimic the shape of distribution of asteroidal distance from the Sun. Track densities in cometary particles, however, should show a range of values. Even though few track densities have yet been measured, Sandford's data suggest that the most likely source of the interplanetary dust collected in the Earth's atmosphere are asteroids. There is no evidence yet that a majority comes from the families.

FINAL DATA PRODUCTS

A set of 15 "final data products" have resulted from the IRAS mission, which will be made available for general information, specific facts and research on asteroids and comets. Here is a capsule summary:

1. IRAS Asteroid Database: contains all of the observations of asteroid-like sources. It will be used to find asteroids with newly-determined orbits, for light curve studies, or any other research where a detailed observation-by-observation study of the data must be made.

2. IRAS Catalog and Database for known Asteroids: contains all observations of known asteroids. It will include fluxes in each band, coordinates, color temperatures and intrinsic variability.

3. IRAS Database of Previously Unknown Asteroid-Like Sources: similar to FDP 2, but for unknown asteroids.

4. IRAS Catalog and Database of Known Asteroids: a distilled subset of FDP 2, it is designed for users whose interest is only casual. It presents the "best" parameters which have been adopted for each known asteroid.

5. IRAS Asteroid Population Models and Survey Parameters: brings together all the information needed to characterize the completeness and reliability of the IRAS asteroid survey. It includes sky coverage as a function of heliocentric distance, ecliptic latitude vs. longitude plots and asteroid number density vs. a variety of parameters including albedo, diameter, flux and motion vector.

6. Completeness Estimate and Summary: brings together all of the information on the status of data and observations of all the known asteroids. It will be used in evaluating the completeness, reliability and bias of the IRAS asteroid survey.

7. IRAS Composite Catalog of Comet Observations.

8. IRAS Catalog and Database of Fast Moving Asteroids: a small subset of FDP 3, plus known fast-moving asteroids.

9. IRAS Catalog and Database of Known Asteroid LRS spectra: a catalog of low resolution spectra organized by asteroid number.

10. Catalog and Database of Previously Unknown Asteroid LRS Spectra: contains all the LRS spectra for asteroid-like sources other than known asteroids and comets.

11. JPL-IRAS Asteroid Database: contains all IRAS observations and other databases, including the 8–color asteroid survey, light curve parameters, and taxonomic classification.

12. JPL–IRAS Composite Asteroid Catalog: a subset of FDP 11 organized by IAU and United Kingdom-Caltech Asteroid Survey number.

13. JPL–IRAS Catalog of Known Asteroids: a subset of FDP 12, it presents the "best" parameters which have been adopted by the Asteroid Analysis Group for each known asteroid.

14. JPL–IRAS Deep Sky Asteroid Catalog: includes additional results derived from deep sky observations for known and previously unknown asteroids.

15. Non-Asteroid Reject Database: a set of asteroid-like observations that failed to pass the tests designed to

identify asteroids.

16. Asteroid Names: contains the names and provisional designations as well as pointers to identify the types of data available in the Ground-Based Data file.

17. Ground-Based Data: includes the eight-color survey, lightcurves, polarimetry, the 24-color spectrophotometry survey, and UBV photometry

18. Non-Asteroid Reject Database: a set of asteroid-like observations that failed to pass the tests designed to identify asteroids.

Table 17–1 contains the most comprehensive collection of data ever compiled on the asteroids. Most of the data in this table were obtained from E. F. Tedesco's MS DOS floppy disk version of the IRAS Asteroid Catalog published in the Infrared Astronomical Satellite Asteroid and Comet Survey (1986, D. Matson, editor). From left to right, the columns are asteroid number (NO.), weighted, mean visual, geometric albedo (Pv), weighted, mean diameter (D), absolute magnitude on the IAU system (H), slope parameter in the IAU system (G), rotational period in hours (Per) and taxonomic type on the Tholen system (Type). If an asteroid does not have an albedo listed, the D, H and G data are not from IRAS, but rather from ground-based data. The H values in this case are in the V band, while H values from IRAS are in the B band. For non-IRAS data, the D values come from the asteroid rotation list compiled by Alan Harris in 1985. These values should be considered approximate only. The rotational periods are taken from the Ground-Based data set, which in turn was abstracted from Lagerkvist et al (1985). The compositional types without an asterisk are taken from David Tholen's PhD thesis (1984b). Types followed by one asterisk are taken from the Harris rotation list, which used a system based on data from Tedesco in 1984. Types followed by two asterisks were taken from the TRIAD file, published in 1979. Data on the reliability of each number listed in the table can be found in the sources just listed. The table is complete up to 3317, the highest-numbered asteroid observed by IRAS.

			IRAS			
ID/1.	PV	D	H	G	Per	TYPE
1	0.10	913	4.04	0.111	9.075	G
2	0.14	523	4.79	0.148	7.811	B
3	0.22	244	6.12	0.300	7.213	S
4	0.38	501	3.96	0.338	5.342	V
5	0.14	125	8.07	0.672	16.812	S
6	0.25	192	6.53	0.240	7.274	S
7	0.21	203	6.61	0.509	7.135	S
8	0.22	141	7.37	0.327	13.6	S
9		146	6.32	0.29	5.079	S
10	0.075	429	5.96	−0.039	17.495	C
11	0.15	162	7.47	0.272	10.77	S
12	0.16	117	8.11	0.240	8.654	S
13	0.099	215	7.22	−0.020	7.045	CG
14		158	6.27	0.09	9.35	S
15	0.19	272	6.06	0.199	6.081	M
16	0.10	264	6.69	0.217	4.196	S
17	0.15	93.2	8.60	0.134	12.275	S
18	0.22	148	7.26	0.175	11.572	S
19		219	7.09	0.10	7.445	G
20	0.19	151	7.33	0.263	8.098	S
21	0.20	99.5	8.04	0.163	8.137	M
22	0.12	187	7.19	0.215	4.147	M
23	0.21	111	7.92	0.370	12.308	S
24		197	7.07	0.10	8.38	C
25	0.22	78.2	8.72	0.095	9.945	S
26	0.16	98.7	8.49	0.400	10.60	S
27		101	7.07	0.25	8.5	S
28	0.15	126	8.02	0.221	15.695	S
29	0.16	219	6.67	0.208	5.390	S
30	0.13	104	8.61	0.413	13.686	S
31	0.070	248	7.20	0.150	5.531	C*
32	0.25	82.6	8.36	0.110	9.443	S
33		54	8.43	0.24	18.601	S
34	0.057	118	9.07	0.035		C
35	0.058	108	9.24	0.150		C
36	0.076	109	8.96	−0.054	9.930	C*
37	0.17	112	8.12	0.251	7.33	S
38	0.058	120	9.03	0.054		C
39	0.29	159	6.83	−0.029	5.138	S
40	0.20	111	7.99	0.307	9.136	S
41	0.073	182	7.89	−0.057	5.988	C
42	0.12	107	8.63	0.587	13.59	S
43	0.28	65.3	8.76	−0.048	5.751	S
44	0.49	73.3	7.75	0.440	6.422	E
45	0.048	214	7.93	0.150	5.700	FC
46	0.046	131	9.08	0.106	21.04	P
47	0.072	133	8.52	0.125	13.	C
48	0.064	225	7.55	−0.047	11.89	CG
49	0.051	154	8.66	0.389	10.42	CG
50		88	9.20	0.15	100	EMP
51	0.086	153	8.13	0.061	7.785	CU
52	0.057	312	6.91	−0.004	5.631	CF
53	0.045	119	9.32	−0.101	26.85	CEMP*
54	0.050	171	8.40	0.149	7.04	C
55	0.32	67.5	8.37	0.347	4.804	M
56	0.062	117	8.99	0.150	13.7	P
57	0.21	116	7.78	0.071		S
58	0.056	97.7	9.48	0.150		C
59	0.048	173	8.39	0.014	13.69	CP
60	0.15	61.6	9.53	0.332	25.208	S
61	0.21	83.6	8.51	0.076	11.45	S
62	0.090	99.3	8.95	0.250		BU
63	0.17	108	8.25	−0.018	9.297	S
64		65	7.65	0.37	8.752	E
65	0.057	245	7.46	0.150	6.07	P
66	0.050	78.3	10.10	0.150		C
67	0.21	60.3	9.22	0.247	15.89	S
68	0.20	127	7.68	0.110	14.848	S
69	0.12	143	7.80	0.153		M
70	0.070	127	8.73	0.150	15.87	C
71	0.28	87.3	8.08	0.370	28.8	S
72	0.056	89.3	9.78	0.232		TDG*
73	0.21	45.5	9.82	0.250		−
74	0.034	123	9.53	0.150	9.0	C*
75	0.12	58.3	9.73	0.250	8.92	M
76	0.029	190	8.78	0.438		P
77	0.13	71.0	9.32	0.259	9.012	MU
78	0.064	125	8.82	0.079	7.22	C
79	0.27	68.8	8.71	0.178	5.979	S
80	0.15	81.7	9.00	0.300	14.05	S
81	0.046	124	9.20	0.150		C
82	0.17	63.6	9.32	0.336	12.999	S
83	0.069	84.2	9.59	0.301	10.16	EMP
84	0.070	83.0	9.64	−0.224		C**
85	0.068	157	8.22	0.053	6.875	FC
86	0.043	127	9.22	0.115	16.634	C
87	0.040	271	7.65	0.275	5.186	P
88		210	7.05	0.17	6.042	CF
89	0.16	159	7.45	0.144	11.387	S
90	0.051	125	9.06	0.260		C
91	0.042	114	9.52	0.150	6.025	CP*
92	0.20	132	7.48	0.326	15.94	EMP
93	0.085	146	8.20	−0.113	5.979	CU
94	0.038	212	8.21	0.085	7.22	CP
95	0.062	145	8.55	0.078	8.688	C
96	0.038	174	8.74	0.150		−
97	0.19	87.1	8.40	0.255	35.	M
98	0.041	109	9.67	0.150		CG
99		79	9.42	0.15	30	C

			IRAS			
ID/1.	PV	D	H	G	Per	TYPE
100	0.16	92.0	8.62	0.250	>20.	S*
101	0.15	68.3	9.32	0.497	23.16	S
102	0.049	86.0	9.95	0.150		P
103	0.17	95.2	8.45	0.107	23.74	S
104	0.052	127	8.99	0.196	9.	C
105	0.032	123	9.59	0.292	>20.	C
106	0.083	152	8.16	0.168		G
107	0.060	237	7.50	−0.173		C
108	0.19	67.2	9.13	0.250		S
109	0.060	91.6	9.60	0.110	26.3	GC
110	0.17	89.1	8.50	0.184	10.927	M
111	0.064	139	8.59	0.043	22.2	C
112	0.037	75.5	10.50	0.150		C**
113	0.27	47.6	9.57	0.263	9.935	S
114	0.084	103	9.00	0.098		T
115	0.25	83.5	8.37	0.144	7.241	S
116	0.22	75.5	8.73	0.250	13.7	S
117	0.040	154	8.86	0.484		EMPC
118	0.20	45.7	9.87	0.250	7.78	S
119	0.17	60.7	9.50	0.574		S
120	0.045	178	8.43	0.172	>20.	C
121	0.042	217	8.11	0.150	6.1	C
122	0.20	86.5	8.46	0.250		S**
123	0.19	49.8	9.78	0.250	10.04	S*
124	0.15	79.5	8.98	0.311	9.921	S
125	0.18	47.5	9.74	0.357	3.969	M
126	0.15	46.5	10.18	0.250		S**
127		128	8.48	0.15	12	EMP*
128	0.045	194	8.23	0.150	39.	C
129	0.17	125	7.77	0.366	4.957	M*
130	0.089	189	7.61	−0.036		G
131	0.095	43.3	10.76	0.250		SU
132	0.14	47.0	10.03	0.117		M
133	0.21	70.1	8.97	0.242	12.708	SR*
134	0.041	122	9.35	0.064		C
135	0.13	82.0	8.91	0.194	8.40	M
136	0.13	41.7	10.45	0.250	11.5	M*
137	0.048	150	8.74	0.098	>20.	C
138	0.18	47.5	9.92	0.250		S*
139	0.051	162	8.49	0.150	41.8	CP*
140	0.071	114	8.92	0.150	>20.	P*
141	0.036	135	9.22	0.150		C**
142	0.042	57.1	10.88	0.145		F
143	0.041	92.8	9.98	0.150		C**
144	0.059	146	8.59	0.081	13.810	C
145	0.044	155	8.74	0.013	20.6	C
146	0.052	137	8.83	0.135	18.54	C
147	0.029	137	9.45	0.150		C
148	0.14	104	8.46	0.130	20.664	GU
149	0.15	22.0	11.70	0.250		S*
150	0.034	157	9.03	0.150	8.14	CEMP*
151	0.14	46.7	10.21	0.250		S**
152		54	8.58	0.25	5.282	D
153	0.060	175	8.13	0.031		P
154	0.070	192	7.89	0.150		C*
155	0.021	49.5	12.02	0.150		CMEU**
156	0.040	126	9.31	0.150	22.5	C
157	0.15	19.1	12.04	0.150		−
158	0.17	39.8	10.29	0.250		S
159	0.061	131	8.76	0.150		C
160	0.059	85.0	9.76	0.150		C*
161	0.12	45.7	10.27	0.731	7.288	M
162	0.047	105	9.60	0.250		STU*
163	0.047	76.5	10.21	0.150		C*
164	0.053	110	9.28	0.011	13.66	CEMP*
165	0.069	160	8.23	0.150		CD*
166		51	9.85	0.15	9.5	GC*
167	0.21	42.2	10.02	0.250	16.	S
168	0.050	154	8.68	0.155		C
169	0.19	36.5	10.45	0.250		S
170	0.14	46.2	10.31	0.250		S
171	0.053	121	9.08	0.244	13.44	C
172	0.12	64.5	9.70	0.250		S**
173	0.053	159	8.49	0.121	5.93	C
174	0.14	71.7	9.26	0.250		S**
175	0.065	107	9.13	0.150		−
176	0.053	125	9.12	0.150		−
177	0.048	75.3	10.27	0.150		C
178	0.21	37.8	10.31	0.250		S*
179	0.14	81.0	9.03	0.250	11.173	S
180	0.11	32.7	11.22	0.250		S**
181	0.12	107	8.57	0.053	7.	S
182	0.16	45.3	10.19	0.296	80.	S*
183	0.16	36.0	10.62	0.250	11.77	S*
184	0.18	68.2	9.00	−0.060	6.7	EMP
185	0.053	165	8.41	0.273	10.83	S
186	0.15	52.3	9.92	0.287	19.6	C
187	0.053	135	8.87	0.128		S
188	0.19	41.3	10.20	0.250		S
189	0.18	38.5	10.41	0.250		S
190			7.67	0.15		P
191	0.041	105	9.66	0.150		−
192	0.21	107	8.07	0.029	13.622	RS
193			9.80	0.15		−
194	0.050	174	8.39	0.150	15.67	C
195	0.053	89.7	9.74	0.150		C
196	0.18	146	7.50	0.475	8.333	S
197	0.27	32.6	10.33	0.250		S**
198	0.19	58.7	9.43	0.373		S
199	0.13	63.0	9.60	0.150		−

		IRAS				
ID/1.	PV	D	H	G	Per	TYPE
200	0.053	132	8.91	0.059	19.	C
201	0.14	70.5	9.19	0.139	3.747	M
202	0.17	85.5	8.69	0.250		S**
203	0.029	120	9.78	0.150	23.3	DCEMP*
204	0.17	50.8	9.82	0.250		S
205	0.061	83.5	9.73	0.150		C**
206			8.65	0.10		C
207	0.050	60.7	10.69	0.150		C**
208	0.21	44.3	9.85	0.250		S
209	0.044	149	8.84	−0.086	8.	C
210	0.041	90.0	9.99	0.150		CF
211	0.059	148	8.56	0.032	18.375	C
212	0.046	140	8.92	0.150		C**
213	0.072	84.6	9.47	0.150		F
214	0.40	26.8	10.15	0.480	6.835	E
215	0.18	37.3	10.46	0.250		S**
216	0.088	140	8.23	0.247	5.385	M
217			9.87	0.15		CMEU**
218	0.15	62.0	9.54	0.250	6.636	S*
219	0.15	43.6	10.30	0.250	29.76	S
220	0.066	30.6	11.94	0.250		CEU**
221	0.12	110	8.48	0.157	10.436	S
222	0.082	58.0	10.18	0.651	7.	BU
223	0.022	90.7	10.66	0.150		EMP
224		66	8.71	0.25	18.933	M*
225	0.041	124	9.28	0.150		F
226	0.13	39.2	10.64	0.150		C*
227	0.056	90.1	9.77	0.150		–
228	0.12	10.7	13.59	0.250		S
229	0.037	96.0	10.00	0.250		BCU
230	0.14	113	8.32	0.354	24.	S
231	0.042	85.1	10.20	0.150		–
232	0.045	55.2	10.97	0.150		C
233	0.073	108	9.08	0.168	19.70	T
234	0.22	44.6	9.84	0.043	26.5	S
235	0.15	60.2	9.66	0.250	17.56	S*
236	0.10	90.5	9.14	0.192		S
237	0.15	44.0	10.22	0.250		–
238	0.032	156	9.11	0.507	8.99	C
239	0.054	43.0	11.42	0.150		–
240	0.039	108	9.69	0.134		C
241	0.062	169	8.19	0.043		CP
242	0.14	41.5	10.41	0.150		–
243	0.16	32.5	10.83	0.203		S
244	0.10	13.8	13.15	0.250		–
245	0.16	84.8	8.76	0.393	14.38	S
246	0.13	63.8	9.73	0.400	16.222	A
247	0.059	137	8.69	0.073	12.10	CP*
248	0.057	52.0	10.94	0.150		S*
249	0.041	37.2	12.02	0.250	42.62	S*
250	0.18	85.5	8.52	0.705	5.105	M
251	0.17	31.1	10.86	0.150		–
252	0.052	72.1	10.33	0.150		–
253	0.036	61.0	11.10	0.150		–
254	0.13	14.1	12.93	0.250	6.0	S
255	0.038	58.3	11.03	0.150		CMEU**
256	0.044	66.1	10.70	0.150		–
257	0.070	73.5	9.94	0.250		C**
258	0.15	67.7	9.33	0.461		S
259	0.037	185	8.53	0.150		CMEU**
260	0.034	101	9.97	0.150		C**
261	0.10	52.6	10.19	0.250		B
262			11.72	0.25		–
263	0.14	28.0	11.32	0.250		–
264	0.27	53.5	9.24	0.250		S
265	0.054	30.5	12.16	0.250		–
266	0.054	113	9.23	0.150		C
267	0.034	53.6	11.43	0.250	5.9	SDU*
268	0.038	142	9.04	0.150	6.	FC
269	0.068	54.7	10.64	0.150		–
270	0.19	52.2	9.66	0.250	15.06	S*
271	0.058	61.2	10.48	0.150		C**
272	0.10	29.0	11.59	0.150		–
273	0.12	32.1	11.11	0.150	23.	C*
274	0.17	30.3	10.92	0.250		–
275	0.036	121	9.54	0.150		EMP
276	0.041	127	9.28	0.154		EMP
277	0.21	29.5	10.79	0.250		S
278	0.21	38.0	10.18	0.150		–
279	0.030	135	9.52	0.520		D
280	0.033	48.6	11.67	0.150		–
281	0.14	13.1	13.03	0.399	4.348	SU*
282	0.043	40.5	11.61	0.250	6.42	BFU
283	0.025	150	9.44	0.150	6.888	EMP*
284	0.055	55.1	10.76	0.150		CEMP*
285	0.037	48.3	11.58	0.150		–
286	0.043	96.5	9.77	0.150		C**
287	0.16	70.1	9.19	0.295	7.603	S
288	0.11	37.5	10.93	0.438		S
289	0.14	41.5	10.65	0.400		A
290			12.1	0.25		–
291	0.14	17.5	12.28	0.250	4.32	S*
292	0.11	35.0	11.08	0.150		–
293	0.055	58.0	10.67	0.150		–
294	0.045	59.6	10.91	0.150		–
295	0.15	30.6	11.08	0.250		S**
296			12.63	0.25		S
297	0.14	45.8	10.23	0.150		–
298			11.24	0.25		–
299	0.081	21.1	12.52	0.250		–

		IRAS				
ID/1.	PV	D	H	G	Per	TYPE
300	0.033	79.1	10.63	0.150		–
301	0.056	55.5	10.83	0.150		–
302	0.045	40.5	11.59	0.150	>10.	F
303	0.047	103	9.68	0.150		–
304	0.047	68.5	10.47	0.089	18.36	C
305	0.16	50.7	9.91	0.250		S**
306	0.17	49.2	9.91	0.509	8.75	S
307	0.053	58.0	10.67	0.150		C**
308	0.043	148	8.97	0.283	12.032	T
309	0.037	54.7	11.29	0.150		–
310	0.087	36.3	11.27	0.150		–
311	0.20	27.8	10.92	0.250		S*
312	0.18	51.0	9.77	0.250		S**
313	0.050	101	9.57	0.045	10.080	C
314	0.057	61.6	10.57	0.150		–
315			13.43	0.25		–
316	0.018	49.3	12.32	0.150		–
317	0.29	22.6	10.85	0.400	8.17	E
318			9.27	0.15		C**
319	0.028	73.3	10.97	0.150		–
320			10.63	0.25		–
321	0.15	31.2	10.99	0.250	2.870	S*
322	0.080	73.8	9.74	0.150		EMP
323	0.16	37.7	10.57	0.250	10.	S
324	0.057	242	7.52	0.104	29.43	CP*
325	0.073	78.0	9.70	0.250		M*
326	0.039	100	9.84	−0.109		C
327	0.11	35.5	11.03	0.150		–
328	0.028	120	10.00	0.250		S*
329	0.037	80.5	10.35	0.150		C
330			12.7	0.25		–
331	0.040	78.5	10.33	0.150		C**
332	0.17	45.0	10.04	0.150	7.	C*
333	0.042	81.5	10.26	0.150		C**
334	0.064	170	8.18	−0.057		C
335	0.053	93.6	9.57	0.140		FP
336	0.042	72.0	10.51	0.173	13.70	D
337	0.13	63.2	9.45	0.250	4.610	EMP
338	0.17	62.1	9.24	0.250		M
339	0.16	43.7	10.11	0.249		S
340	0.11	32.5	11.18	0.250	7.7	S*
341	0.26	16.6	11.88	0.250		S**
342	0.036	65.0	10.86	0.150		C**
343	0.099	20.6	12.32	0.150		CSGU*
344	0.053	138	8.82	0.172	10.75	CSU
345	0.056	100	9.47	0.150	12.371	C
346	0.13	110	8.44	0.570		S
347	0.14	54.1	9.71	0.250		M
348	0.036	88.3	10.30	0.150		–
349	0.34	143	6.91	0.325	4.701	R.
350	0.047	123	9.17	0.150		C
351	0.20	44.3	9.96	0.250		S**
352	0.31	22.5	11.01	0.250	6.7	S
353			11.22	0.15		–
354	0.19	162	7.27	0.321	4.277	S
355	0.16	25.7	11.29	0.150		–
356	0.062	135	8.72	−0.081	31.82	C*
357	0.048	110	9.43	0.150	>20.	CEMP*
358	0.050	91.8	9.86	0.150		–
359	0.15	47.5	9.99	0.250	7.3	CEMP
360	0.052	121	9.09	0.150	6.21	C
361	0.039	149	9.02	0.150		DP
362		97	8.95	0.10	18	EMPC*
363		95	8.97	0.15	15	EMPC*
364	0.20	31.0	10.74	0.250	9.155	S
365	0.029	110	9.99	0.299		EMP
366	0.076	98.1	9.26	0.150		–
367	0.14	22.3	11.75	0.250		S**
368	0.032	74.5	10.72	0.150		D
369	0.17	62.2	9.26	0.219		M
370			10.69	0.25		C**
371	0.16	56.7	9.61	0.250		–
372	0.054	195	8.13	0.150	8.67	BFC*
373	0.038	99.6	9.84	0.150		C
374	0.19	48.2	9.80	0.250		S
375		200	7.43	0.23	16.83	C*
376	0.22	37.0	10.29	0.250	7.74	S
377	0.051	94.5	9.73	0.305	15.	PD*
378	0.17	31.6	10.83	0.250		S**
379	0.045	96.1	9.75	0.250	6.6	B
380	0.051	76.3	10.14	0.150		C
381	0.045	124	9.17	0.150		C
382	0.13	60.6	9.55	0.250		M
383	0.072	49.7	10.65	0.244	6.4	B
384	0.16	38.5	10.53	0.250		S**
385	0.20	94.1	8.36	0.184		S*
386	0.063	173	8.16	0.228	9.763	C
387	0.16	106	8.36	0.237	16.	S
388	0.053	120	9.13	0.150		C
389	0.20	81.6	8.63	−0.062		S
390	0.19	26.8	11.04	0.150		–
391			11.1	0.25		S**
392	0.051	64.6	10.59	0.150		C*
393	0.069	106	9.14	0.150	38.7	C**
394	0.16	36.2	10.58	0.278		S
395	0.041	54.2	11.15	0.259		C**
396	0.17	34.8	10.57	0.150	12.	C*
397	0.15	46.0	10.17	0.220	15.48	S*
398	0.045	50.5	11.26	0.150		–
399	0.14	52.8	9.94	0.150		–

			IRAS			
ID/1.	PV	D	H	G	Per	TYPE
400	0.14	34.3	10.80	0.250		–
401	0.030	103	10.15	0.150		–
402	0.12	57.6	9.86	0.163		S
403	0.12	51.3	10.24	0.250		S**
404	0.041	101	9.71	0.189	8.93	C
405	0.045	129	9.12	0.121	10.08	C
406	0.043	53.8	11.11	0.150		P
407	0.050	97.6	9.62	0.150		C
408	0.12	45.5	10.41	0.150		–
409	0.057	168	8.32	0.284	9.03	CEMP*
410	0.054	128	9.01	0.083	32.50	C
411	0.006	79.6	9.86	0.150		–
412	0.043	93.3	9.99	0.150		MEU**
413	0.12	34.3	10.92	0.250		MEU**
414	0.047	75.2	10.30	0.150		C
415	0.049	80.1	10.09	0.315		C**
416	0.15	89.5	8.75	0.257		S
417	0.17	43.3	10.07	0.250		EMP
418	0.13	38.5	10.53	0.250		M
419	0.044	133	9.03	0.145		F
420	0.038	146	9.04	0.042		P
421			11.87	0.25		S
422		15	10.89	0.40	20	EM*
423	0.038	217	8.15	0.681	4.622	C
424	0.030	90.5	10.43	0.150		–
425	0.046	66.8	10.63	0.150		–
426	0.037	134	9.27	0.150		C**
427	0.26	33.8	10.21	0.150		–
428	0.067	21.0	12.73	0.250		–
429	0.044	70.3	10.51	0.150		C
430	0.10	34.6	11.20	0.150		–
431	0.048	97.7	9.61	0.250		B
432	0.17	48.6	9.96	0.250	8.287	S*
433		21	10.74	0.25	5.270	S
434		10	11.47	0.38	26.51	E
435	0.077	43.0	10.93	0.150		–
436	0.048	63.0	10.71	0.150		–
437	0.56	14.3	11.24	0.250	12.	S*
438	0.045	63.6	10.58	0.150		–
439	0.036	79.3	10.44	0.150		C**
440			11.82	0.25		–
441	0.14	73.2	9.09	0.250	10.35	M*
442	0.044	67.5	10.56	-0.015		C
443	0.17	28.3	11.13	0.250		S
444	0.044	170	8.53	0.226	6.214	C
445	0.044	89.8	9.93	0.150		C**
446	0.35	43.0	9.60	-0.374		A
447	0.052	82.0	10.03	0.150		–
448	0.050	49.7	11.05	0.243		CU**
449	0.031	88.6	10.36	0.150		C
450	0.099	35.6	11.15	0.250		–
451	0.073	230	7.30	0.204	9.727	CU
452			12.3	0.25		–
453	0.14	24.2	11.61	0.250		S**
454	0.059	84.5	9.72	0.150	7.7	CB*
455	0.060	87.5	9.66	0.150		C**
456	0.10	43.1	10.70	0.150		S
457			11.19	0.15		–
458	0.17	40.0	10.39	0.250		S**
459	0.15	27.5	11.33	0.250	6.38	S
460			10.76	0.15		–
461	0.051	45.7	11.15	0.150		–
462	0.30	38.0	9.85	-0.080		S
463	0.077	21.5	12.44	0.250		C**
464	0.046	76.5	10.19	0.150		FEMPU*
465	0.037	76.6	10.57	0.150		–
466	0.056	121	9.00	0.150		C
467	0.036	47.5	11.66	0.150		–
468	0.050	71.7	10.27	0.150	8.3	CPF*
469	0.030	129	9.54	0.150		EMP
470	0.19	28.5	10.99	0.250		S
471	0.20	139	7.44	0.285	7.105	S
472	0.24	47.6	9.64	-0.007		S
473			10.0	0.25		–
474	0.077	37.5	11.32	0.250		S*
475	0.033	31.0	12.56	0.150		EMP
476	0.039	121	9.42	0.150		P
477	0.21	25.2	11.14	0.250		S
478	0.16	82.0	8.85	0.139		S
479	0.041	77.5	10.43	0.150		–
480	0.17	58.0	9.58	0.471		S
481	0.041	116	9.45	0.150		C**
482	0.15	51.6	9.96	0.250		S*
483	0.13	73.5	9.31	0.250		S
484		38	10.09	0.15		–
485	0.12	68.2	9.49	0.150	17.59	S*
486	0.11	24.5	11.83	0.250		–
487	0.22	64.2	9.06	0.078		S**
488	0.052	158	8.53	0.150		C
489	0.038	144	9.05	0.150		C**
490	0.057	121	9.07	0.150		C**
491	0.052	101	9.61	0.150		–
492	0.047	54.5	11.06	0.250		–
493	0.036	52.0	11.45	0.150		–
494	0.059	89.1	9.67	0.094		C**
495	0.041	41.7	11.77	0.250		S*
496	0.10	17.5	12.75	0.250		S
497	0.385	45.3	10.71	0.107	4.620	M
498	0.073	84.8	9.57	-0.049		M
499	0.033	86.0	10.31	0.420		P

			IRAS			
ID/1.	PV	D	H	G	Per	TYPE
500	0.15	45.1	10.17	0.150		–
501	0.068	80.1	9.82	0.150		–
502	0.20	20.7	11.63	0.250	10.5	S*
503	0.071	79.5	9.70	0.150		C**
504	0.16	31.2	10.88	0.150		–
505		117	8.80	0.15	8.179	FC
506	0.044	109	9.53	0.107		EMPC
507	0.12	48.5	10.28	0.150		–
508	0.039	147	9.03	0.150		C
509	0.20	59.0	9.33	0.250		S
510	0.065	59.3	10.44	0.150		PD*
511	0.053	337	6.89	0.020	5.130	C
512	0.15	23.3	11.73	0.250	5.582	S
513	0.083	52.5	10.53	0.250	5.23	S*
514	0.029	110	9.90	0.150	>20.	EMPC
515	0.031	43.0	12.11	0.150		I
516	0.15	75.7	8.99	0.250	7.	M*
517	0.034	95.5	10.09	0.221		C**
518	0.15	17.6	12.24	0.150		S
519	0.12	53.1	10.07	0.250		S
520	0.081	30.3	11.67	0.250		CGU*
521	0.036	121	9.52	0.536	>24.	C
522	0.027	113	9.95	0.364		EMP
523	0.18	36.7	10.42	0.150		–
524	0.038	74.1	10.53	0.150		C**
525			12.55	0.25		RU**
526	0.058	46.7	11.00	0.250		B
527	0.043	55.2	11.11	0.150		–
528	0.054	86.2	9.90	0.150		–
529	0.10	38.2	10.94	0.250		S
530	0.043	89.3	9.92	0.150		F
531	0.19	17.8	11.92	0.150		–
532	0.16	231	6.63	0.247	9.406	S
533	0.19	34.8	10.58	0.250		S*
534	0.14	37.5	10.64	0.250	9.	S*
535	0.047	77.0	10.24	0.150		C**
536	0.042	158	8.77	0.150		EMP
537	0.23	47.5	9.61	0.150		C**
538	0.051	77.8	10.19	0.150		–
539	0.066	55.3	10.65	0.150		–
540	0.19	21.0	11.66	0.250		S
541	0.041	59.1	11.02	0.150		–
542	0.19	43.5	10.02	0.250		SU**
543	0.13	44.2	10.37	0.150		–
544	0.22	26.0	10.98	0.150		–
545	0.050	115	9.25	-0.095	7.2	CD*
546	0.049	69.7	10.45	0.150		CU**
547	0.042	73.0	10.49	0.150		MEU**
548			11.43	0.25		S
549	0.16	20.5	11.87	0.250		S
550	0.22	39.8	10.06	0.250		S**
551	0.041	81.2	10.21	0.150		EMPC
552	0.034	81.0	10.56	0.150		–
553			12.41	0.25		–
554	0.051	98.5	9.55	0.150	13.63	FC
555	0.060	42.5	11.33	0.150		–
556	0.21	39.5	10.15	0.250	4.283	S
557			12.21	0.25		–
558	0.10	61.6	9.80	0.250	10.	M
559	0.046	80.0	10.18	0.150		C
560	0.060	41.0	11.40	0.150		CMEU**
561	0.067	25.7	12.24	0.250		–
562	0.13	35.8	10.82	0.360		S
563	0.21	54.8	9.48	0.250	5.69	S
564	0.047	50.7	11.15	0.150		C**
565	0.076	29.6	11.86	0.250		SU**
566	0.032	175	8.85	0.431		C
567	0.035	97.0	9.98	0.150		CU**
568	0.038	89.7	10.20	0.150		–
569	0.028	75.6	10.84	0.088		C**
570	0.052	106	9.48	-0.044		ST
571	0.019	44.5	12.56	0.250		S
572	0.080	30.8	11.60	0.250		C**
573	0.11	50.5	10.22	0.250		–
574	0.19	8.81	13.44	0.250		S**
575	0.10	23.1	12.02	0.250		–
576	0.025	86.8	10.73	0.150		–
577	0.10	44.2	10.64	0.150		–
578	0.054	71.6	10.31	0.150		–
579	0.17	89.6	8.60	0.051	13.	S
580	0.069	54.7	10.63	0.150		–
581	0.058	67.1	10.37	0.150		–
582	0.19	47.0	9.92	0.250		S
583	0.052	86.0	9.82	0.150		C
584	0.17	56.2	9.63	0.339		S
585	0.035	60.3	11.04	0.150		C**
586	0.049	85.0	9.90	0.150		CU**
587			12.4	0.25		–
588	0.030	147	9.36	0.150		DU
589	0.049	92.5	9.78	0.150		C**
590	0.095	40.5	10.94	0.435		C*
591	0.030	54.7	11.43	0.150		MU**
592			9.63	0.15		–
593	0.053	78.2	9.98	0.067	9.89	C
594	0.15	10.0	13.41	0.150		–
595	0.080	114	8.89	0.150		–
596	0.036	117	9.61	0.150		–
597	0.22	37.7	10.13	0.150		–
598	0.044	74.7	10.39	0.150		C**
599	0.14	69.6	9.36	0.250	9.566	S

IRAS

ID/1.	PV	D	H	G	Per	TYPE
600	0.17	28.3	11.04	0.150		SG*
601	0.042	76.0	10.32	0.150		CEU**
602	0.045	130	9.11	0.308		C
603	0.049	15.2	13.76	0.150		
604	0.075	65.3	10.16	0.150		
605	0.058	72.0	10.22	0.150		
606	0.076	40.0	11.17	0.150		TSD
607	0.050	65.5	10.59	0.150		−
608			10.69	0.25		−
609	0.054	56.3	10.84	0.150		−
610			12.1	0.25		−
611	0.091	59.0	10.18	0.250		S**
612	0.036	40.5	11.99	0.150		−
613	0.031	82.0	10.47	0.150		P
614	0.089	29.0	11.73	0.150		−
615	0.051	49.5	11.08	0.150		C**
616	0.15	23.5	11.63	0.250		S**
617	0.043	149	8.87	0.150		P
618	0.058	124	8.94	0.150		C
619		32	10.20	0.46		S*
620			11.37	0.40		CMEU**
621	0.10	31.2	11.25	0.150	>10.	FCEMP*
622		24	10.30	0.25	47.5	S
623	0.037	46.0	11.58	0.250		C**
624		221	7.47	0.15	6.924	D
625	0.12	31.3	11.20	0.150		CEMP
626	0.041	104	9.69	0.150		CMEU**
627	0.062	51.0	10.78	0.150		
628	0.14	51.2	10.00	0.250	13.5	SD*
629			9.67	0.15		
630	0.13	20.3	12.08	0.150		−
631	0.12	60.5	9.83	0.586	5.92	S
632		15	11.74	0.15	4.6	SC*
633	0.12	38.8	10.73	0.250		S*
634	0.040	69.1	10.71	0.150		−
635	0.042	100	9.74	0.150		C
636	0.039	78.3	10.46	0.150		C*
637	0.037	43.5	11.80	0.150		
638	0.048	68.0	10.55	0.150		−
639	0.14	74.5	9.19	0.431		S
640	0.063	84.8	9.72	0.150		G
641		10	12.5	0.25	8.9	S*
642	0.10	40.0	10.94	0.250		S**
643	0.036	76.1	10.54	0.314		P
644	0.14	23.2	11.72	0.250		S*
645	0.17	32.0	10.86	0.250		S*
646			13.1	0.25		−
647			11.49	0.25		CMEU**
648	0.046	70.5	10.40	0.150		EMPC
649			12.30	0.15		
650			13.03	0.15		−
651	0.12	36.8	10.87	0.035		S
652	0.092	22.1	12.27	0.250		
653	0.17	43.3	10.15	0.250		S
654	0.043	132	9.11	0.054	31.9	C
655	0.11	37.2	10.96	0.150		
656	0.075	57.5	10.44	0.250		
657	0.040	43.6	11.72	0.150		SC*
658	0.15	26.0	11.43	0.250		SU**
659	0.040	115	9.52	0.150		EMPC
660	0.15	44.2	10.30	0.250	7.92	S
661	0.091	52.0	10.45	0.250		S
662	0.15	27.2	11.26	0.150		−
663	0.033	104	9.91	0.150		EMP
664			9.99	0.15		EMPC
665	0.21	56.1	9.32	0.150		
666	0.005	29.7	11.60	0.150		−
667	0.057	83.5	9.92	0.150		−
668	0.032	28.0	12.93	0.150		−
669	0.10	36.5	11.06	0.250		SU*
670	0.24	36.5	10.13	0.150		−
671	0.031	63.7	11.15	0.150		−
672	0.040	34.8	12.21	0.150		−
673	0.089	39.3	11.05	0.250		C**
674	0.18	101	8.31	0.250	>30.	S*
675		74	8.05	0.25	7.717	S
676	0.042	82.6	10.26	0.150		C**
677	0.25	29.3	10.54	0.150	>10.	C*
678	0.30	44.0	9.49	0.150		−
679		114	9.01	0.15	7.625	
680	0.040	86.7	10.10	0.150		CMEU**
681			10.73	0.25		−
682	0.082	15.5	13.17	0.150		
683	0.050	116	9.35	0.150	4.322	C*
684		23	10.92	0.25		−
685	0.20	13.0	12.58	0.250		−
686	0.11	44.1	10.59	0.250		S
687			11.72	0.15		EMP
688	0.057	44.0	11.31	0.150		SC*
689	0.10	15.0	12.90	0.150		C**
690	0.078	140	8.32	0.150		CEU**
691	0.037	92.6	10.09	0.150		C**
692	0.18	47.7	9.94	0.250		S
693	0.076	69.1	9.99	0.250		CU**
694	0.051	92.7	9.73	0.150		CP*
695	0.16	51.2	9.90	0.250		S
696	0.052	79.3	10.12	0.150		CMEU**
697	0.037	82.5	10.34	0.150		C**
698			10.7	0.25		−
699		11	11.99	0.40	3.656	S
700	0.16	17.1	12.23	0.250	6.	−
701	0.15	46.0	9.99	0.150		CU**
702	0.056	202	7.89	0.130	8.36	C
703			12.5	0.25		−
704	0.064	333	6.64	0.019	8.723	F
705	0.038	139	9.16	0.150		EMP
706	0.075	32.0	11.70	0.150		−
707			12.90	0.25		
708	0.15	25.0	11.53	0.250		SU**
709	0.045	99.6	9.72	0.150	52.4	EMP*
710	0.065	30.8	11.94	0.150		−
711			12.10	0.25		−
712	0.046	132	9.08	0.064	11.87	C
713	0.041	109	9.56	0.150		C
714	0.24	41.0	9.97	0.250		S
715	0.18	31.5	10.77	0.150		−
716	0.12	25.5	11.67	0.250	>17.	S*
717	0.051	36.5	11.74	0.150		CMEU**
718	0.038	76.5	10.56	0.150		−
719			15.7	0.25		−
720	0.18	37.8	10.34	−0.225		S*
721	0.050	82.6	10.06	0.150		D
722			12.17	0.25		−
723	0.12	38.3	10.79	0.150		−
724			13.6	0.25		−
725	0.037	31.8	12.43	0.150		CSU
726	0.038	47.2	11.58	0.150	13.04	S*
727	0.14	37.5	10.65	0.150		−
728			12.7	0.25		−
729	0.11	53.3	10.14	0.250		−
730			13.6	0.25		−
731	0.12	46.6	10.19	0.150		C**
732	0.058	39.0	11.56	0.250		−
733	0.049	92.0	9.75	0.150		CF
734	0.028	78.6	10.83	0.150		−
735	0.044	77.0	10.27	0.150		C**
736	0.11	19.0	12.45	0.250	6.7	S*
737	0.23	46.3	9.67	0.250	14.13	S*
738	0.044	64.8	10.72	0.150		−
739	0.030	110	9.91	0.935	15.9	EMP
740	0.049	94.5	9.74	0.150		CEMP
741	0.11	32.5	11.19	0.150		CMEU**
742	0.11	46.7	10.43	0.250		S**
743	0.046	55.7	11.02	0.150		−
744	0.039	62.0	10.85	0.150		−
745			10.38	0.15		P
746	0.038	75.5	10.50	0.150		PC*
747	0.047	178	8.39	0.150	9.40	P
748	0.039	107	9.68	0.150		S**
749			11.85	0.25		F
750	0.043	24.0	12.73	0.150		C
751	0.047	115	9.32	0.150		−
752	0.033	65.7	11.02	0.250		
753		25	10.34	0.25	9.84	S*
754	0.047	89.1	9.88	0.150		C**
755	0.11	41.0	10.63	0.523		M
756	0.031	73.8	10.86	0.150		−
757	0.11	34.0	11.06	0.250		EMPF
758	0.10	86.5	9.13	0.150		−
759	0.038	52.7	11.35	0.150		−
760	0.16	74.8	9.18	0.250		S**
761			10.91	0.25		SC
762	0.032	142	9.23	0.496		F
763	0.064	17.3	13.19	0.250		
764	0.077	60.5	10.21	0.150		C**
765			12.29	0.15		−
766	0.12	37.1	10.80	0.250		MU*
767	0.073	40.6	11.21	0.150		−
768			10.19	0.15		EMP
769	0.049	102	9.64	0.150		−
770	0.22	18.5	11.81	0.250		
771	0.14	30.5	10.99	0.250		EMP
772	0.055	123	8.99	0.150		C
773	0.033	99.1	10.04	0.150		D
774	0.15	57.0	9.66	0.150		S
775	0.096	35.0	11.25	0.250		
776		174	7.68	0.34	7.672	C
777	0.037	68.7	10.82	0.150		−
778	0.057	67.3	10.20	0.008	11.659	F
779	0.12	72.7	9.35	0.150		SC*
780	0.047	97.1	9.79	0.150		−
781	0.082	60.0	10.24	0.150		CEU**
782	0.23	13.5	12.33	0.250		
783	0.042	41.3	11.78	0.250		C**
784	0.049	90.0	9.93	0.150		
785	0.13	52.1	9.88	−0.003		M
786	0.067	93.2	9.40	0.150		C
787	0.15	30.3	11.02	0.150		−
788	0.076	109	9.03	0.150		−
789			11.09	0.15		P
790	0.034	176	8.75	0.150	10.37	C
791	0.029	107	10.04	0.150		
792	0.039	63.5	10.93	0.150	9.17	M*
793	0.15	30.8	10.99	0.150		−
794	0.035	41.0	12.00	0.150		
795	0.034	78.7	10.61	0.150		EMPD*
796	0.18	46.7	9.81	0.150	7.75	S*
797		24	10.45	0.25	5	M
798	0.11	46.2	10.33	0.237		−
799	0.059	46.5	11.15	0.150		

		IRAS				
ID/1.	PV	D	H	G	Per	TYPE
800			11.60	0.25		S**
801	0.039	35.3	12.12	0.150		EMPC
802			12.4	0.25		-
803	0.087	51.8	10.49	0.150		-
804	0.049	161	8.58	0.221	7.426	PC
805	0.043	73.0	10.42	0.150		CEMP
806	0.020	65.2	11.61	0.150		-
807	0.10	31.3	11.47	0.298		S*
808	0.21	34.3	10.42	0.150		-
809			12.08	0.25		-
810			13.0	0.25		-
811	0.14	23.6	11.68	0.250		S
812			11.3	0.25		-
813	0.084	16.1	13.07	0.250		C**
814	0.031	116	9.76	0.524	35.8	C*
815	0.13	24.5	11.62	0.150		-
816	0.036	62.5	11.05	0.150		-
817	0.13	25.0	11.00	0.150		-
818	0.11	53.0	10.15	0.150		-
819			12.09	0.25		-
820	0.033	61.1	11.18	0.150		-
821			11.84	0.15		C
822			12.18	0.15		-
823	0.11	20.2	12.26	0.250		-
824	0.089	36.0	11.31	0.250		S**
825	0.21	12.5	12.70	0.250		S**
826	0.085	21.5	12.43	0.150		-
827			12.98	0.25		-
828	0.044	55.8	10.93	0.150		-
829	0.034	44.0	11.87	0.150		-
830	0.14	47.1	10.26	0.250		S**
831			12.4	0.25		-
832			11.20	0.25		-
833			11.1	0.25		-
834	0.068	69.2	10.08	0.150		-
835	0.037	41.3	11.92	0.150		-
836			13.2	0.25		-
837			11.9	0.25		-
838	0.039	63.1	10.84	0.150		P
839	0.17	22.3	11.57	0.250		S**
840	0.34	30.0	10.20	0.150		-
841		8	13.02	0.25	3.39	S*
842	0.054	43.2	11.41	0.150		-
843			13.1	0.25		-
844	0.055	66.1	10.47	0.150		-
845	0.035	57.5	11.26	0.150		-
846	0.039	54.2	11.08	0.150	>24.	CBU*
847	0.13	32.1	11.17	0.250		S**
848			11.09	0.15		-
849		105	8.19	0.25	4.119	M
850	0.038	84.5	10.33	0.150		-
851	0.17	14.2	12.61	0.250		S
852	0.25	24.6	10.96	0.250	4.56	S*
853	0.048	28.0	12.41	0.250		C**
854			12.41	0.25		-
855			12.05	0.25		-
856	0.037	52.0	11.42	0.250		S*
857	0.17	16.5	12.01	0.250		-
858	0.28	23.1	10.97	0.250		S**
859	0.032	77.5	10.71	0.150		-
860	0.11	32.8	11.02	0.250		M
861	0.039	70.1	10.71	0.150		-
862	0.18	29.2	10.93	0.150		-
863	0.39	31.5	10.21	0.400		A
864			12.98	0.25		S
865	0.059	20.7	12.90	0.250		-
866	0.036	91.7	10.22	0.150		-
867	0.087	28.5	11.79	0.150		-
868	0.050	54.7	10.88	0.150		C**
869	0.057	21.0	12.92	0.150		-
870			11.8	0.25		-
871	0.10	12.2	13.39	0.250		-
872	0.16	33.5	10.68	0.250		CMEU**
873	0.044	33.5	12.07	0.150	10.6	PC
874	0.064	58.3	10.57	0.150		-
875	0.15	14.8	12.55	0.250		-
876	0.11	25.8	11.76	0.250	>14.	S*
877	0.047	39.6	11.58	0.398		F
878			15.4	0.25		-
879			11.6	0.25		-
880	0.036	36.0	12.08	0.150		F
881			12.4	0.25		-
882	0.042	48.8	11.41	0.150		-
883			12.86	0.25		-
884			8.89	0.15		D
885	0.060	37.0	11.63	0.150		-
886	0.079	93.3	9.32	0.150		-
887		3.9	14.20	0.25	73.97	S
888	0.13	44.8	10.40	0.250		S**
889	0.080	22.6	12.38	0.250		-
890	0.095	30.0	11.56	0.250		-
891	0.050	53.6	11.03	0.150		-
892	0.048	78.5	10.25	0.150		-
893	0.036	78.2	10.42	0.150		CMEU**
894	0.12	40.8	10.60	0.150		-
895	0.029	147	9.44	0.150		CMEU**
896	0.16	14.5	12.59	0.250		-
897	0.21	24.0	11.23	0.250		S
898			12.3	0.25		-
899	0.16	30.0	10.85	0.150		CMEU**
900	0.057	22.7	12.74	0.250		S*
901			11.79	0.25		S
902			12.4	0.25		-
903	0.056	65.7	10.45	0.150		-
904	0.036	62.5	11.04	0.150		-
905	0.076	21.0	12.60	0.250	10.	S*
906			9.98	0.15		-
907	0.057	65.8	10.35	0.150		C
908	0.099	28.0	11.69	0.250		-
909	0.037	120	9.50	0.150		EMP
910	0.054	53.0	10.97	0.150		-
911	0.041	175	8.65	0.150		D*
912	0.053	86.6	9.92	0.150		-
913			12.6	0.25		-
914	0.084	79.0	9.56	0.150	>14.	CU
915			11.97	0.25		-
916	0.032	36.5	12.35	0.250		-
917	0.047	30.5	12.31	0.150		-
918	0.13	24.5	11.64	0.150		-
919	0.055	30.5	12.13	0.150		-
920	0.082	26.7	11.99	0.150		-
921	0.047	60.5	10.83	0.150		-
922			11.94	0.15		-
923	0.037	33.6	12.35	0.150		-
924	0.040	87.6	10.11	0.150		C**
925	0.23	57.0	9.25	0.250	7.92	S
926	0.043	50.5	11.31	0.150		-
927	0.068	70.0	9.98	0.150		C**
928	0.033	69.7	10.90	0.150		-
929			12.42	0.25		-
930	0.032	39.1	12.19	0.250		-
931	0.12	52.6	9.94	0.250		M
932			10.05	0.15		C**
933	0.024	26.0	13.40	0.250		-
934	0.040	57.1	11.13	0.150		-
935	0.11	8.69	14.07	0.250		-
936	0.084	44.1	10.88	0.250		-
937	0.049	27.5	12.64	0.250		S
938	0.072	28.0	12.04	0.150		-
939	0.083	17.8	12.99	0.250	>20.	S*
940			9.33	0.15		-
941			11.55	0.15		C**
942	0.11	32.7	11.18	0.150		-
943	0.044	72.0	10.51	0.250		-
944		39	10.75	0.15	10	D*
945	0.18	29.5	10.90	0.250		S
946	0.044	50.0	11.17	0.150		FU
947	0.19	27.7	10.97	0.150		-
948			11.42	0.15		-
949	0.051	71.0	10.39	0.150		-
950	0.17	17.5	12.11	0.250		-
951	0.15	15.5	12.54	0.250		S
952	0.055	84.5	9.92	0.150	7.51	C*
953	0.12	31.5	11.20	0.150		-
954	0.052	59.7	10.56	0.150		-
955	0.12	18.7	12.33	0.150		-
956			12.61	0.25		-
957	0.034	76.6	10.65	0.150		-
958	0.031	53.7	11.56	0.150		ERU**
959	0.026	59.1	11.50	0.150		-
960			13.12	0.25		-
961	0.032	39.3	12.19	0.150		-
962	0.026	39.5	12.43	0.250		S
963	0.12	11.5	13.45	0.250		S**
964			10.94	0.15		-
965	0.048	54.5	11.03	0.150		-
966	0.23	27.3	10.89	0.250		S**
967	0.076	14.7	13.36	0.250		-
968	0.17	31.0	10.92	0.250		SU**
969	0.038	20.5	13.21	0.150		FEMPU
970			12.3	0.25		-
971	0.043	66.7	10.71	0.150		-
972	0.045	79.0	10.30	0.150		-
973	0.067	54.7	10.66	0.150		-
974	0.19	24.8	11.30	0.250		S
975			10.38	0.25		S**
976	0.043	86.6	10.09	0.150		C**
977	0.050	67.0	10.45	0.150		C**
978	0.034	82.5	10.39	0.150		CMEU**
979	0.10	40.6	10.83	0.150		-
980	0.17	89.0	8.67	0.058		SU
981	0.083	31.2	11.46	0.150		CFU*
982			10.27	0.15		-
983	0.043	77.3	10.32	0.150		CMEU**
984	0.31	33.6	10.03	0.150	5.781	C*
985			13.08	0.25		-
986	0.10	53.0	10.23	0.150		-
987	0.14	44.6	10.26	0.150	>10.	C*
988	0.064	29.0	12.09	0.150		-
989	0.11	14.3	13.02	0.150		-
990	0.097	20.3	12.41	0.150		-
991	0.043	34.5	12.01	0.150		CU**
992	0.082	30.8	11.68	0.150		-
993			12.02	0.25		-
994	0.18	27.2	11.08	0.150		S*
995	0.11	32.6	11.17	0.150		-
996	0.060	34.1	11.69	0.250		B
997	0.056	23.5	12.69	0.150		-
998	0.057	35.0	11.81	0.150		-
999	0.18	21.2	11.59	0.150		

			IRAS			
ID/1.	PV	D	H	G	Per	TYPE
1000	0.051	54.0	10.99	0.150		–
1001	0.044	78.3	10.25	−0.060		MEU**
1002	0.023	57.1	11.74	0.150		–
1003			10.57	0.15		
1004	0.035	76.6	10.54	0.150		–
1005	0.057	62.7	10.53	0.150		–
1006	0.030	35.7	12.44	0.150		–
1007	0.071	24.6	12.32	0.150		–
1008	0.063	41.0	11.36	0.150		–
1009			14.1	0.25		–
1010	0.043	45.2	11.56	0.150		–
1011			12.85	0.25		S**
1012	0.039	23.0	12.99	0.150		F
1013	0.16	35.6	10.57	0.150		C**
1014			11.92	0.15		–
1015	0.039	101	9.79	0.150		C**
1016			12.22	0.25		–
1017	0.043	39.0	11.87	0.150		–
1018	0.24	16.7	11.81	0.150		S*
1019	0.15	9.55	13.67	0.244		S
1020			12.06	0.15		–
1021	0.046	103	9.55	0.039		F
1022	0.16	31.1	10.94	0.150		–
1023	0.062	60.2	10.47	0.150		–
1024	0.055	43.2	11.38	0.150		–
1025			12.87	0.40		E
1026			13.4	0.25		–
1027	0.068	36.1	11.54	0.150		–
1028	0.052	76.3	10.09	0.150		C
1029	0.12	24.5	11.74	0.342	14.4	S*
1030	0.028	65.5	11.22	0.150		–
1031	0.043	78.0	10.24	0.150		C**
1032	0.055	59.1	10.70	0.150		–
1033	0.096	25.5	11.92	0.250		–
1034	0.21	8.85	13.36	0.250		–
1035	0.032	56.8	11.39	0.150		–
1036	0.17	41.0	10.26	0.307		S
1037			13.24	0.25		–
1038			10.82	0.15		DTU
1039			11.22	0.15		–
1040	0.097	42.5	10.81	0.150		–
1041	0.048	60.6	10.81	0.150		–
1042	0.025	76.7	11.01	0.150		–
1043	0.14	37.3	10.74	0.250		S**
1044	0.19	20.0	11.67	0.150		–
1045			13.09	0.25		–
1046			10.41	0.15		–
1047			12.00	0.25		S
1048	0.045	72.5	10.39	0.150		C**
1049	0.029	58.2	11.45	0.150		–
1050			12.7	0.25		–
1051	0.042	68.6	10.67	0.150		–
1052			12.02	0.25		S**
1053			12.56	0.15		–
1054	0.045	49.6	11.29	0.150		–
1055			12.10	0.25		S**
1056			11.62	0.25		–
1057	0.027	49.1	11.86	0.150		–
1058	0.13	14.6	12.79	0.250		S**
1059			10.56	0.15		–
1060			13.2	0.25		–
1061			12.07	0.15		C
1062		55	10.10	0.15		C*
1063	0.14	18.0	12.21	0.250		S*
1064	0.15	19.8	11.95	0.150		–
1065			12.7	0.25		–
1066			12.34	0.25		–
1067			10.83	0.15		–
1068	0.14	26.8	11.38	0.150		C*
1069	0.13	43.2	10.42	0.150		–
1070	0.048	40.0	11.71	0.150		–
1071	0.058	52.7	10.90	0.150		–
1072	0.037	46.5	11.67	0.150		C*
1073			11.46	0.15		–
1074	0.052	53.8	10.96	0.150		–
1075	0.089	40.5	10.97	0.250		–
1076	0.029	24.5	13.14	0.495	7.336	F
1077			12.8	0.25		–
1078			11.61	0.25		–
1079	0.099	23.7	12.05	0.250		S*
1080	0.027	27.8	12.94	0.150		F
1081	0.024	40.3	12.45	0.150		–
1082	0.055	47.0	11.11	0.150		C**
1083			12.8	0.25		–
1084	0.091	32.0	11.49	0.150		–
1085	0.044	72.3	10.52	0.150		–
1086	0.054	70.5	10.35	0.150		–
1087	0.12	40.8	10.60	0.250		S
1088			11.45	0.25		S
1089	0.17	14.1	12.58	0.250		–
1090			12.9	0.25		–
1091	0.067	36.3	11.55	0.150		–
1092	0.044	47.6	11.41	0.150		C*
1093	0.036	120	9.50	0.150		C**
1094	0.083	18.1	12.82	0.150		–
1095	0.11	29.5	11.39	0.250		C*
1096	0.069	46.2	11.00	0.150		–
1097	0.057	25.3	12.51	0.150		–
1098	0.12	28.5	11.40	0.150		–
1099	0.13	35.8	10.84	0.150		–

			IRAS			
ID/1.	PV	D	H	G	Per	TYPE
1100			11.25	0.25		–
1101	0.047	41.0	11.68	0.150		–
1102	0.12	43.5	10.41	0.150		C**
1103			12.49	0.40		E
1104	0.033	24.2	13.20	0.150		–
1105	0.081	42.5	10.97	0.250		ST
1106			11.8	0.25		–
1107	0.070	81.0	9.76	0.150		–
1108			11.88	0.15		CEMP
1109	0.035	69.5	10.64	0.150		–
1110			12.16	0.25		–
1111		37	10.74	0.15		FEMPU*
1112	0.095	40.3	10.93	0.250		S*
1113	0.13	44.7	10.32	0.150		–
1114	0.057	63.0	10.52	0.150		–
1115	0.066	71.1	10.11	0.150		–
1116	0.14	40.7	10.45	0.150		–
1117			12.13	0.25		–
1118	0.033	80.7	10.59	0.150		–
1119	0.022	44.8	12.31	0.150		–
1120			12.2	0.25		–
1121			11.4	0.25		–
1122	0.20	13.8	12.44	0.150	20	S*
1123			11.62	0.25		–
1124	0.10	28.6	11.49	0.150		EMP
1125			12.01	0.15		–
1126	0.085	13.7	13.40	0.250		–
1127	0.030	50.3	11.62	0.150		C**
1128	0.052	40.2	11.59	0.150		–
1129	0.11	38.3	10.82	0.250		S*
1130			12.1	0.25		–
1131			14.2	0.25		–
1132	0.056	34.2	11.87	0.150		–
1133			12.30	0.25		S
1134			13.66	0.15		–
1135	0.047	51.5	11.17	0.150		–
1136	0.094	27.2	11.80	0.150		–
1137	0.089	26.1	11.96	0.250		S*
1138			11.1	0.25		–
1139			12.55	0.25		S
1140	0.13	31.5	11.24	0.250		S**
1141	0.056	11.6	14.21	0.250		–
1142			10.48	0.15		–
1143	0.041	135	9.23	0.150		D
1144			10.12	0.15		D
1145	0.098	25.5	11.90	0.250		–
1146	0.17	34.5	10.48	0.150		EMP
1147			12.04	0.25		–
1148	0.16	31.7	10.96	0.250		S
1149	0.041	57.3	11.09	0.150		–
1150			13.3	0.25		–
1151	0.012	22.0	14.51	0.250		–
1152	0.18	18.2	11.93	0.250		–
1153			12.26	0.25		–
1154	0.027	64.3	11.16	0.150		FEMPU
1155	0.14	15.2	12.61	0.250		–
1156			12.8	0.25		–
1157			10.09	0.15		–
1158	0.14	21.7	11.83	0.250		–
1159	0.044	31.0	12.34	0.250		–
1160			11.14	0.25		–
1161	0.040	39.0	11.94	0.150		–
1162	0.080	56.8	10.35	0.250		P
1163	0.082	34.8	11.42	0.150		–
1164			13.16	0.25		–
1165	0.032	54.6	11.45	0.150		–
1166	0.078	24.0	12.28	0.150		–
1167	0.039	69.0	10.68	0.150		D
1168	0.12	12.5	13.21	0.150		S*
1169			13.2	0.25		–
1170	0.11	12.3	13.38	0.250		S
1171	0.038	73.6	10.53	0.150		P
1172	0.038	151	8.99	0.150		D
1173	0.026	135	9.62	0.150		P
1174			11.7	0.25		–
1175			10.41	0.15		–
1176	0.064	32.0	11.88	0.150		–
1177	0.039	95.5	9.92	0.150		EMPFU
1178	0.070	21.6	12.62	0.150		CDFP*
1179			13.9	0.25		–
1180			9.15	0.15		P
1181			11.5	0.25		–
1182	0.14	18.0	12.24	0.250		–
1183	0.068	20.6	12.76	0.250		–
1184			11.39	0.15		–
1185			12.11	0.25		S
1186	0.18	39.0	10.31	0.250		–
1187	0.037	37.0	12.15	0.150		–
1188	0.13	13.8	12.91	0.250		–
1189	0.053	58.3	10.78	0.150		–
1190	0.065	20.1	12.87	0.250		–
1191	0.052	45.6	11.34	0.150		–
1192		8.4	12.93	0.25	6.558	S*
1193			12.1	0.25		–
1194	0.031	56.8	11.42	0.150		–
1195			13.4	0.25		–
1196	0.11	33.8	11.16	0.150		–
1197	0.064	49.0	10.95	0.150		C*
1198			15.6	0.25		–
1199	0.089	35.5	11.25	0.250		C**

ID/1.	PV	D	IRAS H	G	Per	TYPE
1200	0.054	42.0	11.48	0.150		–
1201	0.030	38.3	12.30	0.150		–
1202	0.033	66.3	11.01	0.150		–
1203	0.017	44.7	12.56	0.150		–
1204		11	12.27	0.25	7.90	S*
1205			14.1	0.25		
1206			9.48	0.15		–
1207	0.074	27.7	12.02	0.250	8.4	C*
1208	0.036	111	9.69	0.150		FCU
1209			10.4	0.25		–
1210	0.13	34.5	10.91	0.250		SM**
1211	0.043	41.6	11.74	0.150		–
1212	0.038	90.7	10.08	0.150	>16.	P
1213	0.036	43.2	11.84	0.150		–
1214	0.051	37.0	11.81	0.150		
1215			11.39	0.40		S
1216			12.73	0.25		–
1217			13.4	0.25		–
1218			13.08	0.25		–
1219	0.14	13.1	12.91	0.250		S*
1220		34	11.1	0.25	737	C*
1221			18.0	0.25		–
1222	0.055	22.0	12.86	0.150		–
1223		34	10.66	0.25	8.6	S*
1224	0.19	15.5	12.37	0.250	10.	S*
1225			12.5	0.25		–
1226	0.074	18.5	12.91	0.150		–
1227	0.058	48.2	11.08	0.150		–
1228			11.6	0.25		–
1229	0.070	31.0	11.84	0.150		–
1230			13.5	0.25		–
1231	0.084	22.0	12.38	0.150		–
1232	0.093	39.6	11.01	0.150		–
1233	0.048	34.5	12.02	0.150		–
1234	0.10	28.3	11.57	0.250		C*
1235			12.96	0.15		–
1236	0.043	26.3	12.68	0.250	>72.	T
1237	0.046	42.0	11.65	0.150		SC*
1238	0.059	22.5	12.71	0.150		–
1239	0.056	17.1	13.37	0.150		–
1240	0.058	60.5	10.60	0.150	7.	C*
1241	0.039	86.2	10.20	0.150		C**
1242	0.055	49.2	11.11	0.150		–
1243	0.037	75.5	10.60	0.150		–
1244	0.049	31.2	12.21	0.250		–
1245	0.20	28.3	10.88	0.488	4.855	S
1246	0.22	19.8	11.57	0.150		–
1247	0.059	40.6	11.32	0.150		C**
1248			9.84	0.15		–
1249	0.15	14.6	12.65	0.250		S
1250	0.046	21.7	13.06	0.150	3.92	S*
1251			10.71	0.40		E
1252			10.97	0.25		–
1253	0.027	30.1	12.92	0.150		–
1254	0.031	49.2	11.72	0.150		–
1255	0.10	34.6	11.21	0.150		–
1256	0.039	78.0	10.42	0.150		D
1257		14	11.90	0.25		–
1258	0.048	47.5	11.33	0.150		–
1259	0.063	36.2	11.63	0.250	12.	C*
1260			11.8	0.25		–
1261	0.077	34.2	11.53	0.150		–
1262	0.043	58.7	10.98	0.150		C*
1263	0.044	50.7	11.21	0.150		C**
1264	0.037	77.5	10.54	0.150		–
1265			10.80	0.25		–
1266	0.060	76.0	10.00	−0.079		P
1267	0.030	26.8	13.07	0.250	5.5	S*
1268	0.040	97.5	9.83	0.150		P
1269	0.047	109	9.50	0.150		D
1270	0.15	9.58	13.53	0.250		–
1271	0.045	49.5	11.32	0.150		–
1272			12.4	0.25		–
1273	0.011	30.5	13.85	0.250		–
1274			11.89	0.25		S**
1275	0.084	33.0	11.42	0.150		EMP
1276	0.068	36.2	11.53	0.150		–
1277	0.070	30.0	11.85	0.150		C
1278			11.05	0.25		–
1279		10	12.57	0.25		S*
1280	0.044	55.3	10.97	0.150		EMP
1281			11.51	0.15		–
1282	0.053	55.7	10.87	0.150		–
1283	0.093	29.8	11.62	0.150		–
1284	0.088	40.2	11.00	0.150	>18.	T
1285	0.068	45.5	11.04	0.150		–
1286	0.083	33.8	11.52	0.250		S**
1287	0.090	27.0	11.86	0.250		–
1288	0.034	39.2	12.13	0.150		C*
1289		24	10.64	0.25		S*
1290			12.6	0.25		–
1291		51	10.36	0.25		C*
1292			11.41	0.15		–
1293	0.059	8.52	14.83	0.250		–
1294	0.074	38.5	11.31	0.150		–
1295	0.040	52.0	11.34	0.150		–
1296	0.061	26.5	12.32	0.250		–
1297	0.012	66.0	12.08	0.150		–
1298	0.034	47.3	11.70	0.150		–
1299			11.91	0.15		–

ID/1.	PV	D	IRAS H	G	Per	TYPE
1300	0.061	32.1	11.91	0.150		–
1301	0.15	24.7	11.48	0.150		–
1302			10.8	0.25		–
1303	0.041	88.8	10.13	0.150		–
1304	0.16	47.8	9.99	0.150		–
1305	0.13	29.5	11.29	0.150		C*
1306	0.052	69.5	10.47	0.250		S**
1307			12.33	0.25		S
1308	0.043	45.0	11.56	0.150		–
1309	0.039	59.8	11.04	0.150		–
1310			11.55	0.25		S
1311			12.7	0.25		–
1312	0.047	38.3	11.82	0.150		–
1313			11.8	0.25		–
1314	0.071	14.1	13.60	0.250		S**
1315	0.043	65.5	10.75	0.150		–
1316			13.7	0.25		–
1317		62	9.93	0.15	7.048	EMP*
1318	0.12	14.5	12.83	0.250		–
1319			10.6	0.25		–
1320	0.041	45.6	11.59	0.150		–
1321	0.10	36.3	11.09	0.150		C*
1322			13.0	0.25		–
1323	0.038	60.1	11.06	0.150		–
1324			12.5	0.25		–
1325	0.16	12.5	12.91	0.150		–
1326			10.96	0.25		–
1327	0.021	33.5	12.97	0.150		–
1328	0.036	59.6	11.05	0.150		–
1329	0.11	27.5	11.67	0.250		SU**
1330	0.044	58.0	10.85	0.150		M**
1331	0.094	37.0	10.99	0.250	>10.	BC*
1332	0.059	49.5	11.02	0.150		–
1333			11.71	0.15		–
1334	0.21	28.3	10.81	0.150		–
1335			13.8	0.25		–
1336	0.11	25.1	11.74	0.250		S
1337	0.042	41.0	11.80	0.150		–
1338			12.91	0.25		–
1339	0.10	27.6	11.63	0.250		–
1340	0.060	29.5	12.12	0.150		–
1341	0.10	30.7	11.27	0.150		CMEU**
1342	0.11	20.1	12.16	0.250		EMP
1343	0.059	28.3	12.22	0.150		–
1344			13.00	0.25		–
1345	0.036	79.3	10.45	0.150		EMP
1346	0.23	15.1	12.09	0.150		SC*
1347	0.028	36.0	12.53	0.150		–
1348			11.2	0.15		–
1349			10.66	0.15		–
1350	0.14	26.1	11.47	0.250	6.	S
1351	0.037	67.1	10.85	0.150		–
1352	0.097	24.0	12.05	0.150		–
1353	0.12	37.5	10.80	0.250		–
1354	0.048	52.5	11.12	0.150		–
1355			13.18	0.25		EMP
1356	0.031	67.2	11.06	0.150		–
1357	0.033	45.1	11.76	0.150		–
1358	0.030	24.0	13.32	0.250		–
1359	0.035	55.5	11.25	0.150		C**
1360	0.054	31.0	12.12	0.150		–
1361	0.040	34.7	12.20	0.150		–
1362	0.066	31.1	11.82	0.150	7.	CP*
1363			11.60	0.25		–
1364	0.084	29.3	11.77	0.250		S**
1365			12.23	0.25		–
1366	0.12	31.7	11.19	0.150		C*
1367			13.1	0.25		–
1368	0.14	22.3	11.76	0.150		S*
1369	0.045	45.5	11.49	0.150		–
1370			13.8	0.25		–
1371	0.049	35.2	11.96	0.150		–
1372			11.6	0.25		–
1373			13.1	0.25		–
1374			13.6	0.25		–
1375	0.055	23.7	12.68	0.250		–
1376			12.48	0.25		–
1377			13.1	0.25		–
1378			12.25	0.25		–
1379	0.16	21.0	11.76	0.150		S*
1380			12.0	0.25		–
1381	0.050	24.0	12.76	0.250		–
1382			12.26	0.25		–
1383	0.059	24.2	12.57	0.150		–
1384	0.045	29.0	12.46	0.150		–
1385	0.12	25.0	11.72	0.150		–
1386			13.6	0.25		–
1387			13.2	0.25		–
1388	0.074	29.3	11.90	0.250		SM**
1389	0.049	28.1	12.44	0.250		C*
1390	0.033	104	9.95	−0.221		P
1391			12.08	0.25		S
1392	0.040	30.0	12.48	0.150		MEU**
1393			12.28	0.25		–
1394			11.89	0.25		–
1395	0.095	20.8	12.37	0.150		–
1396	0.16	14.0	12.67	0.250		–
1397		20	11.49	0.15		SC*
1398	0.11	34.5	11.11	0.250		–
1399			14.1	0.25		–

ID/1.	PV	D	H	G	Per	TYPE
1400			11.8	0.25		–
1401			12.29	0.25		S**
1402			12.94	0.15		–
1403			11.29	0.15		–
1404	0.049	92.0	9.87	0.150		–
1405			12.52	0.25		–
1406	0.054	31.0	12.12	0.150		–
1407	0.10	23.1	12.02	0.150		–
1408	0.046	41.0	11.70	0.150		–
1409	0.077	36.8	11.37	0.150		–
1410	0.10	22.6	12.12	0.250		–
1411	0.066	34.3	11.68	0.150		–
1412			12.5	0.25		–
1413	0.077	25.0	12.21	0.250		–
1414	0.039	20.0	13.44	0.150		–
1415	0.064	17.0	13.29	0.250		S**
1416		34	10.47	0.25	4.3	–
1417			11.19	0.15		–
1418	0.22	11.0	12.93	0.250		S
1419	0.14	17.5	12.27	0.250		–
1420	0.064	23.8	12.52	0.150		–
1421			10.36	0.15		–
1422			13.43	0.25		S
1423	0.056	31.8	12.03	0.250		–
1424	0.052	74.0	10.28	0.150		–
1425			11.7	0.25		–
1426	0.21	18.5	11.75	0.150		–
1427	0.059	39.2	11.52	0.150		–
1428	0.035	60.0	11.16	0.150		–
1429		12	12.1	0.25	28	S*
1430			12.1	0.25		–
1431			11.4	0.25		–
1432			12.26	0.25		–
1433			11.7	0.25		–
1434	0.12	31.0	11.23	0.250		S
1435	0.035	20.0	13.56	0.150		–
1436	0.023	63.6	11.50	0.150		–
1437	0.029	171	9.00	0.150		DP*
1438	0.033	41.7	12.02	0.150		–
1439	0.027	60.1	11.40	0.150		EMPFU
1440			11.7	0.25		–
1441	0.035	17.6	13.83	0.150		–
1442			11.62	0.25		S
1443			11.2	0.25		–
1444	0.069	31.2	11.84	0.150		–
1445			11.85	0.15		C
1446			13.18	0.25		–
1447			11.12	0.15		–
1448	0.017	23.0	13.99	0.250		–
1449			12.6	0.25		S**
1450	0.11	17.2	12.59	0.150		–
1451			12.7	0.25		–
1452			11.9	0.25		–
1453			12.58	0.25		S
1454			13.1	0.25		–
1455			13.3	0.25		–
1456	0.036	45.5	11.61	0.150		C**
1457			11.3	0.25		–
1458	0.11	18.7	12.44	0.150		–
1459	0.079	33.2	11.56	0.150		–
1460			12.6	0.25		–
1461	0.11	38.2	10.78	0.250		M
1462	0.072	31.5	11.79	0.150		–
1463	0.028	51.7	11.72	0.150		–
1464	0.082	27.5	11.94	0.250		–
1465			11.0	0.25		–
1466	0.022	23.5	13.72	0.250		–
1467	0.054	112	9.27	0.150		GC
1468	0.022	17.7	14.29	0.250		–
1469	0.060	60.2	10.57	0.150		–
1470	0.039	40.5	11.89	0.150		–
1471	0.050	33.1	12.06	0.150		–
1472			12.63	0.25		–
1473	0.052	19.0	13.22	0.150		–
1474			12.61	0.15		–
1475			13.0	0.25		–
1476			13.7	0.25		–
1477	0.042	31.0	12.31	0.150		–
1478		11	12.75	0.25		S*
1479			11.71	0.15		–
1480			13.38	0.25		–
1481	0.085	36.6	11.27	0.150		C*
1482			10.97	0.25		–
1483			11.70	0.15		–
1484	0.029	46.3	11.92	0.150		–
1485	0.072	26.3	12.17	0.150		–
1486			13.47	0.25		–
1487	0.085	35.6	11.33	0.150		–
1488			10.9	0.25		–
1489	0.046	31.5	12.27	0.150		–
1490	0.058	20.5	12.95	0.250		–
1491	0.061	27.3	12.27	0.150		–
1492	0.051	15.0	13.78	0.250		–
1493	0.069	26.1	12.07	-0.203		F
1494			13.16	0.25		–
1495			11.72	0.15		–
1496			12.46	0.25		–
1497			11.8	0.25		–
1498			11.9	0.25		–
1499	0.036	36.2	12.24	0.150		–

ID/1.	PV	D	H	G	Per	TYPE
1500			13.12	0.25		S**
1501	0.12	12.2	13.23	0.150		–
1502	0.033	34.8	12.40	0.150		–
1503	0.18	23.0	11.44	0.150		–
1504	0.11	16.5	12.77	0.250		S*
1505	0.086	23.8	12.19	0.150		–
1506			12.04	0.15		–
1507			13.5	0.25		–
1508			11.90	0.25		BCF
1509	0.095	12.1	13.63	0.250		S
1510	0.067	27.0	12.20	0.150		–
1511	0.020	23.8	13.77	0.250		–
1512	0.032	90.0	10.31	0.150		P
1513		7	13.40	0.25	30	S*
1514			12.4	0.25		–
1515			12.8	0.25		–
1516	0.046	24.2	12.84	0.150		–
1517	0.046	38.7	11.82	0.150		–
1518			12.42	0.25		–
1519	0.065	29.6	12.03	0.150		–
1520	0.039	56.5	11.17	0.150		–
1521			12.1	0.25		–
1522		10	12.54	0.25		S*
1523		11	12.54	0.25	5.33	S*
1524	0.043	45.8	11.54	0.150		–
1525	0.096	13.6	13.27	0.150		–
1526			13.6	0.25		–
1527			12.07	0.25		–
1528			12.4	0.25		–
1529			10.04	0.15		P
1530			13.4	0.25		–
1531			11.9	0.25		–
1532	0.085	28.5	11.85	0.250		SU**
1533	0.072	32.3	11.72	0.250		S*
1534	0.053	24.3	12.68	0.150		–
1535	0.044	29.0	12.50	0.150		–
1536			13.07	0.25		–
1537	0.12	15.0	12.76	0.150		–
1538			14.4	0.25		–
1539			11.12	0.15		–
1540	0.042	47.5	11.49	0.150		–
1541	0.10	22.2	12.10	0.150		–
1542	0.049	50.1	11.20	0.150		–
1543			12.4	0.25		–
1544	0.052	24.2	12.69	0.250		–
1545	0.085	21.7	12.40	0.150		–
1546			10.6	0.25		–
1547			10.75	0.15		–
1548	0.043	29.5	12.49	0.150		–
1549	0.13	11.3	13.30	0.250		–
1550			11.80	0.15		–
1551	0.031	23.3	13.34	0.250		–
1552	0.093	21.5	12.33	0.150		–
1553			11.6	0.25		–
1554			11.57	0.15		–
1555			11.55	0.15		–
1556	0.10	30.8	11.28	0.150		EMPC
1557			11.25	0.25		–
1558	0.029	68.1	11.09	0.150		–
1559			12.0	0.25		–
1560	0.075	21.0	12.62	0.150		–
1561	0.071	33.1	11.68	0.150		–
1562	0.20	12.8	12.60	0.250	8.2	S*
1563			12.7	0.25		–
1564			10.87	0.15		EMP
1565			12.6	0.25		–
1566		1.7	16.65	0.25	2.273	C**
1567	0.052	71.0	10.29	0.150		–
1568			12.0	0.25		–
1569	0.019	36.5	12.89	0.150		–
1570	0.099	16.2	12.87	0.250		–
1571	0.023	34.5	12.83	0.150		–
1572			10.05	0.15		–
1573	0.11	12.0	13.40	0.250		–
1574	0.030	64.2	11.20	0.150		–
1575			12.6	0.25		–
1576	0.065	31.7	11.70	0.250	6.7	BU
1577			14.1	0.25		–
1578	0.040	57.0	11.12	0.150		D
1579	0.040	48.5	11.33	0.150		F
1580		6.5	14.55	0.02	6.130	C*
1581	0.049	40.0	11.54	0.250		BCU
1582	0.048	39.6	11.73	0.150		–
1583	0.051	109	9.41	0.150		D
1584	0.13	24.7	11.70	0.250	10.3	S
1585	0.042	52.1	11.26	0.150		C*
1586	0.074	16.0	13.21	0.250		–
1587			11.7	0.25		–
1588			11.0	0.25		–
1589			12.13	0.25		–
1590	0.14	14.8	12.67	0.250	6.7	S*
1591	0.065	21.5	12.71	0.250		–
1592	0.16	15.5	12.42	0.150		–
1593		6.6	13.50	0.25	47	S*
1594	0.12	13.1	13.08	0.250		–
1595	0.037	28.0	12.60	0.150		–
1596	0.037	51.1	11.46	0.150		–
1597			12.2	0.25		–
1598	0.043	14.5	14.02	0.250		–
1599	0.036	44.0	11.81	0.150		–

ID/1.	PV	D	H	G	Per	TYPE
1600			13.1	0.25		—
1601			12.50	0.25		S
1602	0.11	12.2	13.49	0.250		RU**
1603	0.048	39.3	11.74	0.150		
1604	0.090	33.8	11.33	0.245	8.	EMPSCU
1605	0.098	38.5	11.01	0.250		
1606	0.041	26.1	12.72	0.150		C
1607	0.15	14.8	12.56	0.150		—
1608			12.62	0.25		—
1609	0.087	32.2	11.52	0.150		S*
1610			13.6	0.25		—
1611			10.7	0.25		—
1612			11.0	0.25		—
1613	0.072	22.0	12.55	0.150		—
1614	0.048	49.5	11.25	0.150		—
1615	0.048	32.3	12.05	0.250	>18.	B
1616	0.079	28.0	11.94	0.150		
1617			10.9	0.25		
1618			11.6	0.25		
1619			12.21	0.25		S
1620			15.82	0.25	5.22	S**
1621	0.32	11.0	12.54	0.250		S**
1622			12.3	0.25		
1623	0.081	34.1	11.48	0.150		—
1624	0.072	28.0	12.04	0.150		—
1625			10.32	0.15		C
1626			11.40	0.25		
1627			12.88	0.25		S
1628	0.048	59.1	10.86	0.150		C*
1629	0.10	11.0	13.70	0.250		—
1630	0.083	23.8	12.22	0.150		—
1631	0.13	11.5	13.27	0.250		—
1632	0.046	30.7	12.31	0.150		—
1633	0.072	40.3	11.24	0.150		—
1634			12.94	0.25		—
1635	0.078	22.5	12.42	0.150		—
1636	0.14	12.1	13.08	0.250		S**
1637	0.062	49.7	10.96	0.150		—
1638			11.7	0.25		—
1639	0.043	41.0	11.65	0.150		C**
1640			13.5	0.25		—
1641	0.11	29.0	11.48	0.250		C*
1642	0.085	26.1	12.00	0.150		—
1643			12.6	0.25		—
1644		19	12.01	0.25	5.156	S
1645			11.5	0.25		—
1646		14	12.05	0.25	69.2	S*
1647	0.028	72.0	11.00	0.150		—
1648			12.63	0.25		—
1649	0.049	28.7	12.40	0.150		—
1650	0.042	31.6	12.19	0.150		F
1651			12.3	0.25		—
1652			12.6	0.25		—
1653			11.6	0.25		—
1654	0.078	30.8	11.74	0.150		—
1655			11.03	0.15		EMPFU
1656	0.11	9.31	13.90	0.250		R**
1657	0.14	9.61	13.65	0.250		—
1658			11.41	0.25		—
1659	0.16	31.6	10.88	0.150		—
1660	0.033	18.1	13.83	0.250		—
1661	0.058	14.5	13.70	0.250		—
1662			11.9	0.25		—
1663	0.034	13.2	14.48	0.250		—
1664	0.018	29.7	13.40	0.250		—
1665			11.88	0.25		S
1666			12.91	0.25		—
1667			11.95	0.25		—
1668			12.4	0.25		—
1669	0.051	41.5	11.48	0.150		CU**
1670	0.072	28.1	12.02	0.150		—
1671			12.40	0.15		—
1672			11.9	0.25		—
1673			11.0	0.25		—
1674	0.076	29.6	11.85	0.150	8.1	S?*
1675	0.15	13.5	12.76	0.250	5.3	S*
1676	0.070	12.3	13.83	0.250		—
1677			12.2	0.25		—
1678	0.038	45.2	11.68	0.150		—
1679			10.4	0.25		—
1680	0.19	16.3	12.10	0.150		—
1681	0.083	22.0	12.48	0.250		S**
1682			12.89	0.25		—
1683			11.7	0.25		—
1684	0.093	29.5	11.65	0.150		—
1685	0.030	12.2	14.84	0.034	10.196	S*
1686	0.063	36.3	11.62	0.150		—
1687	0.084	42.6	10.95	0.250	6.3	C?*
1688			12.2	0.25		—
1689		15	11.73	0.25	145	S*
1690	0.071	36.1	11.50	0.150		—
1691	0.044	40.6	11.63	0.150		CU
1692	0.037	38.5	12.08	0.150		—
1693	0.044	39.5	11.77	0.150		CBU
1694			12.13	0.15		—
1695	0.069	21.0	12.70	0.150		—
1696			13.2	0.25		—
1697			12.1	0.25		—
1698			11.1	0.25		—
1699			13.2	0.25		—

ID/1.	PV	D	H	G	Per	TYPE
1700	0.032	23.5	13.21	0.250		EMP
1701	0.13	29.7	11.20	0.150		—
1702	0.050	36.8	11.77	0.150		MU**
1703	0.086	10.8	13.90	0.250		—
1704			12.7	0.25		—
1705	0.071	12.0	13.90	0.250		—
1706			12.8	0.25		—
1707		8.7	12.61	0.25	>10	S*
1708	0.036	33.5	12.40	0.150		—
1709			12.98	0.25		—
1710			13.4	0.25		—
1711			11.04	0.25		S
1712	0.044	66.2	10.70	0.150		—
1713			13.1	0.25		—
1714	0.10	19.2	12.44	0.150		—
1715	0.042	24.5	12.90	0.250	>11.	S*
1716	0.035	29.3	12.70	0.150		—
1717			12.44	0.25		—
1718			13.6	0.25		—
1719	0.10	21.0	12.20	0.150		—
1720			13.2	0.25		—
1721	0.052	44.3	11.40	0.150		—
1722	0.025	26.2	13.33	0.150		—
1723	0.13	35.0	10.86	0.250		S*
1724	0.037	38.2	11.98	0.150		CFBU
1725			11.1	0.25		—
1726	0.034	30.0	12.70	0.150		—
1727			13.1	0.25		—
1728			11.6	0.25		—
1729			12.4	0.25		—
1730			11.6	0.25		—
1731	0.061	56.2	10.70	0.150		—
1732	0.14	24.2	11.59	0.150		—
1733			13.0	0.25		—
1734	0.048	31.0	12.25	0.150		—
1735	0.058	66.0	10.40	0.150		—
1736	0.026	30.1	13.00	0.250		—
1737	0.10	26.5	11.80	0.150		—
1738			12.6	0.25		—
1739	0.090	8.71	14.33	0.250		—
1740			13.25	0.15		F
1741	0.064	26.2	12.30	0.150		—
1742		33	11.88	0.25		C*
1743	0.050	20.5	13.11	0.250		S*
1744	0.027	14.1	14.56	0.250		—
1745			12.1	0.25		—
1746			9.91	0.15		D
1747	0.11	8.11	14.66	0.250		—
1748			10.52	0.15		D
1749	0.012	115	10.90	0.150		—
1750			13.52	0.25		S**
1751	0.11	14.3	13.00	0.150		—
1752			13.5	0.25		—
1753		35	11.1	0.25	8.8	C*
1754	0.033	82.6	10.41	0.150		P
1755	0.10	29.0	11.73	0.250		—
1756			12.8	0.25		—
1757		6.9	13.45	0.25	4.89	S*
1758	0.11	29.0	11.50	0.150		—
1759		10	13.15	0.15	29.25	SC*
1760	0.028	40.1	12.30	0.150		—
1761			11.5	0.25		—
1762			11.7	0.25		—
1763			13.1	0.25		—
1764	0.064	30.1	12.00	0.150		—
1765	0.090	45.8	10.67	0.150		CMEU**
1766	0.048	24.5	12.77	0.150		—
1767			12.26	0.25		C**
1768			12.45	0.15		F
1769			12.7	0.25		—
1770			12.39	0.25		—
1771	0.047	58.7	10.90	0.150		—
1772		12	12.93	0.15		S*
1773			11.42	0.25		—
1774			12.2	0.25		—
1775			12.2	0.25		—
1776	0.044	39.7	11.80	0.150		—
1777			11.8	0.25		—
1778			11.8	0.25		—
1779			14.3	0.25		—
1780	0.093	31.7	11.49	0.250		—
1781			12.7	0.25		—
1782	0.073	33.1	11.65	0.150		—
1783	0.043	26.3	12.74	0.150		—
1784	0.13	15.5	12.61	0.250		—
1785			12.8	0.25		—
1786	0.12	23.5	11.80	0.150		—
1787	0.060	29.8	12.10	0.150		—
1788			11.7	0.25		—
1789		7.3	12.54	0.25	5.8	S*
1790			12.61	0.25		—
1791	0.032	29.3	12.80	0.150		—
1792			12.05	0.15		C**
1793	0.046	18.6	13.40	0.250	7.0	S*
1794	0.035	43.1	11.78	0.150		C
1795	0.036	28.7	12.73	0.150		—
1796	0.041	76.5	10.34	0.150		EMPFCU
1797			12.8	0.25		—
1798			12.6	0.25		—
1799	0.067	28.2	12.10	0.150		—

	IRAS					
ID/1.	PV	D	H	G	Per	TYPE
1800			12.7	0.25		–
1801			11.2	0.25		–
1802			11.7	0.25		–
1803			12.2	0.25		–
1804			12.3	0.25		–
1805	0.051	33.7	12.00	0.150		–
1806			12.7	0.25		–
1807			12.7	0.25		–
1808	0.078	17.0	13.03	0.150	4.0	C*
1809			11.7	0.25		
1810			12.8	0.25		
1811			11.1	0.25		
1812	0.056	26.6	12.42	0.150		
1813	0.022	27.8	13.32	0.150		
1814			13.1	0.25		
1815	0.044	34.0	11.98	0.150		F
1816			13.6	0.25		
1817	0.081	17.0	13.00	0.250		–
1818			14.1	0.25		
1819	0.046	44.6	11.50	0.150		–
1820			13.5	0.25		–
1821			13.7	0.25		–
1822			13.04	0.25		
1823			13.0	0.25		–
1824	0.072	22.6	12.50	0.150		–
1825			11.8	0.25		–
1826	0.042	27.6	12.64	0.150		–
1827			12.41	0.15		
1828	0.069	30.5	11.90	0.150		–
1829			12.6	0.25		
1830			12.53	0.25		S**
1831	0.040	17.8	13.64	0.250		
1832	0.041	36.3	12.08	0.150		–
1833			11.97	0.15		
1834			11.6	0.25		–
1835			11.6	0.25		–
1836			11.5	0.25		–
1837			13.47	0.25		–
1838	0.054	39.5	11.60	0.150		–
1839			11.6	0.25		–
1840			11.7	0.25		–
1841	0.018	53.3	12.17	0.150		–
1842			12.75	0.25		S
1843	0.056	28.0	12.30	0.150		–
1844			11.2	0.25		–
1845			11.8	0.25		–
1846	0.041	12.7	14.34	0.250		–
1847	0.13	26.5	11.50	0.150		–
1848			11.41	0.25		–
1849			11.1	0.25		–
1850			13.1	0.25		–
1851	0.065	20.7	12.80	0.150		–
1852			10.7	0.25		–
1853	0.17	25.3	11.30	0.150		–
1854			12.89	0.15		–
1855			12.7	0.25		–
1856			12.3	0.25		–
1857			12.6	0.25		–
1858			11.7	0.25		–
1859	0.034	48.6	11.64	0.150		–
1860			11.5	0.25		–
1861			11.8	0.25		–
1862		2.0	16.23	0.12	3.065	Q
1863		1.8	15.81	0.40		SU
1864		3.3	15.02	0.25	8.57	SQ
1865		1.6	16.91	0.25	6.80	S
1866			13.2	0.25		–
1867	0.037	131	9.32	0.150		D
1868			9.6	0.25		–
1869			11.2	0.25		–
1870			10.8	0.25		–
1871			11.2	0.25		–
1873	0.024	64.8	11.40	0.150		–
1874			11.0	0.25		–
1875			12.2	0.25		–
1876			14.7	0.25		–
1877	0.021	50.3	12.10	0.150		–
1878	0.070	21.0	12.68	0.250		–
1879			13.0	0.25		–
1880	0.036	26.2	12.93	0.150		–
1881	0.072	31.2	11.80	0.150		–
1882	0.12	23.8	11.80	0.150		–
1883			13.2	0.25		–
1884	0.059	12.5	14.00	0.250		–
1885			13.6	0.25		–
1886	0.094	20.7	12.40	0.150		–
1887			11.53	0.25		–
1888			12.0	0.25		–
1889	0.068	36.8	11.50	0.150		–
1890	0.060	31.1	12.00	0.150		–
1891	0.10	18.8	12.50	0.150		–
1892		12	12.28	0.25		S*
1893	0.11	21.2	12.10	0.150		–
1894			12.3	0.25		–
1895	0.048	20.6	13.14	0.150		–
1896			13.7	0.25		–
1897			13.79	0.25		–
1898			12.2	0.25		–
1899			12.7	0.25		–
1900			12.2	0.25		
1901			11.2	0.25		
1902	0.028	101	10.19	0.150		EMP
1903	0.10	29.7	11.50	0.150		–
1904	0.085	20.7	12.50	0.150		–
1905			13.54	0.25		
1906			12.7	0.25		
1907			12.1	0.25		
1908	0.085	26.1	12.00	0.150		–
1909	0.056	19.5	13.10	0.250		–
1910	0.078	36.0	11.40	0.150		–
1911	0.023	83.0	10.81	0.150		P
1912			12.0	0.25		–
1913			11.2	0.25		–
1914			12.5	0.25		–
1915		0.7	19.05	0.16	4.9	SMU
1916			15.03	0.25		–
1917			15.2	0.25		–
1918			11.2	0.25		–
1919			13.77	0.40		EMP
1920			14.34	0.40		EMP
1921			14.5	0.25		–
1922			11.8	0.25		–
1923	0.026	16.2	14.34	0.250		–
1924	0.046	14.0	14.04	0.250		–
1925			12.2	0.25		–
1926			12.1	0.25		–
1927			11.8	0.25		–
1928		8.7	12.95	0.25		S*
1929			12.2	0.25		–
1930	0.071	28.6	12.00	0.150		–
1931			13.4	0.25		C**
1932			13.5	0.25		–
1933			13.3	0.25		–
1934	0.27	7.25	13.50	0.250		–
1935			13.3	0.25		–
1936	0.085	26.2	12.00	0.150		–
1937	0.095	15.5	13.00	0.250		–
1938			12.7	0.25		–
1939	0.074	35.3	11.50	0.150		–
1940	0.039	38.6	12.00	0.150		–
1941			11.2	0.25		–
1942	0.046	14.8	13.90	0.250		–
1943			15.83	0.25		S
1944			13.7	0.25		–
1945			12.2	0.25		–
1946		8.4	12.7	0.25	10.223	S*
1947	0.12	35.0	11.00	0.150		–
1948			12.2	0.25		–
1949			13.5	0.25		–
1950			13.84	0.25		–
1951	0.026	4.98	16.90	0.250		–
1952	0.062	40.5	11.33	0.150		C**
1953			11.8	0.25		–
1954			12.1	0.25		–
1955			12.08	0.25		–
1956			11.7	0.25		C*
1957		38	11.53	0.25		C*
1958	0.039	42.6	11.80	0.150		–
1959			12.7	0.25		S*
1960	0.038	28.8	12.65	0.150		–
1961	0.019	55.5	12.00	0.150		–
1962			12.2	0.25		–
1963	0.036	46.5	11.63	0.150		C
1964			13.4	0.25		–
1965			12.3	0.25		–
1966			14.0	0.25		–
1967			12.15	0.25		–
1968			11.7	0.25		–
1969	0.066	25.8	12.30	0.150		–
1970	0.029	28.5	13.00	0.150		–
1971			12.3	0.25		–
1972		35	13.2	0.25		C?*
1973			11.7	0.25		–
1974	0.039	26.6	12.80	0.150		–
1975			12.1	0.25		–
1976			13.49	0.25		–
1977	0.014	60.8	12.10	0.150		–
1978			13.1	0.25		–
1979			13.6	0.25		–
1980	0.024	13.0	15.03	0.250		–
1981			16.9	0.25		–
1982			12.90	0.25		–
1983			12.7	0.25		–
1984	0.038	39.3	12.00	0.150		–
1985	0.038	39.3	12.00	0.150		–
1986	0.011	49.5	12.80	0.150		–
1987	0.11	16.8	12.60	0.250		–
1988	0.011	23.6	14.40	0.250		–
1989			12.2	0.25		–
1990			13.15	0.25		S
1991			13.5	0.25		–
1992			12.1	0.25		–
1993			12.2	0.25		–
1994	0.035	26.0	13.00	0.150		–
1995			12.6	0.25		–
1996			12.1	0.25		–
1997	0.11	8.53	14.10	0.250		–
1998			12.50	0.25		–
1999	0.065	37.6	11.50	0.150		–

ID/1.	PV	D	IRAS H	G	Per	TYPE
2000			11.36	0.25		S**
2001			12.96	0.25		EMP
2002	0.068	18.5	13.00	0.250		–
2003			11.8	0.25		–
2004			12.8	0.25		–
2005			12.2	0.25		–
2006			13.0	0.25		–
2007	0.057	25.3	12.50	0.250		–
2008	0.058	52.5	10.90	0.150		–
2009	0.043	40.5	11.80	0.150		–
2010			11.54	0.25		BU
2011			12.7	0.25		–
2012			13.2	0.25		–
2013			12.1	0.25		–
2014			12.54	0.25		–
2015			12.3	0.25		–
2016	0.094	25.0	12.00	0.150		–
2017			12.71	0.25		–
2018			14.5	0.25		–
2019	0.077	17.3	13.00	0.250		–
2020	0.068	25.6	12.29	0.250		–
2021			13.6	0.25		–
2022	0.035	26.5	12.94	0.150		–
2023			11.6	0.25		–
2024			13.3	0.25		–
2025	0.046	45.0	11.50	0.150		–
2026			13.2	0.25		–
2027			11.7	0.25		–
2028			14.1	0.25		–
2029			13.2	0.25		–
2030			13.6	0.25		–
2031			13.3	0.25		–
2032	0.023	42.0	12.40	0.150		–
2033			13.7	0.25		–
2034			12.7	0.25		–
2035			12.78	0.40		–
2036			12.7	0.25		–
2037			13.7	0.25		–
2038			12.2	0.25		–
2039	0.019	27.5	13.50	0.150		–
2040	0.031	34.3	12.50	0.150		–
2041			12.5	0.25		–
2042			12.9	0.25		–
2043	0.029	49.6	11.80	0.150		–
2044	0.14	7.87	14.00	0.250		–
2045			12.3	0.25		–
2046	0.094	27.3	11.80	0.150		–
2047			13.7	0.25		–
2048			13.79	0.40		E
2049			15.1	0.25		S
2050			12.79	0.25		–
2051	0.057	25.2	12.50	0.150		–
2052	0.087	35.1	11.36	0.250		S
2053			12.14	0.15		–
2054	0.029	24.5	13.33	0.150		–
2055			13.5	0.25		–
2056			12.2	0.25		–
2057			14.7	0.25		–
2058	0.092	31.7	11.50	0.150		–
2059			14.7	0.25		–
2060			6.62	0.25		B
2061			16.7	0.25		C**
2062			16.96	0.25		S**
2063			17.6	0.25		–
2064			13.7	0.25		–
2065	0.048	22.0	13.00	0.150		–
2066	0.024	21.6	13.80	0.250		–
2067	0.044	50.3	11.15	0.150		P
2068	0.029	35.7	12.50	0.150		–
2069	0.037	40.0	12.00	0.150		–
2070			13.6	0.25		–
2071			13.2	0.25		–
2072		9.6	12.64	0.25	4.4	S*
2073			12.7	0.25		–
2074			13.8	0.25		–
2075			13.7	0.25		–
2076			14.2	0.25		–
2077			13.2	0.25		–
2078			12.7	0.25		–
2079			12.2	0.25		–
2080			13.6	0.25		–
2081	0.036	26.1	12.73	0.150		F
2082			12.7	0.25		–
2083			13.33	0.25		–
2084	0.037	22.0	13.30	0.250		–
2085		26	11.85	0.15	32	SC*
2086			11.9	0.25		–
2087			13.2	0.25		–
2088		11	12.48	0.25	10.37	S*
2089			11.25	0.25		–
2090	0.041	41.2	11.89	0.250		S
2091	0.077	34.7	11.50	0.150		–
2092			11.6	0.25		–
2093			13.2	0.25		–
2094			12.79	0.25		–
2095			12.8	0.25		–
2096			13.2	0.25		–
2097			11.7	0.25		–
2098	0.080	17.8	12.90	0.250		–
2099			15.44	0.25		–

ID/1.	PV	D	IRAS H	G	Per	TYPE
2100		3.5	16.12	0.17	19.79	C
2101			18.2	0.25		–
2102			16.3	0.25		–
2103	0.17	24.0	11.43	0.150		–
2104			9.9	0.25		–
2105	0.034	24.0	13.20	0.250		–
2106			11.7	0.25		–
2107	0.11	17.8	12.50	0.150		–
2108	0.080	23.5	12.30	0.250		–
2109		18	11.91	0.15	32	SC*
2110			13.6	0.25		–
2111	0.11	30.1	11.33	0.250		S
2112			12.6	0.25		–
2113			13.23	0.25		–
2114	0.055	32.6	12.00	0.150		–
2115	0.095	24.8	12.00	0.150		–
2116	0.045	22.8	13.00	0.150		–
2117			11.7	0.25		–
2118			11.87	0.15		–
2119			13.7	0.25		–
2120	0.055	43.0	11.40	0.150		–
2121			12.5	0.25		–
2122			12.1	0.25		–
2123			11.05	0.25		–
2124			12.05	0.25		–
2125	0.058	15.8	13.51	0.150		–
2126			12.4	0.25		–
2127	0.023	42.5	12.36	0.150		–
2128			14.0	0.25		–
2129			14.0	0.25		–
2130	0.018	18.0	14.50	0.250		–
2131	0.14	9.01	13.84	0.400		S
2132	0.051	34.0	12.00	0.150		–
2133			13.5	0.25		–
2134			13.0	0.25		–
2135			18.0	0.25		–
2136			11.6	0.25		–
2137	0.029	44.5	12.00	0.150		–
2138	0.16	15.5	12.40	0.150		–
2139			12.81	0.15		F
2140	0.054	36.0	11.80	0.150		–
2141	0.081	26.7	12.00	0.150		–
2142	0.077	21.8	12.50	0.150		–
2143			14.1	0.25		–
2144	0.13	18.0	12.34	0.250		–
2145	0.081	37.0	11.30	0.150		–
2146			10.4	0.25		–
2147	0.032	33.7	12.50	0.150		–
2148			11.1	0.25		–
2149			11.8	0.25		–
2150			13.4	0.25		–
2151	0.22	20.2	11.50	0.150		–
2152	0.024	49.0	12.00	0.150		–
2153	0.090	20.2	12.50	0.150		–
2154	0.035	21.5	13.40	0.150		–
2155	0.022	29.5	13.20	0.150		–
2156	0.029	22.7	13.59	0.250	5.62	S
2157			11.5	0.25		–
2158			11.4	0.25		–
2159			12.16	0.25		–
2160			11.96	0.25		–
2161			12.2	0.25		–
2162			12.7	0.25		–
2163			11.6	0.25		–
2164			11.9	0.25		–
2165			11.5	0.25		–
2166			14.3	0.25		–
2167		9.6	11.7	0.25	7.0	S*
2168			12.9	0.25		–
2169	0.064	20.0	12.90	0.150		–
2170			13.5	0.25		–
2171			13.3	0.25		–
2172			11.5	0.25		–
2173			11.4	0.25		–
2174			13.3	0.25		–
2175			14.5	0.25		–
2176			12.2	0.25		–
2177			11.7	0.25		–
2178			13.5	0.25		–
2179	0.069	23.1	12.50	0.150		–
2180			11.1	0.25		–
2181			12.2	0.25		–
2182	0.060	31.2	12.00	0.150		–
2183	0.035	37.5	12.20	0.150		–
2184	0.10	29.7	11.50	0.150		–
2185	0.12	20.2	12.14	0.150		–
2186			12.4	0.25		–
2187			13.48	0.15		–
2188			12.0	0.25		–
2189			12.4	0.25		–
2190	0.020	18.0	14.38	0.250		–
2191	0.12	21.2	12.00	0.150		–
2192	0.062	30.6	12.00	0.150		–
2193	0.027	51.5	11.76	0.150		–
2194			12.6	0.25		–
2195			12.6	0.25		–
2196	0.036	62.2	10.91	0.150		CFEMPU
2197	0.076	26.6	12.08	0.150		–
2198			14.5	0.25		–
2199			13.1	0.25		–

			IRAS			
ID/1.	PV	D	H	G	Per	TYPE
2200			12.7	0.25		–
2201	0.33	1.90	16.21	0.250	24	S*
2202			16.3	0.25		–
2203			12.01	0.15		
2204	0.018	27.5	13.60	0.150		–
2205			11.7	0.25		–
2206			11.6	0.25		–
2207	0.058	92.6	9.60	0.150		D
2208	0.036	45.2	11.71	0.150		D
2209	0.15	19.2	12.00	0.150		–
2210			14.4	0.25		–
2211			13.9	0.25		–
2212			14.0	0.25		–
2213			13.8	0.25		–
2214	0.045	28.5	12.50	0.150		–
2215	0.13	17.2	12.40	0.150		–
2216	0.12	21.8	12.00	0.150		–
2217	0.066	29.8	12.00	0.150		–
2218	0.037	31.5	12.50	0.150		–
2219	0.046	45.0	11.50	0.150		–
2220			12.0	0.25		–
2221			13.1	0.25		–
2222	0.073	28.2	12.00	0.150		–
2223	0.027	105	10.20	0.150		DU
2224			11.9	0.25		–
2225			12.0	0.25		–
2226			11.75	0.25		–
2227			13.8	0.25		–
2228	0.036	29.7	12.65	0.150		–
2229			13.2	0.25		–
2230			12.0	0.25		–
2231			12.5	0.25		–
2232			12.0	0.25		–
2233			12.69	0.25		–
2234			12.2	0.25		–
2235	0.019	54.6	12.06	0.150		–
2236			12.4	0.25		–
2237	0.10	23.6	12.00	0.150		–
2238	0.078	21.6	12.50	0.150		–
2239	0.025	43.1	12.26	0.150		–
2240	0.048	27.6	12.50	0.150		–
2241	0.040	123	9.40	0.150		D
2242			13.9	0.25		–
2243			12.9	0.25		–
2244	0.026	29.6	13.00	0.150		–
2245	0.052	33.6	12.00	0.150		–
2246	0.034	52.1	11.45	0.150		D
2247			13.6	0.25		–
2248	0.074	30.0	11.86	0.150		–
2249	0.023	46.0	12.20	0.150		–
2250			11.6	0.25		–
2251	0.047	29.5	12.40	0.150		–
2252			12.85	0.15		–
2253			13.1	0.25		–
2254			12.5	0.25		–
2255	0.071	28.5	12.00	0.150		–
2256			11.9	0.25		–
2257			13.1	0.25		–
2258	0.048	27.6	12.50	0.150		–
2259	0.024	25.0	13.50	0.250		–
2260	0.064	85.0	9.74	0.150		DTU
2261			13.43	0.25		–
2262			12.7	0.25		–
2263	0.10	23.5	12.00	0.150		–
2264	0.10	30.8	11.39	0.150		–
2265			13.3	0.25		–
2266	0.029	53.6	11.56	0.150		D
2267	0.036	16.0	14.00	0.250		–
2268			11.9	0.25		–
2269	0.10	30.2	11.50	0.150		–
2270			10.81	0.15		–
2271	0.079	34.1	11.50	0.150		–
2272			14.04	0.25		S
2273			13.34	0.25		–
2274			12.70	0.25		–
2275			13.60	0.25		–
2276			13.0	0.25		–
2277			12.11	0.15		–
2278			14.27	0.15		FC
2279	0.040	17.0	13.59	0.150		F
2280			14.14	0.25		–
2281			13.5	0.25		–
2282			13.4	0.25		–
2283			12.70	0.25		–
2284			12.7	0.25		–
2285			13.7	0.25		–
2286			13.2	0.25		–
2287			13.1	0.25		–
2288			11.3	0.25		–
2289			13.4	0.25		–
2290			12.16	0.15		–
2291	0.068	38.5	11.41	0.250		–
2292			11.8	0.25		–
2293			10.8	0.25		–
2294			11.4	0.25		–
2295			12.2	0.25		–
2296			11.4	0.25		–
2297	0.069	29.1	12.00	0.150		–
2298			12.9	0.25		–
2299			13.4	0.25		–

			IRAS			
ID/1.	PV	D	H	G	Per	TYPE
2300			11.76	0.25		–
2301			11.5	0.25		–
2302			12.20	0.41		–
2303			11.5	0.25		–
2304			12.22	0.15		–
2305			11.8	0.25		–
2306	0.035	23.3	13.22	0.150		–
2307	0.029	45.1	11.99	0.150		–
2308	0.081	19.6	12.67	0.150		–
2309			11.4	0.25		–
2310			12.1	0.25		–
2311	0.029	61.0	11.30	0.150		D
2312	0.039	60.0	10.97	0.150		D
2313	0.032	17.6	13.92	0.150		–
2314			12.8	0.25		–
2315	0.13	26.0	11.50	0.150		–
2316			12.57	0.25		–
2317			13.46	0.15		–
2318			13.85	0.25		–
2319			12.15	0.25		–
2320	0.056	40.5	11.50	0.150		–
2321	0.075	22.0	12.50	0.150		–
2322	0.042	18.7	13.50	0.250		–
2323			11.1	0.25		–
2324			11.64	0.15		–
2325			12.05	0.15		–
2326	0.048	45.6	11.41	0.150		–
2327			13.76	0.25		–
2328	0.073	14.1	13.50	0.250		–
2329			15.1	0.25		–
2330	0.061	39.0	11.50	0.150		–
2331	0.046	20.7	13.17	0.250		–
2332	0.083	34.2	11.44	0.150		–
2333	0.055	23.8	12.68	0.150		–
2334			13.5	0.25		–
2335			13.1	0.25		–
2336			11.44	0.15		–
2337	0.042	25.2	12.85	0.150		–
2338			11.9	0.25		–
2339			13.55	0.15		–
2340			20.2	0.25		–
2341			12.7	0.25		–
2342			11.97	0.15		–
2343			13.6	0.25		–
2344			12.0	0.25		–
2345	0.067	35.5	11.61	0.250		S
2346			12.1	0.25		–
2347			11.42	0.15		–
2348			12.5	0.25		–
2349	0.089	21.5	12.38	0.150		–
2350	0.043	14.7	14.00	0.250		–
2351			13.1	0.25		–
2352			10.79	0.15		–
2353			11.9	0.25		–
2354			11.4	0.25		–
2355	0.11	22.5	12.00	0.150		–
2356	0.039	49.2	11.47	0.150		–
2357	0.042	103	9.71	0.150		D
2358			11.2	0.25		–
2359			12.93	0.25		–
2360			12.43	0.15		–
2361			11.91	0.15		–
2362			13.6	0.25		–
2363	0.066	91.7	9.50	0.150		D
2364	0.17	22.3	11.57	0.150		–
2365			11.96	0.15		–
2366			13.95	0.25		–
2367			13.75	0.25		–
2368		2.4	15.6	0.25	5.9	SQ*
2369			12.00	0.15		–
2370	0.44	18.0	11.00	0.150		–
2371			12.72	0.25		–
2372	0.061	24.6	12.50	0.150		–
2373			12.6	0.25		–
2374			11.21	0.15		–
2375			10.71	0.15		D
2376	0.052	40.6	11.58	0.150		–
2377			12.44	0.25		–
2378	0.072	37.7	11.39	0.150		–
2379	0.071	32.5	11.58	0.150		C
2380			13.2	0.25		–
2381	0.30	13.8	12.00	0.150		–
2382			11.5	0.25		–
2383			13.47	0.25		–
2384			12.40	0.30		–
2385			13.4	0.25		–
2386	0.15	15.5	12.50	0.150		–
2387			11.58	0.25		–
2388			12.97	0.25		–
2389			13.1	0.25		–
2390			12.33	0.15		–
2391			12.5	0.25		–
2392			13.39	0.25		–
2393	0.039	50.8	11.40	0.150		–
2394	0.014	56.0	12.29	0.150		–
2395			12.4	0.25		–
2396			11.36	0.15		–
2397			11.25	0.15		–
2398			13.58	0.25		–
2399			13.27	0.25		–

IRAS						
ID/1.	PV	D	H	G	Per	TYPE
2400			12.43	0.25		–
2401			12.3	0.25		–
2402			13.30	0.25		–
2403			12.4	0.25		–
2404			11.14	0.15		–
2405	0.030	29.3	12.79	0.250		BCU
2406			13.6	0.25		–
2407			10.77	0.15		C
2408	0.023	25.3	13.50	0.150		–
2409			13.04	0.25		–
2410			12.99	0.25		–
2411			12.98	0.25		S
2412			11.9	0.25		–
2413	0.13	26.6	11.43	0.250		–
2414	0.068	33.5	11.70	0.150		–
2415			12.13	0.15		–
2416	0.090	27.8	11.80	0.150		–
2417			12.25	0.15		–
2418			12.6	0.25		–
2419			13.45	0.25		–
2420			11.8	0.25		–
2421	0.044	43.3	11.62	0.150		–
2422			13.6	0.25		–
2423			13.7	0.25		–
2424			13.0	0.25		–
2425			11.72	0.25		–
2426	0.053	28.2	12.35	0.150		–
2427			13.2	0.25		–
2428	0.061	31.0	12.00	0.150		–
2429			12.33	0.25		–
2430			12.2	0.25		–
2431			12.8	0.25		–
2432	0.10	10.0	13.88	0.250		–
2433			11.88	0.33		–
2434			11.61	0.15		–
2435			14.9	0.25		–
2436			12.2	0.25		–
2437			13.5	0.25		–
2438			13.69	0.25		–
2439	0.10	23.8	12.00	0.150		–
2440			13.6	0.25		–
2441	0.065	11.8	14.00	0.250		–
2442			12.73	0.25		–
2443	0.092	35.1	11.27	0.250		–
2444			11.86	0.15		–
2445			12.94	0.25		–
2446			12.99	0.25		–
2447			13.05	0.15		–
2448	0.073	33.2	11.65	0.150		–
2449			14.47	0.40		E
2450	0.035	35.0	12.35	0.150		–
2451			12.02	0.15		–
2452			12.02	0.15		–
2453	0.031	45.7	11.89	0.250		–
2454			13.68	0.25		–
2455			11.78	0.15		–
2456	0.035	103	10.00	0.150		–
2457			12.9	0.25		–
2458	0.052	28.0	12.39	0.150		–
2459	0.062	24.3	12.50	0.150		–
2460			11.96	0.25		–
2461	0.072	28.5	12.00	0.150		–
2462			13.98	0.25		–
2463	0.14	12.6	13.00	0.150		–
2464	0.075	20.0	12.72	0.150		–
2465	0.047	22.2	13.00	0.150		–
2466	0.038	24.6	13.00	0.150		–
2467			12.65	0.25		–
2468	0.16	9.53	13.50	0.250		–
2469			12.1	0.25		–
2470			11.7	0.25		–
2471			11.66	0.15		–
2472			13.5	0.25		–
2473			13.51	0.25		–
2474	0.082	21.1	12.50	0.150		–
2475			11.1	0.25		–
2476	0.11	24.8	11.79	0.250		–
2477			12.01	0.15		–
2478			12.54	0.25		–
2479	0.037	20.0	13.50	0.250		–
2480			13.49	0.25		–
2481			13.93	0.15		–
2482			12.4	0.25		–
2483	0.021	53.3	11.98	0.150		–
2484	0.060	12.3	14.00	0.250		–
2485			12.54	0.15		–
2486			12.98	0.25		–
2487			13.2	0.25		–
2488			14.0	0.25		–
2489			12.00	0.15		–
2490	0.12	13.6	12.99	0.150		–
2491			13.74	0.25		EMP
2492	0.086	26.5	11.96	0.150		–
2493			12.8	0.25		–
2494	0.028	57.7	11.50	0.150		–
2495			15.6	0.25		–
2496			13.5	0.25		–
2497			13.28	0.15		–
2498			12.03	0.15		–
2499			12.25	0.15		–

IRAS						
ID/1.	PV	D	H	G	Per	TYPE
2500			12.84	0.25		–
2501			12.15	0.25		A
2502	0.11	18.8	12.36	0.150		–
2503			14.1	0.25		–
2504			11.93	0.15		–
2505			11.31	0.15		–
2506			11.86	0.25		–
2507			11.63	0.15		–
2508			13.5	0.25		–
2509			13.15	0.15		–
2510			12.28	0.25		S
2511	0.041	18.0	13.62	0.250		–
2512			12.8	0.25		–
2513			13.5	0.25		–
2514	0.019	24.5	13.75	0.150		–
2515			12.34	0.15		–
2516			13.76	0.25		–
2517	0.016	47.5	12.55	0.150		–
2518			13.69	0.25		–
2519			11.40	0.15		–
2520			11.73	0.15		–
2521			11.7	0.25		–
2522			11.58	0.25		–
2523	0.073	23.6	12.38	0.250		–
2524	0.048	36.7	11.88	0.150		–
2525			10.76	0.15		–
2526			12.1	0.25		–
2527			13.04	0.15		–
2528			11.6	0.25		–
2529			13.1	0.25		–
2530			11.8	0.25		–
2531	0.10	25.6	11.81	0.250		–
2532			12.7	0.25		–
2533			11.76	0.15		–
2534	0.081	34.2	11.47	0.150		–
2535			12.64	0.33		–
2536			13.11	0.25		–
2537			12.8	0.25		–
2538			13.76	0.34		–
2539			14.39	0.25		–
2540			13.2	0.25		–
2541			12.1	0.25		–
2542	0.040	33.6	12.28	0.137		–
2543			11.8	0.25		–
2544	0.14	10.1	13.50	0.250		–
2545			13.21	0.25		–
2546	0.070	18.2	13.00	0.150		–
2547			13.7	0.25		–
2548			12.7	0.25		–
2549			12.8	0.25		–
2550			11.34	0.15		–
2551			12.40	0.43		–
2552			14.98	0.25		–
2553			11.1	0.25		–
2554			12.91	0.13		–
2555			12.03	0.31		–
2556			13.70	0.25		–
2557			12.49	0.25		–
2558			13.87	0.25		–
2559	0.025	30.5	13.00	0.150		–
2560			11.81	0.15		–
2561			13.12	0.25		–
2562	0.17	24.5	11.36	0.250		–
2563	0.041	34.0	12.22	0.150		–
2564			13.53	0.25		–
2565			14.6	0.25		–
2566			12.71	0.25		–
2567	0.058	24.5	12.55	0.150		–
2568			13.4	0.25		–
2569	0.047	33.0	12.14	0.150		–
2570	0.026	30.0	13.01	0.150		–
2571			13.21	0.25		–
2572			13.4	0.25		–
2573			11.3	0.25		–
2574			12.56	0.25		–
2575	0.026	18.8	14.00	0.250		–
2576			11.22	0.15		–
2577			12.7	0.25		EU
2578			11.70	0.25		–
2579			13.1	0.25		–
2580			13.49	0.25		–
2581			13.3	0.25		–
2582	0.064	37.8	11.50	0.150		–
2583	0.028	18.8	13.92	0.250		–
2584	0.043	11.8	14.45	0.250		–
2585			12.6	0.25		–
2586			13.10	0.25		–
2587			11.19	0.15		–
2588			13.43	0.15		–
2589			12.05	0.25		–
2590			12.84	0.25		–
2591			11.58	0.15		–
2592			11.7	0.25		–
2593			14.01	0.25		–
2594			11.7	0.25		–
2595	0.014	38.2	13.17	0.150		–
2596			12.9	0.25		–
2597			11.74	0.15		–
2598			12.59	0.15		–
2599			12.27	0.15		–

	IRAS					
ID/1.	PV	D	H	G	Per	TYPE
2600			11.29	0.25		–
2601	0.10	22.7	12.10	0.150		
2602			13.08	0.15		–
2603			11.98	0.15		
2604	0.045	18.0	13.50	0.250		
2605			12.7	0.25		–
2606			11.42	0.15		–
2607			13.47	0.25		
2608		1.0	17.57	0.25	8.0	S*
2609			13.27	0.25		–
2610			13.5	0.25		–
2611			11.96	0.15		
2612			11.20	0.15		–
2613			11.38	0.15		–
2614			13.3	0.25		–
2615			12.9	0.25		
2616	0.23	9.01	13.20	0.250		–
2617	0.027	59.2	11.46	0.150		–
2618	0.022	32.6	13.00	0.150		–
2619			12.6	0.25		–
2620			12.61	0.25		
2621	0.035	50.1	11.55	0.150		–
2622			11.6	0.25		–
2623			13.3	0.25		–
2624			10.6	0.25		–
2625			13.4	0.25		
2626			11.9	0.25		–
2627			11.93	0.15		–
2628			12.7	0.25		–
2629			14.76	0.25		–
2630			11.68	0.15		
2631	0.029	34.0	12.59	0.150		–
2632	0.054	32.7	12.00	0.150		–
2633			13.02	0.25		–
2634	0.058	46.5	11.16	0.150		–
2635			13.25	0.25		
2636			11.46	0.15		–
2637	0.024	19.6	14.00	0.250		–
2638			12.4	0.25		–
2639			13.34	0.25		–
2640			13.31	0.25		
2641			13.16	0.25		–
2642			12.5	0.25		–
2643			14.8	0.25		–
2644			13.86	0.25		–
2645	0.075	17.5	13.00	0.250		
2646	0.073	28.2	12.00	0.150		–
2647			12.80	0.25		–
2648			13.02	0.25		–
2649	0.031	33.1	12.59	0.150		–
2650			11.7	0.25		
2651			12.4	0.25		–
2652			11.8	0.25		–
2653	0.055	20.5	13.00	0.250		–
2654	0.043	23.1	13.00	0.150		–
2655	0.032	40.7	12.10	0.150		
2656			13.84	0.25		–
2657			11.93	0.15		–
2658			12.6	0.25		–
2659	0.063	31.0	11.95	0.150		–
2660	0.14	13.3	12.89	0.150		
2661			11.6	0.25		–
2662	0.052	10.5	14.50	0.250		–
2663			13.86	0.25		–
2664	0.034	13.1	14.50	0.250		–
2665			13.34	0.25		
2666	0.024	39.3	12.50	0.150		–
2667	0.029	28.5	13.00	0.150		–
2668			13.52	0.25		–
2669			12.77	0.15		–
2670			10.70	0.15		
2671			13.7	0.25		–
2672	0.044	21.5	13.14	0.150		–
2673			12.5	0.25		–
2674	0.041	102	9.81	0.150		D
2675			12.45	0.25		
2676			12.7	0.25		–
2677	0.062	22.5	12.67	0.150		–
2678			12.6	0.25		–
2679			12.0	0.25		–
2680			13.5	0.25		
2681			12.58	0.15		–
2682			13.76	0.25		–
2683			11.97	0.15		–
2684			11.79	0.15		–
2685			12.36	0.15		
2686			11.6	0.25		–
2687		13	12.07	0.15		S*
2688	0.069	21.5	12.64	0.150		–
2689			13.87	0.25		–
2690	0.20	21.2	11.50	0.150		
2691			13.61	0.25		–
2692			12.33	0.15		–
2693			13.22	0.25		–
2694			13.94	0.25		–
2695			12.10	0.15		
2696			12.1	0.25		–
2697	0.034	54.0	11.42	0.150		–
2698			12.15	0.15		–
2699			12.0	0.25		–

	IRAS					
ID/1.	PV	D	H	G	Per	TYPE
2700			12.31	0.25		–
2701			12.4	0.25		–
2702			11.5	0.25		–
2703			13.46	0.25		–
2704			12.93	0.25		–
2705	0.062	9.71	14.50	0.250		–
2706			11.9	0.25		–
2707	0.046	29.7	12.40	0.150		–
2708			11.98	0.32		–
2709	0.018	20.2	14.24	0.250		–
2710			13.43	0.15		–
2711			11.88	0.25		–
2712			14.4	0.25		–
2713			11.68	0.25		–
2714			12.86	0.25		–
2715	0.098	15.0	13.04	0.150		–
2716			13.5	0.25		–
2717			12.76	0.25		–
2718	0.043	29.2	12.50	0.150		–
2719			13.5	0.25		–
2720	0.042	9.39	15.00	0.250		–
2721			12.0	0.25		–
2722			12.27	0.15		–
2723			12.93	0.15		–
2724	0.022	30.7	13.12	0.150		–
2725	0.053	42.0	11.49	0.150		–
2726	0.020	34.0	13.00	0.150		–
2727			12.4	0.25		–
2728	0.048	18.5	13.39	0.150		–
2729	0.083	21.8	12.42	0.250		–
2730			11.71	0.15		–
2731	0.029	51.1	11.70	0.150		–
2732			12.27	0.15		–
2733			13.39	0.33		–
2734	0.081	26.8	12.00	0.150		–
2735			14.41	0.25		SDU
2736			12.98	0.25		–
2737			11.8	0.25		–
2738			12.0	0.25		–
2739	0.090	13.6	13.35	0.250		–
2740	0.087	26.0	12.00	0.150		–
2741			11.6	0.25		–
2742	0.062	21.1	12.80	0.150		–
2743			12.35	0.15		–
2744			15.09	0.25		S
2745			13.37	0.25		–
2746			13.68	0.25		–
2747			11.5	0.25		–
2748			13.0	0.25		–
2749			12.26	0.15		–
2750			12.85	0.25		–
2751	0.037	20.0	13.50	0.250		–
2752			11.4	0.25		–
2753	0.079	20.5	12.61	0.150		–
2754			13.6	0.25		–
2755			11.9	0.25		–
2756			13.19	0.15		–
2757			11.56	0.15		–
2758			13.85	0.15		–
2759	0.041	73.3	10.57	0.150		–
2760	0.043	62.6	10.76	0.150		EMP
2761	0.025	32.3	12.88	0.150		–
2762			13.69	0.25		–
2763			12.43	0.25		–
2764			13.48	0.25		–
2765	0.017	46.6	12.50	0.150		–
2766			12.2	0.25		–
2767			11.60	0.25		–
2768			12.79	0.25		–
2769			12.12	0.15		–
2770			13.1	0.25		–
2771			13.03	0.15		–
2772			13.43	0.25		–
2773			13.24	0.25		–
2774	0.043	39.0	11.88	0.150		–
2775			13.5	0.25		–
2776			12.62	0.25		–
2777			13.40	0.25		–
2778			13.06	0.25		–
2779			13.53	0.25		–
2780			13.3	0.25		–
2781			12.03	0.15		–
2782	0.013	26.8	14.00	0.150		–
2783			13.2	0.25		–
2784			13.1	0.25		–
2785			12.0	0.25		–
2786			12.1	0.25		–
2787			11.4	0.25		–
2788			13.0	0.25		–
2789			13.7	0.25		–
2790			12.85	0.15		–
2791			11.5	0.25		–
2792			13.00	0.25		–
2793	0.087	32.5	11.50	0.150		–
2794			13.1	0.25		–
2795			13.19	0.25		–
2796			12.51	0.50		–
2797	0.046	123	9.31	0.150		–
2798			13.0	0.25		–
2799	0.011	18.1	15.00	0.250		–

			IRAS								IRAS			
ID/1.	PV	D	H	G	Per	TYPE	ID/1.	PV	D	H	G	Per	TYPE
2800			12.9	0.25		−	2900			12.9	0.25		−
2801			12.31	0.15		−	2901			12.28	0.25		−
2802			10.7	0.25		−	2902			14.43	0.25		−
2803			11.7	0.25		−	2903			12.1	0.25		−
2804	0.086	26.0	12.00	0.150		−	2904			11.70	0.15		−
2805			12.3	0.25		−	2905			11.99	0.15		−
2806	0.057	20.1	13.00	0.250		−	2906	0.060	62.0	10.50	0.150		−
2807			12.6	0.25		−	2907			11.6	0.25		−
2808			11.44	0.25		−	2908	0.034	33.7	12.45	0.150		−
2809			13.69	0.25		BEMPF	2909	0.066	26.0	12.29	0.250		−
2810			12.3	0.25		−	2910			13.91	0.25		−
2811			12.11	0.25		−	2911			11.4	0.25		−
2812			13.51	0.25		−	2912			12.8	0.25		−
2813	0.036	36.7	12.21	0.645		−	2913			12.5	0.25		−
2814			12.44	0.25		−	2914			13.95	0.25		−
2815			13.12	0.25		−	2915			13.39	0.15		−
2816	0.046	26.1	12.67	0.150		−	2916			13.5	0.25		−
2817			13.91	0.25		−	2917			11.89	0.15		−
2818			13.89	0.25		−	2918			12.1	0.25		−
2819	0.12	13.3	13.00	0.150		−	2919			12.09	0.15		−
2820			13.1	0.15		−	2920	0.034	123	9.63	0.150		−
2821			13.4	0.25		−	2921			13.4	0.25		−
2822			12.53	0.15		−	2922	0.065	12.0	14.00	0.250		−
2823			13.3	0.25		−	2923			13.3	0.25		−
2824			13.58	0.25		−	2924			11.9	0.25		−
2825	0.046	17.7	13.50	0.250		−	2925			14.2	0.25		−
2826	0.023	42.0	12.40	0.150		−	2926			13.6	0.25		−
2827			12.2	0.25		−	2927			12.23	0.15		−
2828			13.7	0.25		−	2928	0.035	33.0	12.47	0.250		−
2829	0.029	47.3	11.88	0.150		−	2929			11.70	0.43		−
2830			12.55	0.25		S	2930			12.52	0.15		−
2831			12.15	0.25		−	2931			11.82	0.25		−
2832			12.5	0.25		−	2932	0.015	48.7	12.50	0.150		−
2833			12.15	0.25		−	2933	0.068	24.0	12.44	0.150		−
2834			12.0	0.25		−	2934	0.058	31.7	12.00	0.150		−
2835	0.033	30.6	12.70	0.150		−	2935			13.30	0.15		−
2836			11.1	0.25		−	2936			12.43	0.15		−
2837			11.94	0.25		−	2937			13.09	0.25		−
2838			14.27	0.25		−	2938			11.44	0.15		−
2839			12.7	0.25		−	2939			12.69	0.25		−
2840			12.96	0.25		−	2940			14.1	0.25		−
2841			12.8	0.25		−	2941			13.54	0.25		−
2842			11.9	0.25		−	2942			13.49	0.25		−
2843			12.94	0.25		−	2943			12.74	0.25		−
2844			13.61	0.25		−	2944			12.6	0.25		−
2845			13.51	0.25		−	2945			12.1	0.25		−
2846	0.10	31.6	11.40	0.150		−	2946			13.24	0.25		−
2847			12.6	0.25		−	2947			12.9	0.25		−
2848	0.070	25.2	12.30	0.150		−	2948			12.9	0.25		−
2849	0.056	17.7	13.30	0.150		−	2949			13.69	0.25		−
2850			12.0	0.25		−	2950	0.081	17.8	12.88	0.150		−
2851			12.36	0.25		−	2951	0.054	52.1	11.00	0.150		−
2852			12.2	0.25		−	2952			14.1	0.25		−
2853			13.61	0.25		−	2953			11.68	0.15		−
2854			13.0	0.25		−	2954			13.83	0.25		−
2855			13.1	0.25		−	2955			13.19	0.25		−
2856	0.078	27.2	12.00	0.150		−	2956			12.40	0.15		−
2857			12.7	0.25		−	2957	0.17	29.0	11.00	0.150		−
2858			13.8	0.25		−	2958			12.2	0.25		−
2859			13.5	0.25		−	2959	0.036	42.1	11.89	0.150		−
2860			13.02	0.25		−	2960			13.9	0.25		−
2861			12.73	0.25		−	2961			13.0	0.25		−
2862			13.57	0.25		−	2962			11.39	0.15		−
2863			12.31	0.15		−	2963			12.50	0.25		−
2864	0.042	18.8	13.48	0.150		−	2964			12.4	0.25		−
2865	0.14	17.5	12.30	0.250		−	2965			13.7	0.25		−
2866			11.79	0.15		−	2966			13.58	0.25		−
2867			12.81	0.25		−	2967	0.047	35.5	11.98	0.150		−
2868	0.014	25.3	14.02	0.150		−	2968			14.9	0.25		−
2869			12.37	0.15		−	2969			12.63	0.25		−
2870			12.92	0.25		−	2970			12.76	0.15		−
2871	0.036	19.6	13.55	0.250		−	2971			13.6	0.25		−
2872	0.056	16.7	13.42	0.150		−	2972			14.13	0.25		−
2873			13.13	0.39		−	2973			12.53	0.25		−
2874			13.58	0.25		−	2974			13.9	0.25		−
2875			12.39	0.15		−	2975			12.8	0.25		−
2876			12.68	0.15		−	2976	0.044	42.1	11.68	0.150		−
2877	0.017	37.0	13.00	0.150		−	2977			12.73	0.15		−
2878			11.57	0.15		−	2978			11.7	0.25		−
2879	0.057	32.0	12.00	0.150		−	2979	0.039	30.0	12.55	0.150		−
2880	0.043	18.5	13.50	0.250		−	2980			13.2	0.25		−
2881			13.64	0.25		−	2981			11.83	0.15		−
2882			12.03	0.22		−	2982			12.00	0.25		−
2883			13.19	0.25		−	2983	0.055	33.7	11.92	0.150		−
2884			12.1	0.25		−	2984	0.013	27.2	13.96	0.178		−
2885			14.2	0.25		−	2985			12.29	0.25		−
2886			13.5	0.25		−	2986	0.051	23.0	12.84	0.150		−
2887			13.07	0.25		−	2987			11.83	0.15		−
2888			13.2	0.25		−	2988			11.9	0.25		−
2889			11.50	0.25		−	2989	0.050	14.5	13.85	0.250		−
2890			12.96	0.25		−	2990			13.3	0.25		−
2891			11.11	0.15		−	2991			13.77	0.25		−
2892	0.043	58.5	11.00	0.150		−	2992			13.0	0.25		−
2893	0.055	92.8	9.72	0.150		D	2993	0.099	12.2	13.47	0.150		−
2894			12.2	0.25		−	2994			14.2	0.25		−
2895			9.23	0.15		−	2995	0.062	15.3	13.50	0.150		−
2896			12.85	0.25		−	2996			11.87	0.15		−
2897			13.79	0.25		−	2997			13.16	0.15		−
2898			12.7	0.25		−	2998			14.4	0.25		−
2899			13.57	0.25		−	2999			13.36	0.18		−

		IRAS				
ID/1.	PV	D	H	G	Per	TYPE
3000			13.2	0.25		–
3001			12.40	0.25		–
3002			12.8	0.25		–
3003	0.061	28.3	12.18	0.150		–
3004			14.4	0.25		–
3005			13.88	0.25		–
3006	0.051	11.1	14.41	0.250		–
3007			12.76	0.25		–
3008			11.88	0.15		–
3009	0.10	7.10	14.62	0.250		–
3010			12.43	0.15		–
3011			11.9	0.25		–
3012	0.022	64.1	11.50	0.150		–
3013	0.044	12.3	14.34	0.250		–
3014			13.18	0.25		–
3015			11.15	0.15		–
3016			12.22	0.15		–
3017			11.99	0.25		–
3018			12.92	0.25		–
3019			11.95	0.15		–
3020			12.17	0.15		–
3021			11.93	0.15		–
3022			13.5	0.25		–
3023			13.75	0.43		–
3024	0.053	41.1	11.54	0.150		–
3025	0.014	52.1	12.50	0.150		–
3026	0.062	21.3	12.79	0.150		–
3027			12.9	0.25		–
3028	0.11	28.5	11.50	0.150		–
3029			13.2	0.25		–
3030			14.4	0.25		–
3031			13.14	0.25		–
3032	0.065	27.5	12.18	0.150		–
3033			12.51	0.25		–
3034			12.28	0.25		–
3035			12.62	0.15		–
3036	0.11	44.8	10.50	0.150		–
3037	0.11	21.2	12.13	0.150		–
3038			13.45	0.25		–
3039			12.6	0.25		–
3040			14.7	0.25		–
3041			12.52	0.12		–
3042			13.6	0.25		–
3043			13.75	0.25		–
3044	0.063	24.2	12.50	0.150		–
3045			11.45	0.15		–
3046	0.056	20.2	13.00	0.150		–
3047			12.91	0.15		–
3048			13.75	0.25		–
3049			11.48	0.15		–
3050			14.65	0.25		–
3051	0.055	16.2	13.50	0.150		–
3052	0.050	13.6	14.00	0.250		–
3053			12.53	0.25		–
3054	0.059	28.0	12.26	0.637		–
3055			12.6	0.25		–
3056			12.69	0.25		–
3057			13.48	0.25		–
3058			14.4	0.25		–
3059			13.63	0.25		–
3060			13.3	0.25		–
3061	0.042	26.5	12.72	0.150		–
3062	0.094	27.7	11.76	0.150		–
3063	0.037	125	9.50	0.150		–
3064			13.13	0.15		–
3065			12.09	0.15		–
3066			11.39	0.15		–
3067			13.2	0.25		–
3068			13.3	0.25		–
3069			13.9	0.25		–
3070			14.11	0.25		–
3071			11.9	0.25		–
3072			13.57	0.25		–
3073			13.57	0.25		–
3074			13.60	0.25		–
3075			14.0	0.25		–
3076			13.84	0.25		–
3077			12.96	0.40		–
3078	0.045	31.6	12.27	0.150		–
3079			13.22	0.15		–
3080			11.67	0.15		–
3081			14.07	0.25		–
3082			12.38	0.15		–
3083			13.95	0.25		–
3084			13.54	0.25		–
3085			13.39	0.25		–
3086			13.60	0.25		–
3087			12.9	0.25		–
3088			11.63	0.15		–
3089	0.058	39.8	11.50	0.150		–
3090			12.1	0.25		–
3091			13.8	0.25		–
3092	0.065	38.0	11.48	0.150		–
3093			11.6	0.25		–
3094	0.061	24.5	12.50	0.150		–
3095			11.5	0.25		–
3096			12.49	0.15		–
3097	0.034	25.0	13.11	0.150		–
3098			14.8	0.25		–
3099			11.16	0.15		–
3100			14.0	0.25		–
3101			13.4	0.25		–
3102		1.8	16.04	0.25	148	–
3103			14.7	0.25		–
3104	0.12	22.3	11.97	0.150		–
3105			13.0	0.25		–
3106			10.81	0.15		–
3107			13.8	0.25		–
3108			13.9	0.25		–
3109	0.099	24.2	12.00	0.250		–
3110			12.96	0.15		–
3111			14.0	0.25		–
3112			13.55	0.25		–
3113			13.17	0.25		–
3114			14.13	0.25		–
3115	0.14	20.5	11.98	−0.049		–
3116			12.34	0.25		–
3117			12.31	0.15		–
3118	0.048	37.5	11.83	0.150		–
3119			12.24	0.15		–
3120			11.86	0.15		–
3121			13.62	0.25		–
3122			14.3	0.25		–
3123			13.36	0.15		–
3124			13.24	0.15		–
3125			12.11	0.01		–
3126			12.30	0.15		–
3127	0.025	31.0	12.96	0.150		–
3128			11.34	0.15		–
3129			12.51	0.15		–
3130			12.9	0.25		–
3131			12.03	0.15		–
3132	0.024	39.0	12.52	0.150		–
3133			13.53	0.25		–
3134	0.041	55.8	11.14	0.150		–
3135			14.1	0.25		–
3136			11.7	0.25		–
3137			13.4	0.25		–
3138			13.07	0.25		–
3139	0.044	45.6	11.50	0.150		–
3140	0.082	29.7	11.76	0.346		–
3141	0.078	43.5	11.00	0.150		–
3142			12.43	0.15		–
3143			12.6	0.25		–
3144	0.012	28.2	14.00	0.250		–
3145			14.4	0.25		–
3146			13.06	0.25		–
3147	0.011	29.0	14.00	0.150		–
3148	0.014	51.5	12.50	0.150		–
3149			13.75	0.25		–
3150	0.065	33.5	11.77	0.150		–
3151			11.99	0.15		–
3152	0.047	35.1	12.00	0.150		–
3153			13.11	0.25		–
3154			12.62	0.15		–
3155			12.4	0.25		–
3156	0.040	32.5	12.36	0.150		–
3157	0.032	34.2	12.47	0.150		–
3158			12.54	0.15		–
3159			12.53	0.15		–
3160			13.71	0.40		–
3161	0.087	15.6	13.09	0.150		–
3162			11.46	0.15		–
3163			13.7	0.25		–
3164	0.090	19.8	12.54	0.150		–
3165			13.0	0.25		–
3166	0.10	12.0	13.50	0.250		–
3167			11.5	0.25		–
3168	0.034	30.3	12.68	0.150		–
3169			12.32	0.15		–
3170			12.1	0.25		–
3171	0.041	47.3	11.50	0.150		–
3172			13.36	0.25		–
3173			13.3	0.25		–
3174			11.9	0.25		–
3175	0.030	17.6	14.00	0.250		–
3176	0.066	37.3	11.50	0.150		–
3177			12.12	0.15		–
3178			11.9	0.25		–
3179			11.9	0.25		–
3180			14.6	0.25		–
3181			13.0	0.25		–
3182	0.031	27.5	13.00	0.150		–
3183			12.7	0.25		–
3184			12.90	0.15		–
3185			13.8	0.25		–
3186			12.52	0.15		–
3187	0.050	17.0	13.50	0.250		–
3188			13.4	0.25		–
3189			13.1	0.25		–
3190			13.01	0.15		–
3191			12.39	0.15		–
3192			13.8	0.25		–
3193	0.014	25.2	14.06	0.147		–
3194	0.10	18.8	12.50	0.150		–
3195			12.61	0.15		–
3196			12.4	0.25		–
3197	0.050	25.0	12.68	0.332		–
3198			13.53	0.25		–
3199			15.03	0.25		–

		IRAS				
ID/1.	PV	D	H	G	Per	TYPE
3200	0.089	5.23	15.45	0.250		–
3201	0.011	22.7	14.50	0.250		–
3202			10.4	0.25		–
3203			14.17	0.25		–
3204			12.29	0.15		–
3205			13.22	0.15		–
3206			13.6	0.25		–
3207	0.040	19.6	13.44	0.150		–
3208			12.17	0.15		–
3209			13.50	0.25		–
3210			11.28	0.15		–
3211	0.014	32.5	13.50	0.150		–
3212			13.89	0.25		–
3213			12.28	0.15		–
3214	0.10	29.5	11.50	0.150		–
3215			12.3	0.25		–
3216			13.87	0.02		–
3217			14.5	0.25		–
3218			13.6	0.25		–
3219			11.8	0.25		–
3220			13.3	0.25		–
3221			13.28	0.25		–
3222	0.042	33.5	12.22	0.150		–
3223	0.083	24.5	12.17	0.150		–
3224	0.042	34.8	12.15	0.150		–
3225			13.40	0.25		–
3226			13.2	0.25		–
3227			12.8	0.25		–
3228			12.5	0.25		–
3229			12.4	0.25		–
3230	0.051	26.8	12.50	0.150		–
3231			13.1	0.25		–
3232			11.82	0.15		–
3233			13.0	0.25		–
3234	0.026	30.0	13.00	0.150		–
3235			13.1	0.25		–
3236			13.81	0.25		–
3237	0.061	31.0	12.00	0.150		–
3238	0.037	15.6	14.00	0.150		–
3239			14.66	0.25		–
3240			9.9	0.25		–
3241	0.060	20.6	12.89	0.150		–
3242			12.2	0.25		–
3243			11.6	0.25		–
3244			14.1	0.25		–
3245			13.0	0.25		–
3246			11.47	0.15		–
3247	0.035	17.7	13.81	0.250		–
3248	0.029	50.1	11.77	0.150		–
3249			13.56	0.25		–
3250			11.1	0.25		–
3251			12.2	0.25		–
3252			12.14	0.15		–
3253			13.51	0.25		–
3254			10.99	0.15		–
3255			13.72	0.30		–
3256	0.023	29.0	13.18	0.150		–
3257			13.50	0.25		–
3258			13.36	0.25		–
3259	0.10	37.5	11.00	0.150		–
3260	0.041	18.1	13.59	0.250		–
3261			11.77	0.15		–
3262			10.83	0.15		–
3263			13.11	0.25		–
3264	0.036	24.1	13.12	0.150		–
3265			13.25	0.49		–
3266			13.50	0.25		–
3267			12.90	0.25		–
3268			13.4	0.25		–
3269			12.74	0.15		–
3270			14.7	0.25		–
3271			16.9	0.25		–
3272			13.6	0.25		–
3273	0.045	35.8	12.00	0.150		–
3274			12.2	0.25		–
3275	0.025	16.0	14.39	0.250		–
3276			12.01	0.15		–
3277			11.27	0.15		–
3278	0.046	35.6	12.00	0.150		–
3279			13.78	0.25		–
3280			12.4	0.25		–
3281			12.8	0.25		–
3282			13.5	0.25		–
3283	0.061	15.5	13.50	0.250		–
3284			12.84	0.15		–
3285	0.19	10.0	13.19	0.150		–
3286			13.06	0.15		–
3287			14.3	0.25		–
3288			15.34	0.25		–
3289			14.2	0.25		–
3290			11.5	0.25		–
3291			12.2	0.25		–
3292			12.2	0.25		–
3293			13.7	0.25		–
3294			12.6	0.25		–
3295			12.9	0.25		–
3296			13.04	0.15		–
3297			12.52	0.15		–
3298	0.032	16.8	14.00	0.250		–
3299			13.4	0.25		–

		IRAS				
ID/1.	PV	D	H	G	Per	TYPE
3300			10.5	0.25		–
3301			13.2	0.25		–
3302			12.9	0.25		–
3303			11.8	0.25		–
3304			13.0	0.25		–
3305			12.4	0.25		–
3306			12.6	0.25		–
3307	0.038	13.5	14.30	0.250		–
3308			11.72	0.15		–
3309			13.9	0.25		–
3310	0.12	27.1	11.50	0.150		–
3311	0.047	22.3	13.00	0.150		–
3312	0.034	32.7	12.50	0.150		–
3313			12.2	0.25		–
3314			14.02	0.25		–
3315			12.50	0.15		–
3316	0.075	23.5	12.37	0.150		–
3317	0.050	127	9.15	0.150		–

HOW TO
OBSERVE
ASTEROIDS   18

Locating one asteroid among a couple of thousand is not as easy as finding Trafalgar Square in London—especially against the star-crowded backdrop of the galaxy.

Robert Heinlein, 1939

Observing asteroids can be great fun, but a dedicated program of positional, occultation or photometric observations demands a lot of hard work. The time spent planning an observation and then analyzing the data far exceeds the time spent at the telescope finding the little beasties.

The choice of which of the following observing programs you engage in will depend on the equipment available to you, observing site, and finances. Simply finding asteroids can be done with an inexpensive pair of binoculars, but a program of photoelectric photometry can cost $5,000 to $10,000 or more.

Visual tracking of asteroids: Binoculars or small telescopes will suffice to find the brightest asteroids. All you need for this project is a finder chart showing the path of the asteroid against the background stars (Fig. 18–1). These can be obtained from Jahn (see Appendix 1). Such charts can also sometimes be found in the popular magazines *Astronomy* or *Sky & Telescope*.

One interesting test you might try involves the brightest asteroid, 4 Vesta. At opposition, Vesta can be glimpsed by the unaided eye under excellent observing conditions. To avoid any bias in your judgment, try to see it without first looking at it in binoculars. For those who are willing to be patient, another asteroid will become bright enough (magnitude 6) to see under excellent conditions. This is 3200 Phaethon, the parent of the Geminid meteor shower, which will pass only 1.6 million km away in 2287 AD. (Fox *et al*, 1984).

Positional measurements: After you have acquired some skill in finding asteroids, the next logical step is to record your observations, noting both the position and the time of observation. Armed with a small telescope (15–20 cm aperture) and a good star atlas (*Atlas Stellarum*, which goes down to magnitude 14 is the best), you can plot and find hundreds of asteroids. The annual *Ephemerides of Minor Planets* provides coordinates for all asteroids near their time of opposition (See Appendix 1).

It is just this challenging program that I began when I

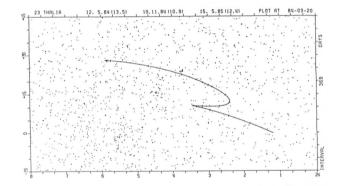

Fig. 18–1. *A chart prepared by Jost Jahn showing the path of 23 Thalia over an interval of 369 days. Along the top of the chart is the name of the asteroid and first date with magnitude, opposition date with magnitude, ending with the date the chart was plotted.*

was 13 years old. Ten years later (having acquired a lot of valuable observing skill in the process), I was making hundreds of positional measurements each year. Some nights I was able to find 25 asteroids or more!

By carefully noting the position of the asteroid with respect to nearby stars, you can measure its coordinates to within $1'$ in declination and $0\cdot1$ in right ascension. It is most important to make at least two observations on the same night or on subsequent nights, to ensure that the object you plotted really was the asteroid. Stars that are variable can occasionally confuse the interpretation of a star field.

Report forms for such observations are available from Professor Frederick Pilcher, Recorder of the Minor Planets Section of the Association of Lunar & Planetary Observers. Each year the observations you make, along with those of all other visual observers, are published in tabular form in the Minor Planet Bulletin. You may find that one of the asteroids you plotted was seen by no one else at that opposition.

Among the most avid asteroid hunters in the world is G. Roger Harvey of Concord, North Carolina. Since he began using a 29-inch telescope (Photo 18-1) in June, 1984, he has logged more than 500 asteroids. This brings his lifetime total to more than 1,600—about half of all the known asteroids.

A step up from these approximate positional measurements are precise ones, accurate to 1 second of arc. This can be accomplished with the aid of a micrometer or a camera. A photograph is preferred, as this provides an objective record that can be reexamined later. Timing of the exposure must be accurate to within a minute with an accuracy of 1 second. Merton (1977) gives the mathematical formula necessary to interpolate the position of the asteroid on the photograph with respect to two reference stars. Such accurate positions can be used to improve the orbital elements of asteroids (Hodgson, 1978).

There is a particularly dedicated group of amateurs in Germany, led by Dr. Frevert in Wetzlar, who have reported some 1,000 positional measurements to the Minor Planet Center. Asteroids down to magnitude 16 have had their coordinates measured on plates (Frevert, 1981). One member of the group, Fr. Seiler, observes with a 30 cm Newtonian from the Reintal Observatory. "The observatory does not look like one because it's in a house that looks like a barn. However, the dwelling has a tower which makes it look like a castle. The estate was originally situated in Munich around 1900, but the previous owner moved all the buildings by railway and with horse-drawn carriages to its present location." Seiler, who was looking for an observing site 20 years ago, made a deal with the owner to rent the tower for an observatory. (*Sterne und Weltraum*, 1981). Another member of the group is Kurt Ressel, a retired engineer in Bendestorf on the southern edge of the Harburger Mountains. His observatory is equipped with a 180 mm refractor, 250 mm Cassegrain, and a Schmidt camera for asteroid photography. A typical run using AGFA 400 film involves taking six exposures of 10 minutes each to show the asteroid's movement with a blink comparator. (*Sterne und Weltraum*, 1983).

Search and Recovery Work: Skilled astrophotographers with access to a Schmidt camera (preferably 36 cm or larger) can do much more than take pretty pictures of deep-sky objects or constellations. Dozens of asteroids on the critical list (see Chapter 4) are in need of photographic recovery work. By taking two photos of the same field twice on the same night, you can determine the motion and direction of any asteroid in the field, and maybe even find a new one! The chances of finding a new asteroid are very remote, of course, but Takeshi Urata, an amateur astronomer in Japan, discovered one in 1978. It was named 2090 Mizuho in honor of his daughter (Gunter, 1985).

Meteor Observing: Logging the passage of meteors through the Earth's atmosphere requires no optical aid, and is a good way to become familiar with star patterns. Most meteor showers recur regularly each year and are often associated with comets, but the close match in orbital elements of the strong Geminid meteor shower and the

Photo. 18-1. *G. Roger Harvey of Concord, North Carolina has seen more asteroids than anyone else- about 1,600, nearly half the total numbered population.*

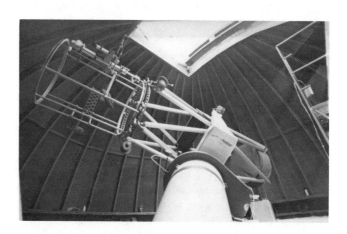

Photo. 18-2. *The 29-inch telescope Harvey has been using since 1984 to find asteroids. This replaced a 20-inch instrument he used for six years.*

asteroid 3200 Phaethon has added a new wrinkle to an old subject.

Jack Drummond (1982) has calculated the radiants (points in the sky where meteors appear to emanate from) of Earth-crossing asteroids, and he emphasizes that the task of monitoring these radiants falls to visual observers. "The rates will probably be low, if a radiant is active at all, and must be determined over many nights." He cautions that only experienced meteor observers should seriously attempt to detect meteors, but the "association of asteroids with visual meteor showers has far-reaching implications." Interested observers should contact Dr. Drummond at the Steward Observatory, University of Arizona, Tuscon, AZ 85721.

Appulses: The passage of minor planets through star clusters is not only visually interesting but scientifically advantageous. Three useful aspects have been noted by Welch *et al* (1984).

1. A higher probability of occultations.

2. All bright clusters have photoelectric sequences available, thus affording an opportunity for photoelectric photometry.

3. Positions are more easily obtained due to the number of stars near the asteroid.

Passages of asteroids near bright stars or variable stars also offers some possibilities for visual photometry (Sventek, 1984).

Occultations: Unlike the other observing programs described here, occultation work requires travel—perhaps hundreds of kilometers for important events. Despite the difficulties, occultation chasing is becoming quite popular. Before 1977, only seven asteroid occultations had ever been seen, but that number has increased sixfold since then (Maley, 1984).

Occultations can either be recorded visually (with a tape recorder and audible time signals), photographically (a stationary camera will show a break in a star's trailed image at the moment of occultation), or photoelectrically. The latter method requires a portable telescope and photometer capable of high-speed photometry and data recording. Oswalt & Rafert (1985) describe a portable system which consists of only four commercially available subsystems: a Celestron 14 telescope, Starlight 1 photometer, Commodore SX–64 portable computer, and a Honda portable generator. Cost of the complete system is $12,000, within reach of small institutions and serious amateurs. Detailed observing methods are given by Harris (1983), and regional occultation coordinators are listed in Dunham & Kristensen (1983). Observers interested in this work should contact Jim Stamm, director of the Asteroid Research Project (International Occultation Timing Association), Rt 13, Box 109, London, Kentucky 40741. Amateurs are also actively observing asteroid occultations from Europe, a successful event having taken place in Denmark and Germany on 19 January 1983. Observations of 106 Dione yielded a diameter of 145 km (Reimann, 1983).

Visual Photometry: Magnitude estimates for most asteroids are based on photographic observations, but in transforming to the standard B magnitude, errors of 0.5 magnitude or more may be made. If an asteroid passes through a field covered by a star chart prepared by the American Association of Variable Star Observers (AAVSO), its V magnitude can be estimated. By applying a B–V correction of 0.8 magnitude, any discrepancies can be noted and corrected (Binzel, 1984a). Pilcher (1981) provides details on this technique.

An equally important project that can be done with visual photometry is the determination of the rotational period and the phase coefficient of asteroids. Only asteroids with large amplitudes and relatively fast rotation periods (less than 12 hours) are amenable to visual photometry, but it has been done with notable success (Pilcher, 1983). Visual photometry was successfully employed on 216 Kleopatra, which has an amplitude of more than a magnitude. Making magnitude estimates every 20 minutes

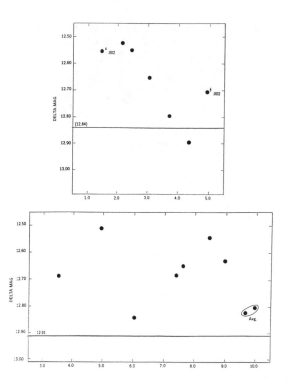

Fig. 18–2. and –3. *Sample lightcurves of an asteroid used to determine its rotational period. The horizontal line is a line of constant brightness- since an asteroid can brighten or dim by several magnitudes over a few months, this permits the lightcurve from one night to be superimposed upon those of other nights. Two points had to be shifted in this example because of standard star variations, and two other points were averaged.*

Photo. 18–3. *Friedrich Frevert, a German astronomer from Wetzlar. Dr. Frevert organized the Minor Planet Working Group in 1975, a group of 25 amateur astronomers who make positional measurements of asteroids.*

167

Photo. 18–4. *Jack Drummond of the University of Arizona Steward Observatory has pioneered the use of speckle interferometry in asteroid research, and he encourages amateur astronomers to search for meteors associated with Earth-crossing asteroids.*

with respect to 3 comparison stars, the time of minimum light was recorded to within two minutes of the predicted time by an amateur in Germany (Kersken, 1982). Remarkably enough, only binoculars (and a lot of experience estimating magnitudes!) were used by Roy Panther in England to determine the phase coefficient of 18 Melpomene. These remarkable observations should inspire others who seek a real challenge with modest equipment (Panther & Binzel, 1984).

Photoelectric Photometry: Scientifically useful photometry on asteroids can likely be done with telescopes as small as 25 cm aperture, but a telescope 36 cm or larger is recommended. There are probably several hundred asteroids bright enough for instruments of this class to observe photoelectrically. The first asteroid you gather data on should be one that is already well-observed. This will allow you to compare your results with what should be expected, and thus "iron out" any bugs in your equipment or observing procedures before tackling an unknown lightcurve (Cunningham, 1983c; Fig. 18–2).

To choose an asteroid for observation, scan the Russian Ephemerides of Minor Planets to find which objects are within range of your telescope. Considerations here include magnitude of the asteroid, declination of the asteroid, phase of the moon, and proximity of the moon to the asteroid. Next, check your candidate asteroids in the TRIAD file and the Asteroid Lightcurve Catalogue (see Appendix 2). The most poorly observed asteroid should be your target. Important candidates are also regularly listed in the Minor Planet Bulletin.

When you have selected an asteroid, the next step is to choose the comparison and check stars. If you plan to observe the asteroid for a few weeks or months, two or more sets of such stars will be needed. If the asteroid is near the celestial equator, choose stars from the UBV photoelectric sequence given by Landolt (1973) for the selected areas 92–115. If it is not near the equator, choose your stars

from the SAO Catalog, or the photoelectric catalogues of Blanco *et al* (1968) or Nicolet (1978). Try to eliminate any variables from your selection by checking them against the Russian Variable Star Catalogues (Cunningham, 1984 d).

After collecting the data, programs to reduce and analyze it can be found in Kaitting (1984), Cunningham (1983d) and Cunningham & Kaitting (1982b). All these programs are written in BASIC for an Apple II+ computer, and are designed to be user friendly, with numerous remark statements.

One of the fundamental properties of an asteroid that can be determined by photometry is its rotational period. Once you have collected several nights data on an asteroid, it is usually possible to estimate its period to within a few minutes. Several techniques can be used in such an analysis, but all must be used with care. Particularly in the case of an asteroid whose period is not already approximately known, it is advisable to have your results confirmed by a professional astronomer who has experience in period determination. (Cunningham, 1985c).

The author has modified and corrected a Fourier harmonic analysis program presented by Ghedini (1983) which can be used in some cases. In general, such a method is best suited for regularly spaced data. Such a period search even on a small data set can take 10 hours or more on a micro computer.

Another useful method is the trial period technique based on constructing good light curves. These are good for widely-scattered data for singly periodic objects, and for cases in which the light curve is quite non-sinusoidal. Typical of such numerical techniques, they may give spurious or alias periods. Details can be found in Stellingwerf (1978) for the "bin method" and Dworetsky (1983) for the "string length method".

One of the most widely used techniques for finding an asteroid's period does not rely on any of this fancy mathematics, however. It consists of fitting parts of light curves together. The first step is to prepare plots for each night of your delta magnitudes versus time, which you obtained from the reduction program.

Next, you must determine by what amount the magnitude of the asteroid is changing from night to night. Pick your longest or best night's data as a zero point, and correct all other nights relative to it. To calculate the correction, use the relation

$$\text{total correction} = 5(\log r\Delta) + \alpha\beta.$$

For C–type asteroids, the phase coefficient β is 0.0359. For S–types, it is 0.0293. An example constructed for a C–type from such data is given in Table 18–1. On your plot of the best night, draw a horizontal line at any convenient δ magnitude, and shift the line by the appropriate relative correction on all the other plots.

An example is given in Figs. 18–3 and 18–4. On a night we will call 'one', a line has been drawn at 12.91, marking the zero point. The next night of available data was taken 48 hours later, night 'two'. Here, the line has been shifted 0.06 magnitude. These are lines of constant brightness—when overlaying the plots, keep these lines on top of one another.

Asteroid light curves are usually doubly periodic—that is, they have two maxima and two minima during a full rotational phase. On night one, two maxima are clearly separated by about 3.5 hours. This is an important clue, as it indicates the likely period is double that, some 7 hours. To confirm it, overlay the plots so that 8 hours on night one lines up with 1.5 hours on night two. Next calculate the time interval, in this case 41.5 hours. Finally, some simple division is necessary (Table 18–2). Take a series of small integers and divide the time interval by them, thus producing a series of possible periods. In this case, the correct answer is obviously 6.9 hours.

Some cases may not be so simple of course. For some asteroids it may be necessary to make another table similar to Table 18–2, but using half-integer numbers instead. It is also helpful to have more than two nights data, preferably consecutive, to check the solution and refine it. Two other things must be mentioned. In the plot of night one, an average of the last two data points was made before a final composite light curve was constructed. The first and last data points of a night are traditionally suspect; in any case an average of two closely spaced data points often "cleans up" or improves the visual appearance of a light curve. The other aspect of light curve fitting is shown in the plot of night two. Both the first and last points should be raised by 0.02 magnitude in the composite light curve. The change is being applied because of a slight non-linearity of the comparison star. It is important to plot the instrumental magnitude of the comparison star versus time for each night. An occasional "dip or bump" from a straight line will be reflected in the asteroid plot, and should therefore be corrected (Cunningham, 1984d).

The other data necessary for an analysis of your target asteroid can be obtained from the computer programs detailed in Cunningham and Kaitting (1983a) and Cunningham (1983d).

Photo. 18–5. *The author and the 36.2 cm telescope at the Dance Hill Observatory in Ontario with which he began asteroid photometry in 1980. The observatory was officially opened by Dr. Helen Hogg, professor emeritus of the University of Toronto. Photo by Dance Hill co-founder Murray Kaitting of the Tardis Observatory.*

TABLE 18–1				
	Corrections			
Date	$r\Delta$	α	Total	relative
May 11/12	2.08	0.57	2.65	0
9/10	2.08	0.53	2.61	−0.04
10/11	2.08	0.55	2.63	−0.02
12/15	2.09	0.63	2.72	+0.07

TABLE 18–2	
N	P
4	10.3
5	8.3
6	6.9
7	5.9

PROFILES   19

From what has gone before, the reader will readily infer that these minor planets are of no sort of interest to the casual amateur who dabbles in astronomy; and indeed that they are of very little interest to anybody.

George Chambers, 1913

George Chambers' cynical attitude most certainly does not pertain today, more than 70 years later. The following profiles of asteroid researchers, both professional and amateur, attest to this flowering of interest. Based on interviews and letters, these profiles provide insights into the human factors that are just as much a part of scientific investigation as data points and equations.

ALFVEN, Hannes was born in Norrkoping, Sweden in 1908. He studied at Uppsala University from 1926, and earned a PhD in philosophy in 1934. In 1937 he became a research physicist at the Nobel Institute for Physics in Stockholm, and from 1940-73 was a professor at the Royal Institute of Technology. Since 1967 he has been a professor at the University of California in San Diego. Dr. Alfven has received numerous honors, including the Nobel prize in 1970.

"My interest in asteroids goes back to 1942, when I demonstrated that the asteroids could not be due to one or more 'exploded planets' but represented a 'planetesimal state' in a slow formation of planets."

In more than 250 scientific papers, Dr. Alfven has made significant advances in our knowledge of the structure and evolutionary history of the solar system and the role of the asteroids in that development from the perspective of plasma physics.

ALVAREZ, Luis W. Born in San Francisco in 1911, Luis Alvarez developed an early interest in scientific apparatus. He served two summers as an apprentice in the Mayo Clinic instrument shop in which institute his father served as a physiologist. He received his degree in physics from the University of Chicago and joined the Berkeley Radiation Laboratory in 1936.

Dr. Alvarez has made major contributions to several branches of physics. He discovered nuclear beta decay via electron capture, made the first measurement of the magnetic moment of the neutron, and helped develop the radar system used by the Allies in World War II. At Los Alamos, he worked on detonator research used in the development of the first atomic weapon.

After the war, he designed the first proton linear accelerator, making several major discoveries in high energy particle physics. Dr. Alvarez also led a joint Egyptian-American team that "X-rayed" the Second Pyramid at Giza, using cosmic rays, in a search for the burial chamber of the Pharoah Cephren.

"In 1978, with my geologist son Walter, and with Frank Asaro and Helen Michel, I initiated a program to find out what caused the great extinctions, 65 million years ago, that wiped out most of the life on earth, including the dinosaurs. We found large enhancements of iridium in a thin layer of clay, worldwide, that we attributed to the impact of an asteroid or comet."

Dr. Alvarez draws a parallel between this not being noticed by paleontologists, and another major scientific discovery. "From my own field of nuclear physics, we all know that the discovery of fission was missed by 'all the people who should have, and could easily have made it,' and was instead made by two nuclear chemists, Hahn and Strassmann, who used the terribly complicated and time consuming techniques of fractional crystallization, to separate Barium from Radium. When I heard the results, a week later, I confirmed the discovery in less than one hour, using the techniques of nuclear physics instrumentation."

Dr. Alvarez won the Nobel prize in 1968, has received ten other medals and awards, and six honorary doctorates. He is a past president of the American Physical Society.

BARUCCI, M. Antoinetta was born in Rome in 1957, and earned her PhD in mathematics at the University of Rome. She spent two years at the Observatoire de Meudon in Paris with an ESA (European Space Agency) fellowship, and three months at JPL and Palomar Observatory. She is currently working at the Istituto di Astrofisica Spaziale in Rome.

"I began to study asteroids with photoelectric photometry observations. To resolve the problems in the inversion of the lightcurve function, in order to define the physical parameters of an asteroid, I designed with my colleague Marcello Fulchignoni an experimental device called SAM (System for Asteroid Models) to simulate in the laboratory asteroid observations. These laboratory simulations in asteroid-like models of different shape, composition and morphology, have been carried out in order to separate the overlapping effects on the lightcurves."

BELL, Jeffrey F. Born in Tecumseh, Michigan in 1955, Dr. Bell received his BSc degree from the University of Michigan (1977) and his MSc and PhD from the University of Hawaii (1979, 1984). His research interests include infrared spectral surveys of asteroids; interpretation of asteroid spectra by means of lab simulations; and reconstruction of meteorite parent bodies by integration of astronomical and geochemical data. Dr. Bell is an assistant scientist, Planetary Geosciences Division, Hawaii Institute of Geophysics; and assistant director, Pacific Regional Planetary Image Facility.

"I began asteroid work from the 'pure astronomy' perspective but have gradually come around to the view that traditional astronomy training and technology is inadequate, possibly even harmful, to someone who wants to deal with the composition of asteroids. Many workers in the past who took this approach were tripped up by the vast community of meteorite researchers who have their own notions about asteroids. To bridge this gap I have joined the Meteoritical Society and am immersing myself in the meteorite literature. I think that the main area where the pure astronomer can still contribute is in measuring lightcurves and pole positions, which is a thankless task that few professional astronomers want to be saddled with. I hope you emphasize in your book the contribution that the new-style 'high-tech' amateur astronomers can make in this area."

"I chose asteroid work for basically unscientific reasons—namely that they are the planetary bodies most likely to play an important role in the future exploitation of space. Many people in the field are similarly motivated, though reluctant to say so in public."

BELSKAYA, Irina N. Born in Kharkov, USSR in 1958, Irina Belskaya graduated from Kharkov State University in 1980 and began work at the observatory there in the department of physical investigations of the Moon and Planets.

"Being a student I was fond of the physical investigations of asteroids. My course and diploma works were devoted to the photometry and polarimetry of the M-type asteroids. Now I'm preparing a thesis on that topic."

BINZEL, Richard P. Born in Washington Court House, Ohio in 1958, Richard Binzel earned his BA from Macalester College, St.Paul, Minnesota (1980) and an MA and PhD from the University of Texas at Austin (1982, 1986). His thesis was on the photometric properties of small asteroids. In 1980 Binzel won the Apker award, the highest award of scientific merit at the college level in the United States.

"I was an amateur astronomer since I was 9, but by the time I was 13 I was completely bored with it because I'd seen all the Messier objects and other amateur projects. So I came to a point of decision where either I would do something else or I would start making scientific observations to contribute to astronomy in a direct way. And asteroids were a convenient outlet to do that. In terms of the asteroids being in our own backyard, we will eventually be out among the asteroids and utilizing them. That's why the preliminary study and understanding of them now is timely."

BOWELL, Edward L. Born in London, England in 1943, Edward Bowell graduated with a BSc degree from University College London and joined the faculty as Lecturer in Astronomy. He earned a doctorate in astrophysics from the University of Paris (1973). While working at Meudon Observatory, he became interested in asteroids and how their diameters could be derived by means of polarimetry and photometry.

Dr. Bowell joined the staff of Lowell Observatory in Arizona in 1973. Together with Kari Lumme, he has developed a theory relating to the magnitude of asteroids. "I got interested in asteroids about 1970. Their polarization properties intrigued me, and I thought it might give a handle on diameters. I realized it would be nice to do a photometric survey to get broadband colors, so I worked with Zellner from 1975-79 trying to map out the geography of 500-600 asteroids.

"In 1979-80 I had the realization there was still life in the subject of determining asteroid positions, so I got involved in astrometry and orbital theory. Employing a scanning microdensitometer is a good way of extracting position and brightness data, and I now do more positions than anyone, about 4,000 a year. Just recently I started using a CCD camera in the stare mode. One of the goals is trying to get improved orbits of earth-approachers. Their positions are very ill-determined when far from Earth, which is where a spacecraft will encounter them. In three or four minutes, the 2 meter telescope can see down to blue magnitude 22."

BOYNTON, William. Born in Bridgeport, Connecticut in 1944, William Boynton earned his BA from Wesleyan University in Middletown, Conn. (1966) and a PhD in chemistry from Carnegie-Mellon University in Pittsburgh (1971). He then spent three years at both Oregon State University and UCLA. He has been at the University of Arizona since 1977.

"When I took my first post doc at Oregon State I started getting interested in applying my chemistry to outer space studies. The big advantage of the asteroids is that they're probably the least processed material available in the solar system, so they probably have preserved a record of what the early solar system was like.

"Unfortunately we can't exploit those properties until we actually have an asteroid sample return mission. The future in this area is going to be along the lines of the space missions. I hope it happens soon enough that I'm alive to see it. It's in the talking stages now, but it's been in the talking stages for 10 years and NASA doesn't have a lot of money for these kind of scientific studies."

CHAPMAN, Clark R. Born in New York in 1945, Clark Chapman earned his bachelors' degree from Harvard College (1967), an MS in meteorology from the Massachusetts Institute of Technology (1968) and a PhD in planetary science from MIT (1972). Since then he has been a senior scientist at the Planetary Science Institute in Tucson. Dr. Chapman has been president of Commission 15 of the IAU since 1982, and was chairman of the Division for Planetary Sciences of the American Astronomical Society (1982–83). Many of Dr. Chapman's 120 scientific papers have addressed the problems of asteroid collisional evolution and asteroid mineralogy.

In his book *Planets of Rock and Ice* (1982), Dr. Chapman writes "One afternoon in August 1974, I graphed the sizes of the S–type asteroids separately from the C–types and I noticed that most S–types were between 100 and 200 kilometers in size.

"On that broiling August day in Arizona, my thoughts turned to memories of my boyhood winters in Buffalo, New York, for an analogy that might explain the asteroid size. Two brothers who lived on the block had tendencies toward delinquency. Occasionally they made snowballs with rocks in the centers. I well remember my playmates being chased through the neighborhood by irate drivers of dented cars. The asteroid analogy, however, concerns the fate of the snow and the central rocks. The snow, of course, splattered everywhere when the missiles struck a car, but the rocks remained intact. It seemed to me the same might be true for asteroids, whose solid metallic cores were much stronger than their rocky outer layers. Over eons in the celestial demolition derby, the odds would be against survival of the rocky outer layers of the once-melted Vesta-like asteroids, but their strong metallic cores would have remained whole: split apart at their core/mantle interfaces, they would appear to be stony-iron asteroids of 100 to 200 kilometer sizes.

"I published an article on my idea. Then it began to fall apart. As more asteroids were classified and measured, the differences in size distributions of S– and C–type asteroid vanished. The nugget of my snowball idea may yet be salvaged, however. Although Vesta-sized bodies cannot be stripped to 150–kilometer cores, my associate Richard Greenberg and I now think that stony-iron meteorites may be derived from denuded 30–kilometer-diameter cores of parent bodies originally less than 100 kilometers in size. If a few percent of the asteroids of all sizes had melted and formed cores, most of the smaller ones would have had their rocky mantles stripped away."

CHERNYKH, N. S. was born in 1931 in the town of Usman in the Lipetsk region of the USSR. He studied at the Irkutsk Pedagogical Institute and from 1958 to 1961 worked in the Irkutsk Laboratory of Time. Later he was a postgraduate student at the Leningrad Institute for Theoretical Astronomy (ITA), and in 1971 received the degree of Candidate of Science for the thesis *A Determination of the Mass of Jupiter from the Modern Observations of Minor Planet 10 Hygiea*. "Since 1963 I have been on the staff of the Crimean Astrophysical Observatory where I run the program of astrometric observations of minor planets and comets with the Zeiss double 40-cm astrograph. This program was initiated by me at the request of the ITA, and has been jointly carried out since 1965 by some members of the ITA staff and me.

"For the year we usually photograph 500–600 numbered minor planets. During 20 years we have observed almost all minor planets with permanent numbers: 97% within 2,000 about 95% within 3,000. Every year we discover about 500–600 unnumbered minor planets. By the beginning of April, 1985, 351 minor planets with permanent numbers had been discovered by our observing group; 164 of them were discovered by myself. Annually we determine from 2,000 to 3,000 positions of minor planets. During 20 years we have obtained altogether about 40,000 positions."

CRUIKSHANK, Dale P. Born in Des Moines, Iowa in 1939, Dale Cruikshank received his BSc degree from Iowa State University (1961) and his MSc and PhD from the University of Arizona (1965, 1968). In 1970 he joined the staff of the Institute for Astronomy of the University of Hawaii, and has pursued a program of infrared and photometric studies of the planets, satellites, asteroids and comets in support of NASA's missions to these objects.

"I got interested in astronomy at the age of 14 as I made plans to see the total solar eclipse of 30 June 1954. My first interest was in the Sun, but quickly transformed to the planets, which I observed with my own telescopes for many years in Iowa and then in Arizona. Kuiper influenced me strongly in my interest in the planets, and I followed him to Tucson in about 1960 or 61. I published my first papers (professionally) in 1964, and have been at it since that time. I came to Hawaii because there was a large (88–inch) telescope dedicated in part to planetary studies here—now there is also the NASA IRTF 3–meter telescope and parts of the 3.6 and 3.8 meter telescopes. The future promises the University of California 10–meter, to which I will also have access, and very likely several other many-meter telescopes in the relatively near future." Cruikshank serves on various NASA committees and working groups, is an Associate Editor of Icarus, and a member of the Board of Directors of the Canada-France-Hawaii Telescope Corp. He is author or co-author of more than 130 scientific papers published in journals and books. His hobbies are philately and music.

DAVIS, Donald R. Born in Concord, North Carolina in 1939, Donald Davis earned his BSc degree from Clemson University in South Carolina (1962) and his PhD in physics from the University of Arizona. He has been at the Planetary Science Institute in Tucson since 1962. Dr. Davis won the Presidential Medal of Freedom in 1970.

"I spent four years working on the Apollo program, in developing computer code for the real time system that calculated trajectories to bring the Apollo spacecraft back to Earth. My interest in dynamical processes combined with my colleagues here at PSI who had observational expertise in asteroids. Ten years ago I began studying the collisional history of the asteroid belt. One of the most interesting results that has come out of asteroid research in recent years is this mapping out of the various compositions and type of asteroids in the belt. And the discovery that there seems to be fairly discrete zones where most compositional types tend to be concentrated. One of the major problems is to understand why it is that some asteroids melted and other asteroids did not."

DEBEHOGNE, Henri P. G. Born in Namur, Belgium in 1928, Henri Debehogne joined the astronomy staff of the Royal Observatory of Belgium in 1963. He received his PhD in mathematical science in 1965 from the University of Brussels. Since 1977, he has been a visiting professor at the Universidade Federal do Rio de Janiero.

Dr. Debehogne has made several major advances in the theoretical and practical aspects of astrometry and celestial mechanics. He and his team have made more than 250 asteroid discoveries at the European Southern Observatory, La Silla, Chile. "B. G. Marsden has given, for various research and for the development of the astrometrical work in South America, the name Debehogne to the minor planet 2359. Photometric work is performed in collaboration with Turin and Uppsala and by means of the 50 cm telescope at La Silla two times each year—at first for asteroids, but also on comets and variable stars."

DERMOTT, Stanley F. was born in Ormskirk, England in 1942 and emigrated to the United States in 1977. He is currently a professor at the Center for Radiophysics and Space Research at Cornell University.

"I was never an amateur astronomer, but became interested in astronomy while teaching high school shortly after graduation. My interest was aroused by my discovery of Bode's Law and this led to an interest in the dynamics of resonance. I left teaching and took a research job at the Royal Military College of Science in England.

"There I was fortunate in that I was left completely to my own devices for five years and this was long enough to launch me on a research career." Dr. Dermott's recent research has dealt with the nature of the Kirkwood gaps, asteroid rotation rates, and the identification of two subclasses of S–type asteroids.

DRAKE, Michael J. Born in Bristol, England in 1946, Michael Drake earned his BSc at Manchester University (1967) and PhD at the University of Oregon (1972). He then became a research assistant at the Smithsonian Astrophysical Observatory in Cambridge, Massachusetts for a year. He has been at the University of Arizona since 1973 and was associate director of the Lunar & Planetary Laboratory from 1978–80.

"I became interested in asteroids largely through the Apollo program which from a research point of view was something of a hobby. It got me interested in objects that had traditionally been considered astronomical objects which were now slowly but surely becoming geologic objects in that we were beginning to get rocks from them.

"The University of Arizona is a unique institution. In addition to the traditional astronomical approaches to studying the solar system, there is a broad range of chemists, physicists and geologists as well as astronomers, all of whom are working on different aspects of studying the solar system. That interaction is really a remarkable synergistic kind of interaction that's very exciting. One of the reasons I have an interest in asteroids is because we think certain classes of meteorites come from asteroids, and I discovered that the kind of work I could do as a geochemist studying meteorites in the laboratory interfingered very elegantly with the infrared reflectance spectroscopy of asteroid surfaces."

FARINELLA, Paolo. Born near Ferrara, Italy in 1953, Paolo Farinella earned his doctorate degree from Pisa University in 1975, where he worked until 1977. After five years at the Observatory of Merate near Milan, he returned

to Pisa as a university researcher. His asteroid work has been in the fields of celestial mechanics and physical properties.

"Research in celestial mechanics is important to understand the Kirkwood gaps and to get better-defined families in order to have better constraints on collisional models. Until 10 years ago most people believed asteroids were in stable orbits, but now we have Chiron, Hidalgo and the Apollo-Amors, which are unstable with regard to collisions and dynamics. A significant increase in our understanding has resulted from the coupling of classical celestial mechanics and numerical integration methods.

"With regard to families, we are simulating them numerically and integrating the separate orbits to see the evolution of fictitious families and compare them to real ones. In collisional work, we are trying to work out quantitatively reliable models of catastrophic collisions of asteroids. There are two ways to do this—laboratory experiments to measure the size distribution and velocity of the fragments; and trying to understand from a theoretical point of view how to scale up to real asteroids."

FROESCHLE, Claude was born in 1939 in Dakar, Senegal, and received his bachelor's degree in mathematical science at Besancon (1962). He obtained his Doctorate of Science at Nice (1971). Dr. Froeschle has been an astronomer at Nice Observatory since 1968, where he has pursued research into the dynamical evolution of the asteroid belt.

Froeschle did a study of resonances among the asteroids, developing a theory concerning the stability of their orbits. In collaboration with Fricke and Scholl, he studied the collisional evolution of asteroids that exist in large numbers outside the domain of resonance. More recently, he has studied non-gravitational effects in the motions of asteroids.

With Hans Rickman of Uppsala University, at the Nice Observatory in 1978, Froeschle studied statistical properties of the evolution of the orbits of the Jupiter family of comets by a Monte-Carlo method. The study of the lifespan of different models compared to actual observations allowed a judgment on the composition of the comet core. They are now working on the relationship between comets and the Apollo and Amor asteroids.

FULCHIGNONI, Marcello was born in Rome in 1943. He earned doctorate degrees in physics and math from the University of Rome (1967, 1969), and started at the CNR in Italy in 1970. In 1971 he took a chair in statistics in Rome, and since 1982 has been the director of the Institute of Space Astrophysics.

"I remember my grandfather when I was 5 or 6 telling me the story of the constellations and their mythology. Maybe that was the seed of my interest. My first professional interest was in moon samples, and then Mars and Mercury. After the Viking mission in 1977, our group at CNR grew to 10 people, and we started studying asteroids from a laboratory point of view. We also observe lightcurves using the 1 and 2 meter telescopes at Pic du Midi, the 1.5 meter in Bologna, the 1 meter French telescope in the Alps and the 0.9 meter in Catania.

"The lab work is done with SAM—the System for Asteroid Models. It consists of a parallel light source and a moving arm which represents the Earth. The support at the centre can change the rotation axis, aspect (from 0 to 45°) and obliquity. We can also change the shape of the model (which is usually 10–16 cm), its morphology and surface coating. When you want to study regular shapes it can be done analytically, but put a mountain or crater on it and it's easier to use the model. But many craters produce a problem of roughness, which is not easy to handle in the model. One important result from SAM is that an object with a crater one-third the size of the object has no effect on the lightcurve at least out to 30° of phase. I was surprised by the result. In the past, when there was something strange in a lightcurve, people often said it was due to a crater."

GAFFEY, Michael J. was born in Meadville, Pennsylvania in 1945. He obtained a BA and MS from the University of Iowa (1968; 1970), and a PhD in earth and planetary science from MIT (1974). Since then he was a member of the research staff at MIT (1974–77), an astronomer at the University of Hawaii (1977–84), and a senior research associate at the Rensselaer Polytechnic Institute in Troy, New York. Dr. Gaffey is also associate editor of the Journal of Geophysical Research.

"My interests in geology and astronomy date back to my early childhood. In first and second grade, I was collecting the wide variety of rocks and minerals present in the glacial deposits on which our farm was situated. And my parents, who were very encouraging toward education, gave me a 3.5 inch reflecting telescope for Christmas when I was nine—after a long campaign on my part, triggered by a wonderful book *The Golden Book of Astronomy* and fed by the series of animated TV shows called "Man In Space" that were aired on the Walt Disney Show in the early fifties. Sputnik, when I was 11, made my interest in such far-out stuff respectable.

"My major interests have been and continue to be the nature of the asteroids and what their properties can tell us about the origin and evolution of the inner solar system. Exploration of their relationships to the meteorites, the development of improved interpretive techniques to analyze spectral data, and specialized asteroid observational programs (e.g. characterization of rotational spectral variations) constitute my major areas of work at the moment. My wife and I are in the process of writing a book on the geological applications of spectroscopy."

GEHRELS, Tom was born in Haarlemmermeer, The Netherlands in 1925. He earned his bachelor's degree at Leiden University (1951). He moved to the United States in that year, and got his PhD from the University of Chicago (1956). Later he became a research associate at McDonald Observatory in Texas and moved to the University of Arizona in 1961. Dr. Gehrels was instrumental in organizing the 1971 and 1979 Tucson asteroid conferences, and edited the textbooks following these meetings. He is now director of the Spacewatch project at the University of Arizona, and Sarabhai professor and Fellow at the Physical Research Laboratory in Ahmedabad in India.

"I was raised in a strict Protestant faith and began to doubt its tenets, and I decided at a young age to become a scientist to find out for myself the origin of people." This search is described in his book *On The Glassy Sea: An astronomer's journey*, written in 1649:

> Witness this new-made world, another heaven
> From heaven gate not far, founded in view
> On the clear hyaline, the glassy sea;
> Of amplitude almost immense, with stars
> Numerous, and every star perhaps a world
> Of destined habitation.

GRADIE, Jonathan C. Born in Putnam, Connecticut in 1951, Jonathan Gradie obtained his BS and PhD degrees from the University of Arizona (1973; 1978). Since then he has been a research associate at Cornell University, and is now at the University of Hawaii at Manoa, where he studies the mineralogy of asteroids.

"My interests in astronomy began when I was a small child about the age of 5. I remember that my father brought over a friend who had a small telescope with which I was able to view the Moon. I have never forgotten the feeling of amazement that it gave me. My next big step in astronomy was getting my brothers and sisters to help me finance a telescope purchased through an ad in *Boy's Life*. The telescope was a cardboard telescoping spyglass. Through it I learned about chromatic aberrations and the Milky Way! I and a friend, Richard Stockdale, built an 8–inch telescope and 'dome' at my house in Putnam, CT during our high school days. Then I went to the University of Arizona, where I was employed by Tom Gehrels as a data processor and later an observer. My interest in asteroids was stimulated by Gehrels and my dissertation advisor, Ben Zellner."

GREENBERG, Richard was born in New York City in 1947. He earned his BSc from MIT (1968) and a PhD from MIT (1972). Dr. Greenberg was an assistant professor at the University of Arizona from 1972-76, then PSI and has now returned to U of A.

"I didn't get into asteroids until graduate school at the department of earth and planetary sciences at MIT. It struck me that certain problems in celestial mechanics could be addressed by asteroid work. The orbital resonances that are important in governing the history of the asteroids was the door that led me into the subject." "I'm not convinced most eucrites have to come from Vesta. We could be seeing examples of a 'Vesta' that doesn't exist anymore."

GUNTER, Jay U. Born in Sanford, North Carolina in 1911, Jay Gunter received his AB degree from the University of North Carolina (1931) and MD degree from Jefferson Medical College in Philadelphia (1936). He achieved the rank of Lt. Cmdr. in the U.S. Navy Medical Corps in World War II, and was a pathologist and director of the Laboratories at Watts Hospital in Durham, N.C. between 1947 and his retirement in 1976. In 1983, Dr. Gunter received the Amateur Achievement Award of the Astronomical Society of the Pacific.

Dr. Gunter began writing magazine columns on asteroids in 1971, and the additional information he mailed out to interested readers evolved into the popular publication *Tonight's Asteroids*. Nearly 700 people now subscribe to the bi-monthly newsletter. Dr. Gunter retired as editor in 1986.

His interest in astronomy began in 1968. "I had a good deal of interest in comets, the way they moved and changed positions among the stars. There were relatively few comets that could be seen, but there were asteroids, with similar celestial dances. I've often called asteroids the poor man's comets. There are not really many people interested in asteroids. Maybe 2 percent of amateur astronomers; but the ones who are, are fascinated."

HARRIS, Alan W. Born in Portland, Oregon in 1944, Alan Harris earned his BS in geophysics from the California Institute of Technology (1966), and an MS and PhD from the University of California at Los Angeles (1967, 1975). He worked at Rockwell International, taught at the NATO Advanced Study Institute and has been a guest investigator at the Hale Observatories.

Dr. Harris was a visiting associate professor at both the University of California at Santa Barbara and the University of California at Los Angeles. Since 1974, he has been a member of the technical staff of the Jet Propulsion Laboratory, where he is engaged in photometric studies of asteroids.

HARTMANN, William K. was born in New Kensington, Pennsylvania in 1939. He earned his BSc in physics from Penn State (1961), MS in geology from the University of Arizona (1965), and a PhD in astronomy from UA (1966). He has been at the Planetary Science Institute since 1971. Dr. Hartmann is author of *Moons And Planets* (2nd ed 1983). He is also co-author of the books *The Grand Tour* (1981) and *Out of the Cradle* (1984), and is a noted space artist.

"I developed an interest in astronomy from reading books as a teenager, building telescopes, and being inspired by Chesley Bonesteel paintings of space." His interest in asteroids began in graduate school where a determination of the age of the Moon from crater counts led to consideration of the number of asteroids available to hit the Earth and inner planets.

Since then he has worked on the collisional history and size distribution of asteroids, and concentrated on the outer asteroids, notably Hektor. "It could have been white on one side and black on the other like Iapetus. But Cruikshank and I showed it wasn't."

HARVEY, G. Roger. An amateur astronomer from Concord, North Carolina, Roger Harvey has observed more asteroids than anyone (1,565 by mid-1986). His education was in mechanical engineering at George Washington University, and he has been a corporate pilot since 1968. Harvey also teaches an astronomy lab at the University of North Carolina in Charlotte.

His interest in astronomy began when his eighth grade science class saw Saturn through the 26-inch refractor at the U. S. Naval Observatory in 1953. He soon began making telescope mirrors, and by 1973 installed a 10-inch re-

flector in a 25-foot diameter observatory in his back yard. About this time his interest in asteroids was sparked by a talk given by Dr. Gunter, editor of *Tonight's Asteroids*.

"Soon I was hooked. After 129 asteroids with the 10-inch I commissioned a 20-inch and added 901 more in six years. In May, 1984, with 1031 asteroids under my belt I decommissioned the 20-inch." Harvey has since begun observing with his 29-inch telescope, one of the largest privately owned instruments in the world.

"Motivation doesn't readily crystalize into words. Certainly the 'thrill of the hunt' in finding asteroids I haven't seen before keeps the fires burning. If the position or magnitude is not as advertised then the observations contribute something to science. Visually establishing rotation periods is not only useful scientifically but fun. My best night was confirming by magnitude, position and motion 21 asteroids."

HELIN, Eleanor F. Born in Pasadena, California, Eleanor Helin graduated from Occidental College and the California Institute of Technology, where she became a member of the Lunar Research Lab in 1960. Her research on the numbers and characteristics of Apollo asteroids began in 1968, when she began a four-year term at the U. S. Geological Survey. Returning to Caltech in 1972, she initiated the planet-crossing asteroid survey at Palomar Mountain the following year. Since 1980, Helin has been a member of the technical staff at the Jet Propulsion Laboratory.

"As a geologist, I have always been interested in the history and evolution of our planet Earth, so my early work on meteorites, lunar geology, and planetary cratering provided the necessary background for understanding the dynamical aspects of this history. It was a natural step to want to know more about the objects which are the probable parent bodies of the meteorites and the objects responsible for the cratering and impact features found on Earth as well as the other terrestrial planets. Hence, the result was the initiation of the Palomar Planet-Crossing Asteroid Survey (PCAS) in collaboration with Eugene Shoemaker."

HUBBARD, William B. Born in Liberty, Texas in 1940, Dr. Hubbard grew up partly in Colombia, South America. He earned his BSc from Rice University in Houston and a PhD from the University of California at Berkeley. After a post doctoral position at Caltech, Hubbard became an assistant professor at the University of Texas. He has been at the University of Arizona since 1972, where he is a full professor and former director of that university's Lunar and Planetary Laboratory (1977–81). He is author of the book *Planetary Interiors* (1984), and more than 80 scientific papers.

"I was an amateur astronomer as a kid, but didn't decide to become a professional astronomer until I received my bachelor's degree in physics. One of my sidelines is observation of occultations and I noted that one has fairly frequent observational opportunities for asteroid occultations. We've had a project here for quite a few years to go out and observe asteroid occultations. The purpose of that exercise is to try to measure their sizes accurately, and what we're really after is trying to see if we can find any evidence for companions to asteroids. So far we haven't.

"The main importance of asteroid research is to shed light on the origin of the solar system. The asteroids seem to show an interesting gradient in composition with respect to heliocentric distance that may be related to the way in which solid particles formed when the solar system was first forming."

KRESAK, Lubor. Born in Topolcany, Czechoslovakia in 1927, Lubor Kresak earned his MA at Charles University in Prague (1951), a PhD at the Czechoslovak Academy of Sciences (1957) and a DSc from the same institute in 1967. Since 1955 he has been at the Slovak Academy of Sciences in Bratislava. Dr. Kresak was president IAU Comission 20 (1973-76), and has received numerous awards including the Gottwald National Prize for Science by the Czechoslovak President (1970), the Gold Medal for Merit in Natural Sciences by the Slovak Academy of Sciences (1977) and the Copernicus Medal by Charles University (1973).

"I got interested in astronomy at the age of 15, and as a high-school student I was an amateur meteor observer. During my university studies in Prague, I used to spend almost every vacation at the Skalnate Pleso Observatory, which at that time became known worldwide for comet discoveries.

"My first small contribution to astronomy was the identification of Object Benitez with the asteroid 247 Eukrate in 1947. At that time, after the break-up of the ephemeris service during the Second World War, all asteroids were virtually lost; and also, the time spent in computing orbits with mechanical calculators was quite uncomparable with the present high-speed computers.

"In my opinion, all the different types of objects present in the solar system deserve great attention, because (1) they constitute our broader environment already accessible to the spacecraft technique and, on a long time scale, responsible for catastrophic events affecting the Earth and the life on it, and (2) they constitute a broad variety of object types which may be present everywhere in the Universe, but are so far observable only within the Solar System. Each kind of object, from micrometeorites to the giant planets, displays its own characteristic features. A weak point of the asteroids is that a single observation (say, photographic image or spectrum) contains much less information than, e.g., a similar observation of an active bright comet. A strong point is that only for the asteroids do we have a statistical sample of thousands of objects, much less affected by observational selection than those of other objects, and with an accuracy and stability of orbits allowing for a long-term extrapolation of their dynamical history. But even so, some of these thousands of objects are entirely unique in some sense. This is why still broader statistics have to be aimed for, and new surprising discoveries have to be expected."

LAGERKVIST, C.-I. Born in Nassjo, Sweden in 1944, C.-I. Lagerkvist earned his BSc and PhD from Uppsala University (1971, 1977). Together with Dr. Rickman, he organized the Asteroid Comet Meteor conferences in Uppsala in 1983 and 1985; and he has edited both the *Asteroid Lightcurve Catalog* and the *Atlas of Photometric Asteroid Lightcurves*.

"I got interested in asteroids around 1971. Quite by coincidence I saw the book from the Tucson meeting and decided to devote my PhD thesis to that work. The resulting Studies of Small Asteroids was mainly composed of photographic photometry of small asteroids. I am mostly interested in the rotational properties of asteroids. From 1978–80 I did a survey by photographic photometry of several hundred asteroids down to 18th magnitude. From this I hope to see if small asteroids are collisional fragments or more like the original planetesimals. If they are fragments, they should be more elongated."

"We need to learn more about the compositions of asteroids. What we see is only scattered light from the surface. If we really know something about the composition, we will know much more about the origin of the solar system."

LEBOFSKY, Larry A. Born in Brooklyn, New York in 1947, Larry Lebofsky spent his early years in Connecticut. He earned his BSc from Caltech (1969) and a PhD in planetary sciences from MIT (1974). He spent three years at the Jet Propulsion Laboratory and has been at the University of Arizona since 1977, where he has pursued spectroscopic and infrared studies of asteroids.

"A friend of mine worked at the planetarium and I developed an interest in astronomy through him. My interest in planetary astronomy developed when I started working with Bruce Murray on the Mariner flyby of Mars. In graduate school I worked with Tom McCord and did a lot of research on Saturn's rings. My real interest in asteroids started when I went to JPL".

"I would have said at one point the greatest contribution of asteroid research was just our basic knowledge of the evolution and formation of the solar system. Now, I see the asteroids being important in the context of mining of asteroids for their minerals. And so I'm beginning to get involved with that. It has many implications for strategic metals and defense interests."

LEVY, David Born in Montreal, Canada in 1948, David Levy earned his bachelor of English degree from Acadia University, Wolfville, Nova Scotia (1972) and a Masters degree in English from Queens University, Kingston, Ontaro (1979). He has been an observing assistant for the Planetary Science Institute since 1982, and is recorder of both the comets and meteors sections of the ALPO. Levy discovered a comet in 1984 and has one of the largest private collections of telescopes in the world.

"Before an observing run I make sure of the rising and setting time of each asteroid, plot them on a chart, and make sure the Moon will not get in the way of our asteroids or standard stars. When we get up on the mountain on Kitt Peak I'm responsible for the setting up of the equipment. During each observing night I operate the data system, so I do the technical commands of punching in the requested data for each star or asteroid. A very important part of my work is to make sure the data that are coming in are proper.

"Occasionally I will switch places with the observer and

go to the telescope. It can involve quite a lot of hectic work. It's all right when it lasts an hour or two, but when it lasts for 13 hours on a cold winter night it can be very tedious. But it's fun, it's interesting, and the most exciting part of it is watching in real time our data appear on the television screen."

LEWIS, John S. Born in Trenton, New Jersey in 1941, John Lewis graduated from high school in Pennsylvania. He earned his BSc from Princeton (1962) MSc at Dartmouth in Hanover, New Hampshire (1964) and a PhD in chemistry from the University of California (1968). He was at MIT from 1968–82, and is now a professor at the University of Arizona where he is pursuing research related to the exploitation of asteroidal resources for mining and defense applications.

Dr. Lewis has served on numerous scientific committees, and is currently an associate editor of *Icarus*, a member of the NASA Advisory Committee on the Detection of Extrasolar Planetary Systems, and director of the Arizona Centre for Space Resources. He is also co-author of the book *Planets and Their Atmospheres* (1984).

"My interest in space exploration goes back to 2nd grade when my parents bought me the little *Golden Book of Stars*. One of the things that fascinated me was that there were tables of data on the planets in the book, and the tables were chock full of question marks where numbers should have been. I directed my career toward space exploration from that time on.

"The reason I became interested in asteroids is that my work over the last 15 years has been devoted to the study of the origin of the solar system. We, living here on Earth, are accustomed to a planet that has been recycled so many times by geological activity that the clues to its origin are exceedingly difficult to find. Asteroids and comets appeal to me enormously because many of them are very primitive objects that have been sitting around in cold storage since the solar system formed."

LUPISHKO, Dmitrij P. Born in the Sumskaya region of the Ukraine, USSR in 1942, Dmitrij Lupishko graduated from Kharkov State University in 1969. Since then he has been at the Astronomical Observatory of Kharkov University, and is now the deputy-director. "In 1971–75 I carried out an extensive photoelectric and photographic observations of Mars. In 1975 I defended a thesis and in 1977 published with my colleagues the book *The Absolute Photometry of Mars* in 1971, 1973 and 1975." Since 1977 Dr. Lupishko has been engaged in the physical investigations of asteroids.

MARSDEN, Brian G. was born in Cambridge, England in 1937. He earned his BA degree from Oxford University (1959), an MA from Oxford (1963) and a PhD from Yale University (1965). He has been at the Smithsonian Astrophysical Observatory since 1965, and since 1978 Dr. Marsden has been director of the Minor Planet Center at SAO.

Dr. Marsden, who first got interested in astronomy at the age of five, developed a keen interest "in the possible connection between minor planets and comets. But I discovered there was a lack of information about minor planet orbits." Largely through his efforts, our knowledge of such orbits has been put on a secure basis, but he feels there has not yet been a proper evaluation of how electronic machines should handle orbit computations and perturbation calculations.

"Nobody has the essence of how to do it. Gauss understood the problem perfectly. He invented things that some people thought they subsequently invented." When he took over the MPC, he "did not get much in the way of records. Each provisional designation had a card file, but I never got it." Beginning in 1978–79, Dr. Marsden established 13 loose-leaf books to record provisional designations, with 25 objects per page. While most data are now stored in computer, "the names of the discoverer associated with each provisional designation are not in the computer. It is a bookkeeping nightmare, but we have it well organized. We waste more time trying to get general orbits from a few nights' observations than anything else we do."

In addition to his invaluable expertise in orbit determinations of new asteroids and comets, Dr. Marsden publishes the *Minor Planet Circulars* ("every batch is like a 100–page scientific paper"), and is largely responsible for policy matters on Commission 20 of the International Astronomical Union.

McFADDEN, Lucy-Ann. Born in New York City in 1952, Lucy McFadden earned her BA degree from Hampshire College, Massachusetts (1974); MS from M.I.T. (1977) and PhD in geology and geophysics from the University of Hawaii (1983). She is currently a research associate at the University of Hawaii and the NASA/Goddard Space Flight Center.

McFadden was introduced to planetary science by Dr. Brian O'Leary, and was selected to work for the Mariner 10 TV science team at the Jet Propulsion Laboratory in 1973. She began observational work on the asteroid Vesta while at MIT, in order to determine a more precise compositional analysis of the pyroxene chemistry. McFadden moved to the University of Hawaii along with the MIT research team in order to take advantage of the excellent observing conditions on Mauna Kea.

"When I entered the Ph.D. program in the Department of Geology and Geophysics at the University of Hawaii in 1978, I had decided to study the near-earth asteroids under the supervision of Dr. Michael Gaffey, in an effort to determine their mineralogical composition and their relationship to other objects in the solar system. At this time, Dr. Gaffey and I were approached by Dr. Hiroshi Takeda of the University of Tokyo to measure the reflectance spectra of unusual meteorites found by Japanese expeditions in Antarctica. I have taken primary responsibility for this project which has run in parallel with my asteroid work."

McMILLAN, Robert S. was born in Pittsburgh, Pennsylvania in 1950, and earned his BS degree from Case Institute of Technology (1972), an MA from the University of Texas (1974) and a PhD from UT (1977). From 1977–79 he was a research associate at the Marshall Space Flight Center. Since 1979 he has worked at the Lunar & Planetary Laboratory, University of Arizona. Dr. McMillan is now a senior research associate in charge of development of the asteroid detection camera for the Spacewatch project.

MILLIS, Robert L. was born in 1941, and earned his BA degree from Eastern Illinois University in Charleston (1963) and PhD from the University of Wisconsin, Madison (1968). Since then he has been a staff astronomer at Lowell Observatory in Flagstaff, Arizona and adjunct professor at Ohio State University in Columbus. From 1981 he has also been a co-investigator on the International Ultraviolet Explorer satellite.

His specialty is high-time resolution photometry and observation of occultations using portable equipment. His investigation of asteroids, ring systems, and planetary atmospheres through observation of stellar occultations has resulted in more than 40 scientific papers.

OSTRO, Steven J. Born in 1946 in Somerville, New Jersey, Steven Ostro earned a BS and AB degrees from Rutgers University (1969), Master of Engineering from Cornell University (1974) and a PhD in Planetary Sciences from MIT (1978). He was an assistant professor of astronomy at Cornell from 1979 to 1984, when he moved to JPL.

Dr. Ostro's specialty is planetary radar astronomy. In more than 25 scientific papers, he has made major advances in the radar detection of asteroids, Galilean satellites, Saturn's rings and Mars.

"For a solar phase angle of zero, if the albedo is uniform (i.e., if color is constant) as far as you can tell, then we could argue that odd harmonics in the lightcurve indicate a non-equatorial aspect. Hence, you can get a constraint on a pole direction from one lightcurve. The form of the constraint is exclusion of the pole from the great circle 90° from the asteroid's direction. All of Russell's work involved opposition lightcurves. From an ideal set of such lightcurves, one can find the asteroid's line of equinoxes, and the absolute value of the angle between the asteroid's pole and orbit plane, and the sense of rotation."

PAOLICCHI, Paolo. Born in Pisa, Italy in 1950, Paolo Paolicchi graduated in 1972 from the University of Pisa and Scuola Normale Superiore. Since 1975 he has been a staff astronomer at the Brera Observatory in Merate, Italy. In 1984, he became an associate professor of astronomy at the University of Pisa. Dr. Paolicchi began his asteroidal studies in 1979, with a paper on binary systems. He has more recently concentrated on families of asteroids.

PEROZZI, Ettore. Born in Naples, Italy in 1957, Ettore Perozzi received his doctorate in physics from the University of Rome (1981). Since then he has been a research fellow at the Planetology branch of the Space Astrophysics Institute in Rome and a visiting scientist at the European Space Operations Center in Darmstadt, West Germany. At ESOC, Dr. Perozzi is involved in the planning of two possible joint space missions between ESA and NASA: the Multiple Flyby Asteroid Mission and the Saturn Orbiter/Titan probe.

Dr. Perozzi's interest in asteroids was sparked by a children's book, *Le Petit Prince* by Antoine de Saint-Exupery. "When I first came to know the story of the Small Prince (at that time I was not even able to read a book by myself) it was also the first time I came to know the existence of the asteroids." He tells an amusing anecdote relating to asteroid names. "One day I was looking through the TRIAD, but this time not for working reasons: I wanted to find out how many friends of mine were included in the list, to whom I could tell that somewhere above their heads there was an asteroid bearing their name spinning across the sky. Then my attention was caught by number 1198: its mythical name was Atlantis; but what surprised me was to read also beside the name, the comment: 'Lost' ... poor old asteroid, with a name like that, it couldn't have shared a different fate."

PILCHER, Frederick. Born in Calgary, Alberta, Canada in 1939 of American parents, Frederick Pilcher earned his BS degree from Washburn University in Topeka, Kansas (1959) and an MS degree in physics from the University of Kansas (1962). Since then he has been chairman of the physics department at Illinois College, Jacksonville, Illinois. By mid-1986, Professor Pilcher had observed 1,400 asteroids. In 1973 he co-authored the *Tables of Minor Planets* with Jean Meeus, which book will be issued in a much-expanded revised edition. In 1983, he became recorder of the Minor Planets section of the Association of Lunar & Planetary Observers.

"I see the studies of asteroids as interesting in themselves. Each is a world to be explored. Each becomes recognized as an individual different from all the rest as it becomes better known. I do not know what brilliant intuition may come in the future from this amassed knowledge, but the history of science is unequivocal. Insights and applications yet dimly perceived will enrich humanity from the study of this plurality of worlds."

SCHOBER, Hans J. born in Holenbrunn, Germany in 1944, Hans Schober moved to Austria in 1950. He entered the University of Graz in 1962, and was employed as a research assistant at the Institute for Astronomy in Graz from 1967–1971. He earned his PhD in geophysics and experimental physics in 1971, and continued his work at the Institute, becoming its director in 1981. In more than 75 scientific papers, Dr. Schober has added greatly to our knowledge of the photometric properties of asteroids.

"I started my career from electronics and electromechanics, switching over to astronomy (I was interested in solar-terrestrial relations) and getting a student job I started with construction of photometers and telescopes. After getting my PhD I was looking for an astronomical topic and started with observations at OHP in France of the asteroid 89 Julia—which was fascinating to see (1972); a one-year stay at the astronomical institute at Bochum, Germany with connections to ESO in Chile was useful to learn modern methods of observing and the effective use of good climate conditions. My main interest became the asteroid field—in 1975 we had an asteroid meeting in Graz, Austria and I came in personal touch with Gehrels, the Van Houtens, Scaltriti and Zappala, Lagerkvist and Degewij. International cooperation started and culminated for me personally in the Tucson Asteroid meeting 1979, when I met everybody working in the States on that topic, who had not come in 1976 to Grenoble or Lyon (France) for the IAU meetings.

"As far as asteroids are concerned I was interested in the individual properties of the single asteroids, to derive as precisely as possible all the information we can get. On the other hand there were many other observers—and my results could be used for statistical purposes, too. My main interest behind the observations are of course to see the growing importance of the field in connection with the origin and evolution of the entire solar system. But of course the individual studies were of interest, as I personally was involved with preparations of suitable asteroids for a possible asteroid space mission."

SCOTTI, James V. Born in Bandon, Oregon in 1960, Jim Scotti lived in Michigan, Massachusetts and New York before moving to Arizona. He earned a BSc degree in astronomy from the University of Arizona (1983), and has been a research assistant on the Spacewatch project there since 1982. In addition to observing, he has been largely responsible for Spacewatch software development, enabling asteroids to be quickly distinguished from stars and other objects. Scotti is also assistant recorder for both the comets and meteor section of the Association of Lunar & Planetary Observers.

Even though he "started out more interested in galaxies and stars," Scotti has gained personal knowledge of asteroids through his "hands-on experience with Spacewatch. Asteroids are important to the study of the solar system and other solar systems. A good sampling of orbits down to small sizes will provide the statistics necessary to make further progress in solar system studies."

SHOEMAKER, Eugene M. Born in Los Angeles in 1928, Eugene Shoemaker earned his BSc and MSc from the California Institute of Technology (1947, 1948) and a PhD from Princeton (1960). He has been a geologist with the U.S. Geological Survey since 1948 and has also been a professor at Caltech since 1969. Dr. Shoemaker has been an investigator on the television experiments of the Ranger, Surveyor and Viking spacecraft, and in 1965 established the Center for Astrogeology at Flagstaff, Arizona. In 1973, he initiated the Palomar Planet-crossing asteroid survey. Dr. Shoemaker has received numerous honors, including two honorary doctorates and the NASA Medal for Scientific Achievement (1967).

"I got into asteroids initially in order to try to understand the cratering rate on Earth. They are primarily of interest to me now as remnants of the planetesimals from which the planets accumulated. I view the asteroid belt as a kind of zoo, where planetesimals from all parts of the solar system have been preserved (in a unique, dynamically safe refuge). Understanding how these 'rare beasts' arrived in this refuge will provide insight into the dynamics of accretion.

"At the present time my work on asteroids is carried out in collaboration with my wife, Carolyn S. Shoemaker. Carolyn works full time on our asteroid survey. She has discovered more than 150 asteroids, among which 16 are now numbered."

SHOR, Victor was born in Kharkov, USSR in 1929. He graduated from Kharkov University in 1952, and taught in high school for four years before joining the staff of the

Institute for Theoretical Astronomy as a doctoral student. He earned his PhD in 1962. Since then he has worked in the Minor Planets, Comets and Satellites Department of the ITA, now headed by Prof. Yu. Batrakov. Dr. Shor is currently deputy chairman of the editorial staff of the *Ephemerides of Minor Planets*. "I am engaged in compiling the routine for improvement of preliminary predictions of stars by minor planets. Our experience shows that the accuracy of such predictions can be substantially increased. It is especially true in the case when positions of the planet as well as the star are measured on the same plate taken a few days before the event. We intend to organize a regular service with that end in view, at first for occultations which could be seen from the territory of the USSR and then, maybe, for other regions."

SONETT, Charles P. Born in Pittsburgh, Pennsylvania in 1924, Dr. Sonett earned his BSc at the University of California at Berkeley (1949) and his PhD in nuclear physics at UCLA (1954). After graduating he went to work in industry for TRW.

"We were the Air Force system contractor for the early ICBM program. When Sputnik happened (1957) there was a crash to start putting things in space, and I developed the instrumentation for some of those early shots. I spent 6 years doing that, then I went to NASA headquarters for 2 years as head of the Lunar & Planetary science program. Then I went to NASA/Ames Research Center and organised the Space Science Division and I spent 11 years there." In 1973, Dr. Sonett organised the planetary science department at the University of Arizona, where he has been since.

"Asteroids are important as markers of the early solar system and what we can learn about the solar system that's essentially frozen into asteroids. It's unfortunate we have to do it by remote at the moment. Why is there this vast belt of small objects between Jupiter and Mars? It's a little bit anomalous. From a more personal standpoint there's the problem of thermal metamorphosis that we think we see in the asteroids and we definitely see in the meteorites. I've been working for about 15 years on electromagnetic heating."

TAYLOR, Gordon E. Born in Birmingham, England in 1925, Gordon Taylor is a staff astronomer at the Royal Greenwich Observatory. In 1958 he made the first observation of the occultation of a star by an asteroid (Vesta). He has published more than 60 scientific papers on various aspects of planetary research, and is a past president of the British Astronomical Association.

"My main interest in this field goes back to the early 1950s when I realized that with improved accuracy of the ephemerides of Ceres, Pallas, Juno, and Vesta it was becoming possible to predict occultations of stars by these bodies with some chance of securing observations and also to lunar occultations of these minor planets.

"My own interest in determining the sizes and shapes of the minor planets using the occultations technique goes back over 30 years. We believe that minor planets may be primordial material left over from the time of formation of the solar system. In order to obtain some insight into the composition of these bodies we need to know the density which is derived from the mass and size. Hence my attempts to obtain accurate sizes for these bodies."

TAYLOR, Ronald C. Born in New Jersey, Ronald Taylor earned his bachelor's degree from Miami University in Ohio, an MSc from Montclair College in New Jersey (1960) and a second MSc from the University of Arizona (1964). He started working at the University of Arizona in 1967, and is currently a high school teacher in Tucson.

"Under Tom Gehrels' direction I have a wide range of latitude to pursue my specialty of pole determination of asteroids. (I had a dream once that Tom had sent me to the Moon to observe, and I got clouded out.) As the building blocks of the solar system, the more and the sooner we know about asteroids, the sooner we will know about the formation of the solar system. From a more practical point of view perhaps the eventual voyage to the asteroids and using their natural resources will be their greatest contribution. I'm a great believer in the spinoffs that occur from this type of work."

TEDESCO, Edward F. was born in Brooklyn, New York in 1947. He earned his BSc degree from St. John's University (1969), an MS in physics from Fordham University (1973) and a second MS in astronomy from New Mexico State University (1978). His PhD is also from New Mexico State (1979). Dr. Tedesco was a research associate at the University of Arizona from 1979–81, and is now a member of the asteroid science group at the Jet Propulsion Laboratory.

Dr. Tedesco's doctoral dissertation, on the photometric properties of the Hirayama families, has been followed by several important papers on asteroid lightcurves, rotation rates, and pole positions, related visual and IR observations of comets and planetary satellites. He is editor of the IRAS asteroid workshop reports.

THOLEN, David J. born in Hays, Kansas in 1955, he received BSc degrees in physics and astronomy from the University of Kansas (1978) and a PhD in planetary science from the University of Arizona (1984). He is currently an assistant astronomer at the University of Hawaii. An indefatigible observer of asteroids and distant solar system objects, Tholen was instrumental in developing the eight-color asteroid survey. His 'News Notes' are a regular contribution in the *Minor Planet Bulletin*.

"I'm concentrating on small bodies which include asteroids, comets and outer planetary satellites, all of which are atmosphereless with the possible exception of Pluto. Despite the fact people think of them as vastly different entities, I like to study them to discover how they are related. They all formed out of the same solar nebula, so what do they have in common? I see a connection between Pluto and comets, comets and asteroids, and asteroids and planetary satellites—the primary variable being heliocentric distance.

"Phobos and Deimos, the outer Jovian satellites and Phoebe are all candidates for being captured objects. I don't think you can state conclusively they are captured objects. We don't have a crystal ball to look back in time to see what happened, but we are using the best of our ability to reconstruct the past."

WEIDENSCHILLING, Stuart J. Born in New Jersey in 1946, Stuart Weidenschilling earned his BSc and MSc in aeronautical engineering from MIT (1968, 1969) and a PhD in planetary science from MIT (1976). He took a post doctoral position at the Carnegie Institute for 2 years, and has been at the Planetary Science Institute in Tucson since 1978.

"I was not particularly interested in asteroids at that time (1978). I was much more interested in the formation of the solar system and asteroids seemed to be a minor problem compared to making planets. When we began this observational program I found to my surprise that I enjoyed doing it, at least when the nights are not terribly cold! There are two aspects of asteroids which are important. One is that we get samples of them that can be analyzed in great detail and give clues to the chemistry and physical state of the primitive solar nebula. And also perhaps there is a clue to the large scale structure of the solar nebula and the overall processes that shaped the solar system in that it is anomalous that we have an asteroid belt there rather than a planet. The reasons for that are not clear at this time."

WETHERILL, George W. was born in Philadelphia in 1925. He was a radar technician in the Navy from 1943–46, and was educated at the University of Chicago where he earned a Ph.B. (1948), S.B. (1949), S.M. (1951) and Ph.D. (1953) in physics. He joined the technical staff of the Department of Terrestrial Magnetism at the Carnegie Institution in Washington in 1953, and in 1960 was appointed professor of geophysics and geology at the Univ. of California at Los Angeles. He was chairman of the UCLA department of planetary and space science from 1968–72. Since 1975, Dr. Wetherill has been director of the Department of Terrestrial Magnetism at Carnegie.

From his first asteroid-related paper in 1967, Dr. Wetherill has made major advances in our understanding of the dynamics of Earth-crossing asteroids. "The question as to whether the meteorites come from Earth-approaching asteroids or main-belt asteroids is based on a misconception. It's all part of the same story. Multiple fragmentation events can be detected in large meteorites, but most people look at small ones. They see no evidence for it, and invoke Occam's Razor to say it doesn't happen."

Dr. Wetherill has led many organizations and won numerous awards: president of the Meteoritical Society, Geochemical Society and the International Association of Geochemistry and Cosmochemistry; editor of the Annual Review of Earth and Planetary Science; fellow of the American Academy of Arts and Sciences; and awarded the Leonard Medal of the Meteoritical Society.

WILKENING, Laurel L. Born in Richland, Washington in 1944, Laurel Wilkening earned her BA from Reed College, Portland, Oregon (1966) and a PhD in chemistry from the University of California, San Diego (1970). From 1972–73 she was a research associate at the University of Chicago, and since then has been at the University of Arizona, where she is a professor and vice-provost. Dr. Wilkening has also served on several government committees, most recently chairing the NASA Comet Rendezvous Science Working Group.

"I'm interested in origins, which is why I got interested in meteorites—how the solar system got started. I am particularly interested in asteroids because of their potential as remnant material left over from the formation of the solar system.

"It is important to know what they are made of and why they are not all the same composition. If we actually understood why Ceres is like Ceres and why Vesta is like Vesta we would probably understand quite well why the asteroids don't all have the same composition."

ZAPPALA, Vincenzo Born in Biella, near Torino, Italy in 1945, Vincenzo Zappala earned his PhD at Torino University in 1970. In 1981 he became an associate professor of astronomy. A specialist on the rotational properties of asteroids, his most recent work is in the study of collisional fragmentation.

"As an astronomer, I began my researches on positions of asteroids in 1970 at the Torino Observatory, located at Pino Torinese, compiling a new program for plates' reduction and calculation of the positions. This kind of work on asteroids was an old 'institutional' program of the Observatory. From 1970 to 1974 my interest was mainly devoted to the orbital study of minor planets and comets, together with some analyses about parallaxes of stars by means of the 105–cm astrometric reflector."

"However, starting from 1974, with the collaboration of F. Scaltriti, researcher on eclipsing binaries, a program of photoelectric lightcurves began, using the 45 and 105–cm reflectors of our institute. Obviously it was mainly devoted to bright asteroids for new period determinations and for phase curve detections. After an observational period, I started to analyse the data statistically and theoretically, with the aim of outlining an evolutionary history of the belt."

ZELLNER, Ben H. Born in Forsyth, Georgia in 1942, Benjamin Zellner earned his BSc at the Georgia Institute of Technology (1964) and a PhD in astronomy from the University of Arizona (1970), where he worked until joining the Space Telescope Institute in 1985.

Zellner developed an interest in asteroids in the early 1970's. "Very few people had ever seen the satellites of Mars in a telescope. I had a polarimeter which I used to get a polarization phase curve of Deimos. Tom Gehrels had a few such curves of asteroids, so I decided to go and get some more. And I started getting very interesting results like the bi-modality in the albedos—C–types and S–types and so forth. That was one of the things in 1971–72 that really launched the new science of asteroids." Zellner is especially interested in small asteroids. "What are the very small objects like? We don't know. We've looked at a few very small Earth-approaching objects, but it's hard to say whether or not they are like the main belt objects because we haven't looked at main-belt objects that small. We have looked at some small objects in the Nysa family and found something new we had never seen before—they have spectra unlike anything we've seen anywhere else. Is it possible the small asteroids are very different? I wouldn't

think so, but it needs to be checked out."

ZHOU, Xing-hai. "I was engaged," writes Dr. Zhou, "in determining positions of asteroids, when I worked at Quingdao Observatory. After doing so there for 20 years, I moved to the Purple Mountain Observatory in 1978, and since then, I have been doing photometry of asteroids. At present, I am interested in the problem of collisional evolution of asteroids." He has also been involved in statistical investigations, notably the magnitude distribution of main belt asteroids.

ZIOLKOWSKI, Krzysztof was born in Biala Podlaska, Poland in 1939. He earned his MSc in astronomy (1962) and PhD (1968) from Warsaw University. He is currently chief of the comet and asteroid orbits laboratory in the Space Research Centre of the Polish Academy of Science in Warsaw; editor of the Polish monthly astronomical journal *Urania*; and vice-president of the Polish Association of Amateur Astronomers.

Dr. Ziolkowski's main scientific interests are the dynamics of comets and asteroids. His most recent investigations have led to the discovery of "nongravitational effects" in the motion of asteroids. "My unexpected results created some controversy. But I feel sure that at least in two cases—1221 Amor and 1862 Apollo—these anomalies really exist. I have the evidence of their non numerical origin. The existence of nongravitational effects in the motion of asteroids leads to the conclusion that some minor planets—especially Apollo-Amors types—can be extinct comets as have been supposed by some astronomers."

APPENDIX I
REFERENCE
MATERIAL

For the latest research on asteroids, both observational and theoretical, the reader should consult the major journals. Asteroid papers are most often found in *Icarus, Astronomy & Astrophysics, Astronomical Journal, Nature* and *Science*. Other journals that occasionally publish papers on asteroids include *Monthly Notices* of the Royal Astronomical Society, *Astrophysical Journal, Moon and Planets* and *Astronomische Nachrichten*. Popular astronomy magazines, notably *Sky & Telescope*, and *Astronomy*, also publish short notes or articles on asteroids. Various other magazines, such as *Scientific American* and *Natural History* have published feature articles on the subject. Both the Planetary Society (110 S. Euclid Ave., Pasadena, CA 91101) and the L5 Society (1060 E. Elm, Tucson, AZ 85719) publish asteroid articles in the magazines sent to members.

The World Space Foundation (PO Box 4, South Pasadena, CA 91030) is a non-profit organization that sponsors the Asteroid Project with major funding support from the Planetary Society. The Asteroid Project provides additional support to Eleanor Helin's International Near-Earth Asteroid Survey (INAS), which is primarily funded by NASA. The standard reference book on the positions of asteroids, published yearly by Leningrad Observatory, is the *Ephemerides of Minor Planets*, available from the Minor Planet Center, Smithsonian Astrophysical Observatory, 60 Garden St., Cambridge, MA 02138, USA.

Also available from the Minor Planet Center are the *Catalogue of Discoveries and Identifications of Minor Planets*; and *Catalogue of Orbits of Unnumbered Minor Planets*. Both were published in 1982.

The *Minor Planet Circulars* provide rapid dissemination of announcements of discovery and orbital elements, as well as newly-designated names of asteroids. A subscription to these highly technical circulars is available from the Center, as is a computer tape containing minor planet observations. The third edition, prepared in 1984, contains 322,203 observations: 236,220 of the numbered asteroids; 69,416 of the unnumbered; and 16,567 of comets. The tape is available as 9-track, ASCII, unlabeled, 1600 bpi, 80-byte record size, 8000-byte block size. The cost is $300.

In late 1984, the Minor Planet Center instituted a phone-in service via computer. For a $4.50 monthly fee, subscribers can get notifications of new asteroids and comets, orbital elements and ephemerides.

A useful database for photometrists is available from Dr. C.-I. Lagerkvist, Astronomiska Observatoriet, Box 515, 751 20 Uppsala, Sweden. The *Asteroid Lightcurve Catalogue* contains extensive information about all published lightcurves of asteroids; and the *Atlas of Photometric Asteroid Lightcurves* contains all published lightcurves normalized to the brightness at maximum.

Finding charts to aid in photographing asteroids are available from Jost Jahn, Rosenweg 2, D–2410 Moelln/Lbg., Federal Republic of Germany. Each chart plots the path of an asteroid for up to several months. Interested observers should send a minimum of DM 16 to cover costs of copies and postage.

Two other publications deserve special mention. *Tonight's Asteroids*, a popular level bi-monthly publication, reproduces star charts with the paths of bright asteroids plotted on them. It was founded in 1971 by Dr. J. U. Gunter and edited by him until he "retired" in 1986. *Tonight's Asteroids* is now edited by Joseph and Diane Flowers. To subscribe, send a few self-addressed, stamped envelopes 1 ounce first class postage to Route 4, Box 446, Wilson, North Carolina 27983.

Essential to all asteroid astronomers, both amateur and professional, is the *Minor Planet Bulletin*. It is a quarterly publication of the minor planets section of the Association of Lunar and Planetary Observers, and is edited by Richard Binzel, Planetary Science Institute, Suite 201, 2030 E. Speedway, Tucson, Arizona 85719. Papers for publication should be sent to him, while subscriptions are handled by Derald Nye, Route 7 Box 511, Tucson, AZ 85747.

Books Devoted Primarily or Exclusively to Asteroids

ASTEROIDS (edited by Tom Gehrels). University of Arizona Press, 1979; 1181 pages. The largest and most comprehensive work ever published on minor planets, it includes the complete TRIAD file. Professional level.

THE ASTEROIDS by Alan E. Nourse. Franklin Watts Publishers, N.Y., 1975; 59 pages. Excellent introduction for the young reader.

THE ASTEROIDS by Daniel Kirkwood. J. B. Lippincott Co., 1888; 360 pages. First book ever written on asteroids, by the man whose name is associated with the gaps in the asteroid belt.

ASTEROIDS, COMETS, METEORIC MATTER (edited by Cornelia Cristescu, W. J. Klepczynski, & B. Millet). 22nd Colloquium of the International Astronomical Union, 1974, 350 pages. A professional review concentrating on celestial mechanics. Partially in French.

ASTEROIDS: AN EXPLORATION ASSESSMENT (edited by David Morrison & William Wells). NASA Conference Publication 2053, 1978; 300 pages; softcover. Deals mainly with meteorites, mineralogy, and space missions to the asteroids. Professional level.

BETWEEN THE PLANETS: Comets, Asteroids, Meteorite by Hermann-Michael Hahn. Franckh'sche Verlagshandlung, West Germany, 1984; 208 pages. Written in German by a science journalist, most of the text deals with comets.

THE CALCULATION OF THE ORBITS OF ASTEROIDS AND COMETS by Kenneth P. Williams. Principia Press Inc., Indiana, 1934; 214 pages. Classic work on celestial mechanics. Professional level.

DWARF PLANETS by E.L. Krinov. State Publication of Technical-theoretical Literature, 1956; 31 pages. A brief popular review, in Russian.

GEOLOGICAL IMPLICATIONS OF IMPACTS OF LARGE ASTEROIDS AND COMETS ON THE EARTH (edited by Leon T. Silver & Peter H. Schultz). Special Paper 190, The Geological Society of America, 1982; 528 pages. A professional review.

GLI ASTEROIDI (The Asteroids) by P. Farinella, P. Paolicchi and V. Zappala. Il Castello Collane Tecniche, Milan, Italy, 1983; 127 pages. Volume 1 in a series of astronomy books in Italian.

MINOR PLANETS by I.I. Putilin. Technical-Theoretical Institute, Moscow, 1953, 412 pages. An excellent book in russian, largely devoted to orbital work but containing a wealth of historical data Professional level.

ON THE DETERMINATION OF THE GENERAL PERTURBATIONS OF THE MINOR PLANETS OF THE MINERVA GROUP by N. V. Komendatov. United Scientific & Technical Publishing House, Moscow, 1935; 75 pages. Mathematical treatise on celestial mechanics. Professional level.

PHYSICAL STUDIES OF MINOR PLANETS (edited by Tom Gehrels). U. S. Govt. Printing Office, 1971; 687 pages. Proceedings of the first Tucson asteroid conference; superseded by ASTEROIDS. Professional level.

PROJECT ICARUS, MIT Students System Project. MIT Press, 1979; 162 pages; softcover. Not about asteroids per se, it describes a hypothetical space mission to prevent Icarus from colliding with Earth. Professional level.

THE SYSTEM OF MINOR PLANETS by Gunter Roth. Faber & Faber Ltd, London, 1962; 128 pages. Written largely from a European perspective for the advanced amateur; well written, with a particularly good historical section.

THE NAMES OF THE MINOR PLANETS by Antonio Paluzie-Borrell. Published by Jean Meeus, Kesselberg Sterrenwacht, 1963.

TABLES OF GENERAL PERTURBATIONS FOR A GROUP OF MINOR PLANETS by Sophia L. McDonald and Armin O. Leuschner, Berkeley, 1952, 210 pages.

TABLES OF MINOR PLANETS DISCOVERED BY JAMES C. WATSON by Armin O. Leuschner. National Academy of Sciences Vol. 10, 7th Memoir, 1910.

TABLES OF MINOR PLANETS by Frederick Pilcher and Jean Meeus. Privately published, 1973; 104 pages. An important compilation of facts and figures about asteroids.

THE TINY PLANETS by David C. Knight. William Morrow & Company, N.Y., 1973; 95 pages. Another excellent book for the young reader; includes a glossary.

Some Books With Chapters on Asteroids

ASTEROIDS COMETS METEORS (edited by C.-I. Lagerkvist & H. Rickman). Uppsala University, Sweden, 1983; 455 pages. Recent European asteroid research is presented in 200 pages of this excellent book. Professional level.

ASTEROIDS COMETS METEORS II (edited by C.-I. Lagerkvist & H. Rickman). Uppsala University, Sweden, 1985. Proceedings of the international conference. Professional level.

ASTRONOMY by David Brewster. Edinburgh, 1811. The first four asteroids are reviewed on pages 126-133.

BETWEEN THE PLANETS by Fletcher G. Watson. Harvard University Press, 1956; 222 pages. Chapters 2 & 3 review the history and physical nature of asteroids. Amateur level.

BETWEEN THE PLANETS: COMETS, ASTEROIDS, METEORITE by Hermann-Michael Hahn. Franckh'sche Verlagshandlung, West Germany 1984; 208 pages. Written in German by a science journalist, most of the text deals with comets.

THE CLOUDY NIGHT BOOK by George Mumford. Sky Publishing Corp., 1979; 115 pages. Designed to occupy astronomers on cloudy nights, this book includes a crossword puzzle on page 24 featuring the names of the first 100 asteroids.

COMETS, METEORITES, and ASTEROIDS by Franklyn M. Branley. Thomas Crowell Company, N.Y., 1974. Chapter 2 gives a short overview of asteroids for the young reader.

COMETS, METEORS AND ASTEROIDS: How they affect Earth, by S. Gibilisco. John Wiley & Sons, 1985; 208 pages. Another popular level book on impacts and their affect on Earth's climate and life.

COSMIC DEBRIS by John Burke. University of California Press, 1986. A review of meteorites in history, it includes a section of collision-catastrophe theories. Professional level.

COSMIC IMPACT by John K. Davies. St. Martin's Press, N.Y., 1986; 197 pages. Covers many aspects of asteroid and comet collisions with Earth. Popular level.

DYNAMICAL TRAPPING AND EVOLUTION IN THE SOLAR SYSTEM (edited by V. V. Markellos & Y. Kozai). D. Reidel Pub. Co., 1983; 424 pages. Includes sections on asteroids and trapped motion in the three-body problem (Trojans). Professional level.

DYNAMICS OF THE SOLAR SYSTEM (edited by Raynor L. Duncombe). D. Reidel Publishing Company, 1979; 330 pages. Part V includes nine papers on asteroids. Professional level.

ELEMENTS OF ASTRONOMY by John Davis. J. B. Lippincott & Co., Philadelphia, 1868; 343 pages. Good review of our scant knowledge of the asteroids in the mid-19th century. Popular level.

THE FLAMMARION BOOK OF ASTRONOMY. Simon & Schuster, N.Y., 1964; 669 pages. Good section on history, names and orbits. Popular level.

HISTORY OF ASTRONOMY 6th revised edition by Patrick More. MacDonald and Co. Ltd., London 1983; 327 pages. Chapter 17 is an insightful history of asteroid discovery at the popular level.

INTRODUCTION TO PLANETARY GEOLOGY by Billy Glass. Cambridge University Press, 1982. Chapter 10 deals with asteroids and comets. Professional level.

THE JOY OF GAZING by David H. Levy. Montreal Centre. RASC, 1982; 62 pages; softcover. Chapter 8 briefly mentions asteroid occultations. Young reader level.

MOON AND PLANETS by William K. Hartmann. Wadsworth Publishing Company, 1983. Chapter 7 presents a wide-ranging survey of asteroids. Advanced level.

NEW WORLDS FOR OLD by Duncan Lunan. William Morrow & Co. Inc., 1979; 268 pages. Chapter 8 looks ahead to the exploration and mining of asteroids.

ON THE ORIGIN OF THE SOLAR SYSTEM by Hans Alfven. Oxford University Press, 1954; 191 pages. Chapter 7 draws parallels between the ring system of Saturn and the asteroid belt. Professional level.

OUR WORLD IN SPACE by Robert McCall and Isaac Asimov. New York Graphic Society, 1974. Chapter 5 explores the possibilities of colonizing Ceres. Popular level.

PIONEERS OF SCIENCE by Sir Oliver Lodge. Macmillan and Co. Ltd., 1893. Lecture XIII covers the history of asteroids. Popular level.

PLANETS OF ROCK AND ICE by Clark R. Chapman. Charles Scribner's Sons, N.Y., 1982.; 222 pages. Chapter 4 looks at the origin and composition of asteroids. Amateur level.

THE RIDDLE OF THE DINOSAUR by John Noble Wilford. Alfred Knopf, N.Y., 1985, 304 pages. The dinosaur extinction debate is well covered in several chapters.

THE ROMANCE OF MODERN ASTRONOMY by Hector MacPherson. Seeby & Co. Ltd., 1911. Chapter 9 gives a good survey of asteroids.

THE SOLAR SYSTEM by Zdenek Kopal. Oxford University Press, 1972; 152 pages; softcover. Chapter 8 primarily considers the orbital properties of asteroids. Amateur level.

SECRETS OF THE HEAVENS by I.I. Lieprov. Moscow, 1904. Details the discovery circumstances of the first 300 asteroids. Russian text.

SOLAR SYSTEM PHOTOMETRY HANDBOOK (edited by Russell M. Genet). Willmann-Bell Inc., 1983. Chapters 1 & 8 cover asteroid photometry and occultations for advanced amateurs.

SPACE DEBRIS, ASTEROIDS AND SATELLITE ORBITS (edited by J. Kessler, E. Grun, & L. Sehnal). Pergamon Press, 1985, 229 pages. Proceedings of two workshops and the COSPAR Commission P meeting, held in June-July, 1984. Professional level.

SPACE GARBAGE by Jack Meadows. George Philip Pub., London, 1985; 160 pages. Dr. Meadows of the University of Leicester writes about all the material left over after the formation of the planets: asteroids, meteorites, comets and dust.

SPACE MANUFACTURING 5: Engineering with Lunar & Asteroid Materials (edited by B. Faughnan & G. Maryniak). AIAA, N.Y. 1985; 268 pages. A professional review.

STORY OF THE SOLAR SYSTEM by George F. Chambers. D. Appleton & Company, 1913; 188 pages. A disparaging look at asteroids in the early 20th century. Popular level.

SURFACES AND INTERIORS OF PLANETS AND SATELLITES edited by A. Dollfus. Academic Press, London, 1970. Pages 317-175 cover photometry of asteroids.

THE NEW GUIDE TO THE PLANETS by Patrick Moore. W.W. Norton Co., N.Y., 1974. Chapter 2 gives a short overview of asteroids for the young reader.

THE NEMESIS AFFAIR by David M. Raup. W.W. Norton & Co., 1986; 220 pages. A survey of the dinosaur extinction debate by professional paleontologist. Popular level.

SUN AND PLANETARY SYSTEM (edited by W. Fricke & G. Teleki). D. Reidel Pub. Co., 1982. Several professional papers on asteroids.

SPACE PUZZLES by Martin Gardner. Archway paperback, 1972, 129 pages. Chapter 5 poses some puzzles about comets and asteroids. Popular level.

WATCHERS OF THE SKIES by Willy Ley. Viking

Press Inc., N.Y., 1963; 528 pages. Chapter 13 is a
superb historical survey of asteroid discovery. Popular
level.

GLOSSARY

a—see semi-major axis.

absolute magnitude—the magnitude of an asteroid at a distance from the Earth and the Sun of 1 astronomical unit.

absorption bands—dark lines superposed on a continuum spectrum.

achondrite—a stony meteorite that lacks chondrules.

AGORA—Asteroidal Gravity, Optical and Radar Analysis spacecraft, proposed by the European Space Agency in 1983.

albedo—the percentage of sunlight that an object reflects from its surface.

alpha(α)— see phase angle.

Amors—a class of earth-approaching asteroid, whose orbits do not overlap the Earth's.

aphelion distance,*Q*—the maximum distance between an object and the primary body it orbits.

Apollos—a class of earth-approaching asteroid, whose orbit overlaps the Earth's.

argument of perihelion, ω (omega)—angle between the ascending node and the perihelion, measured in the direction of motion.

asteroid belt—a region of space between Mars and Jupiter where the great majority of asteroids are located.

astrograph—a refracting telescope designed to give a field of view of 10° degrees or more.

Atens—a class of earth-approaching asteroid, whose orbits overlap Earth's orbit at aphelion.

AU—astronomical unit, the average distance between the earth and sun, 149,597,870 km (approximately 93 million miles).

B(1,0)—absolute magnitude in the blue band.

ballistic spacecraft—travels without propulsion after being launched.

beta (β)—see phase coefficient.

Bode's law—a numerical relationship giving the distances of the planets from the Sun.

Bond albedo—see albedo.

breccia—rock composed of broken rock fragments cemented together by finer-grained material.

carbonaceous chondrite—a rare type of meteorite characterized by the presence of carbon compounds.

carbonyl—any of a series of metal compounds containing the CO radical.

charged coupled device (CCD)—an array of thin-film semiconductors used to rapidly generate a picture of an area of the sky. The term CCD refers to the mechanism by which the photoelectrically converted electrons are read off the chip as a signal.

color index—the difference in magnitudes between any two spectral regions.

coma—a region of diffuse gas that surrounds the nucleus of a comet.

commensurability—an orbital configuration in which two bodies orbit a common barycenter (the Sun) when the period of one is a rational fraction of that of the other.

contact binary—a dumbbell-shaped asteroid composed of two spherical asteroids in contact. A possible model of 624 Hektor and 216 Kleopatra.

Cretaceous-Tertiary—a geologic boundary dated at 65 million years, likely caused by an asteroid impact.

Darwin ellipsoid—tidally elongated ellipsoids nearly in contact, resulting from fission of a Jacobi ellipsoid. A possible model of 624 Hektor.

Differentiation—the general process of formation of different types of igneous rocks from a common parent magma.

Earth-crosser—a type of asteroid whose orbit occasionally intersects that of the Earth as a result of distant perturbations by the planets.

eccentricity—the amount by which an elliptical orbit deviates from circularity.

elongation—the angle minor planet-Earth-Sun. An elongation of 0° is a conjunction; one of 180° is an opposition.

ephemeris—a list of computed positions occupied by a celestial body over successive intervals of time.

equinox—either of two points on the celestial sphere where the celestial equator intersects the ecliptic.

families—groups of asteroids with almost equal values of the orbital elements *a*, *e* and *i*.

feldspars—common aluminous silicate minerals in meteorites.

FK5—The fifth catalogue of fundamental stars in which the precise positions and proper motions are listed for a given epoch.

Fourier analysis—the analysis of a periodic function into its simple harmonic components.

Galilean satellites—the four largest satellites of Jupiter, discovered by Galileo.

Galileo—American spacecraft.

geocentric distance, *d*—distance between the Earth and an asteroid.

geometric albedo—see albedo.

gravity assist—a means of accelerating a spacecraft by flying it past a larger world.

greenhouse effect—a phenomenon whereby an environment

is heated by the trapping of infrared radiation.

heliocentric distance, r—distance between a celestial body and the Sun.

Hildas—a class of asteroids at the 2/3 resonance.

Hipparcos—an astrometry spacecraft due for launch by the European Space Agency in 1988.

Hirayama family—see families.

IAU—International Astronomical Union, founded in 1919.

inclination, i—the angle between an asteroid's orbit and the plane of the ecliptic.

interferometer—an instrument which splits a light beam into two or more parts and subsequently reunites them.

Jacobi ellipsoid—an equilibrium figure with axis ratios of approximately $b/c = 1.5$, $a/c = 2$ to 4. See also Maclaurin spheroid.

JD—Julian Day number, the number of days that have elapsed since Greenwich noon on 1 Jan. 4713 B.C..

Kirkwood gaps—voids in the asteroid belt where the orbital period of the asteroids are at certain fractions of the period of Jupiter.

Lagrangian points—Five points in the orbital plane of two massive bodies in circular orbits around a common center of gravity, where a third body can remain in equilibrium.

libration—angular motions about the center of mass of a celestial body caused by gravitational torques.

lightcurve—a plot of magnitude values versus time.

longitude of ascending node—angular distance measured eastward in the plane of the Earth's orbit from the vernal equinox to the point where the asteroid crosses the ecliptic from S to N.

longitude of perihelion—the sum of the argument of perihelion and the longitude of the ascending node.

Maclaurin spheroid—a spheroidal equilibrium figure with axis ratios $a = b > c$, where a/c ranges from 1 to 1.7. At higher values it becomes a Jacobi ellipsoid.

magnetite—an opaque mineral commonly found on C–type asteroids.

magnitude—the brightness of an astronomical object. A difference of five magnitudes corresponds to an intensity difference of 100.

Maksutov telescope—a reflector whose primary mirror is spheroidal instead of parabolic, and which has a corrector lens to remove spherical aberration.

Mars crosser—asteroids that cross the orbit of Mars, at about 1.5 AU.

megaton—a thousand tons of TNT, equivalent to 4.19×10^{22} ergs.

metamorphism—the petrologic and chemical change induced in a rock by exposure to elevated temperature.

meteor—an extraterrestrial rock that burns up during its passage through Earth's atmosphere. Swarms of meteors, some associated with comets, produce annual meteor showers.

meteorite—a meteor that survives passage through the Earth's atmosphere.

micrometer—an instrument for measuring small distances in the field of an eyepiece.

Monte Carlo method—a technique for resolving problems in statistics by the use of random sampling.

Nemesis—a red dwarf star, which has been proposed as a companion of our Sun, and implicated in mass extinction events on Earth.

obliquity—the angle between a planet's axis of rotation and the pole of its orbit.

occultation—the passage of one celestial object in front of another, as seen from a particular place.

olivines—common rock-forming silicate minerals in meteorites.

Oort cloud—a region extending to more than 100,000 AU (1 light year) from the Sun, postulated as the birthplace of comets.

opposition effect—the apparent surge in brightness of an asteroid at small phase angles.

opposition magnitude—the brightness of an object at opposition; see also elongation.

osculating elements—orbital elements calculated without considering the perturbing forces of other planets.

Paleontology—the science of extinct organisms.

parent body—planet- or comet-like solar system bodies in which meteorites were formed or stored.

perihelion distance, q—the point in the asteroid orbit closest to the Sun.

phase angle, α—the angle subtended at the asteroid by the direction to the Sun and Earth.

phase coefficient, β—the rate at which the magnitude of an asteroid varies with phase angle, in units of mag/degree.

photometry—the measurement of the brightness of a celestial object. It can take the form of visual, photographic, or photoelectric photometry, the latter being the most accurate.

photosynthesis—a biological process occurring in plants, whereby the radiant energy of sunlight is stored as chemical energy.

phyllosilicate—a mineral in which silicon and oxygen are linked so as to form sheets of indefinite extent; the ratio of silicon to oxygen is 2:5.

planetesimal—bodies between 1 and 100 meters size, most of which finally accreted to larger bodies. See also parent body.

polarimetry—an observational technique based on an empirical relation of the variation with phase angle of polarized light from asteroids.

precession—a slow, periodic conical motion of the rotation axis of a spinning body.

proper elements—orbital elements which include the perturbing effects of other planets.

pyroxines—a group of common rock-forming silicates which have ratios of metal oxides to silicon dioxide of 1:1.

Q—see aphelion distance.

q—see perihelion distance.

Radar—an acronym for radio detecting and ranging.

radiometry—a diameter-measuring technique based on the reflectivity of asteroids.

reduced magnitude—the brightness an asteroid would have at a distance of 1 AU from both the Earth and Sun.

Reflector telescope—also known as a Newtonian telescope, it uses two mirrors to form a magnified image of celestial objects.

Refractor telescope—a telescope that uses a single lens.

regolith—a layer of fragmented rocky debris that forms the surface terrain of at least some asteroids; it is produced by meteoritic impact.

resonance—the natural vibration frequency of a physical system. Resonance phenomena are exhibited by all systems in motion—in the case of asteroids, by the Kirkwood gaps. See also secular resonance.

Schmidt telescope—a type of reflecting telescope used as a large camera.

secular resonance—occurs when the period of precession of a node or an apse is a small rational fraction of a similar period for a major planet (see also resonance).

semi-major axis—the distance from the center of an ellipse to the edge, through the intervening focus.

sidereal period—the time it takes for an object to make one complete circuit of its orbit relative to the stars.

solar parallax—angular size of the Earth's radius as measured from the center of the Sun.

Spacewatch—a telescope on Kitt Peak that is used, in part, to search for Earth-approaching asteroids.

spallation—an impact-generated process whereby 'plates' of crustal matter are flaked or chipped off an asteroid's surface.

speckle interferometry—a technique whereby the resolving power of a telescope is improved by a large factor.

subduction—a process whereby one of the Earth's crustal plates slides below another plate.

synodic period—the period of revolution of one body about another with respect to the Earth.

terrestrial planets—the four rocky planets closest to the Sun: Mercury, Venus, Earth and Mars.

TRIAD—Tucson Revised Index of Asteroid Data, a compilation of scientific data on the asteroids.

Trojans—asteroids that occur in two of the Lagrangian points that precede and follow Jupiter in its orbit.

type—that element of a taxon with which the name is permanently associated.

BIBLIOGRAPHY

The following abbreviations are used in the References:

AA—Astronomy and Astrophysics

AAS—Astronomy and Astrophysics Supplement

ACM—Asteroid Comets Meteors (ed. C.-I.Lagerkvist & H. Rickman)

AJ—Astronomical Journal

ApJ—Astrophysical Journal

Asteroids—Asteroids (ed. T. Gehrels)

BAAS—Bulletin of the American Astronomical Society

JBIS—Journal of the British Interplanetary Society

JHA–Journal of the History of Astronomy

JRASC—Journal of the Royal Astronomical Society of Canada

JRASNZ—Journal of the Royal Astronomical Society of New Zealand

LPS—Lunar and Planetary Science

MNRAS–Monthly Notices of the Royal Astronomical Society

MPB—Minor Planet Bulletin

PASP—Publications of the Astronomical Society of the Pacific

PSMP—Physical Studies of Minor Planets (ed. T. Gehrels)

Special Paper 190—Geological Implications of Impacts of Large Asteroids and Comets on the Earth (ed. L. Silver & P. Schulz)

ST—Sky and Telescope

Alexander, Stephen (1851). AJ 1, 181.

Alfven, H. (1964). Icarus 3, 52.

Alfven, H. and Arrhenius, G. (1970) Science 167, 139.

Allen, David A. (1970). Nature 227, 158.

Allen, David A. (1984). ST 67 (6), 493.

Alvarez, Luis W. (1983). Proc. Natl. Acad. Sci. 80, 627.

Alvarez, Luis W., Alvarez, Walter Asaro, Frank and Michel, Helen V. (1980). Science 208, 1095.

Alvarez, Walter (1985). The Galaxy and the Solar System conference, Tucson.

Alvarez, Walter and Muller, R. A. (1984). Nature 308, 718.

Alvarez, Walter, Alvarez, Luis W., Asaro, Frank and Michel, Helen V. (1982). Special Paper 190, 305.

Alvarez, Walter, Kauffman, Erle G., Surlyk, Finn, Alvarez, Luis W., Asaro, Frank and Michel, Helen V. (1984). Science 223, 1135.

Anderson, Charlene M. (1984). Planetary Report 4 (3), 3.

Andre, Ch. (1901). Astron. Nach. 155, 27.

Archibald, J. David and Clemens, William A. (1982). American Scientist 70 (4), 377.

Argelander, F. (1856). AN 42, 339.

Argelander, W. M. (1883). Astron. Nachr. 982.

Arlot, J. E., Lecacheux, J., Richardson, Ch. and Thuillot, W.(1985). Icarus 61, 224.

Armitage, Angus (1949). Popular Astronomy 57, 326.

Asaro, Frank, Alvarez, Luis W., Alvarez, Walter and Michel, Helen V. (1982). Special Paper 190, 517.

Ashbrook, Joseph (1970a). ST 40 (6), 361.

Ashbrook, Joseph (1970b). ST 40 (4), 213.

Asimov, Isaac (1953). Lucky Starr and the Pirates of the Asteroids. Doubleday and Co. Inc., Garden City, N.Y.

Asimov, Isaac (1972). Asimovs' Biographical Encyclopedia of Science and Technology, pg 207. Avon Books.

Aumann, H. (1985). Astronomical Society of the Pacific meeting, Flagstaff.

Baade, Walter (1934). PASP 48, 54.

Baier, G. and Weigelt, G. (1983). AA 121, 137.

Bailey, Solon I. (1913). Harvard Annals 72 (5), 165.

Balazs, B. A. and Szecsenyi-Nagy, G. (1984). Briefe Franz von Zachs in Sein Vaterland. Publ. Eotvos Univ. no. 7, Budapest.

Balogh, A. (1984). Spaceflight (26), 242.

Barber, G. A. (1985). ACM II, Uppsala.

Barnard, E. E. (1895). MNRAS 56, 55.

Barton, Samuel G. (1916). AJ 30 (6), 41.

Barucci, M. A. (1983). AAS 54, 471.

Barucci, M. A., Fulchignoni, Marcello, Burchi, Roberto, and D'Ambrosio, Viriol (1985). Icarus 61, 152.

Barucci, M. A., Bockelee-Morvan, D., Brahic, A., Clairemidi, S., Lecacheux, J. and Roques, F. (1986). AA 163, 261.

Bauer, G. and Weigelt, G. (1983). AA 121, 137.

Beatty, J. Kelly (1985). ST 69 (2), 127.

Beck, R. A. (1981). Irish Ast. J. 15, 87.

Bell, J. F., Gaffey, M. J. and Hawke, B. R. (1984b). LPS XV.

Bell, J. F., Hawke, B. R., and Gaffey, M. J. (1984a). LPS XV, 46.

Bell, J. F., Hawke, B. R., Gradie, J. C., McCord, J. B. and Gaffey, M. J. (1985). PASP 97, 892.

Bell, J. F., Hawke, B. R., Singer, R. B. and Gaffey, M. J. (1984c). LPS XV, 48.

Benton, Michael J. (1985). Nature 314, 496.

Beyer, M. (1953). Astron. Nachr. 281, 121.

Bianchi, R. and 7 co-authors (1984). AA 139, 1.

Bien, Reinhold (1980). Moon and Planets 22, 163.

Binzel, Richard P. (1978). MPB 6 (2), 18.

Binzel, Richard P. (1983a). Solar System Photometry Handbook (ed.Russell M. Genet).

Binzel, Richard P. (1984a). MPB 11 (1), 4.

Binzel, Richard P. (1984b). Icarus 57, 294.

Binzel, Richard P. (1984c). Icarus 59, 456.

Binzel, Richard P. (1985). Icarus.

Binzel, Richard P. (1986). PhD thesis, University of Texas.

Binzel, Richard P. and Mulholland, J. Derral (1983). Icarus 56, 519.

Blake, Robert (1984). Illustrated London News 272, 64.

Blanco, V. M., Demers, S., Douglass, G. G., and FitzGerald, M.P.(1968). Publ. U.S. Naval Obs., Second Series, 21.

Bobrovnikoff, N. T. (1929). Lick Obs. Bull. 407, 18.

Bohor, B. F., Foord, E. E., Modreski, P. J., and Triplehorn, D. M. (1984). Science 224, 867.

Borngen, F. and Kirsch, K. (1983). Die sterne 59, 344.

Bowell, Edward, Chapman, Clark R., Gradie, Jonathan C., Morrison, David, and Zellner, Benjamin (1978). Icarus 35, 313

Branham, Richard L. (1980). Celestial Mechanics 22, 81.

Bray, A. A. (1985). Modern Geology 9, 397.

Briggs, F. H. (1973). ApJ 184, 637.

Brooks, Robert R. and 7 co-authors (1984). Science 226, 539.

Brouwer, Dirk (1935). AJ 44, 57.

Brouwer, Dirk and Ashbrook, Joseph (1951). AJ 56.

Brown, E. W. (1925). Trans. of the Astronomical Observatory of Yale University 3, 1.

Brown, R. Hamilton, Morrison, David and Telesco, C. M. (1982). Icarus 52, 188.

Brownlee, D. E., Bates, B., and Beauchamp, R. H. (1983). Chondrules and their Origins, pg. 10.

Brownlee, Donald E. (1981). Natural History 90 (4) 73.

Brownlee, Donald E. (1984). Planetary Report 4 (2), 9.

Bryant, Robert (1889). AJ 8, 185.

Burchi, R. and Milano, L. (1983). Moon and Planets 28, 117.

Burchi, R., D'Ambrosio, V., Tempesti, P. and Lanciano, N. (1985). AAS 60, 9.

Burns, J. A. and Tedesco, E. F. (1979). Asteroids, 494.

Butterworth, P. S. and Meadows, A. J. (1985). Icarus 62, 305.

Cailliatte, C. (1956). Bulletin Astron. Paris 20, 283.

Cailliatte, C. (1960). Publ. Observatory Lyon 6(1), 259.

Calder, William A. (1936). Bulletin Harvard College Obs. 904.

Capaccioni, F., Cerroni, M., Farinella, P., Flamini, E., Martelli, G., Paolicchi, P., Smith, P. N., and Zappala, V. (1984). Nature 308, 832.

Capaccioni, F., Cerroni, P. Coradini, M., DiMartino, M., Farinella, P., Flamini, E., Martelli, G., Paolicchi, P., Smith, P. N., Woodward, A. and Zappala, V. (1986). Icarus 66, 487.

Carusi, A. and Massaro, E. (1978). AAS 34, 81.

Carusi, A. and Valsecchi G. B. (1982). AA 115, 327.

Catullo, V., Zappala, V., Farinella, P. and Paolicchi, P. (1984). AA 138, 464.

Cellino, A., Pannunzio, R., Zappala, V., Farinella, P. and Paolicchi, P. (1985). AA 144, 355.

Chaikin, Andrew (1984). ST 67, 18.

Chandler, S. C. (1898). Observatory 21, 449.

Chandrasekhar, S. (1969). Ellipsoidal Figures of Equilibrium; Yale Univ. Press, New Haven, Conn.

Chang, Y. C. and Chang, C. S. (1962). Acta Astron. Sinica 10, 101.

Chang, Y. C. and Chang, C. S. (1963). Acta Astron. Sinica 11, 139.

Chapman, Clark R. (1976). Geochim Cosmochim Acta. 40, 701.

Chapman, Clark R. (1984). The Planetary Report 4 (5), 22.

Chapman, Clark R. (1985). IAU report.

Chapman, Clark R. and Davis, Donald R. (1975). Science 190, 553.

Chapman, Clark R., Williams, James G., and Hartmann, William K. (1978). Ann. Rev. Astron. Astrophys. 16, 33.

Chapman, Clark, Johnson, Torrence and McCord, Thomas (1971). PSMP, pg. 51.

Chapman, C. R., Morrison, D. and Zellner, B. (1975). Icarus 25, 104.

Charlier, C. V. L. (1906). Astr. Nachr. 4094.

Chernykh, N. S. (1970). Bull. Inst. Theor. Astron. 12, 127.

Clarke, Arthur C. (1950). JBIS 9 (6), 261.

Clarke, Arthur C. (1973). Rendezvous with Rama (Harcourt Brace Jovanovich, Inc., N. Y.), pg. 1.

Clarke, Arthur C. (1984). 1984: Spring (Ballantine Books, N. Y.), pg. 139.

Clayton, Robert N., Mayeda, Toshiko K. and Brownlee, Donald E. (1986). Earth and Planetary Science Letters 79, 235.

Clemence, G. M. (1965). Ann. Rev. of Astron. & Astrophys. 3, 93.

Clemens, William A. (1982) Special Paper 190, 407.

Clemens, William A. (1985). Geological Society of America conference, Orlando.

Clemens, William A. (1986). Dynamics of Extinction, pg. 63.

Clerke, Agnes M. (1887). A Popular History of Astronomy in the 19th Century, pg. 92.

Cochran, Anita L. and Barker, Edwin S. (1984). Icarus 59, 296.

Combes, M.- A. (1975). MPB 3 (1), 4.

Combes, M.- A. (1976) MPB 3 (3), 36.

Combes, M.- A. (1977). MPB 4 (3), 26.

Cosmovici, C. B., Schmidt, E. and Stanggassinger, U. (1983) ACM, pg. 187.

Covault, Craig (1985). Aviation Week & Space Technology, 1 Apr. 1985, pg. 18.

Croft, Steven K. (1982). Special Paper 190, 143.

Cruikshank, Dale (1985). DPS meeting, Baltimore.

Cruikshank, Dale P. (1977). Icarus 30, 224.

Cruikshank, Dale P. and Hartmann, William K. (1984). Science 223, 281.

Crum, W. L. (1918). AJ 31, 173.

Cunningham, Clifford J. (1983a). MPB 10 (4), 26.

Cunningham, Clifford J. (1983b). MPB 10 (1), 4.

Cunningham, Clifford J. (1983c). JRASC 77(3), 121.

Cunningham, Clifford J. (1983d). Microcomputers in Astronomy (ed. Russell M. Genet), pg. 214.

Cunningham, Clifford J. (1984a). MPB 11 (1), 3.

Cunningham, Clifford J. (1984b). MPB 11 (3), 27.

Cunningham, Clifford J. (1984c). IAPPP Comm. 15, 18.

Cunningham, Clifford J. (1984d). IAPPP Comm. 17, 50.

Cunningham, Clifford J. (1985a). MPB 12, 13.

Cunningham, Clifford J. (1985b). MPB 12, 29.

Cunningham, Clifford J. (1985c). ACM II, Uppsala.

Cunningham, Clifford J. (1985d). DPS meeting, Baltimore.

Cunningham, Clifford J. and Kaitting, Murray K. (1982a). MPB 9 (1), 1.

Cunningham, Clifford J. and Kaitting, Murray K. (1982b). JAAVSO 11 (1), 10.

Cunningham, Clifford J. and Kaitting, Murray K. (1983a). MPB 10 (2), 11.

Cunningham, Clifford J. and Kaitting, Murray K. (1983b). JRASNZ 30 (5), 346.

Cutler, Andrew and Hughes, Mari (1985). Space Manufacturing With Lunar and Asteroidal Materials (ed. Faughan and Maryniak). AIAA.

d' E. Atkinson, R. (1982). JHA 13, 77.

David, Leonard (1980). OMNI 2 (6), 46.

Davidson, M. (1932). MNRAS 92, 46.

Davies, J. K., Eaton, N., Green, S. F., McCheyne, R. S., and Meadows, A. J. (1982). Vistas in Astronomy 26, 243.

Davies, J. K., Green, S. F., Stewart, B. C., Meadows, A. J. and Aumann, H. H. (1984). Nature 309, 315.

Davies, John (1984). New Scientist 104, 46.

Davies, John K. (1985). ST 70, 317.

Davis, Donald R., Chapman, Clark R., Weidenschilling, Stuart J., and Greenberg, Richard (1985). Icarus.

Degewij, J. and Tedesco, Ed (1982). Comets (ed. L. Wilkening) pg. 665.

Degewij, J. and Van Houten, C. J. (1979). Asteroids, pg. 417.

Degewij, J., Tedesco, E. F. and Zellner, B. (1979). Icarus 40, 364.

Dermott, S. F., Gradie, J. and Murray, Carl D. (1985). Icarus 62, 288.

Dermott, S. F. and Murray, C. D. (1983). Nature 301, 201.

Dermott, S. F. and Murray, C. D. (1985). Icarus.

Dermott, S. F., Nicholson, P. D., Burns, J. A., and Houck, J. R. (1984). Nature 312, 505.

Dermott, Stanley and Murray, Carl (1982). Nature, 296, 418.

Dermott, Stanley F. (1979). Icarus 37, 575.

Dermott, Stanley F. and Murray, Carl D. (1981). Nature 290, 664.

Dermott, Stanley, F., Harris, Alan W., and Murray, Carl D. (1984). Icarus 57, 14.

Dermott, S. F., Gradie, J. and Murray, Carl D. (1985). Icarus 62 (2), 289.

Dicke, R. H. (1965). AJ 70 (6), 395.

Dicke, R. H. and Goldenberg, H. Mark (1967). Nature 214, 1294.

Dickel, John R. (1979). Asteroids, 212.

Dietz, R. S. (1964). J. Geol. 72, 412.

Dobrovolskis, A. R. and Burns, J. A. (1984). Icarus 57, 464.

Dogett, L. E. (1971). AJ 76, 486.

Dollfus, Audouin (1971). PSMP, 95.

Dollfus, Audouin, and Zellner, Ben (1979). Asteroids, 170.

Dollfus, Audouin, Mandeville, Jean-Claude, and Duseaux, Mark (1979). Icarus 37, 124.

Donnison, J. R. (1979). MNRAS 186, 35.

Donnison, J. R. and Sugden, R. A. (1984). MNRAS 210, 673.

Drexler, K. Eric (1978). L-5 News 3 (4), 7.

Dreyer, J. L. E. and Turner, H. H. (1923). History of the Royal Astronomical Society.

Drummond, J. D., Cocke, W. J., Hege, E. K., Strittmatter, P. A., and Lambert, J. V. (1985a). Icarus 61, 132.

Drummond, J. D., Hege, E. K., Cocke, W. J., Freeman, J. D., Christou, J. C., and Binzel, R. P. (1985b). Icarus 61, 232.

Drummond, Jack D. (1982). Icarus 49, 143.

Dunbar, R. S. and Helin, E. F. (1983). BAAS 15 (3), 830

Dunham, D. W. (1979). Occ. Newsl. II, 12.

Dunham, D. W. and Maley, P. D. (1977). Occ. Newsl. 1, 115.

Dunham, D. W., Van Flandern, T. C., Millis, R. L., Chapman, C. R., Maley, P. D., and Povenmire, H. (1983). BAAS 15 (3), 822.

Dunham, David W. and Kristensen, L. K. (1983). ST 66, 238.

Dunham, E. W. and 9 co-authors (1984). AJ 89 (11), 1755.

Dunlap, J. L. (1971) PSMP, 147.

Dunlap, J. L. (1974). AJ 79 (2), 324.

Dunlap, J. L. (1976). Icarus 28, 69.

Dunlap, J. L. and Gehrels, T. (1969). AJ 74, 796.

Dunlap, J. L., Gehrels, T., and Howes, M. L. (1973). AJ 78, 491.

Dyson, F. W. (1912). MNRAS 72, 352.

Emiliani, C., Kraus, E. B., and Shoemaker, E. M. (1981). Earth Planetary Science Letters 55, 317.

Everhart, Edgar (1979). Asteroids, pg. 283.

Faggart, Billy E., Basu, Asish R., and Tatsumoto, Mitsunobu (1985). Science 230, 436.

Farinella, P., Paolicchi, P, and Zappala, V. (1981b). AA 104, 159.

Farinella, P., Paolicchi, P., Tedesco, E. F., and Zappala, V. (1981a). Icarus 46, 114.

Farinella, Paolo, Paolicchi, Paolo, and Zappala, Vincenzo (1982). Icarus 52, 409.

Fayet, G. (1949). Ann. Bureau des Longitudes Paris 12, 156.

Feierberg, Michael A. and Drake, Michael J. (1980). Science 209, 805.

Feierberg, Michael A., Larson, Harold P., and Chapman, Clark R. (1982). ApJ 257, 361.

Feierberg, Michael A., Larson, Harold P., Fink, Uwe and Smith, Howard A. (1980). Geochim Cosmochim. Acta. 44, 513.

Feierberg, Michael A., Lebofsky, Larry A., and Larson, Harold P. (1981). Geochim Cosmochim Acta 45, 971.

Feierberg, Michael A., Lebofsky, Larry A., and Tholen,

David J. (1985). Icarus.

Feierberg, Michael A., Witteborn, Fred C. and Lebofsky, Larry A. (1983). Icarus 56, 393.

Fesenkov, V. G. (1942). Report of the Soviet Academy of Sciences 24 (6), 163.

Fiala, A. D. (1968). Dissertation, Yale.

Field, George and Chaisson, Eric (1985). The Invisible Universe, Birkhauser Publishers.

Fischer, A. G. (1984). Catastrophes and Earth History (eds. Berggren, W. A. and Van Couvering, J. A.), Princeton Press.

Fish, Robert A., Goles, Gordon G., and Anders, Edward (1960). ApJ 132, 243.

Fisher, Arthur (1983). Popular Science 222 (2), 36.

Fox, Ken, Williams, Iwan P. and Hughes, David W. (1984). MNRAS 208, 11p.

Frederick, Donald J. (1984). Space World, pg. 24.

Fricke, Walter (1982). AJ 87 (9), 1338.

Friedman, Louis and Sagan, Carl (1984). Science Digest 92 (3), 58.

Fujiwara, Akira (1982). Icarus 52, 434.

Fujiwara, Akira, Kamimoto, Goro, and Tsukamoto, Akimasa (1978). Nature 272, 602.

Fulchignoni, M. and Barucci, M. A. (1984). BAAS 16.

Gaffey, Michael J. (1984). Icarus 60, 83.

Gaffey, Michael J. (1985a). LPS XVI, 231.

Gaffey, Michael J. (1985b). DPS meeting, Baltimore.

Gaffey, Michael J. (1986). Icarus 66, 468.

Galle, A. (1875). AN 85, 257.

Ganoe, William H. (1984a). L 5 News 9 (4), 3.

Ganoe, William H. (1984b). Space World, 22.

Gault, D. E. and Sonett, C. P. (1982). Special Paper 190, 69.

Gauss, Karl (1809). Theoria Motus.

Gehrels, T. (1955). ApJ 123, 331.

Gehrels, T. (1967). AJ 72 (8), 929.

Gehrels, T. (1977). Comets, Asteroids, Meteorites (ed. A. H. Delsemme). pg. 323.

Gehrels, T. (1984). Bull. Astron. Soc. India 12, 16.

Gehrels, T. (1986). Icarus 66, 288.

Gehrels, T. and Mc Millan, R. S. (1982). Sun and Planetary System, 279. (W. Fricke and G. Teleki ed.).

Gehrels, T. and Owings, D. (1962). ApJ 135, 906.

Gehrels, T. and Taylor, R. C. (1977). AJ 82, 229.

Gehrels, T., Roemer, E., Taylor, R. C., and Zellner, B. H. (1970). AJ 75, 186.

Gehrels, Tom and Binzel, Richard P. (1984). MPB 11 (1), 1.

Gerver, Joseph L. (1984). J. of Differential Equations 52 (1), 76.

Giffen, R. (1973). AA 23, 387.

Gill, D. (1894). MN 54, 344.

Gill, D. (1897). Annals Cap. Obs. 6.

Gilmore, A. C. and Kilmartin, P. M. (1984). JRASNZ 30 (6), 391.

Gilvarry, J. J. (1953). PASP 65, 173.

Glass, Billy (1982). Introduction to planetary geology, Cambridge University Press, pg. 336.

Goldstein, R. M. (1968). Science 162, 903.

Goodwin, Harold (1962). Space: Frontier Unlimited, D. Van Nostrand Company Inc., pg. 16.

Gould, B. A. (1854). AJ 2, 80.

Gould, B. A. (1856). AJ 4, 166.

Gradie, J. and Tedesco, E. (1982). Science 216, 1905.

Gradie, J. and Zellner, B. (1977). Science 197, 254.

Gradie, Jonathan and Veverka, Joseph (1980). Nature 283, 840.

Gradie, Jonathan and Veverka, Joseph (1981). LPS 12B, pg. 1769.

Gradie, Jonathan C., Chapman, Clark R., and Williams, James G. (1979). Asteroids, 359.

Gradie, J. and Veverka, J. (1986). Icarus 66, 455.

Green, S. F., Meadows, A. J., and Davies, J. K. (1985). MNRAS 214, 29p.

Greenberg, Richard and Chapman, Clark R. (1983). Icarus 55, 455.

Greenberg, Richard and Chapman, Clark R. (1984). Icarus 57, 267.

Grey, Vivian and Grey, Jerry (1962). Space Flight Report To The Nation, Basic Book Inc., N.Y., pg. 45.

Grieve, R. A. (1982a). GEOS 11 (4), 1.

Grieve, Richard (1982b). Special Paper 190, 25.

Groeneveld, Ingrid and Kuiper, Gerard (1954). ApJ 120, 200.

Gunter, Jay U. (1985). Mercury 14 (1), 9.

Gustafson, B. (1985). ACM II, Uppsala.

Hahn, Gerhard, and Rickman, Hans (1985). Icarus 61, 417.

Hall, Douglas, and Genet, Russell (1984). ST 67 (3).

Hallam, A. (1984). Nature 308, 686.

Hansen, Olav (1977). Icarus 32, 229.

Harrington, W. W. (1883). American J. of Science 26, 461.

Harris, A. W. (1985). ACM II. Uppsala.

Harris, Alan W. (1983a). AAS 15 (3), 828.

Harris, Alan W. (1983b). Solar System Photometry Handbook (ed. Russell M. Genet).

Harris, Alan W. and Burns, Joseph A. (1979). Icarus 40, 115.

Harris, Alan W. and Young, J. W. (1983). Icarus 54, 59.

Hartmann, William (1983). Moon And Planets, Wadsworth Inc., Belmont, CA, pg. 203.

Hartmann, William K. and Cruikshank, Dale P. (1978). Icarus 36, 353.

Hartmann, William K., and Cruikshank, Dale P. (1980). Science 207, 976.

Hartmann, William K., Cruikshank, Dale P., and Degewij, Johan (1982). Icarus 52, 377.

Hartmann, William K., Cruikshank, Dale P., Degewij, Johan and Capps, R. W. (1981). Icarus 47, 333.

Hege, G. (1980). BAAS 12, 662.

Heinlein, Robert (1978). Masterpieces of Science Fiction (ed. Thomas Durwood and Armand Eisen), Ariel Book /Ballantine Books, pg. 53.

Helin, Eleanor and Shoemaker, Eugene (1979). Icarus 40, 321.

Helin, Eleanor F. and Hulkower, Neal D. (1981). World Space Foundation, Foundation Astronautics Notebook 2.

Hellings, R. W., Adams, P. J., Anderson J. D., Keesey, M. S., Lau, E. L., Standish, E. M., Canuto, V. M., and Goldman, I. (1983). Physical Review Letters 51 (18), 1609.

Hemenway, Paul (1980). Celestial Mechanics 22, 89.

Henson, Carolyn (1979). L-5 News 4 (5), 5.

Heppenheimer, T. A. (1975). Icarus 26, 367.

Heppenheimer, T. A. (1978). AA 70, 457.

Heppenheimer, T. A. (1978). Moon and Planets 18, 491.

Herbert, Floyd and Sonett, Charles P. (1979). Icarus 40, 484.

Herget, Paul (1950). MNRAS 110, 167.

Herget, Paul (1968). The Names of the Minor Planets, Cincinnati Observatory.

Herget, Paul (1971). PSMP, 9.

Herrick, Samuel (1953). AJ 58, 156.

Herschel, John (1866). Outlines of Astronomy, 9th ed.

Herschel, William (1802). Phil. Trans. Royal Society.

Hertz, H. G. (1968). Science 160, 299.

Hertzsprung, E. (1911). Potsdam Pub. 22, 39.

Heward, Edward Vincent (1912). Contemporary Review CI, 403.

Hildebrand, A. R., Boynton, W. V., and Zoller, W. H. (1984). Meteoritics.

Hildebrand, Alan R. (1984). NASA Summer Study on Extraterrestrial Resources.

Hill, G. W. (1873). Collected Mathematical Works. (Johnson Reprint Corp., New York, 1965).

Hinks A. R. (1910). MNRAS 70, 588.

Hinks, A. R. (1909). MNRAS 69, 544.

Hirayama, K. (1923). Jap. J. of Ast. and Geophysics 1, 55.

Hirayama, Kiyotsugu (1918). AJ 31, 185.

Hoag, Arthur (1985). ST 69 (3), 214.

Hodgson, Richard G. (1978a). MPB 6 (2), 17.

Hodgson, Richard G. (1978b). MPB 5 (4), 27.

Hoffman, A. and Ghiold, J. (1985). J. Geol. Mag. 122, 1.

Hogg, Helen Sawyer (1950). JRASC 44, 163.

Holden, Edward S. (1896). PASP 8, 23.

Horz, Friedrich and Schaal, Rand. B. (1981). Icarus 46, 337.

Horz, Friedrich, McKay, David S., Morrison, Donald A., Brownlee, Donald E., and Housley, Robert M. (1981). LDEF First Mission Experiments (ed. Lenwood G. Clark) pg. 107.

Housen K. R., Wilkening, L. L., Chapman, C. R. and Greenberg, R. J. (1979). Asteroids, 601.

Housen, Kevin R. (1981). LPS 12B, 1717.

Hsu, Kenneth J. McKenzie, Judith A., and He, Q. X. (1982). Special Paper 190, 317.

Hughes, David (1982). MNRAS 199, 1149.

Hut, Piet (1984). Nature 311, 638.

Huth, Johann S. (1807). Berliner Jahrbucher.

Ip. W.-H. (1979). Icarus 40, 418.

Ip. W.-H. and Mehra, R. (1973). AJ 78 (1), 142.

Ishida, Keiichi, Mikami, Takao, and Kosai, Hiroki (1984). Pub. Astron. Soc. Japan 36, 357.

Jablonski, David (1986). Science 231, 129.

Janiczek, P. M., Seidelmann, P. K., and Duncombe, R. L. (1972). AJ 77 (9), 764.

Jastrow, Robert (1983). Science Digest 91 (9), 51.

Johnson, E. L. (1951). MNASSA 10, 58.

Johnson, T. V., and McGetchin, T. R. (1973). Icarus 18, 612.

Jones, Eric M., and Kodis, John W. (1982). Special Paper 190, 175.

Jurgens, R. F. and Bender, D. F. (1977). Icarus 31, 483.

Kaitting, Murray K. (1984). JAAVSO 13 (1), 3.

Kastner, Miriam, Asaro, F., Michel, H. V. and Alvarez, W. (1983). Meeting on Glass in Planetary and Geological Phenomena (Alfred University, N. Y.).

Kelly, Kenneth (1986). MPB 13 (2), 11.

Kepler, J. (1596). Mysterium Cosmographicum. In Prodromus Dissertationum

Kerr, Richard A. (1981). Science 211, 1333.

Kersken, Hans-Peter (1982). Stem zeit 3, 75.

Kester, F. E. and Alter, D. (1919). AJ 50, 50.

Khatib, Ahmad R., Anderson, John D., Hellings, Ronald W., and Moffat, John W. (1985). Proposal to JPL.

Kiang, T. (1962). MNRAS 123, 509.

King, Elbert A. and King, Trude V. (1979). Icarus 40, 439.

King, T. V. V., McFadden, L. A., Gaffey M. J. and McCord, T. B., (1983). BAAS 15 (3), 825.

Kirkwood, Daniel (1867). Meteoric Astronomy, pg. 110.

Kirkwood, Daniel (1867). Proceedings of AAAS 15.

Kirkwood, Daniel (1868). MNRAS 29, 96.

Kirkwood, Daniel (1888). The Asteroids. J. B. Lippincott Co..

Kirkwood, Daniel (1890). PASP 2, 49.

Kirkwood, Daniel (1891). Pop. Astron. 1, 19.

Kitchell, J. A. and Pena, D. (1984). Science 226, 689.

Klepczynski, W. J. (1969). AJ 74 (6), 774.

Klepczynski, W. J. (1974). IAU Coll. 22, pg. 97.

Klepczynski, W. J., Janiczek, P. M. and Fiala, A. D. (1971). AJ 76, 939.

Klose, A. (1928). Vjschr. Astron. Ges. 63, 333.

Knezevic, Z. and Zappala, V. (1982). Sun and Planetary System (ed. W. Fricke and G. Teleki), pg. 299.

Knight, David C. (1973). The Tiny Planets. William Morrow Co.

Knight, J. D. (1984). Science 223, 1180.

Kolcum, Edward H. (1984). Aviation Week and Space Technology 120 (26), 100.

Komensaroff, M. M. (1984). Proc. Astron. Soc. Australia 5, 457.

Koroleva, L. S. and Orelskaya, V. I. (1982). Sun and Planetary System (W. Fricke and G. Teleki ed.), pg. 449.

Kowal, C. T., Liller, W., and Marsden, B. G. (1979). Dynamics of the Solar System (ed. R. L. Duncombe), pg. 245.

Kozai, Yoshihide (1979). Asteroids, 334.

Kozai, Y. (1979). Dynamics of the Solar System (ed. Duncombe). D. Reidel Pub.

Kresak, L. 1977). Bull. Astron. Inst. Czech. 28, 65.

Kresak, Lubor (1979). Asteroids, pg. 289.

Kresak, Lubor (1984). Space Science Reviews 38, 1.

Kresak, Lubor (1979). Asteroids, pg. 289.

Kresak, Lubor (1984). Space Science Reviews 38, 1.

Kristensen, L. K. (1981). Astron. Nachr. 302, 43.

Kristensen, L. K. (1984). Astron. Nachr. 305 (4), 207.

Krug, W. and Schrutka-Rechtenstamm, G. (1936). Z. Astrophys. 13, 1.

Kuiper, G. P., Fujita, Y., Gehrels, T., Groeneveld, I., Kent, J., Van Biesbroeck, G., and Van Houten, C. J. (1958). ApJ Suppl. 32 (3), 289.

Kyte, Frank T. (1984). Meteoritics 19, 257.

Kyte, Frank T. and Wasson, John T. (1982). Special Paper 190, 235.

Kyte, Frank T. and Wasson, John T. (1983). Meteoritical Society.

Labeyrie, A. (1970). AA 6, 85.

Lagerkvist, C.-I. (1983). ACM, pg. 11.

Lambert, John V. (1983). Southwest Regional Conference for Astronomy and Astrophysics, pg. 13.

Landolt, Arlo (1973). AJ 78 (9), 959.

Larson, Harold P., Feierberg, Michael A. and Lebofsky, Larry A. (1983). Icarus 56, 398.

LaViolette, P. A. (1983). Meteoritics 18 (4), 336.

Lazovic, J. and Kuzmanoski, M. (1979). Publ. Dept. Astron., Univ. of Belgrade, no. 9.

Le Bertre, T. and Zellner, B. (1980). Icarus 43, 172.

Lebofsky, Larry A. (1980). AJ 85 (5), 573.

Lebofsky, Larry A., Lebofsky, Marcia J. and Rieke, George H. (1979). AJ 84 (6), 885.

Lebofsky, Larry A., Tholen, David J., Rieke, George H. and Lebofsky, Marcia J. (1984). Icarus 60, 532.

Leone, G., Farinella, P., Paolicchi, P. and Zappala, V. (1984). AA 140, 265.

Leuschner, A. O. (1916). Popular Astronomy 25, 385.

Leuschner, A. O. (1936). PASP 48, 55.

Levin, B. and Bronshten, V. A. (1986). Meteoritics 21, 199.

Levy, David H. (1983). Deep Sky 1 (4), 28.

Levy, David H., Davis, Donald R., Weidenschilling, Stuart J., Chapman, Clark R., and Greenberg, Richard (1984). MPB 11 (4), 31.

Lewis, John S., and Meinel, Carolyn (1983). Defense Science 2000+ 2 (3), 33.

Lewis, John S., Watkins, G. Hampton, Hartman, Hyman and Prinn, Ronald G. (1982). Special Paper 190, 215.

Ley, Willy (1963). Watchers of the Skies. Viking Press.

Lieske, Jay and Null, George (1969). AJ 74 (2) 297.

Lindsay, and Gill (1877). Dun. Echt. Obs. Publ. 2

Linke, Felix (1948). Kosmos.

Liu, L. and Innanen, K. A. (1985). AJ 90 (9), 1906.

Low, F. J. and 16 co-authors (1986). Icarus 65, 70.

Lowell, Percival (1917). AJ 26, 171.

Lowman, P. D. and Webster, W. J. (1984). BAAS 16, 442.

Lumme, Kari and Bowell, Edward (1981). AJ 86 (11), 1705.

Lunan, Duncan (1979). New Worlds For Old, William Morrow and Company, Inc., pg. 165.

Lupishko, D. F. and Bel'skaya, I. N. (1983). Solar System Research 16, 153.

Lupishko, D. F., Akimov, L. A., and Belskaya, I. N. (1983). ACM, pg. 63.

Lupishko, D. F., Kiselev, N. N., Chernova, G. P., and Bel'skaya, I. N. (1980). Pis'ma Astron. Zh. 6, 184.

Lupishko, D. F., Velichko, F. P., Tupieva, F. A., and Chernova, G. P. (1981). Sov. Astron. Letters 7 (4), 241.

Macdougall, J. R., McPherson, P. H., Mount, K. E., and Thomas, G. R. (1984). JBIS 37 (7), 337.

Maddox, John (1984). Nature 308, 685.

Magnusson, P. (1983). ACM, pg. 77.

Maley, Paul (1984). Astronomy 12 (2), 51.

Maley, Paul D. (1982). Revista Mexicana de Astronomia y Astrofisica 5, 213.

Mandeville, J.-C. (1981). LDEF First Mission Experiments (ed. Lenwood G. Clark), pg. 120 and 124.

Marsden, Brian (1970). AJ 75 (2), 206.

Marsden, Brian (1977). JRASC 71 (4), 309.

Marsden, Brian G. (1979). Asteroids, 77.

Marsden, Brian G. (1980). Celestial Mechanics 22, 63.

McAdoo, David and Burns, Joseph (1974). Icarus 21, 86.

McCall, Robert and Asimov, Isaac (1974). Our World In Space, New York Graphic Society, pg. 126.

McCheyne, R. S., Eaton, N., Green, S. F., and Meadows, A. J. (1984). Icarus 59, 286.

McCheyne, R. S., Eaton, N., Meadows, A. J. (1985). Icarus 61, 443.

McFadden, Lucy (1983). PhD thesis, Univ. of Hawaii.

McFadden, Lucy A., Gaffey, Michael J. and McCord, Thomas B. (1985). Science 229, 160.

McFadden, Lucy A., Gaffey, Michael J., and McCord, Thomas B.(1984). Icarus.

McKinnon, William B. (1982). Special Paper 190, 129.

McLaren, Digby (1983). New Scientist 100 (1385), 588.

McMahon, James H. (1978). MPB 6 (2), 14.

Mease, K. D., Anderson, J. D., Wood, L. J. and White, L. K. (1982). AIAA 20th Aerospace Sciences Meeting.

Meissinger, H. F. and Greenstadt, E. W. (1971). PSMP, pg. 543.

Melosh, H. J. (1982). Special Paper 190, 121.

Merton, G. (1977). MPB 4 (3), 27.

Metcalf, Joel H. (1912). Popular Astronomy 20, 201.

Milani, A., Murray, C. D. and Nobili, A. M. (1985). ACM II, Uppsala.

Miller, T. W. (1956). J. British Astron. Assoc. 66, 97.

Millis, R. L., Bowell, E., and Thompson, D. T. (1976). Icarus 28, 53.

Millis, R. L., Wasserman, L. H., Bowell, E., Franz, O. G. and Klemola, A. (1983). BAAS 15 (3), 822.

Millosevich (1880). Astr. Nachr. 2363.

Milne, David H., and McKay, Christopher P. (1982). Special Paper 190, 297.

Moffat, John (1981). Proc. of 7th International School of Gravitation and Cosmology (ed. v. de Sabbata).

Monck, W. H. S. (1888). Sidereal Messenger, pg. 334.

Moore, Patrick (1976). Comets: An Illustrated Introduction, Scribners.

Moore, Patrick (1983). History of Astronomy. Macdonald & Co., pg. 102.

Moore, Patrick (1984). ST 68 (5), 400.

Morrison, David (1973). Icarus 19, 1.

Morrison, David (1977). Icarus 31, 185.

Morrison, David (1979). Scientific Research with the Space Telescope, IAU Colloquium 54, pg. 77.

Morrison, David and Lebofsky, Larry (1979). Asteroids, 184.

Muller, G. (1893). Publ. Astrophys. Obs. Potsdam 30, 355.

Murray, Carl D. (1986). Icarus 65, 70.

Napier, W., and Dodd, R. . (1974). MNRAS 166, 469.

Narayan, C. and Goldstein, J. I. (1985). Geochim. Cosmochim. Acta 49, 397.

Neugebauer, G. and 11 co-authors (1984). Science 224, 13.

Newburn, Ray L. (1961). Advances in Space Science and Technology vol. 3 (ed. Frederick Ordway), pg. 195.

Newcomb, S. (1862). Mem. Amer. Acad. Arts Sci. 8, 123.

Nicholls, Peter. (1983). The Science in Science Fiction (Alfred A. Knopf, Inc.) pg. 23.

Nicholson, Seth B. (1961). ASP leaflet no. 381.

Nicolet, B. (1978). AAS 34, 1.

Niehoff, John C. (1977). Icarus 31, 430.

Niehoff, John C. (1978). Asteroids: An Exploration Assessment (ed. David Morrison), pg. 225.

Noteboom, E. (1921). Astron. Nachr. 214, 153.

O'Dell, C. R. (1986). Icarus 67, 71.

O'Handley, D. A. (1967). Astron. Pap. Am. Eph. 20, 319.

O'Keefe, John D. and Ahrens, Thomas J. (1982). Special Paper 190, 103.

O'Keefe, John D. and Ahrens, Thomas J. (1985). Icarus 62, 328.

O'Leary, Brian (1977). Science 197, 363.

O'Leary, Brian (1980). OMNI 2 (8), 22.

O'Leary, Brian (1983). Advances in the Astronautical Sciences 53 (ed. James D. Burke and April S. Whitt), pg. 375.

O'Leary, Brian, Gaffey, Michael J., Ross, David J. and Salkeld, Robert (1979). Space Resources and Space Settlements, NASA SP-428, pg. 173.

Oberth, Hermann (1957). Man Into Space. Harper Brothers Publishers, N.Y.

Officer, C. B. and Drake, C. L. (1985). Science 227, 1161.

Olbers, W. (1803). Ann Physik 14, 38.

Olbers, W. (1805). Monthly Correspondence 6, 88.

Oort, J. H. (1950). Bull. Astron. Inst. Netherlands 11 (408), 91.

Opik, Ernst (1958). Irish Ast. J. 5, 34.

Opik, Ernst (1970). Irish Ast. J. 9, 283.

Opik, Ernst (1976). Irish Ast. J. 13, 22.

Opik, Ernst (1978). Moon and Planets 18, 327.

Ostro, Steven (1983). Review of Geophysics and Space Physics 21 (2), 186.

Ostro, Steven J. (1985a). Proceedings of the International School of Physics "Enrico Fermi", Italy.

Ostro, Steven J. (1985b). PASP 97, 877.

Ostro, Steven J., Campbell, Donald B., and Shapiro, Irwin I. (1983). AJ 88 (4), 565.

Ostro, Steven J., Campbell, Donald B., and Shapiro, Irwin I. (1985). Science 229, 442.

Ostro, Steven, and Connelly, Robert (1984). Icarus 57, 443.

Oswalt, T. D. and Rafert, J. B. (1985). IAPPP 20, 18.

Overby, Dennis (1984). Discover 5 (5), 26.

Panther, Roy and Binzel, Richard P. (1984). MPB 11 (4), 34.

Paolicchi, P., Farinella, P., and Zappala, V. (1982). Sun and Planetary System, 295.

Paolicchi, P., Farinella, P., and Zappala, V. (1983). Adv. Space Research 2, 235.

Parkhurst, Henry M. (1890). Harvard Annals 18 (3), 29.

Perozzi, E. (1983). ACM, 149.

Pickering, Edward (1903). Popular Astronomy 11, 181.

Pierce, D. A. (1971). AJ 76, 177.

Piironen, J. O., Poutanen, M., DiMartino, M., and Zappala, V. (1985). AAS 61, 299.

Pike, R. J. (1978). LPS 9, 901.

Pilcher, Frederick (1981). MPB 8 (2), 10.

Pilcher, Frederick (1983). MPB 10 (3), 18.

Pilcher, Frederick (1984). Tonight's Asteroids 83, 1.

Pilcher, Frederick and Meeus, Jean (1973). Tables of Minor Planets.

Pillmore, C. L., Tschudy, R. H., Orth, C. J., Gilmore, J. S. and Knight, J. D. (1984). Science 223, 1180.

Playford, P. E., Mclaren, D. J., Orth, C. J., Gilmore, J. S. and Goodfellow, W. D. (1984). Science 226, 437.

Plummer, J. (1916). MNRAS 76, 378.

Porter, J. G. (1950). Journal British Astron. Assoc. 61, 2.

Pospieszalska-Surdej and Surdej (1985). AA 149, 186.

Pournelle, Jerry E. (1983). Citizens Advisory Council on National Space Policy, Executive Summary Report, pg. 17. L-5 Society.

Poutanen, M., Bowell, E., and Lumme, K. (1981). BAAS 13, 725.

Preston-Thomas, H (1952). JBIS 11, 173.

Project Icarus: MIT Students System Project (1968). MIT Press.

Putilin, I. (1952). News of the Observatory, Odessa State Univ. 2, 7.

Rabe, Eugene (1950). AJ 55, 112.

Rabe, Eugene (1961). AJ 66 (9), 500.

Rabe, Eugene (1967). AJ 72, 852.

Rabe, Eugene (1971). PSMP, 13.

Rampino, M. R. and Reynolds, R. C. (1983). Science 219, 495.

Rampino, Michael R., and Stothers, Richard B. (1985). The Galaxy and the Solar System conference, Tucson.

Raup, David and Sepkoski, John (1984). Proc. Natl. Acad. Sci 81, 801.

Raup, David M. (1986). Science 231, 1528.

Raup, David M. and Sepkoski, John J. (1986). Science 231, 833.

Reasenberg, R. D. (1983). Phil. Trans. Royal Soc. London A 310, 227.

Reijnen, Gijsbertha C. (1981). Utilization of Outer Space

and International Law. Elsevier Scientific Pub. Co., Amsterdam.

Reimann, Ingo (1983). Stem zeit 3, 70.

Reitsema, Harold J. (1979). Science 205, 185.

Rice, Hugh (1937). Popular Astronomy 45, 149.

Richardson, Robert S. (1967). Getting Acquainted with Comets. McGraw-Hill Book Co., N. Y.

Roach, F. E. and Stoddard, L. G. (1938). ApJ 88, 305.

Robinson, Leif J. (1984). ST 67 (1), 4.

Rosenhagen, J. (1932). Mitt Wien. Sternw. 1 (2), 45.

Roseveare, N. T. (1982). Mercury's Perihelion from Le Verrier to Einstein, Clarendon Press.

Ross, Stanley (1966). Space Flight Handbook vol. 3, part 5. ASA SP-35.

Rothblatt, Martin A. (1981). American Institute of Aeronautics and Astronautics, pg. 89.

Russell, C. T., Aroian, R., Arghavani, M., and Nock, K. (1984). Science 226, 43.

Russell, Henry Norris (1906). ApJ 24 (1), 1.

Sadler, H. (1895). English Mechanic and World of Science no. 1584, 533.

Sandford, Scott (1986). Icarus 68, 377.

Sather, R. E. (1976). AJ 81 (1), 67.

Scaltriti, F. and Zappala, V. (1980). AA 83, 249.

Scaltriti, F., and Zappala, V. (1976b). Icarus 28, 29.

Scaltriti, F., Zappala, V. (1976a). AAS 23, 167.

Scaltriti, F., Zappala, V., and Stanzel, R. (1978). Icarus 34, 93.

Scherbaum, L. M. and Kazantsev, A. M. (1985). Astronomicheskii Vestnik 19, 195.

Schmadel, L. D. (1980). Astron. Nachr. 301, 251.

Schmadel, L. D. (1981). Sterne und Weltrum 9, 335.

Schmadel, L. D. and Kohoutek, L. (1982). Astron. Nachr. 303, 139.

Schober, H. J. (1982). The Scientific Aspects of the Hipparcos space astrometry mission, ESA SP-177, pg. 169.

Schober, Hans Josef, Scaltriti, Franco and Zappala, Vincenzo (1980). Moon and Planets 22, 167.

Scholl, Hans (1982). Formation of Planetary Systems (ed. A. Brahic), pg. 835.

Scholl, H. and Froeschle, Ch. (1985). ACM II, Uppsala.

Schroeter, John (1807). Phil. Trans. Royal Society, pg. 245.

Schroll, A., Haupt, H. F., and Maitzen, H. M. (1976). Icarus 27, 147.

Schubart, J. and Zech, G. (1967). Nature 214, 900.

Schubart, Joachim (1971). PSMP, 33.

Schubart, Joachim (1982). Celestial Mechanics 28, 189.

Schubart, Joachim and Matson, D. L. (1979). Asteroids, pg. 84.

Schweizer, F. (1969). AJ 74, 779.

Scott, Edward (1984). Nature 311, 708.

Sekanina, Zdenek (1983). AJ 88 (9).

Shkuratov, Yu G. (1983). Sov. Astron. 27 (5), 581.

Shoemaker, E. M. (1977). Impact and Explosion Cratering (ed. Roddy, D. J., Pepin, R. O. and Merrill, R. B.), pg. 1.

Shoemaker, E. M. and Wolfe, R. F. (1984). Meteoritics 19, 313.

Shoemaker, Eugene M. (1983). Ann. Rev. Earth Planet Sci. 11, 461.

Short, Nicholas M. (1975). Planetary Geology, Prentice-Hall pub., pg. 16.

Showalter, M. R. Ostro, S. J., Shapiro, I. I. and Campbell, D. B. (1982). BAAS 14, 725.

Simon, Cheryl (1984). Science News 125, 250.

Singer, S. Fred, Stanley, John E. and Kassel, Philip C. (1981). LDEF First Mission Experiments (ed. Lenwood G. Clark), pg. 112.

Sitarski, G. (1983). Acta Astronomica 33 (2), 295.

Sloan, Robert E., Rigby, J. Keith, Van Valen, Leigh M., Gabriel, Diane (1986). Science 232, 629.

Slusser, George Edgar (1978). The Space Odysseys of Arthur C. Clarke. Borgo Press, San Bernardino, California.

Smit, J. and Hertogen, J. (1980). Nature 285, 198.

Smit, J. and Van der Kaars (1984). Science 223, 1177.

Smith, Dale W. (1985). IAPPP Communications 21, 3.

Smith, Dale W., Johnson, Paul E. and Shorthill, Richard W. (1981). Icarus 46, 108.

Soberman, Robert K., Neste, Sherman L. and Petty, Alan F. (1982). PSMP, pg. 617.

Spencer-Jones, H. (1941). Memoirs Royal Ast. Soc. 66, 1.

Stableford, Brian and Langford, David (1985). The Third Millenium, Metheun.

Staley, D. O. (1970). J. of Geophysical Research 75 (28), 5571.

Staude, N. M. (1925). Russian Astron. J. 2, 45.

Stetson, D. S., Lundy, S. A. and Yen, C. L. (1984). AIAA-84-2016. Astrodynamics Conference.

Stewart, B. C., Davies, J. K. and Green, S. F. (1984). JBIS 37, 348.

Stobbe, J. (1940). Astron. Nachr. 270, 1.

Stone, E. J. (1867). MNRAS 27, 302.

Stracke, G. (1941). Astron. Nachr. 271, 281.

Stroobant, P. (1920). Ann. Obs. Roy Belgique. Nouvelle Serie 14, 147.

Sventek, Paul L. (1984). JAAVSO 13 (1), 45.

Sweet, A. R. & Jerzykiewicz, T. (1985). GEOS 14 (4), 6.

Sykes, Mark V. and Greenberg, Richard (1986). Icarus 65, 51.

Sykes, Mark V. and Greenberg, Richard (1985). PASP 97, 904.

Tacchini (1880). Astr. Nachr. no. 2363.

Taff, G. (1985). Celestial Mechanics. Wiley and Sons, pg. 216.

Taylor, Gordon (1981a). Journal British Astron. Assoc. 92 (1), 13.

Taylor, Gordon (1981b). AJ 86 (6), 903.

Taylor, Gordon (1983). ACM, 107.

Taylor, R. C. (1973). AJ 78 (10), 1131.

Taylor, R. C. (1977). AJ 82, 441.

Taylor, R. C. (1978). AJ 83, 201.

Taylor, R. C. and Tedesco, E. F. (1983). Icarus 54, 13.

Taylor, R. C., Gehrels, T., and Capen, R. C. (1976). AJ 81, 778.

Taylor, Ronald C. (1979). Asteroids, 480.

Taylor, Ronald C. (1985). Icarus.

Taylor, Ronald C., Tapia, S., and Tedesco, Edward F. (1985). Icarus.

Tedesco, E. F. , Veeder, G. J., Matson D. L. and Lebofsky, L. A. (1983). BAAS 15 (3), 825.

Tedesco, E. F. and Sather, R. E. (1981). AJ 86, 1553.

Tedesco, E. F., and Zappala, V. (1980). Icarus 43, 33.

Tedesco, E. F., Gradie, J. and Tholen, D. G. (1985). in preparation.

Tedesco, E. F., Veeder, G. J., Matson, D. L. and Tholen, D. J. (1983). BAAS 15 (3), 825.

Tedesco, E., Drummond, J., Candy, M., Birch, P., Nikoloff, I., and Zellner, B. (1978). Icarus 35, 340.

Tedesco, Edward F. (1979). Icarus 40, 375.

Tedesco, Edward F. (1979). Science 203, 905.

Tedesco, Edward F. and Taylor, Ronald C. (1985). Icarus.

Tholen, D. J. (1983). BAAS 15 (3), 829.

Tholen, D. J. (1985). ACM II. Uppsala.

Tholen, David J. (1984a). MPB 11 (4), 26.

Tholen, David J. (1984b). PhD thesis, Univ. of Arizona.

Tholen, David J. (1986). MPB 13 (2), 23.

Tholen, David J. and Zellner, B. (1984). Icarus 58, 246.

Thomas, G. R. (1983). JBIS 36, 38.

Thomas, P. and Veverka, J. (1979). Icarus (special Asteroid issue).

Thomas, P. and Veverka, J. (1980). Satellites of Jupiter (ed. D. Morrison). University of Arizona Press.

Titius von Wittenburg, J. D. (1766). Betrachtung uber die Natur.

Toon, O. B., Pollack, J. B., Ackerman, T. P., Turco, R. P., McKay, C. P., and Liu, M. S. (1982). Special Paper 190, 187.

Tschermak, G. (1875). Sitzungsber. Akad. Wiss. Wien, Math- naturw 71, 661.

Van Flandern, T. C., Tedesco, E. F. and Binzel, R. P. (1979). Asteroids, 443.

Van Houten-Groeneveld, I., and Van Houten, C. J. (1958). ApJ 127, 253.

Van Houten, C. J., Herget, P. and Marsden, B. G. (1984). Icarus 59, 1.

Veeder, G. J., Matson, D. L. and Tedesco, E. F. (1983). Icarus 55, 177.

Veeder, G. J., Matson, D. L., Hoover, G. and Kowal, Charles (1983). AJ 88, (7), 1060.

Vesely, Carl D. (1971). PSMP, pg. 133.

Vogel, H. C. (1874). Research of the spectra of the planets, pg. 23, Leipzig.

Von Zach, F. (1789). Berliner Jahrbucher, pg. 156.

Von Zach, F. (1801). Monthly Correspondence 3, 602.

Von Zach, F. (1802). Monthly Correspondence 5, 172.

Vsessviatsky, S., and Filippov, J. (1935). Ast. J. of the Soviet Union 12, 434.

Wallentinsen, Derek (1979). MPB 6 (4), 34.

Walz, Marjorie A. (1981). L-5 News (12), 8.

Wasson, John T. (1985). Meteorites. W. H. Freeman and Co., pg. 199.

Wasson, J. T. and Wetherill, G. W. (1979). Asteroids, pg. 926.

Watson, F. (1937). Harvard College Obs. Circular 419, 1.

Watson, Fletcher (1956). Between The Planets. Harvard Univ. Press.

Watson, William W. (1977). MPB 5 (3), 22.

Webster, W. J. and Lowman, P. B. (1984). BAAS 16, 442.

Weidenschilling, S. J. (1977). Astrophysics and Space Science 51, 153.

Weidenschilling, S. J. (1980). Icarus 44, 807.

Weissman, Paul R. (1984). Science 224, 987.

Weissman, Paul R. (1985). Nature 314, 517.

Welch, Douglas, Kaitting, Murray and Cunningham, Clifford (1984). MPB 11 (3), 24.

West, R. M., Madsen, C., and Schmadel, L. D. (1982). AA 110, 198.

Wetherill, G. W. (1984). Meteoritics 19 (1), 1.

Wetherill, G. W. (1985). Asteroidal Source of Ordinary Chondrites.

Wetherill, G. W. and Williams, J. B. (1968). J. of Geophysical Research 73 (2), 635.

Wetherill, George (1979a). Icarus 37, 96.

Wetherill, George (1979b). Scientific American 240 (3), 54.

White, Wayne N. (1984). L-5 News 9 (2), 9.

Wijesinghe, Mahendra P. and Tedesco, Edward F. (1979). Icarus 40, 383.

Wilde, Pat, Berry, William B., Quinby-Hunt, Mary S., Orth, Charles J., Quintana, Leonard R., and Gilmore, James S. (1986). Science 233, 339.

Williams, J. G. (1971). PSMP, 177.

Williams, J. G. (1984). Icarus 57, 1.

Williams, J. G. and Wetherill, George (1973). AJ 78 (6), 510.

Williams, Steve (1982). L-5 News 7 (8), 5.

Wisdom, J. (1982). AJ 87 (3), 577.

Wisdom, Jack (1983). Icarus 56, 51.

Wisdom, Jack (1985). Nature 315, 731.

Witt, G. (1905). Untersuchung uber die Bewegung des Planeten (433) Eros, thesis.

Witt, G. (1908). VJS Astron. Ges. 43, 295.

Witt, G. (1933). Astron. Nachr. 9 (1), 1.

Wolbach, Wendy S., Lewis, Roy S., and Andrew, Edward (1985). Science 230, 167.

Wood, Charles A. and Ashwal, Lewis D. (1981). LPS 12 B, pg. 1359.

Wright, J. L. (1982). Asteroid Program, a JPL report by CME Research, Pasadena.

Wyse, Arthur B. (1938). ASP leaflet, no. 114.

Yamada, Yoshiro (1982). JBIS 35, 459.

Zappala, V. and Knezevic, Z. (1984). Icarus 59, 436.

Zappala, V. and Van Houten-Groeneveld, I. (1979). Icarus 40, 289.

Zappala, V., Barucci, M. A., and Fulchignoni, M. (1984b). BAAS 16.

Zappala, V., Debehogne, H., Lagerkvist, C. I., and Rickman, H. (1982). AAS 50, 23.

Zappala, V., Di Martino, M., Scaltriti, F. Djurasevic, G. and Knezevic, Z. (1983a). Icarus 53, 458.

Zappala, V., Di Martino, M., Scaltriti, F., Burchi, R., Milano, L., Young, J. W., Wahlgren, G., and Pavlovski, K., (1983b). AA 123, 326.

Zappala, V., DiMartino, M., Hanslmeier, A., and Schober, H. J. (1985). AA 147, 35.

Zappala, V., Farinella, P., Knezevic, Z. and Paolicchi, P. (1984a). Icarus 59, 261.

Zappala, Vincenzo (1980). Moon and Planets 23, 345.

Zappala, Vincenzo (1984). Icarus.

Zappala, Vincenzo, Scaltriti, Franco, Farinella, Paolo and Paolicchi, Paolo (1980). Moon and Planets 22, 153.

Zappala, V. and Knezevic, Z. (1986). Icarus 65, 122.

Zellner, B., Tholen, D., and Tedesco, E. F. (1985a). Icarus 61, 355.

Zellner, B., Leake, M., Morrison, D. and Williams, J. G. (1977). Geochim Cosmochim Acta 41, 1759.

Zellner, B., Thirunagari, A., and Bender, D. (1985b). Icarus 62, 505.

Zellner, Ben (1976). Icarus 28, 149.

Zellner, Ben (1979). Asteroids, pg. 783.

Zellner, Ben, Gehrels, Tom and Gradie, J. (1974). AJ 79 (10), 1100.

Zessewitsche, W. (1937). Observatory 60, 289.

Zhou, Xing-hai and Wu, Zhi-xian (1983). Pub. of Purple Mt. Obs. 2 (3), 10.

Zhou, Xing-hai and Yang, Xiu-yi (1981). Acta Astron. Sinica 22 (4), 378.

Zhuravlev, S. G. and Kiryushenkov, V. N. (1982). Sov. Astron. 26 (3), 349.

Zielenbach, J. W. (1968). AJ 74, 567.

INDEX

3/94 9

A Little Boy's
PRAYER

Other works available by
Stephen Marshall

Off The Record—
DVD

Life Times Seven—
Audio Music CD

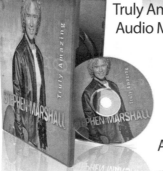

Truly Amazing—
Audio Music CD

You Make My Day—
Another Inspiring Book!

Formula Won—
Audio Teaching & Music CD
for Your Day-to-Day Winning

Purchase these items online at
www.StephenMarshall.net

A Little Boy's
PRAYER

STEPHEN MARSHALL

A Little Boy's Prayer

Cover by Lindsay Allison
LindsayHamiltonDesigns.com
Editing: Cristel Phelps & Mary Ann Woodcock

Published by Marshall Books a division of MH Media Group
P.O. Box 991
Brentwood, TN 37027

PROMOTING A MESSAGE OF HONOR AND TRUTH TO THIS GENERATION.

Printed in the United States of America

Library of Congress Cataloging-In-Publication Data

Marshall, Stephen
A Little Boy's Prayer / by Stephen Marshall
ISBN-10: 0-615-40695-5
ISBN-13: 978-0-61540-695-4

Dedication

To everyone who longs to be covered by the hand of
The Father.

To my beautiful wife Pam who championed this story
and never tired of encouraging me to write it.

And to my Mom who made amazing sacrifices as a single
mother for me, Lindsay and Angela. She made Christmas
a gift from God, and God the Gift of Christmas.

About The Author

Abandoned by his father at a young age, Stephen Marshall began a journey like many others to discover his true identity. He is a prolific songwriter and recording artist. Other singers have used his songs on the their albums, in their concerts, and churches around the world have incorporated his music into their worship services. Stephen has used his platform as a Christian singer and musician to encourage audiences around the globe. He has been on national television shows as a guest and as a co-host with his wife Pam Thum. Together they have founded a women's conference called *Born To Win* and the men's event *I Am A Son*. As thankful as he is for all these great opportunities, Stephen's passion and testimony remain the same. His life does not exist in the doing, but in the being. His being ... that is entirely in God. "In Jesus Christ, I am a son!" (John 1:12)

A Little Boy's Prayer
The Musical

Don't wait until December to make plans to go experience
the timeless musical production based on this great story
you're reading now. For information on a theater or church
performing the play near you, go to
www.aLittleBoysPrayer.com

You will find it to be a heart warming, entertaining adventure
for the whole family. Many of your favorite Christmas
songs will carry you on a journey into a world where the true
meaning of Christmas once again breathes childlike hope into
your heart.

If you're church is looking for something new, fresh and
exciting to offer to your community, go to the *Musical* page
on the website for more information.

www.aLittleBoysPrayer.com

A Little Boy's Prayer

Chapter 1

Dear God, I just want my Dad to come home for Christmas. We're gonna build a tree house together and stuff. I know he's got work to do but ... I need him to help me break in my catcher's mitt. Thanks God.

Time and years trudge by slowly, but then too quickly for some. What once seemed impossibly far off for even a boy has now become the same man's reality.

It had all the makings of a perfect day. The morning sun uninterrupted allowed for an inspiring view of the hillside with its blazing arrangement of colors. A light breeze choreographed just enough movement to make one stare, if you were so inclined. It had almost the same effect as watching the glowing embers in a fireplace. Rob touched the mug of hot coffee to his mouth and took a sip. It was Friday and he favored it for the imposed characteristic of being a day to tie up loose ends. The round face of the thermometer attached just outside the window read sixty-one degrees already and it was only seven thirty. A few little patrons fluttered around the bird feeder that Elle kept well supplied. It was a beautiful world from where he was sitting.

He smiled when he remembered the first time that he and Elle had walked through this house and she discovered the natural landscape outside the bay window of this breakfast nook. It had been early in the spring and they were still about a month from getting married. The window had framed a vibrant green with a cloudless

topping of blue sky that day. Elle was sold that very
second. Rob loved that about her. She was spontaneous
and inspired but at the same time committed to her choices
and decided. It's not at all that she was ever stubborn …
no, not at all. On the contrary Elle was probably one of
the most giving, understanding and adaptable people on
the face of the earth.

She was the reason he was here in Forrester. Even
though he grew up in this beautiful little town, his
ambition for success told him if he was ever going to
be someone he needed to go east to the big cities. They
had been high school sweethearts and Elle had genuinely
encouraged him to go after his dreams even if it meant
moving away. Rob had moments of great clarity though
and he knew that this town and Elle were a package deal.
You may want an orange tree in your backyard but that
brings you to the choice of either moving to Florida or
going with a tree that belongs in upstate New York. For
him the choice was not simple but Elle was the prize he
was unwilling to live without. He loved her.

He still wrestled with the nagging feeling that
something big was missing in his life and there was some
contest beyond these hills that would make him authentic.
He was a lawyer that had graduated at the top of his class
with all kinds of offers but it meant little to him now. He
secretly felt it was like having a rocket; parking it on a lot
somewhere and running a hotdog stand out of it. It was
just too typical of the small town thinking he grew up in.
He worried that a part of him was becoming so numbed
that he might never even be able to recognize greatness.
Under no circumstances could he ever let Elle know he
thought this way and that made his burden even heavier.
Even if he failed his own ambitions he couldn't fail her.

From the other side of the house came the thump of
about 45 pounds jumping off the last step of the staircase
followed by the shuffle of little stocking feet coming down
the hall toward the kitchen. A smile spread across Rob's

lips as he took another sip of his coffee and took in one more glance at the fresh painting of the hills.

"Hi Daddy!" clipped Brodie's raspy little voice.

Instantly Rob filed any career remorse he had wrestled with and came to life. "Good morning Catcher! Are you ready for some breakfast?"

Brodie just grinned his sleepy little grin and kept marching toward Rob. Catcher was Rob's idea for a middle name for Brodie, being a huge baseball fan. At six years old Brodie recognized his father's occasional use of that name as a rallying cry for sport activities, adventures and just getting the day started.

The top of his light brown hair bobbed around the kitchen counter just in time to have Rob turn in his chair and give him the once over.

"Well look at you. Mommy has you looking pretty sharp today." Hoisting him up on his lap. "Is there something special going on at school?"

Elle always had her boy looking sharp but with Brodie there was always something special going on. Elle came around the corner just in time to catch her husband messing up Brodie's hair with his morning manhandling of their son. Suddenly Rob's quiet morning got lively.

"Yeh Dad! Today I want to bring Grampy's hammer to school and show all the kids and …"

"Rob, I just got his hair looking good …", Elle sighed with her good-natured dimples countering any possible sting from her mild scold.

With both mother and son sputtering away at the same time Rob went into his organizer role, "Wait, wait a sec here you guys!" Rob was laughing at the pair.

"Mommy's getting me in trouble for messing up your hair and what's all this about you taking a hammer to school?"

Elle was already going to work on Brodie's and her breakfast. She loved listening in on this energetic exchange between father and son in the morning. It seemed to be the most pure time Rob and Brodie shared. With all of Rob's responsibilities weighing on him and especially the pressure of his new law practice, the days seemed to drain him of precious resources that their little boy longed for.

"Dad I want to bring the hammer that Grampy gave me to school to show everyone. Mrs. Hatcher said we could all bring a toy or a picture or a present that we got and tell what it means to us. She said just to make sure that it was okay with our parents and not to bring anything too big. Can I Dad, can I?" Brodie was right in his face now with the best appeal expression he could muster.

Rob liked being in control as much as he hated being out of control. Just the mention of his own father and that trademark hammer yanked a patch off the wound he kept forgetting that was still there. Maybe it was the lawyer side of him but he prided himself in not showing what he felt. For some reason, this was a tough one.

"My concern son is that one of the other children might want to try it out and accidentally damage some property or worse, they could hurt themselves or one of the other students."

Daddy always calls me "son" when he's saying something really smart and hard to understand, Brodie thought.

Usually he would just nod his head even if he didn't have a clue as to what it all meant but this time it was really important. Elle knew this was more than just *Show and Tell* for Brodie and so she started to speak but was cut off by his earnest little tone.

"Dad I won't let no one touch it and it's real important 'cause when I think of Grampy I think of this hammer and how he would always help people with it! And that's important right Dad? And Grampy gave me his hammer right before he went to heaven and that means I'm going to be like him and help people. Right Dad? That's really important, right Dad?"

Rob felt bombarded by this raspy little fella's cross-examination. He was past trying to hide his feelings as he could feel the hot moisture gathering in the corners of his eyes. He glanced out the window at what was now just a blur of color.

Clinton Larson had passed away almost a year ago and it was a sad day for the town of Forrester. Clint had been considered the local handyman although he was an excellent wood craftsman and a self-employed building contractor. Still no job was too small for his consideration or free advice. He was one of the most giving and kind pillars of the community.

Rob looked back on the sudden transformation of his father from a healthy, strong man to almost overnight, lying in a hospital bed with only weeks to live. With composure he did his best to comfort his Mom and others at his father's funeral. He didn't cry, not one tear.

A little hand suddenly patted lightly on his and he heard Brodie's voice get closer and quietly intense, "Daddy, it is important isn't it? It's Grampy's hammer and I'm going to grow up and help people too."

It was like this little person had found something that Rob had searched for all his life. There was such an assured quality to his young voice it was like their roles suddenly got reversed. He was done. The knot in his throat was so high he could barely breathe let alone talk.

Elle was a little startled by the scene but quickly came over to rescue Rob from the emotional moment. She knew there was much undone business in this realm of his life. "Hey Brodie, Daddy knows it's important and I think if you promise to keep the hammer in your backpack and only bring it out when Mrs. Hatcher tells you to and then put it away until you get back home, that should be safe." The whole time she was leading Brodie to his breakfast of scrambled eggs and toast at the counter.

"Oh I promise Mom. I won't bring it out for no one but when Mrs. Hatcher says." He slurped his milk, turned with a faint white moustache and smiled at his Dad, "Dad, did you hear that? I'll be real safe k?"

Rob managed a smile as he got up and patted his shoulder walking out of the kitchen.

The excited mother-son conversation gradually quieted as he slipped his arms into his suit coat, grabbed his keys, briefcase, and gently closed the front door behind him.

Whew! How did that happen? He thought as his car started and he slipped it into gear. One minute everything is neat and in order, and then the next my life feels like a tangled heap on the ground. *What's happening to me?* Rob was feeling completely frustrated with himself and this emotional tide that was tossing him around. Brodie's tender questions had felt like a violent collision with his heart.

"Daddy, it is important isn't it?" He could still hear his son's voice as he turned out of his neighborhood and onto the road that shortly slowed into Main Street. It was a strangely difficult thing for Rob to see so much of his father coming out of his son.

It used to be that anytime there was a need for wisdom around town you could be sure to hear among different ones, "What does Clint say?" He was strong of character and equally as humble. Clint had a knack for leading people to the answers they were looking for with a series of off handed questions. By the time the conversation was over, most people weren't sure if he had actually advised them on the matter or if they had figured it out by themselves.

That wasn't satisfactory for Rob and it may have had something to do with the silent contention that distanced him from the town sage.

He had complicated feelings about his Dad. He always admired his calm wisdom but at the same time was driven to not be like him. He believed his father could have been a much bigger success but his soft heart got in the way. It takes courage to make the hard decisions and Rob had concluded when he was a teenager that his Dad just wasn't strong enough. That seemed like such a foolish thought now. Seeing that at this vulnerable moment he longed to soak up some of that courage from that soft heart of his.

If Clint's legacy was asking the right questions, Rob wasn't conscious of it, but he was laboring to counter his father's life by being the one *with all the answers*. Pretty ambitious he supposed … or quite arrogant he suspected. Maybe that was the balancing act Rob was trying to perform here. He never felt like his Dad got what was due him for all that he'd given. This town needed him and he came through for them for many years, but where was the honor he'd deserved in all of it?

Something to this line of reasoning reminded him a little too much of his father and his son's approach of getting to the truth. *That's enough of that*, he thought. *Probably enough emotional evaluation for a lifetime.*

Elle had just cleaned up the counter after her and Brodie's breakfast. Hurriedly she got the last dishes in the dishwasher and was calling out, "Brodie are you ready?" When she heard his famous little bounce off of the last step.

"Ready Mom!" Came his carefree voice.

As she slipped on a light jacket, she began to run down her checklist for her son. "Okay, you've got your backpack?"

"Yup."

"Here's your lunch."

"Is there oatmeal cookies Mom?"

"Yes sweetie."

"Enough for Jesse too?"

"Yes and yes I made your sandwich with brown bread."

"Thanks Mom", he was grinning now.

"Brodie did you put Grampy's hammer safely in your backpack?"

"Yup."

It was a little too carefree for Elle's taste. "You remember what Daddy and I said; it only comes out when Mrs. Hatcher is there and tells you to, okay?" They were heading out the door for their daily ride together to school and Elle's work.

"Okay Mom." Then quickly jumping to another thought, "Mom did you see how important it was to Daddy? You could tell by the way he looked. Right?"

Elle always marveled at how perceptive her little boy was. She felt so thankful for this child and always enjoyed his enthusiastic approach to every discovery.

"Brodie, it's all very important to Daddy and you are very important to Daddy."

He got a satisfied look on his face as she reached over and gave a quick tug on his already buckled seatbelt, and then started the car. The ride to school was filled with all kinds of chatter about what they might do this weekend and then the conversation intensified in mutual tandem over the coming Christmas season. They were truly a pair and could always play off of each other's excitement.

By the time Elle dropped him off at school they were both talking wildly about decorations, the coming snow, the Forrester Christmas Pageant and late night hot chocolates.

As Brodie marched into the front doors of the one-story school, he was deep in an imaginative state about the season to come and had a musing smile on his face. He was sure he wouldn't be able to concentrate at all on school until he heard a couple of his classmates call out his name. Suddenly he remembered that today was a great day and he had something to share with his world!

Chapter 2

Turning into one the diagonal parking spots in front of the old brownstone building that housed his office, Rob glanced over at the diner adjoining his place. Evelyn's Diner had been a town fixture for many years and the unofficial social download center for just as long. This made it unusual for Rob to visit of his own choice but he felt that even a little town gossip might help to clear his head.

Most of the time he only ended up at Evelyn's when Harry Carson, the town's mayor, insisted on a business luncheon. Rob found these meetings barely tolerable. Harry was filled with a sense of self-importance and used these opportunities to grandstand any business they had in front of the locals. In contrast, Rob strongly leaned toward being low-key and discreet about such matters. It was all part of the game though and Rob put up with it because his young firm depended on the town's business.

Things were hopping today as he pushed open the old wooden framed glass door with an *OPEN* sign tilted just slightly at eye level. The familiar sound of the little shop bell ringing seemed to initiate a barrage of chatter. The heads that turned at the sound of the innocent little ringing reminded Rob of his secret desire to bend that contraption past the point of recognition and ever being heard again. For some reason that thought put a big grin on his face, which curious onlookers interpreted as, *It's so good to see each and every one of you.*

There was something unusual going on though because the diner's easily distracted cliental was quite focused indeed. Most of the time it seemed like folks were just waiting for someone to walk in the door of Evelyn's and entertain them with some tidbit of unimportant information, or even just an interesting color choice of wardrobe. Not today though.

The atmosphere was anxious and almost intense especially for this sleepy little town. It seemed like everyone had their elbows up on the table and was leaning into their opponent to best address some deep confabulation. This was a better distraction then Rob had expected.

He walked across the diner to the row of faded maroon stools lining the serving counter and sat down with a little half-spin in but still partly eyeing the array of occupied booths. The seat-yourself policy was as natural as breathing, which was probably a good thing today. For some reason the customers seemed surprisingly plenty, but service seemed scant.

Rob could see through the long narrow order window that Freddy was putting everything into meeting the demands of the stack of breakfast tickets. Their eyes met for a second but Freddy seemed too busy to engage in their traditional exchange of waves and smiles.

"Hi Mr. Larson." Melissa seemed almost out of breath as she came up with her pot of coffee. Rob didn't even have a chance to respond to the young waitress before she flipped a coffee cup upright, began pouring the brew and at the same time starting spilling the news, "Did you hear what happened to Ms. Jenny?" Without waiting she jumped ahead to her conclusion of the whole thing, "Oh

it's just awful Mr. Larson. I feel so bad for her. It's just
not fair she works so hard you know?"

Rob had a pretty fast mind but even this was moving a
little too fast for him. "Hold up Melissa. Now what are
you talking about?" He was very easy with his tone.

He and Elle really liked this girl. She was a senior
at Forrester High and they sometimes used her to look
after Brodie. So he was pretty familiar with her between
running into her at the diner and her babysitting for those
few special outings that wouldn't work for a little boy.
Rob knew Melissa to be animated but honest and reliable.
In fact he was wondering why she wasn't in school as she
usually only worked evenings and Saturdays.

Before she could get another word out Evelyn scooted
down the back of the counter and gave her immediate
orders. "Melissa I need you to coffee up all the tables
along the back wall and please take out all these orders for
table six. I'm sorry dear to make you work so hard."

"Oh it's no problem Ms. Evelyn." She hurried off
quickly and happily like she instantly had no thought of
the crisis that she was about to uncover for Rob.

Evelyn too, had the signature coffee pot in hand and
now even began to add another little sip to Rob's freshly
poured, full and untouched cup of coffee that he never
asked for. A big sigh came out of her, as she seemed to
find the perch that she had been frantically waiting to land
on.

"Oh Rob, am I ever glad to see you. I've been planning
to come over and see you at your office this morning
but as you can see, it's so busy I don't know if I'll get a
chance."

Evelyn was a petite and spunky little woman of
probably sixty some years old. Proof that opposites
attract, she married her high school beau Chuck Spence
who became the town sheriff. Chuck was a thoughtful and
slow moving lumberjack of a man, sometimes a little too
sleepy Rob thought.

With her hair tied up on top of her head, Evelyn consistently moved faster than most teenagers. Her motherly hen way was a signature of the diner and not just the tasty fast food. Of course the price was always right for even the most conservative of budgets.

"Good morning Evelyn. Is there something wrong with Jenny?" Rob asked with his concerned professional tone.

"You see! You're such a smart young man. You've already figured out that something's wrong. My!"

Rob had to focus to keep from allowing the corners of his mouth to turn up and maintain his concerned look. He'd never gotten such rave reviews for hearing such a little bit of gossip.

"Well I really don't know much of what's happened. Do you want me to make an appointment to see you this afternoon and you can come over and tell me privately of the matter?" He was trying to keep his voice low because the counter of solitary patrons, all men, was also pretty full and that made for a lot of ears.

"Oh gracious dear, you're here now so let's get this ball rollin'."

This wasn't the context Rob ever imagined having a client disclose the details of any matter of concern, but he was learning in this town to adjust. He knew his professors back at law school would look on disapproving. *Oh well*, he thought, *this isn't Boston is it?*

"What seems to be the problem?" he said quietly, wondering at the fine line between being a lawyer and a part of the chin wagging chain.

Evelyn leaned over looking almost eye-to-eye with Rob where he sat and she put down her coffee pot. This was serious. "Last night after Jenny and the girls closed up, it was about 10:30 when she got home to her place up on Porter Street. Well if the dear didn't go and trip over something on her walkway and break her hip. I guess her outdoor light wasn't working and that walk is concrete you know. My but she could have hurt herself worse you know Rob, but it's still bad. Very bad."

Evelyn looked away for a moment as if to imagine the unfortunate accident of her friend and employee. Jenny was about ten years younger than her but about ten times more experienced in regrettably difficult circumstances.

Rob didn't mind thoughtful pauses but this wasn't in the controlled environment of his office and potential interruptions were backing up all around them. "That's too bad Evelyn. I feel real bad for her." Again he was maintaining his concerned look although he genuinely felt sorry for Jenny. He didn't know her that well but she had waited on him many times and he recalled her quiet but friendly face. He always thought that she seemed sad to him.

"Well Rob dear, it's more than just Jenny you know. It's that little fella Drew that's got nobody but her. He's only four you know?" She furrowed her brow with so much anxious expression that it almost made Rob feel like he needed to run out of the diner that second and save the world.

Coming up with answers and solutions was the business Attorney at Law Rob Larson was in and he always had this conviction that everything was somehow made to fit in a neat box. With that basic belief system being his inspiration, he proceeded with some calm and leading questions that he figured would quickly defuse any emotional content as he felt that would only clutter up *the box*.

"Do you know who is her next of kin? Surely she has some family that can care for the boy in the meantime."

"Well that's just it. There is no one and I mean, no one! Her niece Kerry signed over legal custody of Drew when he was born and then she took off straight from the hospital for a 'better life' somewhere else in the world. Her and Jenny never had much of a relationship, even though Jenny raised her when her own momma wouldn't, and now since the boy's come along, Kerry has made a point of purposely staying away. Jenny's never had a clue of where she's living and no contact since. And as for any other family, well, me and the girls here at the diner, we're it. Jenny's had a hard life and a lonely one you know."

"Who's looking after the boy right now?" Rob was trying not to think like a father but Brodie kept coming to his mind.

"He's still with Mrs. Gillespie, Jenny's neighbor. She's been a real sweetheart you know. She was at the house babysitting when Jenny came home last night and if it wasn't for her hearing Jenny calling for help, I just hate to think of how long she might of laid there. Poor dear!" Evelyn looked away again like she was giving the whole matter some respectful thought.

"Excuse me Evelyn!" called a heavyset man at a booth directly behind Rob. "We only got a few more minutes for our breakfast and then we got to be back on the site." He was speaking for his three other hungry companions too. Obviously construction guys and they all looked like they could eat their weight in pancakes for which Evelyn was famous.

"Sorry Bobby! I'll be right there. Thank you boys for waiting!"

She grabbed her coffee pot and gave me a busied little smile. "She needs your help Rob." And then in an almost casual voice as she started for around the counter added, "they're going to take him away you know."

Take him away? Caught at Rob's attention and he was uncertain now as to what she meant. He swiveled around on the hard stool as she came up on his side of the counter to wait on the hungry and impatient table. With a slight lean toward Rob, not wanting to detour too much from the adjacent table, she caught his question, "Who?"

With an almost startled look, "The Child Services that's who. They want to take little Drew away and put him in a home. You gotta help them Rob. They need a professional."

It was like she dropped this silent bomb and then
without a second thought jumped to a different world and
began her 'good-morning' banter with this suddenly happy
foursome. Rob was baffled. What just happened? What
kind of mess was just thrown into his lap and what in the
world could he do?

He wasn't responsible for this woman Jenny's difficulty
and as for her nephew, it was a sad turn of events but
maybe it was best for the authorities to take over his care.
*And why is none of this reasoning seeming to answer my
second emotional burst of day!* Rob thought as he walked
in a daze out of the diner. He kept seeing Brodie's face
and all that did was further fuel the irrational heart-rending
feelings he couldn't contain.

After Elle dropped off Brodie at school she stopped by
her mother's place and they drove the short distance to
work.

Joanne had started Murdock's Café when Elle was
just a little girl. Her husband Frank had encouraged her
to follow her dreams and so the coffee shop became a
mother-daughter labor of love. For Elle it had always
been a special place of connection with so many people in
Forrester.

The café was located on the south end of Elm Street
with a perfect view of the historic old mill sitting like a
picture at the top of the pond. The pond itself was the
jewel of Gordon's Park and always a big part of the town's
Christmas celebrations. There was family skating and
sledding, and the evenings showcased an elaborate light
display. It was definitely the place to be.

As Elle unlocked the front door and held it open
for her Mom she couldn't help but smile at the perfect old
building. Her Dad had wisely advised her Mom to buy it
back in the first few years of the business and helped to
put together the deal with old Mr. Scott. The Murdock
family had been friends with the Scotts for years so the

whole thing came together quite favorably for Joanne.
She always told Elle that this place was a gift from God,
for them, and for all the folks who sought a few moments
of solace from a busy world.

There was such a warm atmosphere inside with
comfortable high back chairs and little round-topped tables
spaced loosely across the vintage wooden floor. The
original wood-burning fireplace from when the structure
was first built in 1896 dominated the design along the
far wall and the high ceilings were part of the magic that
allowed for the magnificent big windows showcasing the
view to the park.

It was much more than a café though. Because
of Joanne and Elle's great love for books they had
a wonderful collection of classics filling the built in
bookcases along the back wall. It was truly a rare find
for any of the fortunate tourists who happened upon
Murdock's Café while in town and as for many of the
longtime residents, it was a treasure.

Elle and her Mom played the perfect hosts, often
working the room with light conversation and encouraging
words that some might pay a therapist for of the less
authentic sort. Here it came free with a cup of Earl Grey
or a fresh scone and cappuccino. Some would appreciate
a quiet moment in the comfort of one of the parlor chairs
facing the park. With a worn copy of a Dickens title in
one hand, a thin curl of steam lifting from the French
pressed coffee beside them, it was the perfect escape for
many at Murdock's Café.

"Dear did you make it to the bank last night in time?"

"Oh yeh Mom. I made it just in time to make the
deposit and caught Mrs. Casey right in the parking lot as
she was leaving for the day. She told me to thank you for
the box of oatmeal cookies you sent and of course you
know, they're her favorite." Elle tilted her head and gave
her famous squinted smile combination.

Joanne absolutely loved her daughter. This was her

and Frank's only child and they were united in their full
appreciation and love for this girl.

"Mom, something really weird happened this morning
at breakfast."

Joanne continued tying up her apron and signaled Elle
to go on with an "Oh?"

"When I was fixing some toast and eggs, Rob was
sitting at the kitchen table having his coffee and then
Brodie started in on wanting to take his Grampy Clint's
hammer to school for a kind of show-and-tell thing that his
class is having. Mrs. Hatcher told the kids that she wanted
them to bring something from home that had a story they
could tell about it."

"How did Rob respond?" Joanne was intently listening
but had gone to work brewing coffee.

"That's just it Mom," Elle was getting her animated
face on now that made her such a great storyteller. "Rob
started this cute concerned-father speech about taking the
hammer to school but there was way more to it than that."
Her voice went long and dramatic when she almost sang
the word "way".

"I don't think I remember ever seeing Rob get so
emotional and …" She paused as if to try to figure it
out herself, looking down in thought. "And lost." She
continued, almost whispering now, "Mom he almost
seemed like a little boy himself. Lost. With his own son
standing right there."

Elle went to the fridge and pulled a bowl of dough to
roll out for their now famous scones. Purposely leaving
some space in the conversation for her Mom to respond
for she knew it wouldn't be a quick response. She was
a wise woman and Elle was well accustomed to her
mother's way of never giving a quick answer or a careless
comment. Joanne really was a virtuous woman and
now she considered the scene. Elle hadn't asked for her
thoughts but this was familiar territory for the two and

neither had a need to define the lingering pause. Both still busied with the preparations of running the finest café around and to an outsider, as if they'd both lost all train of thought for the conversation.

As if all at once back on track Joanne straightened up from sliding trays of treats onto the display rack and turned to face Elle.

"Dear, Rob is a wonderful man but he's been running from something that's been his all along and yet he can't seem to recognized it. He thinks what he's always dreamed of is out there someplace." Her delicate hand made an elegant sweep in the direction of the impressive floor to ceiling panes, as if to indicate the whole wide world.

"He can't earn this Elle. He can't win it. It's already his but he's got to see it and receive it. It's his heritage." Elle was all ears and watching every move her mother made. She just loved it when this grace would come over her.

With muted breath and a few thoughtful nods she concluded, "Brodie gets it, and that's what shakes Rob's world. His own little boy can see what he can't and somehow deep down inside he knows it."

Elle didn't say a word. She didn't need to. She would ponder these thoughts through the responsibilities of the day and let them roam freely around her heart. Not like some burden or thing to be rid of, but cherishing them like found pieces to the puzzle of her life and knowing that these truths always led to what was good and sure. Maybe, even what would become mysteriously wonderful!

Chapter 3

Brodie gave the loose rock an uneven stuttered kick like a little boy would still unsure of which foot would get to enjoy the pleasure. The little stone rolled forward in an unpredictable line coming to rest on the street just in front of Josh. The older homes they strolled past belonged to one of the finer neighborhoods in the town of Forrester. There were no sidewalks here, but something in the mature trees and the history of family that shaded the avenue seemed to assure that it was a safe place for children to be children. Both boys were deep in conversation with heads down. They were unmindfully taking turns at kicking this stray stone, as chance rolled it in front of one or the other.

"Yeh Brodie that was so cool when you told how your Gramp used that hammer to save those people's lives. Is that really the hammer he used?" Josh looked up curiously, squinting hard with one eye because of the sun.

"Josh, for sure this is it! He told me himself before he went to heaven."

Josh gave a quiet and thoughtful "Wow", as his eyes blankly aimed for another kick of the shared grey target.

"But how do you know? I mean you didn't see what he did for real did you?" Josh simply wondered.

This was Brodie's best friend and he knew Josh well enough by now to know that he was just trying to fill the blanks in for things he found hard to imagine.

Brodie had an easy, almost spontaneous way of believing things. Elle could totally relate to this ability and Rob secretly envied this power.

"Josh I've seen the pictures of Grampy working on that hospital over in Africa. There's one with him working with this hammer outside and you can even see some of the sick kids there!"

Brodie had a natural animation that helped stir his friend's thinking and at the same time he was shaking his thumb over his shoulder at his backpack. Of course they both knew this was where the protected relic was being transported back to its resting place.

"And besides you know where Mrs. Miller lives. You can ask your folks about the winter that the snow was so heavy it broke in her roof. She lives alone you know and she would've died in the cold but Grampy came over and fixed it ... in the middle of the storm ... with this ... exact ... hammer!" Brodie turned up the gusto with a few well-placed pauses and now both thumbs forcing Josh to stare at his backpack with a look of awe.

"Man Brodie, can you believe it's really yours?" Now Josh was officially convinced of the authenticity of the hidden tool's great historic accomplishments. Now his own voice pitched up one half an octave, "Isn't it cool that your Gramp used that same hammer to make your tree house in the backyard?"

Now they were both facing each other with not a spare bit of attention for another kick of the stone that had traveled with them from outside the schoolyard, almost to the far end of Mayfair Avenue.

Almost at the same time you could hear, "Come on!"
"Let's go!"

Like they both knew the plan was to get to Brodie's
backyard as fast as possible to investigate every bruised
board where Grampy Clint had expertly driven a nail to
secure his grandson's boyhood adventures. The little
feet that had practiced so long on that stone were now
pounding across every possible shortcut they could find to
make the final dash down Rainbow Boulevard where both
boys lived.

Brodie, loaded down with his precious burden, would
start to fall behind but Josh kept adjusting his speed so
they could keep the adventure in perfect tandem. After all,
his spirited friend would surely help him see far past the
nail heads set in the wood of their fort. That's what Brodie
had always called it, "their fort". Now Josh was anxious
to learn of another of the hidden gems this special man had
stashed away for them before his journey on to another
mysterious, faraway place.

Brodie was always able to see the picture that the
insignificant dots made. It wasn't just Josh who felt this
but all their other friends would become absorbed in the
process of those fresh green eyes staring past them into
an invisible world and dictating the marvel of something
bigger than they could've dreamed. A little smaller than
the other boys his age, Brodie had a way of leading that
wasn't typical for his years.

Elle had instilled in her son a fearless love of life and
an appreciation for the modest things. Maybe that too
was part of the reason why at six years old when size is
typically a forceful concern, it had absolutely no influence
on this polite, but durable little boy who was compelled to
invite others to share in his discoveries and questions …
no matter who they were.

Racing into the backyard with shouts of delighted
entitlement, the backpacks fell off mindlessly as both
boys began their ascent to the coveted world above in the

treetops. Well … it seemed to be the treetops to these
fellas.

Clint had in fact made sure that the perfect tree was
the roost for his cherished grandson and friends. The
main branches of the big maple that supported the tree
house from its floor were only about seven feet off the
ground. That was still too risky for a grandfather to allow,
not to mention Brodie's parents, so Clint had constructed
the climb with an open stair that angled up sharply to a
platform that completely circled the diameter of the tree at
slightly better than three feet from the ground.

The tire swing that hung a good distance out from
the trunk, could easily be pulled over to this advantage,
and often was, to get that sudden rush of speed. On
the opposite side of the platform from the stairs, was a
nautical like network of rope ladders making up a real
boy's climbing dream and every parents hopeful safety
guarantee. This net fanned out from the whole back half
of the platform up to the fort's floor access through a good
size hatch.

The fort itself had an abundant supply of windows,
all big enough to pop your head through but not so a
six year old could get his shoulders through and most
visitors under ten, tried. Outfitted with skylights on each
side of the pitched roof, that was really just old camper
vents Grampy Clint had picked up at the junkyard, the
boys would crank them open on sunny days or close tight
for those rainy conferences that stewed into satisfactory
schemes for tomorrow.

Elle heard the whooping and commotion from in the
living room where she was entertaining a new friend and
her daughter. Grateful that she could either pickup Brodie
from school on the rainy and snowy days, or be waiting at
home for him on fair weather afternoons, she was mindful
that it was a modern day privilege to be the one greeting
her son after school.

Many of her friends had to use daycare or a finely tuned network of mothers and babysitters alternating a vanload of children. These were truly the kinds of liberties that Elle celebrated in lavishing on herself. It was very important to Rob too and of course Joanne wouldn't have it any other way. Her grandson got the best and that was Elle.

It had always been a unanimous family notion, even when Brodie was just a baby and Elle would bring him with her to the café for a few hours everyday. Perched on top of one end of the counter in his car seat or napping in the crib Joanne had put in the small office, Brodie unconsciously enjoyed each day fully with his mother either at home or in the wonderful world of Murdock's Café.

True, there was also those exciting walks in the park and around town in his stroller with this perky voice coming from behind him announcing everything like it a tour of the seven wonders of the world. And all of this was going on before the little tot could even say a single word. It surprised no one in the family that he started to talk before most children his age. Elle later invested so much time at the café taking Brodie through the many children's books that he was far ahead of his class in reading skills.

"That would be Brodie and his friends," laughed Elle. "He really likes school but when he gets out in the afternoon, he's ready to play and spend some of that saved up energy from sitting all day."

She was talking to the new friend she'd recently made while waiting on her at the café that summer. Meredith was a reserved young woman in her late twenties. She had dark hair, almost black that came down to her shoulders in a bob and was quite beautiful Elle thought. Although she dressed very plain and wore very little makeup, she was petite; probably the same size as Elle and had a great smile that she didn't use near enough.

"He must bring a lot of excitement to you and your husband," she said with a faint hint of that smile.

"Are you kidding Mare? That boy keeps me and Rob jumping, and we love every second of it!"

Meredith found this spunky woman to be a breath of fresh air to her already weary heart. Even the way Elle casually began calling her 'Mare' in place of her full name helped to kindle a few flames of comfort. Right now that was priceless.

She had moved here to Forrester early in the summer from Bailey City, which was only about an hour's drive but felt like a universe away. Not only was Bailey City twenty five times the size and population of Forrester, but more than that it also held all of the life she'd ever known, including her newly divorced husband and a world of shattered dreams still smoldering behind her in a heap.

Moving her and her four-year-old daughter was the hardest and smartest thing she could do. The avalanche of circumstances surrounding her and Nick's breakup was coming in on Lacey, and that Meredith could not stand for. As for visitation rights, Nick couldn't care less and basically opted out of any parental privileges so he could pursue his new freedoms. Meredith, though relieved of any fight over her dark haired little angel, could never comprehend how a father could simply abandon this, his own child.

"Lacey. Here honey, do you want another cookie? Is that okay Mare? I'm not going to mess up meal plans am I?"

Elle's pretty eyes sparkled with warmth for both of them as she held out the plate of too many choices. There was chocolate chip, peanut butter and all out chocolate walnut.

Lacey's tiny hand moved out and hovered over the plate as she turned her head to look up, "Can I Mom?"

It was the sweetest voice with just a faint hint of a lisp. Meredith loosened up with a laugh as she looked into the hazel eyes of her sweet girl, "Oh, what else can I say when you and Mrs. Larson gang up on me with those pleading looks?"

She reached out her hand and ran it lovingly down the back of Lacey's head. "I guess you can have just one more but you be sure to thank Mrs. Larson," all the while she kept stroking her hair.

Lacey smiled big and looked across at Elle who was bent over serving her. "Thank you Misth Larsum" and with that her hand came down decisively on a rich, dark chocolate cookie that looked too big for her hand.

"Thank you Elle", whispered Meredith. It wasn't so much for the cookie but for the sincere kindness this woman had offered her and her daughter at a time when friendships she had once thought sure, splintered into a thousand sharp bits and cut her deep into the soul.

It was the end of June when she got moved into the small apartment on the northeast side of Forrester, which was considered the less than favorable side of town, but rent was cheap. She walked into Murdock's Café around the middle of July, hot and discouraged after two weeks of getting nowhere trying to find a job. Sitting down at one of the tables facing Gordon's Park, Meredith sipped a small ice tea and stared at the beautiful fountain bubbling up out of the pond feeling totally hopeless. Just then a sweet voice to her side said, "Hi. My name is Elle." And when Meredith unlocked her weary eyes from her trance and turned her head, there was that friendly smile with a hand stuck out just waiting to be shaken.

Meredith wasn't going to make any of the same mistakes she'd made back in Bailey City and that included trusting anyone, but there was something about Elle that just made you want to empty your heart on the table and have her assess the contents. It was at that very first introduction that Meredith took a chance and told Elle she was having a hard time to find work.

Without nosing into any personal affairs, Elle easily

gathered any helpful facts that Meredith could give her that might hint toward an ideal position. After what seemed like only a few minutes, the grand hostess of Murdock's Café was placing calls to key people she knew of that could use Meredith's bookkeeping skills. By the time she stepped out into the cooler afternoon, she was armed with two names, their numbers and two appointments for the next day.

She ended up taking the job with Mr. Carter who had his offices across the hall from Rob's law firm. Carter and Associates was a full service accounting and bookkeeping firm.

Dale Carter was an untidy man to look at but very sharp with numbers and business. He surrounded himself with extremely organized people, which Meredith easily fell into that group, and was quick to reward those he came to trust.

Meredith suspected that Elle asked Rob to pull a few strings, but either way, she was thankful and secretly hoped she had found a true friend. Could there really be any other kind?

Just then a commotion of entertaining proportions broke in from the back of the house. Squeaky runners gave just enough announcement on the hardwood of the hall floor, that all the ladies of the tea party turned their heads in a focused gaze at the double French door entrance like it was an empty stage about to be filled with the featured show. Along with the percussive sounds of four energetic boys feet, was the musical lilt of a raspy, high voice. "Mom! Maaauuuummm! Mom! Maaauuuummm!" Repeatedly like a songbird that sings the same pattern of notes over and over. There were some other indistinct words but that was the motif of this spontaneous piece.

The boys were both obviously caught of guard when they came around the corner and found themselves center stage, for Elle had given them no warning when she had called out initially, "In here!" Eyes went wide to the pleasure of all the girls.

Josh immediately grabbed his own hands, dropped his head slightly and backed to the wall between the opened door and the fireplace.

Brodie on the other hand recovered quickly, his face relaxing into a friendly smile. "Hi Mom," he said, suddenly composed.

"Brodie you remember Ms. Meredith and her pretty daughter Lacey, don't you?" It was intentional that Elle avoided using Meredith's last name Fletcher and the title of Mrs. The little things made up the whole of a matter. If one intended to be a friend and protect any flickering embers of hope, it would be the least of things, that when cherished, would rekindle a future.

"Hello Ms. Meredith. Hello Lacey."

Just then Lacey put up her hand and squeezed her fingers together like she was catching the wind. "Hi Bowdie," she said with her face all lit up and her other finger pulling at her lower lip shyly.

Brodie didn't bother correcting her because he knew she was quite young and besides, he knew much better than to be like that. He did struggle with the feeling however that Lacey seemed to have a thing for him and that made him uncomfortable. Didn't she know she was just too young for him? She was only starting pre-school and he was already in grade one, putting in a full day. He figured her mom should have a talk with her about this but that was her business. That's what Elle had sternly warned anyway on a previous occasion when the subject came up.

As if saved by the recollection of why he came in the house to begin with, Brodie turned with a burst of intensity that cut off Meredith's greeting. "Mom! Can me and Josh have an apple and a knife and some coleslaws to take up to our fort?"

Elle started to giggle and the whole scene pleased Meredith. There was such lightness in the air. "Brodie!"

Elle was shaking her head and laughing, "What in the world do you want all that for?"

Josh had relaxed the grip on his hands now and was enjoying his freedom from any attention. Brodie gave Josh a glance, "Mom we're hungry and we're havin' a real important meeting …" Then his voice trailed off low, "that's kind of a secret." Which meant he didn't want to say anymore in front of a certain company.

"Ooooh", she drew out, "I see." Elle got a little more serious, if that was even possible, while sporting her mischievous grin. "Okay, well first of all, I think Ms. Meredith was trying to say 'hello' to you when you got excited and interrupted her."

Taking that as a cue, Meredith quickly interjected, "Oh, I don't want to get in the way of a couple of hungry men. It's nice to see you again Brodie", she added with a smile.

"Now what about introducing your friend Josh?" Elle said as she walked over to give the unintentional outsider some support.

"Oh yeh, I'm sorry. Everyone this is my best friend Josh we've known each other for, like all of our lives!" Brodie couldn't help but develop the introduction with such color. "Ms. Meredith, do you want to know something?" He asked intensely.

"Of course," she responded trying to come up to his level of potency.

"Well Josh is *the fastest* runner in our grade AND he knows how to whistle with his fingers in his mouth and it's real loud!" It was like he was detailing the world record of an Olympic champion. Josh turned a slight red from the praise but the discomfort was well worth the public affirmation of being called Brodie's best friend, plus he enjoyed his abilities being celebrated.

"Isn't that something Lacey?" Meredith took the chance to bring her into the discussion.

Lacey scooted a bit closer to her mom, finger still pulling at her lip and now resting her other hand on her mom's knee. She didn't take her eyes off of the boys but gave a quiet, "Un-huh".

"Do you want to hear him whistle?" Brodie's eyes got wide. Josh's fingers automatically started to move to his mouth.

"Okay just wait", Elle jumped in, "let's hold off on the whistling for now." She smiled big at Josh with her hand resting on his shoulder. "I've heard Josh whistle," directing her comments to Meredith and Lacey, "and Brodie's right. He is so loud that it would probably hurt your ears bad if we had him do it indoors."

Josh grinned and looked down sheepish at the burden of more praise.

"So let's save that for a baseball game or sometime when we're all outdoors." Elle kept it positive. "Now about your meeting in the tree house; how about if you guys grab an apple each in the kitchen, they're on the counter, and that should be good enough to hold you for the rest of your talks. Supper is in a few hours and Josh, I'm sure your mom has a good meal planned for you." Josh looked up nodding.

"Can we take a knife to cut up our apple Mom?" That was one of Brodie's new favorite ways of eating certain fruit.

Elle would allow him the use of a table knife to bluntly cut off slices, feeding his mouth and his innate desire to do anything like a boy. She felt the need to clarify to her new friend that she didn't allow her six year old to run around with sharp blades. "I let him use a dull dinner knife to slice his apple up," came the quiet footnote so to not nick the sense of ownership Brody had of this privilege, but she could tell he didn't like it being said.

"Mom, it's still pretty sharp." Brody said it almost lamenting what he felt was an attack on his grownup-ness.

"Well Honey that's why I prefer that you only use that in the house when you're sitting at the table, right?" She hoped that helped retrieve the sense of importance to the privilege.

Satisfied, Brodie whirled around with his manliness intact. "K. Thanks Mom!" He said without looking back. "Bye." His arm went up over his head in a lazy wave back toward the room's guests and he kept moving. "Come on Josh," he called.

Elle patted Josh's shoulder as he turned to follow his pal, "have a good time guys." And with that the entertainment squeaked back down the hall toward the kitchen.

Meredith waited until she was sure they were out of earshot. "Coleslaw?"

Elle wrinkled up her nose, shrugging her shoulders and the two broke out into laughter. Lacey relaxed and just stared at the opening where the boys disappeared, filled with admiration for "Bowdie". A big smile spread across her beautiful, angelic face. She didn't know that the women were now snickering at the dreamy look of her little telltale expression.

Chapter 4

Rob had been pensive most of the weekend and that
was only starting to become usual. He had always tried
to make a conscious effort to let go of work related
responsibilities and be a fulltime family man starting
Friday night through the weekend. In fact six and seven
years ago when he left work for the day, he would
mentally shut the door on all those second hand cares to
focus on family.

Elle never mentioned it but he knew that in the few
short years of Brodie's life, his thoughts were becoming
increasingly conditioned with priority on the things that'd
started out at the outer edges of his living. Now the
very nucleus of his world seemed to do the unthinkable
and flip-flop to that lesser and dutiful place of his
consideration. Didn't he still love his family? "Of course
I do!" he would answer in defense to the accusations his
heart would pile up against him.

Elle was especially perceptive but she never even
hinted at knowing she and Brodie had been replaced or
demoted. Some might call that melodramatic but when
something else has taken your place, what else do you call
it? Her attentions for him were always with encouraging

words and she would thank Rob with the most sincere appreciation for what he knew was his second best, if not less than that. This only armed him with more self-disgust and a drive to do something big to atone for his shortcomings.

How could he have every expression of Elle's face so perfectly memorized and still not know that it was the precious, immaterial things that mattered most to her? He wanted to believe that his personal sacrifice was for her and Brodie, but truthfully, it was all about him. They were the ones sacrificing for the one they loved and he was the one wiping his mouth without a word of thanks. He would have known that but the walls he used to defend himself were so high, he couldn't see out or in.

This weekend had gone sort of rough for some reason. He had to postpone a hiking trip with Brodie to work on some details for the township, which Mayor Carson was pressing him for.

"This could be big I tell you, BIG!" said Carson. Shifting his toothpick quickly from one side of his mouth to the other.

It was potentially big for Forrester seeing how it was plans for a new retirement village along the Brunswick River and there were already three successful contractors from outside bidding on the job. But even now the thought of Harry adjusting that toothpick around his mouth frustrated the importance of what he was doing at the cost of failing his son.

Adding to the whole misdeed was the exuberant appearance of Elle first thing Saturday morning dressed in a red flannel shirt, sleeves rolled up, hiking boots on and a picnic basket in hand. Her plan was to set up a chow station with a campfire at a suitable point along Tucker Trail and then when the men felt so inclined to take a break from exploring, they could roast some grocery supplies explorer-style.

Rob dropped the bomb right there with a wince and

said, "Sorry Elle, I've got to work." The surprise was, he was the one who felt totally let down. His heart was on fire.

Elle simply smiled and said, "That's okay Rob. Brodie will understand." With that she set the woven basket down and went upstairs to break the news to Brodie.

There it sat; a basket alone in the hallway quietly indicting him. He knew Elle didn't do it intentionally but it was distasteful evidence. *What a coward I am*, he remembered thinking as he heard her climb the stairs to his bedroom. He just couldn't stand the idea of looking into his face and breaking his word ... again.

The door was mostly open and Elle stepped into Brodie's cheerfully decorated bedroom. There was a paper border around the top of the walls with a collage of everything to do with the game of baseball. Bats, gloves, little boys in uniform and of course, baseballs made a vibrant crown to the still blue walls Elle had first christened the room with when finding out she was carrying a boy. Brodie was just buttoning up his plaid blue shirt from the outfit Elle had laid out for him earlier and jerked his head up with an excited smile at her appearance.

"Hi Mom, I just got to get my boots on and get my compass and then I ..."

"Dear..." Elle interrupted him, "it looks like we're going to do something different today. Daddy has to take care of some important work that's come up."

Brodie still had that sleepy look on his face but he was quick enough to know what he'd just been told. "But Mom," was all he said with the most sad face, as he turned away sitting on the edge of his bed. His voice had gone from a fast excitement to a slow, drawn out moan.

"You'll see Brodie, we'll have a great time today!" Elle tried to sound happy but her heart was breaking at the sight of her little boy. He had a hot pool of tears brimming at the bottom of his eyes and he couldn't explain it, but

suddenly a lump had formed in his throat and it ached.
It wasn't the loss of a fun hiking trip that upset him the
most but something strange between him and his dad. He
felt like he was losing the confidence he once had that he
mattered more than anything to him.

Just then, something happened. He wiped at his eyes
hard and took a deep breath. He wasn't going to cry,
not this time. He wasn't sure why the abrupt stance but
he felt empowered by a new sharp feeling that helped
counterbalance the other feelings of distance he felt forced
on him. He felt angry and he didn't need to cry about this
anymore.

Elle sensed the forceful tide. She saw the sweetness
leave her son's face and a hard twist purse his lips as he
built his first little wall to protect himself. *What on earth
is going on?* Elle thought to herself. *I hope this thing
is not catching*, thinking mostly about the other 'fence
builder' downstairs.

Getting down on her knees beside Brodie where he sat
on his bed just staring off, Elle began to speak to this deep
feeling heart that beat inside this six-year-old boy. "I think
I know how you're feeling right now." She paused and he
didn't move a muscle.

She got quieter, "When I was young my Daddy told
me one year that he was going to get me something very
special that coming Christmas, something I'd always
wanted."

Brodie's eyes blinked a few times as though to say he
was listening.

"Every night when I'd go to bed, I'd fall asleep wishing
for Christmas to come. I was so excited I just couldn't
stand it. Everyday I'd smile and pretend like the gift was
already here! Do you know what I mean dear?" She tried
to pull him into her story and away from the slope of his
thoughts.

Brodie went for it. "Well yeh Mom but what was it
you wanted?" His breath had that uncontrolled hitch of

emotion but he didn't even notice he was so distracted.

"Okay, I'll tell you but you got to promise not to laugh." She pretended to look around for anyone who might overhear her.

"Mom I won't laugh." Then with raised eyebrows, "why? Was it something really funny?"

Elle continued pulling him into the scene of her world. "It wasn't funny to me," she said with a serious face. "Brodie this was everything to me. It was going to be my dream-come-true present."

"What Mom? What was it?" He couldn't take it anymore.

She gave just the right amount of determined thought and then spoke it like the deciding point from which there was no retreat. "My Daddy told me ... he was going to get me a pony!" She said with as much drama as she could deliver.

Brodie's eyes went wide. "For real! You got a pony for Christmas?"

"No honey. I said my Daddy told me he was going to get me one for Christmas. You see that's not the end of the story."

Elle changed her position to sit on the bed beside Brodie. He was not taking his eyes off of her now and ready to ride that pony himself. "I woke up on that Christmas morning and there were some nice presents under the tree for me, but they were little things. I waited and waited. I kept hoping that at some point a truck would show up at our little farm or that my Daddy would bring a beautiful pony out from somewhere he'd been hiding him, but ... nothing." Elle let her head drop with her voice, sadness on her face.

"That's no fair Mom!" Brodie furrowed his brow. "You should've got your pony 'cause he promised."

Elle looked up and right into his bright eyes, "And you know what Brodie? My dad never said anything about it over the rest of the Christmas holidays or the weeks after."

She could see that Brodie was speechless. "Do you know how I felt?" She didn't wait for him to answer, "I felt sad and hurt, and I felt angry." She could see her little boy's jaw set in firm empathy toward her. "I never said anything to my mom or dad, I just went on feeling those feelings and thinking about how bad my dad let me down." Brodie just sat trying to process it all.

"One night I was laying in bed and now instead of dreaming and being happy with all my good thoughts, I was crying and being sad with my hurt thoughts. I guess my mom heard me and she came in my room in the dark and sat on my bedside and asked me what was the matter. I just couldn't hold it in anymore Brodie. I told my mom how disappointed I was that Daddy didn't get me my pony like he said he would and then I told her that I didn't want to talk to him anymore. Do you know what she told me?"

Lost in the time warp of his Mom's account he could only whisper, "What?"

"She took my hand", with that Elle grabbed his, "and said, Elle your daddy loves you very much. You may not understand this but your Daddy wanted to get you that pony more than you even wanted to have it, but something happened that you don't know about. Daddy lost his job at the mill because they're closing it down in the next few years and that's why he didn't get you the pony. He didn't have near enough money to buy the pony, feed him, get him all his shots AND be able to look after you and me."

Elle pulled out of character for a second, "and then do you know what my Mom said? She said, Elle honey, your Daddy got big tears in his eyes when he realized he couldn't get you that pony for Christmas. It broke his heart to let you down and now it breaks his heart because you don't want to sit beside him anymore."

She sat there for a moment still holding Brodie's hand. "Can you believe that? I didn't want to sit with my daddy anymore." She paused and let him try to respond to the scene.

"I guess sometimes, …" he said slowly, trying to think his way through this, "us kids don't know what stuff is going on for moms and dads." Elle waited because there was more. "Things hurt and I don't like them but … did you love your dad anymore Mom?"

Elle flashed a big smile and said, "I made sure to love him everyday after that. In fact I helped my Mom make him his favorite breakfast the next morning, French toast and I sat right close beside him. The whole time I kept thanking my daddy for all the sweet presents he and Mom did get me that Christmas."

"Did you ever get your pony?" Brodie was swinging his feet back and forth now, which was a real good sign, kind of like a dog wagging his tail.

"Nope," she said matter-of-factly. "My dad gave me something way, way better."

"Better?" Brodie spit it out like she was messing with the impossible.

"Way better. My dad gave me and my mom … Murdock's Café!" Elle opened up her arms like she was presenting the finale.

For Brodie, that more than made up for the pony because if there was anyplace full of mystery and wonder, it was the café he'd practically been brought up in. The intrinsic air that prodded a boy's imagination made this place a doorway to castles, adventures and dreams beyond what the citizens of Forrester could ever know. It was here with the warm smell of roasted coffee beans and the eclectic sounds of unpopular music, that he learned what few do; stories are not to be just read or heard, but unfolded in the darkroom of the imagination. The thought that a child, even if it was his Mom, whom he thought the world of, could be given such an awesome gift. It was just all the more beyond his great ability to think the impossible.

Jumping up off the bed he squeezed out an excited cry, "Mom! Is it true? Did you really get the café instead of the pony?" His hands were even waving now.

"It wasn't instead of the pony Brodie. That's what I'm trying to tell you. Sometimes things that we hope for grow into bigger hopes and dreams that end up not looking anything like the smaller things we started with." She wasn't sure if that last statement wasn't too broad for him because he was still looking expectantly at her for the punch line.

"Yeh okay, but Grandpa Frank is your daddy right and he gave you the store." Brodie often called the café a bookstore because of the picturesque collection of vintage books displayed and for sale on the back shelves. In a way he was right and considering that he didn't drink any coffee, you could understand his assessment of the place.

"To me and Gramma-Jo. Yes, Grandpa Frank is my daddy and he gave the 'bookstore' to me and Gramma-Jo to share."

This well told story made a groundbreaking impression on Brodie's understanding of the adult world. It was more complicated then he ever thought. The idea that a little girl's pony was somehow connected to a father's job was serious. It was serious for kids and for adults too. On the other hand, that a pony lost could be a bookstore found was a like a gleaming trophy of relentless hope.

Rob had no clue of the process and journey Elle walked Brodie through but he marveled at his son's forgiveness and encouraging attitude toward him that morning. Of course it didn't ease Rob's guilty conscience but it impressed him to believe that his son knew something that he didn't. Hardly did Daddy know, but the little boy had just cashed in his "pony", so to speak.

Brodie and Elle were in great spirits and seemed to be making the most of the perfect fall weekend. They didn't see much of Rob that Saturday after they came down and smothered him with hugs, grabbed a quick breakfast and took off for an inspired treasure hunt in the big town of Forrester.

Brodie added a little encouragement after wolfing down a piece of bagel and then heading for the door. "Dad", Rob was seated behind his desk in the home office, head leaning on one hand.

"Daddy you're doin' a great job of working and me and Mommy we're talkin' about how good a job you do. Thanks for everything and it's no problem that we couldn't go exploring today 'cause me and Mommy we're gonna go on a treasure hunt in town and find cool stuff for Christmas. Okay?" He added with lots of gusto.

The defense had to rest because counsel didn't have a clue where he stood in the least. "Thanks Brodie. I love you son and I know you'll have fun looking for treasure today." Rob meant every word of it but it fell out of him lamely. "Come here and give me a hug," he said pushing his high back leather chair sideways to his desk.

Brodie was quick to oblige, mouth full and wiping his hands free from any crumbs. "I love you," came the raspy voice almost muted by the mouthful of food.

"Love you too Catcher." Brodie smiled and ran off encouraged at hearing his nickname.

When the door slammed shut behind the pair and their enthusiastic conversation faded from the neatly organized walls of Rob's office, he heaved a sigh. Not a satisfied one but in reality, a signature belonging to a burdened man.

He wrestled with peculiar feelings for someone in his position and what position was that? He was the husband and the father, and yet he felt strangely jealous of the twosome. He missed the friendship and the time he used to spend with his beautiful Elle. On the other hand he coveted the trust and admiration he saw Brodie give to his mom. Oh how he longed for both!

One side of him knew that they were his, in the freest sense of love's entitlement to one another, but on the other hand, something in his own heart choked his power to indulge in what was right there in front of him. He didn't really need to be working all day so what was keeping him from being with his two favorite people? Rob looked at all the books on his shelves, organized to perfection and arrayed for legal battle. Something he could not see though, was more out of place than he could bear.

He felt like he had spent his lifetime insulating himself against this very thought but now the faint whisper of a desperate voice that sounded a lot like his own came up on the inside, *Something's wrong and I just can't seem to fix it*! His hands pushed through his dark wavy hair and locked behind his neck as though to support his burden.

Rob jerked his thinking back into hand, grabbed the contracts and threw himself into a furious work mode. "Harry won't know what hit him when I drop this on his desk Monday morning," he said out loud to himself. Discipline and diligence had been his stay for so long, and so he comforted himself with the idea that this was only another day. That's all it was, right? This unconscious reasoning had been guilty of spilling days like diamonds for too long.

Rob was unaware of his own disregard for the priceless gift that expired with each sunset. Time has never been merciful since its beginning. No such virtues were reserved as an option for a soul. On the other hand, time was only a broker of absolutes measuring those choices. Whether it seemed fair of not, time would always tell.

It's a peculiar thing how there can be such a difference of experience even under one roof. Brodie had an exciting weekend exploring the nooks and crannies of every shop in Forrester unmindful of the failed promise of his father.

Elle enjoyed the energy of Brodie's constant, "Mommy, what about this?" and "Mom, look at this!" It made her smile and helped distract her mind from a nagging concern for Rob. Somehow she knew her precious home was at a crossroad and the outcome of whatever was going on in Rob's heart would determine where they would all go from here. Today she let it all go and threw herself into the search of Christmas decorations with her most favorite little boy.

Elle had a gift for finding lost treasure in second hand stores and consignment shops. She wasn't a random shopper who could be easily seduced by a 'sale' sign. She laid out the plan for Brodie and so they focused their search for figurines of people and animals that would help tell the Christmas story. Always keeping their eyes open for the hope of finding a very special angel to go on top of the tree. They were fussy and not just anything would do but patience was rewarded with a few rubber shepherd boys, some sheep and a unique ceramic star that would be perfect just about anywhere.

They made a day of it including a lunch break with Gramma-Jo at the café, a stroll through Gordon's Park on the way to more shopping and of course, a stop at Fred's ice creamery. It was a day of laughter and fun as they took it and lived it for what it could be.

Already on the shortlist for culprit of the weekend, Rob figured there was no need to bother pandering to his current irreparable image by going to church Sunday morning. Of course this was all in his mind but he was on a roll anyway playing the misunderstood warrior. All in all, he saw no redeeming benefit in sitting through one of Pastor Hunston's sermons right now.

Last week he preached a message on "casting all your care on the Lord", which really irritated Rob. Well that might be fine for some, he thought, but quite foolish for those of us with responsibilities and maybe even a hint of ambition. His own arrogant judgment escaped this same review.

As outdated as the older Pastor's thoughts were though, they patiently kept knocking at the door of Rob's fact driven mind. Even worse, this idealistic way of dealing with life had seeped into a most vulnerable place in Rob's interior and was now testing his beliefs. It was very discomforting and for some reason it kept bringing him back to thoughts about his dad. After really thinking about it, he was confident that his family would be better off if he skipped church this time.

Sunday afternoon things took a turn for the better and the clouds that seemed to hover over Rob gave way to the sunshine of a brisk fall day. Deciding to throw himself into something physical, he wasn't long raking up leaves in the backyard when his faithful troops showed up.

"Hey do you want some help?" Elle said wrinkling up her nose into a big smile, her long blonde hair pulled back and a rake already in hand. She walked right over to Rob and leaned into his chest.

He grinned and took in a deep breath, enjoying the light fragrance that was so feminine. Her sweater was soft like her and he couldn't help but take pleasure in how beautiful she was in her blue jeans and hiking boots.

"Daddy I got my rake too." Brodie called out with a sucker in his mouth making it hard to understand.

"Wow, this is more help than a fella could ever hope for," Rob was beaming at the interruption of his aloneness. Elle closed her eyes and leaned in for another squeeze as Brodie excitedly flung his yellow plastic rake into the leaves.

"Can we jump into the pile when we get it really big?" Brodie had one hand holding his sucker close to his mouth and the other dragging approximately two whole leaves in his rake toward the pile Rob had been working on.

"I don't see why not," and then Rob let go of his rake letting it fall carelessly and his eyes half closed in a most mischievous look, "in fact I think Mommy needs to be the first thrown in!" With that he scooped her light frame up, swinging her around and started stomping toward the colorful heap.

"Don't you dare Rob!" Elle demanded, throwing her

head back and laughing.

Brodie instantly threw down his rake and screamed with excitement, "Yehhhh, do it Daddy!" Still holding his sucker with one hand, he was pushing Rob from behind and thrilled with the wildness of the moment. Everyone was either yelling or laughing as the threesome hit the autumn mound of leaves. Rob had turned halfway as he pretended to throw Elle so she landed safely on top of him and Brodie needed no encouragement to pile on. They yelled and giggled with leaves flying everywhere. It was the postcard picture of a perfect family.

That night they ordered takeout Chinese food and enjoyed the fireplace for the first time that season. The family room was dim, mostly lit by the crackling fire. Everyone had a sleepy look on their face from all the afternoons fresh air, the one slice too many and the hypnotic dance of the flame coming from the embers inside the stone surround.

The board game lay in the middle of the plush rug waiting indefinitely for another play. Brodie's eyes would not stay open any longer but he was aware of how contented he felt cuddled up between his mom and dad as they sat on the floor. Rob looked down at him and smiled.

"Elle," he was stroking their son's hair.

"What Rob?" she almost whispered.

"This is good," he paused and then continued, still staring at Brodie, "children should feel loved and safe, shouldn't they?"

It was such a simple thing to ask but she knew he wasn't asking the obvious as much as he was appreciating the order of the way things were supposed to be.

Watching him as he gently brushed a strand of hair from the sleeping face between them she responded, "Yes Rob. I wish every child could know that." Something turned in her heart and she smiled a thankful look.

Chapter 5

"Good morning Rob."

"Good morning Dorothy." Rob had just stepped into the main entrance of his office building and pulled the door closed behind him.

Dorothy Kyle was an excellent receptionist and secretary that he had generously inherited from Dale Thompson's office. Thompson was a respected barrister and had made the decision to shut down his own law practice upon accepting the appointment of judge for the Franklin District, which included Forrester. Dorothy had been with him for fifteen years and of course Dale wanted her to continue but it would have required her moving. That was not an option for Dorothy. She and her husband had deep roots in her hometown of Forrester so the job opening with Rob was perfect timing and a perfect fit. Rob felt so a thousand times over as Dorothy, had being in her early fifties, was efficiently experienced, professional and sometimes reminded him of the aunt he never had. Always professionally dressed, today she had on a beige pantsuit with a white blouse that neatly contrasted her dark short hair and complimented the fine black beads that hung loosely around her neck. From head to toe she was the picture of composure and organization.

"Did you have a good weekend?" he asked.

"Yes we did. Phil and I took a trip over to Georgetown to see our daughter and her husband. How about you?" Dorothy had poured Rob a coffee and was following him into his office with her laptop. She always arrived a good fifteen minutes before Rob usually started so she could have the lights and coffee on.

Rob was unloading his brief case onto his desktop and answered absent mindedly, "Yes, it was a good weekend. Nice weather. Yes, good weather." Still sorting through his files, Rob didn't see the knowing look on Dorothy's face as she interpreted his politeness.

"Hmmm, that sounds like fun." Dorothy said it with kindness and dedicated herself to the laptop's screen getting ready for business. Rob wasn't really sure what her comment meant but it caught him off guard. Looking up he saw her busy in the chair across his desk, her round-rimmed glasses fixed on her work and seemingly unaware of how unsettled her words made him.

"Yes … ummm … it was a fun weekend," he said distracted now, "well, I had quite a bit of work on these land deal contracts and zoning proposals for Mayor Carson." His tone got much more sure when he departed from the personal realm and spoke of his workload.

Dorothy had a big-sister affection for Rob. Not a motherly affection as she was very discreet about her age and would not want anyone to regard her as old enough to be Rob's mother. Nevertheless, she quickly decided to ease any personal pressure Rob felt and focus on work. After all, that was the agenda for the present moment.

"That's great Rob. I will make copies of the files

you've already sent me and have them ready for Mayor Carson's nine o'clock meeting this morning."

"Good, good. Alright then, we've got about a half an hour before he gets here so let's take a look at the ..." Rob was interrupted by a quick knock on the outside door and then it opening to a woman's voice speaking softly to someone.

"Come on Drew. Just take my hand honey." It was Evelyn from the diner next door. She had on her full serving uniform right down to the white nylons and what looked like nurses shoes. The only thing extra to her uniform and apron was a three quarter length coat that was unbuttoned and a young boy holding her hand. He had the blondest hair Rob had ever seen. It was almost white and perfectly straight. Rob's office door was open halfway and at the perfect angle to the front door for him to take it all in. It was also the perfect angle for him to be seen by the visitors.

Already up without a word from Rob, Dorothy quickly and gently closed his office door behind her. With a friendly smile she glided into her role as the helpful receptionist. In the meantime, Rob cleared his desk of the files he'd brought from home and wondered what the unexpected visit was about. Maybe it was for Dorothy but somehow he didn't think so. He could hear the muffled voices talking outside his heavy oak door.

"Hello Evelyn. It's good to see you and who's this little fellow?" Dorothy asked as she slid behind her desk.

"Hi Dorothy. This here is Andrew, and he lives with his Aunt Jenny." What a strange introduction Dorothy thought. Most children are introduced as being someone's child.

"Hello Andrew," Dorothy noticed he was half hiding behind Evelyn's leg. He must be only four or five she thought. "How old are you dear?" But he didn't answer.

Evelyn looked down at him and tried to encourage him. "She's a nice lady Drew. Tell her how old you are." He just looked up at the smiling secretary without blinking an eye.

"That's okay Andrew. I'm glad to meet you and my name is Dorothy."

"You know I'm not really sure myself how old he is but I think Jenny said he had turned four not too long ago."

Dorothy kept smiling but sat down behind her desk and in so doing she somehow transposed the moment from a cordial welcome to important business. "How can I help you today Evelyn?"

Without hesitation Evelyn jumped into the matter. "Well you see, I need to talk to Rob somethin' desperate. I told him last week at the diner that there was gonna be a problem with Ms. Jenny and the situation with her accident. You did hear about her fallin', didn't you Dorothy?"

Dorothy tried to speak but Evelyn barreled on. "Oh it's just awful, awful! And you know we're trying not to say too much around ...", her voice got a little quieter as she tilted her over and nodded at Andrew who was still staring at the confident face across the desk.

Dorothy seized her opportunity and took control. "Evelyn, why don't you and Andrew come with me and I'll seat you in our conference room. You two can make yourself comfortable and I know Mr. Larson will want to speak with you himself." As she was talking, she had gracefully guided both down a short hall and into a comfortably furnished room with a small table in the middle. "Can I get you a cup of coffee or tea?" Dorothy asked Evelyn.

"Oh that would be great," she said throwing her coat over a chair and plopping down in the one beside it.

"And what about you Andrew?" She crouched down in front of him so that she was almost eye level, "I make a pretty good cup of hot chocolate. Would you like some if I made it for you?"

Dorothy found the key to his strongbox and she

managed to get one word. "Okay" came a soft, timid voice.

"Very good," she responded and without missing a beat grabbed Evelyn's coat. "I'll hang this up for you." Heading for the door she turned, "Evelyn, Mr. Larson already has a full schedule of appointments this morning but let me speak with him and see what he can do right now. I'll be back with your coffee and hot chocolate so please just relax." With that she closed the door to the room and made her way to Rob's office.

She knocked and waited to hear Rob's voice, "Come in." Stepping in she closed the door behind her, as their practice was to always pursue every measure of discretion.

"Rob, Evelyn says that it's very important that she see you regarding the accident Jenny Richards had last week and I believe it has something to do with the little boy Andrew, which I understand is Jenny's nephew."

Rob let out a sigh. He was secretly hoping this whole unpleasant thing would just go away because it was the least of all reasons for which he even went to law school. He knew so little of the matter and yet everything in him said this was messy. Business was his business and a predictable safety net. Matters of the heart were cumbersome. Something about even the thought of this boy warned him to avoid this with all his power.

Quietly noticing the hesitation in Rob's eyes, Dorothy noted what an unfamiliar look this was for him, especially in this office. She appreciated the decisive counsel this talented young lawyer brought to his clients, his gifted ability to negotiate and above all, his ethical stand regardless of the consequences or profits. She had been around this legal world enough to know the opportunities provided for someone in Rob's position to enjoy nearly untraceable kickbacks, perks and options that many found easy to justify. The confusing thing was, that the same virtue that kept him from taking a bribe seemed to be the very gap in his armor that disqualified him from doing what he really longed for, to help people.

"I told her that you were already booked up this morning and that I'd see what you could do. Would you like me to make an appointment for her this Thursday? You have an opening in the afternoon."

Rob thought about it for just a second and as tempting as that was, something told him that this wasn't going away. Looking past Dorothy and deep in thought, he resigned himself to it. "Tell her I'll be in to see her in a few minutes. Please remind her that I don't have much time and when Mayor Carson comes in, bring him in here and make him comfortable."

Rob was so lost in thought that he didn't even hear her respond, "Yes of course".

Dorothy was out the door and busy before Rob was aware of being alone again. He was thinking of his father. This was just the kind of thing that he was so good at handling. Somehow he came up with these simple remedies that Rob had still not been able to find a workable substitute for in his expensive textbooks. He stood up slowly and found himself longing for even just one of those old fashioned 'fixes'.

Rob stepped into the small conference room. It was not overly furnished but not sterile either. Elle had helped him decorate his entire office and this room featured an oil painting of a lake in the foreground of a rugged mountain range. Dorothy was already serving his guests and had naturally put a cup of coffee and water on the table where he would sit. Rob was armed with just a pad of paper and a pen.

"Will that be all Mr. Larson?" Dorothy was the model of proficiency and was backing out the door with a tray in her other hand.

"That's great. Thank you Dorothy." With that she smiled and gently pulled the door closed.

"Good morning Evelyn." With that Rob extended his hand across the table.

Evelyn grabbed his hand and could only say, "Good morning." The formalities of the last ten minutes had so disorientated her to the familiarity of Rob her diner customer, to the constant references of him as "Mr. Larson" the lawyer.

Rob faced down the giant he had felt intimidating him now and looked into the blue eyes of the pale small face across from him. This chocolate mustached boy, who was staring right back at Rob, represented all the needs and questions Rob had failed to come to terms with. "And good morning to you young man." Immediately Rob thought, 'what a stupid thing to say. He's just a small child!' "What's your name?" He asked with every ounce of kindness he could communicate with his face.

"Andrew," came his whispery voice so quickly that he actually intercepted Evelyn's help. All she got out was a breath in.

Rob narrowed his eyes and repeated his name, "Andrew … that's a good name."

The boy tapped his tiny hands on the table and smiled slightly, "yup".

Rob didn't know why but he greatly admired his response. His blonde hair was dirty. He could see that his hands were dirty and his clothes didn't fit him right. His jacket was too thin for the cooler fall weather and too big to really be his. His stripped shirt was stained and too small, and Rob knew if he could stand him up that his shoes and pants were probably every bit trash ready. He lived with his aunt who could barely take care of him and she was now in the hospital with who knows what kind of money problems. If what Evelyn said in the diner the other day was correct he was one inch from being tossed into the government's child services program and therefore increasing his odds of being some kind of negative statistic by the time he turned sixteen. Here he was now sitting in a lawyer's office in the care of a woman he barely knew and being introduced to some man, who probably in his

young eyes, looked like he owned the world. Despite all
of this, he seemed to have some confidence of a goodness
in his given name.

Suddenly Rob flashed to something he'd always heard
his father say. "A good name is preferred above silver and
gold." The thought only distracted him for a moment for
then the breath that Evelyn had been holding let loose.

"Now Rob, here's what the problem is and we just
don't know what's gonna happen to ..." Normally Rob
would never interrupt anyone but he had a protective
instinct for Andrew as he watched him sip another bit of
the hot chocolate.

"Now hold on just for a second Evelyn." Rob's hand
had gone up in an effort to help conduct the woman to a
halt. Proceeding gently and quietly he said, "I want to
be sensitive to Andrew here so let's not go back over the
details of the accident or any negative potential you feel
that Children's Social Services might have in this matter.
Tell me what it is you think I can do to help and ...", he
paused directing his full attention on Evelyn now, "and
keep in mind, I'm a lawyer Evelyn, not a family counselor
and neither do I run an adoption agency".

As soft spoken as his words were, they stung Evelyn.
Typically quick with a reply she sat there feeling rebuked
and speechless. This town was very special to her because
it was an island of community in a world of indifference.
Most of these people she served day after day weren't just
customers, they were friends and family. These few words
of Rob's were the seeds of indifference that could destroy
the world she loved from the inside out. She was a simple
woman but she recognized the destructive force of Rob's
fear to engage and take a stand for what was right.

Uncharacteristically, she lowered the tone of her
voice and slowed her words as though to weigh each one
carefully. "Your daddy was a friend of mine and a mighty
big man too. He fixed more than the brick and shingles
of the homes we live in. He cared about people and he

cared about this town. Maybe he didn't have a big fancy education like he helped you get, and maybe he didn't have the fancy office like this here, but he had answers and courage he was willing to share with folks that needed help."

As if punctuating that last line she nodded her stern face toward Andrew. "Look I don't care if you're a lawyer or a carpenter with a hammer and a saw, I'm hopin' there's somethin' of your daddy in you that can influence this town to help someone who needs helpin'!" Now her voice was back up to full volume and a little extra.

Evelyn had no intention of being that blunt or forceful. It always saddened her to see some of the old faithful guard retire from this life but she did have much hope for these sons and daughters who were the truest riches Forrester possessed. Sometimes they needed some straight talk though and she figured she would be more than obliged to give it to them. She'd kept her eye on Rob ever since the passing of his father and watched him shrink back from the opening. Yes, today she did her old friend Clint Larson an honor and reminded his kid that it was time to be a man. Of course she didn't have a clue as to what the solution was to Jenny and Andrew's predicament, but she was sure this was an opportunity for Rob to be a champion.

Falling back into that faraway look, which seemed to be in the general direction of the shaded window behind Evelyn, Rob weakly reconciled himself to the issue, "I'll tell you what Evelyn; I'll stop into the hospital later today and see Jenny. Maybe there's something I can help her with or advise her on that might help ease these concerns. After all she is Andrew's legal guardian."

Rob saw that at least this agreeable fact got him off the hook with Evelyn although he doubted that Jenny could tell him anything that would help her or Andrew.

Satisfied enough that Rob would do something, she

turned to Andrew with her hostess charm back in place, "Come along Hon, we got to get back to the diner."

Getting up she helped her small companion out of his chair and wiped his mouth with a no-nonsense rub. Rob had already opened the door for them and stood courteously waiting when the five foot two inch woman stopped in front of his much taller frame.

"You'll do the right thing Rob and thank you for letting me speak my mind." With that she tugged Andrew down the hall, chattering away lightly and then reconnected with Dorothy at the reception area to pick up her coat and a friendly goodbye.

There was no time to think about what had just happened because Mayor Carson was already in his office and had been waiting for ten minutes. The problem was that's all Rob did for the rest of the day was think about Evelyn's scolding, the boy, and his own sense of deficiency. This meeting with Harry was something he had looked forward to as a payoff, especially considering the sacrifices he'd made at home. It was far more than what he billed the township for in work down, but that the town's elected officials always applauded his diligent expertise and gave him the sense that he'd moved mountains. That was the high Rob was now addicted to.

However, today did not go as planned. Sure Mayor Carson was absolutely excited with Rob's work, *for the people.* In fact he got Wayne Doyle, the president of Mountain National Bank, Tom Selman, the town's treasurer and Scott Burgess, the head of tourism and marketing for Forrester to meet them for a presumptive victory lunch at The Red River Steakhouse. It was one of two restaurants in town with linen table clothes and napkins, catering to the discreet pallet and not so discreet wallet.

It was like high school boys congratulating each other over an exhibition football game they won by default because the other team didn't show up. It had no effect on the season and none of it mattered to life. The whole thing was hollow and meaningless.

Rob found himself wishing for all the time back with Elle and Brodie that he'd sacrificed for this weak honor, a t-bone that was too well done and company that were too anxious for their next glass of wine. The guys were slapping each other on the back over a victory that merely fit in a ledger book somewhere and was never inspired to help anyone but the bottom line. Rob groaned inside when he thought of his boy telling him what great work he did and hoped that Brodie never saw him sitting at a table like this.

It wasn't really the outward appearance of this luncheon that so offended Rob with himself. In fact he had bused tables like this as a teenager and been a waiter in his college years to help pay for school. It was more than just the tips that drew him, but the atmosphere of importance that seemed to surround these modern day round tables where kings and knights would meet. So intoxicating was this picture of power and prestige that unknowingly it diminished Rob's own perceptions of his father's value.

Clint Larson could never be found smoking a cigar and waxing in the grease of his own self-importance at one of these grandstands. Without realizing it, Rob had been seduced into forsaking pure wisdom in exchange for the chase of an empty image and a place at this table. This was not what he wanted, not at all.

The guys continued to talk and laugh over their food, not noticing that Rob had quietly retired his membership from their virtual world. He was amazed at how easy it was to put in a few words here and there just to keep the gab going and so fill his role at this important meeting.

What scared him the most was the thought that it might be too late. The idea of standing at a crossroad makes you think that you have a choice. Maybe he was so far past this point now, that all there was in front of him was the road under his feet.

He immediately thought of his father and the decisiveness of that day and hour. It was one year ago, five months and about a week. Yes he knew it well. There wasn't a day that went by that he didn't wrestle with the futility of all his ambition after he knelt beside his father's grave and buried his dreams. Dreams that would only have been complete with the approving smile his father could give him. To maintain now would be easy but that wouldn't do.

Elle needed a whole husband and Brodie needed a dad. It seemed that the people of Forrester needed a Clint Larson. "A good man leaves something lasting", he remembered his father saying. It was time for Rob to find out what that was and see if he could wrap his hands around it in some way.

Chapter 6

"Elle, I have a meeting tonight. I'll probably be a couple of hours." Rob folded his napkin and laid it beside his mostly unfinished dinner. He hadn't changed into his casual clothes as he usually did when he got home from work, but only took off his navy blue striped tie.

Elle knew that was one of his 'power ties' that he used to leverage himself for important meetings. Rob never wore a suit without a tie, just like he never did anything halfway.

Something about his look told his wife that this man that she knew so well had suddenly resigned from something on the inside of him. Was it good or bad? She didn't know but it made her nervous. He didn't eat hardly any of the roast chicken dinner she had made, which was one of his favorites. There had been few words since he got home and Elle had been hopeful that the business of the day would have reversed his sullen mood. Even Brodie was instinctively giving his dad a wide leeway.

"Okay Honey." She said it as cheerful as she could in hopes to impress on his distracted and faraway mind that she was here for him, adding, "Do you want me to make you something special for dessert for when you get home?"

There was a delay and then, "Umm ... sorry, what did you say?" And then before she could say anything he clicked back for a moment of muttered reality, "Uh no ... no thanks Elle. I'm not all that hungry today." He looked at her and could see the concern she was trying to hide on her face.

"Hey it's okay." He said in a more soothing tone and stepping toward her. "I had a kind of rough day."

Shaking his head now with a strained laugh, he said more to himself, "Like that's something new." Elle reached out and touched his arm knowing that he'd say only as much as he wanted to say.

"I've got a client ..." he paused, "well a potential client that I tried to see earlier today who's in the hospital, but it didn't work out with visiting hours and the doctor needing to see her or ... something like that." Elle knew that Rob was frustrated and spent.

"I have an idea," she said quickly. "How about if Brodie and I tag along, and keep you company. You know it's a good half hour ride to the hospital."

Rob smiled at this girl he was instantly so thankful for. Brodie was still sitting at the table and would have approved but he was too busy eating his dessert, brownie and vanilla ice cream.

"Ohhh," Rob closed his eyes and hugged her, "that's really tempting ... live entertainment the whole way there and back ... mmm."

Elle looked up at him hopeful that she could do something to make it all better.

Then deciding, "But I think I'll give you guys the night off." Elle pretended to pout which only made Rob laugh. "Hey besides it'll be too boring for Brodie and you sitting around a waiting room." Which he knew wasn't true. These two could have fun anywhere.

Rob kissed her lightly and said, "I'll take care of this and be home in a couple of hours. Okay?" He said it tenderly as if Elle needed assurance of something more.

Looking up he said, "See you in a while Brodie."

"Bye Daddy!" Brodie managed with a mouth full of ice cream and chocolate from ear to ear.

Rob smiled at the picture of his son like this and it occurred to him how important it was. Grabbing his car keys off the wall table in the hallway, he headed out the door into the cool evening.

It only took Rob twenty minutes to get to the hospital. Of course there was little to no traffic and combined with his fast driving, the trip north of town was made short. Rob was frugal in many things but not his clothes or car. He saw them as necessary accessories to the big picture of who he was and his profession. German engineering and Italian designs seemed to suit his taste best.

The drive was beautiful lasting for the duration of the sunset and dividing distances between parallel runs along the Brunswick River and the famed rolling hills of the area. He passed the popular ski hills that fueled Forrester's commerce for a solid five months of the year. These five months were additionally important as they helped market the town as a desirable tourist-stop for the other seven months of the year.

Williamson's County Hospital was built five years ago and was not only meant to be advancement medically but a strategically located solution for the area. Geographically it was north of Forrester about a fifteen-minute drive and almost the same distance south of Bolin Forge. The ski resorts had fastest access to the new facility but with the combined talent and resources of the whole area, it was in everyone's best interest. Being such a big hospital in a rural area made it an employment opportunity of choice to many doctors, nurses and staff from around the country.

Rob had not been here since he had said goodbye to his father and it didn't please him any to be pulling into the too familiar parking lot. It was dark now and the sterile looking lines of the structure had a halogen glow. Rob forced one foot in front of the other as he made his way into the lobby of the building. So was the way of discipline he thought, it had a way of taking you places you really didn't want to go.

After a few inquiries he was on the elevator headed to the fifth floor, which the receptionist referred to as 'medical'. Even the antiseptic odor triggered a feeling of hopelessness in Rob.

The nurse at the floor's main desk directed him to a common area at the end of the hall saying, "She's waiting for you in the leisure room Mr. Larson."

Rob didn't know what to expect or for that matter what he could say. The only reason he was even here was because of the compelling case Evelyn made for him to get involved. Again he asked himself, *and what is it I'm getting involved in here?*

Rob ambled down the hall with a weary droop to his shoulders. Unconsciously he must have run his hand through his hair five or six times by the time he rounded the corner into the open lounge area.

The leisure room was furnished in the manner of a high-end coffee shop or a reading area in a library. There was lots of window to the outside world on the far end facing east and also to the south side, which would be most pleasing in daylight because of the view to the river and the amassing hills with their abundance of now colorful forest.

Rob had seen Jenny many times at Evelyn's Diner and had even spoken to her casually because she had waited on him or refilled his coffee cup. Still he didn't really know her at all. He wasn't even aware that she was caring for her young nephew. The room wasn't that crowded but Rob was having a hard time to find her at first.

Then he caught a wave out of the corner of his eye and saw Jenny rolling her wheelchair out of a glass enclosure along the windowless wall. Rob bounced over to hold the door for her as she exited the smoking suite. It was one of very few places in the entire hospital where you could have a cigarette.

Jenny was wearing what looked like a new housecoat, probably a gift from Evelyn he thought, and she had her pack of cigarettes and lighter on her lap. Her grey roots were neglected and the familiar blonde hair didn't look so natural in here. Like Evelyn she was a thin woman who spent her life running from table to table. Rob thought it might be the trauma she'd been through but she looked older than her boss even though she was almost ten years younger at fifty-three.

"Thank you Mr. Larson. I appreciate that." She wheeled over to a nearby set of chairs and table.

"Can I get you anything Ms. Richards?" Rob asked motioning to a couple of vending machines along the wall. She seemed uncomfortable especially in the role reversal the circumstances seemed to have put them both in.

"Oh … yeh, that would be great. How about a diet coke of some kind? And Mr. Larson you can just call me Jenny, if you don't mind?"

Rob smiled a tired smile. "Sure Jenny and you can just call me Rob." With that he walked over and popped a few bills in the vending machine and waited for the cans to roll out at the bottom.

Sitting down across from her, Rob handed her a soda and then slumped into a relaxed pose, snapping open his own apple juice. "Well Ms. Jenny," he started, "I am very sorry for the accident you've had. I hope the staff here is treating you well and giving you some encouragement."

Jenny seemed nervous and was fidgeting with her lighter. "Well I guess it's my lot in life Mr. Larson …" she looked up and corrected herself with a slight laugh, "uh, sorry. Rob."

He just smiled back and let the moment linger. This was something that he'd learned from his father. If you let people just have some space, they'll usually say what's really on their heart.

She continued, "You … uh, you caught me enjoying one of my few pleasures." She looked down and thumbed the blue pack of cigarettes. Rob settled in and enjoyed another sip of his juice and let her continue. "Yes I guess the doc is treating me alright. You know he said that I'm probably the youngest patient he's ever done a full hip replacement on."

She seemed to brighten up at that last remark and Rob wasn't sure if it was because she was considered the youngest at something or that she actually got a full hip replacement. He figured it was the first though.

"Did he say when you'd be ready to leave?"

"Oh, he figures in a couple of days. I had a few complications but nothing serious outside the actual surgery." She took a nervous sip of her coke and then looked down, "Look," she hesitated. "Rob. I know Evelyn pressured you to come see me and I appreciate that. She's always been good to me you know, and she just cares. That's the way she is."

Jenny's voice was low and raspy, partly from the years of smoking and probably the stress she was under. "The truth is I don't have any money to pay you and even if I did, I'm not sure there's anything you could do."

Rob waited for just a few seconds and then said, "Ms. Jenny I'm not sure that I can do anything to help but if you want to tell me what the problem is involving your nephew Andrew, I'll keep the matter confidential and maybe, just maybe, I might be able to help you with some advice."

She looked at him now, "You mean you're not going to send me a bill for today?" Rob gave a genuine grin now, "This is a free house call Jenny; no charge." The gesture seemed to put her at ease.

"That's good news in the middle of a lot of bad news. I don't know how much Evelyn has told you but I've been having a hard time financially. I've borrowed against every ounce of equity I managed to build up in that ole house of mine and as you might guess, I've got some serious new medical bills now. Well, the truth is, I can't go on like I have been anymore." She dropped her eyes on that last line so there was more to it then just that.

"What do you mean when you say 'I can't go on like I have' Jenny?" Rob asked.

"Well, just that, I'm not as young as I used to be you know and if I'm gonna have any kind of life … well I have to do it now, there isn't any 'after' left." She said with an abruptness that caught at him.

"So what does that mean for Andrew?" Rob could feel this going somewhere foreign to his whole thought process.

"Do you have any children?" Jenny quizzed Rob.

"Yes, I have a little boy, six years old."

"Then you know how much time it takes and how much money it takes to look after a child."

Rob had a confused look on his face. "Are you saying that you can't afford Andrew anymore so you're thinking of giving him over to Child Services?"

Jenny sighed deeply. It was like she'd carried this debate in her heart all of her life. Tiredly she began, "Rob, my mother died when I was fifteen. My dad left us when I was only five. I think it was the news that mother was expecting again. He was gone before my baby sister Mary was born. Anyway, there was no else around when mother died so I had to quit school and go to work to take care of Mary and me. I raised her from the time she was around eight years old and then she got pregnant by some smooth talking high school quarterback when she was seventeen. That's when my niece Kerry came along and one year later Mary took off for good to leave me to raise another child. Maybe I did a little better job with Kerry because she didn't get pregnant until she was twenty one, but still not good enough because she didn't want anything to do with Drew and she signed over legal custody of him to me."

"Does she ever come home to see Andrew?"

Jenny gave a sarcastic huff, "Are you kidding? I don't think she even knows his name and besides, she's in no shape at all to be a mother to him."

Rob didn't feel like he needed any more detail of Kerry's life. It was hard to imagine a mother forgetting her child but it happened all the time. The things people chased to comfort and fill their lives were often capable of controlling their entire personality. He was the furthest thing from a family counselor but he knew the force of rejection somehow found its way from one generation to the next.

"So where does that leave you now Ms. Jenny?" Rob asked but felt certain of the answer.

"I'm at the end." She said plainly. "I'm broke. The bank has given me a second foreclosure notice. Child Services has already filed complaints against me for what they feel is neglect and I'm tellin' you, I've done my best for all those kids!" She got hard when she came to her own defense.

Then as though she saw Andrew's face, "That boy is a sweet boy." She put her head down and suddenly began wiping tears away and then just as quickly, cleared her throat and looked up with a determined smile. "But I can't look after him any more."

The words slammed at Rob's heart.

"I've already told Evelyn all of this and she begged me to hold off calling Child Services until I talked with you. I don't want you to feel like this is your problem and no offense, but I doubt you can help me. Or for that matter little Andrew."

It was Rob's turn to feel nervous. He shifted uncomfortably in his chair trying to gather some kind of intelligent thought. "Ms. Jenny," he started slowly, "I am going to give this matter some thought. I need to look into a few things and I promise to be discreet."

He pushed his chair back slowly and stood up. Reaching out his hand he added, "I hope you're feeling much better soon."

She took his hand and gave him a smile like he remembered at the diner, "Thank you for coming Rob and … I hope I didn't waste too much of your time."

Jenny felt apologetic now for all she'd dumped on Rob but he smiled back, "Oh it was a pleasure Jenny and I will be in touch with you."

Rob couldn't wait to get out of there. *It was a pleasure?* He recited his parting words. *What in the world!* It was anything but a pleasure. What a stupid thing to say.

The whole way home he thought about Andrew being entirely alone in the world. The boy had no father, no mother and now his only relative in the whole world was deserting him. Rob couldn't imagine being four years old and utterly forsaken.

Unexpectedly he began to think of when his father got recalled to active military duty. Rob was only seven and his dad had been his ultimate hero until then. For the next three years, because of the priority and various locations of Clint's missions, Rob didn't see his dad scarcely at all.

He remembered how cold he was toward his dad that first Christmas Clint got leave to come home. As Rob sped past the "Welcome to Forrester" sign it occurred to him that he never remembered letting go of the deep offense he felt toward his father for deserting him to save the world.

Funny, he thought, *every boy wants to believe his dad can save the world, but just don't leave me in the process of doing it.*

No, things were never the same between Rob and his dad after that. In his mind Rob chalked it up to maturing and learning to take care of himself. He'd never realized until now that he became critical of his father for all the things that he had once admired him for.

It all happened the day he felt truly abandoned by his father. Clint had a dedication to what was right and honorable. He justified the sacrifice of those years as being for the sake of his family and country, but he himself never got over the sorrow he lived in for the loss of his son's heart. Rob never comprehended that. He was so fixated on what he believed to be the injustice he was dealt, his eyes were blinded to the courageous acts of love his hero marked the world with.

Right now all Rob could think about was holding his little boy. Something in the memory of Andrew's expressionless face made Rob fear the unthinkable, that he'd broke a trust with Brodie that he might never get back.

He turned the last few corners too fast and knew Elle would never approve if she were in the car with him, but there was an urgency, like every second counted. He couldn't stand the thought of Brodie taking those rejections deep into his heart and then locking him out … forever.

Elle had just put Brodie in bed and was coming down the stairs when Rob walked in the front door. She would have asked Rob more about his meeting at the hospital but Rob seemed anxious to say 'goodnight' to Brodie before he fell asleep. Giving her a quick kiss, he touched his hand softly to her cheek and then hurried quietly upstairs.

Elle just stood on the stairs for a moment and held her hand to her cheek thinking of how long it had been since she had seen that impulsive tender side of Rob.

"Hey is everyone asleep in here?" Rob whispered as he pushed through the crack in the bedroom door.

"Yup. Everyone's asleep, 'cept me Daddy." Brodie whispered back in an exaggerated hush.

Rob couldn't help chuckle.   He sat on the side of Brodie's bed and ran his hand over his little head. "So

Mr. Lion, Buster and Shaggy are all gone ni-nite?" Still whispering Rob reached over and patted on the stuffed animals that were such perfect company for sleeping.

"Daddy, his name's not Shaggy, it's Ralphy." Brodie was trying to keep in a whisper but Rob's attention and teasing was getting him excited.

They both laughed as quiet as they could and then Rob leaned over hugging his boy. It was a beautiful sight that no one would see by the dim night-light, but God.

"Brodie, I love you son." Rob could feel a lump in his throat.

"Daddy I love you too!" The comeback was so natural and runaway. Just the way it should be Rob thought and he breathed a deep sigh.

"Catcher, Daddy has something he has to ask you for?"

Brodie sat up and instinctively pulled Buster onto his lap, "What Dad? What do you want? You can have anything."

It touched Rob's heart to feel so welcome in his boy's unrestrained affections. "Well ...", it wasn't easy scrapping up even enough humility to deal with a six year old size person, "You may not understand all of what I want to say ..." the words came slow, "but I want to tell you that I'm really sorry."

Suddenly Rob's heart opened up and things he needed to say were said. "Daddy is sorry for all the times he let you down; for all the times I said I'd do something with you and then changed everything at the last minute. I'm sorry for doing that to you and Mommy. I feel bad for getting your hopes up to go on an adventure and then not doing what I said I'd do with you. I want you to know that you mean more to me than work or any of that other stuff I do."

He paused for a second and then finished, "Brodie, Daddy needs to ask you ... will you forgive me for all my mistakes?"

Rob wasn't certain that his boy could even understand

all he was saying or asking. Brodie looked deep into Rob's eyes with a concerned look and then a big grin lit up his face.

Reaching up with both hands he held Rob's face and drew him closer saying, "Sure Daddy. You're the best daddy in the whole world!" With that he pulled Rob's face right to his own, gritting his teeth and squeezing his eyes shut in the ultimate display of affection spilling over the sides of his tiny being.

Rob could feel it too and he squeezed his own eyes shut to keep any displays of emotion from escaping. Throwing his arms around his treasured son, he gave a muffled, "thank you son. Thank you."

Without any warning Andrew's face came to Rob's mind. "Hey Brodie."

"Yeh Daddy?" They were facing each other now, with Rob still sitting on the side of the bed.

"Did Mommy say your prayers with you tonight?" That had always been one of the jobs that Elle took care of.

"Yup and we prayed for you too Daddy."

"Wow. I think I owe you and Mommy a lot of thanks for all those prayers."

Brodie just smiled, not sure how he could collect. Still perplexed about Andrew, Rob felt a peace in this moment like he had never experienced and so he chased it.

"There's a little boy that's about two years younger than you and right now he needs some help."

"What's wrong with him Dad?"

"There's nothing wrong with him physically. What I mean is, he's not hurt. Well ... he's not hurt with a cut or a broken arm, but ..." Rob was trying to make it as simple and easy to understand for Brodie as he could.

"His name is Andrew and right now he needs a big answer to a big problem in his life."

Brodie grabbed Rob's arm, "Daddy you could help him! Right?"

Rob thought for a moment, "I'm going to try Brodie but it's such a big problem that he needs more help than just me." Rob felt small and now he amazed himself, "I thought maybe you could pray for Andrew and see if God could help him."

"Yeh Daddy! Me and you can do that!" Brodie was excited at the chance to do something important with his dad and that night something of a miracle began in the Larson home.

Chapter 7

The phones were already ringing when Rob stepped into the office. He had on a light brown suit and carried an optimism that Dorothy picked up on immediately. She was on a call so she smiled and mouthed, "you look sharp" with one thumb up for approval.

It was an overcast day but Rob felt like breathing was coming easier than it had in a long time. He wasn't thinking about the contracts that he could hear Dorothy fielding calls regarding. There was a new consideration for his life and a sense of order that didn't make sense to his routine thought process, yet the priority shift sounded in his core like an answer he had been looking for too long. Still, mixed in with all of this was the persisting and gaping trouble chained to the slightest figure of a boy, Andrew. Where to even begin to find the remedy?

Just then his phone rang with an intercom call from Dorothy's desk. "Good morning Rob. Mayor Carson's on line two. Just to give you a 'head's up', he's next door at Evelyn's and is wondering if you have a few minutes to pop over to meet someone."

Normally Rob tried to avoid these casual appointments with Harry at coffee shops and diners because of his tendency to grandstand the over importance of any meeting. Today though, Rob was up for just about anything.

"Good morning Mayor Carson." Rob greeted him solidly knowing how much Harry loved his title.

"Rob! I'm glad I caught you. Listen, I'm right beside you here at Evelyn's and I have a guest with me from out of town. Can you spare a few minutes to come over and meet him?"

Rob was positive, "Sure, I'll be right over."

"Great!" Carson came back. "See you in a couple of minutes."

With that Rob stepped back into the reception area where Dorothy was stationed and quickly reviewed the morning schedule before stepping out.

Harry Carson was a comical man who was both proud and humble at the same time, if that was possible. Some folks in town thought the mayor was quite proud because he tended to be too loud, too obvious and too easily impressed with himself. On the other hand, Harry was easily led, which Rob knew could be good or bad, depending on who was leading, and he was quickly impressed with people, which also could cut both ways. He had a struggle with the short man syndrome and the fact that he was generously overweight didn't help either.

Harry would periodically look at Rob's trim shape and then slap his own stomach saying, "You know Rob, I've always been a big-boned fella." Rob enjoyed those entertaining moments with the mayor. One thing for sure, Harry was passionate about Forrester and his job as mayor.

Stepping in the front door of Evelyn's Diner, Rob got the usual welcome with every head, ever so obviously, turning for the three-second gawk. He wasn't long finding Harry because today he was in full parade with his signature plaid sport coat and his lovely wife Madge. Now Madge was a perfect match for Harry in anyone's opinion. She had a pile of bleached blonde hair stacked on top of her head, which Rob never knew how much was her own, compared to Harry's balding long dark strands that seemed no less attention grabbing. Madge had a cute face and a knack for fitting her plump figure into clothes that were at least two sizes too small for her. Being the first lady of Forrester, she had her own design motif that she was locally famous for and that always included faux animal prints. The combined design power of the two together just about reached out and grabbed Rob from across the room.

Harry bellowed out a big, "Over here Rob!" A routine Rob knew he couldn't avoid.

Approaching the booth they were sitting in Rob immediately calculated that this seating arrangement was not well thought out. The couple was tightly squeezed in across from the visitor, whose back was to Rob as he approached.

"Mayor Carson, it's good to see you." Harry beamed at the sound of the endorsement in front of his guest. "And it's good to see you too Madge." Rob knew she wouldn't appreciate being called, "Mrs. Carson". It would have interfered with her image; whatever that was.

"Good to see you Rob," Harry said as he managed to wiggle himself out from behind the table and stand up to shake his hand.

Madge said hello and stuck out her hand so that Rob wasn't sure if he were to shake it or kiss it. Rob opted as usual for a gentle handshake.

"Rob I'd like you to meet Mr. Stuart Jenkins. He is a top reporter for the *America Now* paper. And Mr. Jenkins, this is Rob Larson the finest lawyer in our town."

Rob turned and was not sure if he was more amused with the Mayor's use of adjectives in front of their job titles or the careless look of the "top" reporter of one of the nation's biggest papers.

"It's a pleasure to meet you Mr. Jenkins," Rob said as he shook his hand.

"Yeh, good to meet you," he said completely disinterested and then motioned to the end of the bench he was sitting on, "Have a seat." His voice was completely empty of expression, like he was still asleep.

Rob sat down as Stuart comfortably continued eating his breakfast. Harry had managed to work himself back in beside Madge and plopped his elbows on the table with a huge smile.

Looking directly at Rob, as Mr. Jenkins was deeply engrossed in his pancakes he started, "Mr. Jenkins is here to do a story on the upcoming Christmas pageant and Forrester's reputation for being Christmas Town U.S.A. Isn't that great?" There was no denying that Harry was excited.

This could be worth millions of dollars alone in advertising and if it was done right, it could have an extremely positive effect on their economy's growth almost immediately. There was also the prestige hanging like ripe fruit on a vine in front of Harry's round pudgy face and that part of it so tickled Rob that he almost laughed looking at his delirious grin.

Something did bother him about Jenkins though. Rob had inherited a solid ability from his father it seemed to quickly assess people. He didn't like to think of it as judging character, after all he was a lawyer not a judge, but there was something unsettling in these first few seconds of meeting him. First of all he didn't have the look or attitude of someone who could even pull off a story like this – something of moral goodness and family value.

Secondly, Rob knew enough about facts and details that it made all the difference how and who told them in regard to how the outside world would perceive them.

"So Stuart," Rob used his first name intentionally, "when did you get into town?"

Still working on his last few morsels he barely looked up. "I got in last night. Checked into The Kingston Hotel and the next thing your Mayor was callin' me up."

Rob looked back at Harry as Stuart continued.

"Yup this town's got quite the information loop. I wasn't in my room but a half an hour and he phoned to welcome me and ask if he could help with anything."

Harry was a little embarrassed but he was in such a good mood he just chuckled saying to Rob, "Colleen works the front desk and she used to work for me when

I was manager out at the clubhouse. Anyway, she must have seen the press I.D. or somethin' and next thing you know ..." he gave another nervous laugh. "Oh you know the way I am Rob. I like to keep my ear to the ground and help folks anyway I can."

Madge saved Rob from even thinking about it and rolled her eyes dramatically giving a low, "oh boy."

Harry cheerfully ignored her and turned his attention on their guest as he continued, "And Mr. Jenkins I want you to know that my office is at your disposal. An-y-thing we can do to help you get your story, it'll be our pleasure."

Rob wished he could pull Harry back but that would be no use and besides, what reason could he give? It was just a gut feeling he had that said, "CAUTION".

"Thanks Mayor. I don't plan on being here long. I'm just gonna nose around a bit, grab a few pictures and see if I can come with an angle for my story." Stuart had finally straightened up from his feeding frenzy and was cradling a black coffee. Rob figured he was anything but the top reporter for his paper. He looked like he was in his late twenties to early thirties, no wedding ring, dressed like he didn't mean to get dressed, and all of about one hundred and fifty pounds at five foot nine. He had an air of being even less interested with his head up then it was when it was down.

Not that any of this disqualified him to be a great reporter, but Rob was sure that a big paper wouldn't send one of their top guns to put together a minuscule article in the back of the travel or social section. There was no story but Harry went on bragging about Forrester's iconic position as the American postcard Christmas town.

Rob saw Evelyn headed their way so he flipped his coffee cup over. He was comfortable knowing that he'd at least got his feet wet by going and visiting Jenny last night. She didn't have on her usual smile walking up to the table Rob thought, but maybe she didn't know of his visit.

"Good morning Evelyn," Rob smiled, "How are you?"

"It's not going so well this morning Mr. Larson."

Her tone was cold and the sound of her calling Rob, *Mr. Larson*, even stopped Harry mid-speech.

Not that this was the time or place; Rob had no choice, "What's wrong Evelyn?"

Despite her apparent anger with Rob she instinctively filled every coffee cup on the table while talking, "I don't know what you said to Jenny last night but you've done it now." Evelyn's lips were tight and she was frowning.

Rob's neck was feeling hot, "What ... what happened?"

This was not the way to handle such a sensitive matter and Rob knew it. He found himself despising the familiarity of a smaller population at that moment. Even this reporter couldn't come into town without everyone knowing and the Mayor phoning him.

"Rob I should have known better than to let you get involved in this!" He could feel the pressure now.

Harry and Madge just stared at him. Madge had a big wad of breakfast gum that she just kept chewing with her wide-eyed gawk. It was bovine in quality.

Rob put on his best game face for negotiation and smiled, "Evelyn what's the problem and is this something we should talk about over at my office?"

She responded with a disgusted, "Humph! A lot of good that did. I'm not gonna bother wastin' any more time going over there and lookin' for your help."

Rob could feel the stranger at his elbow waking up from his bland stupor and taking it all in which made him feel more trapped.

"You know who showed up at Mrs. Gillespie's when I dropped Drew off this morning?" Before Rob could even begin to wonder Jenny let it fly, "Social Services! That's who Rob." Evelyn looked around the table for a second, as though to include everyone. "And do you know what Jenny said when I called her? She said that she had called them herself this morning."

Evelyn had an astonished look on her face to add to the effect of what she'd just said. "Apparently after talking to you she felt like there was nothing that could be done, it was hopeless, and so she's gonna turn little Drew over to some government agency. I can't begin to imagine what's going to happen to him!"

Rob could see she was really upset now and had an urge to defend himself. In as calming of a voice as he could find he tried to settle her down, "Evelyn, I never encouraged her to do any of this and it's just as much a shock to me as it is to you. I'm really sorry about this."

Everyone was quiet. Some of the tables close by had grown silent to better hear what the fuss was about, though that would not have been hard to predict. She picked up her coffee pot from off of the table and gained her composure with a tired smile.

"Rob, it's not that you said anything wrong. It's just that … you didn't say anything right." With that she moved away and through the swinging doors that went back into the kitchen.

Quickly Rob excused himself, "Harry I've got to go make some calls. It was nice to meet you Stuart and all the best on your article. Madge …" he nodded to them and headed out without looking back.

He didn't want to give Harry a chance to ask all the questions that he could see were just bubbling to come out of him. Besides wanting to exit from a very uncomfortable atmosphere, Rob was genuinely concerned about the welfare of Andrew. What was going to happen to this suddenly homeless four-year old?

Elle was on her familiar run by the school on the way to the café so that she could drop Brodie off. It was typically a time of mother and son talk, and today was especially interesting for Elle. "So what did Daddy say when he came in your room last night to say 'good night'?"

"Oh … he called Ralphy, Shaggy." Then Brodie giggled remembering how funny that was to him that his dad always got Ralphy's name wrong.

Elle laughed along at the enjoyment of her boy, "So is that all he said Sweetie?"

Brodie had a pocket size figurine in his hand of a soldier and was moving him around on his lap preoccupied. Without looking at her he said, "Nope. Daddy said he was sorry for not doin' the adventures with me and …" he had to think for a moment. "And for you too Mommy, and he said I'm more important then his work."

He said all this while dancing his toy soldier around on his lap, not noticing the awe his words had transferred onto Elle's face.

"So that's it? And then he said 'goodnight'?" She had just pulled up in front of his school where there was a constant flow of traffic and junior pedestrians.

Brodie was already so settled into the routine of the 'drop-off' that he enthusiastically undid his seatbelt and grabbed the car door handle.

"Oh just a minute Brodie," Elle wasn't done her motherly interview. "Now tell Mommy if there was anything else Daddy said last night." Brodie pinched his lips together in deep thought and rolled his mouth from side to side making the most distracting faces.

Then slowly he recounted his dad's words, "He said, 'forgive me for my mistakes' and I said 'sure' and told him he was the best daddy." With that Brodie gave one of his modest smiles that usually accompanied an accomplishment he was proud of. Then his eyes got wide because now he remembered what really interested him, "And you know what else Mom?"

Elle reciprocated in hopes of keeping the momentum going, "What, please tell me?" She asked eagerly.

"Daddy said we need to pray for a boy named Andrew that's way littler than me and he needs help!" Brodie was fully alert now and continued, "He doesn't have a broken arm or somethin' but Daddy says he's got a big problem and needs a lot of help ... the kind of stuff he figures God can fix you know."

Elle was speechless. Rob had seemed different when he came downstairs from saying goodnight to Brodie but she couldn't put her finger on it. She had asked him how his meeting at the hospital went and he'd responded with, "Alright I guess," which she knew meant he wasn't up to talking about it. Still, he seemed peaceful and when she came into the kitchen this morning he was cheerfully attentive to both her and Brodie. It reminded her of when they were first married.

She couldn't imagine Rob doing everything her child had just told her but she knew he wasn't lying. Brodie couldn't make up something like this in his wildest imaginations.

After leaving the school Elle headed straight for the café, playing her own imaginary images of the story Brodie told her of last night. Elle always carried a belief that there was greatness in Rob. That he could find the courage to express an apology to their son, regardless that he was just a child, confirmed her idea of true strength.

And on another note, who was this boy Andrew?

Elle was so overly hasty when she pulled into the parking lot behind the older building that her SUV bounced back and forth as she snapped the gear up a touch prematurely. Hurriedly she jumped out almost forgetting her bag and then reaching back to grab it.

The fresh autumn air was pushing her blonde hair across her face and her high-heeled boots clicked on the brick pavers' stone. For a second she glanced up toward the sound of crows cawing but quickly focused and marched toward the rear entrance of the café. She was anxious to sort this out. Maybe her mom would have an idea what it all meant.

Joanne, ever the picture of a traditional homemaking mother, was already loading cinnamon twists, scones and other treats onto the racks behind the display glass. Elle knew she had just pulled them out of the oven and the smell of hot baked goods filled the air with the aroma of comfort and nurturing. Closing her eyes she took in a deep breath and smiled at how easily it reminded her of her wonderful childhood.

"Mom, I never get tired of the yummy smell of your baking."

Joanne had her hands full transferring the goodies and so she continued saying, "Good morning dear. I'm glad you like it. Someone sounds to me like they're in a good mood this morning."

No one, not even Rob, would be able to tell the difference between Elle having a good day or a blah day, but this mother knew her child well and turned to look at her.

Unable to conceal her excitement, Elle spontaneously crinkled up her nose, flashing her beautiful smile she said, "Mom, last night something amazing happened with Rob and Brodie …"

Patiently Joanne listened as her daughter told the facts she knew and then conjectured on all the rest. She laughed a few times because Elle was so dramatic which confirmed again where Brodie got his sense of flair.

After all was told and Joanne took her pause of thought, she said just one thing to Elle, "It's not over dear. Something big has begun."

Chapter 8

The front door swung open followed by the sound of a backpack being dropped and the scuffle of little feet. Rob was at his desk working on a few edits to a legal brief and he smiled wide. He had planned this morning that if he could move his schedule at all, he was going to be waiting for Brodie when he got home from school. He looked at the clock and it was three thirty right on the button.

"Mom! I'm home Mom!" came his high raspy voice.

"Catcher, I'm in here!" Rob shouted back. Instantly he could hear his son's steps run toward the French doors.

"Dad! What are you doin' home? Are you sick or somethin'?" Brodie was excited to see Rob and ran right over to him.

Rob had already changed out of his suit into a black turtleneck sweater and blue jeans. He grabbed Brodie and gave him a playful hug nuzzling his head with his chin.

"Nope, I'm not sick and I didn't fire myself … yet!" he said grinning. "I came home early just so I could hang out with my coo-ool son!"

The pleasure was all over Brodie's face. "Wow! Ever cool Dad!"

There was no doubt in Rob's mind but that he had greatly impressed his son by showing up. It wasn't easy either. He had to inconvenience his work ethic some and he struggled to force a few 'hot button' issues to the back of his mind, but he was determined that his apology the night before was more than just talk. Truthfully, he needed this time with Brodie and had been looking forward to it all day, especially after the incident in the diner.

"So what do you want to do together? Do you want to go to the park, or … how about if we go out back and toss the ball around? What do you think?" Rob had pulled him up on his lap now and Brodie loved even the opportunity of deciding what to do together. What could be better than planning something fun with your dad?

With a moment of deep consideration, he all of a sudden stuck his pointer finger straight up in the air blurting out, "I know what we could do Daddy!" and then Brodie waited for his father's reply.

Rob knew he was waiting and thought it was cute how expectantly he stayed on pause holding out for a reply.

"Okay, what son?" Rob was up for just about anything.

Taking his finger and touching Rob's chest lightly he laid out the plan methodically. "Let's me and you get some coleslaws and apples and go up in the tree fort and camp out."

The gigantic smile at the end told Rob that this was the ultimate desire of his heart right now, and right now was all that mattered. Even though he didn't have a clue what the deal was with the coleslaw, he had his sights set on making up some distance toward his son.

With an excited voice Rob announced, "Coleslaw and apples and tree house, here we come!" and then he threw Brodie in the air catching him in a bear hug. Brodie was so excited he squealed and could barely process the sudden bonanza.

Conveniently for Rob, Elle had picked up a couple of readymade bags of coleslaw and so he emptied one into a plastic bowl and mixed the dressing in. Meanwhile he had Brodie bag a couple of apples.

"Daddy we need to bring a knife too. Can we?"

"Sure," Rob responded, "I'll tell you what, how about if I grab my jackknife and you grab your backpack, then we'll put all our camping supplies in there. Does that sound good?" Of course it sounded good.

Brodie shouted, "Yay!" and ran out of the kitchen to get his bag. Once they emptied his school supplies out and loaded up the provisions, including Rob's jackknife and a butter knife for Brodie, they were out the back door and walking hand in hand toward the big maple tree.

Brodie was chattering away like some of the chipmunks that scurried around the yard. There was already a thin covering of dry leaves on the ground replacing the piles they had raked up on the weekend, but it was fun to hear the swish of the path they kicked through them.

Brodie had on his bright yellow and blue jacket with his favorite camouflage backpack. His jeans were rolled at the bottom so you could plainly see his construction looking boots. That was a must for him and a painful thing when his mother would force him to wear anything else. Rob had thrown on a tan jacket that unintentionally looked great with his black turtleneck. They were a good-looking pair traveling across the big open yard, landscaped with the various coniferous and hardwood trees.

It was a sight heaven smiled on because of the thousand words unspoken and the simple essence of purpose. Man has always ambitiously reached for the stars and yet steadily moved away from the light … away from the path Rob and Brodie were just now discovering.

A strange sensation came over Rob as he stepped up on the first tier that ascended into his son's world. He had never been here before. It suddenly occurred to him that he'd never seen the inside of this tree house and now he knew that he had purposely avoided it.

The conclusions he had rehearsed last night came vividly to his mind and he realized that the wall he had long ago assigned against his father, shut out even these uncomplicated expressions of love. For the first time Rob looked up and around at the care his dad had invested into this wooden wonderland.

"Come on Daddy!" Brodie yelled back as he scurried up the taunt rope net leading to the main lodge. Rob leaned his weight onto the ropes and looking up he could see how skillfully the whole project was designed and accomplished.

All the wood was cedar and the smell was still strong. Rob knew enough about woodworking to know that this tree fort, as Brodie called it, was made to last and deliver a lifetime of safe fun.

Climbing up to the opening in the floor, he could see the exactness of every measurement and masterful skill used to work with the great arms of the tree, but without inflicting wounds on the branches that might lead to rotting wood. Brodie was already sitting cross-legged on the floor and grinning ear to ear when Rob's head popped up in the corner to stare.

"Come on all the way Daddy," he said excitedly. There was an excitement in his heart that he hadn't felt since the day his Grampy announced that his tree house was finished and it was time for the grand tour.

Brodie didn't know it but Clint was extremely weak and in pain for most of its construction. His doctor thought he was crazy taking on such a task and none of his family understood, but it had to be done. Something in Clint's heart needed to be poured out, and as insignificant as it appeared, this was his final offering.

Rob was surprised at how big the structure was on the inside and the light, it seemed to come from everywhere. Brodie jumped up and began showing off his place.

Climbing up a ladder built right into the wall he started cranking the vents in the ceiling, "See this Dad? It makes it so I can see what the birds are doin' way up high and plus it makes it even more sunnier in here. Cool right?"

Rob was impressed, "For sure this is really cool," and he meant it, looking around in awe. When Brodie scrambled back down the ladder, jumping past the last two steps, he flung open the door that led to a deck about five feet by five feet. Rob was standing up now, not quite straight, but he was comfortably able to walk over to the door, bend down a little more and step out.

It was beautiful. Not in the sense of being some architectural sensation, but in the natural canopy the branches provided with their golden yellow leaves rustling aloud with every breeze. Yes the view and breeze up here made it like a whole other world within a world.

Brodie sat down on the deck with his feet swinging over the edge. Rob almost stopped him but then realized the rope netting continued under the deck, making it another safety feature.

Tapping his hand on the planks beside him, Brodie said, "Come on Daddy, sit down like this, it's fun." Rob believed him.

"That does look like fun Brodie." The whole experience was almost magical to him. Sitting down beside his boy he looked around. They were only about seven feet off the ground but life looked different from here. It was a perspective that was both familiar and exotically déjà vu.

"It's nice right?" Brodie asked looking up at him.

"Yes" he answered looking around, "I'd say it's close to perfection."

"I'm really glad you came up here with me today 'cause this is the first time ever," squeaked his raspy voice in appreciation.

Rob was going to apologize again for taking so long to share this experience but then Brodie cut in on his regret.

"Daddy! Do you want to have our snack sitting out here?" he asked eagerly, his eyes wide with expectation.

"Why not? This is a perfect place."

And with that Brodie was up like a shot and ran into the tree house to grab his backpack.

"Okay here's your knife Daddy," Brodie passed him his closed jackknife, "and here's mine knife," he looked up and smiled at Rob as he placed it on the deck beside him. "And here's our apples ... and some coleslaws!" he announced as if it was the crowning ingredient.

When the contents began coming out on the deck, the strangeness of the coleslaw finally got the best of Rob.

"You must really like coleslaw a lot." Rob said chuckling as Brodie passed him the bowl.

Brodie just shrugged his shoulders as he tilted his head and said, "I don't know. I guess it's alright."

Rob was puzzled. "Alright? What are you talking about? You made it sound like this was the perfect snack to have in the tree house." Rob was enjoying the pursuit of this doubtful reasoning.

Brodie thought for a moment and then said matter-of-factly, "you see Grampy liked me to bring him a snack when he first started working on our tree fort. Mommy gave me chicken and coleslaws to bring to him and he really liked it. He wanted me to get him more coleslaws and I did. He said it was good for his hammerin' hand. And he was right Daddy 'cause you should of seen how hard he hit those nails!"

Rob was quiet. He found himself imagining his dad swinging a muscular arm to build the floor he now sat on.

After a moment Brodie's voice got abnormally quiet, "Grampy didn't want any snacks after a while though. I brought him coleslaws and stuff and he seemed happy I brought it out to him but Daddy I saw, he never ate any of it." He extended his little hands, palms up and shrugged his shoulders still wondering why.

"I could tell too that he didn't eat any coleslaws 'cause

his hammerin' hand got shaky and the nails didn't go in fast anymore."

He paused as though trying to figure it all out, "you know after Grampy finished our fort he went to the hosspidel to go away with the angels."

This could have been a really difficult moment for Rob as he could feel the flood of emotion and regret beginning to wash over him, but then all of a sudden Brodie jumped up and shouted like the house was on fire, "Daddy! Daddy!"

Startled, Rob jerked his feet up on the deck, "What is it son?" His brow furrowed as he twisted his head all around trying to find the problem.

"I just remembered something!" he said dramatically. Rob was just a little bit irked with his boy's version of shock therapy at such a vulnerable moment, but at the same time he was relieved.

"What is it?" he said with a slight tone of impatience.

"Daddy I remember now! When Grampy gave me his hammer after making the tree fort, he put it in a red toolbox remember? It's the one I keep under my bed. Remember?"

"Sure Brodie. How could I ever forget? That's all you seem to talk about is that hammer and Grampy. Don't you ever want to talk about anything else?" Rob's tongue was sharp and it surprised him how mean-spirited he had suddenly become. He hoped Brodie was undiscerning to this ugly attitude but he could see the expression change on his young face. He looked at his dad trying to decide how to answer because he longed for his approval and he obviously said something wrong.

"Yeh I like to talk about other stuff Daddy." He said it so cautiously that Rob knew he bruised the moment.

"Brodie, I ... I know you thought a lot of Grampy and that's good son." He dropped his feet back over the deck and relaxed with a deep breath before continuing. "You see your Grampy was my dad and so when he ...

you know … went to heaven, well things were kind of complicated between us."

Looking Rob right the eyes Brodie asked, "Did you love him, you know, like I love you?"

Slowly he began to nod his head but the words came hard, "Yes … I did love him, like you love me."

There was no sense going any further and telling him of how it soured into the very bitterness he just got a taste of. It was this poison Rob needed a remedy for. His hand went instinctively to Brodie's shoulder as he sat beside him.

Brodie had a satisfied look on his face judging Rob's answer as good enough to make the whole matter all better. "That's good Dad," he said patting Rob on the back.

Wanting to get back on track and enjoy the moment Rob reached around and grabbed the bowl of coleslaw.

"Okay then, how about some good ole coleslaw for the boys?"

Brodie responded cheerfully, "Yeh," and reached down to grab an apple and a table knife. Like it was a natural part of the plan all along, he began to cut off raggedy junks of apple and drop them into the bowl of salad.

Rob laughed, "So let me guess, this is what Grampy always did?"

Brodie hesitated, still stung from the last tribute to his beloved grandfather. "Aw … it tastes a lot better with apple you know."

Rob tousled the already wind blown head of his boy and assured him, "Brodie it's okay son. I know Grampy liked apple in his coleslaw. I lived with him you know?" Brodie grinned with relief.

They both had their knives out and were trimming pieces of apple into the common pot.

"So how do we eat this stuff now?" Rob asked already knowing the answer.

Brodie took delight in the simplicity of his reply, "like

this" and he grabbed the slaw with his fingers dropping it into his mouth.

"Oh so that's how you woodsmen do it."

This only pleased Brodie further and seemed to restore his confidence in their relationship. "Daddy is now a good time to tell you what I remembered?" He said it calmly, taking a different tact this time.

Rob had a mouth full of coleslaw and apple, having to admit to himself it was better then he thought it would be. "Sure you tell me what it is you remembered."

"Well like I was sayin', when Grampy gave me his hammer after buildin' the fort, he put it in the red toolbox. Before he shut the box he showed me the secret place inside and said I shouldn't show no one 'cause it was our secret. But he put a letter in the secret place and said it was for you and even put your name on it."

Rob's mouth was hanging open and his heart felt like it forgot to beat.

Brodie went on, "He said to keep it in the secret place until the first day that you come up into the tree fort, and today's the first day! Right Daddy?"

Brodie was excited again and Rob was utterly speechless. Nothing in life had prepared him for the vulnerability he felt right now.

"Grampy said it might take a long time for you to want to come up here but he said that's okay and for me to just forget about our secret until today. But I remembered!"

Rob sat in disbelief. "It couldn't be," he thought. "It's just not possible."

Brodie dropped his knife on the deck and started for the doorway. Rob turned his head, "Where you goin'?" he asked with an expressionless face.

"I'm gonna go get the toolbox for you Daddy. Is that okay? 'Cause I won't open it. I'll let you. Okay?" Brodie stood in the doorway of the cabin and it seemed to Rob like it was the gateway back to another world.

"Sure ... that would be good ... you do that." Rob's

voice trailed off like the sound of Brodie's steps across the floor and then quiet until he heard him pounding on the ground underneath of him.

"Be right back Dad. Don't leave!" came his call as he sped across the yard on his secret mission.

It took Brodie maybe five minutes to run back to the house, run upstairs, grab the toolbox out from under his bed and make his way back to the tree house. The delayed moments were filled with apprehension for Rob.

When someone gets into a new car they look for familiar controls like a steering wheel, a brake, and the accelerator. There was nothing familiar about this moment, neither were there any controls.

His mind was working frantically to find some thread to grab onto but everything was foreign. *It just can't be*, he reasoned in his mind. With no comprehension in sight he was swiftly brought back into the here and now when he looked in the direction of the pounding little boots.

Brodie came to a stop right just in front of him and beamed up at him from below. Both arms were wrapped around the bright red toolbox.

"I got it!" and with that he ran under the deck to begin his climb.

Any other time Rob would have jumped up to help him but he was numb from the shock of what message the box could possibly carry.

With effort, Brodie scrambled up through the hatch and worked at his delivery. Rob didn't even turn around at the sound of him coming up behind and panting for breath. He was motionless, staring off through the branches of the sugar maple into the distance.

Brodie emphasized his breathing in hopes of winning his father's attention but finally had to add, "I got it Dad! Here it is. See?" Holding it out to his dad he lifted his eyebrows to encourage what he felt was the anticipation of a treasure found.

Rob moved slowly lifting the regular sized rectangular toolbox out of his son's hands.

"Go ahead and open it up," Brodie chirped. Rob set the box on his lap and unlatched the front, flipping the lid open. Sitting in the tray at the top was the now famous hammer, a measuring tape, a combination square and a wood plane, absent the sharp blade. All of these tools were familiar to Rob being staples to his father's handiwork.

"Daddy what you do is lift that handle right there and it'll open up to an underneath secret box." He leaned over pointing his little finger at the handle of the toolbox's tray. Rob looked up at him for a second and then returned his stare to the contents of the small chest.

Not saying a word, he lifted up the tray and set it beside him on the deck. There in the bottom was a plain white envelope with 'Rob' penned in his father's handwriting, nothing else. Reaching for it he picked up the sealed note and could tell whatever its contents; they were brief but maybe not light.

When he saw it was safely delivered, Brodie turned and started to walk away. Almost as if he was afraid of being alone with the message, Rob looked back to where Brodie was heading toward the loft exit, "Are you leavin'?"

Turning around he said, "Grampy said it was very important that once you got the secret letter I should let you be alone to read it."

A gust of wind rustled all the leaves around them and Rob suddenly felt very alone. He didn't want Brodie to go and yet he knew it was better.

Staring blankly, he watched his son dutifully march across the natural setting of their backyard toward the house. Rob could hear the sound of his thin voice humming some child's melody and then it faded into the wind. He couldn't help but wonder at this little boy and the carefulness in which he handled his grandfather's wishes. There was a confidence in Brodie that startled him at times and yet he admired it.

The paper between his fingers made him feel burdened and troubled. It was almost like this was the thing that he'd been running from all his life and now it was upon him. He held in his hand a mysterious message that his father had sent to him as if from another world, and now he had to step out past all the safe boundaries of reasoning to do what he'd never dreamed.

Chapter 9

Rob's breathing had unconsciously sped up and become shallow as he unfolded his jackknife and ran the blade neatly down the spine of the envelope. Setting the knife down on the deck beside him, he cautiously looked inside the opening as if he wasn't sure what to find. And that was the truth, Rob was probably never so unsure in his life and the feeling was traumatic.

He grabbed at the few folded pages inside as if to push back the fears that had ambushed him. Strangely he felt some anger rise up toward his father. *How could he be doing this to me now? If he wanted to tell me something why didn't he talk to me when he had the chance?* Rob could feel a strong argument mounting in his head against even reading the letter, but his hands were on autopilot and even now they began to unfold the letter.

His eyes scanned the inked pages immediately validating it as his father's handwriting. Taking a deep breath Rob began to read:

Dear Rob,

My days here are growing short and I'm getting kind of tired. I wish I could talk to you face to face instead of writing this letter, but I take full responsibility for the broken road between us. There are things on my heart that I need to say to you, now more than ever, and yet I know you're not in the place to hear them, at least not as of the writing of this.

I want you to know that I'm very proud of you Rob. You're my son and I can't begin to tell you the joy I've experienced watching you grow up. I remember watching you graduate from school with honors. I remember the day you proposed to Elle and showed me her engagement ring. It was a dream come true to see you marrying such a wonderful girl. You've made many strong choices and as your father, I want you to know I admire the character and quality I see in you.

When you were a boy I figured I had done my time in the military and could devote myself to family. Things happened in the world though. I felt like I needed to do my duty and invest for your freedom. You were about seven when I left for those three years and it was the toughest and loneliest decision of my life. I was a young man and thought I was doing the right thing for my family and country. The truth is son even now I'm not sure I made the right decision. Not because the service wasn't noble but it cost me a bond with you I've never gotten back. Something broke and I just can't seem to fix it. Now I'm trusting God for the impossible.

Maybe you don't remember but I had promised to make you a tree house the year I got called back for active duty. You wanted it for Christmas and it was going to be our project to work on together. I only got home for a few days that Christmas and then I had to leave. You were really disappointed with me and I can't blame you. By the time those three years were up, it felt like I had lost the most important thing in my life ... you. You were ten but it seemed like you were going on eighteen and the promise of making you a tree house had suddenly expired with you growing up. You've always been a good son Rob. It just seemed like you didn't trust me anymore, didn't need me and at times, didn't want me. You're a successful man now with your own family so this may seem too little and too late, but I'm sorry Rob. I regret never having the chance to build that tree house with you and never being able to heal the road between us.

Since you're reading this letter you're probably sitting somewhere up in the tree house I built for Brodie. He's a beautiful boy and I love him. You're a great father Rob and again you've made me proud of you. Just between us though, with everything in me I really built this tree house as a gift to you. You see son, one thing I've learned with all the building I've done is that everything has to have a foundation, and a good one if it's going to last. Like this tree house you're sitting in, I did my best to make it strong and safe for Brodie and his friends, but ultimately it's only as sure as the tree it's resting in.

I had a dream of sitting in a tree house, something like this one, and telling my boy of the most important things I'd learned in life. Well this is going to have to do son and I'm believing that you and these words being read up here will mend some distance between earth and heaven.

Look at this tree. As strong and beautiful as it is, it didn't make itself. Like everything, it had a beginning and even now it still depends on the rain, the sunshine and this ground it's anchored to. You've always been independent, self-motivated and ambitious Rob, but believe me when I tell you this; there is no such thing as a self-made man. You came from somewhere and even now your life is dependent upon more things unseen than you could imagine. Wise men speak of a 10 and 20-year plan for life but from where I'm standing right now, you best have at least a 100-year plan.

Ask yourself right now, what is my life built on and

*will it last? I've always held onto the truth I got from
the Bible. It says in Proverbs chapter 24 that through
Wisdom is a house and a life built, and by understanding
it's established on a strong foundation. There is no Wisdom
greater than God's. The life you build on that foundation
will last. I pray that every time you look out in your
backyard and see this tree house, you'll remember me and
think about what you're building your life on.*

God bless you always son. With all my love ... Dad.

The tears rolled freely down Rob's face and splashed
on his sleeve. He could hear the very timber of his
father's voice in every word and he realized how much he
missed him.

For the next hour Rob sat there undisturbed with a
voice that had been too long silenced from his heart. Over
and over he would re-read a paragraph of the letter and
then let his emotions flow freely. Something was moved
inside of him and there would be no turning back from this
place.

Never in the galaxies of all that exists had there seemed
to be so much tearing down of ancient barriers and in their
place, expansive new paths to endless possibilities. Rob
was both free from one thing and now joyfully bound to
another; like a man who had believed a lie all his life and
suddenly found the truth.

Just then a lone snowflake floated down in front of
Rob. He watched it as it gently fell to the ground. Within
seconds there were dozens and then it was official. The
first snow of the season was upon Forrester and Rob knew
that his dad would have had it no other way.

"You must have prayed for this Dad". Then he
laughed, "I guess it's a good thing I didn't climb up this
tree in the summer. You and God might have had to some
explaining to do to the world."

With that he laughed and felt a fulfillment like he'd
never known. He felt like a seven-year-old boy and swung

his feet from high above to say so.

Jumping up he carefully folded his father's letter back into the envelope and put it in his inside jacket pocket. The cool snow felt good on his face as he climbed down from the tree house and started walking back to the house. Rob looked at his home and felt newly excited about his little family. A smile came to his face as he thought about Elle and Brodie.

Without warning his full heart pushed him into a run and he started yelling, "Elle! Brodie! It's snowing! Come on outside!"

Elle had come home about an hour ago and was busy putting away all the groceries she had picked up that afternoon. She figured since Rob was with Brodie she'd take advantage of the break in her usual routine and get a list of things done for the home. Brodie had met her in the kitchen and was just beginning to fill her in on his afternoon with Daddy when they both heard Rob calling them from outside.

"What's your dad doing? I thought you guys were together." Elle started walking to the back kitchen window and then saw the beautiful, white flakes already accumulating into a good snowfall.

"Oh, Daddy was out in my tree fort ..."

"Look Brodie! It's snowing out!" Elle interrupted. Completely excited by the sight of the first snow.

Brodie quickly forgot what he was saying and ran to the window with a shout, "Yeaaa!"

Elle swung her head to look at Brodie who was captivated now with the already salt and pepper world. "Honey did you say your dad was up in your tree house?"

"Yup," he said looking at her with a firm smile.

Just then the back door opened and they could hear Rob's excited voice, "Hey you guys it's snowing! Elle ... Brodie!"

They both jumped from their place at the window and hurried to the back door.

"Isn't it cool Dad?" Brodie was shouting.

"It's awesome!" Rob shouted back and then he started to laugh.

Elle was all smiles but was unusually reserved. Never could she remember being the ballast for these two. Despite her excitement over the first snow she was puzzled at Rob's enthusiasm over the snow, and did she hear Brodie correctly? Was Rob really up in the tree house? There was a sudden barometer change in the atmosphere of her home and her mind was reeling to keep up with it.

"Come on you two! Let's go for a walk and celebrate the first snow of the season."

Brodie responded with an affirmative, "yes!" and instantly started pulling on his boots.

Elle couldn't help it but crinkled up her nose with a sense of pleasure at Rob's spontaneity. Opening up the coat closet, they were only minutes getting outfitted with wool hats, mittens, scarves and winter jackets. Soon they were strolling from sidewalk to pathway and leaving fresh prints of a family making memories in a new white world.

They stayed out playing until the streetlights all came on, waving at many of their neighbors as they came home from work. Since there was no one home to cook Rob suggested that they order a pizza and find a Christmas movie to watch together. Elle and Brodie didn't need any persuasion. It was almost Thanksgiving anyway, and with the new snow on the ground it was officially time to get into the spirit of the season.

Elle could not remember the last time that her and Rob had laughed so much together. It was wonderful. Yes, that was the perfect word for it, wonderful.

"What a great story," Rob commented as the movie ended and the musical finale played out to the words 'The End'. It was Elle's favorite Christmas movie, a classic called, *It's a Wonderful Life*.

"Yes I never get tired of that old movie. It always

speaks to me," she said sleepily.

"Me too," Brodie chimed in, already in his pj's.

Rob and Elle instantly exchanged a look and both grinned. "So that movie really speaks to you, does it?" Rob asked Brodie with an amused air, and put his hand around the back of his fine neck as he sat cuddled up between him and Elle.

"Yeh," Brodie responded in a drowsy tone, "it's nice when everybody loves each other at the end."

Rob smiled and sat back thinking, his gaze resting on the burning embers in the fireplace. Just then came a friendly pop followed by a soft sounding sizzle and crackle from the flickering opening. It was like a miniature band shell where all the performers danced and leapt in perfect sync to the myriad of sounds, offering their lights to anyone discerning enough to recognize their stage.

Neither Rob nor Elle knew it of the other, but they were both deep in thought considering the moment. Rob felt like a man that had been blind and was just now beginning to see all that he had to be thankful for. He was thankful to be thankful, and that realization stunned him. Like a man who just started breathing and wondered how he existed before that first breath, he was amazed at what was already in his life; what was already in that warm family room beside him.

Elle was having a parallel awakening of her own. Not sure of what was going on in her husband's heart, but sure of a profound dawning in their lives, she felt like some of the supernatural extract of her favorite Christmas movie had spilled over into her reality. It wasn't as much about what she could see, but the strength of what she couldn't see. Whatever was going on, it was strong and actually made her a little nervous. A woman has a way of feeling the wind change in her life even before a leaf blows.

"Hey I've got an idea," came Rob's tired and gentle voice into the cozy, dim room. As he forced himself up from his restful position, being careful not to disturb the other two, he started toward the bookcase. "When I was a boy my Dad would read to me out of a very old book about mysteries and secrets that didn't belong to this world."

He was squinting in the dim light, scanning the shelves for one specific selection. Rob couldn't see the immediate reaction his words triggered in Brodie but as soon as his little ears heard the words, "mysteries and secrets", every ounce of sleep left him and he sat straight up watching his dad.

"There it is," Rob said straining to grab at a thick old leather bound book from off the top shelf.

"That looks really old and heavy Daddy."

"Well you're right. It is old and pretty heavy. Your Grampy gave me this book when I got out of school and before that he got it from his Dad, which would have been your Great Grampy."

"Wow!" Brodie exhaled low with his eyes expressing a sudden awe he possessed for the book.

"That must be really old, right Daddy? Like maybe a hundred years or something."

"It's old that's for sure." Rob slumped back down beside Brodie who was now up on his knees and intensely focused on the worn and ancient looking book.

Being a lawyer he was subconsciously aware that perception was reality for most people. Feeling like he'd already lost precious time and opportunity, Rob wanted an introduction of the truth for his son to be unrestrained by tired grownup notions and traditions. Besides, he felt a sudden realization himself of the infinite value of this volume, now that his offence was leveled and he could see.

"Hey Daddy that's a Bible, isn't it?" His little hands reaching across Rob's to touch the dry leather cover.

"You're right, this is a Bible, but it's even more." Brodie's eyes quickly looked up to search Rob's face.

"This Bible is a book of secrets," he paused, "mysteries", his voice got even lower, "and wisdom."

"Wisdom," Brodie repeated like he was in a trance and trying to wrap his tired brain around such a concept.

"Yes wisdom. It's like a power to know what to do and make the right choices, even when others don't understand what you're doing. This wisdom is for boys and daddies …" Slowly looking over at Elle, who was probably more entranced than Brodie could possibly be, "and mommies. These secrets are for anybody who is willing to look inside and study it."

Unbeknownst to everyone sitting there in front of the fireplace, history was in the making at that moment in the Larson home. Life would never and could never be the same. A father's prayers and a boy's prayers had found their mark that day, and life from beyond this world was already growing.

"Are you going to open up that book and share some of those mysteries with your wife and son?" Elle sounded playful and was smiling.

"Yeh Daddy, can you tell us some secrets?"

Rob grinned, "Well you guys are pretty special people to me so I guess I could find you something to think about while you drift off to sleep tonight. Let's see here … hmmm." Flipping the heavy cover back he started turning pages in chunks and then narrowed his search somewhere closer to the middle of the volume.

"Ah here it is." The pages stopped with one leaf still cradled in his right hand.

"What did you find Daddy?" Brodie was up on his knees with both hands on his father's forearm.

"This is the book of Proverbs and my Dad used to read me awesome things out of this when I was just a boy. Here are a couple of lines I remember that I think you'll really like."

Just then Rob turned and looked right at Brodie. "Always remember this son, these are mysteries and so they're not meant to be ..." He paused looking for the right picture, "they're not meant to be like unimportant things just laying around on the floor. These are treasures and they're hidden, so the mystery part of them makes them something to be investigated and not easy to find."

"Remember how Mommy did a treasure hunt for you and the guys at your last birthday party?"

"Yeh it was so cool!"

"That's right it was so cool but it was a challenge too. It wasn't easy but you guys just kept searching because you knew there was something worth finding. That's sort of the way things are in this book except it's a million times more."

Rob tried to sound a little dramatic although that was more Elle's specialty, but coming from him it registered big with his audience.

Clearing his throat just before he read made Elle smile. She knew her husband well enough to know this was an old reflex of his used to cover up any discomfort. It was true. Rob did feel a peculiar nervousness as he ventured out, leading his family into a whole world that until now, he had ignored.

"Proverbs chapter three, verses five and six says, 'Trust in the Lord with all your heart and lean not on your own understanding. In all your ways acknowledge Him and He will direct your paths.' Hmmmm." Rob paused thoughtfully. It seemed that the words triggered a specific thought for him.

Brodie looked from the pages up to his dad's face and seized on the quiet moment with keen interest. "Dad you're right!" he said emphatically.

"I am?" Rob grinned breaking from his deep train of thought. "What am I so right about son?" wondering at what inspired Brodie's inference.

"It's just like you said Dad," and with all the optimism his face could muster he gave his most positive thought on his father's scripture reading. "Everything you just read is like a total mystery to me and I can tell it's gonna be real hard to figure out."

Both Elle and Rob were stunned for a second and then broke into laughter. Brodie was instantly pleased with himself having inspired such a reaction and so he threw himself into the family hysterics with pleasure.

It was the end of a big day for Rob and his family. Whether it was the warmth of the fireplace, the late hour of the evening, the weight of the freshly unfolded words from his father or all of the above, there was a sense of intoxication with life in the Larson home.

Rob's mind drifted into a restful sleep that night, content with the overwhelming peace and surprisingly unconcerned with his inability to understand it all. With the end of the day came a secret transfer of confidence from all his own ambitious plans to an infinite design. What amazing hope lay in his heart. What an unspeakable rest now secured his soul.

Chapter 10

"Good morning, good morning everyone!" Rob
strolled into the kitchen with a cheerful energy and headed
straight for Elle, giving her a loving kiss.

"Mmmm, hi you," he almost whispered.

"Well good morning to you mister," Elle came back
happily ruffled and love struck, almost forgetting the eggs
she was tending. Brodie watched the whole thing smiling
quietly over his bowl of cheerios.

"I was just about to send Brodie upstairs to get you out
of bed for work," Elle mockingly scolded, shaking her
spatula in the air.

"I know. I don't think I ever remember having such a
deep sleep," he said as he started peeling an orange. Then
like he came to a sudden conclusion, "Yes I feel great
Elle."

"Good for you," she laughed looking at him and
shaking her head. He was like this different man but yet it
was the same Rob.

"How are you this morning Catcher?"

"Great Dad." Brodie had a mouth full of cereal and milk went flying with each word. "I beat you to breakfast today right?" His chipmunk cheeks were in a pinched grin trying to hold their contents.

"You're a winner son," Rob patted his head pulling up a chair beside him and gave a satisfied sigh, "ahhh man I slept great."

"Yeh me too Dad."

"Good."

Neither Brodie nor Elle knew that Rob had not slept in but instead; he woke up alert to a desire to search the ancient manuscript for more. A fire was kindled in his heart now that burned strong. It interrupted the very temperament of his previously trusted thought process and that was saying a lot considering the amount of confidence Rob had invested in his own intellect.

"Okay so what's the plan today?" enthusiastically rubbing his hands together Rob directed his gaze at his six year old boy busily shoveling cereal in his tiny mouth.

His eyes went big with desire to reply to his Dad's question but with the timing of the question and his mouth at full capacity, Elle jumped in moving to the table with a plate full of bacon and eggs for her and Rob.

"Well, here's what I've got going on today: first I'm going to drop Brodie off at school and then head to the café; Meredith is going to meet me at the café for lunch and I'm going to try to persuade her to join the choir for the Christmas production because we need some more altos; and then I'm going to come home and make my two favorite guys a big dinner. What do you think about that?" She finished just in time to put her first fork full of breakfast and look searchingly at the other two.

Rob never had a chance to respond because Brodie had just come up for air from his cereal bowl with a burst.

"Okay, okay I'll tell you what. Guess what? Guess what I'm doing Daddy? And you can listen to this too

Mommy." They both exchanged a playful but subtle snicker as they enjoyed their breakfast, and their chirpy son.

"Alright we're listening," Rob encouraged him on.

"First of all like Mommy said, she's gonna drive me to school and I hope we get there early enough for me to play in the snow a little bit before the bell rings." Brodie had a big grin on his face and looked right at Elle when he said that last part as if to tweak her schedule in his favor.

Just as Brodie was about to fill his parents in on the rest of his imaginary calendar the doorbell rang.

Brodie jumped up running for the door and Elle slowly got up to follow him looking at Rob, "Were you expecting anyone?"

"Nope." He responded carelessly digging into another egg. "It's probably one of Brodie's buddies all excited about winter's first snow."

Brodie got to the door by way of the long hallway and yanked open the door.

"Hey Josh, what's going on?" He asked with much more interest than usual. It could have been the surprise of seeing his friend mixed with the totally new white landscape and the sudden chill of the wind racing across the snow into the front door.

Just then Elle caught up to the scene. "Hi Josh. You look like you're dressed warm."

"Hi Mrs. Larson. I'm walking to school this morning 'cause it's really cool, all the snow." His little frame was almost as wide as it was tall with all the winter gear he had on.

It wasn't hard for Elle to smile broadly at Josh because he looked so comical. "Well I agree that this snow is cool because I'm freezing right now," she said as she had one arm wrapped around herself and pulled Brodie back from the threshold of the door, shivering.

"Come on in Josh." As he stepped in Elle quickly shut the door behind him.

116

"I just came by to see if Brod wanted to walk with me in the snow to school." He was looking right at Brodie but seemed to be asking Elle figuring she was truly the deciding factor.

Brodie immediately turned, "Can I Mom?" His hands clenched in front of him almost like a prayer.

Elle saw it coming a mile away and had already been making a mental list of the snow armor she expected him to wear in defense of the winter conditions.

"Okay but here's the deal, you get all your snow suit on that you had on last evening with me and Daddy ...",

Brodie was already running back down the hallway shouting, "Come on Josh!"

"Hold it Brodie! Let me finish." Brodie and Josh respectfully froze in motion awaiting Elle's orders. "Make sure you have dry gloves, scarf and toque. And bring me an extra pair of mitts so I can put them in your backpack in case you need some dry ones to play with for lunch. Okay ... go."

Like a shot the boys were headed for the mudroom off the back entrance where the family stash of outdoor clothes were warehoused.

"Hey Mr. Larson." Josh sung out as both boys rushed past the breakfast nook where Rob was still calmly finishing breakfast.

The excitement in the boys' voices as they sorted through Brodie's suiting up for the journey to school was music in Rob's ears. He thought about the genuine appreciation these young lives had for the beauty of the winter wonderland and the contrasted bland, unthankful and even annoyed regard many adults grew into for the white stuff.

That thought triggered a business observation with consideration of Forrester. It was a reflex for Rob, kind of like connecting the dots. The same snow many adults considered a nuisance was a big part of the context that made this town a viable tourist attraction. That in turn was more than just money, but a successful and strong economy for this whole area.

Across town that same subject was intensely on the mind of another man, but not in such a pleasant manner. Mayor Carson held the thick, big city paper up to his face so close that all Madge could see was a curl of cigar smoke rolling above him. His stocky pajama clad legs were crossed flipping one slipper violently below.

She could tell something was wrong. He had been so excited about getting today's copy of *America Now* that he had arranged with Sam at the newsstand to make sure it was at his door first thing. Now he was just grunting and puffing on his cigar at a ridiculous tempo.

Suddenly he smashed the paper down onto the table in a heap and between clenched teeth declared, "That's it Madge! We're ruined!" He pulled the cigar out of his mouth and locked it between his stubby fingers, gesturing widely as if to include everything. "All I've worked and sacrificed to build for this town is … pluuuggggh," his tongue stuck out with a rude noise signifying – down the drain.

Madge knew it was serious but as accustomed as she was to the sight of Harry in the morning with his long strands of hair standing up on end, she couldn't help but giggle, not sure if it was his resemblance to all three stooges at once or the audacity of his reference to his work and sacrifice.

Madge knew better than anyone, although it wasn't really considered a secret. Harry didn't work at being the Mayor of Forrester but rather he worked at enjoying the privileges of being mayor. That was the extent to which his finely tuned constitution could bear anything remotely considered as work.

"This is serious Madge!" He didn't appreciate her giggle. Not when his world was falling apart.

"Oh alright, what's the problem now Harry?" Madge

resigned from her amusement and shuffled her furry
slippers over to the coffee pot.

Not forsaking her trademark animal print, she had on
an uncomfortably tight looking tiger print negligee with
a sheer housecoat over top. Radical yes, but even now it
seemed to work its magic on her husband as he easily got
distracted from tragedy he was spiraling into.

"Harry?"

"Whaa? Oh yeh, it's terrible, just terrible. Look at
this Madge! I just knew there was something about
that reporter Jenkins." He almost spit his name out
with a bitter snarl. "Didn't I say there just seemed to be
something about that big city jerk I didn't trust?" His
hands were out like he was just hoping she'd remember.

Stirring her coffee she pursed her lips and looked up
trying to recall, "Nope, I never heard you say anything like
that" she whined. "In fact you said …".

Harry quickly interrupted her, "Never mind what I said
Madge, just look at this right on page six of a national
paper. A national paper for Pete's sake! I'm telling you
we're done."

He moaned and shook his head. Madge shuffled over
to the table, coffee in hand and began reading under the
heading he pointed to.

Christmas Town U.S.A. Abandons Orphan. She
glanced to the bottom of the article where it gave credit
for the article and sure enough, by Stuart Jenkins. Harry
was staring right through her and seemed to be holding his
breath.

"Will you just relax Harry and eat something. I can't
read with you having a heart attack in front of me," she
sort of sang in her nasally tone. Madge's voice was as
unmistakable as her hiccup laugh.

Impatiently Harry grabbed a sausage off the plate with
his fingers and began biting at it angrily, grunting every
once in a while. It was a wonder how he could tell the

difference between his fingers and the swollen meat.

Madge couldn't help but spy on him from under the blonde curls that hung down in front of her face. It wasn't that the piece wasn't of great concern to her but her man was just so ... undeniably Harry Carson, the original.

"What can I get you ladies for lunch?" Elle's dimples were such a warm welcome to Meredith and Lacey as they stepped into Murdock's Café.

"Oh I just love your smile Elle." This was a rare expression coming from the usually quiet and conservative woman. Her own beautiful smile being such an uncommon sight only further egged on the perky blonde hostess.

Looking down over the counter at Lacey, whose hand was tightly clutching her mother's, "Lacey I've got tuna salad sandwiches, chicken sandwiches, I've got peanut butter and jam sandwiches, aaaannnnd ... I've got Brodie's favorite sandwich of all time." Just the mention of Brodie's name shook all the timidity out of our tiny frame.

"You got Bodie's fav'rite sam-mich?"

"Yes, I sure do. Do you want to know what it is?"

Lacey had her free hand offering a finger to her mouth and she nodded eagerly, exposing her baby teeth.

Elle absolutely enjoyed Lacey. She often wondered what the sex of her baby was that she carried after Brodie. It was about a year and a half after he was born that she found out she was expecting again. The joy only lasted about four months until she miscarried but the sorrow has silently dragged on these past four years. She needed to deal with the whole matter in a strong way, which until now had not included Rob.

Brodie's simple faith and expectation in seeing his younger sibling had brought more hope and healing than anything else. It was like he could freely see both sides of life and often imagined Grampy Clint bouncing the little one on his knee.

"It's a peanut butter and banana sandwich!" She found herself going on autopilot for just a split second but her power to live in the moment broke through.

"Yes, dat's what I want Mommy," her big eyes looking up to Meredith.

"All right Honey, you tell Mrs. Larson that's what you'd like and remember to say 'please'".

"Ms. Larson, that's what I like. The peanut butter and nana. Peez."

"Sweetie by all means that's what you're going to get." Looking up to Meredith, "She's such a darling Mare."

Just then Joanne came up to the counter for a peak. "Hi beautiful. Would you like some milk with your sandwich?"

Lacey was getting her confidence up now and responded quickly, "Yes peez".

Meredith looked down at the precious life in her hand and was overwhelmed with thankfulness despite all the heartbreak and challenges she'd been through to get to this place. This was a safe place such as she hadn't known in a long time.

After finishing up with the lunch order, Elle insisted that her guests sit down and relax. Meredith wanted to pay for her own ticket but knew she wasn't going to argue with those dimples of Elle's.

Especially when Joanne chimed in, "Meredith you and Lacey go sit down and let me serve you. You too Elle! I've got this and you need to take a break." She emphasized her words with a mock sternness.

Laughing, Elle pulled off her apron and dropped it behind the counter. "Okay you heard her Mare. We better do what Momma says or we're going to get in trouble."

For the next hour the two and a half ladies enjoyed a delicious lunch of soup, sandwich, salad, and ended off with Joanne's famous scones and loose-leaf tea. Time went quickly as they connected on a level beyond commonplace chatter. Neither cared much to discuss material things or people and their doings. They found themselves meeting in the arena of idea and principle. It wasn't the usual conversation one would expect between two friends and they sensed that they had the genesis of something special that they'd both longed for.

Elle took the opportunity to apply some pressure and recruit Meredith for the choir. "Okay I know you're busy and have a lot of stuff going on but I want you to think about joining our choir and singing in the Christmas production at our church."

"I don't know Elle. That really sounds like a big commitment and besides, I've never sung in a choir before. I don't know how to read music and the truth is, I'm not sure I can pull it off."

She was gently wiping around Lacey's mouth and it was obvious she was used to the process.

"Mare. There's no sense trying to fool me. I've been around you enough to know that every time there's music playing you start humming or singing the alto part. Like just a few minutes ago you were doing backups for James Taylor when Lacey and I were talking about her new shoes."

Both girls laughed and Lacey kicked up her one shoe for another look.

Sweetly persistent, Elle knew that now was the time if Meredith was going to join because they really only had four weeks left before the church began its weeklong musical presentation. The Christmas production was always a big deal with people of Forrester. The church Elle and Rob attended was known for its choir production while on the other end of town the Forrester First Baptist always had a great Christmas play. Almost all the townsfolk, whether they were church going people or not, found their way to at least one presentation of each production. It was the official baptism of the town into the spirit of Christmas for that year.

The general thought was basically that the united contributions of its people in honor of the true meaning of Christmas resulted in the commercial blessing on the town's secular efforts. Strangely enough, this thinking sat well with a variety of people. Of course those with a Christian faith found it a most natural fit but even the superstitious found it parallel to throwing salt over their shoulder or knocking on wood. No one cared to argue with the prosperity the town from being known as Christmas Town U.S.A. and a great place to go skiing.

"Okay Elle. Where do I sign up?" She relented.

"Oh do you mean it?" Elle clapped her hands and bounced in her seat. Her excitement was worth the answer Meredith thought as she enjoyed the sight of Elle's flashing smile and wrinkled nose.

"Well what else can I say? You're the most determined salesperson I've ever had to deal with," she said laughingly.

"Stop Mare." Elle protested with a fun pout. "I wasn't hard on you was I?"

And before Mare could admit to her excitement about singing with her friend, Elle went to work justifying her hard sell. "It's true we need the help, and especially in the alto department, but truthfully, I think you need this opportunity Mare." She smiled and nodded her head.

"I knew that's why you were encouraging me to join. That's why you're such a good friend Elle and I appreciate it."

"Awwww!" Elle spontaneously half stood up and reached over Lacey to hug her friend.

Meredith responded gratefully and thankfully. She quietly thanked God for what had become a trusted island of comfort in her life. "Whew, okay, now reality is setting in and I just got a wave of nervousness."

Elle laughed at her. "Girl you're going to do great. I just know it."

They finished their lunch making plans to get together with the music director that night. Elle had already cleared things with Angela Berry concerning Meredith before she even asked her and Angela was quite excited to think they possibly had another alto, not an easy thing to come by in this small town.

Angela had taught music many years and made the younger woman feel at ease as she progressively took her through some simple scales and intervals. Elle sat by quietly supportive and hopeful. She held Lacey on her knee so Mare could concentrate.

The audition ended with an obvious affirmation when Angela spun around on her piano bench and exclaimed, "Well praise the Lord, we've got a new alto in the choir and I think we just may have another soloist too!"

Elle erupted into a celebrative dance with Lacey and Meredith couldn't help but release the biggest smile she'd accomplished in a long time.

"Oh my. My goodness Ms. Berry! Do you really think so?" Unconsciously she was patting herself as if to calm her heart from all the excitement.

That night Angela spoke some much-needed confidence into Meredith. Elle celebrated with her like a true friend. It was an uncommon appreciation for another human being's success. The kind that is unhindered by any jealousy, envy or vanity. It was a pure seed of impression realized for another's gift.

Angela was truthful in her appraisal with no false compliments. She advised her in the areas she felt she could improve and then handed her a stack of sheet music along with a CD to practice with.

Before Meredith could protest about not being able to read, Angela encouraged her, "Now most of my choir can't read a note so don't worry if you can't read music. Just listen to the CD over and over and memorize your part. That'll be much more effective anyway and then you can just concentrate on singing from your heart."

Meredith was so excited she could hardly get to sleep that night. She finally fell asleep whispering prayers of blessing on her friend Elle.

"Father God thank you for bringing Elle into our life. She's been such a good friend and blessing. Please bless her God. Bless her with the thing that she desires most. Thank you God. Thank you."

Chapter 11

Rob's day was already off to an unusual start with Elle and Brodie out the door before he even finished his coffee. It was perfect though because he was enjoying both the quiet of the moment and the unusual peace he felt around him. It was like a protective layer he had always longed for but somehow never knew existed. There was no denying it was here now. He smiled to himself just as his cell phone rang.

"Rob. It's Carson."

He knew before he answered who it was from the caller I.D. As was Rob's habit though, he answered with the suitable greeting of that time of day and then his full name. Harry secretly found it irritating that he had to introduce himself after hearing, "Good morning. This is Rob Larson. Can I help you?" He figured he was too important to not be quickly and easily identified, especially by Rob, and this morning it was especially frustrating.

"Did you happen to get a look at the *America Now* today?" There was a sharp bite to his voice that was unusual.

"No Mayor I'm still at home and I don't get that paper."

"Well you need to get a copy as fast as you can and read our friendly Mr. Stuart Jenkins' article on page six. It's about our fair town of Forrester and you should be so happy that it's ... NOT ON THE FRONT PAGE!" His voice bawled over the phone.

Rob was taken off guard because never before had Harry ever lost it to the point of going into a shouting frenzy. Something was wrong in paradise. He didn't even have a chance to inquire of the matter because Mayor Carson maintained his roaring decibel and laid out the whole jest of Jenkins' article.

"He's told the whole nation that Christmas town U.S.A. has no room for this UNFORTUNATE," his tenor was viciously sarcastic, "little orphan boy, who's been rejected by his family and now the community that so arrogantly heralds itself as having the sole license on the spirit of Christmas! Oh it gets better!"

"Listen to this and I quote: 'There is an odd parallel between the traditional tale of the Bethlehem-ish version of the winter holiday and modern day Forrester. As legend has it there was no room in the Inn for what we understand was an unwed mother and her child. Here's hoping for something better than a manger, or some shack for this forsaken four year old. Hope may not be enough though. Mayor Carson proudly gives his assurance that every inch of available real estate is already dedicated to the well paying tourists fueling the town's economy. To reflect its true spirit, Forrester might more aptly wear the informal moniker *Commercial Town U.S.A.*'"

"Can you believe that? I never said such a thing! Never!" He shouted his defense as though the whole world stood pointing a condemning finger.

When Harry finally needed to suck in a much-needed

breath, Rob interjected an empathetic "That's terrible!" In hopes that it would help pacify his stout, troubled client. It really was a potentially very bad thing for the whole area and Rob's mind could quickly forecast the fallout of such a media assault on the town's image.

The strange thing was that the explosive nature of the matter seemed to have no effect him. Not in a careless or irresponsible way, but Rob was assured that the calm was greater than the storm. It was probably a good thing he couldn't see Mayor Carson on the other end of the exchange, still in his shiny tight robe, pacing his kitchen floor, beet red and puffing his cigar like a mad man. The unflinching calm Rob had mixed with the cartoon like picture at Carson's house might have just pushed him over the edge into pure laughter. Harry's wound could not have tolerated that strong of salt.

For a half an hour Mayor Carson scolded and blamed Rob for the whole article. The premise of his accusation being that as a lawyer he should have more professionally and discreetly handled Evelyn's complaint in the diner. Rob noticed the unfamiliar ground he personally held and that he felt absolutely no need to defend himself.

Occasionally he heard himself say, "I understand Mayor" and "I regret the concern this has caused you". For the most part though he was growing into the awareness of how secure he now felt. Even when Mayor Carson began threatening to pull the whole account of Forrester's legal work from him, Rob calmly took Harry's side and said, "I'd I hope you wouldn't Mayor but I understand you want to do the best for the township."

That seemed to finally pull the plug on the fury Harry had erupted into. He stopped pacing and could feel his blood pressure abate. The line was quiet for a moment because for the first time, Harry didn't quite know what to say.

Feeling the need to strike some kind of resolution, his tone normal now, "Rob, we've got to do something and we've got to do it fast." For the first time in probably years, he made a completely honest statement. "You know better than anyone in this town what this kind of publicity could turn into. You're a smart guy Rob and me ... well ... even I know how this thing could snowball into a disaster the town might never recover from."

Rob could almost hear the man's shoulders drooping over the phone. "Mayor, if you would, give me chance to come up with some ideas and then let's meet in a quiet place with the executive. As your council, let me advise you not to talk to anyone until we get together."

All of sudden Harry felt like a whipped pup. "Yeh okay. Trust me I won't be talking to anyone."

Rob had a thought, "Have the guys clear their schedule for a couple of hours tomorrow morning and all of you meet me at Murdock's Café around eight. They don't open until nine thirty and we'll be mostly away from any onlookers." There were other reasons too, but that was enough for the distraught Mayor to process.

The reply was simple. "Yup. Okay. See you tomorrow."

Harry took Rob's advice about not talking to anyone to the utmost. He phoned Janice his secretary and had her make the confidential appointments with the town's executive, which was three phone calls: Tom Selman, Scott Burgess and Wayne Doyle. He also gave her strict charge not to bother him with absolutely anything the rest of the day. He briefly told her what had been printed in *America Now* with next to zero emotion and then told her he could not be disturbed the rest of the day so he could focus on a solution to this crisis. That amounted to him staying hidden in his house all day, wrapped up in his robe and following Madge around like a sad puppy.   Unfortunately for Janice, she had to field dozens and dozens of calls that ranged from outraged business owners, to fearful citizens all concerned about the misrepresentation of themselves circulating around the country. It was as if the Grinch had just showed up on the doorsteps of City hall. Janice was quite sharp, in contrast to her boss, and more accurately filled the position of an executive assistant considering that she ran his office for the better part. This situation though was another matter entirely and she found herself deferring wholly to the absent figure head in hopes that Carson would be able to find a Christmas miracle.

Rob literally climbed a tree. He phoned Dorothy at the office and gave her a brief outline of what was happening. She already knew because her and Phil did have a subscription to the paper and had read the abrasive piece that morning over their early breakfast.

"I won't be coming into the office today so please make my apologies and reschedule my appointments for another day. I hate to dump this on you Dorothy but I need some time to sort this thing out."

"It's no problem at all Rob and please let me know if there's anything else I can do."

As they hung up he thought of how grateful he was for her. She did excellent work and above all, she was trustworthy.

Swinging his long legs over the edge of the deck Rob thought, if the world could see him right now they'd think he was crazy, considering everything that was going on. He'd quickly changed out of his suit into a pair of jeans and flannel shirt after his conversation with Mayor Carson. Like his movements were pre-arranged he threw on a warm jacket, grabbed the ancient manuscript and marched out the back door to the tree house. The cool breeze off the snow mixed with the warm sun on his face added to the feeling he already possessed of being in the perfect place at the right time. Lightly caressing the old leather cover on his lap he looked up, much like a boy who felt at ease talking to his father.

"I'm thankful to You God. I'm thankful for the things

I've come to understand in these last few days." He paused, "I think it's taken me far too long to come to this place and I've missed out on … I've missed precious moments with the people I love."

Rob's head dropped just for a moment but then like the regret was quickly washed away, his face lifted with a smile. "You've blessed me God. You've given me this chance to live and …", he weighed his words, "I know you've given me this time to love." He patted the Bible resting closed, "It's like this Book has come to life but I know, it's always been there for me. I guess it's me who has come alive to Your Word."

He let the thought of what he'd just said bounce around in his heart while he calmly appreciated the winter scene of his back yard. The snow glistened and sparkled at countless points while the busyness of tiny birds feeding acted like a moving ornamental display, their vibrant colors such a contrast against the white backdrop.

"Father God, I need help. Well it's not so much for me that I'm concerned, it's this town and the people in it. It's this little boy Andrew who seems to have no one, and it's even people like Harry Carson. I can tell he's scared God and I know what it feels like to feel alone."

Rob felt confident he was talking to the right Person so his vulnerability was natural and not guarded with any of his own intellectual offerings. "The truth is I really don't even know what the problem is so how do I ask You for the answer? Sure I know that this article looks like a direct attack on Forrester and its people, but … there's something more, isn't there God?"

His head cocked to one side and looking up, he had to squint because of the sunlight. It was a picture that would have been the delight of his father. And between a great cloud of witnesses and God who delights in His children, it's not so difficult to believe that the picture is circulating in heaven. Clint believed for it.

Clearing his throat and focusing on the worn Book, he

grabbed it on both sides, "I need direction from Your Word God. Please help me and I'll take what You give me and try to help others."

Flipping open the large Bible he automatically began navigating toward the book of Proverbs. The pages made a light, cheerful sound in the wind. His eyes fell on a verse that had been underlined by either his father or grandfather he figured. Proverbs 11:14 "Where no counsel is, the people fall: but in the multitude of counselors there is safety." He thought about how his father's counsel, even from the grave, had moved mountains for him personally.

The scheduled meeting tomorrow morning included the Mayor and his sidekicks. Rob wasn't being critical of them but on the other hand he had no confidence that these men contained anything that would mirror this type of counsel.

"Okay God. We need wise counsel, but who?"

Instantly his mind went to a man whom probably a few days ago he would never have considered. Pastor James Hunston. Although he was the pastor of The Hope Center where he and his family attended, Rob had been quietly critical of his philosophy. Now, out of the blue, Rob realized a new respect and appreciation for the man.

The thought of Pastor Hunston precipitated into another face and that was of Dr. David Murphy. Rob had done some legal work a few years ago for Forrester First Baptist Church and in the process had several meetings with the church's older pastor. He was of a more traditional background, but Rob learned that the clerical collar he wore could fool you into thinking he was dry and irrelevant. Dr. Murphy was anything but unconnected to the modern world and its people. He had a dry wit that he used well, he spoke three different languages that he had exercised usefully in his early years abroad as a missionary, and despite his senior office he loved to play with the children.

Perfect, Rob thought. Funny how these guys were right under my nose all the time. Still someone was missing. He couldn't escape the feeling that there was someone else.

Just then a breeze caught the yellowed pages. His place lost in Proverbs, he looked down to see more lines and notes in the book called Ecclesiastes. It was the ninth chapter and his eyes were drawn to the word 'wisdom' in verse fifteen. "Now there was found in it a poor wise man, and he by his wisdom delivered the city; yet no man remembered that same poor man."

A contented pause quietly rested in front of Rob. He could feel his expectation growing. There was something to what he'd just read that was more linked to the solution than his mind could grasp and he knew it. Suddenly a name came to him that he hadn't heard in years, maybe since he was a boy. It was his father's old friend Kenneth Henry. That was it!

Clint Larson met up with Kenneth Henry when he first joined the military as a young man. Kenneth was almost ten years older but the two became fast friends. They had been moved around a lot in occupational assignments for those three years, which meant they got to experience many new places and things together.

It could be very lonely for a young man on those long tours overseas and some gave into the temptations that ended with cruel consequences. It wasn't that way for these two buddies. They shared the same faith and became an influential force among their fellow soldiers.

Their friendship continued after getting out of the military and was such a strong bond that Kenneth left his southern roots for a spread about ten miles west of Forrester. He came from a farm in Mississippi and decided to make a 'go of it' on a combination ranch-farm in the rolling hills that surrounded the town. It wasn't a popular idea being that the area had such a long history of commerce in lumber. Still that didn't bother the independent thinking southerner.

Rob remembered seeing him often in the early years of his life. In fact he was Uncle Ken to him in those days. Taller than his father, he must have been at least six foot two and lean as a rake but there was a rugged strength to his athletic build. If it wasn't for his dark skin you would have thought Clint and Ken were brothers the way they were together. Rob was startled at how much he remembered of the quiet man.

In those days things were changing fast for the area. It was the mid-seventies and the industry that everyone around Forrester had come to depend on was not reviving as hoped but now most certainly found itself at its end. A town hall meeting had been called because the leaders were panicking, much like today. People were moving out of town in a mass exodus and the bank had to foreclose on the family dream. The pessimism in the air was growing into a death sentence for the town.

A town hall meeting would be more or less a last stand for the presiding mayor and a forum to excuse himself from any responsibility for the inevitable demise of the things. It was the most negative and hopeless speeches anyone could endure. When the floor was opened up for questions or comments, the room was painfully silent except for one man.

Kenneth Henry had been seated at the back of the room and now he stood up stretching out his lanky form. His calm baritone voice resonated easily as he addressed the room.

"It seems to me that y'all are fixed on what cha' don't have instead of what cha' do. Sure anyone can see that the mill don't have the business it used to have but changin' times jus' mean we got to change the way we see things. Take my garden now. I got to go at diff'r'ent today then three months ago when it was jus' turned dirt."

A few of the town's folk chuckled at Ken's simple approach but he went on anyway.

134

"Here's what I see and you can do what 'cha want with it. Ya'll pulled down a pretty piece of timber off those mountains. Some folks from the outside think you turned what God made beautiful into an eye sore but you fed your children and made a life. Now it looks like you got just a bunch a' bare hills." Kenneth rubbed his chin hard while some even began to turn in their chairs to listen.

"Well now, the last time me and Clint Larson saw bare hills like that was over in Europe. And you know what those folks did? They set up lodges and little boxes on cables to carry skiers up the slopes, and charged them money to do it! Now I'm not sayin' that's what 'cha ought' a do. That's just one fella's mind on the matter but I do know that there ain't nothing good gonna come out' a rollin' over and givin' up. I said my piece."

With that he turned and gently walked out of the school auditorium. Kenneth didn't get to enjoy the uproar that quickly ensued after his departure.

The room was almost immediately split. Some were mocking the man's over simplified solution to their demise but others had their faith ignited and instantly began to see a light at the end of the tunnel. The outcome of the meeting is history now.

A select few caught a hold of the dream and invested in the town's future as a winter resort get-away. Those few were well rewarded for their ability to see what others couldn't. The naysayers on the other hand lost any investment they did have in Forrester and became a part of the faded history, much like the quiet old mill in Gordon's Park.

The town was resuscitated with a renewed vision and purpose. The economy of the area boomed and soon caught the attention of the whole nation as the postcard perfect place to celebrate the holidays and enjoy winter sports. Business savvy storefront owners responded in kind with chalet and North Pole themed décor as the new Forrester vogue. It worked for everyone.

The mysterious chapter of the whole account is that it seemed no one remembered the man who with a few words turned the fate of the entire region from certain demise to brilliant success. It was the kind of idea that CEOs and company presidents become famous and celebrated for. The kind of celebration that translates into huge paychecks and lavish year-end bonuses.

The parallel between the account of the man in the book of Ecclesiastes and Kenneth was remarkable Rob thought.

He warmed in the absolute sense of direction he had for the meeting tomorrow morning, and yet it didn't bother him in the least that he still didn't have a material answer for the crisis they were all in.

"It's all going to work out," he thought and then suddenly he got an inspiration that had completely nothing to do with the imposing problems at hand.

Rob laughed like a little kid as he whirled around on the platform, pulling up his feet and sitting cross-legged. There was a look of mischief on his face, his eyes darting from branch to board and from trunk to maze of grid shaped rope. He scanned every opening in the fort as if making mental measurements and even when he was hurrying back to the house he kept spinning around for last mental snapshots.

"Oh this is going to be great," he said chuckling out loud.

The early afternoon went by quickly for Rob as he spent his time searching two hardware stores and Gables Department store for all the supplies he needed. He gave Elle a quick call and she was taken off guard to find out that he didn't go into the office. Rob neatly smoothed it over with the simple rationale that it was an easy day and he could make the calls from home. It was totally true. He admitted to himself that a short time ago it would have been a horrible day but now everything was different. It was a great day!

Rob told Elle that since he was off he would pick up Brodie, which worked out perfect for her. After having lunch with Meredith and Lacey things had got really busy at the café and she could use an extra hour or two to help her Mom.

"That's great Honey. You take all the time you need. Catcher and I will be just fine."

"Hey son. How was school?" Rob almost yelled through the open passenger window as he sat parked right in front of Brodie's school. Josh was at Brodie's side and they were deep in some conversation until he heard his father's voice.

"Dad!" Instantly Brodie ran up to the window with Josh right behind him. "What're you doin' here Dad?" He had a big grin on his face and his nose was already running.

"Guys I've got the coolest project in the world going on, but I need a couple of helpers."

Brodie yanked the door open, "We could help you Dad. Me and Josh!"

"Are you serious? Would you boys help me out?" Rob was acting like one of them. Josh just stood there grinning. He'd never seen Mr. Larson like this so it was a welcome change.

"Do you wanna help Josh?" Brodie was already leaning in the front seat.

"Yeh sure. What do we got to do?"

Turning back to his Dad, "Yeh Dad, what are we doin'?"

Rob didn't give them any details because he was enjoying the prolonged excitement and sense of adventure that had overtaken them. "You'll see. It's going to be crazy fun and AWESOME!"

With that both boys shouted and bounced into the car. The boys were so hyped that Rob had a difficult time communicating with Josh's mom when he called to let her know that he picked them up and was heading home.

"Okay guys come around back here and check this out." They had all piled out of the black sedan, now parked in front of the house.

"What it is Dad? Are we gonna ... whoa!"

Rob could see the wonder in their eyes when he popped the trunk and the westerly sun glinted on all the packages.

"Wow. These are Christmas lights and ..."

"Look Brod! It's a giant star!"

"Cool." The two breathed out in synchronized pleasure.

"Do you guys want to know what we're doing?"

"Yeh!"

"I bet 'cha I know," said the other.

"Grab as many boxes as you can because we're going to light up the tree house like you can't imagine."

"Yes!" Brodie exclaimed like he just won a game, bringing his clenched fist and elbow down into the air. Of course with the big mitts you had to guess that there was a fist in there.

Rob had bought so many lights, cables and decorations, that it took all three of them close to a half an hour just to get all their supplies into the back yard. Once everything was lying on the ground at the base of the tree Rob reviewed the project with his partners and then gave them a loose plan. It was loose because this was new for all of them.

"Okay guys, I'll go get the big ladder. Josh how about if you start taking all the red lights up into the fort and Brodie, I think we're going to need Grampy's hammer. Do you mind if we use it on this project?"

Brodie's mouth was open. This was too good to be true. Working on a project with his Dad and best friend, and now a reason to use Grampy Clint's hammer. He was already running to the house when he shouted back, "I'll go get it right now!"

The three of them worked the rest of the afternoon and

finally had to call it quits around suppertime. They all decided to keep their adventure a secret until they could officially plug it in for the big reveal.

"When are we gonna finish Dad?"

"Well tomorrow's Friday so then we have the whole day Saturday to work on it. How does that sound?"

"Cool! I know we'll get it done before it gets dark and then we'll light it up. Right?" Brodie was looking up as they walked toward the backdoor of the house.

"You got it Son. But now remember; let's not say a word about this to your Mom, okay? That way she'll be so surprised when we hit the switch."

"For sure. Oh I can't wait!" Brodie giggled with excitement as he tamed himself down enough to come in for the night.

It was good for the tree-house gang that Elle was preoccupied with her plans to go pick up Meredith for a choir audition. The Larson men felt confident that given the busy night she had away from home, it would work to their advantage in keeping the extreme Christmas makeover in the backyard top secret. Anything really good always has a sense of timing.

Chapter 12

It was a somber group that was gathering at Murdock's Café. Joanne had arrived at six thirty to start on her baking for the day but knowing that Rob was having a special business meeting, she had the coffee and some croissants already waiting. Mayor Carson was actually one of the last of his crew to arrive. Tom Selman, the town treasurer, was one of the first to show up. Though he was usually a reserved, pensive man, today his aim seemed to be to unburden his soul of all that ailed him. And with Tom that always had something to do with money.

"Oh good morning everyone." He sputtered like it was something he always had to say but resented more so today. "Rob did you did you hear that The Kingston and Martha's Landing have had their phones ringing off the hook?"

"Oh?"

"Not with bookings, no, but with cancellations and long time customers threatening to cancel!"

His browed furrowed deeply emphasizing his pinched face and long nose. He was not a handsome man but the fear he now wallowed in, made him most unpleasant Rob thought. He was just about to say more when Joanne rescued the moment by butting in.

"Tom you must be cold. Would you like a fresh cup of coffee and how about a croissant with some jam? I just made them."

Tom was always cold and Joanne's coffee sounded good, but the temptation of the breakfast pastry completely distracted him. His tall, poker thin figure was misleading because Tom loved food almost as much as he did money.

Rob was relieved to have him otherwise minded and winked at Joanne as she served him.

Wayne Doyle and Scott Burgess showed up in just as foul a mood as Tom, but none of them came close to the gloomy sulk the honorable Harry Carson walked in with. He wore a felt hat pulled down low on his forehead and long coat that made him look even shorter. Though he usually sported a toothpick when in the public eye, today he was hanging on to his private vice of smoking cigars. He needed all the comfort he could get.

He gave no greeting when he walked in.

Rob cheerfully said, "Good morning Harry."

He just looked over at him while hanging up his coat on the coat rack and grunted. Rolling his cigar around in his mouth he shuffled across the floor to where they were gathering at a long table made up several pulled together.

Some of the other guys gave a sullen 'hello' and 'good morning' as he sat down. Wayne was a refined man and it suited him as the president of a bank. He looked up from his coffee and peering over his square shaped glasses he half whispered, "Ah Harry, you're going to have to put out that cigar in here."

He didn't seem to hear because he took another puff and started into lamenting with the worst looking pout on his face.

Joanne walked up to the table with a big smile on her face and a full serving tray. "Good morning Harry. Here's a coffee for you and a fresh pastry. The cream and sugar are on the table, and here, just put your cigar in here and I'll get rid of that for you."

She stuck an old looking bowl right in front of him and rested her other hand on his back. Harry became like an eight year old freshly reprimanded for not having wiped off his shoes at the door.

"Aw sure ... aw ... thanks Joanne," he mumbled. Harry felt awkward and glanced around the table at the others.

Wayne gave him a look like, *I told you so.* The others took note and reminded themselves that they weren't in a boy's club.

Joanne marched the doomed cigar right out back of her place and threw it in the dumpster. She didn't even want it in the trash in case it kept stinking up her place. She wasn't trying to be hard on Harry and would never intentionally embarrass anyone but on the other hand, she and Harry had a different relationship. From infant to a toddler, Joanne had babysat him many times. Harry had his reasons for not frequenting Murdock's Café and it wasn't because he didn't love the food there.

A surprised look flashed on all the men's faces when Pastor James showed up. He was his usual cheerful self and Rob was already thankful for his attendance for just that reason. As he was taking his seat and thanking Joanne for a coffee the door opened again. This time it was Dr. David Murphy and he was holding the door open for a middle aged woman that none of them recognized.

"Dr. Murphy it's good to see you and thank you for coming." Rob stepped over at once to greet the older man with a handshake and a smile. "And you must be Debbie Eastman?"

"Yes I am," she replied. There was nothing notable about Ms. Eastman. Her appearance and manner were as plain as her expression. She had on a dark grey pantsuit with a light colored blouse and looked much like the schoolteacher everyone's had at some point or another.

"Thank you for coming on such short notice."

"Not a problem."

After he hung up their coats, Rob directed the newcomers to a few empty seats at the table.

Mayor Carson had a strange look on his face and was whispering across the table asking Scott and Tom, "Who in the world is she?" Each of the guys carelessly shrugged their shoulders.

"Most of you know one another but I'd like to

introduce you to Debbie Eastman. Debbie is the director of social services for this area, which includes Forrester. I felt that her expertise and knowledge would be most helpful to us and with any questions we might have. Of course I believe you all know, or at least should know," he was grinning, "the pastors of our churches. This is Dr. David Murphy and Reverend James Hunston." He conducted his hand in the direction of each man respectively as he looked toward Debbie.

Just as Rob was finishing the rest of the introductions the heavy wooden door of the café opened again. A tall gentleman stepped inside and immediately removed his wool knit hat revealing a tight crop of wiry white hair. Glancing about the room he quickly locked in on Rob, the only person standing at the table.

"I apologize for being late. There was quite a snow that fell last night and it's still difficult gettin' around them hills." His voice was soft but low and booming. Kenneth Henry would never tell them that he had stopped to help a young woman who had slid into a ditch trying to drive her children to school.

"It's good to see you." Rob came across the room with his hand outstretched. He felt slightly uncomfortable because this man had always been *Uncle Ken* to him growing up but at his father's memorial he had purposely avoided him for reasons he still didn't fully understand.

He was put at ease though when Kenneth's face lit up flashing his pearly white smile. "Oh my goodness! It's wonderful to see you Rob." He grabbed his right hand almost covering it again with his left. "My, my, my … you look more and more like your pa." There was a great sense of affection coming from him for the younger man.

The reunion was so warm and welcome to Rob's heart that he almost forgot where he was and the business at hand. Out of the corner of his eye he caught a movement from the group to his side. Mayor Carson had his neck craned around almost like an owl and the look on his face was just about as wide-eyed.

"Kenneth I'm so glad you came. Would you please join us?" Rob led him to chair right beside his own and Joanne was already pouring him a coffee.

"Oh thank you dear. That's just what these cold bones could use." He was a most gracious man Rob thought.

"I'm sorry to interrupt Rob but I thought we were going to have a meeting this morning to discuss a critical and confidential problem we're having with … you know … that very critical and confidential *civic* matter."

The mayor's voice had a hoarse, impatient strain to it. Tom joined in now that his belly was full. "Yes Harry needs …", a sharp look corrected him from across the table, "Mayor Carson needs all the *qualified* …", he seemed to throw a skeptical glance in the direction of Kenneth, "people of his team to come together to stem these outrageous accusations and stop the hemorrhaging of our economy."

Mayor Carson cleared his throat as if Tom had already said too much and then taking the reigns again, "I think what Tom's saying is, that maybe you misunderstood the serious nature of …"

"There's no misunderstanding at all Mayor Carson." Rob interrupted with the most respectful and cheerful tone he could muster. He didn't want to allow Harry enough lead so that he might offend the very people that could help him, and with Harry that was a very real possibility.

"Everyone here at this table, who is not on the town counsel, has been brought in at my request, and I thank them all for coming. Not to minimize the problem, let me give a brief summary of what has taken place so everyone can understand the uniqueness of this gathering."

"A little boy by the name of Andrew Richards, who doesn't have any parents, has been living with his Aunt Jenny. Ms. Richards has recently run into some hard times and broken her hip. The doctors believe she will fully recover but this has compounded other hardships

Ms. Richards has endured. She now feels that she can no longer look after her nephew Andrew."

"Obviously that leaves this little boy in a very sad and difficult place. He is not quite five years old. The strange thing is the matter has snowballed into a dramatic public story. The national paper *America Now* has run an article showcasing Andrew as the poster boy for the town of Forrester's heartless neglect of its orphan's. The article if you haven't already seen it is titled, *Christmas Town U.S.A. Abandons Orphan.*" He exhaled a hint of contempt.

"There has already been a flood of cancellations and complaints coming into the hotels, the resorts and rental companies. I've found out from Sheriff Dole that there are more reporters coming into town looking to develop the story and probably hoping to develop the whole 'no room in the inn' angle for their paper or television network."

Mayor Carson had been stone quiet up to this point but now he groaned, "Television? Ohhh!" His voice trailed off in misery. The look on his face was humorous although obviously it best reflected his dispair. His jowls hung loosely around his open mouth with his upper lip slightly protruding and his nose was curled up as puggish as could be. Harry was a sight to behold.

"I'm not going to lie to you," Rob continued, "the way this story is being spun in the media, it's the chink in a moral fabric that these guys love to tear open. Most of them need some kind of Christmas angle for their outlet and this is like blood in the water for a bunch of sharks. They say there's no such thing as bad press but if we try to ignore this and stay quiet, I believe the damage to the character of everything Forrester symbolizes will be its end."

There was just a slight hesitation in his voice now and he smiled. "My Dad always told me and I wish I had listened more, 'A good name is to be chosen above silver and gold.'" Kenneth got a big smile on his face and Rob seemed to feel his approval.

Quickening his pace now for the conclusion of his opening remarks, "There you have it. One little boy's dire circumstances have evolved into a critical state for this whole town."

Suddenly a leading came up into Rob's heart and though he didn't have time to weigh it, he knew it was the right way to go. "All of you are leaders in different respects in the community and I know that each of you can sympathize with the weight of concern Mayor Carson has right now because as you know if this thing continues to spiral downward taking the town of Forrester with it, the media will no doubt want to nail this thing to our leadership."

With a slight pause for a taste of the dramatic as he could see the charge was already being felt at the other end of the table. He finished off, "Mayor Carson will unfairly become the fall guy for this whole mess, and I really don't think anyone of us want it to come to that."

Rob said it rhetorically and saw that he achieved his goal. The table was suddenly united, for different reasons, but nonetheless, united.

Mayor Carson almost came out of his seat. "Okay so now does everyone get it? This is serious! We need to pull together here for the sake of this great town and ... and this little fella. We need to put our heads together and show these people who we really are. We're a great town and we stick together and ... and we stand up for the right thing ... and each other!"

His husky whine sounded more like a panicked plea than a mustering of the troops but it was just the response Rob hoped for, and besides, it was pleasantly odd to hear Harry use the word 'we' that much.

Up until then Mayor Carson and his guys were obviously snubbing the guests Rob had invited. He knew any wisdom they might offer would only be scorned, but now they all seemed desperate for the shelter of even regular town folk.

"Alright then you heard it from the Mayor himself, we need to stand together as a town and do the right thing. Kenneth? What's your take on the situation?"

Rob not only had a confidence that the older man had something to offer but he was sincerely curious to hear what he'd say. It could have been that he was the most senior person at the table or the intangible quality he possessed from years of leadership in the military, but there was an obvious signal that it was Kenneth's turn to come to bat.

In his usual thoughtful manner, his voice seemed to take over the table. "Well now, with all respect," and he nodded in a few directions around the table, "it seems to me that we're a lookin' at the whole matter upside down. This newspaper fella' has done us all a favor by drawin' our attention to a need that it seems, we didn't know about. Now just imagine if this young boy were to be forgotten and neglected by us. My! The crime against this town would be somethin' shameful."

His eyes closed and he shook his head as if to imagine the effect. The depth of expression in Kenneth's face was irresistible.

"No sir! This man done us a good turn. For if this were to be laid to our account … my, my, my! Even the angels couldn't save this town."

He didn't need a lot of words and now straightened up to drive his conclusion home. "The fact is this whole thing needs to be fixed right at the root. We need to help that boy, look after 'im and we need to do it now." His words were like a bucket of ice-cold water on a sleeping soul.

"I couldn't agree more." Dr. Murphy backed the bold remarks. "And I have to say I'm saddened that we needed this wake-up call to care for our own."

"That's my heart too Dr. Murphy and thank you Kenneth for your great insight," Pastor Hunston chimed in. "I think we all agree that we need to make up for lost time and do something collectively to help this young lad."

There was now a hearty and vocal agreement that spread around the table. The miserable look on the town counsels face was now replaced with a doe-eyed look of complete dependence.

"Well that's all fine and good, but what do we do?" Being a bank manager, Wayne's focus was the bottom line and he was no doubt summing up the others' thoughts.

"Yes, we need a plan of action," Mayor Carson added trying to sound like the confident leader.

"Debbie where is Andrew right now?" Rob asked.

"He's staying at one of the only two foster homes I have here in town, but it's only for a few days until I find another home for him, which will be in another county."

"Why do you need to move him out of town so quickly?"

"The families I have here in town all have older children in their teens and without going into details, it's unsuitable for a five year old in either case. There is no place else so I am forced to take him outside the county for more permanent care."

She had been very business-like in her mood up to this point but now her demeanor changed. "He's the sweetest little boy and I have to tell you this is the part of my job I find most painful because the truth is, I don't really see a hopeful future for him."

Mayor Carson saw a light and jumped in, "So then if you can find him a home outside the county, then we're all set! Right? I mean everything is taken care of. Right?"

His face had an ignorant look of glee on it but even his colleagues couldn't hide the distaste they felt for his viewpoint. Dr. Murphy whirled his head to look down the table with the most appalled look on his face and would have let loose with a reprimand but Joanne had just walked up to the table with a hot plate of scones and a fresh pot of coffee.

"Oh come on Harry. Please tell me you didn't just say what I think you did." There was disgust in her voice.

He suddenly reverted to his open mouthed, bewildered look again. "What do you mean?" came his whine.

"I mean you're acting so thick headed it's like you're in a different world. Did you not just hear what these folks said?" Joanne left him no time to reply. Not that he would have anyway.

"The town's only hope and your only hope, that is if you want to keep on being mayor; is that boy! And if they have to take him away from town to get him a home somewhere else, well mister, you can just kiss any hope you've got of coming out of this as Mayor, good bye. Is that plain enough Harry?"

He just gawked at her, mouth still open.

She set the serving items down daintily and then in her usual warm manner said, "I apologize for the interruption everyone," and then turned back toward the kitchen.

The rest the table just looked after her with silent gratitude because it needed to be said and who better than one of the women who had changed many of Harry's diapers. Since his mother wasn't there to reprimand him, Joanne was a fine replacement.

The meeting quickly recovered with that out of the way and soon there were some great ideas put on the table. It was determined that some kind of community event could be used as a fundraiser to set up Andrew's Aunt Jenny so that she could retain custody and keep her home. The more they discussed it, the more the event seemed to naturally tie itself to the Christmas celebration, for many reasons. Both Pastors quickly offered to bring their respective church productions together for a united community effort.

There was a temporary stall on where the event could be held until Kenneth swung his long arm around pointing out the window. "Why it's so natural folks, the answer's right in front of you."

Gordon's Park would be the place and both Pastors determined to work together in morphing Forrester First Baptist's play and The Hope Center's cantata into a community Christmas outdoor musical. No small feat but there was an instantaneous enthusiasm and energy between the two leaders. The town's counsel got on board quickly and soon began presenting solutions freely drawing on their own contacts and resources.

Mayor Carson sat for the first half hour of planning like a spanked brat but even he started to feel the hope that was rising in the room. Not wanting to be left out he volunteered to be the master of ceremony for the big production but Rob quickly and gently prevented that run-away disaster. He thanked Harry but sold the point that considering the delicate nature of the crisis; Dr. Murphy and Pastor Hunston would best host the event in a show of town unity and 'spiritual harmony'.

"Oh, of course, you're right Rob. That makes perfect sense." He was determined not to get in trouble again.

"Hey I got an idea!" Tom lit up. "Mayor Carson could come out at the end of the whole thing in a Santa suit with a big sack full of candy and run around throughout the crowd handing out candy to all the kids."

"Tom! What's that gonna do?" Harry was obviously repelled by the idea and hoping everyone else would help him quickly squash it.

"No, no, that's a great idea Harry." Wayne said.

Then Scott Burgess added his marketing spin on the whole thing. "Seriously Harry, it might be the best light for you to be in since you're kind of being tagged as Scrooge right now. This way you can have more of a hands-on connection with the kids and help repair the town's image."

Mayor Carson looked stunned but by now felt whipped into submission. "Sure, sure. Yeh I'll do the Santa thing. Whatever you guys say."

Rob just chuckled and he could see the amusement on the pastors' faces.

"There's still one problem y'all haven't considered," came Kenneth's deep drawl. "Ms. Eastman here's got to move Andrew now and if that boy leaves town, ain't no program gonna turn the tide of what that news will do. The boy needs to be safe now, not tomorrow." There was a rebuke in his tone and everyone heard it.

"He'll stay with us."

Everyone's head swung around to the counter where Elle stood with her apron on. She had come to the café after dropping Brodie off at school and as always, came in the back entrance through the kitchen. No one had noticed she was even there, not even Rob, but now it was his turn to shock everyone, including himself.

"That's right, Andrew will stay with us until we get everything worked out for Jenny Richards." Looking at Debbie he quickly asked, "Can we make this happen Debbie with some kind of temporary custody order that will satisfy your office?"

"Hey you're the lawyer. Can you pull some strings and make a miracle happen with Judge Thompson? He's not a last minute kind of guy you know and he likes things *by the book.*"

Debbie emphasized the later part as though to create some doubt, but Rob smiled broadly.

"Oh I think Judge Dale Thompson will be happy to see me." With that he looked across the room grinning at Elle who stood there with an amazed look on her face. She looked strikingly beautiful Rob thought.

Chapter 13

As would be expected the first thing Rob did after the meeting was call Jenny. She was still in the hospital because of some minor complications but he had no trouble getting her on the phone.

"That's really great," she responded in a monotone voice as Rob told her of the town's plan to help her and Andrew. Although she didn't sound very excited, he reasoned that the heavy medication she was on would not only dampen the pain but any reaction she might have to good news. The bottom line was, she was on board. After all, why wouldn't she be?

In the months that followed folks would often say they didn't even remember Thanksgiving happening because of the mad dash they found themselves in. The flurry of activity that hit the town almost instantaneously after that meeting was as sudden as a northwester snowstorm. Things typically got busy for Forrester as the town approached Christmas but no one had seen this coming. The usual happenings were set aside to devote all resources to the success of this new benefit, and that was not going over big with everyone in town.

Mayor Carson had more than one fire to put out. Several angry Forresters preferred to keep things the way they had always been. Even though they understood the crisis at hand, they felt his office should be able to make a call, push a button or something to fix the problem. Anything but not "compromise the Forrester Christmas they'd come to hold so dear", as the uppity and ever socially concerned Mrs. Thacker put it. Tradition was not a means but the end for her.

Fortunately there were many that wholeheartedly jumped at the opportunity of helping someone in need and quickly stepped up to the challenge. After all, Christmas was all about giving and shouldn't the people of Forrester epitomize that spirit?

Probably the most fired up person in town was Brodie and with good reason. Not only did he love Christmas but also he took great pleasure in the grand scheme of making something wonderful happen for someone else. The attachment between Brodie and Andrew came naturally and in the mysterious framework of a closeness that seemed as though it was predestined.

Drew was quite shy around men so when Rob met Debbie at the McLaughlin's place to pick him up, he looked scared standing at the front door with his little suit case already packed. Rob considered the fact that the boy's whole world had been turned upside down in the last couple of weeks. Here he was staying with people he didn't know and a myriad of other unknowns he faced alone.

"Hi Drew. It's nice to see you again." Rob tried to sound as pleasant as he could but Andrew's eyes were down and fixed on the stone path in front of him. He didn't move except to squeeze his stuffed puppy even harder to his chest. "Drew we would love it if you'd come stay at our house for a while until your Aunt Jenny is feeling better."

At the name of his Aunt he looked up and Rob thought he could see a glimmer of hope. He had on a new pea coat that the foster family must have given him. He made the foot-high snow banks that lined the path look large, as he seemed to contemplate his future.

"Hey my son Brodie came with me and he's about your age. He's over in the car and he's really been looking

forward to meeting you. Can you see him over there
Drew?"

That was all it took. Andrew took one look over at
Rob's car parked at the end of the driveway and saw
Brodie in front seat waving cheerfully. A big smile crept
across his face that seemed to power his tiny green rubber
boots forward with courage, and that was the beginning of
Brodie and Drew.

Elle had made a few modifications of the guest
bedroom in hopes of making Andrew more comfortable
but his fascination with Brodie soon changed all of that. It
was quickly determined that Drew was happiest and most
comfortable on a rollaway cot they brought into Brodie's
room. It was a relief to Elle and Rob to see him so quickly
at ease in their home.

On the other side of town, it was equally a relief to
Mayor Carson that Drew was now in the Larson home.
In fact he called a town hall meeting of sorts in the
main lobby of The Kingston Hotel. Hoping of course
that any of the visiting media would show up for his
announcement. He had Scott introduce him to the small
crowd. Partly because Scott had some flair for that kind
of thing and the only other option was Tom, and he knew
Tom would say something stupid.

"Alright everyone can I have your attention? Mayor
Carson has a few announcements to make that I believe
you will find of great interest and importance. Afterwards
he will be happy to take a few questions. If you're with
the media please feel free to come down front here.
Please, let's give a hand for Mayor Harry Carson."

Harry came from around the corner and took a few
steps up on the hotel's grand staircase to give himself a
platform. There actually was a light trickle of applause
from a few hot spots mixed into the audience, including
Madge who Harry had personally coached on being
enthusiastic. Several reporters were there, including Stuart
Jenkins, and there were even a couple of flashes from

cameras. The atmosphere was big for a small town.

"Thank you, thank you everyone." Harry smiled big, his plump face shining with a reddish hue. These were the moments he lived for.

"Now as many of you know, the town of Forrester is a wonderful community of people that care about others. Especially ..." his emphasis was further punctuated with a glance at Jenkins, "those less fortunate. I mean that's how we've been given the great honor of being known as *Christmas Town U.S.A.* It's because that true Christmas spirit of giving lives here with us." His whiny voice and overuse of dramatic pause made it very easy to hear every word.

"I was deeply disturbed when it came to my personal attention that a young boy in our town had come on hard times. You can't imagine how painful it was for me to hear that little Andrew Richards had no place to live and was being turned over to the Child Care Services. Why, our greatest hope for any kind of future is to be a hope for others, especially the little ones!"

In a peculiar way Mayor Carson really did represent the people of Forrester. It was obvious to anyone who knew Harry that these weren't his own thoughts or feelings, but they did belong to the people behind the plan. As he shared the vision of a consolidated effort by the town to put on a Christmas production in Gordon's Park, he borrowed words and ideas from every decent person he'd heard on the matter. His intense craving for the spotlight though, that was the fuel for his passionate delivery. All in all, it made for a pretty convincing speech. Even Jenkins stopped rolling his eyes after a few minutes.

"And so every penny of money raised at the outdoor Christmas production will go toward *Andrew's House.* This will be a four unit building that I've insisted be right alongside the brand new development that overlooks the scenic Brunswick River. Andrew's House will be dedicated toward helping families in difficult times

giving them a chance to get back on their feet." Harry
had no shame in taking full ownership of everyone else's
benevolence. Some might say he had the makings of a
real politician.

"Now, I'd like to open it up to any questions?"

Stuart Jenkins didn't hesitate. "Yeh Mayor Carson,
where is Andrew Richards at this time? The last I heard
he was in Child Services care and on his way to some
orphanage outside of your county." Jenkins didn't like
anything about Forrester and it showed as he curled his lip
in disdain and anticipated pleasure over the certain ruin of
this hick-mayor.

"Mr. Jenkins! It's good to see you." Harry was
beaming at him and this totally caught Stuart off guard.

"I'm so glad you asked me about Andrew." Harry
had purposely not spoken of his whereabouts hoping
that Jenkins would lead off the questions and give him a
chance to put him in his place. The moment was playing
delightfully in his favor.

"Of course when I found out that little Andrew was
without a home, I knew I had to act fast and pull this
child to safety. My darling wife and I talked of opening
our own home but then one of my key leaders, a well
respected citizen of Forrester, reminded me that he and his
wife already had a boy Andrew's age and he practically
insisted that he come live with them."

The smug look on Mayor Carson's face as he starred
down Stuart in front of everyone was cliché as in the cat
who ate the mouse.

It was Saturday morning but that was nothing special
to Drew for his life was foreign to most typical routines or
constants. In fact the only consistency in his world was
that everyday he would brace himself for the loneliness
that was sure to come. He had to admit though that he felt
quite cozy between the flannel sheets of his bed.

It was around six in the morning and he could see

Brodie sound asleep, with his face scrunched up on his pillow. It was a short distance from his bed to Brodie's. He liked his new friend and wondered if he'd ever get to see him again after the changes that were sure to come with the new day. For now he'd pretend that he belonged and clutching his stuffed puppy, snuggled into the blankets and watched Brodie for a sign of when the day would start.

Elle was torn about leaving so early this morning. She wanted to stay and make sure that Drew felt at home but she knew her Mom really needed her help preparing for a huge catering order. Joanne had insisted that she would be fine but Elle knew that her Mom would need assistance. Rob assured her that he and Brodie would do a great job of making Drew feel welcome and well taken care of.

"Hey are there any hungry boys in here?" The bedroom door opened slowly and Drew almost instinctively pulled himself like a turtle into his shell, down into the covers. Rob had on one of Elle's unmanly aprons pulled over his dusty blue v-neck sweater and faded blue jeans.

"Hi Daddy," came Brodie's scratchy voice as he sat up in bed. His eyes were barely opened and the corners of his mouth were already divulging his happy mood. "Are you making breakfast this morning?"

Rob could barely understand the question because of the simultaneous yawn.

"Yup I'm making you guys a hungry man's breakfast this morning because we have a lot of work to do today."

Brodie suddenly remembered that he had a roommate and his eyes sharpened as he pushed himself up on his knees to stare over at Drew, who was still unsure about coming out of the covers.

"Drew! Did you hear that? Dad's gonna make us a big breakfast 'cause we got a lot of stuff to do!" His voice was excited.

Crawling toward the bottom of his bed Drew could see the horse and cowboy print all over his pajamas. The whole package was more than enough to lure him out of his protective shell.

"Drew, I know the work Daddy has for us to do today. Do you want to know what it is?"

Drew didn't make a peep but nodded his head *yes*.

"We're going to finish decorating the tree fort with Christmas lights and stuff and then we're gonna turn them on tonight and light up the whole thing!" His arms were moving in wide motions giving as dramatic of a presentation as possible. "Isn't that right Dad?"

"Yes, you are exactly right and that's why you sleepy heads need to get up now. I've got a big breakfast already going for you guys so just keep your pajamas on for now and you can change after you eat."

Rob tousled Brodie's hair and gave him warm pat on the shoulder.

"All right men, get up and get your faces washed and meet me downstairs in the kitchen. Brodie, please make sure Drew feels at home. You show him around the bathroom and where he can get a face cloth, soap and all that stuff. Okay?"

"Sure thing Dad! Come on Drew, I'll show you what to do."

Rob hardly got turned around toward the door when two sets of little feet outran him and did a hard turn into the adjacent bathroom.

Breakfast was noisy and fun, even though Brodie was doing most of the talking. Drew was already so enamored with his older friend that it was obvious to Rob that everything Brodie did, Drew tried to imitate. His face lit up when Rob suggested they put one of Brodie's winter coats on him so he'd be plenty warm while working on the tree house.

The move to the backyard was an exploit for each one of them in their own way. Brodie had grabbed his Grampy Clint's hammer and was focused on finishing this Christmas masterpiece today. For Drew the whole adventure was beyond anything he'd ever imagined. As they came up on the big maple tree cradling the complex fort in its mighty hands, he concluded that there couldn't be a more fun place in the world. It was just such an awesome sight for his wide eyes to take in.

Rob found his time with the boys almost unearthly. For obvious reasons, this tree house was now as special to him as it was to his son Brodie. He would pull a fresh line of colored lights out and consult with the fellows, trying to steer the plan toward something in the ballpark of Brodie's imagination that was actually possible. The whole time the boys were working, Rob found himself staring. He was enjoying the delight he saw in their faces, but he was soaking up the overpowering aura of peace he felt.

He had to help Drew up and down for the most part because his movements were so restricted with the bigger winter jacket and the bulky snow pants on. Rob noticed that the first time he picked up the boy, he seemed tense but with the need to relocate him over and over so he could keep up with Brodie, he started to automatically reach out his hands for help. A trust was being forged in the very place Rob had his own restored.

The more they worked on the project the bigger it seemed to become. They had the fort structure pretty well outlined and trimmed with lights by noon but Rob's vision of doing up the rest of the tree was looking like too big of a job, even though Josh had joined them mid-morning.

"Now you fellas look like you has been a workin' mighty hard. My, my! That's gonna be one pretty sight when you light her up, I declare."

Rob was half way up the tree struggling on the ladder with an armload of lights when he heard Kenneth's booming voice.

"Hey Uncle Ken," Rob instinctively responded before he even had a chance to think about it. "Good to see you. What are you doing out here?"

Kenneth's face was already lit up with a huge grin.

"Well now it's like this; I came by earlier just to see how you all was makin' out and you was so busy workin' with your crew here that no one even noticed me. So I said to myself if I'm gonna get noticed around here, what do I need to do? Then out of the blue it hit me. What does hard workin' men never have enough of? Good food, that's what!" He held up two huge brown bags in each hand.

Brodie, Drew and Josh were positioned up in the tree house and all of them were standing absolutely still and gawking at Kenneth.

"Any you boys up there like hamburgers and french fries?"

Brodie snapped out of the trance and shouted, "Yeh we do! Come on up!" Suddenly the whole fort came to life again.

Kenneth laughed and started for the climb that led up into the fort. "Are you sure it's alright boys? Do I need to know some password or special hand signal to get past the perimeter?"

"The primeter? What's that?" Brodie threw his question toward the cabin where the older man had set down the lunch bags on the floor and was now hoisting himself up through the deck.

"Guys I'd like you to say hello to Mr. Kenneth Henry. He was a real soldier in the U.S. military and he knows all about forts and being on guard. And Brodie you should know that Mr. Kenneth was probably Grampy Clint's best friend."

Rob had managed to step off the ladder onto a branch and step over to the porch surrounding the fort. He pulled off his glove and grabbed the visitor's rough muscular hand, "Welcome and this is very generous of you."

Ken pulled the younger man to himself and gave him a quick hug.

After a quick introduction to each of the boys Ken said, "Now first of all, I'd feel a whole lot better with this setup if all you boys would just call me 'Uncle Ken'. Is that okay Rob if the boys call me that? 'Cause if I'm gonna tell these here fellas military secrets we got to be closer than them calling me Mr. Ken."

"You know it is." He replied decidedly.

"Alright then you fellas heard the boss, I'm Uncle Ken. So now why don't we sit a spell and get some nourishment, and I'll explain to you the vital necessity of a perimeter when you got yourself such a fine outpost like you got here."

He was already sitting down with his feet hanging off the deck. All the boys gathered around him and seemed to be at quick ease with him Rob noted. In fact he found himself anticipating what the authoritative character would say next.

"Who's the captain of this here outfit?"

Josh offered up an answer, "That's probably Brodie 'cause his Grampy built this place for him and he lets all of us guys come over and play in it and hang out."

"Well that's mighty fine of you Brodie and since you're the captain of this here place, would you mind sayin' a word of blessin' and thanks for these here burgers and fries?"

"Yeh sure. I can do that." This totally reminded Brodie of being with Grampy Clint because he would always have one of them say grace before they would eat together.

Brodie along with the others bowed his head and prayed the prayer of thanksgiving he had been taught.

God you're good, You give us life
Food and family, and all that's right
Thank You for the gifts you give
The love and strength for each to live
Amen

Lunch was great and not just because Evelyn's Diner made some of the best burgers and fries around. Uncle Ken broke into all these military stories as he explained to the boys what a perimeter was and the extreme value in maintaining that border so to not compromise your base. Rob found himself enthralled in the lesson being taught.

Afterwards the five of them made an awesome team in wrapping up the decorating job. Uncle Ken was fearless when it came to heights and also had a few long ladders he always carried in his three quarter ton pickup, which he drove up easily from the back of the property right to the tree. What was impossible to reach before now became easy from the back of his truck. Rob couldn't help but drift off in thought for a while, considering how that the right people can bring impossibilities within reach.

"Won't you stay for dinner tonight Uncle Ken?" Rob asked.

"Yeh pleeeeease?" Brodie pleaded. "You got to stay and see us throw on the switch after dark."

"Oh my! That's awful temptin' and you can be sure that I wish I could but I got to get on home and help feed the critters."

"The critters?" Josh furrowed his brow into a question. "What's that?"

"That's my cows and horses and mules and a bunch a' other livestock."

"Can we come and see them?" Brodie asked excitedly.

"Certainly you can. But if you can wait for a few days, I'm supposed to bring in a truck load of those critters for the Christmas play everyone's doin' in town."

"You are?" All the boys blurted out at once.

"In fact I'm gonna bring in my camel and my sheep too. And wait 'til you fellers meet ole Charlie. He's the most stubborn and loveable camel in these hills."

"He's probably the only camel in these hills," Rob added laughing.

"You know, you probably right." Ken admitted with a sly smile.

After loading up all the tools and everyone congratulating each other on the fine Christmas decorating job, Kenneth gave special attention to saying goodbye to each of the boys.

When he came to little Andrew he got down on one knee and said, "Drew it was a pleasure spendin' time with you today and I hope we get to do it some more. Now I want you to know somethin', your Uncle Ken here is gonna be prayin' for you 'bout everyday. Okay? So you remember that."

Drew hadn't said hardly a word all day and the truth was, it was beyond anything he'd ever experienced. Looking up into the dark brown eyes of the big man in front of him he said in a voice that reminded Ken of a newborn colt, "I never had a Uncle before."

It caught him off guard but he quickly wrapped the tiny boy in his big arms and whispered, "You do now son. I'll be your Uncle Ken for as long as you want me." The tough old warrior could feel the sting in the corner of his eyes.

Arrangements were made for Josh to stay over for dinner so he could be a part of the official commencement of their light display. Things weren't so good at home between Josh's parents so any invitation he got to be at the Larson home was an indulgence he gladly jumped at. Although he was fairly athletic, he was a little bit of an outsider at school until he and Brodie became great friends. Brodie was a natural leader and his fearless personality was already refined enough by his mother's meticulous training that he easily drew other kids to himself. That automatically put Josh on the winning team.

"Don't you guys all look comfy!" Elle laughed at the sight of Rob sitting on the couch with Brodie, Drew and Josh. They were watching some animated show about talking vegetables dressed up like pirates. She heard the giggling way down the hall.

"Hey Mom! Us guys are just relaxing." Brodie was up on his knees and head almost entirely spun around so he could get a visual on her.

"Yes I can see you're relaxing." She walked over to

the end where Rob was sitting and put her hand on his shoulder. "So is this how you guys spent the day? Having fun sitting around while I worked hard at the café?" Elle was obviously teasing them all and hoping they had a playful time.

"No Mom we …"

Rob wasn't sure what Brodie was going to say and since they'd already decided they were going to surprise Elle with the light display, he interrupted.

"That's right son we weren't just having fun sitting around all day but we also had a lot of fun doing guy things on secret missions." Turning and looking at the boys with an emphatic look he said, "Isn't that right boys? We've been keeping the perimeter, right?"

Instantly all the guys got it and began to nod their head unanimously, "Yeh that's right," elbowing each other like they were part of a secret fraternity.

Elle didn't have a clue what they were talking about and figured it was some kind of guy-code talk, but in any case, they all seemed quite happy with themselves.

Her voice got very gentle, "Hi Drew. How are you doing? Did you have a nice day with everyone?"

He looked up at her and gave one of his rare but compact smiles, and then nodded his head without saying a word.   He was neatly stuffed right between Josh and Brodie, and seemed to be as content as he could be.

"Oh … now I've got to figure out what to feed you guys. Everyone must be hungry by now."

Rob grabbed her arm, "Honey don't you worry about it. I figured you'd have worked hard all day and the last thing you needed to do was come home and feed us guys, so I took the liberty of ordering some takeout. It should be here any minute."

"That's wonderful Rob. Thank you."

"And guess what it is Mom? It's your favorite."

Rob and Brodie had discussed this before hand and decided that it would be extra special if they built up to the big Christmas light reveal with some of Elle's favorite comfort food, *Mezzaluna's*. It was the best Italian food around for at least a hundred miles.

"Oooooo, yummy. This is going to be fun. Can you stay and eat with us Josh?"

"Yes Mrs. Larson. I already phoned my Mom and she said it was okay."

"That's great. We'll have a real party, right Drew?" Elle wanted to involve the shy boy in as much conversation as possible. "Do you like Italian food Drew? Things like spaghetti and meatballs, lasagna, fettuccini and oh … did you get some of their garlic bread Rob?"

"But of course Signora." He replied with his best Italian impersonation.

"Do you like any of that kind of food Drew?"

Everyone was looking at him waiting for his answer. He felt awkward and under pressure but he managed to squeak out, "I like hotdogs."

Brodie and Josh started to giggle but Elle took the lead knowing that they meant no harm, "I'll tell you what Drew, if you don't like any of this Italian stuff I'll make something just for you, okay?"   He gave his usual quiet nod looking up from under his bangs.

Dinner was a great success and everyone ate like they hadn't eaten in weeks. Rob suggested they stay in the family room since he knew the kitchen overlooked the backyard and he figured the boys could possibly let the cat out of the bag. Elle had put a plate together for Drew of spaghetti with a meatball, garlic toast and a little lasagna. He must have forgot about the hotdogs because she'd never seen so much food stuffed into such a tiny package.

"Before we get into dessert I thought we'd take a break and have some fun," Rob announced. "Does that sound good to everyone?"

Brodie rubbed his hands together in excitement and almost whispered, "Here we go."

Then he shouted along with the others,

"Yay, let's have some fun!"

Elle added her voice to the cheerful clamor but had no idea that her joy was the subject of their mysterious planning. Brodie and Rob knew how much she loved everything Christmas so their hopes were high that she'd be delighted.

Rob pulled out a blindfold and said, "Okay here's what were going to do, I'm going to blindfold Elle and then we're going to lead her to a place in the house. Then she has to guess where she is and what she'd be looking at when we take off the blindfold. Does that sound like fun?"

The guys all roared, "Yehhh!"

Elle tried to fake some enthusiasm but actually couldn't understand why anyone thought that would be fun.

When Rob came at her with the scarf she even made a funny expression that only made him laugh the more. "You trust me, right dear?"

In the midst of the childish humor and playing, Elle sensed a tenderness she wasn't used to coming from Rob. Once she was blindfolded, he put his arm around her waist and taking her left hand, led her from behind. There was a vulnerability to the woman in his arms that surprised him and that he also enjoyed. Elle found herself liking the game much more than she thought she would and was disappointed when they stopped.

"We've arrived," he said without releasing his arm from around her waist or her hand. "Now all you have to do is guess where we are and what you think you're looking at."

Elle didn't want to disappoint anyone by making the game too easy. She knew exactly where she was, the breakfast nook just off the kitchen. As for what she was looking at, that was just a bit harder because Rob had done a few turns with her when they stepped into the room.

"Let me get my bearings here." She could hear the boys whispering and trying to restrain their laughter. "Are we in the ... attic?"

She could hear the giggling increase and Brodie whisper too loudly, "She thinks she's in the attic!"

"Wait, wait a second. No that's not right. It can't be the attic or I'd be smelling Daddy's old musty baseball uniform."

Rob countered, "Hey it hasn't been that long."

After making a few more guesses for the kids' sake she got a sudden revelation, "Okay I know where I am now. We're in the breakfast nook. I'm sure of it because I can smell the toast that Daddy burnt this morning." Her dimples were deep and her smile huge.

Rob thought what a beautiful picture she made and then in a serious tone he asked, "Are you serious Elle? Can you really smell the toast?"

"Just a little," she whispered.

"If you are in the breakfast nook then tell me what you would see when we take off your blindfold?" Rob said it as if he was on a stage and speaking to an audience. Elle caught the playful quality in his voice and responded in kind.

"I believe sir that I would see a great window over looking our dark backyard with a few plants on the window sill that desperately need watering."

"Is that your final answer my fair lady?" Rob bellowed.

"Yes it is!" Elle had lowered her voice trying to sound like Rob who was already untying the scarf from around her head.

The blindfold off, her eyes quickly adjusted to the darkened room and she could see that her guess was perfectly correct, except the plants looked better than she had supposed. "Okay so what do I win you guys because I was right?"

"Brodie, let's give your Mom her prize."

Brodie smiled a toothy grin and then hollered, "Josh! Go ahead and hit it!"

Elle hadn't noticed but Josh had slipped away during the final part of her guessing, prompted by a signal from

Rob. They had worked it out earlier that Josh would turn on the lights. It was considered a real honor to throw the switch but since Brodie really wanted to be in the room with his Mom when she first saw the display, Josh got the gig.

Suddenly the pitch-black window that Elle was staring into came alive with a burst of light and movement. The sugar maple tree was transformed into an animated fantasy world. Even Rob found himself breathing a low, "Whoa." It was the first time any of them had seen the display in the dark and it was awesome to say the least.

From the trunk of the tree widening out to many of the branches came an exciting flowering of solid blue lights. Rob couldn't believe how high Uncle Ken had gotten some of the strands. The fort itself was alive with lights, completely outlined in red with clear icicle lights hanging from the roof. The nautical rope lattice was overlaid with a web of multicolored mini-lights and motion racing rope lights were used to make the ladder and deck stand out. Like fruit hanging from a tree, yellowish ornaments trimmed several of the branches. Topping off the spectacular exhibition was a huge glowing white star.

Elle gasped. Rob recognized it wasn't embellished for the children, but genuine awe.

"I … I can't believe it. It's absolutely beautiful and WONDERFUL!" She shrieked.

"Whoa," Rob laughed covering his ear closest to Elle.

"Mom, do you like it? Do you?" Brodie was thrilled with the glowing fantasy world and his mother's excitement over it.

"Oh Honey, it's perfect. I just can't believe it! You guys. Just look at this Christmas miracle you made!" Her heart was dancing as she squeezed Rob's arm even tighter.

Drew pushed his little face up against the window with a reverential wonder over what he was looking at. It was beyond his comprehension and his heart beat rapidly as he tried to take in the dreamland outside, and in. He turned and looked up at the single shape of this man and woman embracing each other in the dimness of the room. It felt safe.

A hand came up on Drew's shoulder and he immediately looked down at it. Turning his head the opposite way he came face to face with Brodie.

"Do you like it Drew?"

"It's pretty," he responded.

"I think we all did a great job together. And now you're a part of our tree house club. Do ya wanna be?" Came his melodic voice.

Drew stared at his new friend and nodded his head in agreement as if making an oath. "I really do Brodie."

Chapter 14

It didn't take long for news to spread around town about the *Christmas Tree House* in the Larson's backyard. That's what Marvin Johnson officially named it when he came out to do his article for the *Forrester Gazette*. He was a young man in his early twenties with unruly short hair and an inquisitive nature that just wouldn't quit.

"Mr. Larson how many lights do you figure you have in this display?"

"That's a really good question Marvin. Hmmm ... I'm just guessing but from the ridiculous number of packages I bought, I would estimate oh, maybe ten thousand."

"How much would you say you paid for the whole shot?" Marvin asked, his pen ready for an answer.

"I wouldn't." Rob came back grinning, "That's for me to know and you to hopefully never find out."

The reporter in Marvin wasn't amused by the dead end.

After a few more light questions and Rob giving most of the credit to each of the boys and Kenneth Henry, Marvin finished off by taking some pictures that made it to the second page of the *Gazette*. Brodie made sure to get

y of the paper the next day so he could cut out the
for his scrapbook.

Christmas seemed to be coming at the Larson home this year from every angle. The tree house was drawing all kinds of attention with cars driving by every night for a look-see. The maple tree was situated so that it could be easily seen from either the north or south side of the street they lived on. Some neighbors even honked their horn as a way of saying hi which Rob never understood but tried to tolerate.

Elle was caught up in a busy schedule of making holiday treats for the café, decorating at work and at home, buying gifts for Christmas which was now less than three weeks away, and all the regular things a wife and mother are involved in. On top of all that, she now had Drew to look after, choir practice for the town production and Rob to figure out.

She always knew that there was this other side to her husband. A side she longed to see and longed for him to discover. These days brought something different about Rob and it wasn't that he'd changed really. It was rather that he'd been freed of an obligation he could never fulfill, a burden that had relentlessly censured his existence. There was an easiness and strength to him now.

Although Elle delighted in Rob's discovery of everything good about their life, it was not without its pressures. When a woman has to shelve her desire for affection, she quietly puts layers over parts of her heart so she can be the responsible wife without living out of her need. Elle found herself awkward at times with his revived attention and tenderness.

One day at Murdock's Café Rob swung by to pick up Drew on his way to get Brodie from school. Just as he was leaving he stepped behind the counter and pulled her close kissing her long on the mouth.

"You get more beautiful everyday Elle," he whispered in her ear. Then taking Drew's hand they marched out the front door.

"Okay little man let's go pickup your best buddy from school." His cheerful chitchat faded against the dinging of the bell as she looked on.

Flustered and not knowing where to look, Elle wrapped her arms around herself nervously and tried to avoid eye contact with any of the onlookers in the busy café. She was admittedly uncomfortable.

"It's okay dear. He's your husband you know?" Joanne had just stepped out from the back with a tray of fresh baking. She had watched the whole scene through the window of the swinging door to the kitchen. Elle just gave a nervous laugh.

Setting down the hot cinnamon rolls and walnut scones on the counter, she wiped her hands on her apron and stood close to her daughter looking around the room.

"You know Elle, getting your prayers answered isn't particularly easy. When good things come our way it usually requires a letting go of the old things we once used to fill that space."

The younger woman looked deep into the caring eyes of her mother and Joanne touched her still crossed arms.

"You know what I mean. Like letting go of that independent state of heart that *seems* to protect you from disappointments."

She punctuated those last words with a knowing squeeze of her hand. "It's time to open up and let the sunshine in Sweetie."

Then abruptly she changed tracks, "Gracious! Don't those rolls smell delicious?"

Giving her girl one more reassuring squeeze she began refilling the display under the counter with the supply of goodies.

Elle mumbled, "They sure do Mom. Thank you." Off she retreated to the kitchen to get another load of fresh baking and sort out the complicated tangle of her heart. Mechanically she put on the oven mitts and opened the oven door to a heat wave of aroma. Perfectly uniform gingerbread men laying obediently on the hot metal sheets just waiting for orders. For a moment Elle admired their predictable design and then thought; *why do feelings have to be so complicated.*

To say things were developing with the Forrester Christmas production was an understatement. Scott Burgess had phoned Mayor Carson on the Monday after Thanksgiving very excited. He had been talking to a couple of his friends who booked bus tours and they expressed interest in possibly putting together a special tour to see Forrester's Christmas show. It would be a budget excursion and the agents thought it would appeal to their last-minute customers looking for a fun outing.

The idea exploded and before Rob could rein Mayor Carson in, he had contracted with *Premier Tours Inc* six performances starting the week before Christmas and the last one being on Christmas Eve. When they had first agreed on the cooperative town effort it was decided that there would be two performances one week before the twenty-fifth on the weekend. Mayor Carson became so enthused when the first two nights sold out in a day that he conspired with Scott to add four more nights.

There were too many pulls for Harry to resist and he easily sold most of the key business owners on the development before news ever got to Rob. The obvious advantages would be the heavy boost in tourist traffic, which all the shop owners recognized as potential business. Other upsides were the group rate of twenty-five dollars a head toward the *Andrew's House* benefit fund, free advertising for the town of Forrester and the two main hotels would be included in the overnight package.

Premier Tours let Scott know that they had booked up all their vacancies by the end of the week, something they'd never seen on such short notice. With two buses per show and fifty-five people on each bus, Mayor Carson felt obligated to initiate the executive order.

"Harry do you realize that none of these people involved in this Christmas production are professional? And none of them are getting paid. They're all busy people volunteering their time for Pete's sake!" Rob was emphatic but not too forceful, as Harry had strategically dropped this bomb on him in the most public place, Evelyn's Diner.

Rubbing his fat hands together in pure pleasure he seemed to not even notice Rob's concern.

"Rob this is genius I'm telling you. Pure genius. Not only is it punching up the town's business but hey … I'm helping you solve this problem you've got with that little boy and his Mom or Aunt or, or whatever. Right?" He snickered with pure pleasure in himself.

Rob just shook his head in disbelieve. This pudgy little man was so outrageous in how he thought that Rob could only sigh and laugh as he sunk his face into his hands.

"You're unbelievable Harry. And by the way, it's his Aunt. Can you remember that please in case you actually talk to another reporter about what's going on?"

"Oh sure, sure. No problem." Then he reached across the table and patted Rob on the arm as if to console him, his face becoming serious, "Listen my friend, you need to just relax. Old Harry's got it all under control. You'll see it's all gonna work out just fine." With that he pulled his hand back while shifting his toothpick back and forth in to a self-assured smile.

Just then they were interrupted and Rob was pleased to be rescued.

"Good afternoon fellas. What'll it be today?" Evelyn was already topping up their coffees.

"Good to see you Evelyn," came Harry's gruff official voice. Then leaning forward he asked in a much quieter, boy-like manner, "Ev do you have anymore of that great apple pie of yours?"

"You know I do Mayor. You want the usual with an

extra scoop of ice cream and a slice of cheese?"

"Perfect!" Came his recovered official voice.

"You celebrating something Harry?" Rob couldn't resist but before the man could reply Evelyn offered the truth.

"Celebrating?" She taunted. "If he's celebrating, then just about everyday he's finding somethin' to get happy about."

Harry sat back with a defensive look on his face and gave a nervous laugh, "Come on you guys! That's not true." He spread his meaty palms out in front of himself in an effort to solicit leniency but none was given.

"Oh Harry! There's no need to be embarrassed." Evelyn's voice was getting louder.

In a quick defensive move Harry tried to divert the attention onto Rob. "Evelyn isn't it just wonderful what Rob and his family is doing looking after your friend's son, I mean nephew? And hey, are you excited about the whole Christmas in the park idea? It's going to be great for business."

Before Evelyn could get a word in Harry jumped to yet another thought. "Oh that reminds me Rob, we needed a catchy name for the whole deal. You know, marketing and all that. So we came up with, *A Forrester Christmas in the Park*." His arms stretched out as if unveiling an invisible marquee just above his head.

"So who's this 'we'?" Rob asked and then added, "And don't you think it's a little bit long?"

He was frustrated with Harry and was having a hard time hiding it. The mayor was having his moment but Rob was concerned about the demand this commitment would put on the good people in this town.

"Well ... you know, me and Scott Burgess, and the guys who work for Premier. Rob they needed to start marketing this thing and we didn't have time to call a town meeting and take a vote. Hey when opportunity knocks you've got to open the door and say, 'come on in!'

and light the cigars. Right?"

Harry often took a common adage and twisted it to suit his pleasure and right now he was pleased as punch with himself and it showed.

"Well I like it." Evelyn had been standing there in her practiced stance with pencil pressed hard to the order pad. "It sounds perfect and I think you're on to something special for this here town Mayor."

Harry crossed his arms in a satisfied pose and looked smugly across the table. "Thank you Evelyn for appreciating my hard work," he said flatly. Rob just stared back trying to swallow what was obviously impossible.

"Okay, I think we're done here Mayor. I'll leave you to enjoy your pie." Rob slid out of the booth.

"Come on Rob. We've got more business we need to go over." That wasn't the truth. The only thing Harry hated more than being alone, was eating alone.

"Well I've got work to do and probably some damage control to take care of. Have you told the Pastors and key organizers of this *Forrester Christmas In the Park* that you've single-handedly quadrupled their workload and made plans for everyone's Christmas Eve?"

Harry got a sheepish look on his face. "No, I haven't yet," he murmured.

Rob started for the door.

"Oh Rob, I almost forgot. Jenny's been staying with me since she's got out of the hospital."

"That's great Evelyn. How's she feeling now?"

"Much better."

"She probably wants me to bring little Drew by to see her."

Evelyn hesitated which Rob wasn't aware that was even possible with her personality. "It's funny you know, she hasn't really asked about him much. But she's still on a lot of pain medication so that makes a person kind of loopy, you know."

He didn't really understand so he just nodded to

acknowledge the sentiment. "Please tell her I'm glad to
hear that she's doing better and if ...", now it was his turn
to hesitate because he was thinking of Andrew and he felt
protective of the boy. "If she'd like me to bring him by for
a visit anytime, I'd be happy to do that."

"That would be sweet Rob and I'm sure when she's
feeling better, she'll want that. She did tell me if I ran into
you to ask if you'd mind coming over to see her just for a
few minutes. Do you think you could do that sometime?"
Evelyn was trying to talk around the patrons coming and
going because Rob had kept the conversation moving
toward the front door and away from Harry's curious ears.

"Sure I'll be happy to do that Evelyn. It'll probably be
the beginning of next week but I'll call and set a time to
come see her. How does that sound?"

"Oh Rob, you're such a dear! Thank you hon." Before
Rob could grab the front door handle; the petite woman
grabbed him and gave him a one-armed hospitality hug
still holding her order pad.

Once out in the fresh air, Rob thought it all over.
*Harry was going to be Harry. What can you do with a
guy like that? As for Jenny, the idea of not asking to see
Drew seemed strange but maybe she has good reason and
that's why she wants to speak with me in person. That's
it. At least this visit will be much easier than the ordeal I
endured at the hospital when we first met.*

Looking both ways he stepped out across the street
toward his office. He had a lot of phone calls to make and
much explaining.

Driving home that evening was especially rewarding
for a man who had spent all afternoon calming anxiety
attacks and tempers aimed at the town counsel and
particularly Harry Carson. Rob tried breaking the news
to Pastor Hunston and Dr. Murphy of the vamped up
schedule over phone but within fifteen minutes they were
both sitting in his office. Once they got on board with the
new itinerary Rob realized he had another rough edge to

sand off. Each pastor was used to being the host of his own Christmas presentation and so the question was, who would be the MC for this merger?

On an inspiration, Rob suggested that they act as co-hosts introducing the production each night and welcoming the audience. After that Rob used some artful diplomacy to gently suggest that because of their busy schedule it would be better to relinquish all narration to someone in the community with a fitting voice. At first he could sense he was meeting resistance from both great men until he mentioned the name Kenneth Henry. When Rob said his name, the leaders looked at each other and simultaneously their faces lit up in agreement. It was amazing to Rob the favor that a good man could procure at just the mention of his name.

The rest of the organizers were either calmed or persuaded over the phone and soon everyone was on board for *A Forrester's Christmas In the Park*. Rob shook it off as he drove in the driveway and stepped out into his garage.

There was something about the busyness that made him savor the solace he discovered in the most unusual times, and this was one of them. Looking across the court to the side entrance of the house he unexpectedly thought of his father's letter. He'd read the letter so many times parts of it were memorized.

He could hear his father's voice saying, *I'm proud of you son.* A gentle breeze blew a dusting of snow that sparkled magically in the outdoor lights. *I had a dream of sitting in a tree house, something like this one, and telling my boy of the most important things I'd learned in life.*

These were his father's dreams and prayers, and now Rob felt closer to him than ever before. The letter was safely tucked in the old leather bound volume he poured over every morning. Something in those ancient words went beyond his understanding and brought a clarity he'd never known. He gladdened suddenly at the feel of the heavy bronze door handle under his hand.

That night Rob took the boys out in the backyard after dinner for some snowman building lessons. Not being the ideal snow for such art they soon found themselves sitting up in the brightly lit tree house and watching the cars drive by. Drew was as content as could be and simply sucked the snow off of his woolen mittens while Brodie asked a million questions.

"Daddy, Drew says he doesn't have a Mommy or a Daddy. Why do some kids not have a Mommy or a Daddy?"

Rob looked at Drew concerned that the question might be upsetting to him but he could see that his popsicle-like mittens were the perfect pacifier.

"There's no easy response to that Brodie." Rob thought for a moment.

"I suppose people wish they could do right but they can't. Not on their own anyway. If they don't get help to do what's right, then they get hurt somehow and they end up leaving little boys and girls without a Mommy or Daddy." The answer seemed to satisfy Brodie because he quickly moved on.

"Guess what?"

"What?" Rob played along.

"Mommy's been teaching Drew to say his prayers at night 'cause he didn't know how. Daddy he didn't even know what bedtime prayers was."

Drew was still distracted by the passing car lights and frosty mitts. The wool hat was hanging heavy over his eyes and he looked cozy inside the bulky snowsuit sitting on the wooden deck.

"Well Brodie, a lot of children out there have never been taught things like that."

Tilting his head back Rob enjoyed the myriad of twinkling colors. The branches glowed under the blue lights and seem to reach forever into the heavens. He

knew his dad would have gotten great pleasure out
of seeing him now in this picture and the truth is Rob
believed his faith was such that he had seen it.

"When I was a boy my dad taught me to say my
bedtime prayers."

"Grampy Clint?" Brodie wanted to be sure he was
imagining the scene perfectly.

"That's right, it was Grampy Clint."

Brodie interrupted and leaned across his dad toward
Drew who didn't seem to be paying attention anyhow.
"Drew that's my Grampy we're talkin' about. He lives in
heaven now instead of here anymore."

He was very matter of fact about it. Drew took it for
what it was and responded with, "Oh", and went back
to watching cars. Rob chuckled at the simple way these
boys processed mysteries that the world wrestled with for
thousands of years.

"Anyway, what I started to say before you guys got all
intellectual on me ..." with that he gave Brodie a playful
roughing up which Drew could only semi-ignore.

"When my dad, your Grampy, went away into the army
I prayed a prayer for something almost every night that he
was gone. Do you want to know what it was?"

This appeared to grab Drew's attention and Brodie
was instantly on pins and needles. "What was it Daddy?
Somethin' really cool, right? Like your own laptop or a
go-cart? Was that it?"

"Nope. None of those things." Rob swung his feet
back and forth from the fort's deck in a playful way.
"What about you Drew? Do you want to guess at what I
was praying for when I was a boy?"

Whenever he could involve him in something, Rob
tried to swing the door wide so the shy boy would feel
welcome but never forced.

Looking up into Rob's face the boy squinted for a
moment as though he could see something in his eyes and
then he whispered, "Your Daddy."

At first Rob was dazed by the lad's perception and then troubled at the reality that this young life was so accustomed to perceiving need.

"That's right Drew. You hit it right on." He gave him an affirming rub on the back and was again reminded of how tiny he was. "In fact, here's the whole truth. I prayed for my dad to come back home and build this here tree house for me and now look, here it is!"

"Yeh but how come it took so long? You didn't get to play here when you were a boy 'cause Grampy made this when you were big." Brodie sounded genuinely concerned about the legitimacy of this so-called answer to another boy's prayer.

"You know what I just recently discovered? My prayer was answered when I was just a boy. My dad came home to me and wanted to build me this tree house back then but I was so angry. I was angry with him for leaving and I was angry with God for not giving me what I wanted when I wanted it."

Both boys were staring at Rob now.

"I got so used to looking at what I didn't have that I stopped believing God heard me. When my prayers didn't look like they got answered I couldn't even see what I wanted anymore."

It took Rob close to twenty-five years to figure this out so he wasn't sure how much of what he said made sense to these two. He hoped the story would at least help to keep them from making the same mistake he'd made. As the three of them sat there in the quiet frosty night they each pondered on pieces of the truth. Brodie wondered at how his wonderful Daddy could have been the angry boy he just heard about.

The lawyer in Rob began to outline a case against the dangers of believing that prayers were unanswered.

Maybe it was better to never have prayed than to live life offended, he reasoned.

If heaven were measuring, the smallest of the three

was juggling the weightiest piece of truth. Drew sat motionless but concluded that he'd come upon the doorway of making what seemed impossible a reality. The difference between himself and this other boy Rob spoke of; he would see the answer when it came and not wait until he was all grown up.

Chapter 15

"Elle this is just so exciting I feel like I'm coming unglued at the seams!"

Meredith was sitting at a round petite table for two tight up against the front window in Murdock's Café. She had ordered her favorite blend of coffee but had hardly been able to touch it as she chattered on to Elle about every aspect of the production.

"I've never seen you so happy Mare and you don't know how happy that makes me." They were genuine words from a devoted friend.

"And I think I'm officially in everyone's good books for scouting out one of the great vocal talents of all time for our choir."

That was not an exaggeration either as everyone in the choir was finding out; Meredith had a unique and beautiful voice. Angela Berry was no slouch of a teacher either. When she discerned a diamond in the rough, she wasted no time in drawing it out with some exercises and instruction. Meredith was a diligent student and threw herself into it.

"You're so sweet Elle. I think of you often and how thankful I am for your friendship. I just feel like …

well, like you've given me so much and I wish I had more to give to you."

"You're silly Mare!" Elle's curly blonde hair was tied up on top of her head and her nose pinched as she giggled. Meredith thought again of what a beautiful woman her friend was.

"We're friends and it's me that's grateful to have you and Lacey in my life. Besides it's true. You are giving so much to this whole town by using your beautiful voice in this production. Oh I can't wait for everyone to hear you. I told Rob how great you were and he said 'good', he was going to quit being a lawyer and become your manager."

Meredith closed her eyes and laughed nervously. "Elle don't even joke like that 'cause I'm already nervous enough about the concert and it's almost one week away from the first performance!"

Elle's face got instantly serious. "Oh I know. I'm not even singing any solos and I get butterflies in my stomach every time I think about it."

She paused and then mockingly slapped her hands lightly on the table, "Okay let's change the subject. Have you done any Christmas shopping for Lacey yet?"

Groaning she answered and almost sang her answer, "No Elle. Isn't that terrible? What am I going to do? Mr. Carter has been so good to give me the whole week off before Christmas so I can concentrate on the production, but right now I'm busy day and night with work and practicing."

As they worked out a plan to get together the next week and go shopping for the children, the picture from the outside looking in seemed like a Christmas postcard. The snow lightly spiraled down onto the wet sidewalk while the two friends laughed and talked over their steaming hot cups.

Across Elm Street Gordon's Park was a flurry of activity with town employees and volunteers busying themselves like Santa's helpers trying to get ready for the big day. Carpenters were converting two parallel flat bed transport trailers into a stage with a vaulted ceiling. For a temporary stage it was actually looking quite impressive. Then there was a network of trim experts armed with ladders and instructions from the park superintendent as to what tree got what lights. The old mill always got special attention and looked like something from the North Pole when it was done.

A few things that were typically a part of the seasonal setup in the park worked perfectly into the ambitious planning for the production. Gordon's Park was always the focus of the town's Christmas decorating and so they had built up quite a warehouse store of lights, and the complex arrangement was already mapped out.

The pond descended from the mill with a shallow meandering bank carving out an open area reserved for family skating in the winter months. There was already a standing arrangement for bleachers from the local high school to be set up around the pond. It was quite easy for a few men to slide them into place, anchoring them in front of the stage in a perfect semicircle. It was as though the town had been planning for this all along.

Any visitor coming into town for the first time would already be impressed with the extensive planning seemingly invested in *A Forrester Christmas In The Park*. A couple of the workers impressed with the results said, "We should have done something like this a long time ago." The stage was set in more ways than one for this little town. Most of its people didn't have a clue how much was at stake and with reporters like Jenkins quietly prowling around, the threats of yesterday were now out of sight and out of mind. One way or the other, things would never be the same again come Christmas day.

Elle took Rob's arm as they stepped up on the porch of the older colonial cottage style home belonging to Evelyn and Chuck Spence. The place was in great shape and well kept they noticed. White shutters contrasted attractively against a modern taupe and the four square pillars gave the entrance a charming feel. Rob didn't see a doorbell so he reached for the doorknocker in the middle of the spruce wreath and let it tap a couple of times lightly.

Jenny opened the door and shuffled sideways with the help of her walker making way for her visitors.

"Hello Mr. Larson. Please come in."

"Hi Jenny. This is my wife Elle. Elle this is Jenny Richards, Andrew's aunt."

Elle naturalized the moment instantly, "Oh it's good to see you again Jenny. I remember you from Evelyn's Diner. You're such an excellent waitress and that is a really demanding job isn't it?"

Jenny warmed to Elle's dimples and easy conversation, "Yes I guess but you know I've been doing it so long I don't even think about it." She looked down at the walker and then added, "Well until this. Now all I think about is what I used to be able to do and hoping I'll be able to get around like I used to."

Once they hung their own coats up in the entrance they followed Jenny into a living room at the front of the house. It was modestly furnished but comfortable. Rob figured that Chuck must have swung by earlier and started a fire in the fireplace for her. Maybe he was just hoping that it would offset the cigarette smoke seeing how that neither of them smoked. There was a Christmas tree in the corner of the room and older looking decorations neatly placed cheered the space. A discerning eye could see that these homeowners were thrifty people who maintained everything and threw away nothing.

"Can I get you a tea or coffee?" Jenny offered.

"No thank you. You just relax Jenny." Rob kindly instructed her.

Elle jumped in, "That's right. You need to get your rest right now so you tell us if there's anything we can do for you."

Jenny was an uncomplicated woman and figured Elle's

offer was as good an open door as needed. "How's Drew doing?" She asked with her eyes shifting down Rob noticed.

Elle responded cheerfully, "Oh he is such a wonderful boy. Thank you for letting him stay with us while you're recovering and all these details are being worked out. He's becoming such good friends with my son who's six. Brodie just thinks the world of little Drew and … we do too."

Elle looked at Rob who was not taking his eyes off Jenny, but studying her response to Elle's report.

"It's so sweet at night time when I tuck him into bed, he says his prayers and always prays for his Aunt Jenny. Your injury has made an indelible impression on his young life because he always prays for all the people with broken legs and broken arms."

Her voice broke up and Rob turned his head, caught by the emotional burst. Quickly Elle covered it by laughing.

"Oh dear. He's probably going to be a doctor with a love like that for people."

Recovering quickly or at least looking and sounding the part she went on.

"The cutest thing Jenny is how he ends his prayers every night. Rob's father Clint built my son a tree house in the backyard just before he passed away. Drew seems to love it out there as much as Brodie does. You know, it's a special boy place where they go to play and dream big dreams."

Elle leaned forward and Rob could see how excited she was in telling these things to Jenny.

"Anyway, at the end of his prayers he always says, 'God make it so me and Aunt Jenny can live in Brodie's tree house all the time.' I thought about telling him that you couldn't live in a tree but then it hit me, when you both move into your new home he'll see that as even a better answer. Don't you think?"

The room was uncomfortably quiet. Jenny had

something to say but she was looking into the fireplace as if hoping to find a direction.

Still avoiding both of their eye contact she cleared her throat, "Mr. Larson, when you met me in the hospital, I never said anything to make you think that I wanted the town folks to give me a place to live did I?"

Rob answered calmly, "No you didn't."

Now her eyes came up to look directly into Rob's, "And I don't." She said flatly. "It's not that I don't think what you're trying to do isn't great. I mean it's wonderful if that's what a person wanted but it's not what I want. Maybe you didn't understand me when we spoke that day."

There was anger in her voice or maybe it was fear.

"Sure I lost my house to the bank and yes, I got some money problems going on along with these physical challenges." She gave the walker a nudge with her strong leg.

"I've spent close to thirty-five years raising children, since I was just a kid myself, and now I've got nothing left to give. No town counsel can fix that. Putting me in some little town house, paid for by someone else ain't gonna give me back all those years and it sure won't help Drew."

Rob was lost for words and he had a troubled look on his face. "I see."

"Look, I never signed up to be the wicked witch of the west here but it seems you've left me with no choice. Can't you understand that I can't afford this town's charity? And now this thing has become so public that as soon as I can, I've got to get away from here and start over somewhere else where no one knows me."

Elle had tears in her eyes and was obviously upset.

"Oh Jenny we don't want that for you and we're so sorry for making things worse."

The lawyer in Rob quickly came to the front and he needed time to think before anything more was said.

"Have you told anyone else what you've just said to us?"

"No. Evelyn has an idea that something is up but I haven't said anything because I'm afraid of getting run out of town. I'd rather wait until I can sneak out with no one watching."

She paused and then said, "I'm scared Mr. Larson. Too many people are giving me attention and I know how it works; I'll have to pay them all back on the other side of this and I just don't have it to give. Not for them and not even for Andrew. I love that boy but I've never been any good for him, and if you knew me, you'd know what I'm saying is true."

There was a tremor in her voice now and Rob knew she was upset.

"Thank you for talking to me about this Jenny. I hear you loud and clear this time. Would you give me a few days to work on this without talking to anyone else? I won't make any moves without talking to you first."

Rob's voice was subdued but confident sounding to her.

"Okay. And something else you should know Mr. Larson. That stupid reporter keeps calling and leaving messages for me. Says he wants to talk to me. He even came to the door the other day when Chuck and Evelyn were at work, but I didn't answer it."

"What ever you do, stay away from him." Rob warned.

"I'm doing my best," she sighed.

"That's great." He encouraged and then trying to ease the tension he said, "And Jenny one more thing, please call me Rob from now on. Is that okay?"

She gave a weak smile, "Sure, Rob."

Standing up Elle immediately gave her a hug assuring that everything would be all right. She didn't have an optimistic look on her face considering that the last time she spoke with Rob she ended up jumping from the frying pan into the fire.

"Please tell Drew that Aunt Jenny sends her love and to be a good boy." Jenny tried to sound upbeat.

Elle smiled back, "I sure will."

Rob didn't say a thing but noticed what he thought might have been a tear in Jenny's eye.

Grabbing their coats and saying a quick goodbye, Rob closed the solid oak door behind them and stepped into the brisk afternoon. The reflection of the sun off the snow was so bright that they both instinctively reached for their sunglasses. Neither of them said a thing as they walked side by side down the sidewalk toward their car. How strange it was that one person's confession could so heavily burden two strong people in a matter of seconds.

Walking toward them was a man in a navy blue winter pea coat, a long scarf wrapped several times around his neck and wool hat stretched on the form of his head. Arriving at their car almost at the same time as them, Rob recognized the stranger as Stuart Jenkins.

"Why it's Rob Larson. What a pleasure meeting you out here. This must be your lovely wife. Elle isn't it?" He knew exactly who she was and put out his hand toward her.

Elle took his hand, "Yes it is. I don't believe I know …".

Rob interrupted her, "Oh that's right you haven't met Mr. Stuart Jenkins. He's that reporter for *America Now*. Maybe you've heard of him? He specializes in telling stories with his own spin on them and then likes to justify it by calling it the truth. His specialty is exploiting people who can't help themselves."

As he spoke he continued to unlock his car doors and open Elle's side for her.

"Come now counselor. You and I know that I've got the facts to back up every word of …".

"Jenkins!" Rob cut him off.

"Don't even bother trying to lecture me on how you manipulate the facts. Save it for your publisher and the people who actually believe the trash you write."

Stuart wasn't fazed in the least and he seemed to take pleasure in the unexpected confrontation. Chuckling he pulled his dark sunglasses off saying, "I see. You're a critic and hey, every writer needs them."

Once Elle was seated, Rob closed her door while she just stared at the two men through the tinted window.

"What are doing down here anyway Jenkins? Do you smell something dead and you're looking for a free meal?" Rob demanded.

"That's good Larson. Real funny." Stuart was smug and put his shades back on. "I don't see that it's really any of your business what I'm doing here."

Rob countered and stepped in closer to the lanky man, "You know that Jenny Richards lives down this street. I represent Ms. Richards and her interests. It's interesting that you came along because she was just complaining to me that you've been calling her and harassing her. If it happens even one more time Jenkins, I'll have to speak with Judge Thompson and I'm sure Sheriff Spence will be more than happy to show you the way out of town."

A big cat grin grew onto Stuart's face, "Hey no problem counselor. I'm just in town to cover your little town's Christmas production."

There was a deep tide of condescension to his tone but Rob didn't care what he thought. Stepping around the front of his car he looked back at the smug looking reporter as he opened his door, "I'm glad we had this chance to talk. Let's pick it up again in the new year, shall we?"

The question was obviously not intended to prompt an answer but a desired distance in their meeting again. With that Rob got into his car and drove off. He noticed in his rearview mirror with satisfaction that Jenkins reversed his direction back down the street.

Nothing was said for a minute as Rob drove faster than he needed to down one street and than the next. Stopping hard and then taking off aggressively. Elle tried to be quiet but finally she couldn't take it anymore and pleaded with him.

"Rob I know you're angry but can you please just take it easy? I know that reporter back there has done and said some bad things but don't you see it's not all his fault. You can be cross at him but it's not going to fix anything for you or anyone else."

She hesitated and then blurted out, "And in case you didn't know, I'm really upset right now and I'm having a hard time with all of this." With that she broke down into sobs.

Rob had a history of running away every time Elle cried. He didn't understand himself; he just knew he couldn't deal with her need in that moment. When Elle miscarried their second child Rob told himself he was giving her lots of space to heal but the truth was he just didn't have the strength to be there for her in those times. Elle learned to hide her tears from him and he pretended to never notice but now the dam broke open with a flood. He'd never seen her like this before and it jerked him out of his own self-interest.

They had just come up on a scenic turnoff from the main road that ran parallel with the Brunswick River. Bare willow trees lined the rivers bank between the parking area and the moving water. Rob skidded the car to a halt in the empty lot and threw his arms around Elle as she pushed her tearstained face into his chest.

She hadn't realized how long she had waited for a safe place to undo her heart until she heard him whisper, "That's alright Honey, you just go ahead and cry. Let it all out." And she did.

Too often, intimacy is something the world has learned from failed instructors who make grand excuses and then make others pay for the lessons. On that sunny December afternoon, Rob and Elle found a beautiful place they'd never known before.

After soaking Rob's shirt with tears she mumbled something about it all being her fault that she lost the baby. It wasn't a dragon or even an evil king, but it was his chance to be a hero and slay the lie that held his wife captive. Rob unburdened his own heart and asked her to forgive him for not being there for her. He expected to feel like a failure at the exposure of his weakness but was amazed at the sudden strength he possessed.

"Oh Rob, I love you." She smiled brightly through swollen eyes and wet strands of hair that hung around her face.

"I love you too Elle and I promise that whatever we do from now on, we do it together."

She laughed unexpectedly and he grinned, "What? What's so funny now beautiful?"

"Well it's like this; I hope you don't take back all those sweet things you've said because somebody has made an absolute mess of your shirt. I mean it's soaking wet and there's makeup all over it and probably some other stuff … eww!"

"I'll make you pay!" he teased as he grabbed her playfully. Elle squealed lightly enjoying the closeness she felt. It went far beyond his physical touch and kiss. She felt her heart relax into an unfamiliar pattern that was open and free.

That night Rob got the bright idea that they were all going out driving around looking at everyone else's light displays. Elle didn't get back from choir rehearsal until about eight thirty so at first she protested the late hour, especially for Drew, but Rob was persuasive and promised to carry anybody to their bed if they fell asleep. Elle threatened that he just may end up carrying all three of them. Finally she conceded on the terms that he would get them an order of fries to go from Evelyn's Diner.

At first the boys started out sitting in the back seat but after picking up their fries and drinks, Brodie begged to sit in front with Rob and Elle.

"What about Drew? You can't leave him in the backseat by himself," Elle reasoned.

"Mommy he can sit beside me. See we can both fit in

one seatbelt." With that Brodie popped out of his place and squeezed up beside Drew putting his arm around his shoulder.

"See how small we are together?" He asked excitedly.

Rob had opted to take the SUV because it was snowing again and figured it was safer for the family's exploring.

Pulling over he flipped up the console, "Okay boys come on up." Brodie instantly stood up in the middle and Rob pulled him over easily.

"Alright who's next?"

Looking back he saw Drew still sitting in his spot. Lightening his voice Rob thought about how big and forceful the world might seem around this tiny figure, "Drew would you like to come up here and sit with all of us?"

His shyness was obvious as he opened up his mouth and nervously licked his mouth. Rob smiled and as if on cue Drew gave a slight nod of his head and lifted his hands.

As he was getting the seatbelt wrapped around the two youngsters Brodie put his hand on his dad's face, "He really likes you Daddy. He's just kind' a quiet you know? Not like me."

Rob was always fascinated with how much his boy saw from behind those hazel eyes.

"He may not talk like you Catcher but he's a good boy like you, isn't he?"

Brodie took the complement fully and nudged Drew with a satisfied look saying, "Dg'yeh hear that?"

The smaller boy didn't say a word but put another fry neatly in his mouth.

The Christmas spirit was brightly glowing around the town of Forrester and the outlying neighborhoods. That is if you could measure it by the decorated homes and buildings. Every street they turned down brought a delightful reaction over the twinkling and blinking displays. Rob had his radio set on the local station that was playing all their favorite Christmas songs.

"Oh Honey! This is our song. Remember?"

Elle turned up the volume up and started singing, "Christmas time is the perfect time for love".

"That's your song?" Brodie asked his dad in disbelief.

"It sure is and you should be pretty thankful for that song." Rob said winking at Elle.

"Why Daddy?"

"It was at Christmas time when I asked your pretty Mom to marry me and this song talking about Christmas being a perfect time for love helped persuade her to say yes. If she didn't get persuaded then we wouldn't have gotten married and there wouldn't be any us. And if there had been no us, there wouldn't be any you."

He tussled Brodie's hair to let him know that just wouldn't do.

Elle looked at this man she loved so much and felt closer to then ever before. She couldn't help herself and reached around the boys to rest her hand on Rob's warm neck. He just kept chatting Christmas light design with the boys and how their tree house was still the best.

Her mind wondered off enjoying her own sweet reflections and decided it was true; *Christmas time is the perfect time for love.*

Chapter 16

A gentle breeze had swept down off the rolling hills
the night before and now an early morning fog pushed its
way into town. The Brunswick River seemed to hold the
cloud like a wrap over Gordon's Park, anticipating the big
reveal.

It was the day before the first presentation of
A Forrester Christmas In The Park and the whole
community was buzzing with excitement, but in this early
hour all was still. The quiet streets lay perfectly patient,
without a doubt the undiscovered inspiration of a master's
brush stroke.

No story is without significance. Yet a tale that lends
sight to goodness beyond ones' experience brings a wealth
that cannot be measured. The eye of a skilled artist is
trained to disregard the conspicuous sights, to uncover the
brilliance hidden in one trivial detail.

From the corner of Elm and Main Street the heart of
this picture-perfect town beat. It was Christmas time and
hope was the affair, whether one could see its light or
not. Of all the many constants of the season, the orbit of

polarized views that mankind possessed for this day were most sure, but the least understood.

It was Rob's habit now to get up even a few minutes earlier than his usual early hour. Although he still slipped into the kitchen for a brewed coffee, he ignored the morning paper on the front step and went directly to the family room still in his robe and slippers. Pulling the heavy leather bound Book that he was becoming so familiar with from the library shelf; he sank down into the rugged overstuffed recliner. A bronze lamp gave off a soft glow through the copper Tiffany glass shade. He sipped the hot black drink and ran his hand over the cracked cover admiring the strength.

For as long as he could remember he disliked this time of year more than any other. He was like many people he guessed. The sight of the decorations only agitated the darkness he felt inside. Christmas had been a secret bone of contention between him and his family, or at least he had wanted it to be unknown, but Elle and Brodie had learned to celebrate in wide circles around him. To say everything was different today would be a glaring understatement. Rob felt excitement and hope in his heart. It was like he had traveled from one side of the universe to the other and found the uncommon denominator of life with his wife and son.

This side of life had not been insulated from complications though. In fact the complexity of the obstacles he presently faced were far beyond the experience of his reason to manage, at least successfully in his estimation.

Jenny had dropped a bomb on him almost a week ago now. Rob was never one to assume anything and so her announcement had come as a shock. Though he had called her within an hour of the initial meeting that had masterminded the charity *Andrew's House*, he scolded himself for not monitoring closely the fragility he recognized in her. Maybe he could have influenced her better if he wasn't so distracted with the unending train of predicaments that Mayor Harry was getting them all into, but in his heart he knew that wasn't the answer. She didn't want to raise Drew and that was plain enough.

"God I need your help. Right now I need more wisdom than I've ever known," he whispered.

Opening the Bible to the place he kept bookmarked with a copy of his father's letter, he began mulling over something in the last paragraph his dad said to him.

I've always held onto a truth I got from the Bible. It says in Proverbs chapter 24 that through Wisdom is a house and life built, and by understanding it's established on a strong foundation.

He flipped through the pages of Proverbs and stopped on chapter twenty-four, staring at the exact words his father had quoted. Instantly it occurred to Rob that wisdom was the beginning of his need but it didn't stop there, he needed understanding too. It wouldn't be enough to build something good but it needed to be established too.

His father's words came to his mind again, *Wise men speak of a 10 and 20 year plan for life but I'm telling you now son, you need to have at least a 100-year plan.*

Not noticing the strength of the morning sun and the lifting fog, Rob turned his head to look out of the two-story set of windows and his eyes suddenly locked on the tree house his father had built. It was a symbol of something to him. More than just a sentimental piece left behind by someone he loved, it was evidence of the truth that God heard and answered prayer. The question it seemed to ask Rob even now was; *do you finally recognize the answer?*

It took Rob twenty-five years to be able to see a lot of things and he wasn't about to let shortsightedness impair his vision for the future any longer. There was a renewed confidence and strength that took hold of him. In fact, a sense of amazement filled him as his whole perspective

shifted from his mortal view of the next few days to
angelic sight of a short century. "Thank you for the
answer. Thank you Heavenly Father."

Jenny was smoking more than usual today although she
knew Evelyn hated it, being a clean freak, but she couldn't
help herself. Despite the fact that the phone calls from Mr.
Jenkins were not as persistent lately, she still felt plenty
justified in biting all her nails off.

Chuck had reported to her a few nights before about the
reporter.

"That boy's been a hoppin' round town like a long
tailed cat in a room full'a rockin' chairs."

Of course neither Chuck nor Evelyn knew anything of
what she'd discussed with the Larsons the week before. It
seemed the only thing anyone wanted to talk about was
the Christmas production and that just churned at Jenny's
nervous stomach as she reached for her cigarettes again.

Just then the phone rang. She grabbed the wireless
like she had been waiting for an important call but
then cautiously checked the caller I.D. The name
came up *Larson, Robert*. Her heart quickened because
unknowingly she had become hopeful that this young
lawyer could open the exit door for her and free her
from the load the town was trying to stick her with. That
sounded harsh but there was no sense in denying what she
felt.

"Hello." She answered.

"Good morning, this is Rob Larson. Is this Jenny?"

"Yes – this is me. I sure hope you got some good news
for me Mr. Larson ... I mean, sorry, Rob. 'Cause I'm on
pins and needles over here and I don't think I can take the
pressure of just sittin' around waitin' anymore." Jenny's
patience had long since expired.

"Okay Jenny, I've been thinking things over and I
believe I have an answer for you, for Andrew and for
the town. Can my wife and I come over to see you this

afternoon about two o'clock?" Rob asked.

"Sure, I guess." Jenny sighed in a dispirited tone. She was hoping more for lightening to strike relieving her of this rebounding obligation.

"I mean isn't this just something you can take care of let me know when it's all done?" She sounded frustrated.

Rob had been as gentle as he could in all his dealings with this troubled woman but the sentiment of this last question struck a dissonant chord and irritated him.

He paused a moment to even his tone and then responded, "Jenny, we're talking about the rest of a little boy's life here and if you really want to walk away from this without a titanic load of regret, I would advise you to cheerfully invest a few more minutes into your nephew's life. What do you think? Can you handle that?"

He bit off the last words making the point that his was not really a question. It was time to act like the adult, even if it was just for one afternoon.

Soundly reprimanded Jenny's reply was meek, "Yes, of course you're right. Two this afternoon; that'll be great," she almost whispered.

"Okay we'll see you then. Goodbye," and Rob hung up the phone.

Now the wheels were in motion and the next step, he would never be able to turn back from, not ever!

This was one of Drew's favorite times of day. He had many favorites and this was already a pattern he'd come to enjoy since being at the Larson home. He could hear her soft steps coming down the hall and then the handle to the bedroom door quietly turn. Brodie was always asleep when the pretty woman would come in to wake them so he'd close his eyes too and pretend like he needed waking. She'd always start with her softest voice and this morning was like all the rest.

"Good morning boys. It's time to get up."

Elle looked at the two little lumps tucked inside their

beds and walked over to the window opening up the curtains. "Look, it's another beautiful day and there's all kinds of adventures just waiting for us!"

Her voice was gentle, bridled excitement and then she did like always and started making up wake-up songs for the boys.

"*Good morning to you, good morning to you. I just want to say good morning Brodie. Good morning to you, good morning to you. I just want to say good morning Andrew.*" Her voice sweetly cooed the youngsters into a celebration of the new dawn.

Brodie moaned happily as he stretched out and kicked his feet under the covers.

"Good morning Mommy," his squeaky voice managed.

Drew was already wide awake but he'd learned that these good morning songs would always have his name in them somewhere and the sound of his name would always synchronize with the tender touch of her hand on his head. That's the moment he would open his eyes and he could never hold back the smile that would bubble up in him looking into her face. She would keep singing her good morning song as she looked down with a look he didn't understand but soaked it up every time.

Breakfast was right on time and everyone was perfectly on schedule in the Larson home, which was especially important today. Rob had informed Elle that there were some new details needing his attention for the production and he really could use her help this morning.

Things were busy at the café but Elle knew that she could call in one of the part-time girls who were always hoping to pickup extra hours, especially around Christmas. Everyone knew the tips were the best in the weeks leading up to the big day.

Rob dropped Brodie off at school and then took Drew to his pre-kindergarten class, which was in an old converted Victorian estate now called Lowell LaPetite School. It had an excellent daycare along with the pre-kindergarten class, and though Drew was apprehensive when Elle first started taking him there for his half days, he'd grown to like his teacher and the students. Today they were coloring pictures of Santa Clause and counting snowmen in pictures.

As Rob walked Drew into his gingerbread looking schoolhouse, he held his hand and thought about Jenny's words. The world was a strange place he thought. He wasn't critical of Jenny because he had no idea what it was like to live her life. Rob remembered the many decisions he had made himself and then the confused sense he had of his own thinking.

What brings the world to a place where there is no room in it for a little boy like this?

The tiny hand in his and the innocent expression on Drew's face seemed to magnify the fault lines his humanity hid under a colorful blanket of its own goodwill.

Just as Rob got back in his car and was heading home his cell phone began ringing. It was Mayor Carson.

"Hello Harry. How are you doing this morning?" Rob asked cheerfully.

"Hi Rob. I'm doing just fine. Everything seems to be falling into place and I'm excited. Kind of nervous you know, but I'm excited. How about you?"

"Oh yes! I'm a bit of both too." He rolled his eyes thinking, *if only he knew what was really going on.*

"Say Rob, I was thinking this morning and I was wondering if you could help me out on this. I'd like to do a press release up for this *Andrew's House* you see, and the guys thought it would be a great idea to get a picture of me with that woman and kid. Can you get them together and maybe bring them over to the office for me? Not now of course, but maybe some time later in the afternoon?"

Rob's eyes bugged out for a second and his brain spun into overdrive, but without a worthwhile thought coming to him.

"Hmmm, okay. That does sound like a good idea Harry."

His mind was reaching out frantically for an answer that would steer the Mayor away from this plan. The situation was too delicate for Rob to handle with Harry in the mix right now and the truth was, Harry was like a bull and this was definitely a china shop.

Just then Rob walked by Roy Garcia all dressed up like Santa Clause heading toward Drew's school, probably as a treat for the kids. Roy had been ringing the bell outside of Gables department store for the Salvation Army now for at least ten years and he was a favorite among the townsfolk and tourists alike. No one had a better *ho-ho Merry Christmas!* The sight of Roy in the Santa suit triggered a thought for Rob.

"Yes sir that's a pretty good idea, but I don't know – that's kind of unfair to you I think."

"Well … w-what do you mean Rob? How's that gonna be unfair to me?" Harry stammered suddenly feeling concerned because if something wasn't going to be good for him that was reason to worry.

"Ah, it's probably nothing and maybe you should just go ahead. Keep it simple and do the shots low-key like the guys suggested."

"Rob you always give me good advice so now, please, just tell me what your concern is about doing this promo shot. I need to hear it."

It was amazing how quickly Harry could go from pushy and cocky, to needy and compliant. It was this paradoxical makeup that made him the endlessly entertaining character he would always be, mayor or not.

"Okay but don't let the guys know it was me that got you thinking this way."

Rob knew there were no *guys*, but it was Harry himself that came up with the idea for the publicity. Nobody else in town cared enough, not even Madge.

"This could be a really big story and if we go and release a stale, boring picture of you and these two in an office or something like that, I just don't feel like it'll give the country the big picture. Come on let's face it Harry, you're the Mayor of this here town and we've got an exciting thing going on right now. It's not every town that does something big like this."

"You're right Rob! So what were you thinking? I mean if I don't do this press release, what should I be doing?" Harry was hopeful that Rob had an even bigger plan.

"I'm glad you asked Harry. Look, let's be frank. There's going to be a lot of people coming to this production over the next week. A lot of people! I think there needs to be a special moment on the last night where you walk out on stage in front of all those people and give one of those huge checks representing all the donations toward Andrew's House. We can have little Andrew on stage and make a big deal of it and that … that is the perfect moment, in front of this huge crowd, the photo op of a lifetime."

Rob was more dramatic than he was comfortable with but he needed to sell this desperately.

There was quiet on the phone. Rob looked to see if he'd lost signal hoping he wouldn't have to call him back and go through that whole thing again.

Finally Harry spoke, "Rob … I can see it."

He chuckled as though delighted by the sudden revelation, "Yup, I can see it and you are absolutely right. It'll be perfect! Christmas Eve, at the big finale, I'll walk out and do Forrester proud. You know it'll probably be a good example for a lot of towns and cities all over the country."

Ah, the pendulum swung wide again and Rob just smiled as he ended the conversation. Harry had to go and work on his speech.

Back at the house Elle was just getting off the phone after making arrangements for someone to fill in for her at the café. When she told her mom that Rob had something come up that needed her help, Joanne had told her not to

206

worry about the café and that she'd take care of it. Elle knew that her mom's version of taking care of it usually meant *going it alone*. That might work on a sleepy summer day but not the week before Christmas. Elle made doubly sure there was lots of help calling in Chloe and Grace. They were part-timers, friendly and great when things were busy.

"Everything all set?" Rob asked.

"No problems at all. Mom agreed to let me bring in Chloe and Grace because I told her I needed her to pick up Drew from school at lunch, and bring him with her to the café."

"How come we can only con your mom out of work with more work?"

Elle laughed. "Yes I know. She's never stopped being a mom and wanting to help me."

She paused and then said, "Speaking of help; what is it I can do for you now Mr. Larson, sir?"

Rob moved toward the closet, still with his own coat on, "If you would be so kind and put your coat on, and please come with me. I've got something I want to show you."

With that he pulled Elle's ski jacket out of the closet and held it open for her to slip into.

Once in their boots, Rob led the way out the back door and across the snow packed yard. It was dimpled from the many little-boy footprints and then hardened as the cycle of mild to freezing weather locked the wet snow into shape. Elle grabbed Rob's arm because it was slippery and her boots were not the best on this icy snow. It pleased her to hold onto his strong arm and walk this close anyway.

"Where are we going?" She asked looking up and shielding the morning sun from her eyes.

"Have you ever been up in the tree house?"

"No. I thought that was just for you boys to play in," she giggled.

Rob looked at her and smiled differently so that it
brought her to attention. "Elle I found something up there
and I want to show it to you."

She didn't bother asking *what*. Instinctively she knew
he was talking about something more than another earthly
possession. His new appreciation for the intangible gave
her a nervous excitement.

It wasn't difficult at all for Elle to find her way up into
the tree house. Rob admired the athletic grace of his wife
as she climbed and crawled her way out onto the deck. All
the while remaining the playful and feminine girl he fell
in love with. It occurred to him that he married far above
the audacious ignorance he possessed. There was no
explanation for it other than his dad's prayers and God's
grace.

Like two children finding a perch to inspect life, they
sat side-by-side on the fort's deck up in the maple tree.

"It's beautiful isn't it?" She exclaimed looking around
at that frosted timberland beyond their property and the
speckled hills of dark and white.

Rob sighed lightly, "Sure is."

Then looking at Elle he continued softly, "You're
beautiful. I think today I realize more than ever before
how blessed I am to have you in my life and yes … Elle
you're beautiful!" He put his arm around her and she laid
her head on his shoulder for a moment soaking it in.

After a minute she broke the silence, "I've got a feeling
you didn't bring me up here to tell me I'm beautiful, but I
sure love hearing it from you."

Rob just smiled. "No I didn't, but it sure helps me
to realize how much I've already been given and I'm
thankful. Today I can see more than ever from up here
and that's what I want to show you. It's like looking at the
road behind us and seeing the goodness that's followed us,
even when I didn't recognize it. I don't want to walk by
another day again and not know what I've been given."

He breathed in the clean, brisk air as if drinking up the day.

"Here I am living in the same home, in the same town and yet it's like my whole world has changed, but it hasn't. I've just had my eyes opened and everything is becoming clear."

He paused to gather his next thoughts. "Elle I believe I can see the road ahead more clear and that's really why I brought you up here. I need to know if we can see the same thing together."

For the next while Rob and Elle lost track of time and everything else. It was as if they were sharing a glimpse of their future through life's kaleidoscope of patterns and lights. The truth is they would never forget what they talked about that day. From the vantage point of a little boy's world, they could see life clearly and they agreed … the picture was beautiful.

It's funny how seeing can be when the blindfolds come off, your whole world changes without moving a thing. That was the way this complicated matter with Jenny and Drew transformed for Rob. Yesterday he dreaded even the thought of the situation, and now today he was anxious to tell Jenny of a sure answer for her and Drew.
The celebration was top secret but the conclusion was profound and destined to be everyone's discovery.

Chapter 17

"Now there's a face I recognize," Came the deep voice.

Rob had just stepped into the large foyer of The Hope Center with Drew in tow. He was hanging up their coats when a large hand rested on his shoulder. Turning around he immediately came face to face with Kenneth's beaming smile.

"Uncle Ken it's good to see you and *Wow*! You look – ummm – you look kingly without a doubt."

They both laughed as Drew nervously backed up behind Rob's leg, still keeping an eye on the sight. Kenneth was in full costume for the final dress rehearsal and what a sight he was. Rob was impressed because Kenneth truly looked every inch a king from the Middle East. Starting with the sparkling stone encrusted turban right down to the long flowing purple and white robe that just covering his strange but authentic looking shoes.

"Are you here to check out the performance and make sure we're up to snuff?" Kenneth teased.

"Please! I've heard from reliable sources that everyone is doing an outstanding job and the town is in for a royal treat."

He chuckled and then added, "Actually I've had a few people tell me that you've found your true calling as an actor and a narrator."

"Oh you know folks Rob. They're just tryin' to encourage an ole fella', but I appreciate all the help I can get you know."

"Dad always said you were too good of man to be so modest." Rob could see that even just the mention of his father brought an unmistakable light to his eyes. His usual booming voice became instantly soft so that Rob had to lean forward to hear him in the crowded lobby.

"T'was Clint that was the good man son, and you be proud to never forget that."

Rob was honored by the remarks coming from such an uncompromising man and war hero. He knew some of Kenneth's history in the military and this was a brave man by standards long forsaken by a soft culture.

"I won't," was all he could say in response.

"Actually Drew and I are here just to catch the beginning of the show where they're running through the shepherd's part. After that us boys have orders to get home and get to bed early so we're rested up for the big day tomorrow. Right Drew? We're here to see Brodie taking care of the sheep."

Rob lightly patted his head. He had gradually relaxed his grip from the back of Rob's leg as he recognized Uncle Ken.

"Oh that's right. Brodie is a great little shepherd boy. And as a matter a fact, those is my sheep he's lookin' after up there. Plus I got my camel and a cow for the manger scene. Say Drew, do you remember what my camel's name is? Do ya remember when we was workin' on the tree house I told you his name?"

The big man bowed over to look into his face.

Drew seemed to be double-checking to make sure that it was Ken under that outrageous outfit.

"His name's Charlie." Both Rob and Ken exchanged impressed glances.

"And do you remember who I am, even with all this getup on?" He was down on his knees now in front of the boy.

"You're Uncle Ken," Drew answered.

It was enough of an invitation for the king to laugh and grab the little fellow in his arms for a hug. Rob was impressed with the gentle warmth that just seemed to flow from Uncle Ken and put the tiniest person at ease. His heart was a true one and the children gave witness to that.

The production had a dramatic opening with beautiful lighting and a deep moving soundtrack like the start of an adventure movie. The audio and stage lighting company the town had hired all the way from Bailey City definitely knew what they were doing.

Scott Burgess told Rob that all the lighting and sound was computerized. This way the tech team could work out the bugs in the past week's rehearsals and then with some slight modifications, plug in to the outdoor setup for the live show. Scott folded his arms presumptuously like there was nothing to it. Rob knew such a complicated feat came with much expertise and admired the excellence.

After what felt like a cosmic journey through stars and galaxies, the music hushed to the strain of a singular string line and a beautiful bluish star appeared overhead. From somewhere a hypnotic low voice began to tell a story of 2000 years ago. One light shone down on the impressive narrator who seemed to ooze with a regal air. Rob was stirred feeling as though he'd been transported through time to this period of humanity's significance. As Kenneth's voice rumbled through the room he described the circumstances surrounding Luke chapter two.

"It was a dark time in history. The Roman government had burdened the people with heavy taxes and now there was a mandatory census. Some would have to travel a great distance just to register. There was much corruption, even among the leaders of the Jewish people and so they prayed for help. They asked God for a deliverer ... a Savior! Listen to the shepherds as they tend their flock in the midnight hour."

Kenneth disappeared into the blackness and suddenly the stage lit up revealing two men sitting cross-legged and sheep lying down beside them. At the same time three shepherd boys came on stage each leading a sheep but Brodie had a little lamb in his arms. The men greeted the younger shepherds and then continued their conversation about the hardship of the times and the constant fear they lived under.

After some thundering sound effects and the blinding effect of flashing lights, Kenneth spoke the words of the messenger angel as the shepherds cowered. It was a compelling vision Rob thought as they had someone dressed in long flowing white robes and lit him so brightly from behind, all you could really make out was the angelic silhouette. Coupled with Kenneth's majestic voice coming from seemingly everywhere, it was quite convincing. Drew even squeezed closer to Rob's side feeling the intimidation of the scene. Rob put his arm around the boy and smiled.

"Brodie's doing a great job isn't he Drew?" Rob asked to hopefully put him at ease.

Drew looked up and suddenly became very expressive. "Brodie's got a baby sheep in his arms."

It was the most excited Rob had ever seen him.

Just as the angel was proclaiming, "For unto you is born this day in the city of David a Savior, who is Christ the Lord!" the music began to swell introducing the familiar melody of Hark the Harold Angels. The lights once again selectively revealed the choir hidden away on either side of the stage. Rob instantly locked in on Elle.

The choir had just begun to sing when from out of

nowhere Mayor Carson walked up on the front of the stage shouting.

"Hold it! Hold it everyone!"

Almost as quickly as Harry appeared, Ernie Jacobs jumped up from the front row. Angela Berry had turned from conducting the choir with a bewildered look on her face.

"Harry, Harry, Harry! What is it now?"

Ernie was Dr. David Murphy's assistant and the aptly appointed director of the town's production effort. It was obvious that Mayor Carson had already done this on several occasions because Ernie was fed up with him. Rob could only imagine what a meddling frustration he must have been to the whole creative process. It could be comparable to an ambitiously sticky fingered child in the kitchen of a fussy chef with no time to waste.

"Well I just got the idea that it would be very effective if the whole choir could step out from their positions and kind of start swaying to the music. You know kind of like this."

Harry started pushing his hips side to side as he worked his way awkwardly forward. Rob knew Ernie would have broken out laughing at the sight if he wasn't so completely irate with the unwarranted interruptions. Rob enjoyed a good chuckle though sitting there in the dark.

"Look Harry, the choir is on risers. It's only the front row that would be able to step out so that wouldn't look right. And besides, tomorrow is the performance and we need to stick to what we've rehearsed! The guys have the lights set for exact placement so please ... PLEASE no more interruptions! We've got to make it all the way through this dressed rehearsal, at least once!"

Ernie was exasperated beyond words.

Mayor Harry took his rebuke and felt only slightly embarrassed.

"Alright good job everyone. It's sounding great." He was backing up and almost fell over one of the sheep lying on the ground.

"Oops! Okay sorry about that."

The choir members were all trying to hold in their laughter but it was hard not to enjoy the comedic routine.

It was only about ten minutes later that Brodie came running out into the foyer already changed out of his shepherd boy's garb and ready to leave. Drew grilled him the whole way home about everything from the lamb he had carried to the thundering sound effects. Brodie assured him from the back seat that it was all so much fun and hopefully next year he would be a shepherd boy too. Rob glanced over at Drew in the front seat and could see he liked the idea very much.

The shoulder strap of the seat belt crossed well over his head and reminded Rob of just how impossible it seemed for this boy to be alone in the world.

With the promise of a bowl of crunchy cereal and a story by the fire, Rob motivated the boys to get ready for bed quickly.

"Awesome Dad! Come on Drew!" He shouted and they took off running down the hall and up the stairs. Drew was quick to lead but he was always mindful of the little guy that would follow him anywhere.

The room was already warm from the fire by the time they came down changed into their pajamas. A bowl of cereal was waiting for each of them on their own cartoon covered TV tray. It pleased Rob to see how excited they could get over sharing such a moment together.

"Guys I was thinking, since Drew had so many good questions about being a shepherd boy, I thought I'd read you the real Christmas story. It's all about angels, shepherds and a very special baby. Do you want hear it?"

"Yeh!" Came the unison response already garbled by milk and cereal.

"Are you gonna read it from your old Bible Daddy?"

Not waiting for a reply Brodie looked at Drew with an intense expression, "That's Daddy's book of secrets Drew.

It tells us stuff like wisdom things and stories from old days so we know what to do. Right Dad?"

"I don't think I could have said it any better son."

It reminded Rob just how intensely young hearts soaked up words and ideas becoming their own reference of truth.

"Okay this amazing story is in a book called Luke inside of this bigger book. It all happened about two thousand years ago when a man named Caesar made a law that everybody had to be registered. He was the ruler of most of the world and so he wanted to know where everybody was born, where they lived now, who their family was and where they worked."

"Now a guy named Joseph went up from Galilee from the town of Nazareth to a town called Bethlehem because that's where his great-grandfather David was from. He had his wife Mary with him and she was getting close to having a baby. While they were in Bethlehem the time came and Mary had her very first born Son."

Rob looked up from the old crinkled pages.

"It's very important for you guys to know that in the chapter before this one, it tells us that this baby was not like other babies. This baby boy was God's only begotten Son. It says here that Mary was very special and highly favored by God so that He chose her to bring His Son into the world. Cool huh?"

Both boys stared at him absorbed in the story and just nodded as they ate sloppily at their cereal.

"Okay. So Mary has God's baby Son and she wrapped Him in swaddling clothes and laid Him in a manger, because there was no room for them in the inn."

"What's swaddle cloth?" Brodie wondered shrugging his shoulders with peculiar look on his face. For some reason this made Drew giggle.

Grinning, Rob enjoyed looking through their eyes at such a famous story.

"Swaddling clothes came from a gauzelike material that

travelers back in those days carried in case they got hurt, or even worse. It was kind of like old-fashioned band-aids, except really big. You see there was no place for them to stay. No homes, no hotels, and nowhere to sleep. So baby Jesus, that's God's Son's name, was born in an old stinky barn with farm animals all around, and they used a feeding trough as his little bed."

"The baby boy had no place to be?" Drew's voice was soft but peaked with interest.

Rob suddenly became aware that Andrew was relating to Jesus' need for a safe place … a place to belong. He cautiously stepped out onto what seemed like a narrow ledge. He hadn't anticipated such a relevant connection with four and a half years of life.

"That's right Drew. Baby Jesus was born into this world with really no place to belong."

"Why?"

He seemed to almost plead and it touched Rob to the very core. Rob could see that even Brodie had his brow furrowed in a troubled expression.

"Why?" Rob repeated.

"You want to know why?" Both boys nodded their heads, spoons still in hand and their bowls forgotten.

"It was so He could take our place boys. You see God the Father in His awesome wisdom sent His own Son so that we could be blessed with the privilege of belonging. It was God's way of making a place for each of us. That's why the story goes on and says that at the same time shepherds were taking care of their sheep in the hills and angels appeared to them. And the glory of God was like a bright light shining all around them and he said, 'I bring you good news of great joy, which shall be for everyone. Unto you is born a Savior, Who is Christ the Lord.'"

"That's what my part is in the play, right?" Brodie was excited to make the connection.

"That's right!"

Rob used Brodie's enthusiasm to bring the story to a climax.

"And it says that the angel told the shepherds that this is how you'll know He's God's own special boy. You'll find him in a manger wrapped in swaddling clothes. Then a whole army of angels appeared in the heavens and they praised God saying, Glory to God in the highest and on earth peace good will to men ... and boys!"

He wasn't the best actor but he tried his best to be dramatic for the boys' sake.

Quieting his voice for effect, "The shepherds went to the city of David and there they found Joseph and Mary, and guess who else."

"Jesus!" The boys shouted.

"Exactly. And the Bible says that the shepherds were so excited when they saw Jesus that they praised God and told people everywhere. Everyone who heard the story was amazed and still to this day, people are amazed to think that God loves us all so much that He would send us His own Son."

The boys went to bed that night with many more questions than Rob could answer but he could tell that the Christmas story made a deep impression on them. Their prayers that night were a random string of petitions to bless others, a few personal desires and the rest seemed like an interview based on the manger scene. At times Rob wasn't sure if the question was directed at him or God.

It didn't take long though for the snuggly blankets to intoxicate the boys with sleep. Their talking slowed and their eyes could not stay open.

What perfect truth for a young mind to drift off to sleep with, Rob thought. *It's the most beautiful story of all.*

The day of the first performance came with a bang. Literally! Rob was studying in the family room at ten after seven and Elle almost had breakfast ready when the doorbell rang followed by a quick pounding. Still in his robe Rob hurried to the front door sensing the urgency of the visitor.

Elle called after him in a hushed tone, "Who do you think it is this early?"

"I don't have a clue," and then he added just before he grabbed the door handle, "but it better be good."

He opened the door just slightly not knowing who or what to expect, as the knocking had continued the whole time. Standing on the front step bundled in an overcoat that was too long for his short frame and a fedora pulled down over his eyes, was Mayor Carson. The cold air rushed in and Rob could see that his bulbous nose was already running.

"Harry what are you doing here?" Rob didn't bother trying to hide his irritation.

"Rob, please! Can I come in and talk with you. It's really important!"

He sounded genuinely upset Rob thought. Even though Harry was given to over reacting and had a bit of the sky is falling mentality, the strain in his voice pulled at Rob.

"Sure come on in," he relented.

Talking his coat and scarf, Rob invited him to follow him back into the kitchen.

"Good morning Harry. Can I get you a coffee?"

"Oh, good morning Elle. Aw no thanks. I ... I'm sorry to intrude on you guys this morning. I just really need to speak to Rob."

He paused for a moment looking a little dazed. Glancing at the breakfast she had going he seemed to revive to the delicious smells.

"Hmmm, you know if it's okay I think I will have that coffee."

"Comin' right up Mayor."

Once the men were seated at the table Harry wasn't long in pouring out the dreadful news that had kept him awake all night.

"Last night I got a call at home from that reporter, Jenkins."

"How did he get your home phone number? Did you give it to him?"

"Well ... actually ... I called him," he said sheepishly. "I was just so excited after seeing the dress rehearsal of the production that I wanted to call that guy up and kind of rub it in his face, you know."

"Harry that guy is dangerous. He's a professional at twisting words and stories. You need to just stay away from him. Period."

Rob emphasized the warning with a point of his finger as if he was instructing a child.

"Well I know that now!" his eyes dropping as if all was lost.

"Okay what's going on?" Rob tried to be patient with the bumbling fellow.

Like a boy trying to blame the other kid for a fight on the playground, Harry's face pleaded as his voice got thin and raspy.

"Rob he just laughed when I told him that this was going to be the best Christmas production in the country and that everyone would see that he was wrong about Forrester. He laughed that stupid, cynical laugh of his! Then he asked, *hey when was the last time you talked with that kid's Aunt Jenny?* So I told him I didn't have any need to because it was all taken care of. He comes back in that smug, know-it-all tone, *oh so you think it's all taken care of ... well maybe you'd better have a chat with Jenny 'cause I think you'll be surprised at what she has to say.*"

Harry's hands were trembling slightly as he took a sip of his coffee.

"So I tried to act like everything was just great but then, the guy threatens me! Can you believe that? He tells me that's he's looking forward to us putting on our first show because he'll be able to write his story about a mayor and a town soliciting donations under false pretenses, and get this ... exploiting orphan children!"

His voice was getting a little too high and too loud now.

Rob put his hands out in front of him, motioning to calm down. He didn't want the boys coming down for breakfast to the Mayor's hysterics. Besides it was too early in the morning for the world to fall apart just yet.

Whispering now, though not sure why, Harry asked, "So is Jenkins right? Have you talked to her Rob, I mean is this whole thing a bust?"

Rob glanced over the kitchen island and caught Elle's eye. She was still busying herself making breakfast and acting like she wasn't hearing a word, but she was intensely aware of the crisis.

The couple exchanged a knowing look and then Rob said to her with a controlled smile, "I guess we're going to have to advance our plans by a few days Honey." Elle's expression instantly radiated joy as a lump filled her throat.

Harry had a confused look on his face as he looked back and forth between the two, "What's going on you two? What's this got to do with the Christmas production?"

Before Rob could say a word, the sound of little feet thumping down the hall announced Brodie and Drew. Their faces still lined from a good night's sleep were indications that the wakeup process had only just begun. Drew was dragging his stuffed puppy by a leg and the blue cotton blanket Elle gave him in the other hand.

"Harry how would like to have breakfast with me and the boys? And after Elle takes them to school, I'll tell you what Mr. Jenkins doesn't know. You'll see that everything is going to be alright."

Harry's eyebrows went up and a doubtful look was on his face.

"I promise you, it's going to be alright," he said in a most assuring manner. It seemed to work because he could see relief spread across the mayor's round face.

"Okay who's ready for some breakfast?" Rob asked, as though pumping up his team for the win.

Of course Brodie rallied to the charge and before
long the kitchen table was filled with food and the most
amusing details Harry ever heard on the Bethlehem story.

At one point he stared back and forth between Brodie
and Rob asking, "Is that really true?"

Rob and Elle couldn't help but laugh as Brodie took
the opportunity to guarantee him, "Oh yeh Mayor Carson,
it's for really real!" Drew just nodded in agreement and
spooned another piece of his pancake that had been pre-cut
into small pieces for him.

Rob had to spend longer than he had hoped with
Harry that morning. It was necessary though and so were
the phone calls he made to ensure that Jenkins hadn't
sabotaged everything. Even though he was confident that
all was in order, Rob was a man of the law and didn't like
assuming on due process. That said; this was one of those
rare times he was happy to oblige the necessity of rushing
things, as long as it didn't compromise the big picture.
And there could be no compromise.

To make sure things didn't get messy, he put together
what he considered a Christmas Sting operation. Sheriff
Spence ran interference with Jenkins starting early that
afternoon.

"Chuck if you can just keep him busy and away from
my office, it would be a huge help to me."

Rob had no idea that Chuck would catch him speeding
and have to take him to the station on suspicion of driving
while under the influence. In the months that followed,
Sheriff Spence enjoyed recounting how furious the big
city reporter got.

"You should have heard him. He kept sayin', *Do you
know who I am? I'm going to bury this little worthless
town? Do you hear me Sheriff? You'll be sorry you
messed with me!*"

Then Chuck would shake his head and enjoy a laugh.

Miraculously every person and detail came into unison
that day to finalize the greatest piece of legal architecture

Rob had ever conceived. The truth is he knew it wasn't his design and much too precious to be considered business.

Miracles happen when people agree to God's plan. The scarcity of the supernatural is not on God's part but mankind's independent will.

Even Judge Thompson said in his gruff manner, "It would seem something is at work here beyond men's intervention or good will."

Everyone that day at the Franklin County Court agreed. There were smiles, hugs and tears of joy. What a unique cast of characters and the world would soon know just what they had come to agree on.

Chapter 18

"Ladies and Gentleman, boys and girls would you please welcome your hosts for this evening; Dr. David Murphy of the Forrester First Baptist Church and Pastor James Hunston of the Hope Center."

The audience was instantly excited as the prerecorded introduction boomed the opening. It was a capacity crowd of about 1,200 and the applause was enthusiastic, mixed with whistles and cheerful shouts. The two ministers walked out on stage smiling and waving.

"Hello and welcome to the premier performance of *A Forrester Christmas in the Park!*"

Dr. Murphy almost shouted in the microphone as the audience responded with a cheer. He was wearing a dark suit under his long overcoat and clerical collar but there was a festive, almost mischievous light in his eyes. The silver haired man had a seasoned instinct for timing and combined with his distinguished look, he commanded attention.

"My esteemed co-host, Reverend James Hunston, and I are confident that you are in for a real treat this evening. You're about to take part in a reenactment of the most awesome story known to mankind and the cast will aspire to take you back in time 2000 years. You will enjoy some of your favorite Christmas carols, and we do encourage you to sing along."

He swung his arm turning to face Pastor Hunston as though handing him the baton.

"Say, you're right Dr. Murphy. Folks take a good look around. Don't you think we've got a great turnout tonight for our very first run of *A Forrester Christmas in the Park?*"

The lights from the frame over the stage seemed to cue instantly and the crowded bleachers lit up to everyone's delight. Again everyone cheered. Much of the open space down in front of the makeshift theater style seating was full of lawn chairs. Blankets were draped over the shoulders of many and the town had the foresight to cover the bleachers with outdoor bench cushions. Propane patio heaters were sporadically placed throughout the crowd on loan from Franks Bar & Grill. It was as comfortable as it could be.

"Now the good thing about you being here for the first performance of this production is that you get to share in a historic moment for the town of Forrester. The bad thing is, we're going to keep getting better every night, sooo …" He could hear the rippled response as some began to snicker.

"Oh. So it's sinking in now is it? Well that just means you're going to have to tell a friend and bring them out another night."

Dr. Murphy seemed to get a concerned look on his face.

"You know I really don't want to sound ungrateful Pastor James but something kind of bothers me as I look out over this wonderful audience."

Pastor Hunston was unlike Dr. Murphy in many ways

and that was obvious even in their clothes. He wore a
three quarter length dark brown leather jacket over a tan
sweater and green corduroy pants. On top of that he didn't
have a dramatic bone in his body but he did his best to
play the straight man to the older man's question.

"Well now what's bothering you about this great crowd
we have here tonight?"

He managed to furrow his brow into an obvious fake
look of something. In this case though his poor acting
only added to the humor.

"I'll tell you what's bothering me. I don't remember
seeing a lot of these people in church last Sunday. What
about you?"

Dr. Murphy drew his hands up on his waist in an
irritated fashion and tapped his foot impatiently.

"Say, you're right Dr. Murphy. Hey, Mr. Light Man!
Turn those lights back up on the crowd for a moment!"

Reaching inside his breast pocket he pulled out a pad
and started writing frantically.

"What are you doing Pastor James?"

"I'll tell you what I'm doing. I'm taking names for
next Sunday. Starting right down front. Look! There's
Mayor Harry Carson and his wife Madge!"

He pointed emphatically as a spotlight swung onto the
couple. Dr. Murphy hastily grabbed his own note pad
and began to point into the audience acting like he too
was collecting names. The crowd broke into laughter and
applause as the First Couple lapped up the attention.

Once everyone settled down and the lights refocused all
attention on the stage, Pastor Hunston began to speak over
a soft bed of music.

"Seriously everyone, it's a blessing for us to be able to
share this night with you.   The music is timeless, the
message is eternal and our hearts are most sincere in what
we desire to accomplish for those who are in great need of
our help."

"Very well said Pastor James and I truly believe that we

will witness a Christmas miracle this evening."

Turning toward the audience Dr. Murphy continued.

"At the end of the performance tonight Mayor Carson will take a few moments to tell you about *Andrew's House.* It is the collective vision of this town to help make a better life for some of the orphaned children and families in crisis. For now though we want you to relax, enjoy the presentation and celebrate with us the greatest gift of all time. Once again, ladies and gentleman, boys and girls please put your hands together for *A Forrester Christmas in the Park.*"

Even as the applause was dying down the mood dramatically changed. Bright stage lights gave way to what looked like a deep blue sky speckled with the most vivid starry hosts. The haunting sound track rumbled and then echoed distant melodic lines from another world. Instantly the wide-eyed and reverent audience was transported to another dimension. Quickly forgotten was the familiarity of Gordon's Park as every ear, young and old, drank in the opening lines of the narrator.

Kenneth suddenly appeared under a single light in full costume, just like in rehearsal except this time the tech team had a mist of fog around him. The scene was mysteriously like a painting and the audible draw of breath from the audience revealed their impression.

"Far, far away ... in another place ... at another time. A people under the burden of a most difficult and hopeless existence struggled to remember a promise. There was a prophecy from God given through Isaiah and many longed to see it fulfilled. The ancient Words sounded like this:

For unto us a child is born, unto us a Son is given: and the government shall be upon His shoulder: and his name shall be called Wonderful, Counselor, The mighty God, The everlasting Father, The Prince of Peace. Of the increase of his government and peace there shall be no end."

As Rob sat in the shadows, exhausted from the bigness

of the day, the words Uncle Ken quoted from Isaiah poured over him like a refreshing wind. The title *of everlasting Father* triggered a joy that involuntarily surged up within and caught at his throat.

Strange he thought. He wasn't used to such outbursts of emotion but than again, his life these last few weeks had been anything but usual, especially today.

The production exceeded everyone's expectation by far. It was said that Ernie Jacobs directed like a general from backstage and via his headset. His manner was calm but the intensity that possessed him made even his amateur colleagues notice.

Pretty much all of the performers were local talent except for the First Presbyterian Hand Bell Choir from Bolin Forge. They were only about a half hour drive away and volunteered to be a part of the evening however Ernie could use them. It proved to be advantageous for everyone. The audience went dreamy at the three beautiful pieces mixed in to the production, and they served perfectly as transitional moments for the stagehands.

The fabricated band shell would go completely dark and the bell choir would come around both sides and stand out front, right on the ground. The audience would gaze hypnotically as the silver bells would flash in the spotlights and ring out haunting refrains of standards like *O Little Town Of Bethlehem.*

As one would suspect, there were subtle cues and performance moments that the cast and singers later critiqued themselves over. The donkey that Joseph led Mary on got a little rebellious when he came to the ramp going up on the stage. The crowd began to chuckle and it was looking like Joseph wouldn't be able to even get Mary to the manger. Kenneth left his post as the narrator and seemed to almost float down onto the ground in his flowing robes. He whispered something into the ear of his mule Jake and then helped the young man lead the animal up on stage with no more incidents.

Once back at his narrator's post, he calmly spoke as if still on script, "Yes, God helped His servant Joseph … even when he had trouble with his donkey."

The crowd roared with laughter breaking into applause and whistles. It all seemed a delightful experience to everyone.

When the choir ended the evening with *Joy To The World* there was an immediate response as the crowd jumped to their feet and applauded. The excitement wasn't just over the success of the production but it was obviously a celebration of the story so well rehearsed. It was beauty not fabricated by man, but brought to light by a small group of courageous townsfolk. Every heart without exception was stirred by the production.

Mayor Carson and Madge walked out onto the platform. The audience was still standing in ovation.

"Wasn't that wonderful?" He shouted and the crowd responded with cheers and whistles.

Madge stood beside her husband wearing a long white coat with dark Dalmatian-like spots all over it and shiny red boots. It was Christmas on heels and Forrester could expect nothing less from its First Lady.

Once Mayor Carson got everyone quieted and sitting back down, his air became unusually reverent and thoughtful.

Taking off his fedora and turning the brim around in his hand he began, "You know … there are a lot of great people in this town. Like you've seen tonight, it takes many folks pulling together to make something special happen. As the mayor of Forrester it's my great privilege to tell you about another project that we've all decided to pull together on."

"Recently it came to my attention …" he paused.

His posture changed and he seemed to correct himself.

"It's actually come to the attention of many fine folks around here that there are some in great need of help. In fact some of those people I'm talking about are little boys and girls. That's where the idea for *A Forrester Christmas in the Park* came from. We wanted to give you the best presentation of the true meaning of Christmas so we could ask you to pull with us on another project. We're calling this new project … *Andrew's House*."

Any of the town's people who had doubted how Harry Carson won the post of mayor were soon reminded again of his infrequent moments of brilliance. He did an excellent work of presenting the mission of *Andrew's House* and giving the town ownership of the idea. People were impressed and even moved to get on board.

"Before we go any further I'd like to invite Rob Larson to come out and make some introductions of his own. Rob is the legal side of our town counsel and a great friend. I think you'll find what he has to say very interesting. Let's give him a welcome."

The audience responded warmly as Rob walked out on stage leading his own miniature parade. Holding onto his arm for support was Jenny Richards who was now able to walk with just a cane. Close behind Elle walked hand in hand with two little boys. Most everyone recognized Brodie who still had on part of his shepherd boy costume.

Elle had managed to slip away unnoticed from the choir formation while Mayor Carson was speaking. Shedding her choir robe she looked elegantly Christmas. Wearing a midnight blue velvet dress with her blonde curls falling on her shoulders, her face was radiant with that dimpled smile. She glanced down and wrinkled up her nose approvingly at each boy as they took their place center stage beside Rob.

"Thank you Mayor Carson, and thank you to everyone who has made the grand dream of *A Forrester Christmas in the Park* this beautiful reality."

There was an audible burst of assent as some clapped and cheered.

"You've been very supportive by attending this first

performance tonight, so I want to thank you and return the favor by keeping this as short as possible."

"Many of you remember my father Clint Larson. Before he passed away he built a first-rate tree house in a large maple tree that grows in our backyard. It was his gift to Brodie, his friends … and yours truly. Dad told me to take a moment and consider that old tree. He said that no matter how good or strong he built that fort, it was only as sound and sure as its foundation … that old maple tree."

"I have to be honest with you. It's only been recently that I've actually listened to what my father said to me. The truth is I've neglected the foundation of life far too long."

Elle pushed closer to her husband, sandwiching the smallest boy between them. Rob turned and taking her hand, smiled knowingly. Reaching down he hoisted the tiny boy up into his arms. He clung shyly to Rob's neck.

"It's my great pleasure to introduce to you some dear people. Of course this is my wife Elle, and that good looking shepherd boy is my son Brodie."

Brodie gave a big wave and unabashedly soaked up the attention.

"Now to my left here is one of the greatest waitresses Forrester has ever had, Jenny Richards."

She looked better than she had in a long time and wore a beautiful plaid coat that Elle had just bought for her late that afternoon.

"Jenny is a very special woman, and also the great-aunt of this precious little boy, Andrew Richards. As you may have guessed, he is the namesake for *Andrew's House*. Now all of his friends call him Drew. Isn't that right Drew?"

Rob gave him a squeeze and Jenny reached over and touched his tiny hand. It seemed to give him the courage he needed to look out at the crowd.

"To be respectful of your time, and some of the unfortunate but private details, I'm going to give you the short end of their story. Miss Jenny here has devoted her life looking after Andrew, but because of some demanding circumstances she has fallen behind. In fact as you may have noticed, she actually has fallen and hurt herself quite badly. This has made it impossible for her to even work at the diner right now. I'm sure you can imagine the chain reaction of complications in her life."

"Jenny and I have had some great conversations. She's told me how much she wants the best for her nephew and asked if anything could be done."

"Ladies and gentlemen, my father's reminder of the importance of foundation has been ringing in my ears. Now, I'm not going to lie to you. When I first became aware of Jenny and Andrew's trouble, I believed two things: there was no solution, and it had nothing to do with me. I was wrong."

"This town of Forrester does not just consist of the buildings or bylaws that govern our local business. It's far greater than that. It's the people and the principals we live by. Much like the Christmas story we've all enjoyed tonight, it's about giving, mercy and kindness. It's the foundation that has brought us through difficult times in the past and it is the answer we have for the future." A thoughtful hush came over the crowd as a sense of anticipation filled the air.

Pausing for a moment, Rob thought of how happy his dad would be right now. He nodded his head knowing that somehow he was, and then cleared his throat.

"With that in mind, my wife Elle and I … and of course Brodie too, we'd like to share some good news with you. Aunt Jenny has given us her blessing and so we have filed to adopt Andrew and make him a part of our family. Tonight I'd like to introduce to you for the first time, our new son and Brodie's new little brother; Andrew Richard Larson!"

Rob hoisted the boy to his shoulder proudly as Elle and Brodie pushed even closer to him. Jenny laughed reaching up to touch the suddenly celebrated life.

As though cued for the grand finale, the music struck a crescendo and the choir broke into a reprise of "Glory To God". The cast still in costume poured onto the stage and began a makeshift parade of sorts around Rob's family. Everyone was trying to get close for a handshake and even more preferably, a big hug. Elle and Rob were laughing at the outpouring of love from both kings and shepherds alike.

Meredith ran out of her place in the choir and was one of the first people to congratulate Elle. Even little Lacey got into the mix, but seemed mostly interested in Brodie's attention. Elle couldn't help notice when Meredith walked away holding Lacey's hand that she was also holding some else's hand. Could it be? Elle's nose wrinkled into a disbelieving smile as she noticed Ernie tenderly leading her back to the choir. They had more to talk about than she had realized.

If ever there was an occasion to remember in Forrester, that clear winter's night was it. To say the crowd went wild would be an understatement. The townsfolk erupted into applause and shouts of joy. Women wept and it wasn't uncommon to see big men wiping tears from their eyes. Visitors from out of town felt immediately fused with the surge of love in the air and everyone wanted to hold a piece of the moment.

The outpouring of charity didn't just end with the roar of applause. The co-hosting ministers quickly directed the kind-hearted folks to do what they could and wasted no time in taking up a collection for *Andrew's House*. The Larson family was obviously doing their part and so everyone jumped at the opportunity to give their best.

The moment was made even more beautiful when a local artist performed a song he had written to commemorate the occasion. Everyone dug deep and passed the hat as Marshall Stevens sang *A Little Boy's Prayer*. It was a moment of great triumph for the town of

Forrester but for reasons that few envisioned.

Mayor Carson kept his word and ran onto the scene dressed like Santa. He and his helpers handed out paper sacks filled with candy to all the little ones. As much as he complained about being forced into the role, he played the part cheerfully and capped off the night perfectly.

Driving off with his family, Rob couldn't wipe the grin from his face. They could all still hear Santa's *ho ho ho* echoing over the sound system.

He and Elle had planned earlier to quietly slip away, knowing that the media would be looking for a follow up story to the smear Jenkins had broke. It wasn't that he didn't want to talk to them but it had been a big day and they all needed some rest, especially the boys.

The week was far from over and as news spread about the Larson family adopting Andrew; the efforts of Forrester became sensationalized with the endearing personal story. Everyone involved insisted on Rob mimicking his speech at each performance as he did the first night. The audience came to expect it and of course it was the perfect inspiration for giving to *Andrew's House.* And give they did!

A Forrester Christmas in the Park had its final performance Christmas Eve. As exhausting as the effort was for many, the joy and kindness that grew with each day overtook the quaint town. Many who had balked at the sacrifice of the usual programs had suddenly found a new favorite tradition. It was a ritual that had more to do with living and loving than with earthly sentiment.

There was also a tradition now only four years old in the Larson home. After Rob got a fire going and the boys were sampling some Christmas cookies, Elle selected two brightly wrapped gift boxes out from under the tree and passed them out. Andrew's eyes got wide and he froze with a cookie almost to his lips.

"Oh yay! I know what this is Mommy. Can we open it

up tonight?" Brodie was bouncing with excitement.

"Okay, okay, but don't say what you think it is. Let's not spoil the surprise for Drew."

"We get to open one present on Christmas Eve Drew. It's allowed 'cause it's our tradition."

Brodie told his new little brother excitedly as he tore into his package. Drew on the other hand held the gift feeling a touch uncertain.

"Go ahead Drew. Just rip the paper off like Brodie does. Have some fun with it." Rob encouraged.

Eventually the newest member of the family got down to the raw box and opened it. Brodie had semi-patiently squirmed around keeping his box closed until they both could experience their gifts together.

"Onesies!" Brodie shouted holding up the red cotton jammies.

Drew was gently touching the material still neatly folded in the box.

"It's soft," he said as he fingered the white snowmen printed on the light blue material.

With Brodie at the lead the boys wasted no time running upstairs and changing for bed. Once everyone was cozy around the fire again, Rob read the famous tale of *The Night Before Christmas*. Drew would have to learn the end of the story next year as he fell fast asleep in Elle's arms.

As Rob closed the colorful book with a quiet, "The End", the sound of the crackling fireplace seemed therapeutic.

"I better get this little guy to bed," Elle whispered starting to lean forward.

Brodie's eyes were half shut but he managed a big smile saying, "Isn't he cute?"

Rob tried to muffle his laughter with his hand and Elle pursed her lips accentuating her dimples. Brodie grinned with pleasure to think he entertained his parents yet again and Elle carried the boy in blue off to bed.

"What do you think sleepyhead? You must be feeling
pretty tired after the big week you've had."

"Yeh I guess I'm ready for bed too," came his lazy
answer. Then livening up a bit he pointed, "Hey look at
that Daddy."

Rob looked out the huge window at the twinkling lights
outlining the tree house. The glow made the falling snow
appear dreamlike in the night.

"That tree house looks as beautiful to me as it does to
you. That's our place. Right son?"

Brodie patted his father on the hand, "That's right. It
belongs to me and you, and Drew, and Grampy."

Rob lay there on the floor beside Brodie for a few quiet
moments. He marveled at how Brodie's faith put little
difference between earthly and heavenly residence. They
both enjoyed the warmth, as their eyes grew heavy with
sleepiness.

Quietly Elle had come back in the room and leaned
over the pair.

"It's Christmas tomorrow so all little boys need to get
to bed."

Rob stirred as she kissed Brodie and pushed his matted
hair away from his face. He wavered between being
asleep and awake.

Scooping up his boy he held him against his shoulder
and Brodie instinctively snuggled closer. In his one-piece
pajamas, he was a picture all in red from his toes up. Elle
paused Rob right at the doorway to grab a picture of him
holding the little package.

"There," she whispered as the flash went off. "We
don't ever want to forget this Christmas."

Gently he climbed the stairs careful to avoid the one
step that always let out a creak or groan, depending on its
mood Rob supposed. Quietly he pushed open the cracked
door to the boys' bedroom. He smiled at the tiny bump
Drew made curled up in his bed. The child was fast asleep
and Brodie was soon to follow.

Pulling the blankets around him, Rob leaned over to kiss his smooth cheek goodnight when suddenly Brodie stirred and wrapped his little arms around his neck. He squeezed his dad with an intensity that caught him by surprise.

"Hey you. I thought you were asleep." Rob whispered.

"I sort of was Daddy, but than I was sort of thinking too."

"There'll be lots of time for 'sort of thinking' tomorrow. Tonight it's time to sleep. Okay?"

"Okay. Daddy? Can I ask you a question?" Brodie whispered in his scratchy voice.

"Alright but then you have to go to sleep."

"Daddy can we … can we have Christmas all year long?"

Rob smiled at his boy's request. He guessed that's what every child dreamed of. Even as he was trying to think of a simple answer to what he thought the question was, Brodie interrupted his thoughts.

"I don't mean the presents. I like them and … and I know it's going to be fun for me and Drew tomorrow, but it's not the toys I really want. You been so nice to Mommy anymore and stuff like that, and you got more time to do things with me. Daddy you even found your old Bible and now you read mysteries to us and I like that. It's just …" he paused as though he could feel the lump in Rob's throat as he whispered in his ear.

"I just don't want Christmas to stop. There's some kind of special feeling in our house now. Ever since you started reading us stories about Jesus everything is different. Even my prayers get answered quicker! Daddy I didn't want to say anything but I knew I was getting a brother. I prayed for him!"

He pushed Rob's tear stained face back to look him in the eye. It was too dark to really see but Rob felt his gaze nonetheless.

Swallowing hard, Rob fell softly forward into the arms

of his little boy. Whispering into his ear he hoped his words would find their worth in Brodie's heart.

"Son whatever it is we've found that makes everyday so special, I promise to never lose it with God's help. And you can pray that Daddy never loses it. Okay?"

"Okay," he whispered feeling content to drift off to sleep.

"So the answer is yes. We can have Christmas all year long."

Rob spoke in a hushed tone, not sure if Brodie was even awake anymore, but realizing his son showed him to the truth again.

Lightly he backed out of the boys' room pulling the door almost closed. Life had suddenly grown in ways he'd never dreamed. Contentment flooded his heart as he realized the fears that once drove him now had no control over him. He softly let go of the bedroom door handle and turned to go.

There she was. Elle had been waiting for him just outside the door.

"I heard everything," she choked as she pushed herself into his arms. "I love you so much Rob."

Cradling her head, he caressed the soft curls. As he looked into her eyes, she gave a rare loving smile reserved for him only. Rob felt a rest sweep over him. He reached down lifting her face and kissed her warmly on the mouth.

"You know sweetheart, I do believe we're about to have Christmas all year long."

Pleased, Elle sighed and laid her head on his chest as he wrapped his arms around her.

A Little Boy's Prayer
Other Products Available

Audio Music CD with Your
Christmas Favorites!

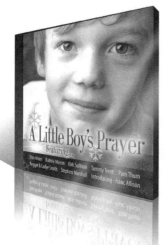

Children's Illustrated Book

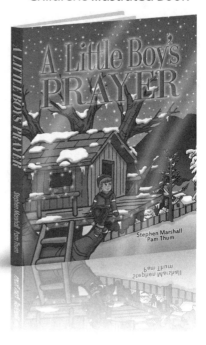

Full Dramatic Performance
Audio CD

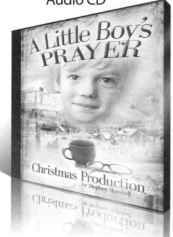

Purchase these items online at
www.aLittleBoysPrayer.com

Jan '91

Compassion

A Reflection on the Christian Life

Text by
Henri J. M. Nouwen
Donald P. McNeill
Douglas A. Morrison

Drawings by
Joel Filártiga

Darton, Longman and Todd
London

Unless otherwise noted, the biblical quotations are taken from or based
upon the Jerusalem Bible published and © 1966, 1967 and 1968 by
Darton, Longman & Todd Ltd and Doubleday & Co. Inc., and are used
by the permission of the publishers.

First published in Great Britain in 1982
by Darton Longman and Todd Ltd
89 Lillie Road, London SW6 1UD

Reprinted 1983, 1984 and 1987

First published in the USA by
Doubleday & Co. Inc., Garden City, New York

ISBN 0 232 51578 6

British Library Cataloguing in Publication Data

McNeil, Donald P.
    Compassion: a reflection on the Christian life.
    1. Christian life   2. Sympathy
    I. Title   II. Morrison, Douglas A.
    III. Nouwen, Henri J. M.
    241'.699   BV4647.S9
ISBN 0 232 51578 6

Printed and bound in Great Britain by
Anchor Brendon Ltd, Tiptree, Essex

THESE REFLECTIONS ARE DEDICATED TO

JOEL FILÁRTIGA

THE COMPASSIONATE PARAGUAYAN DOCTOR-ARTIST
WHO MADE THE DRAWINGS FOR THIS TEXT;
TO HIS COURAGEOUS WIFE

NIDIA;

AND TO THE MEMORY
OF THEIR SEVENTEEN-YEAR-OLD SON

JOELITO

WHO WAS TORTURED
TO DEATH BY A POLICE SQUAD
ON
MARCH 30, 1976

If our life in Christ means anything to you, if love can per-
suade at all, or the Spirit that we have in common, or any
tenderness and sympathy, then be united in your convic-
tions and united in your love, with a common purpose and a
common mind. That is the one thing which would make me
completely happy. There must be no competition among
you, no conceit; but everybody is to be self-effacing. Always
consider the other person to be better than yourself, so that
nobody thinks of his own interests first but everybody thinks
of other people's interests instead. In your minds you must be
the same as Christ Jesus:

> *His state was divine,*
> *yet he did not cling*
> *to his equality with God*
> *but emptied himself*
> *to assume the condition of a slave,*
> *and became as we are;*
> *and being as we are,*
> *he was humbler yet,*
> *even to accepting death,*
> *death on a cross.*
> *But God raised him high*
> *and gave him the name*
> *which is above all other names*
> *so that all beings*
> *in the heavens, on earth and in the underworld,*
> *should bend the knee at the name of Jesus*
> *and that every tongue should acclaim*
> *Jesus Christ as Lord,*
> *to the glory of God the Father.*

(Ph 2:6–11)

Contents

Preface

This book began in a small Greek restaurant in Washington, D.C. As we sat in the empty subterranean dining room expressing our discontent with the individualism and spiritual dryness of our academic lives at Notre Dame, Catholic University, and Yale, the three of us found ourselves scribbling notes on our table napkins. This time, unlike many others, our complaints led not to idleness but to a plan to meet on nine Thursdays in the capital city to study and pray together. Being teachers of pastoral theology and finding ourselves in the city where great political power is sought, acquired, and exercised, the question of how to live compassionately in our world presented itself as the most urgent question for our meetings.

These reflections on compassion have emerged from those nine Thursday meetings. The first formulations of what compassion might mean in our society were born in dialogue with those whom we had occasionally invited to join our discussions: Walter Burkhardt, S.J., theologian and member of the faculty of Catholic University; Parker Palmer, sociologist of religion and Dean of Studies at the Quaker community, Pendle Hill; Mike Heissler, medical student at George Washington University; Patrick Leahy, U. S. Senator from Vermont, and his wife, Marcelle; the late Hubert Humphrey, U. S. Senator from Minnesota; Betty Carroll and Carol Coston, religious sisters working with the Center of Concern and with Network; Jim Wallis and Wes Michaelson, editors of *Sojourners;* and the Little Sisters of Jesus, who live, work, and

pray as contemplatives in the midst of Washington, D.C.
They all shared considerable time with us and offered us
numerous ideas, suggestions, and experiences that became the
rich soil from which this book grew.

Quite a few years have passed since the conclusion of those
meetings. They were years of testing, reformulating, and
reevaluating many of our original thoughts. Now that we
feel confident enough to put our reflections in print, we want
to express our sincere thanks to these "early pioneers" without whom this book would never have been written. Just as
the pioneers of this country would find it difficult to recognize today the country they explored, so our friends may have
a difficult time discerning in these pages the insights they
offered. But those insights are here, and form the backbone
of this book.

We also want to express our deep gratitude to the Paraguayan doctor Joel Filártiga. His powerful illustrations, born
from the tragedy in his own life, add to this book a dimension that far exceeds both our experiences and our words.
The story of Joel, which we tell in the Epilogue, explains
why his drawings have become an integral part of this book.

Introduction

The word *compassion* generally evokes positive feelings. We like to think of ourselves as compassionate people who are basically good, gentle, and understanding. We more or less assume that compassion is a natural response to human suffering. Who would not feel compassion for a poor old man, a hungry child, a paralyzed soldier, a fearful girl? It seems almost impossible to imagine that compassion does not belong among our most self-evident human qualities. Do we not feel deeply offended when someone accuses us of lacking compassion? Does that not sound as if we are accused of a lack of humanity? Indeed, we immediately identify being compassionate with being human. An incompassionate human being seems as inconceivable as a nonhuman human being.

But, if being human and being compassionate are the same,

then why is humanity torn by conflict, war, hatred, and oppression? Why, then, are there so many people in our midst who suffer from hunger, cold, and lack of shelter? Why, then, do differences in race, sex, or religion prevent us from approaching each other and forming community? Why, then, are millions of human beings suffering from alienation, separation, or loneliness? Why, then, do we hurt, torture, and kill each other? Why, then, is our world in such chaos?

Questions such as these suggest that we need to take a critical look at our understanding of compassion. The word *compassion* is derived from the Latin words *pati* and *cum*, which together mean "to suffer with." Compassion asks us to go where it hurts, to enter into places of pain, to share in brokenness, fear, confusion, and anguish. Compassion challenges us to cry out with those in misery, to mourn with those who are lonely, to weep with those in tears. Compassion requires us to be weak with the weak, vulnerable with the vulnerable, and powerless with the powerless. Compassion means full immersion in the condition of being human. When we look at compassion this way, it becomes clear that something more is involved than a general kindness or tenderheartedness. It is not surprising that compassion, understood as suffering with, often evokes in us a deep resistance and even protest. We are inclined to say, "This is self-flagellation, this is masochism, this is a morbid interest in pain, this is a sick desire." It is important for us to acknowledge this resistance and to recognize that suffering is not something we desire or to which we are attracted. On the contrary, it is something we want to avoid at all cost. Therefore, compassion is not among our most natural responses. We are pain-avoiders and we consider anyone who feels attracted to suffering abnormal, or at least very unusual.

Compassion thus is not as natural a phenomenon as it might first appear. We should therefore not be surprised to find some people say without hesitation that a compassionate soci-

ety is a sick society. Peregrine Worsthorne expresses this
"incompassionate" point of view when he writes:

A genuine compassionate society, one that has succeeded in
achieving the ideal of actually putting itself in the shoes of the
unfortunate, will soon find itself marching in the direction of collective solutions inimical to individual freedom. . . . There is a
real and awful danger of people actually beginning to identify
with the world of suffering. . . . No healthy society should
allow itself to see the world through the eyes of the unfortunate,
since the unfortunate have no great interest in perceiving, let
alone exploiting, the highest value of civilization: individual
freedom. Indeed, being for the most part those who have failed
to make use of freedom, either because of fate or circumstances . . . they are likely to be the part of society least enamored of that supremely challenging ideal and most susceptible
to all the temptations to undermine it.[1]

These words probably seem very harsh, but they may be
more representative of our way of living and acting than we
are ready to confess. Although we might not be as eager as
Peregrine Worsthorne to reject compassion in the name of
individual freedom, it is not unlikely that in fact we are close
to his basic conviction that compassion cannot and should not
constitute the core of human motivation. If we give compassion a place at all in our daily concerns, we consider such a
place at best to be on the periphery of our thoughts and actions. Like Peregrine Worsthorne, we too are skeptical about
a world governed by compassion. The idea of such a world
strikes us as naïve, romantic, or at least unrealistic. We
"know" too well that our civilization will not survive if the
crucial decisions are in the hands of truly compassionate people. For those who do not live in a dream world and keep
their eyes open to the facts of life, compassion can at most be
a small and subservient part of our competitive existence.
   This sobering idea was forcefully brought home to us during

the early stages of this book. One day, the three of us visited
the late Senator Hubert Humphrey to ask him about compassion in politics. We had come because we felt he was one
of the most caring human beings in the political arena.
The Senator, who had just finished talking with the ambassador of Bangladesh and obviously expected a complaint,
a demand, or a compliment, was visibly caught off guard
when asked how he felt about compassion in politics. Instinctively, he left his large mahogany desk, over which
hung the emblem reminding visitors that they were speaking
with the former Vice-President of the United States, and
joined us around a small coffee table. But then, after having
adapted himself to the somewhat unusual situation, Senator
Humphrey walked back to his desk, picked up a long
pencil with a small eraser at its end, and said in his famous
high-pitched voice: "Gentlemen, look at this pencil. Just as
the eraser is only a very small part of this pencil and is used
only when you make a mistake, so compassion is only called
upon when things get out of hand. The main part of life is
competition; only the eraser is compassion. It is sad to say,
gentlemen, but in politics compassion is just part of the competition."

Compassion erases the mistakes of life, just as the rubber
end of a pencil removes the smudges on the paper. Perhaps
this is how most of us really feel and think when we are
honest with ourselves. Compassion is neither our central concern nor our primary stance in life. What we really desire is
to make it in life, to get ahead, to be first, to be different. We
want to forge our identities by carving out for ourselves
niches in life where we can maintain a safe distance from
others. We do not aspire to suffer with others. On the contrary, we develop methods and techniques that allow us to
stay away from pain. Hospitals and funeral homes often become places to hide the sick and the dead. Suffering is un-

attractive, if not repelling and disgusting. The less we are confronted with it, the better. This is our principal attitude, and in this context compassion means no more than the small soft eraser at the end of a long hard pencil. To be compassionate then means to be kind and gentle to those who get hurt by competition. A miner who gets caught underground evokes compassion; a student who breaks down under the pressure of exams evokes compassion; a mother on welfare who does not have enough food and clothes for her children evokes compassion; an elderly woman who is dying alone in the anonymity of a big city evokes compassion. But our primary frame of reference remains competition. After all, we need coal and intellectuals, and all systems have their shortcomings!

Thus, what at first seemed to be such a natural human virtue proves to be much less so than we thought. Where does this leave us? Well, it is precisely this ambiguous place of compassion in our lives that provides both the reason for this book and its starting point. Must we simply recognize that we are more competitive than compassionate, and try to make the best of it with a "healthy dose of skepticism"? Is the best advice we can give each other that we should try to live in such a way that we hurt each other as little as possible? Is our greatest ideal a maximum of satisfaction with a minimum of pain?

This book says *No* to these questions, and proposes that in order to understand the place of compassion in our lives, we must look in a radically different direction. The perspective presented here is based on the words of Jesus, "Be compassionate as your Father is compassionate" (Lk 6:36), and is offered in the deep conviction that through compassion our humanity grows into its fullness. This is not said lightly. It is said after years of discussing, reading, writing, and many—often painful—experiences. There have been moments during which we were tempted to drop this project and move to easier subjects. But each time we faced this temptation, we realized that we were doubting the value of a commitment to Christ. As the call to compassion slowly revealed itself to us as the center of Christian life, the thought of ignoring this call—even in writing—increasingly appeared to be a refusal to face directly the radical challenge of our faith.

In the first phase of our work together, we discussed the life, work, and deeds of Jesus Christ on the assumption that all people have a natural desire to be compassionate. Since those days, however, we have become less optimistic and, hopefully, more realistic. National and international events, deeper study of the Scriptures, and the many critical responses of friends, have made us less confident about our "compassionate tendencies" and more aware of the radical quality of Jesus' command: "Be compassionate as your Father is compassionate." This command does not restate the obvious, something we already wanted but had forgotten, an idea in line with our natural aspirations. On the contrary, it is a call that goes right against the grain; that turns us completely around and requires a total conversion of heart and mind. It is indeed a radical call, a call that goes to the roots of our lives.

This increasing awareness of the radical nature of Christ's call to compassion has determined the organization of this book. We want to speak, first of all, about the compassionate God who is revealed to us in Jesus Christ, because God's own compassion constitutes the basis and source of our compassion. Secondly, we want to explore what it means to live a compassionate life as followers of Christ, for it is only in discipleship that we can begin to understand the call to be compassionate as the Father is compassionate. Finally, we want to discuss the compassionate way of prayer and action because it is through these disciplines, which guide our relationships

9

with God and our fellow human beings, that God's compassion can manifest itself. If those who read this book—whatever their particular vocation in life may be—feel deepened in their awareness of the presence of a compassionate God in the midst of an incompassionate world, we will have ample reason for gratitude.

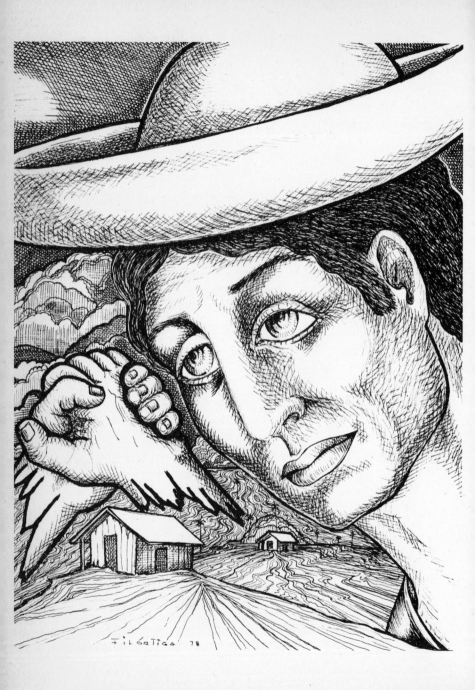

PART ONE

The Compassionate God

1

God-with-Us

IN SOLIDARITY

God is a compassionate God. This means, first of all, that he is a God who has chosen to be God-with-us. To be able to know and feel better this divine solidarity, let us explore the experience of someone being truly with us.

When do we receive real comfort and consolation? Is it when someone teaches us how to think or act? Is it when we receive advice about where to go or what to do? Is it when we hear words of reassurance and hope? Sometimes, perhaps. But what really counts is that in moments of pain and suffering someone stays with us. More important than any particular action or word of advice is the simple presence of someone who cares. When someone says to us in the midst of a crisis, "I do not know what to say or what to do, but I want you to realize that I am with you, that I will not leave you alone," we have a friend through whom we can find consolation and comfort. In a time so filled with methods and techniques designed to change people, to influence their behavior, and to make them do new things and think new thoughts, we have lost the simple but difficult gift of being present to each other. We have lost this gift because we have been led to believe that presence must be useful. We say, "Why should I visit this person? I can't do anything anyway. I don't even have anything to say. Of what use can I be?" Meanwhile, we have forgotten that it is often in "useless," unpretentious, humble presence to each other that we feel consolation and comfort. Simply being with someone is difficult because it asks of us that we share in the other's vulnerability, enter with him or her into the experience of weakness and powerlessness, become part of uncertainty, and give up control and self-determination. And still, whenever this happens, new strength and new hope is being born. Those who offer us comfort and consolation by being and staying with us in moments of illness, mental anguish, or spiritual darkness often grow as close to us as those with whom we have biological ties. They show their solidarity with us by willingly entering the dark, uncharted spaces of our lives. For this reason, they are the ones who bring new hope and help us discover new directions.

These reflections offer only a glimpse of what we mean when we say that God is a God-with-us, a God who came to share our lives in solidarity. It does not mean that God solves our problems, shows us the way out of our confusion, or offers answers for our many questions. He might do all of that, but his solidarity consists in the fact that he is willing to enter with us into our problems, confusions, and questions.

That is the good news of God's taking on human flesh. The Evangelist Matthew, after describing the birth of Jesus, writes: "Now all this took place to fulfil the words spoken by the Lord through the prophet: 'The Virgin shall conceive and give birth to a son and they will call him Immanuel,' a name which means 'God-is-with-us'" (Mt 1:22–23).

As soon as we call God, "God-with-us," we enter into a new relationship of intimacy with him. By calling him Immanuel, we recognize that he has committed himself to live in solidarity with us, to share our joys and pains, to defend and protect us, and to suffer all of life with us. The God-with-us is a close God, a God whom we call our refuge, our stronghold, our wisdom, and even, more intimately, our helper, our shepherd, our love. We will never really know God as a compassionate God if we do not understand with our heart and mind that "he lived among us" (Jn 1:14).

Often we say to each other in a bitter tone: "You do not know what you are talking about because you did not march in protest, participate in the strike, or experience the hatred of the bystanders, because you were never hungry, never knew cold, or never felt real isolation." When we say such things, we express the deep conviction that we are willing to listen to consoling words only when they are born out of solidarity with the condition that was or is ours. God wants to know our condition fully and does not want to take away any pain which he himself has not fully tasted. His compassion is anchored in the most intimate solidarity, a solidarity that allows us to say with the psalmist, "This is our God, and we are the people he pastures, the flock that he guides" (Ps 95:7).

WITH GUT FEELINGS

How do we know this is anything more than a beautiful idea? How do we know that God is our God and not a stranger, an outsider, a passerby?

We know this because in Jesus, God's compassion became visible to us. Jesus not only said, "Be compassionate as your

Father is compassionate," but he also was the concrete embodiment of this divine compassion in our world. Jesus' response to the ignorant, the hungry, the blind, the lepers, the widows, and all those who came to him with their suffering, flowed from the divine compassion which led God to become one of us. We need to pay close attention to Jesus' words and actions if we are to gain insight into the mystery of this divine compassion. We would misunderstand the many miraculous stories in the Gospels if we were to be impressed simply by the fact that sick and tormented people were suddenly liberated from their pains. If this were indeed the central event of these stories, a cynic might rightly remark that most people during Jesus' day were *not* cured and that those who were cured only made it worse for those who were not. What is important here is not the cure of the sick, but the deep compassion that moved Jesus to these cures.

There is a beautiful expression in the Gospels that appears only twelve times and is used exclusively in reference to Jesus or his Father. That expression is "to be moved with compassion." The Greek verb *splangchnizomai* reveals to us the deep and powerful meaning of this expression. The *splangchna* are the entrails of the body, or as we might say today, the guts. They are the place where our most intimate and intense emotions are located. They are the center from which both passionate love and passionate hate grow. When the Gospels speak about Jesus' compassion as his being moved in the entrails, they are expressing something very deep and mysterious. The compassion that Jesus felt was obviously quite different from superficial or passing feelings of sorrow or sympathy. Rather, it extended to the most vulnerable part of his being. It is related to the Hebrew word for compassion, *rachamim*, which refers to the womb of Yahweh. Indeed, compassion is such a deep, central, and powerful emotion in Jesus that it can only be described as a movement of the womb of God. There, all the divine tenderness and gentleness lies hidden. There, God is father and mother, brother and sister, son and daughter. There, all feelings, emotions, and passions are one in divine love. When Jesus was moved to compassion, the source of all life trembled, the ground of all love burst open, and the abyss of God's immense, inexhaustible, and unfathomable tenderness revealed itself.

This is the mystery of God's compassion as it becomes visible in the healing stories of the New Testament. When Jesus saw the crowd harassed and dejected like sheep without a shepherd, he felt with them in the center of his being (Mt 9:36). When he saw the blind, the paralyzed, and the deaf being brought to him from all directions, he trembled from within and experienced their pains in his own heart (Mt 14:14). When he noticed that the thousands who had followed him for days were tired and hungry, he said, I am moved with compassion (Mk 8:2). And so it was with the two blind men who called after him (Mt 9:27), the leper who fell to his knees in front of him (Mk 1:41), and the widow of Nain who was burying her only son (Lk 7:13). They moved him, they made him feel with all his intimate sensibilities the depth of their sorrow. He became lost with the lost, hungry with the hungry, and sick with the sick. In him, all suffering was sensed with a perfect sensitivity. The great mystery revealed to us in this is that Jesus, who is the sinless son of God, chose in total freedom to suffer fully our pains and thus to let us discover the true nature of our own passions. In him, we see and experience the persons we truly are. He who is divine lives our broken humanity not as a curse (Gn 3:14–19), but as a blessing. His divine compassion makes it possible for us to face our sinful selves, because it transforms our broken human condition from a cause of despair into a source of hope.

This is what we mean when we say that Jesus Christ reveals God's solidarity with us. In and through Jesus Christ we know that God is our God, a God who has experienced our brokenness, who has become sin for us (2 Co 5:21). He has embraced everything human with the infinite tenderness of his compassion.

TOWARD NEW LIFE

But what about the cures? Did not the blind see, the lepers become pure, the paralyzed walk again, and the widow see her son come back to life? Is that not what counts? Is that not what proves that God is God and he really loves us? Let us be very careful with our pragmatism. It was out of his compassion that Jesus' healing emerged. He did not cure to prove, to impress, or to convince. His cures were the natural expression of his being our God. The mystery of God's love is not that he takes our pains away, but that he first wants to share them with us. Out of this divine solidarity comes new life. Jesus' being moved in the center of his being by human pain is indeed a movement toward new life. God is our God, the God of the living. In his divine womb life is always born again. The great mystery is not the cures, but the infinite compassion which is their source.

We know too well what it means when cures are performed without compassion. We have seen men and women who can walk again, see again, speak again, but whose hearts remain dark and bitter. We know too well that cures not born out of care are false cures leading not to light but to darkness. Let us not fool ourselves with a shortcut to new life. The many cures by Jesus recorded in the Gospels can never be separated from his being with us. They witness to the infinite fecundity of his divine compassion, and show us the beautiful fruits of his solidarity with our condition. The truly good news is that God is not a distant God, a God to be feared and avoided, a God of revenge, but a God who is moved by our pains and participates in the fullness of the human struggle. The miraculous cures in the Gospels are hopeful and joyful reminders of this good news, which is our true consolation and comfort.

OUR COMPETITIVE SELVES

When we take a critical look at ourselves, we have to recognize that competition, not compassion, is our main motivation in life. We find ourselves deeply immersed in all sorts of competition. Our whole sense of self is dependent upon the way we compare ourselves with others and upon the differences we can identify. When the question "Who am I?" is put to the powers of this world—school officials, church representatives, placement officers, athletic directors, factory managers, television and radio announcers—the answer is simply, "You are the difference you make." It is by our differences, distinctions, that we are recognized, honored, rejected, or despised. Whether we are more or less intelligent, practical, strong, fast, handy, or handsome depends upon those with whom we are compared or those with whom we compete. It is upon these positive or negative distinctions that much of our self-esteem depends. It does not take much reflection to realize that in all family problems, race conflicts, class confrontations, and national or international disputes, these real or imaginary distinctions play a central role. Indeed, we invest much of our energy in defending the differences between people and groups of people. Thus, we define ourselves in ways that require us to maintain distance from one another. We are very protective of our "trophies." After all, who are we if we cannot proudly point to something special that sets us apart from others?

This all-pervasive competition, which reaches into the smallest corners of our relationships, prevents us from entering into full solidarity with each other, and stands in the way of our being compassionate. We prefer to keep compassion on the periphery of our competitive lives. Being compassionate would require giving up dividing lines and relinquishing differences and distinctions. And that would mean losing our

identities! This makes it clear why the call to be compassionate is so frightening and evokes such deep resistance.

This fear, which is very real and influences much of our
behavior, betrays our deepest illusions: that we can forge our
own identities; that we are the collective impressions of our
surroundings; that we are the trophies and distinctions we
have won. This, indeed, is our greatest illusion. It makes us
into competitive people who compulsively cling to our differences and defend them at all cost, even to the point of violence.

A NEW SELF

The compassion Jesus offers challenges us to give up our
fearful clinging and to enter with him into the fearless life of
God himself. In saying, "Be compassionate as your Father is
compassionate," Jesus invites us to be as close to each other as
God is to us. He even asks us to love one another with God's
own compassion. A divine compassion is a compassion without the slightest tinge of competition. Therefore, only God
can be wholly compassionate because only he is not in competition with us. The paradox of God's compassion is that
God can be compassionate because he is God; that is, wholly
other than we are. Because God is wholly other, he can become wholly as we are. He can become so deeply human because he is so fully divine. In short, God can be fully compassionate because he does not compare himself with us and
thus is in no way in competition with us.

Jesus' command, "Be compassionate as your Father is compassionate," is a command to participate in the compassion of
God himself. He requires us to unmask the illusion of our
competitive selfhood, to give up clinging to our imaginary
distinctions as sources of identity, and to be taken up into the
same intimacy with God which he himself knows. This is the
mystery of the Christian life: to receive a new self, a new
identity, which depends not on what we can achieve, but on

what we are willing to receive. This new self is our participation in the divine life in and through Christ. Jesus wants us to belong to God as he belongs to God; he wants us to be children of God as he is a child of God; he wants us to let go of the old life, which is so full of fears and doubts, and to receive the new life, the life of God himself. In and through Christ we receive a new identity that enables us to say, "I am not the esteem I can collect through competition, but the love I have freely received from God." It allows us to say with Paul, "I live now not with my own life but with the life of Christ who lives in me" (Ga 2:20).

This new self, the self of Jesus Christ, makes it possible for us to be compassionate as our Father is compassionate. Through union with him, we are lifted out of our competitiveness with each other into the divine wholeness. By sharing in the wholeness of the one in whom no competition exists, we can enter into new, compassionate relationships with each other. By accepting our identities from the one who is the giver of all life, we can be with each other without distance or fear. This new identity, free from greed and desire for power, allows us to enter so fully and unconditionally into the sufferings of others that it becomes possible for us to heal the sick and call the dead to life. When we share in God's compassion, a whole new way of living opens itself to us, a way of living we glimpse in the lives of the Apostles and those great Christians who have witnessed for Christ through the centuries. This divine compassion is not, like our self-made compassion, part of the competition. Rather, it is the expression of a new way of living in which interpersonal comparisons, rivalries, and competitions are gradually left behind.

Paul gives us a beautiful example of this new-found compassion in his letter to the Philippians. There he writes: God is my witness how much I miss you all with the tender compassion [the *splangchna*] of Christ Jesus (Ph 1:8). Paul feels for his people with the same divine intensity that Jesus felt

for those who came to him with their pain. The mystery is
that Paul loves his people with a divine intimacy. His compassion is thus much more than mere sympathy or emotional
attachment. It is the expression of his new being in Christ. In
Christ, Paul has become capable of the all-embracing and
deeply moving compassion of God. He therefore says, "I miss
you in the *splangchna* of Christ," that is, with Christ's own
most intimate divine interiority. Paul's new life in Christ,
through which he was lifted above rivalry and competition, allowed him to extend divine compassion to his people.
This reveals to us the great mystery of Paul's ministry. He
touched people with God's compassion, a compassion so deep
and so full that it could not fail to bear fruit. This also is the
mystery of our new way of being together. It has become
possible to be together in compassion because we have been
given a share in God's compassion. In and through this compassion, we can begin to live in solidarity with each other as
fully and intimately as God lives with us.

2

Servant God

HE EMPTIED HIMSELF

God's compassion is not something abstract or indefinite, but a concrete, specific gesture in which God reaches out to us. In Jesus Christ we see the fullness of God's compassion. To us, who cry out from the depth of our brokenness for a hand that will touch us, an arm that can embrace us, lips that will kiss us, a word that speaks to us here and now, and a heart that is not afraid of our fears and tremblings; to us, who feel our own pain as no other human being feels it, has felt it, or ever will feel it and who are always waiting for someone who dares to come close—to us a man has come who could truly say, "I am with you." Jesus Christ, who is God-with-us, has come to us in the freedom of love, not needing to experience our human condition but freely choosing to do so out of love.

This mystery of God-with-us in Jesus Christ cannot be grasped. But we can and must enter it humbly and reverently to find there the source of our comfort and consolation. When Jesus was no longer with his disciples, new words were found by the early Christian community to express the mystery of God's compassion. Among the most beautiful and profound of these expressions is the Hymn of Christ which Paul uses in his letter to the Philippians:

> His state was divine,
> yet he did not cling
> to his equality with God
> but emptied himself
> to assume the condition of a slave,
> and became as we are;
> and being as we are,
> he was humbler yet,
> even to accepting death,
> death on a cross.

(Ph 2:6–8)

Here we see that the compassionate God who revealed himself to us in Jesus Christ is the God who became a servant. Our God is a servant God. It is difficult for us to comprehend that we are liberated by someone who became powerless, that we are being strengthened by someone who became weak, that we find new hope in someone who divested himself of all distinctions, and that we find a leader in someone who became a servant. It is beyond our intellectual and emotional grasp. We expect freedom from someone who is not as imprisoned as we are, health from someone who is not as sick as we are, and new directions from someone who is not as lost and confused as we are.

But of Jesus it is said that he emptied himself and assumed the condition of a slave. To be a slave means to be subject

not only to human but also to superhuman powers. It is the
condition of powerlessness in which one feels victimized by
uncontrollable events, anonymous influences, and capricious
agents which surround and elude one's understanding and
control. In the culture in which the Gospel was first proclaimed, these powers were often perceived as antagonistic
and cruel gods. In our day these powers are no longer per-
sonalized, but they remain very real and no less fearful.
Nuclear warheads and power plants, millions of hungry and
dying people, torture chambers and immense cruelties, the
increase in robberies, rapes, and twisted, sadistic plots, all
give us the feeling of being surrounded by a mysterious network of powers that can destroy us any day or hour. The
awareness that we have hardly any influence on our own way
of living and working, and the realization that at any moment
something could happen that could permanently destroy our
life, health, or happiness, can fill us with an all-pervading
sadness and fear.

Is it surprising that, this being our condition, we look away
from our frightening surroundings, away from the here and
now, to something and someone "above" for liberation from
this slavery? In Jesus' day, as well as ours, we find an intense
desire for something unusual, abnormal, and spectacular that
can pull us up out of our misery into a sphere where we are
at a safe distance from the world that threatens to swallow
us.

HE WAS HUMBLER YET

But it is not said of Jesus that he reached down from on
high to pull us up from slavery, but that he became a slave
with us. God's compassion is a compassion that reveals itself
in servanthood. Jesus became subject to the same powers and
influences that dominate us, and suffered our fears, uncertainties, and anxieties with us. Jesus emptied himself. He gave up

a privileged position, a position of majesty and power, and assumed fully and without reservation a condition of total dependency. Paul's hymn of Christ does not ask us to look upward, away from our condition, but to look in our midst and discover God there.

This is not the last word, however. "Being as we are, he was humbler yet, even to accepting death, death on a cross." Here the essence of God's compassion is announced. Not only did he taste fully the dependent and fearful condition of being human, but he also experienced the most despicable, and horrifying form of death—death on a cross. Not only did he become human, but he also became human in the most dejected and rejected way. Not only did he know human uncertainties and fears, but he also experienced the agony, pain, and total degradation of the bloody torture and death of a convicted criminal. In this humiliation, Jesus lived out the full implications of emptying himself to be with us in compassion. He not only suffered our painful human condition in all its concreteness but he also suffered death with us in one of its rawest, ugliest, and most degrading forms. It was a death that we "normal" human beings would hardly be willing to consider ours.

In the Gospel stories of Jesus' healings, we sense how close God wants to be with those who suffer. But now we see the price God is willing to pay for this intimacy. It is the price of ultimate servanthood, the price of becoming a slave, completely dependent on strange, cruel, alien forces. We spontaneously protest against this road of self-emptying and humiliation. We certainly appreciate people who try to understand us. We are even grateful for those who want to feel with us. But we become suspicious when someone chooses to undergo the pain that we would avoid at all costs. We understand conditional solidarity, but we do not understand solidarity that has no limits.

THE DOWNWARD PULL

Jesus' compassion is characterized by a downward pull. That is what disturbs us. We cannot even think about ourselves in terms other than those of an upward pull, an upward mobility in which we strive for better lives, higher salaries, and more prestigious positions. Thus, we are deeply disturbed by a God who embodies a downward movement. Instead of striving for a higher position, more power, and more influence, Jesus moves, as Karl Barth says, from "the heights to the depth, from victory to defeat, from riches to poverty, from triumph to suffering, from life to death."[2] Jesus' whole life and mission involve accepting powerlessness and revealing in this powerlessness the limitlessness of God's love. Here we see what compassion means. It is not a bending toward the underprivileged from a privileged position; it is not a reaching out from on high to those who are less fortunate below; it is not a gesture of sympathy or pity for those who fail to make it in the upward pull. On the contrary, compassion means going directly to those people and places where suffering is most acute and building a home there. God's compassion is total, absolute, unconditional, without reservation. It is the compassion of the one who keeps going to the most forgotten corners of the world, and who cannot rest as long as he knows that there are still human beings with tears in their eyes. It is the compassion of a God who does not merely act as a servant, but whose servanthood is a direct expression of his divinity.

The hymn of Christ makes us see that God reveals his divine love for us in his coming to us as a servant. The great mystery of God's compassion is that in his compassion, in his entering with us into the condition of a slave, he reveals himself to us as God. His becoming a servant is not an exception

to his being God. His self-emptying and humiliation are not a
step away from his true nature. His becoming as we are and
dying on a cross is not a temporary interruption of his own
divine existence. Rather, in the emptied and humbled Christ
we encounter God, we see who God really is, we come to
know his true divinity. Precisely because God is God, he can
reveal his divinity in the form of a servant. As Karl Barth
says, "God does not have to dishonor himself, when he goes
into the far country and conceals his glory. For he is truly
honored in his concealment. This concealment, and therefore
his condescension as such, is the image and the reflection in
which we see him as he is."[3] In his servanthood God does not
disfigure himself, he does not take on something alien to himself, he does not act against or in spite of his divine self. On
the contrary, it is in his servanthood that God chooses to reveal himself as God to us. Therefore, we can say that the
downward pull as we see this in Jesus Christ is not a movement away from God, but a movement toward him as he really is: A God for us who came not to rule but to serve. This
implies very specifically that God does not want to be known
except through servanthood and that, therefore, servanthood
is God's self-revelation.

IN HIS PATH

Here a new dimension of our call to compassion becomes
apparent. If God's compassion reveals itself in the downward
path of Jesus Christ, then our compassion toward each other
will involve following in his path and participating in
this self-emptying, humiliating movement. There is little
doubt that the disciples of Jesus understood their call as a call
to make God's compassion present in this world by moving
with Jesus into positions of servanthood. Peter writes, "Wrap
yourselves in humility to be servants of each other" (1 P
5:5). He thus echoes the many invitations of Jesus to follow
him on his humbling way: "The one who humbles himself
will be exalted" (Lk 14:11). "Anyone who loses his life for

my sake, and for the sake of the gospel, will save it" (Mk 8:35). "The one who makes himself as little as this little child is the greatest in the kingdom of heaven" (Mt 18:4). "If anyone wants to be a follower of mine, let him renounce himself and take up his cross and follow me" (Mk 8:34). "How happy are the poor in spirit . . . those who mourn . . . those who hunger . . . who are persecuted" (Mt 5:3–10). "Love your enemies and pray for those who persecute you" (Mt 5:44).

This is the way of Jesus and the way to which he calls his disciples. It is the way that at first frightens or at least embarrasses us. Who wants to be humble? Who wants to be the last? Who wants to be like a little, powerless child? Who desires to lose his or her life, to be poor, mourning, and hungry? All this appears to be against our natural inclinations. But once we see that Jesus reveals to us, in his radically downward pull, the compassionate nature of God, we begin to understand that to follow him is to participate in the ongoing self-revelation of God. By setting out with Jesus on the road of the cross, we become people in whose lives the compassionate presence of God in this world can manifest itself. As Barth observes, what seemed to be unnatural from the perspective of the world becomes natural for the follower of Christ.[4] Just as in Christ's servanthood God's nature becomes evident, so for those who want to proclaim God's presence in the world, servanthood becomes a natural response. Thus, Paul could say to the Colossians, "It makes me happy to suffer for you, as I am suffering now, and in my own body to do what I can to make up all that has still to be undergone by Christ for the sake of his body, the Church" (Col 1:24). For Paul, servanthood had become natural. It belonged to his new being in Christ.

OUR SECOND NATURE

Our "second nature," the nature we receive in and through Christ, sets us free to live compassionately in servanthood.

Compassion is no longer a virtue that we must exercise in special circumstances or an attitude that we must call upon when other ways of responding have been exhausted, but it is the *natural* way of being in the world. This "second nature" also allows us to see compassion not in moralistic terms, that is, in terms of how we have to behave as good Christians, but as a new way of being in the world. As Christians, we are called to be ambassadors of Christ in whom the reality of God's infinite compassion becomes concrete and tangible (2 Co 5:20). To become humble servants with Christ in discipleship is to become witnesses of the living God. The Christian life is a life of witnessing through servanthood to the compassionate God, not a life in which we seek suffering and pain.

To the outsider, much Christian behavior seems to be naïve, impractical, and often little less than an exercise in self-flagellation. The outsider understandably believes that anyone who feels attracted to suffering and pain and who desires to humble himself or herself to a position of servanthood cannot be taken very seriously. Striving to be a slave seems such a perverted way of living that it offends human sensibilities. Nobody finds anything wrong or strange with attempting to help people who are visibly lacking the basic necessities of life, and it appears quite reasonable to try to alleviate suffering when this is possible. But to leave a successful position and enter freely, consciously, and intentionally into a position of servanthood seems unhealthy. It is a violation of the most basic human instincts. To try to lift others up to our own privileged position is honorable and perhaps even an expression of generosity, but to attempt to put ourselves in a position of disrepute and to become dependent and vulnerable seems to be a form of masochism that defies the best of our aspirations.

Something of this attitude appears in the expression "helping the less fortunate," which frequently can be heard from the mouths of those who ask or offer aid. This expression has an elitist ring to it because it assumes that *we* have made it and have gotten it together while *they* simply have not been able to keep up with us and need to be helped. It is the attitude which says: "Fate is on our side and not theirs. But since we are Christians we have to lift them up and give them a share of our good fortune. The undeniable fact is that the world is divided between the 'fortunate' and the 'unfortunate' ones. So let us not feel guilty about it, but reach out as good people to those who happen to be on the other side of the fence." In this way of thinking compassion remains part of the competition, and is a far cry from radical servanthood.

Radical servanthood does not make sense unless we introduce a new level of understanding and see it as the way to encounter God himself. To be humble and persecuted cannot be desired unless we can find God in humility and persecution. When we begin to see God himself, the source of all our comfort and consolation, in the center of servanthood, compassion becomes much more than doing good for unfortunate people. Radical servanthood, as the encounter with the compassionate God, takes us beyond the distinctions between wealth and poverty, success and failure, fortune and bad luck. Radical servanthood is not an enterprise in which we try to surround ourselves with as much misery as possible, but a joyful way of life in which our eyes are opened to the vision of the true God who chose the way of servanthood to make himself known. The poor are called blessed not because poverty is good, but because theirs is the kingdom of heaven; the mourners are called blessed not because mourning is good, but because they shall be comforted.

Here we are touching the profound spiritual truth that service is an expression of the search for God and not just of the desire to bring about individual or social change. This is open to all sorts of misunderstanding, but its truth is confirmed in the lives of those for whom service is a constant and uninterrupted concern. As long as the help we offer to others is motivated primarily by the changes we may accomplish, our service cannot last long. When results do not appear, when success is absent, when we are no longer liked or praised for what we do, we lose the strength and motivation to continue. When we see nothing but sad, poor, sick, or miserable people who, even after our many attempts to offer help, remain sad, poor, sick, and miserable, then the only reasonable response is to move away in order to prevent ourselves from becoming cynical or depressed. Radical servanthood challenges us, while attempting persistently to overcome poverty, hunger, illness, and any other form of human misery, to reveal the gentle presence of our compassionate God in the midst of our broken world.

JOYFUL SERVANTS

Joy and gratitude are the qualities of the heart by which we recognize those who are committed to a life of service in the path of Jesus Christ. We see this in families where parents and children are attentive to one another's needs and spend time together despite many outside pressures. We see it in those who always have room for a stranger, an extra plate for a visitor, time for someone in need. We see it in the students who work with the elderly, and in the many men and women who offer money, time, and energy for those who are hungry, in prison, sick, or dying. We see it in the sisters who work with the poorest of the poor. Wherever we see real service we also see joy, because in the midst of service a divine presence becomes visible and a gift is offered. Therefore, those who serve as followers of Jesus discover that they are receiving more than they are giving. Just as a mother does not need to be rewarded for the attention she pays to her child, because her child is her joy, so those who serve their neighbor will find their reward in the people whom they serve.

The joy of those who follow their Lord on his self-emptying and humbling way shows that what they seek is not misery and pain but the God whose compassion they have felt in their own lives. Their eyes do not focus on poverty and misery, but on the face of the loving God.

This joy can rightly be seen as an anticipation of the full manifestation of God's love. The hymn of Christ, therefore, does not end with the words about his downward road. Christ emptied and humbled himself:

> But God raised him high
> and gave him a name
> which is above all other names
> so that all beings
> in the heavens, on earth and in the underworld,
> should bend the knee at the name of Jesus
> and that every tongue should acclaim
> Jesus Christ as Lord,
> to the glory of God the Father.

(Ph 2:9–11)

Without these final sentences we would never be able to grasp the fullness of God's compassion. God's compassion as revealed in Christ does not end in suffering but in glory. The servanthood of Christ is indeed a divine servanthood, a servanthood that finds its fulfillment in the lordship of the risen Christ who received the name that is above all other names. The resurrection of Christ is the final affirmation of his servanthood. And with the servant Christ, all servanthood has been lifted up and sanctified as the manifestation of God's compassion. This is the basis of all our joy and hope: Our life of servanthood is lived in union with the risen Christ, in and through whom we have become children of the compassionate Father. Thus Paul can say, "And if we are children we are heirs as well: heirs of God and coheirs with Christ, sharing his sufferings so as to share his glory. I think that what we suffer in this life can never be compared to the glory, as yet unrevealed, which is waiting for us" (Rm 8:17–18).

3

Obedient God

THE INNER LIFE OF GOD

In Jesus Christ, God reveals himself to us as a God of compassion. This divine compassion is God's being with us as a suffering servant. God is with us, he feels with us deeply and tenderly. He allows our human pain to reverberate in his innermost self. He even goes so far as to give up the privileged position of his divine power and to appear in our midst as a humble servant who offers to wash our wounded and tired feet.

But this is not the whole story of God's compassion. There is an element which we need to explore in depth in order to gain yet another glimpse of the mystery of God's infinite love for us. In Jesus Christ, God did not manifest his compassion simply by becoming a suffering servant, but by becoming a suffering servant in obedience. Obedience gives servanthood its deepest dimension.

Often we experience a strong desire to offer our services to our fellow human beings in need. At times we even dream about giving our lives to the poor and living in solidarity with those who suffer. Sometimes these dreams lead to generous actions, to good and worthwhile projects, and to weeks, months, and even years of dedicated work. But the initiative still remains ours. We decide when we go and when we return; we decide what to do and how to do it; we control the level and intensity of our servanthood. Although much good work gets done in these situations, there is always the creeping danger that even our servanthood is a subtle form of manipulation. Are we really servants when we can become masters again once we think we have done our part or made our contribution? Are we really servants when we can say when, where, and how long we will give of our time and energy? Is service in a far country really an expression of servanthood when we keep enough money in the bank to fly home at any moment?

Jesus came to the "far country" because he was sent. Being sent remained uppermost in his consciousness. He never claimed anything for himself. He was the obedient servant who said and did nothing, absolutely nothing, unless it was said and done in complete obedience to the one who sent him.

We are trying to express here what can barely be put into words: In Jesus, God not only reveals his compassion as servanthood but also as obedience. The one through whom all things came to be, became the obedient one. Karl Barth writes, "It belongs to the inner life of God that there should take place within it obedience . . . in himself he is both One who is obeyed and Another who obeys."[5] In Jesus Christ, this inner side of the nature of God becomes visible. In Jesus Christ, we see that God's compassion can never be separated from his obedience. Because through Jesus' complete obedience God made his compassionate entry into our broken, wounded, and painful human condition.

INTIMATE LISTENING

Having said this, however, we must say many other things to prevent our own distorted feelings about obedience from interfering with our understanding of Jesus as the obedient servant. The word *obedience* very often evokes in us many negative feelings and ideas. We think of someone with power giving orders to another without it. We think of orders we follow only because we cannot refuse. We think of doing things others say are good for us but the value of which we do not directly see. We think of the great distance between the one who commands and the one who follows. When we say, "We do this in obedience," we usually imply that we have no real insight into what we do but accept the authority of another regardless of our own desires or needs. Thus the word *obedience* is often tainted by many feelings of hostility, resentment, or distance. It nearly always implies that someone is in a position to impose his or her will on others.

None of these negative associations, however, belongs to the obedience of Jesus Christ. His obedience is hearing God's loving word and responding to it. The word obedience is derived from the Latin word *audire*, which means "to listen." Obedience, as it is embodied in Jesus Christ, is a total listening, a giving attention with no hesitation or limitation, a being "all ear." It is an expression of the intimacy that can exist between two persons. Here the one who obeys knows without restriction the will of the one who commands and has only one all-embracing desire: to live out that will.

This intimate listening is expressed beautifully when Jesus speaks of God as his Father, his beloved Father. When used by Jesus, the word *obedience* has no association with fear, but rather is the expression of his most intimate, loving relationship. It is the relationship with his caring Father who said during his baptism at the river Jordan, "This is my Son, the Beloved" (Mt 3:17), and during his prayer on Mount Tabor, "This is my Son, the Beloved . . . Listen to him" (Mt 17:5). Jesus' actions and words are the obedient response to this love of his Father. We cannot emphasize enough that when Jesus calls God his Father, he speaks about a love that includes and transcends all the love we know. It is the love of a father, but also of a mother, brother, sister, friend, and lover. It is severe yet merciful, jealous yet sharing, prodding yet guiding, challenging yet caring, disinterested yet supportive, selfless yet very intimate. The many kinds of love we have experienced in our various human relationships are fully represented in the love between Jesus and his heavenly Father, but also fully transcended by this same love.

ATTENTIVENESS TO THE FATHER

Thus far, we have primarily used the word *God* to indicate the subject of divine compassion. But it needs to be remembered that Jesus calls this compassionate God *abba*, "beloved Father." Obedience is a listening in love to God, the beloved Father. In this listening there is neither a moment of distance, nor fear, nor hesitation, nor doubt, but only the unconditional, unlimited, and unrestrained love that comes from the Father. Jesus' response to this love is likewise unconditional, unlimited, and unrestrained. We will misunderstand Jesus' going into the world of suffering and pain and his giving himself to us as a servant if we perceive these actions as the heroic initiatives of a son who wants to prove himself to a father whose love has to be earned, or as the anxious fulfillment of a command given by a father whose will must be respected. Rather, we see in these actions a divine listening to a divine love, a loving response to a loving mission, and a free "yes" to a free command.

From the first words Jesus speaks in the Temple, "Did you

not know that I must be busy with my Father's affairs" (Lk
2:49), to his last words on the cross, "Father, into your hands
I commit my spirit" (Lk 23:46), we are made aware that his
first and only concern is to do the will of his Father.
Impressed by Jesus' words and healing acts, we often forget
that his entire ministry was a ministry of obedience. The true
greatness of Jesus' life and words is found in his obedience.
Others have performed miraculous acts, have attracted large
crowds and impressed them with their words, have criticized
the hypocrisy of religious leaders, and have died cruel deaths
to witness to their ideals. If it is men and women of bravery,
heroism, or even generosity that we seek, then many have
spoken words and performed acts at least as remarkable as
those of Jesus. What sets Jesus apart from all other human
beings is his obedience to his heavenly Father. "I can do
nothing by myself . . . my aim is to do not my own will, but
the will of him who sent me" (Jn 5:30). "The words I say to
you I do not speak as from myself: it is the Father, living in
me, who is doing this work" (Jn 14:10). In the moment of his
greatest agony it is to the will of the Father that Jesus clings:
"My Father, if this cup cannot pass by without my drinking
it, your will be done" (Mt 26:42). Jesus' death becomes his
final act of obedience: "He humbled himself and became
obedient unto death" (Ph 2:8 RSV).

It is not surprising that the Apostle Paul considers Jesus'
obedience to be the source of our salvation. To the Christians
of Rome he writes, "As by one man's disobedience many
were made sinners, so by one man's obedience many will be
made righteous" (Rm 5:19). Indeed, just as Jesus' words
gave him divine authority because they were spoken in obedience, so his death made him our divine savior because he
accepted it in obedience.

Thus, the God of compassion is not only a God who serves
but also a God who serves in obedience. Whenever we separate servanthood from obedience, compassion becomes a
form of spiritual stardom. But when we realize that Jesus'

compassion was born of an intimate listening to the unconditional love of the Father, we can understand how servanthood can indeed be the full expression of compassion.
Jesus reaches out to the suffering world from the silent center where he stands in full attentiveness to his Father. Mark's
gospel presents us with a beautiful example of this movement
from intimate listening to compassionate action. There we
read, "In the morning, long before dawn, he got up and left
the house, and went to a lonely place and prayed there" (Mk
1:35). It is from this place, where Jesus was fully attentive to
his beloved Father, that he was called to action. "Everybody
is looking for you," his disciples said, and in obedience to his
Father he answered, "Let us go elsewhere, to the neighboring
country towns, so that I can preach there too, because that is
why I came." And he "went all through Galilee, preaching
in their synagogues and casting out devils" (Mk 1:37–39).

In Jesus, God's compassion is revealed as suffering with us
in obedience. Jesus is not a courageous hero whose act of
emptying and humbling himself earns adoration and praise.
He is not a super social worker, a super doctor, or a super
helper. He is not a great hero who performs acts of self-
denial that no one can imitate. Jesus is neither a spiritual giant
nor a superstar whose compassion makes us jealous and
creates in us the competitive desire to get as far, high, or deep
as he did. No, Jesus is the obedient servant who hears the call
and desires to respond even when it leads him to pain and
suffering. This desire is not to experience pain, but to give his
full undivided attention to the voice of his beloved Father.

WITH HIS LOVE IN US

The emphasis on obedience as an essential characteristic of
the divine compassion brings a new perspective to our lives.
It tells us that following Christ in his compassion does not
mean a search for suffering as a goal in itself. Christians have

been understandably criticized for having an unhealthy attraction to suffering. But suffering is not the issue. Fellowship with Jesus Christ is not a commitment to suffer as much as possible, but a commitment to listen with him to God's love without fear. It is to obedience—understood as an intimate, fearless listening to God's continuing love—that we are called.

We are often tempted to "explain" suffering in terms of "the will of God." Not only can this evoke anger and frustration, but also it is false. "God's will" is not a label that can be put on unhappy situations. God wants to bring joy not pain, peace not war, healing not suffering. Therefore, instead of declaring anything and everything to be the will of God, we must be willing to ask ourselves where in the midst of our pains and sufferings we can discern the loving presence of God.

When, however, we discover that our obedient listening leads us to our suffering neighbors, we can go to them in the joyful knowledge that love brings us there. We are poor listeners because we are afraid that there is something other than love in God. This is not so strange since we seldom, if ever, experience love without a taint of jealousy, resentment, revenge, or even hatred. Often we see love surrounded by limitations and conditions. We tend to doubt what presents itself to us as love and are always on guard, prepared for disappointments. The skeptic in us does not surrender easily. For this reason we find it hard simply to listen or to obey. But Jesus truly listened and obeyed because only he knew the love of his Father: "Not that anybody has seen the Father, except the one who comes from God: he has seen the Father" (Jn 6:46). "You do not know him, but I know him because I have come from him" (Jn 7:28–29).

There is more, however. Jesus did not come into the world clinging to this intimacy with his Father as if it were his private domain. He came to include us in his divine obedience. He wanted to lead us to the Father so that we could enjoy the same intimacy he did. When we come to recognize that in and through Jesus we are called to be daughters and sons of God and to listen to him, our loving Father, with total trust and surrender, we will also see that we are invited to be no less compassionate than Jesus himself. When obedience becomes our first and only concern, then we too can move into the world with compassion and feel the suffering of the world so deeply that through our compassion we can give new life to others. This is what Jesus himself told us in the astonishing words: "You must believe me when I say that I am in the Father and the Father is in me . . . I tell you most solemnly, whoever believes in me will perform the same works as I do myself, he will perform even greater works, because I am going to the Father. Whatever you ask for in my name I will do, so that the Father may be glorified in the Son" (Jn 14:11–13).

WITH EYES ON GOD

By viewing compassion as an obedient response to our loving Father, we avoid the constant temptation to see it as a noble act of self-sacrifice. This temptation is very great. Many Christians have been plagued by the idea that the more they could suffer, the better it would be. Often Christians have gone so far as to afflict themselves with many forms of pain in the false belief that in so doing they were following the way of Jesus Christ. This self-defeating attitude has led to much criticism. Friedrich Nietzsche is probably the best-known critic in this respect. He writes: "Christianity has sided with all that is weak and base, with all failures; it has made an ideal of whatever contradicts the instincts of the strong life to preserve itself . . . at the bottom of Christianity is the rancour of the sick instinct directed against the healthy, against health itself."[6]

This criticism makes us aware of our tendency to restrict our view of Jesus to his voluntary sacrifice on the cross. We forget that this sacrifice was an obedient response to a loving Father who not only sent his son into the world but also raised him from the dead to sit at his right hand. The "journey into the far country," as Barth calls Jesus' mission, is a journey of love. It is this journey that we are called to join. Each time we make participation in human suffering a final goal, a purpose, or an ideal, we distort our Christian vocation and harm ourselves as well as our fellow human beings. This becomes eminently clear in the lives of the saints and of all deeply committed Christians. Their eyes are not focused on pain, but on the Lord. Their question is not, "How can I suffer most for God?" but, "How can I listen best to him?"

A report about the Korean poet Kim Chi Ha shows how true listening leads to an unrelenting cry for justice and an uncompromising commitment to the search for truth. Repeatedly jailed and tortured by the regime of Park Chung Hee for his eloquent criticism of oppression in South Korea, Kim Chi Ha was sentenced to life imprisonment in 1976. Yet his spirit remains firm and his hope undaunted, for beyond his own suffering and the suffering of his people, he sees the suffering of Jesus Christ. In his play *The Gold-Crowned Jesus*, a leper, the most despised of social outcasts in Korea, encounters Jesus imprisoned in concrete by government, business, and church officials. The leper asks, "What can be done to free you, Jesus, to make you live again so that you can come to us?" and Jesus replied: "My power alone is not enough. People like you must help to liberate me. Those who seek only the comforts, wealth, honor, and power of this world, who wish entry to the kingdom of heaven for themselves only and ignore the poor . . . cannot give me life again. . . . Only those, though very poor and suffering like yourself, who are generous in spirit and seek to help the poor and the wretched can give me life again. You have helped to give me life again. You removed the gold crown from my head and so freed my lips to speak. People like you will be my liberators."[7]

We might be impressed by the great compassion we see in

the lives of witnesses like Kim Chi Ha, but they themselves rarely mention it. They do not enjoy suffering, nor are they attracted to it. They want only to alleviate and diminish it. But they are attracted by the love of God with such power that they perceive suffering and pain as only a part of their vocation, a part they will be able to accept when the time for it comes.

WITHOUT FEAR

In our time, so full of cruel persecution, it is understandable that we ask ourselves if we would be able to undergo the severe suffering we read and hear about. We wonder how to prepare ourselves for it and often concern ourselves with a future into which we project many horrors and tragedies. But if our primary concern were to listen carefully to God in our lives and to discern his will for us here and now, these worries would prove to be unjustified and distracting. Much of our inner restlessness, nervousness, and tension is connected with our worries about the unknown future. Sometimes we try to alleviate these worries by far-reaching plans. But our work for the future should be based not on anxiety, but on a vision of something worthwhile in the present. When our schemes for a new world are only an expression of our unhappiness with the present, we risk engaging in what Thomas Merton called "organized despair."

Obedience is listening to a voice that speaks to us today and allowing ourselves to feel the loving care of God in our present lives. Obedience is giving full attention to what the Father says to us in this very moment and responding lovingly to what we perceive, because God is our loving Father in whom nothing that is not love can be found. Apprehension, fear, and anxiety cannot sustain themselves in his presence. Fear always creates distance and divisions. But in the presence of God fear melts away. "In love there can be no fear, but fear is driven out by perfect love" (1 Jn 4:18).

Thus, when we pay careful attention to the loving presence of God, the suffering to which we might be led will never darken our hearts or paralyze our movements. We will find that we will never be asked to suffer more than we can bear and never be tested beyond our strength. When we are led by love instead of driven by fear, we can enter the places of the greatest darkness and pain and experience in a unique way the power of God's care. Jesus' final words to Peter are the strongest affirmation of this truth. After having asked Peter three times, "Do you love me?" and after having been assured three times by Peter of his love, Jesus said, "When you grow old you will stretch out your hands, and somebody else will put a belt around you and take you where you would rather not go" (Jn 21:18). Although Peter did not desire it, he was led to the cross as Jesus was. But because it was love and not fear that led him there, the cross was no longer a sign of defeat, but a sign of victory.

The reality of this love is shown in the stories of Christians who have suffered terrible torture in Latin America. A brother who was arrested and put in prison after working among the poor in Argentina for several years writes: "What characterized our Christian life during this whole time in prison was prayer, and more precisely, prayer of intercession. When you hear the despairing screams of your friends who are in the process of being tortured, and when you experience your total helplessness to do anything, you learn that to pray and to intercede with God is the only worthy human act that one is capable of doing." However, this letter, which describes a darkness few have experienced, is filled with a remarkably victorious tone. In the midst of the darkness, this anonymous brother felt the love of God and compassion for his brothers in such a new and intense way that he closed his letter by saying: "It's not easy to find yourself back in the normal Christian world. It all seems so shabby, formal, less intense, and less calm. For us in prison the gospel was our strength, our weapon against evil, against hate, against oppression." The editor of the *Catholic Worker* who published this letter noted, "The Church in Latin America, and throughout much of the Third World, is being offered a terrible opportunity, which we dare to envy."[8]

This suffering with others in obedience is the way to meet our compassionate God, whose love enables us to live in the midst of the world, serving our brothers and sisters with a deep sense of joy and gratitude.

God is a compassionate God. That is the good news brought to us in and through Jesus Christ. He is God-with-us, who finds nothing human alien and who lives in solidarity with us. He is a servant God who washes our feet and heals our wounds, and he is an obedient God who listens and responds to his divine Father with unlimited love. In fellowship with Jesus Christ, we are called to be compassionate as our Father is compassionate. In and through him, it becomes possible to be effective witnesses to God's compassion and to be signs of hope in the midst of a despairing world.

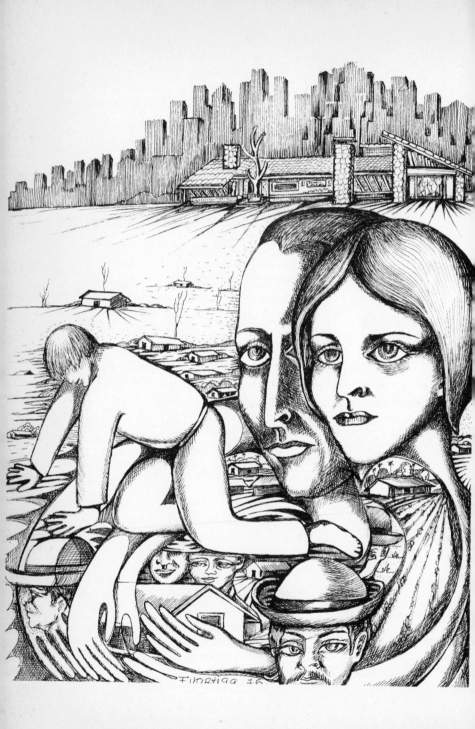

PART TWO

The Compassionate Life

4

Community

NO INDIVIDUAL STARDOM

The main question of the second part of our reflections concerns discipleship. There are many ways to formulate this question: "How can we creatively respond to Jesus' call: 'Be compassionate as your father is compassionate'? How can we make God's compassion the basis and source of our lives? Where can God's compassionate presence become visible in our everyday lives? How is it possible for us, broken and sinful human beings, to follow Jesus Christ and thus become manifestations of God's compassion? What does it mean for us to enter into solidarity with our fellow human beings and offer them obedient service?"

The message that comes to us in the New Testament is that

the compassionate life is a life together. Compassion is not an individual character trait, a personal attitude, or a special talent, but a way of living together. When Paul exhorts the Christians of Philippi to live a compassionate life with the mind of Christ, he gives a concrete description of what he means: "There must be no competition among you, no conceit; but everybody is to be self-effacing. Always consider the other person to be better than yourself, so that nobody thinks of his own interests first but everybody thinks of the other people's interest instead" (Ph 2:3–4). Moreover, Paul stresses that the compassionate life is a life in community: "If our life in Christ means anything to you, if love can persuade at all, or the Spirit that we have in common, or any tenderness and sympathy, then be united in your convictions and united in your love, with a common purpose and a common mind" (Ph 2:1–2).

Precisely because we are so inclined to think in terms of individual greatness and personal heroism, it is important for us to reflect carefully on the fact that the compassionate life is community life. We witness to God's compassionate presence in the world by the way we live and work together. Those who were first converted by the Apostles revealed their conversion not by feats of individual stardom but by entering a new life in community: "The faithful all lived together and owned everything in common; they sold their goods and possessions and shared out the proceeds among themselves according to what each one needed. They went *as a body* to the Temple every day but met in their houses for the breaking of bread; they shared their food gladly and generously; they praised God and were looked up to by everyone" (Ac 2:44–47). God's compassion became evident in a radically new way of living, which so amazed and surprised outsiders that they said, "See how they love each other."

A compassionate life is a life in which fellowship with Christ reveals itself in a new fellowship among those who follow him. We tend so often to think of compassion as an individual accomplishment, that we easily lose sight of its essentially communal nature. By entering into fellowship with Jesus Christ, who emptied himself and became as we are and humbled himself by accepting death on the cross, we enter into a new relationship with each other. The new relationship with Christ and the new relationship with each other can never be separated. It is not enough to say that a new relationship with Christ leads to a new relationship with each other. Rather, we must say that the mind of Christ is the mind that gathers us together in community; our life in community is the manifestation of the mind of Christ. As Paul says to the Romans,

Do not model yourselves on the behavior of the world around you, but let your behavior change, modeled by your new mind. This is the only way to discover the will of God and know what is good, what it is that God wants, what is the perfect thing to do.

(Rm 12:2)

WALKING ON THE SAME PATH

To follow Christ means to relate to each other with the mind of Christ; that is, to relate to each other as Christ did to us—in servanthood and humility. Discipleship is walking together on the same path. While still living wholly *in* this world, we have discovered each other as fellow travelers on the same path and have formed a new community. While still subject to the power of the world and still deeply involved in the human struggle, we have become a new people with a new mind, a new way of seeing and hearing, and a new hope because of our common fellowship with Christ. Compassion, then, can never be separated from community. Compassion always reveals itself in community, in a new way of being together. Fellowship with Christ *is* fellowship with our brothers and sisters. This is most powerfully expressed by

Paul when he calls the Christian community the body of
Christ.

The presence of Jesus Christ, whose lordship resides in
obedient service, manifests itself to us in the life of the
Christian community. It is in the Christian community that
we can be open and receptive to the suffering of the world
and offer it a compassionate response. For where people
come together in Christ's name, he is present as the compassionate Lord (see Mt 18:20). Jesus Christ himself is and
remains the most radical manifestation of God's compassion.

The idea that God's compassion as it revealed itself in Jesus
Christ is represented in time and space by the Christian community raises many difficult questions for us. In our society,
compassion has lost its communal context and therefore has
often degenerated into its opposite. We only need to examine
some of the ways in which human suffering is presented to us
today to come to a better understanding of the communal nature of compassion.

BOMBARDING THE SENSES

One of the most tragic events of our time is that we know
more than ever before about the pains and sufferings of the
world and yet are less and less able to respond to them.
Radio, television, and newspapers allow us to follow from
day to day—even from hour to hour—what is happening in
the world. We hear about armed conflicts and wars, assassi-
nations, earthquakes, droughts and floods, famines and epi-
demics, concentration camps and torture chambers, and
countless other forms of human suffering close to home or
far away. Not only do we hear about them but also we are
daily presented with pictures of starving babies, dying soldiers, burning houses, flooded villages, and wrecked cars.
The news seems to have become an almost ceaseless litany of
human suffering. The question is, do these highly sophis-

ticated forms of communication and this increasing amount of information lead to a deeper solidarity and a greater compassion? It is very doubtful.

Can we really expect a compassionate response from the millions of individuals who read the paper during breakfast, listen to the radio on the way to work, and watch television after returning home tired from their work in offices or factories? Can we reasonably expect compassion from the many isolated individuals who are constantly being reminded in the privacy of their homes or cars of the vast extent of human suffering?

There appears to be a general assumption that it is good for people to be exposed to the pain and suffering of the world. Not only do newspapers and news broadcasts seem to act on this assumption but also most organizations whose main concern is to help suffering people. Charitable institutions often send letters describing the miserable conditions in different parts of the world and enclose photographs of people whose humanity is hardly recognizable. In so doing, they hope to motivate the receiver to send money for relief projects.

We might ask, however, whether mass communication directed to millions of people who experience themselves as small, insignificant, powerless individuals does not in fact do more harm than good. When there is no community that can mediate between world needs and personal responses, the burden of the world can only be a crushing burden. When the pains of the world are presented to people who are already overwhelmed by the problems in their small circle of family or friends, how can we hope for a creative response? What we can expect is the opposite of compassion: numbness and anger.

Massive exposure to human misery often leads to psychic numbness. Our minds cannot tolerate being constantly reminded of things which interfere with what we are doing at the moment. When we have to open our store in the morning, go about our business, prepare our classes, or talk to our fellow workers, we cannot be filled with the collective misery of the world. If we let the full content of newscasts enter into our innermost selves, we would become so overwhelmed by the absurdities of existence that we would become paralyzed. If we try to absorb all that is reported by the paper, radio, or television, we would never get any work done. Our continued effectiveness requires a mental filtering system by which we can moderate the impact of the daily news.

But there is more. Exposure to human misery on a mass scale can lead not only to psychic numbness but also to hostility. This might seem strange, but when we look more closely at the human response to disturbing information, we realize that confrontation with human pain often creates anger instead of care, irritation instead of sympathy, and even fury instead of compassion. Human suffering, which comes to us in a way and on a scale that makes identification practically impossible, frequently evokes strong negative feelings. Often, some of the lowest human drives are brought into the open by a confrontation with miserable-looking people. In the most horrendous way, this was the case in the Nazi, Vietnamese, and Chilean concentration camps, where torture and cruelty seemed easier the worse the prisoners looked. When we are no longer able to recognize suffering persons as fellow human beings, their pain evokes more disgust and anger than compassion. It is therefore no wonder that the diary of Anne Frank did more for the understanding of human misery than many of the films showing long lines of hungry faces, dark buildings with ominous chimneys, and heaps of naked, emaciated human corpses. Anne Frank we can understand; piles of human flesh only make us sick.

How can we account for this psychic numbness and anger? Numbness and anger are the reactions of the person who says, "When I can't do anything about it anyhow, why do you bother me with it!" Confronted with human pain and at the same time reminded of our powerlessness, we feel offended to the very core of our being and fall back on our defenses of numbness and anger. If compassion means entering into solidarity with our suffering fellow human beings, then the increasing presentation of human suffering by the news media does not serve to evoke compassion. Those who know most about what goes on in the world—those who devote much attention to newspapers, radio, and television—are not necessarily the most compassionate people.

Responding compassionately to what the media present to us is made even more difficult by its "neutrality." The evening news offers a good example. Whatever the news correspondent announces—war, murder, floods, the weather, and the football scores—is reported with the same ritualized tone of voice and facial expression. Moreover, there is an almost liturgical order to the litany of events: first the great news items about national and international conflicts, then the more homey accidents, then the stock market and the weather, then a short word of "wisdom," and finally something light or funny. All of this is regularly interrupted by smiling people urging us to buy products of dubious necessity. The whole "service" is so distant and aloof that the most obvious response is to invest no more energy in it than in brushing your teeth before going to bed.

Therefore, the question is, how can we see the suffering in our world and be moved to compassion as Jesus was moved when he saw a great crowd of people without food (Mt 14:14)? This question has become very urgent at a time when we see so much and are moved so little.

COMMUNITY AS MEDIATOR

The Christian community mediates between the suffering of the world and our individual responses to this suffering. Since the Christian community is the living presence of the mediating Christ, it enables us to be fully aware of the painful condition of the human family without being paralyzed by this awareness. In the Christian community, we can keep our eyes and ears open to all that happens without being numbed by technological overstimulation or angered by the experience of powerlessness. In the Christian community, we can know about hunger, oppression, torture, and the nuclear threat without giving into a fatalistic resignation and withdrawing into a preoccupation with personal survival. In the Christian community, we can fully recognize the condition of our society without panicking.

This was convincingly illustrated by Joe Marino, an American theology student who traveled to Calcutta to experience living and working among the poor. The Missionary Brothers of Charity offered him hospitality. There, surrounded by indescribable human misery, he discovered the mediating power of community. In his diary he writes:

One night I had a long talk with Brother Jesulão. He told me that if a brother is not able to work with his fellow brothers and live with them peaceably, then he is always asked to leave . . . even if he is an excellent worker among the poor . . . Two nights later I walked with Brother Willy and he said that to live with his fellow brothers is his first priority. He is always challenged to love the brothers. He stated that if he cannot love the brothers with whom he lives, how can he love those in the street.[9]

In the Christian community we gather in the name of Christ and thus experience him in the midst of a suffering world. There our old, weak minds, which are unable fully to perceive the pains of the world, are transformed into the mind of Christ, to whom nothing human is alien. In community, we are no longer a mass of helpless individuals, but are transformed into one people of God. In community, our fears and anger are transformed by God's unconditional love, and we become gentle manifestations of his boundless compassion. In community, our lives become compassionate lives because in the way we live and work together, God's compassion becomes present in the midst of a broken world.

Here the deepest meaning of the compassionate life reveals itself. By our life together, we become participants in the divine compassion. Through this participation, we can take on the yoke and burden of Christ—which is all human pain in every time and place—while realizing that his yoke is easy and his burden light (Mt 11:30).

As long as we depend on our own limited resources, the world will frighten us and we will try to avoid the painful spots. But once we have become participants in God's compassion, we can enter deeply into the most hidden corners of the world and perform the same works Christ did; indeed, we may perform even greater works (Jn 14:12)!

Wherever true Christian community is formed, compassion *happens* in the world. The energy that radiated from the early Christian communities was indeed divine energy that had a transforming influence on all who were touched by it. That same energy continues to show itself wherever people come together in Christ's name and take on his yoke in humbleness and gentleness of heart (Mt 11:29). This is true not only of Benedict and Scholastica and their followers or Francis and Clare and their brothers and sisters, but also whenever men and women let go of their old, anxious ways of thinking and find each other in the mind of Christ.

Since it is in community that God's compassion reveals itself, solidarity, servanthood, and obedience are also the main characteristics of our life together. Solidarity can hardly be an individual accomplishment. It is difficult for us as individuals to enter into the pains and sufferings of our fellow human beings. But in the community gathered in Christ's name, there is an unlimited space into which strangers from different places with very different stories can enter and experience God's compassionate presence. It is a great mystery that compassion often becomes real for people not simply because of the deeds of one hospitable individual, but because of an intangible atmosphere resulting from a common life. Certain parishes, prayer groups, households, homes, houses, convents, or monasteries have a true healing influence that can make both members and their guests feel understood, accepted, cared for, and loved. The kindness of the individual people often seems more a manifestation of this healing environment than the cause of it.

Servanthood too is a quality of the community. Our individual ability to serve is quite limited. We might be able to help a few people for a while, but to respond in servanthood to all people all the time is not a realistic human aspiration. As soon as we speak in terms of *we*, however, the picture changes. As a community we can transcend our individual limitations and become a concrete realization of the self-emptying way of Christ. This communal realization can then find a specific expression in the daily work of the individual members. Some people work well with teenagers, others with the elderly, others with hospital patients, and others with prisoners. As individuals we cannot be everything to everyone, but as a community we can indeed serve a great variety of needs. Moreover, by the constant support and encouragement of the community we find it possible to remain faithful to our commitment to service.

Finally, we must recognize that obedience, as an attentive listening to the Father, is very much a communal vocation. It is precisely by constant prayer and meditation that the community remains alert and open to the needs of the world. Left to ourselves, we might easily begin to idolize our particular form or style of ministry and so turn our service into a personal hobby. But when we come together regularly to listen to the word of God and to celebrate his presence in our midst, we stay alert to his guiding voice and move away from the comfortable places to unknown territories. When we perceive obedience as primarily a characteristic of the community itself, relationships between different members of a community can become much more gentle. We also realize then that together we want to discern God's will for us and make our service a response to his compassionate presence in our midst.

Thus, God's solidarity, servanthood, and obedience, revealed to us in the life of Jesus Christ, are the marks of the compassionate life lived in community. In and through the community they can slowly become a real and integral part of our individual lives.

A SENSE OF BELONGING

At this point, the question arises, "How can we build community? What do we have to do to make community happen?" But perhaps such questions come from an anxious heart and are less practical and helpful than they appear to be. It seems better to raise the more contemplative question, "Where do we see community occurring?" Once we have become sensitive to the reality of community in our midst, we may find it easier to discover the most appropriate starting point for its growth and development. It makes more sense to sow seeds in soil in which we have already seen something grow than to stand around worrying about how to make the soil fertile.

An illustration from the life of the Trappist monk Thomas Merton might be helpful here. One of the most influential social critics of the sixties, Merton read very few newspapers and never watched television or listened to the radio. Nevertheless, his response to the needs of the world was a compassionate one. Merton could listen to the events of his time and in his solitude discern how to be of obedient service to his fellow human beings. What is important here is to realize that Merton's knowledge of the suffering of the world came not from the media but from letters written by friends for whom particular events had personal significance. To these friends a response was possible. When information about human suffering comes to us through a person who can be embraced, it is humanized. Letters bring life back to a human dimension. In Merton's case, letters came from all over the world and from the most diverse groups of people. They came from monasteries and convents on different continents, from young people wondering what to do with their lives, from novelists such as James Baldwin and Evelyn Waugh, from scholars such as Jacques Maritain and Jean Leclercq, from poets and prophets, from religious, nonreligious, and antireligious people, from cardinals and bishops, from Christians and Buddhists, and from many, many poor people whose names will never be known. In these letters, Merton saw the world with its pains and its joys. He was drawn into a real community of living people with real faces, real tears, and real smiles. Once in a while Merton invited some of his friends to the Abbey, and together they prayed, spoke about the pain of the world, and tried to give each other new hope and new strength. These small retreats proved to be highly significant for those who lived a very active and often dangerous life. They were offered strong mutual support. Many people known today for their courage and perseverance found their inspiration in these experiences of community.

This is just one example to illustrate the importance of community in the compassionate life. Letters and retreats are ways of being in community, but there are many other ways. It is important to keep ourselves from thinking about community only in terms of living together in one house, or sharing meals and prayers, or doing projects together. These might well be true expressions of community, but community is a much deeper reality. People who live together do not necessarily live in community, and those who live alone do not necessarily live without it. Physical nearness or distance is secondary. The primary quality of community is a deep sense of being gathered by God. When Francis Xavier traveled alone across many continents to preach the Gospel, he found strength in the sure knowledge that he belonged to a community that supported him with prayer and brotherly care. And many Christians who show great perseverance in hard and lonely tasks find their strength in the deep bond with the community in whose name they do their work.

Here we touch one of the most critical areas of the Christian life today. Many very generous Christians find themselves increasingly tired and dispirited not so much because the work is hard or the success slight, but because they feel isolated, unsupported, and left alone. People who say, "I wonder if anyone cares what I am doing. I wonder if my superior, my friends at home, or the people who sent me ever think about me, ever pray for me, ever consider me part of their lives," are in real spiritual danger. We are able to do many hard things, tolerate many conflicts, overcome many obstacles, and persevere under many pressures, but when we no longer experience ourselves as part of a caring, supporting, praying community, we quickly lose faith. This is because faith in God's compassionate presence can never be separated from experiencing God's presence in the community to which we belong. The crises in the lives of many caring Christians today are closely connected with deep feelings of not belonging. Without a sense of being sent by a caring community, a compassionate life cannot last long and quickly degenerates into a life marked by numbness and anger. This is not simply a psychological observation, but a theological truth, because apart from a vital relationship with a caring community a vital relationship with Christ is not possible.

Now we must look more closely at the dynamics of community life. We will do so by speaking about the two poles of a mature community life in which God's compassion can become visible: displacement and togetherness.

5
Displacement

MOVING FROM THE ORDINARY
AND PROPER PLACE

The word *community* generally expresses a certain supportive and nurturing way of living and working together. When
someone says, "I miss a sense of community here; something
should be done to build a better community," she or he is
probably suffering from alienation, loneliness, or lack of mutual support and cooperation. The desire for community is
most often a desire for a sense of unity, a feeling of being accepted, and an experience of at-homeness. It is therefore not
strange that for quite a few critical observers of the contemporary scene, the word *community* has become associated
with sentimentalism, romanticism, and even melancholy.

If we want to reflect on community in the context of compassion, we must go far beyond these spontaneous associations. Community can never be the place where God's obedient servanthood reveals itself if community is understood principally as something warm, soft, homey, comfortable, or protective. When we form community primarily to heal personal wounds, it cannot become the place where we effectively realize solidarity with other people's pains.

The paradox of the Christian community is that people are gathered together in voluntary displacement. The togetherness of those who form a Christian community is a being-gathered-in-displacement. According to Webster's dictionary, displacement means, to move or to shift from the ordinary or proper place. This becomes a telling definition when we realize the extent to which we are preoccupied with adapting ourselves to the prevalent norms and values of our milieu. We want to be ordinary and proper people who live ordinary and proper lives. There is an enormous pressure on us to do what is ordinary and proper—even the attempt to excel is ordinary and proper—and thus find the satisfaction of general acceptance. This is quite understandable since the ordinary and proper behavior that gives shape to an ordinary and proper life offers us the comforting illusion that things are under control and that everything extraordinary and improper can be kept outside the walls of our self-created fortress.

The call to community as we hear it from our Lord is the call to move away from the ordinary and proper places. Leave your father and mother. Let the dead bury the dead. Keep your hand on the plow and do not look back. Sell what you own, give the money to the poor and come follow me (Lk 14:26; 9:60, 62; 18:22). The Gospels confront us with this persistent voice inviting us to move from where it is comfortable, from where we want to stay, from where we feel at home.

Why is this so central? It is central because in voluntary

displacement, we cast off the illusion of "having it together" and thus begin to experience our true condition, which is that we, like everyone else, are pilgrims on the way, sinners in need of grace. Through voluntary displacement, we counteract the tendency to become settled in a false comfort and to forget the fundamentally unsettled position that we share with all people. Voluntary displacement leads us to the existential recognition of our inner brokenness and thus brings us to a deeper solidarity with the brokenness of our fellow human beings. Community, as the place of compassion, therefore always requires displacement. The Greek word for church, *ekklesia*—from *ek* = out, and *kaleo* = call—indicates that as a Christian community we are people who together are called out of our familiar places to unknown territories, out of our ordinary and proper places to the places where people hurt and where we can experience with them our common human brokenness and our common need for healing.

In voluntary displacement community is formed, deepened, and strengthened. In voluntary displacement we discover each other as members of the same human family with whom we can share our joys and sorrows. Each time we want to move back to what is ordinary and proper, each time we yearn to be settled and feel at home, we erect walls between ourselves and others, undermine community, and reduce compassion to the soft part of an essentially competitive life.

FOLLOWING THE DISPLACED LORD

Voluntary displacement as a way of life rather than as a unique event is the mark of discipleship. The Lord, whose compassion we want to manifest in time and place, is indeed the displaced Lord. Paul describes Jesus as the one who voluntarily displaced himself. "His state was divine, yet he did not cling to his equality with God but emptied himself

to assume the condition of a slave, and became as we are"
(Ph 2:6–7). A greater displacement cannot be conceived.
The mystery of the incarnation is that God did not remain in
the place that was proper for him but moved to the condition
of a suffering human being. God *gave up* his heavenly place
and took a humble place among mortal men and women.
God displaced himself so that nothing human would be alien
to him and he could experience fully the brokenness of our
human condition.

In the life of Jesus, we see how this divine displacement
becomes visible in a human story. As a child, Jesus is taken to
Egypt to protect him against the threats of King Herod. As a
boy, he leaves his parents and stays in the Temple to listen to
the doctors and ask them questions. As an adult, he goes into
the desert for forty days to fast and to be tempted by the
demon. During the years of ministry that follow, Jesus continuously moves away from power, success, and popularity in
order to remain faithful to his divine call. When the people
are excited because of his healing powers, he confronts them
with their sins and is not afraid to evoke their anger. When
they are so impressed by his ability to give bread that they
want to make him their king, he moves away and challenges
them to work for the food that gives eternal life. When his
disciples ask for a special place in his kingdom, he asks them
if they can drink the cup of suffering, and when they hope
for a quick victory, he speaks of pain and death. Finally,
these displacements lead him to the cross. There, rejected by
all and feeling abandoned by God, Jesus becomes the most
displaced human being. Thus, Jesus' displacement, which
began with his birth in Bethlehem, find its fullest expression
in his death on a cross outside the walls of Jerusalem. Paul
gives words to this mystery by saying, "Being as we are, he
was humbler yet, even to accepting death, death on a cross"
(Ph 2:7–8).

Jesus Christ is the displaced Lord in whom God's compassion becomes flesh. In him, we see a life of displacement lived

to the fullest. It is in following our displaced Lord that the Christian community is formed.

TO DISAPPEAR AS AN OBJECT
OF INTEREST

We must now look more deeply into the way in which displacement becomes a way to compassionate community. At first sight, displacement seems disruptive. Many people who have experienced harsh, cruel displacements can testify that displacement unsettled their family life, destroyed their sense of security, created much anger and resentment, and left them with the feeling that their lives were irreparably harmed. Displaced people, therefore, are not necessarily compassionate people. Many have become fearful, suspicious, and prone to complain. In a world with millions of displaced people, we need to be careful not to romanticize displacement or to make it an easy prescription for people who seek to live compassionate lives.

But we must also say that especially in a world with so many violent and cruel displacements, Jesus' call to voluntary displacement has a very contemporary ring. It is obviously not a call to disruptive behavior, but a call to solidarity with the millions who live disrupted lives.

The paradox of voluntary displacement is that although it seems to separate us from the world—from father, mother, brothers, sisters, family, and friends—we actually find ourselves in deeper union with it. Voluntary displacement leads to compassionate living precisely because it moves us from positions of distinction to positions of sameness, from being in special places to being everywhere. This movement is well described by Thomas Merton. After twenty years of Trappist life, he writes in the preface to the Japanese edition of *The Seven Storey Mountain*, "My monastery . . . is a place in which I disappear from the world as an object of interest in order to be everywhere in it by hiddenness and compassion."[10] To disappear from the world as an object of interest in order to be everywhere in it by hiddenness and compassion is the basic movement of the Christian life. It is the movement that leads to community as well as to compassion. It leads us to see with others what we could not see before, to feel with others what we could not feel before, to hear with others what we could not hear before.

The implications for each of us individually vary according to the specific milieus in which we live and our concrete understandings of God's call for us. The fact that for Thomas Merton voluntary displacement meant leaving his teaching position and entering a Trappist monastery is secondary. For Martin Luther it meant leaving the monastery and speaking out against scandalous clerical practices; for Dietrich Bonhoeffer it meant returning from the United States to Germany and becoming a prisoner of the Nazis; for Simone Weil it meant leaving her middle-class milieu and working in factories as a common laborer; for Martin Luther King, Jr., it meant leaving the "ordinary and proper" place of the blacks and leading protest marches. But for many people it does not even mean physical movement, but a new attitude toward their factual displacement and a faithful perseverance in their unspectacular lives. None of these men and women, whether famous or unknown, desired to abandon the world. They did not want to escape from responsibilities. They did not want to close their eyes to the great pains and problems of their time. They did not want to withdraw into pietism or self-centered introspection. Their sole aim was to disappear as an object of interest—an object of competition and rivalry, an object that can be bought and sold, used or misused, measured, compared, evaluated, and weighed—and thus become real members of the human family by hiddenness and compassion. As long as our primary concern in life is to be interesting and thus worthy of special attention, compassion cannot manifest itself. Therefore, the movement toward compassion always starts by gaining distance from the world that wants to make us objects of interest.

It is worth noting the great role voluntary displacement

has played in the history of Christianity. Benedict went to Subiaco, Francis to the Carceri, Ignatius to Manresa, Charles de Foucauld to the Sahara, John Wesley to the poor districts in England, Mother Teresa to Calcutta, and Dorothy Day to the Bowery. With their followers, they moved from the ordinary and proper places to the places where they could experience and express their compassionate solidarity with those in whom the brokenness of the human condition was most visible. We can indeed say that voluntary displacement stands at the origin of all great religious reforms.

ST. FRANCIS OF ASSISI

The most inspiring and challenging example of displacement is St. Francis of Assisi. In 1209, this son of a wealthy merchant tore his clothes from his body and walked away from his family and friends to live a life of abject poverty. By moving naked out of the fortified city with its power and security and by living in caves and in the open fields, Francis called attention to the basic poverty of humanity. He revealed not only his own nakedness but also the nakedness of all people before God. From this displaced position, Francis could live a compassionate life; he was no longer blinded by apparent differences between people and could recognize them all as brothers and sisters who needed God's grace as much as he did. G. K. Chesterton writes:

What gave him extraordinary personal power was this; that from the Pope to the beggar, from the Sultan of Syria in his pavilion to the ragged robbers crawling out of the wood, there was never a man who looked into those brown burning eyes without being certain that Francis Bernardone was really interested in *him*, in his own inner individual life from the cradle to the grave; that he himself was being valued and taken seriously, and not merely added to the spoils of some social policy or the names in some clerical document . . . He treated the whole mob of men as a mob of Kings.[11]

In the small group of brothers who followed Francis in his

poverty, the compassionate life was lived. These men, who had nothing to share but their poverty and who made themselves fully dependent on God's grace, formed a genuine fellowship of the weak in which they could live together in compassion and extend their compassion to all whom they met on the road. Their communal life of poverty prepared them for unlimited compassion. Chesterton writes that Francis' argument for poverty was "that the dedicated man might go anywhere among any kind of men, even the worst kind of men, so long as there was nothing by which they could hold him. If he had any ties or needs like ordinary men, he would become like ordinary men."[12]

St. Francis offers us an impressive example of displacement that leads to community and compassion. By moving away from their "ordinary and proper places," St. Francis and his followers illuminated the oneness of the human race. They did this not only by the way they lived together but also by the way they created space for others in their common life.

The history of the Franciscan brotherhood, however, also illustrates that as soon as success and wealth seduce people back to their ordinary and proper places, community as well as compassion is hard to find. This was not only true for the Franciscans but also for many other religious groups as well. It is therefore understandable that the history of Christianity is filled with reformers who constantly displace themselves to remind us of our great vocation to a compassionate life.

If we really want to be compassionate people, it is urgent that we reclaim this great tradition of displacement. As long as our houses, parishes, convents, and monasteries are only ordinary and proper places, they will only awaken ordinary and proper responses and nothing will happen. As long as religious people are well dressed, well fed, and well cared for, words about being in solidarity with the poor will remain pious words more likely to evoke good feelings than creative actions. As long as we are only doing well what others are doing better and more efficiently, we can hardly expect to be considered the salt of the earth or the light of the world. In short, as long as we avoid displacement, we will miss the compassionate life to which our Lord calls us.

Those who, like St. Francis, have followed the Lord faithfully have shown us that by disappearing from the world as objects of interest we can be everywhere in it by hiddenness and compassion. Living in the world as objects of interest alienates us from it. Living in the world by hiddenness and compassion unites us with it because it allows us to discover the world in the center of our being. It is not hard to notice that those who are very involved in the world are often out of touch with its deepest struggles and pains, while those who live in solitude and community often have a great knowledge of the significant events of their time and a great sensitivity to the people who are subject to these events.

Thus, displacement makes it possible to be *in* the world without being *of* it. For this Jesus prayed on the evening of his death: "Father . . . I am not asking you to remove them from the world, but to protect them from the evil one. . . . As you sent me into the world, I have sent them into the world" (Jn 17:15, 18).

SOMETHING TO RECOGNIZE

Let us not mistake the idea of voluntary displacement as an invitation to dramatic action. We might think that in order to become compassionate people we must make great farewell gestures to our families, friends, homes, and jobs. Such an interpretation of the call to displacement is more in the spirit of the American pioneers than in the spirit of the disciples of Christ. What we need to understand above all else is that voluntary displacement can only be an expression of discipleship when it is a response to a call—or, to say the same thing, when it is an act of obedience.

Christians whose lives are marked by impressive forms of displacement explain their movements not as self-initiated projects with clear-cut objectives and goals, but as responses to a divine invitation that usually requires a long time to be heard and understood. St. Francis' dramatic gesture of stripping himself and returning his clothes to his father can only be seen as an act of discipleship because it was the climax of many years of inner struggle to discover God's will. Only very slowly after dreams, visions, and years of prayer and consultation did Francis become aware that God was calling him to a life of total poverty. Mother Teresa tells a similar story. She did not leave her community to work with the dying in Calcutta simply because she considered this a good idea or a necessary task, but because she heard God calling her and she found this call confirmed by those from whom she asked advice and guidance. Those who practice voluntary displacement as a method or technique to form new community, and thus to become compassionate, will soon find themselves entangled in their own complex motivations and involved in many conflicts and much confusion.

This is an important consideration, especially in a time when so many forms of self-styled "holiness" are being promulgated. Even the desire to be a saintly person has become subject to false and often destructive forms of ascetical behavior, a fact that reveals more about our needs than about God's call. Saints and "outstanding" Christians should, therefore, never be perceived as people whose concrete behavior must be imitated. Rather, we should see in them living reminders that God calls every human being in a unique way and asks each of us to become attentive to his voice in our own unique lives.

What does this mean for us in terms of voluntary displacement? If voluntary displacement is such a central theme in the life of Christ and his followers, must we not begin by displacing ourselves? Probably not. Rather, we must begin to identify in our own lives where displacement is already occurring. We may be dreaming of great acts of displacement while failing to notice in the displacements of our own lives the first indications of God's presence.

We do not have to look very long or far to find displacements in our lives. Most of us have experienced painful physical displacements. We have moved from one country to another, from West to East, from North to South, from a small town to a large city, from a small, intimate high school to a large, impersonal university, from a playful work milieu to a competitive position; in short, from familiar to very unfamiliar surroundings. Beyond these physical displacements, our lives may be marked by deep inner displacements. As the years go by, familiar images and ideas are often pushed out of place. Ways of thinking, which for many years helped us to understand our world, come under criticism and are called old-fashioned or conservative. Rituals and customs that played central roles in the years of our growth and development are suddenly no longer appreciated by our children or neighbors. Family traditions and church celebrations that have given us our most precious memories are suddenly abandoned and even laughed at as sentimental, magical, or superstitious. More than physical displacements, these inner mental and emotional displacements threaten us and give us feelings of being lost or left alone.

In our modern society with its increasing mobility and pluriformity, we have become the subjects and often the victims of so many displacements that it is very hard to keep a sense of rootedness, and we are constantly tempted to become bitter and resentful. Our first and often most difficult task, therefore, is to allow these actual displacements to become places where we can hear God's call. It often seems easier to initiate a displacement that we ourselves can control than freely to accept and affirm a displacement that is totally out of our hands. The main question is, "How can I come to understand and experience God's caring actions in the concrete situation in which I find myself?" This question is difficult because it requires a careful look at the often painful events and experiences of the moment. "Where have I already been asked to leave my father and mother; where have I already been invited to let the dead bury the dead; where am I already challenged to keep my hand on the plow and not look back?" God is always active in our lives. He always calls, he always asks us to take up our crosses and follow him. But do we see, feel, and recognize God's call, or do we keep waiting for that illusory moment when it will really happen? Displacement is not primarily something to do or to accomplish, but something to recognize.

In and through this recognition a conversion can take place, a conversion from involuntary displacement leading to resentment, bitterness, resignation, and apathy, to voluntary displacement that can become an expression of discipleship. We do not have to go after crosses, but we have to take up the crosses that have been ours all along. To follow Jesus, therefore, means first and foremost to discover in our daily lives God's unique vocation for us.

It is through the recognition of our displacement and the willingness to hear in it the first whispers of God's voice that we start forming community and living compassionate lives. Once we begin to experience our actual physical, mental, and emotional displacements as forms of discipleship and start to accept them in obedience, we become less defensive and no longer need to hide our pains and frustrations. Then what seemed a reason for shame and embarrassment becomes instead the basis of community, and what seemed to separate us from others becomes the basis of compassion.

NO ORDINARY CITIZENS

To say that our main task is to discern God's call in the actual displacements of our lives does not imply passive resignation to sad, distressing, or unjust predicaments. On the contrary, it implies that we must look carefully at our situations in order to distinguish between constructive and destructive forces and discover where God is calling us. Careful attention to God's actions in our lives thus leads us to an even greater sensitivity to his call. The more we are able to discern God's voice in the midst of our daily lives, the more we will be able to hear him when he calls us to more drastic forms of displacement. Some of us are indeed called to move away from our cities and live in caves; some of us are indeed called to sell all we have, give it to the poor, and follow Christ in total poverty; some of us are indeed called to move away from our more familiar milieus and live with the sick and the dying; some are indeed called to join nonviolent communities of resistance, to protest loudly against social ills, to share in the misery of prisoners, the isolation of lepers, or the agony of the oppressed; some are even called to undergo torture and violent deaths. But no one will be able to hear or understand these very blessed calls if he or she has not recognized the smaller calls hidden in the hours of a regular day. Not everyone is called in the way St. Francis, Mother Teresa, Martin Luther King, Jr., Cesar Chavez, Dorothy Day, Jean Vanier, Archbishop Romero, and Dom Helder Camera were called. But everyone must live with the deep conviction that God acts in her or his life in an equally unique way. No one should ever think that he or she is just an "ordinary citizen" in the Kingdom of God. As soon as we start taking ourselves and God seriously and allow him to enter into a dialogue with us, we will discover that we also are asked to leave fathers, mothers, brothers, and sisters and follow the crucified Lord in obedience. Quite often we will discover that we are asked to follow our Lord to places we would rather not go. But when we have learned to see him in the small displacements of our daily lives, the greater call will not seem so great after all. We then will find the courage to follow him and be amazed by our freedom to do so.

Thus, voluntary displacement is part of the life of each Christian. It leads away from the ordinary and proper places, whether this is noticed by others or not; it leads to a recognition of each other as fellow travelers on the road, and thus creates community. Finally, voluntary displacement leads to compassion; by bringing us closer to our own brokenness it opens our eyes to our fellow human beings, who seek our consolation and comfort.

6

Togetherness

THE MIRACLE OF WALKING ON THE FLOOR

The Christian community gathers in displacement and in so doing discovers and proclaims a new way of being together. There are many motives that bring people together. People often come together to defend themselves against common dangers or to protect common values. People also come together because of shared likes or dislikes. Hatred as well as fear can create togetherness. After the resurrection of Christ, the disciples were together in a closed room "for fear of the Jews" (Jn 20:19), and the rulers, elders, and scribes came together in Jerusalem because of their shared annoyance with Peter and his followers (Ac 4:5).

The togetherness of the Christian community, however, is
not the result of shared anger or anxiety; it grows from a
deep sense of being called together to make God's compassion visible in the concreteness of everyday living. In the
Acts of the Apostles, we get a glimpse of this new togetherness: "The faithful all *lived together* and owned everything
in common . . . Day by day the Lord added to their *community* [literally: their togetherness] those destined to be
saved" (Ac 2:44-47). The Christian community is not driven
together but drawn together. By leaving the ordinary
and proper places and responding to the Lord's call to follow
him, people with very different backgrounds discover each
other as fellow travelers brought together in common discipleship.

It is important to realize that voluntary displacement is not
a goal in itself; it is meaningful only when it gathers us
together in a new way. Voluntary displacement, as the
Gospel presents it, leads us to understand each other as
women and men with similar needs and struggles and to meet
each other with an awareness of a common vulnerability.
Therefore, no form of displacement is authentic if it does not
bring us closer together. If we displace ourselves to be special, unique, or outstanding, we simply exhibit subtle forms
of competitiveness that lead not to community but to elitism.
Those entering monasteries or leaving their countries do so
only in the spirit of the Gospel when this brings them closer
to their fellow human beings.

It is remarkable how many people still think of priests,
nuns, monks, and hermits as constituting a spiritual elite. They
speak of them as people living in another world, having their
own mysterious practices, and enjoying a special connection
with God. The danger of this way of thinking is that it divides the people of God into "ordinary" Christians and "special" Christians, with the result that voluntary displacement
no longer leads to togetherness but to separation. True displacement, however, evokes a deep new awareness of solidar-

ity. The criterion for any form of detachment, any form of "leaving home," is the degree to which it reveals the common ground on which we stand together.

This is well illustrated by an event that took place at a circus in New Haven, Connecticut. After many acts of lion tamers and acrobats, the high-wire artist Philipe Petit entered the arena. This agile little Frenchman was going to ask for a kind of attention quite different from that required by the other artists. His act was not as glamorous as you might have expected. In a very playful way, he walked on a steel wire stretched between two small towers, making it seem more like a dance than a balancing act. He acted as if he were conquering the towers and made people laugh with his easy jumps. But then something unusual took place which revealed his real talent. As the end of his performance, he walked down on a wire strung between the tower and the sandy floor. Since this was extremely difficult, everyone followed his movements with special attention. You could see people biting their nails and exclaiming, "How is it possible? How can he do it?"

Attention as well as tension grew and all kept their eyes on his outstretched arms. Everyone was so engrossed in his act that no one realized that for five seconds Philipe had been walking on the safe floor! Only after he himself looked down to the floor with a puzzled face and then up to the stands with happily surprised eyes did the tension break and everyone explode into roaring applause. That indeed was the real artistic moment, because Philipe, the artist, had been able to make his viewers look with admiration at an act that everyone else could do too: walking on the floor! The great talent of this high-wire artist was not so much that he could evoke admiration for an act nobody could imitate, but that he could make us look with amazement at something we can all do together. Therefore, the applause that Philipe received was not simply an expression of excitement over the special feat of dancing between two towers; it was also an expression of gratitude for the rediscovery of the miracle that we can walk together safely on the floor.

This story illustrates how displacement can create a new togetherness. Philipe Petit had to walk on a steel wire to make us see how special it is that we can walk on the floor. The main effect of his being different was to reveal a deeper level of sameness. If we complain that we are not as capable as this artist and only feel less self-confident because of his feat, we have not understood him; but if we come to recognize through his act that we are all part of the same human family, then his displacement is a real service. The Christians who displace themselves by going to monasteries, foreign lands, or places of great need, do not do such things to be special or praised, but to reveal that what separates us is less important than what unites us. And so displacement is the mysterious way by which a compassionate togetherness is realized.

SEEING EACH OTHER'S UNIQUE GIFTS

This new, noncompetitive togetherness opens our eyes to each other. Here we touch the beauty of the Christian community. When we give up our desires to be outstanding or different, when we let go of our needs to have our own special niches in life, when our main concern is to be the same, and to live out this sameness in solidarity, we are then able to see each other's unique gifts. Gathered together in common vulnerability, we discover how much we have to give each other. The Christian community is the opposite of a highly uniform group of people whose behavior has been toned down to a common denominator and whose originality has been dulled. On the contrary, the Christian community, gathered in common discipleship, is the place where individual gifts can be called forth and put into service for all. It belongs to the essence of this new togetherness that our unique talents are no longer objects of competition but elements of community, no longer qualities that divide but gifts that unite.

When we have discovered that our sense of self does not depend on our differences and that our self-esteem is based on a love much deeper than the praise that can be acquired by unusual performances, we can see our unique talents as gifts for others. Then, too, we will notice that the sharing of our gifts does not diminish our own value as persons but enhances it. In community, the particular talents of the individual members become like the little stones that form a great mosaic. The fact that a little gold, blue, or red piece is part of a splendid mosaic makes it not less but more valuable because it contributes to an image much greater than itself. Thus, our dominant feeling toward each other can shift from jealousy to gratitude. With increasing clarity, we can see the beauty in each other and call it forth so that it may become a part of our total life together.

Both sameness and uniqueness can be affirmed in community. When we unmask the illusion that a person is the difference she or he makes, we can come together on the basis of our common human brokenness and our common need for healing. Then we also can come to the marvelous realization that hidden in the ground on which we walk together are the talents that we can offer to each other. Community, as a new way of being together, leads to the discovery or rediscovery of each other's hidden talents and makes us realize our own unique contribution to the common life.

An old Sufi tale about a watermelon hunter offers a fascinating illustration. Once upon a time there was a man who strayed from his own country into the world known as the Land of the Fools. He soon saw a number of people flying in terror from a field where they had been trying to reap wheat. "There is a monster in that field," they told him. He looked and saw that it was a watermelon. He offered to kill the "monster" for them. When he had cut the melon from its stalk, he took a slice and began to eat it. The people became even more terrified of him than they had been of the water-melon. They drove him away with pitchforks crying: "He will kill us next, unless we get rid of him." It so happened that at another time another man also strayed into the Land of the Fools, and the same thing started to happen to him. But, instead of offering to help them with the "monster" he agreed with the Fools that it must be dangerous, and by tip-toeing away from it with them he gained their confidence. He spent a long time with them in their houses until he could teach them, little by little, the basic facts which would enable them not only to lose their fear of melons, but even to cul-tivate them for themselves.[13]

This beautiful tale about obedient service in solidarity well illustrates how compassionate togetherness does not suppress unique talents but calls them forth to fruitfulness. We often think that service means to give something to others, to tell them how to speak, act, or behave; but now it appears that above all else, real, humble service is helping our neighbors discover that they possess great but often hidden talents that can enable them to do even more for us than we can do for them.

SELF-EMPTYING FOR OTHERS

By revealing the unique gifts of the other, we learn to empty ourselves. Self-emptying does not ask of us to engage our-selves in some form of self-castigation or self-scrutiny, but to pay attention to others in such a way that they begin to rec-ognize their own value.

Paying attention to our fellow human beings is far from easy. We tend to be so insecure about our self-worth and so much in need of affirmation that it is very hard not to ask for attention ourselves. Before we are fully aware of it, we are speaking about ourselves, referring to our experiences, telling our stories, or turning the subject of conversation toward our

own territory. The familiar sentence, "That reminds me of
. . ." is a standard method of shifting attention from the
other to ourselves. To pay attention to others with the desire
to make them the center and to make their interests our own
is a real form of self-emptying, since to be able to receive
others into our intimate inner space we must be empty. That
is why listening is so difficult. It means our moving away
from the center of attention and inviting others into that
space.

From experience we know how healing such an invitation
can be. When someone listens to us with real concentration
and expresses sincere care for our struggles and our pains,
we feel that something very deep is happening to us. Slowly,
fears melt away, tensions dissolve, anxieties retreat, and we
discover that we carry within us something we can trust and
offer as a gift to others. The simple experience of being valuable and important to someone else has a tremendous recrea-
tive power.

If we have been given such an experience, we have received a precious kind of knowledge. We have learned the
true significance of Paul's words, "Always consider the other
person to be better than yourself" (Ph 2:3). This is not an
invitation to false humility or to the denial of our own value,
but it is a call to enter Christ's healing ministry with him.
Every time we pay attention we become emptier, and the
more empty we are the more healing space we can offer.
And the more we see others being healed, the more we will
be able to understand that it is not through us but through
Christ in us that this healing takes place.

Thus, in togetherness we call forth the hidden gifts in each
other and receive them in gratitude as valuable contributions
to our life in community.

One of the most impressive examples of this compassionate
togetherness is a community of handicapped people in Rome.
In this community, founded by Don Franco, handicapped

adults and children live together in extended families and call forth talents in each other which before had remained hidden. The beauty of their togetherness is so visible and so convincing that many "healthy" people have joined those who are paralyzed, mentally retarded, blind, spastic, crippled, or deaf and have discovered with them the great gift of community. In this community, there are few people with self-serving complaints, low self-esteem, or deep depression. Instead, they are people who have discovered each other's distinctive talents and enjoy together the richness of their common life.

This new togetherness is the place of compassion. Where people have entered into the mind of Christ and no longer think of their own interests first, the compassionate Lord manifests himself and offers his healing presence to all who turn to him.

GATHERED BY VOCATION

By ceasing to make our individual differences a basis of competition and by recognizing these differences as potential contributions to a rich life together, we begin to hear the call to community. In and through Christ, people of different ages and life-styles, from different races and classes, with different languages and educations, can join together and witness to God's compassionate presence in our world. There are many common-interest groups, and most of them seem to exist in order to defend or protect something. Although these groups often fulfill important tasks in our society, the Christian community is of a different nature. When we form a Christian community, we come together not because of similar experiences, knowledge, problems, color, or sex, but because we have been called together by the same Lord. Only he enables us to cross the many bridges that separate us; only he allows us to recognize each other as members of the same human family; and only he frees us to pay careful attention to each other. This is why those who are gathered together in community are witnesses to the compassionate Lord. By the way they are able to carry each other's burdens and share each other's joys, they testify to his presence in our world.

Life in community is a response to a vocation. The word *vocation* comes from the Latin *vocare*, which means "to call." God calls us together into one people fashioned in the image of Christ. It is by Christ's vocation that we are gathered. Here we need to distinguish carefully between vocation and career. In a world that puts such emphasis on success, our concern for a career constantly tends to make us deaf to our vocation. When we are seduced into believing that our career is what counts, we can no longer hear the voice that calls us together; we become so preoccupied with our own plans, projects, or promotions that we push everyone away who prevents us from achieving our goals. Career and vocation are not mutually exclusive. In fact, our vocation might require us to pursue a certain career. Many people have become excellent doctors, lawyers, technicians, and scientists in response to God's call heard in the community. Quite often, our vocation becomes visible in a specific job, task, or endeavor. But our vocation can never be reduced to these activities. As soon as we think that our careers *are* our vocation, we are in danger of returning to the ordinary and proper places governed by human competition and of using our talents more to separate ourselves from others than to unite ourselves with them in a common life. A career disconnected from a vocation divides; a career that expresses obedience to our vocation is the concrete way of making our unique talents available to the community. Therefore, it is not our careers, but our vocation, that should guide our lives.

The following story about an American family offers a good insight into the difference between a vocation and a career. John, Mary, and their children enjoyed a very ordinary and proper life in a suburb of Washington, D.C. John

was a successful researcher in community development. He
gave workshops, taught at the university, and produced regular reports like any other good researcher. Mary was a creative woman. She found time outside her family obligations for
pottery and weaving. Their children were open and friendly
toward the neighbors. All who knew the family respected
them as caring people, good citizens, and committed Christians. Yet, in the midst of all their successes, life seemed to
lack a dimension that was difficult to articulate. One evening,
when John had come home from a lecture he had just given
on community, he suddenly realized that his own family was
as alienated as most others. The more he thought about it, the
more it struck him that he earned his money by speaking
about ideals he himself did not realize. He felt like a preacher
proudly speaking about humility, angrily pronouncing peace,
and sadly proclaiming joy.

When the contrast between his successful career and his
unsuccessful life became too obvious to deny any longer,
John and Mary took the courageous step of taking their
whole family on a one-year retreat during which they lived
with very little money, social security, and "success." And
there, away from their ordinary and proper place, they discovered life anew. They saw nature as they never had seen it
before; they listened to each other as they had never listened
before; they prayed as they had never prayed before; and
they wondered why it had taken them so long to see what
had always been right before their eyes. In this new situation,
they began to hear more clearly the call inviting them to live
free from the compulsions of the world, but close to each
other and their neighbors, and in continually searching for a
deeper understanding of the mysteries of life. Here they discovered their vocation, a vocation which had always been
there, but which they had not been able to hear before because of the noisy demands of their successful careers.

One of the most remarkable, and in fact unexpected, re-

sults of their "conversion" was that, when their vocation re-
emerged and moved to the center of their attention their
whole world became transformed. Words such as *family*,
friendship, and *love* became new words expressing new experiences of living. Research was no longer an aspect of a competitive academic life, but the expression of the ongoing
search for meaning. Leadership became service, an argument
to convince became an invitation to join, and impressive lectures became compelling challenges. Most of all, their new
way of being together uncovered in the heart of many other
people deeply hidden desires that were never expressed until
they were lived out in the concrete life of this American
family. What for many had been conceived as only a romantic dream suddenly became real enough to be a reachable
goal, an ideal that could be realized. The compassionate life
was no longer a fantasy but a visible reality in the vital community of people who had discovered, through displacement,
a new way of being together.

A vocation is not the exclusive privilege of monks, priests,
religious sisters, or a few heroic laypersons. God calls everyone who is listening; there is no individual or group for
whom God's call is reserved. But to be effective, a call must
be heard, and to hear it we must continually discern our vocation amidst the escalating demands of our career.

Thus, we see how voluntary displacement leads to a new
togetherness in which we can recognize our sameness in common vulnerability, discover our unique talents as gifts for the
upbuilding of the community, and listen to God's call, which
continually summons us to a vocation far beyond the aspirations of our career.

PART THREE

The Compassionate Way

7

Patience

A DISCIPLINE THAT UNVEILS

In this third and final part we want to raise the question: Is there a specific compassionate way that can be practiced day in and day out? In our reflections on the compassionate life the emphasis was on discipleship. Here the emphasis is on discipline.

Discipline and discipleship can never be separated. Without discipline discipleship is little more than hero worship or fadism; without discipleship discipline easily becomes a form of emulation or self-assertion. Discipline and discipleship belong together. They strengthen and deepen each other. Yet we have so many associations, negative as well as positive, with the word *discipline* that it is hard to give it the right emphasis when used in connection with discipleship. When we say that children need more discipline, that there is a lack of discipline in schools, and that without self-discipline no one can reach his or her goal, the word *discipline* suggests a rigorous effort to keep oneself or others under control and to acquire efficiency in human behavior. Even when we use the word *discipline* to designate a field of study and practice, we are still speaking primarily about efficiency and control. When we use the word *discipline* to express the way to a compassionate life, however, these associations become very misleading.

Discipline in the Christian life should never be construed as a rigorous method or technique to attain compassion. Compassion is not a skill that we can master by arduous training, years of study, or careful supervision. We cannot get a Master's degree or a Ph.D. in compassion. Compassion is a divine gift and not a result of systematic study or effort. At a time when many programs are designed to help us become more sensitive, perceptive, and receptive, we need to be reminded continuously that compassion is not conquered but given, not the outcome of our hard work but the fruit of God's grace. In the Christian life, discipline is the human effort to unveil what has been covered, to bring to the foreground what has remained hidden, and to put on the lamp stand what has been kept under a basket. It is like raking away the leaves that cover the pathways in the garden of our soul. Discipline enables the revelation of God's divine Spirit in us.

Discipline in the Christian life does indeed require effort, but it is an effort to reveal rather than to conquer. God always calls. To hear his call and allow that call to guide our actions requires discipline in order to prevent ourselves from remaining or becoming spiritually deaf. There are so many voices calling for our attention and so many activities distracting us that a serious effort is necessary if we are to become and remain sensitive to the divine presence in our lives.

When God calls he gives a new name. Abram became Abraham, Jacob became Israel, Saul became Paul, and Simon became Peter. We must search for this new name because the new name reveals the unique vocation given to us by God. Discipline is the effort to avoid deafness and to become sensitive to the sound of the voice that calls us by a new name and invites us to a new life in discipleship.

Often we cling to our old names because our new names, our new identities, may point us in directions we would rather not go. After all, Abraham, Israel, Paul, and Peter did not have easy lives after they became obedient to God's voice. They had many hard roads to travel and many perils to face. Intuitively, we realize that there are advantages to deafness and that the promises of our own voices are often much more convincing than those offered by God. But we also sense that by remaining deaf we will remain strangers to our deepest selves and never realize our true identities. Without discipline, we might never come to know our true names. And that would be the greatest tragedy of our existence. Deaf people become nameless people who have no destination and remain aimless wanderers, unknown to themselves and their fellow travelers.

Discipline, thus understood, is indispensable in the compassionate life. Without discipline, the forces that call us by our old names and pull us into competitive games are too strong to resist. In the day-to-day practice of living we need to be able to do something that will prevent the seed sown in our lives from being suffocated. We need a concrete and specific way that can provide formation, guidance, and practice. We need to know not only about the compassionate life but also about the compassionate way.

ENTERING ACTIVELY INTO THE THICK OF LIFE

What, then, is the compassionate way? The compassionate way is the patient way. Patience is the discipline of compassion. This becomes obvious when we realize that the word *compassion* could be read as *com-patience*. The words *passion* and *patience* both find their roots in the Latin word *pati*, which means "suffering." The compassionate life could be described as a life patiently lived with others. If we then ask about the way of the compassionate life—about the discipline of compassion—patience is the answer. If we cannot be patient, we cannot be com-patient. If we ourselves are unable to suffer, we cannot suffer with others. If we lack the strength to carry the burden of our own lives, we cannot accept the burden of our neighbors. Patience is the hard but fruitful discipline of the disciple of the compassionate Lord.

At first this may sound disappointing. It really sounds like a cop-out. Each time we hear the word *patience*, we tend to cringe. As children, we heard the word used so often in so many different circumstances that it seemed to be the word that was uttered when no one knew what else to say. It usually meant waiting—waiting until Daddy came home, the bus arrived, the waiter brought the food, school ended, the pain decreased, the rain stopped, or the car was fixed. And so the word *patience* became associated with powerlessness, the inability to act, and a general state of passivity and dependence. It is therefore quite understandable that when anyone in authority—our parents, the priest, the minister, the teacher, the boss—said, "Just be patient," we frequently felt belittled and offended. Often, it simply meant that we were not going to be told what was really happening, that we were being kept in a subservient place, and that the only thing expected of us was to wait passively until someone with power decided to move again. It is sad that a deep and rich word like *patience* has such a perverted history in our minds. With such a history, it is difficult not to consider *patience* an oppressive word used by the powerful to keep the powerless under control. In fact, not a few among those in very influential positions have counseled patience simply to avoid necessary changes in church and society.

But true patience is the opposite of a passive waiting in which we let things happen and allow others to make the decisions. Patience means to enter actively into the thick of life and to fully bear the suffering within and around us. Patience is the capacity to see, hear, touch, taste, and smell as fully as possible the inner and outer events of our lives. It is to enter our lives with open eyes, ears, and hands so that we really know what is happening. Patience is an extremely difficult discipline precisely because it counteracts our unreflective impulse to flee or to fight. When we see an accident on the road, something in us pushes the accelerator. When someone approaches a sensitive issue, something in us tries to change the subject. When a shameful memory presents itself, something in us wants to forget it. And if we cannot flee, we fight. We fight the one who challenges our opinions, the people who question our power, and the circumstances that force us to change.

Patience requires us to go beyond the choice between fleeing or fighting. It is the third and the most difficult way. It calls for discipline because it goes against the grain of our impulses. Patience involves staying with it, living it through, listening carefully to what presents itself to us here and now. Patience means stopping on the road when someone in pain needs immediate attention. Patience means overcoming the fear of a controversial subject. It means paying attention to shameful memories and searching for forgiveness without having to forget. It means welcoming sincere criticism and evaluating changing conditions. In short, patience is a willingness to be influenced even when this requires giving up control and entering into unknown territory.

Jesus and the authors of the New Testament have much to say about this active patience. The Greek word for patience is *hypomonē*. The fact that this word is translated in different places by different English terms such as *patience*, *endurance*, *perseverance*, and *fortitude*, already suggests that we are dealing with a very rich biblical concept. When Jesus speaks about patience, he describes it as the discipline by which God's life-giving presence becomes manifest. Patience is the quality of those who are the rich soil in which the seed can produce "its crop a hundredfold." "These are people," Jesus says, "with a noble and generous heart who have heard the word and take it to themselves and yield a harvest through their perseverance (*hypomonē*)" (Lk 8:8, 15).

It becomes evident that Jesus considers this patience to be central in the lives of his followers. "You will be betrayed even by parents and brothers, relations and friends; and some of you will be put to death. You will be hated by all men on account of my name, but not a hair of your head will be lost. Your endurance (*hypomonē*) will win you your lives" (Lk 21:16–19). Jesus wants his followers not to fight or flee but to enter fully into the turmoil of human existence. He even goes so far as to tell his disciples not to prepare if they should have to defend themselves in court. In the midst of their suffering, they will discover the voice of their compassionate Lord who will give them his wisdom. "They . . . will bring you before kings and governors because of my name . . . Keep this carefully in mind: you are not to prepare your defense, because I myself shall give you an eloquence and a wisdom that none of your opponents will be able to resist or contradict" (Lk 21:12–16).

The active, strong, and fruitful patience about which Jesus speaks is repeatedly praised by the apostles Paul, Peter, James, and John as the mark of the true disciple. Paul in particular offers us a deep insight into the power of patience. He exhorts his friend Timothy to be patient and gentle (1 Tm 6:11) and writes to the Christians at Colossae, "You should be clothed in sincere compassion, in kindness and humility, gentleness and patience" (Col 3:12). He does not hesitate to offer himself as an example of patience (2 Tm 3:10) and to see patience as the source of an intimate solidarity between himself and his people, "When we are made to suffer, it is for your consolation and salvation. When, instead, we are comforted, this should be a consolation to you, supporting you in patiently bearing the same sufferings as we bear. And our hope for you is confident, since we know that, sharing our sufferings, you will also share our consolations" (2 Co 1:6–7). For Paul patience is indeed the discipline of the compassionate life. In a glorious and victorious statement he writes to the Christians in Rome that through patience we are living signs of God's compassionate love: ". . . we can boast about our sufferings. These sufferings bring patience, as we know, and patience brings perseverance, and perseverance brings hope, and this hope is not deceptive, because the love of God has been poured into our hearts by the Holy Spirit which has been given us" (Rm 5:3–5).

This conviction that God's compassionate presence becomes manifest through our patience, endurance, perseverance, and fortitude, is the main motivation for the discipline of patience. This is beautifully expressed by James when he says: ". . . remember it is those who had *endurance* [*hypomeinantas*] that we say are the blessed ones. You have heard of the *patience* [*hypomonē*] of Job, and understood the Lord's purpose, realizing that the Lord is kind and compassionate" (Jm 5:10–11). Thus, the New Testament presents the discipline of patience as the way to a life of discipleship which makes us living signs of God's compassionate presence in this world.

LIVING IN THE FULLNESS OF TIME

Patience as an active entering into the thick of life opens us to a new experience of time. Patience makes us realize that the

Christian who has entered into discipleship with Jesus Christ lives not only with a new mind but also in a new time. The discipline of patience is the concentrated effort to let the new time into which we are led by Christ determine our perceptions and decisions. It is this new time that offers the opportunity and the context to be together in a compassionate way.

In order to explore more fully this distinction between old and new time and to gain a deeper appreciation for the importance of the discipline of patience, let us look at our impatient moments. Impatience always has something to do with time. When we are impatient with speakers, we want them to stop speaking or to move on to another subject. When we are impatient with children, we want them to stop crying, asking for ice cream, or running around. When we are impatient with ourselves, we want to change our bad habits, finish a set task, or move ahead faster. Whatever the nature of our impatience, we want to leave the physical or mental state in which we find ourselves and move to another, less uncomfortable place. When we express our impatience, we reveal our desire that things will change as soon as possible: "I wish he would show up soon . . . I have already been waiting here for an hour and the train has still not arrived. . . . There is no end to his sermon. . . . How much longer before we get there?" These expressions betray an inner restlessness that often shows itself in feet tapping under the table, fingers nervously intertwined, or long, drawn-out yawning. Essentially, impatience is experiencing the moment as empty, useless, meaningless. It is wanting to escape from the here and now as soon as possible.

Sometimes our emotions are so totally dominated by impatience that we can no longer give any meaning to the moment. For example, even though we know that our plane is three hours late and that there is nothing urgent to do, we can be so full of gnawing impatience that we cannot read the novel we wanted to read, write the letters we wanted to write, or have the quiet time for prayer for which we longed. Our sole, all-pervasive desire has become to get away from this place and this time. There is no more hope in the moment.

Those who travel much often complain how little work they get done during their many hours in airports, planes, trains, and buses. Their well-intentioned plans to study their documents, prepare their lectures, or think through their problems are often frustrated even when nothing special distracts them. It seems that the overriding climate of the transportation world is so geared to moving away from the here and now that any real concentration demands more energy than we can normally muster. The transportation business is, in fact, a commercialized impatience. Impatient people might be difficult at times, but too much patience would mean the bankruptcy of many companies. People have to keep moving, so much so that reading a book in an airport coffee shop can hardly be tolerated.

What is the basis of this impatience? It is living in clock time. Clock time is that linear time by which our life is measured in abstract units appearing on clocks, watches, and calendars. These measuring units tell us the month, the day, the hour, and the second in which we find ourselves, and decide for us how much longer we have to speak, listen, eat, sing, study, pray, sleep, play, or stay. Our lives are dominated by our clocks and watches. In particular, the tyranny of the one-hour slot is enormous. There are visiting hours, therapeutic hours, and even happy hours. Without being fully aware of it, our most intimate emotions are often influenced by the clock. The big wall clocks in hospitals and airports have caused much inner turmoil and many tears.

Clock time is outer time, time that has a hard, merciless objectivity to it. Clock time leads us to wonder how much longer we have to live and whether "real life" has not already passed us by. Clock time makes us disappointed with today and seems to suggest that maybe tomorrow, next week, or next year *it* will really happen. Clock time keeps saying, "Hurry, hurry, time goes fast, maybe you will miss the real thing! But there is still a chance . . . Hurry to get married, find a job, visit a country, read a book, get a degree . . . Try to take it all in before you run out of time." Clock time always makes us depart. It breeds impatience and prevents any compassionate being together.

But fortunately for most of us, there have been other moments in our lives too, moments with an essentially different quality in which the experience of patience prevails. Perhaps such moments have been rare in our lives, but they belong among those precious memories that can offer hope and courage during restless and tense periods. These patient moments are moments in which we have a very different experience of time. It is the experience of the moment as full, rich, and pregnant. Such an experience makes us want to stay where we are and to take it all in. Somehow we know that in this moment everything is contained: the beginning, the middle, and the end; the past, the present, and the future; the sorrow and the joy; the expectation and the realization; the searching and the finding. These patient moments can differ greatly from one another. They may occur while we are simply sitting at the bedside of a sick person and realize that being together is the most important thing. They may happen while we are working on a regular task and suddenly recognize that it is good simply to be alive and to work. They may take place while we stand in a quiet church and realize unexpectedly that all is present here and now. We remember these and similar moments with great gratitude. We say: "It seemed that time came to a standstill; everything came together and simply was. I will never forget that moment." These moments are not necessarily happy, joyful, or ecstatic. They may be full of sorrow and pain, or marked by agony and struggle. What counts is the experience of fullness, inner importance, and maturation. What counts is the knowledge that in that moment real life touched us. From such moments we do not want to move away; rather, we want to live them to the fullest.

The following situation illustrates how such moments can be experienced as moments of truth. We are together with a few friends. No urgent subjects are discussed, no plans are made, no people outside the circle are topics of conversation. Few words are spoken. We know each other's wounds. We know of the many unresolved conflicts. But there is no fear. We look at each other with gentleness and patience, and then we realize that we are part of a great event, that all that can happen in our life is happening here and now, that this moment holds the full truth, and that it will stay with us wherever we go. We realize that we are bound to our friends with bonds of love and hope which no distance in time or space will break. We see what unity and peace really are, and we feel an inner strength pervading every fiber of our being. And we hear ourselves say, "This is grace."

Patience dispels clock time and reveals a new time, the time of salvation. It is not the time measured by the abstract, objective units of the clock, the watch, or the calendar, but rather the time lived from within and experienced as full time. It is this full time about which Scripture speaks. All the great events of the Gospels occur in the fullness of time. A literal translation from the Greek shows this clearly: When the time for Elizabeth had *become full* she bore her son John (Lk 1:57); When the days for Mary had been *fulfilled*, she bore Jesus (Lk 2:6); When the days of purification had been *made full*, Joseph and Mary brought him to Jerusalem (Lk 2:22). And the real event always happens in this fullness of time. The words *it happened*—in Greek *egeneto*—always announce an event that is not measured by outer time but by the inner time of maturation. In the days of Herod, *it happened* that Zacharias was the priest to serve in the temple (Lk 1:5). On the eighth day, *it happened* that they came together to circumcise John (Lk

1:59). In those days, *it happened* that a decree was issued by Caesar Augustus (Lk 2:1). While they were in Bethlehem, *it happened* that Mary's time was full to have a child (Lk 2:6). These happenings are all announced as moments of grace and salvation. And thus we see that the great event of God's coming is recognized as the event of the fullness of time. Jesus proclaims, The time has come to its *fullness* and the kingdom of God is close at hand (Mk 1:15), and Paul summarizes the great news when he writes to the Christians of Galatia, When the time had come to its *fullness* God sent his Son, born of a woman . . . to enable us to be adopted as sons (Ga 4:4–5).

It is this full time, pregnant with new life, that can be found through the discipline of patience. As long as we are the slaves of the clock and the calendar, our time remains empty and nothing really happens. Thus, we miss the moment of grace and salvation. But when patience prevents us from running from the painful moment in the false hope of finding our treasure elsewhere, we can slowly begin to see that the fullness of time is already here and that salvation is already taking place. Then, too, we can discover that in and through Christ all human events can become divine events in which we discover the compassionate presence of God.

TIME FOR CELEBRATING LIFE WITH OTHERS

Patience is the discipline of compassion because through patience we can live in the fullness of time and invite others to share in it. When we know that God is offering salvation to us, there is ample time to be with others and to celebrate life together.

As long as we remain the victims of clock time, which forces us into the rigid patterns of time slots, we are doomed to be without compassion. When we live by the clock we have no time for each other: We are always on the way to our next appointment and do not notice the person on the side of the road in need of help; we are increasingly concerned about missing something important and perceive human suffering as a disturbing interruption of our plans; we are constantly preoccupied with our free evening, free weekend, or free month and lose the capacity to enjoy the people we live and work with day in and day out. However, if this clock time loses its grip on us and we begin to live in the inner time of God's abundance, then compassion becomes visible. If patience teaches us the natural rhythm of birth and death, growth and decay, light and darkness, and enables us to experience this new time with all our senses, then we discover limitless space for our fellow human beings.

Patience opens us to many different people, all of whom can be invited to taste the fullness of God's presence. Patience opens our hearts to small children and makes us aware that their early years are as important in God's compassionate eyes as the later years of adults. It makes us realize that it is not the length of one's life that counts, but its fullness. Patience opens our hearts to the elderly and prevents us from the clock-time judgment that their most important years have already passed. Patience opens us to the sick and dying and allows us to sense that one minute of really being together can remove the bitterness of a lifetime. Patience helps us to give a moment of rest and joy to the driven young executive and to create some silence for busy young married couples. Patience allows us to take ourselves less seriously and makes us suspicious every time our many altruistic and service-oriented plans put us back on the time line of our clocks, watches, and calendars. Patience makes us loving, caring, gentle, tender, and always grateful for the abundance of God's gifts.

It is not difficult to recognize people who are patient. In their presence, something very deep happens to us. They lift us out of our anxious restlessness and bring us with them into the fullness of God's time. In their presence, we feel how much we are loved, accepted, and cared for. The many things, both large and small, that filled us with anxiety suddenly seem to lose their power over us, and we recognize that all we really longed for is being realized in this one moment of compassion.

Pope John XXIII was such a patient, compassionate person. In his presence, people felt lifted out of the depths of their entanglements and discovered a new horizon which made them let go of their many fears and anxieties. Many farmers, office workers, students, and housekeepers are also such persons. In their own quiet and inconspicuous ways, they let their friends, their children, and their neighbors take part in the fullness of God's time and thus offer them God's gracious compassion.

Patience, thus, is the compassionate way that leads to the compassionate life. It is the discipline of our discipleship. Since patience must be woven into the very fabric of our daily lives, we need now to explore in greater detail how the discipline of patience assumes texture and shape in a life of prayer and action.

8

Prayer

WITH EMPTY HANDS

The discipline of patience is practiced in prayer and action. Prayer and action are integral to the discipline of patience. In this chapter we want to explore how in prayer we suffer through the here and now and find the compassionate God in the center of our lives.

At first sight, it might seem strange to connect prayer with the discipline of patience. But it does not require much reflection to realize that impatience pulls us away from prayer. How often have we said to ourselves, "I'm really too busy to pray," or, "There are so many urgent things to do that I just don't seem to have the opportunity to pray," or, "Every time I think about going to pray something else demands my attention"? In a society that seems to be filled with urgencies and emergencies, prayer appears to be an unnatural form of behavior. Without fully realizing it, we have accepted the idea that "doing things" is more important than prayer and have come to think of prayer as something for times when there is nothing urgent to do. While we might agree verbally, or even intellectually, with someone who stresses the importance of prayer, we have become children of an impatient world to such an extent that our behavior often expresses the view that prayer is a waste of time.

This predicament shows how necessary it is to view prayer as a discipline. Concentrated human effort is necessary because prayer is not our most natural response to the world. Left to our own impulses, we will always want to do something else before we pray. Often, what we want to do seems so unquestionably good—setting up a religious education program, helping with a soup kitchen, listening to people's problems, visiting the sick, planning the liturgy, working with prisoners or mental patients—that it is hard to realize that even these things can be done with impatience and so become signs of our own needs rather than of God's compassion. Therefore, prayer is in many ways the criterion of Christian life. Prayer requires that we stand in God's presence with open hands, naked and vulnerable, proclaiming to ourselves and to others that without God we can do nothing. This is difficult in a climate where the predominant counsel is, "Do your best and God will do the rest." When life is divided into "our best" and "God's rest," we have turned prayer into a last resort to be used only when all our own resources are depleted. Then even the Lord has become the victim of our impatience. Discipleship does not mean to use God when we can no longer function ourselves. On the contrary, it means to recognize that we can do nothing at all, but that God can do everything through us. As disciples, we find not some but all of our strength, hope, courage, and confidence in God. Therefore, prayer must be our first concern.

Let us now look more closely at the practice of prayer. From all we have said, it is clear that prayer is not an effort to make contact with God, to bring him to our side. Prayer, as a discipline that strengthens and deepens discipleship, is the effort to remove everything that might prevent the Spirit of God, given to us by Jesus Christ, from speaking freely to us and in us. The discipline of prayer is the discipline by which we liberate the Spirit of God from entanglement in our impatient impulses. It is the way by which we allow God's Spirit to move where he wants.

IN THE SPIRIT

Until now we have barely mentioned the Holy Spirit. But we cannot speak about prayer without speaking about the Spirit God sends to draw us into the intimacy of his divine life. The Christian life is a spiritual life precisely because it is lived in the Spirit of Christ. This can easily be misunderstood, as when we say to each other, "Let us do this in the spirit of him who was so good to us." The Gospel, however, speaks in much stronger language. The Spirit is the Holy Spirit sent to us by the Father in the name of Jesus (Jn 14:26). This Holy Spirit is the divine life itself by which we become not only brothers and sisters of Christ but also sons and daughters of the Father. This is why Jesus could say: "It is for your own good that I am going because unless I go, the Advocate (the Spirit) will not come to you . . . But when the Spirit of truth comes he will lead you to the complete truth . . . all he tells you will be taken from what is mine. Everything the Father has is mine" (Jn 16:7-15).

Thus, receiving the Holy Spirit is receiving the life of the Father and the Son. This Spirit makes true discipleship possible, a discipleship that involves not only following in the path of Christ but also participating with Christ in his most intimate life with the Father. Paul expresses this powerfully when he writes to the Christians of Galatia, "The proof that you are sons is that God has sent the Spirit of his Son into our hearts: the Spirit that cries 'Abba, Father,' and it is this that makes you a son . . ." (Ga 4:6. Cf. Rm 8:15). Thus, Paul could also say, ". . . I live now not with my own life but with the life of Christ who lives in me" (Ga 2:20).

Spiritual life is life in the Spirit, or more accurately, the life of the Spirit in us. It is this spiritual life that enables us to live with a new mind in a new time. Once we have understood this, the meaning of prayer becomes clear. It is the expression of the life of the Holy Spirit in us. Prayer is not what is done by us, but rather what is done by the Holy Spirit in us. To the Corinthians Paul writes, "No one can say, 'Jesus is Lord' unless he is under the influence of the Holy Spirit" (1 Co 12:3), and to the Romans he says, "The Spirit . . . comes to help us in our weakness. For when we cannot choose words in order to pray properly, the Spirit expresses our plea in a way that could never be put into words, and God who knows everything in our hearts knows perfectly well what he means, and that the pleas of the saints expressed by the Spirit are according to the mind of God" (Rm 8:26–27). Prayer is the work of the Holy Spirit.

This indicates that prayer as a discipline of patience is the human effort to allow the Holy Spirit to do his re-creating work in us. This discipline involves many things. It involves the constant choice not to run from the present moment in the naïve hope that salvation will appear around the next corner. It involves the determination to listen carefully to people and events so as to discern the movements of the Spirit. It involves the ongoing struggle to prevent our minds and hearts from becoming cluttered with the many distractions that clamor for our attention. But above all, it involves the decision to set aside time every day to be alone with God and listen to the Spirit. The discipline of prayer enables us both to discern the presence of God's life-giving Spirit in the midst of our hectic lives and to let that divine Spirit constantly transform our lives. Having become free, through discipline, to listen patiently to God's Spirit and to follow his divine movements in us, we come to the awareness that this Spirit reminds us of all the things Jesus said and did (Jn 14:26, 16:8), teaches us how to pray (Rm 8:26–27), and empowers us to be witnesses to the ends of the earth (Ac 1:8). Then, too, we understand that the Spirit assures us of the truth (Rm 9:1), brings us righteousness, peace, and joy (Rm 14:17), removes all boundaries to hope (Rm 15:13), and makes everything new (Tt 3:5).

The discipline of prayer makes us stop and listen, wait and look, taste and see, pay attention and be aware. Although this may sound like advice to be passive, it actually demands much willpower and motivation. We may consider the discipline of prayer a form of inner displacement. The ordinary and proper response to our world is to turn on the radio, open the newspaper, go to another movie, talk to more people, or look impatiently for new attractions and distractions. To listen patiently to the voice of the Spirit in prayer is a radical displacement which at first creates unusual discomfort. We are so accustomed to our impatient way of life that we do not expect much from the moment. Every attempt to "live it through" or to "stay with it" is so contrary to our usual habits that all our impulses rise up in protest. But when discipline keeps us faithful, we slowly begin to sense that something so deep, so mysterious, and so creative is happening here and now that we are drawn toward it—not by our impulses but by the Holy Spirit. In our inner displacement, we experience the presence of the compassionate God. Paul writes to Titus:

But when the kindness and love of God our savior for humankind were revealed, it was not because he was concerned with any righteous actions we might have done ourselves, it was for no reason except his own compassion that he saved us, by means of the cleansing water of rebirth and by renewing us with the Holy Spirit which he has so generously poured over us through Jesus Christ our savior. He did this so that we should be justified

by his grace, to become heirs looking forward to eternal life.
This is doctrine you can rely on.

(Tt 3:4–8)

Prayer reveals to us the Spirit of the compassionate God.
As such, it is the discipline that supports discipleship.

AN ALL-EMBRACING INTIMACY

We must now seek a deeper understanding of the way in
which prayer, as patiently attending to the inner movements
of the Holy Spirit, is a discipline of compassion. What has
prayer to do with a compassionate life? Does the compassionate life not demand that we be present to those who
suffer; does it not require that we enter into solidarity with
the poor, oppressed, and downtrodden; does it not motivate
us both to move into the thick of life and to experience the
hardships of existence in solidarity with the outcasts? How
then can prayer be a discipline of compassion?

Many people tend to associate prayer with separation from
others, but real prayer brings us closer to our fellow human
beings. Prayer is the first and indispensible discipline of compassion precisely because prayer is also the first expression of
human solidarity. Why is this so? Because the Spirit who
prays in us is the Spirit by whom all human beings are
brought together in unity and community. The Holy Spirit,
the Spirit of peace, unity, and reconciliation, constantly reveals himself to us as the power through whom people from
the most diverse social, political, economic, racial, and ethnic
backgrounds are brought together as sisters and brothers of
the same Christ and daughters and sons of the same Father.

To prevent ourselves from slipping into spiritual romanticism or pious sentimentality, we must pay careful attention
to the compassionate presence of the Holy Spirit. The intimacy of prayer is the intimacy created by the Holy Spirit
who, as the bearer of the new mind and the new time, does

not exclude but rather includes our fellow human beings. In the intimacy of prayer, God reveals himself to us as the God who loves all the members of the human family just as personally and uniquely as he loves us. Therefore, a growing intimacy with God deepens our sense of responsibility for others. It evokes in us an always increasing desire to bring the whole world with all its suffering and pains around the divine fire in our heart and to share the revitalizing heat with all who want to come. But it is precisely this desire that requires such deep and strong patience. The painter Vincent van Gogh powerfully expresses the discipline of patient prayer when he writes to his brother Theo:

There may be a great fire in our soul, yet no one ever comes to warm himself at it, and the passers-by only see a wisp of smoke coming through the chimney, and go along their way. Look here, now, what must be done? Must one tend the inner fire, have salt in oneself, wait patiently yet with how much impatience for the hour when somebody will come and sit down near it—maybe to stay? Let him who believes in God wait for the hour that will come sooner or later.[14]

One of the most powerful experiences in a life of compassion is the expansion of our hearts into a world-embracing space of healing from which no one is excluded. When, through discipline, we have overcome the power of our impatient impulses to flee or to fight, to become fearful or angry, we discover a limitless space into which we can welcome all the people of the world. Prayer for others, therefore, cannot be seen as an extraordinary exercise that must be practiced from time to time. Rather, it is the very beat of a compassionate heart. To pray for a friend who is ill, for a student who is depressed, for a teacher who is in conflict; for people in prisons, in hospitals, on battlefields; for those who are victims of injustice, who are hungry, poor, and without shelter; for those who risk their career, their health, and even their life in the struggle for social justice; for leaders of church and state—to pray for all these people is not a futile effort to influence God's will, but a hospitable gesture by which we invite our neighbors into the center of our hearts. To pray for others means to make them part of ourselves. To pray for others means to allow their pains and sufferings, their anxieties and loneliness, their confusion and fears to resound in our innermost selves. To pray, therefore, is to become those for whom we pray, to become the sick child, the fearful mother, the distressed father, the nervous teenager, the angry student, and the frustrated striker. To pray is to enter into a deep inner solidarity with our fellow human beings so that in and through us they can be touched by the healing power of God's Spirit. When, as disciples of Christ, we are able to bear the burdens of our brothers and sisters, to be marked with their wounds, and even be broken by their sins, our prayer becomes their prayer, our cry for mercy becomes their cry. In compassionate prayer, we bring before God those who suffer not merely "over there," not simply "long ago," but here and now in our innermost selves. And so it is in and through us that others are restored; it is in and through us that they receive new light, new hope, and new courage; it is in and through us that God's Spirit touches them with his healing presence.

OUR ENEMIES TOO

Compassionate prayer for our fellow human beings stands in the center of the Christian life. Jesus emphasizes the great power of prayer when he says, "Everything you ask for in prayer you will receive" (Mt 21:22), and the Apostle James echoes these strong words when he writes, "The heartfelt prayer of a good man works very powerfully" (Jm 5:16). Compassionate prayer is a mark of the Christian community. Christians mention one another in their prayers (Rm 1:9, 2 Co 1:11, Ep 6:8, Col 4:3), and in so doing they bring help and even salvation to those for whom they pray (Rm 15:30,

Ph 1:19). But the final test of compassionate prayer goes beyond prayers for fellow Christians, members of the community, friends, and relatives. Jesus says it most unambiguously, "I say this to you: love your enemies and pray for those who persecute you" (Mt 5:44); and in the depth of his agony on the cross, he prays for those who are killing him, "Father, forgive them; they do not know what they are doing" (Lk 23:34). Here the full significance of the discipline of prayer becomes visible. Prayer allows us to lead into the center of our hearts not only those who love us but also those who hate us. This is possible only when we are willing to make our enemies part of ourselves and thus convert them first of all in our own hearts.

The first thing we are called to do when we think of others as our enemies is to pray for them. This is certainly not easy. It requires discipline to allow those who hate us or those toward whom we have hostile feelings to come into the intimate center of our hearts. People who make our lives difficult and cause us frustration, pain, or even harm, are least likely to receive a place in our hearts. Yet every time we overcome this impatience with our opponents and are willing to listen to the cry of those who persecute us, we will recognize them as brothers and sisters too. Praying for our enemies is therefore a real event, the event of reconciliation. It is impossible to lift our enemies up in the presence of God and at the same time continue to hate them. Seen in the place of prayer, even the unprincipled dictator and the vicious torturer can no longer appear as the object of fear, hatred, and revenge, because when we pray we stand at the center of the great mystery of Divine Compassion. Prayer converts the enemy into a friend and is thus the beginning of a new relationship. There is probably no prayer as powerful as the prayer for our enemies. But it is also the most difficult prayer since it is most contrary to our impulses. This explains why some Saints consider prayer for our enemies the main criterion of holiness.

As disciples of the compassionate Lord, who took upon himself the condition of a slave and suffered death for our sake (Ph 2:7–8), there are no boundaries to our prayers. Dietrich Bonhoeffer expresses this with powerful simplicity when he writes that to pray for others is to give them "the same right we have received, namely, to stand before Christ and share in his mercy."[15] When we come before God with the needs of the world, the healing love of the Holy Spirit that touches us touches with the same power all those whom we bring before him. Compassionate prayer does not encourage the self-serving individualism that leads us to flee from people or to fight them. On the contrary, by deepening our awareness of our common suffering, prayer draws us closer together in the healing presence of the Holy Spirit.

FAITHFUL TO THE BREAKING OF THE BREAD

As a discipline for living the moment fully and recognizing in it the healing presence of the Holy Spirit, prayer finds its most profound expression in the breaking of the bread. The intimate connection between compassion, prayer, and the breaking of the bread is made clear in the description of the early Christian community: "These remained faithful to the teaching of the apostles, to the brotherhood, to the breaking of bread . . . they shared their food gladly and generously; they praised God and were looked up to by everyone" (Ac 2:42–47). The breaking of the bread stands at the center of the Christian community. In the breaking of bread together, we give the clearest testimony to the communal character of our prayers. Just as discipleship expresses itself above all in a new way of living together, so too the discipline of prayer reveals itself to be first and foremost a communal discipline. It is in the breaking of the bread together that the Holy Spirit, the Spirit sent by Christ and the Father, becomes most tangibly present to the community. The breaking of the

bread, therefore, is not a moment in which we try to forget
the pains of "real life" and withdraw into a dreamlike ceremony, but the festive articulation of what we perceive as the
center of our lives.

When we break bread together, we reveal to each other
the real story of Christ's life and our lives in him. Jesus took
bread, blessed it, broke it, and gave it to his friends. He did so
when he saw a hungry crowd and felt compassion for them
(Mt 14:19, 15:36); he did it on the evening before his death
when he wanted to say farewell (Mt 26:26); he did so when
he made himself known to the two disciples whom he met on
the road to Emmaus (Lk 24:30). And ever since his death,
Christians have done so in memory of him. Thus, the breaking of the bread is the celebration, the making present, of
Christ's story as well as our own. In the taking, blessing,
breaking, and giving of the bread, the mystery of Christ's life
is expressed in the most succinct way. The Father took his
only Son and sent him into the world so that through him the
world might be saved (Jn 3:17). At the river Jordan and on
Mount Tabor he blessed him with the words, "This is my
Son, the Beloved, my favor rests on him . . . listen to him"
(Mt 3:17, 17:5). The blessed one was broken on a cross,
"pierced through for our faults, crushed for our sins" (Is
53:5). But through his death he gave himself to us as our
food, thus fulfilling the words he spoke to his disciples at the
last supper, "This is my body which will be given for you"
(Lk 22:19).

It is in this life that is taken, blessed, broken, and given that
Jesus Christ wants to make us participants. Therefore, while
breaking bread with his disciples, he said, "Do this as a memorial of me" (Lk 22:19). When we eat bread and drink
wine together in memory of Christ, we become intimately
related to his own compassionate life. In fact, we *become* his
life and are thus enabled to re-present his life in our time and
place. Our compassion becomes a manifestation of God's
compassion lived out through all times and in all places. The

breaking of the bread connects our broken lives with God's life in Christ and transforms our brokenness into a brokenness that no longer leads to fragmentation but to community and love. Wounds that are the beginning of the process of decay must remain hidden, but wounds that have become gateways to new life can be celebrated as new signs of hope. Precisely for this reason, compassion, suffering together, can be celebrated in communal prayer.

In the breaking of the bread together, we reclaim our own broken condition rather than denying its reality. We become more aware than ever that we are taken, set apart as witnesses for God; that we are blessed by words and acts of grace; and that we are broken, not in revenge or cruelty, but in order to become bread which can be given as food to others. When two, three, ten, a hundred, or a thousand people eat the same bread and drink from the same cup, and so become united with the broken and poured-out life of Christ, they discover that their own lives are part of that one life and thus recognize each other as brothers and sisters.

There are very few places left in our world where our common humanity can be lifted up and celebrated, but each time we come together around the simple signs of bread and wine, we tear down many walls and gain an inkling of God's intentions for the human family. And each time this happens we are called to become more concerned not only about each other's well-being but also about the well-being of all people in our world.

Thus, the breaking of the bread becomes an expression of solidarity with all who suffer, whether they be nearby or far away. This leads not to cliques, but rather opens us up to the whole of humanity. It brings us into contact with people whose bodies and minds have been broken by oppression and torture and whose lives are being destroyed in the prisons of this world. It brings us into touch with men, women, and children whose physical, mental, and spiritual beauty remains invisible due to lack of food and shelter. It brings us into touch with the dying on the streets of Calcutta and the lonely in the high rises of New York City. It brings us into touch with persons such as Sheila Cassidy in England, Mairhead Corrigan and Betty Williams in Northern Ireland, Kim Chi Ha in Korea, Molly Rush in United States, Jean Vanier in France, and many others all over the world whose cries for justice need to be heard.

These connections are indeed "bread connections" which challenge us to work with all our energy for the daily bread of all people. In this way our praying together becomes working together, and the call to break the same bread becomes a call to action.

9

Action

HERE AND NOW

If the emphasis on prayer were an escape from direct engagement with the many needs and pains of our world, then it would not be a real discipline of the compassionate life. Prayer challenges us to be fully aware of the world in which we live and to present it with all its needs and pains to God. It is this compassionate prayer that calls for compassionate action. The disciple is called to follow the Lord not only into the desert and onto the mountain to pray but also into the valley of tears, where help is needed, and onto the cross, where humanity is in agony. Prayer and action, therefore, can never be seen as contradictory or mutually exclusive. Prayer without action grows into powerless pietism, and ac-

tion without prayer degenerates into questionable manipulation. If prayer leads us into a deeper unity with the compassionate Christ, it will always give rise to concrete acts of
service. And if concrete acts of service do indeed lead us to a
deeper solidarity with the poor, the hungry, the sick, the
dying, and the oppressed, they will always give rise to
prayer. In prayer we meet Christ, and in him all human
suffering. In service we meet people, and in them the suffering Christ.

The discipline of patience reveals itself not only in the way
we pray but also in the way we act. Our actions, like our
prayers, must be a manifestation of God's compassionate presence in the midst of our world. Patient actions are actions
through which the healing, consoling, comforting, recon-
ciling, and unifying love of God can touch the heart of humanity. They are actions through which the fullness of time
can show itself and God's justice and peace can guide our
world. They are actions by which good news is brought to
the poor, liberty to the prisoners, new sight to the blind, freedom to the oppressed, and God's year of favor is proclaimed
(Lk 4:18–19). They are actions that remove the fear, suspicion, and power-hungry competition that cause an escalating
arms race, an increasing separation between the wealthy and
the poor, and an intensifying cruelty between the powerful
and the powerless. They are actions that lead people to listen
to each other, speak with each other, and heal each other's
wounds. In short, they are actions based on a faith that
knows God's presence in our lives and wants this presence to
be felt by individuals, communities, societies, and nations.

Patient action is a hard discipline. Often, our lives get so
overburdened that it takes every bit of energy to survive the
day. Then it becomes hard to value the present moment, and
we can only dream about a future time and place where everything will be different. We want to move away from the
present moment as quickly as possible and create a new situation in which present pains are absent. But such impatient ac-

tion prevents us from recognizing the possibilities of the moment and thus easily leads us to an intolerant fanaticism.
Action as a discipline of compassion requires the willingness
to respond to the very concrete needs of the moment.

THE TEST OF CREDIBILITY

Probably no New Testament writer is as explicit about the
importance of concrete acts of service as James. He writes,
"Pure, unspoilt religion, in the eyes of God our Father is this:
coming to the help of orphans and widows when they need
it, and keeping oneself uncontaminated by the world" (Jm
1:27). With considerable irony, James shows to the "twelve
tribes of the Dispersion"—i.e., the Jewish Christians scattered
all over the Graeco-Roman world—the importance of concrete acts of service.

Take the case, my brothers, of someone who has never done a
single good act but claims that he has faith. Will that faith
save him? If one of the brothers or one of the sisters is in need
of clothes and has not enough food to live on, and one of you
says to them, "I wish you well; keep yourself warm and eat
plenty," without giving them these bare necessities of life, then
what good is that? Faith is like that: if good works do not go
with it, it is quite dead.

(Jm 2:14–17)

James even goes so far as to instruct his readers about how
to speak to those who think that merely having faith in God
is sufficient.

This is the way you talk to people of that kind: "You say you
have faith and I have good deeds; I will prove to you that I have
faith by showing you my good deeds—now you prove to me that
you have faith without any good deeds to show. You believe in
the one God—that is creditable enough, but the demons have the
same belief, and they tremble with fear. Do realise, you senseless
man, that faith without good deeds is useless."

(Jm 2:18–20)

After showing how in the lives of Abraham and Rahab faith and deeds work together, James concludes, "A body dies when it is separated from the spirit, and in the same way faith is dead if it is separated from good deeds" (Jm 2:26).

It is obvious that James does little more than restate in a new context Jesus' emphasis on concrete acts of service. When the disciples of John the Baptist ask Jesus if he is "the one who is to come," Jesus points to his actions, "the blind see again, the lame walk, lepers are cleansed, and the deaf hear, the dead are raised to life, the Good News is proclaimed to the poor" (Lk 7:22–23). His actions are the source of his credibility. The same is true of his disciples. Jesus wants them to be people of action. He leaves little doubt about his opinion, ". . . the one who listens and does nothing is like the man who built his house on soil, with no foundations: as soon as the river bore down on it, it collapsed; and what a ruin that house became!" (Lk 6:49). With great persistence, Jesus stresses that the test of true discipleship lies not in words but in actions: "It is not those who say to me, 'Lord, Lord,' who will enter the kingdom of heaven, but the person who does the will of my Father in heaven" (Mt 7:21–22). Indeed, prayer must yield specific fruits. The final criterion of the value of the Christian life is therefore not prayer but action. In the "wordy" environment of teachers, masters, scribes, and pharisees, Jesus wants his followers to discover for themselves that mere words will not bring them into the kingdom.

What is your opinion? A man had two sons. He went and said to the first, "My boy, you go and work in the vineyard today." He answered, "I will not go," but afterwards thought better of it and went. The man then went and said the same thing to the second who answered, "Certainly, sir," but did not go. Which of the two did the father's will? "The first," they said.

(Mt 21:28–31)

Should there still exist any question in his hearers' minds, Jesus erases the vestiges of doubt when he describes the last judgment, in which concrete acts of compassion are the undeniable sign of "unspoilt religion" (James). Perhaps nowhere else in the New Testament do we find the importance of the discipline of action so clearly presented:

When the Son of Man comes in his glory, escorted by all the angels, then he will take his seat on his throne of glory. All the nations will be assembled before him and he will separate men one from another as the shepherd separates sheep from goats. He will place the sheep on his right hand and the goats on his left. Then the King will say to those on his right hand, "Come, you whom the Father has blessed, take for your heritage the kingdom prepared for you since the foundation of the world. For I was hungry and you gave me food; I was thirsty and you gave me drink; I was a stranger and you made me welcome; naked and you clothed me, sick and you visited me, in prison and you came to see me." Then the virtuous will say to him in reply, "Lord, when did we see you hungry and feed you; or thirsty and give you drink? When did we see you a stranger and make you welcome; naked and clothe you; sick or in prison and go to see you?" And the King will answer, "I tell you solemnly, in so far as you did this to one of the least of these brothers of mine, you did it to me." Next he will say to those on his left hand, "Go away from me, with your curse upon you, to the eternal fire prepared for the devil and his angels. For I was hungry and you never gave me food; I was thirsty and you never gave me anything to drink; I was a stranger and you never made me welcome, naked and you never clothed me, sick and in prison and you never visited me." Then it will be their turn to ask, "Lord, when did we see you hungry and thirsty, a stranger or naked, sick or in prison, and did not come to your help?" Then he will answer, "I tell you solemnly, in so far as you neglected to do this to one of the least of these, you neglected to do it to me." And they will go away to eternal punishment, and the virtuous to eternal life.

(Mt 25:31–46)

This dramatic scene vividly portrays the meaning of the discipline of action. Action with and for those who suffer is the concrete expression of the compassionate life and the final criterion of being a Christian. Such acts do not stand beside the moments of prayer and worship but are themselves such moments. Why? Because Jesus Christ, who did not cling to his divinity, but became as we are, can be found where there are hungry, thirsty, alienated, naked, sick, and imprisoned people. Precisely when we live in an ongoing conversation with Christ and allow his Spirit to guide our lives, we will recognize him in the poor, the oppressed, and the downtrodden, and will hear his cry and respond to it wherever he reveals himself. Thus, action and prayer are two aspects of the same discipline of patience. Both require that we be present to the suffering world here and now and that we respond to the specific needs of those who make up our world, a world claimed by Jesus Christ as his own. So worship becomes ministry and ministry becomes worship, and all we say or do, ask for or give, becomes a way to the life in which God's compassion can manifest itself.

THE TEMPTATION OF ACTIVISM

The disciples speak of their actions as manifestations of God's active presence. They act not to prove their power, but to show God's power; they act not to redeem people but to reveal God's redemptive grace; they act not to create a new world, but to open hearts and ears to the one who sits on the throne and says, "Now I am making the whole of creation new" (Rv 21:5).

In our society, which equates worth with productivity, patient action is very difficult. We tend to be so concerned with doing something worthwhile, bringing about changes, planning, organizing, structuring, and restructuring that we often seem to forget that it is not we who redeem, but God. To be busy, "where the action is," and "on top of things" often seem to have become goals themselves. We then have forgotten that our vocation is not to give visibility to our powers but to God's compassion.

Action as the way of a compassionate life is a difficult discipline precisely because we are so in need of recognition and acceptance. This need can easily drive us to conform to the expectation that we will offer something "new." In a society that is so keen on new encounters, so eager for new events, and so hungry for new experiences, it is difficult not to be seduced into impatient activism. Often, we are hardly aware of this seduction, especially since what we are doing is so obviously "good and religious." But even setting up a relief program, feeding the hungry, and assisting the sick could be more an expression of our own needs than of God's call.

But let us not be too moralistic about it: We can never claim pure motives, and it is better to act with and for those who suffer than to wait until we have our own needs completely under control. However, it is important to remain critical of our own activist tendencies. When our own needs begin to dominate our actions, long-range service becomes difficult and we soon become exhausted, burned out, and even embittered by our efforts.

The most important resource for counteracting the constant temptation to slip into activism is the knowledge that in Christ everything has been accomplished. This knowledge should be understood not as an intellectual insight, but as an understanding in faith. As long as we continue to act as if the salvation of the world depends on us, we lack the faith by which mountains can be moved. In Christ, human suffering and pain have already been accepted and suffered; in him our broken humanity has been reconciled and led into the intimacy of the relationship between the Father and the Son. Our action, therefore, must be understood as a discipline by which we make visible what has already been accomplished. Such action is based on the faith that we walk on solid ground even when we are surrounded by chaos, confusion, violence, and hatred.

A moving example of this was given by a woman who for many years had lived and worked in Burundi. One day she

witnessed a cruel tribal war which destroyed all that she and
her co-workers had built up. Many innocent people whom
she dearly loved were slaughtered in front of her eyes. Later
she was able to say that her knowledge that all this suffering
had been accomplished in Christ prevented a mental and
emotional breakdown. Her deep understanding of God's
saving act enabled her not to leave, but to remain active
in the midst of the indescribable misery and to face the
real situation with open eyes and open ears. Her actions were
not simply an attempt to rebuild and thus to overcome the
evils she had seen, but a reminder to her people that God is
not a God of hatred and violence but a God of tenderness
and compassion. Maybe only those who have suffered much
will understand what it means that Christ suffered our pains
and accomplished our reconciliation on the cross.

NOT WITHOUT CONFRONTATION

But activism is not the only temptation that requires discipline. Impatient action not only leads to overworked and
overcommitted people but also tends to sentimentalize compassion. Therefore, sentimentality is another temptation for
which we need the discipline of action. When we are primarily concerned about being liked, accepted, praised, or rewarded, we become very selective in our dos and don'ts.
We then tend to limit ourselves to those activities that elicit
sympathetic responses. Here we touch on an aspect of compassion that we seldom recognize as such: confrontation. In
our society, the discipline of action frequently requires the
courage to confront. We are inclined to associate compassion
with actions by which wounds are healed and pains relieved.
But in a time in which many people can no longer exercise
their human rights, millions are hungry, and the whole
human race lives under the threat of nuclear holocaust, compassionate action means more than offering help to the suffering. The power of evil has become so blatantly visible in in-

dividuals as well as in the social structures that dominate their lives that nothing less than strong and unambiguous confrontation is called for. Compassion does not exclude confrontation. On the contrary, confrontation is an integral part of compassion. Confrontation can indeed be an authentic expression of compassion. The whole prophetic tradition makes this clear, and Jesus is no exception. Sadly enough, Jesus has been presented for so long as a meek and mild person that we seldom realize how differently the Gospels depict him.

In Passolini's film, *The Gospel According to St. Matthew,* we are faced with an aggressive and abrasive prophet who does not avoid irritating people and who at times even seems to invite a negative response. Although Passolini's portrayal of Jesus is one-sided, there is no doubt that he reminds us again of how often Jesus engaged in confrontation and how unconcerned he was about being tactful and pleasing others.

Honest, direct confrontation is a true expression of compassion. As Christians, we are *in* the world without being *of* it. It is precisely this position that renders confrontation both possible and necessary. The illusion of power must be unmasked, idolatry must be undone, oppression and exploitation must be fought, and all who participate in these evils must be confronted. This is compassion. We cannot suffer with the poor when we are unwilling to confront those persons and systems that cause poverty. We cannot set the captives free when we do not want to confront those who carry the keys. We cannot profess our solidarity with those who are oppressed when we are unwilling to confront the oppressor. Compassion without confrontation fades quickly into fruitless sentimental commiseration.

But if confrontation is to be an expression of patient action, it must be humble. Our constant temptation is to fall into self-righteous revenge or self-serving condemnation. The danger here is that our own witness can blind us. When confrontation is tainted by desire for attention, need for revenge, or greed for power, it can easily become self-serving and cease to be compassionate.

It is not easy to confront compassionately. Self-right-eousness always lurks around the corner, and violent anger is a real temptation. Probably the best criterion for determin-ing whether our confrontation is compassionate rather than offensive, and our anger righteous rather than self-righteous, is to ask ourselves if we ourselves can be so confronted. Can we learn from indignation directed at us? When we can be confronted by a NO from others, we will be more able to confront with a NO. Saying NO to evil and destruction in the awareness that they dwell in our own heart is a humble NO. When we say NO with humility, this NO is also a call for our own conversion. No to racial injustice means a call to look our own bigotry straight in the eye, and NO to world hunger calls upon us to recognize our own lack of poverty. No to war requires us to come to terms with our own violence and aggression, and NO to oppression and torture forces us to deal directly with our own insensitivities. And so all our NO's be-come challenges to purify our own hearts.

In this sense, confrontation always includes self-confronta-tion. This self-confrontation prevents us from becoming alienated from the world we confront. Thomas Merton saw this clearly when he wrote:

The world as pure object is something that is not there. It is not a reality outside us for which we exist . . . It is a living and self-creating mystery of which I myself am a part, to which I am myself my own unique door. When I find the world in my own ground, it is impossible to be alienated by it.[16]

Here we find the key to compassionate confrontation. The evil that needs to be confronted and fought has an accom-plice in the human heart, including our own. Therefore, each attempt to confront evil in the world calls for the realization that there are always two fronts on which the struggle takes place: an outer and an inner front. For confrontation to be-

come and remain compassionate, these fronts should never be
separated.

IN GRATITUDE

Whether they confront evil in the world or support the
good, disciplined actions are always characterized by gratitude. Anger can make us active and can even unleash in us
much creative energy. But not for long. The social activists
of the 1960s who allowed their anger to fuel their actions
soon found themselves burned out. Often they reached a
state of physical as well as mental exhaustion and needed psy-
chotherapy or a "new spirituality." To persevere without
visible success we need a spirit of gratitude. An angry action
is born of the experience of being hurt; a grateful action is
born of the experience of healing. Angry actions want to
take; grateful actions want to share. Gratitude is the mark
of action undertaken as part of the discipline of patience.
It is a response to grace. It leads us not to conquer or destroy,
but to give visibility to a good that is already present. Therefore, the compassionate life is a grateful life, and actions
born out of gratefulness are not compulsive but free, not
somber but joyful, not fanatical but liberating. When gratitude is the source of our actions, our giving becomes receiving, and those to whom we minister become our ministers
because in the center of our care for others we sense a caring
presence, and in the midst of our efforts we sense an encouraging support. When this happens we can remain joyful
and peaceful even when there are few successes to brag
about.

A beautiful example of this attitude was demonstrated by
Cesar Chavez and his staff when they were defeated after a
long campaign for Proposition 14, which tried to secure the
right of farmworkers to organize. Instead of a sense of
depression, there was a party. Instead of a sense of defeat,

there was a sense of victory. A puzzled reporter wrote: "If they celebrate with such joyful festivity when they lose, what will it be like when they win?" What became clear was that Cesar Chavez and the many men and women who had joined him in the campaign for Proposition 14 were so convinced of the righteousness of their actions that the final result became secondary to the value of the action itself. There had been long days of praying and fasting to keep the campaign truthful and honest. There had been hours of singing, scripture reading, and breaking bread together to remind each other that the fruits of all actions come from God. And when finally the action failed and the desired result did not come about, people did not lose hope and courage but simply decided to try again next time. Meanwhile, they had experienced a deep community with each other, had come to know many generous people, and had received a keen sense of God's presence in their midst. They felt that there were reasons to celebrate and be grateful. So no one went home defeated. All had a story to tell, the story of the experience of God's compassion when people gather in his name.

Gratitude is indeed a sign of an action guided by the discipline of patience. Even when there are no concrete results, the act itself can still be a revelation of God's caring presence here and now. Such action is true action because it is born of true knowledge of God's active presence. It grows not from the need to prove anything or to persuade anyone, but from the desire to give free witness to that which is profoundly real. We find this most powerfully put into words by St. John:

> Something which has existed since the beginning,
> that we have heard,
> that we have seen with our own eyes;
> that we have watched
> and touched with our hands:
> the Word, who is life—

this is our subject.
That life was made visible:
we saw it and we are giving our testimony,
telling you of the eternal life
which was with the Father and has been made visible to us.
What we have seen and heard
we are telling you
so that you too may be in union with us,
as we are in union
with the Father
and with his Son Jesus Christ.
We are writing this to you to make our own joy complete.

(1 Jn 1:1–4)

These words are a most eloquent formulation of the meaning of compassionate action. It is the free, joyful, and, above all, grateful manifestation of an encounter that has taken place. The enormous energy with which John, Peter, Paul, and all the disciples "conquered" their world with the message of Jesus Christ came from that encounter. They did not have to convince themselves or each other that they were doing a good thing; they had no doubts concerning the value of their work; they had no hesitation about the relevance of their action. They could do nothing other than speak about him, praise him, thank him, and worship him because it was he whom they had heard, seen, and touched. They could do nothing other than bring light to the blind, freedom to the captives, and liberty to the oppressed because there they met him again. They could do nothing other than call people together into a new fellowship because thus he would be in their midst. Since Jesus Christ had become their true life, their true concern, their true compassion, and their true love, living became acting and all of life became an ongoing expression of thanks for God's great gift of himself.

This is the deepest meaning of compassionate action. It is the grateful, free, and joyful expression of the great encounter with the compassionate God. And it will be fruitful even when we can see neither how nor why. In and through such action, we realize that indeed all is grace and that our only possible response is gratitude.

Conclusion

The great news we have received is that God is a compassionate God. In Jesus Christ the obedient servant, who did not cling to his divinity but emptied himself and became as we are, God has revealed the fullness of his compassion. He is Immanuel, God-with-us. The great call we have heard is to live a compassionate life. In the community formed in displacement and leading to a new way of being together, we can become disciples—living manifestations of God's presence in this world. The great task we have been given is to walk the compassionate way. Through the discipline of patience, practiced in prayer and action, the life of discipleship becomes real and fruitful.

As long as we live on this earth, our lives as Christians must be marked by compassion. But we must not conclude these reflections on compassion without observing that the compassionate life is not our final goal. In fact, we can only live the compassionate life to the fullest when we know that it points beyond itself. We know that he who emptied and humbled himself has been raised high and has been given a name above all other names, and we know too that he left us to prepare a place for us where suffering will be overcome and compassion no longer necessary. There is a new heaven and a new earth for which we hope with patient expectation. This is the vision presented in the Book of Revelation:

Then I saw a new heaven and a new earth; the first heaven and the first earth had disappeared now, and there was no longer any sea. I saw the holy city, and the new Jerusalem, coming down from God out of heaven, as beautiful as a bride all dressed for her husband. Then I heard a loud voice call from the throne, "You see this city? Here God lives among men. He will make his home among them; they shall be his people, and he will be their God; his name is God-with-them. He will wipe away all tears from their eyes; there will be no more death, and no more mourning or sadness. The world of the past has gone."

(Rv 21:1-4)

This is the vision that guides us. This vision makes us share one another's burdens, carry our crosses together, and unite for a better world. This vision takes the despair out of death and the morbidity out of suffering, and opens new horizons. This vision also gives us the energy to manifest its first realization in the midst of the complexities of life. This vision is indeed of a future world. But it is no utopia. The future has already begun and is revealed each time strangers are welcomed, the naked are clothed, the sick and prisoners are visited, and oppression is overcome. Through these grateful actions the first glimpses of a new heaven and a new earth can be seen.

In the new city, God will live among us, but each time two or three gather in the name of Jesus he is already in our midst. In the new city, all tears will be wiped away, but each time people eat bread and drink wine in his memory, smiles appear on strained faces. In the new city, the whole creation will be made new, but each time prison walls are broken down, poverty is dispelled, and wounds are carefully attended, the old earth is already giving way to the new. Through compassionate action, the old is not just old anymore and pain not just pain any longer. Although we are still waiting in expectation, the first signs of the new earth and the new heaven, which have been promised to us and for which we hope, are already visible in the community of faith where the compassionate God reveals himself. This is the foundation of our faith, the basis of our hope, and the source of our love.

Epilogue

The drawings in this book may prove to be more important than the words. Therefore, we will not close this book without telling the painful story that gave birth to these drawings.

One question kept haunting us as we wrote: Are we, well-fed, well-dressed, well-housed, and well-protected people, the ones who should write about compassion? Can we claim that we know to any degree what suffering is, and can we honestly enter into solidarity with those whose lives are literally broken? Although we tried not to become paralyzed by guilt feelings but instead attempted to explore as sincerely as possible our own limited spiritual territories, we still remained painfully aware of the agonizing cries of the millions of people burdened by cruel oppression. As we worked on this book, we read about families dying of hunger and cold, we heard about the systematic killing of indigenous tribes, we were confronted day after day with the imprisonment and torture of men, women, and even children all over the world. Sometimes this knowledge entered so deeply into our hearts that we were tempted to give up writing and to hide ourselves with tears of shame. However, we kept resisting this temptation in the hope that our writing would be an expression not of hypocrisy but of a sincere desire to participate in the confrontation and eradication of the enormous injustices in our world.

In the midst of all these self-doubts and hesitations, a man emerged from the hazy background of our ambiguous feelings and presented himself to us as a representative of the world that seemed to accuse us. His name is Joel Filártiga, a medical doctor living and working with the poorest of the poor in Paraguay. With his wife, Nidia, and the help of his children, he runs a small clinic in Ybyqui, a town two hours' drive from the capital, Asunción. There people come from great distances, walking or riding in little horse-drawn carts, to ask help for their many illnesses. Joel understands his people. He not only knows the illnesses of their bodies but also feels deeply the afflictions in their souls. He speaks their language, Guarani, and listens to the stories of their long struggles, and suffers in his heart with them. While he listens to their souls cry out, he picks up his pencil and draws, draws, draws. From his hands have appeared shockingly powerful drawings in which the agony of the people of Paraguay is expressed and lifted up in an indignant protest. Through his art, Joel Filártiga has become one of the most outspoken defenders of the poor, and one of the sharpest critics of the oppressive Stroessner regime. Through his art he has become much more than a very capable country doctor. He has become a man who, with his pens and pencils, can shout far beyond the boundaries of his country and plead for understanding and support.

The more we heard about Joel, the more we began to realize what compassion is. It is hard work; it is crying out with
those in pain; it is tending the wounds of the poor and caring
for their lives; it is defending the weak and indignantly ac-
cusing those who violate their humanity; it is joining with the
oppressed in their struggle for justice; it is pleading for help,
with all possible means, from any person who has ears to hear
and eyes to see. In short, it is a willingness to lay down our
lives for our friends.

Not long after Joel Filártiga became known to us, we
learned the price he had to pay for his compassion. On
March 30, 1976, the police kidnapped his seventeen-year-old
son, Joelito, and within a few hours, tortured him to death.
Those who had been unable to kill the popular and dearly
loved father did not hesitate to take revenge by the brutal
murder of his teenage son. Joel's and Nidia's grief and
mourning did not drive them into silence and seclusion. Instead, they cried out in acts of fearless protest, doing so at the
risk of their own lives. Instead of dressing their son's elec-
troshocked, burned, and distorted body in fine clothes and
making it look peaceful, they laid it naked on the bloody
mattress on which it had been found. Thus, the hundreds of
people who came to offer condolences were confronted with
the evil attempt to silence a compassionate voice, and were
reminded of Jesus' words, "Because you do not belong to the
world . . . the world hates you" (Jn 15:19).

In August, a few months after Joelito's death, one of us
visited Joel Filártiga in Paraguay and asked him to take part
in our efforts to express for our time the meaning of Jesus'
call to compassion. We felt that this man knew and could
help us to know. In the midst of his grief for Joelito, Joel
found comfort and consolation in the drawings he made for
this book. He drew during the long nights when deep sorrow
kept him awake. He drew after long, anxious sessions with
judges and lawyers to ask for justice, and he drew after hours

of tears. But he drew with hope—hope for himself, his family, his patients, and his people. He drew so that many should know and be converted. He drew so that his dearly-bought compassion would not be quenched but would become a fire that warms the hearts of many to work and pray for justice and peace. It is because of people such as Joel that this book is worth publishing. Therefore, we have dedicated this book to him and to his wife in memory of their beloved son Joelito.

Notes

1. Worsthorne, Peregrine. "A Universe of Hospital Patients. Further Remarks on the British Condition," *Harpers* 251, November 1975, p. 38.

2. Barth, Karl. *Church Dogmatics*, IV/1 (Edinburgh: T. & T. Clark, Sons, 1956), p. 190.

3. Ibid., p. 188.

4. Ibid., p. 191.

5. Ibid., p. 201.

6. Nietzsche, Friedrich. "The Anti-Christ," secs. 5, 51, in *The Portable Nietzsche*, edited and translated by Walter Kaufmann (New York: The Viking Press, 1954).

7. Cited in Chong Sun Kim and Shelly Killen, "Open the Prison Gates and Set My Soul Free," *Sojourners*, April 1979, p. 15.

8. *Catholic Worker*, Vol. XLII, No. 7, September 1977.

9. Marino, Joe. Unpublished diary written in Rome, May 1978.

10. Merton, Thomas. Preface to the Japanese edition of *The Seven Storey Mountain* (*Nanae No Yama*) (Tokyo: Toyo Publishing Company, 1965). Trans. by Kudo Takishi.

11. Chesterton, Gilbert K. *St. Francis of Assisi* (Garden City: Doubleday Image Books, 1957), pp. 96–97.

12. Ibid., p. 101.

13. Shah, Indries. *The Way of the Sufi* (New York: E. P. Dutton & Co., Inc., 1970), p. 207 ff.

14. *The Complete Letters of Vincent van Gogh* (Greenwich, Conn.: New York Graphic Society), Vol. I, p. 197.

15. Bonhoeffer, Dietrich. *Life Together* (New York: Harpers, 1954), p. 86.

16. Merton, Thomas. *Contemplation in a World of Action* (Garden City: Doubleday Image Books, 1971), pp. 154–55.

Acknowledgments

Although we planned this book as the work of three friends, the final text is the result of suggestions, comments, criticisms, and contributions of many people who encouraged us in our work together.

We want to thank all those who helped us in the rewriting of the manuscript by critically reading it or by using it in their teaching. They are: Bob Antonelli, Judith Anne Beattie, Jane Bouvier, Steven Cribari, Agnes McNeill Donohue, James Duane, James Fee, George Fitzgerald, Stacy Hennessy, George Hunsinger, Ben Hunt, Ken and Penny Jameson, Mark Janus, Jay Kenney, Carol Knoll, Mary Meg McCarthy, Kay and Don McNeill, Melanie Morrison, Claude Pomerleau, John Roark, Jim and Mary Ann Roemer, Louis ter Steeg, Naomi Burton Stone, Reg and Ralph Weissert, Vivian Whitehead, Colin Williams, and Gregory Youngchild.

We also want to express our gratitude to Piet van Leeuwen and Mark Fedor for their secretarial assistance; and to Robert Moore, Joseph Núñez, Richard Schaper, and Mich Zeman for their editorial collaboration during the final phases of this book.

To Robert Heller of Doubleday we offer our thanks for his patience and encouragement during the last five years.

Finally, a special word of gratitude goes to John Mogabgab, who not only coordinated much of our work on this book but also made essential contributions to its content and form.

DONALD MCNEILL
DOUGLAS MORRISON
HENRI NOUWEN

ABOUT THE AUTHORS

DONALD P. MCNEILL, a priest in the Congregation of Holy Cross, is presently teaching at the University of Notre Dame, and is the director of the Center for Experiential Learning there.

DOUGLAS A. MORRISON, a priest of the archdiocese of Hartford, Connecticut, is presently teaching at Catholic University in Washington, D.C., and is the director of The Pastoral Center there.

HENRI J. M. NOUWEN, a priest of the archdiocese of Utrecht, the Netherlands, taught at Yale Divinity School for ten years and is presently living as a family brother at the Abbey of the Genesee in upstate New York.

JOEL FILÁRTIGA, a medical doctor in Paraguay, drew the illustrations for this book in memory of his seventeen-year-old son, Joelito, who was tortured to death by a police squad in 1976.